Model Checking

The Cyber-Physical Systems Series
Calin Belta, editor

Model Checking, second edition, Edmund Clarke, Jr., Orna Grumberg, Daniel Kroening, Doron Peled and Helmut Veith

Model Checking

second edition

Edmund M. Clarke, Jr., Orna Grumberg, Daniel Kroening,
Doron Peled and Helmut Veith

The MIT Press
Cambridge, Massachusetts
London, England

For information about special quantity discounts, please email special_sales@mitpress.mit.edu.

This book was set in Syntax and Times Roman by the author.

Printed and bound in the United States of America.

Library of Congress Cataloging-in-Publication Data

Names: Clarke, Edmund M., Jr. (Edmund Melson), 1945– author.
Title: Model Checking / Edmund M Clarke Jr., Orna Grumberg, Daniel Kroening, Doron Peled, and Helmut Veith.
Description: Second edition. | Cambridge, MA : The MIT Press, 2018. | Series: The cyber-physical systems series | Includes bibliographical references and index.
Identifiers: LCCN 2018014965 | ISBN 9780262038836 (hardcover : alk. paper)
Subjects: LCSH: Computer systems–Verification.
Classification: LCC QA76.76.V47 C553 2018 | DDC 004.2/1–dc23 LC record available at https://lccn.loc.gov/2018014965

10 9 8 7 6 5 4 3 2 1

In memory of Helmut Veith

This book is dedicated to
Martha, James, Jonathan, and Jeffrey,
Manfred, Noa, and Hila,
Anna, Theodore, Alexander, and Emilia,
Priva Peled,
Anna and Nikita

Contents

List of Figures xiii

Foreword xix

1 Introduction to the Second Edition 1

2 Introduction to the First Edition 3

2.1 The Need for Formal Methods 3

2.2 Hardware and Software Verification 4

2.3 The Process of Model Checking 6

2.4 Temporal Logic and Model Checking 6

2.5 Symbolic Algorithms 8

2.6 Partial Order Reduction 10

2.7 Other Approaches to the State Explosion Problem 11

3 Modeling Systems 15

3.1 Transition Systems and Kripke Structures 16

3.2 Nondeterminism and Inputs 17

3.3 First-Order Logic and Symbolic Representations 18

3.4 Boolean Encoding 22

3.5 Modeling Digital Circuits 23

3.6 Modeling Programs 26

3.7 Fairness 33

4 Temporal Logic 37

4.1 The Computation Tree Logic CTL* 37

4.2 Syntax and Semantics of CTL* 39

4.3 Temporal Logics Based on CTL* 43

4.4 Temporal Logic with Set Atomic Propositions and Set Semantics 47

4.5	Fairness	47
4.6	Counterexamples	48
4.7	Safety and Liveness Properties	50

5 CTL Model Checking — 53

5.1	Explicit-State CTL Model Checking	53
5.2	Model-Checking CTL with Fairness Constraints	58
5.3	CTL Model Checking via Fixpoint Computation	60

6 LTL and CTL* Model Checking — 71

6.1	The Tableau Construction	72
6.2	LTL Model Checking with Tableau	74
6.3	Correctness Proof of the Tableau Construction	76
6.4	CTL* Model Checking	80

7 Automata on Infinite Words and LTL Model Checking — 85

7.1	Finite Automata on Finite Words	85
7.2	Automata on Infinite Words	87
7.3	Deterministic versus Nondeterministic Büchi Automata	88
7.4	Intersection of Büchi Automata	89
7.5	Checking Emptiness	91
7.6	Generalized Büchi Automata	95
7.7	Automata and Kripke Structures	96
7.8	Model Checking using Automata	97
7.9	From LTL to Büchi Automata	98
7.10	Efficient Translation of LTL into Automata	100
7.11	On-the-Fly Model Checking	108

8 Binary Decision Diagrams and Symbolic Model Checking — 113

8.1	Representing Boolean Formulas	113
8.2	Representing Kripke Structures with OBDDs	119
8.3	Symbolic Model Checking for CTL	121
8.4	Fairness in Symbolic Model Checking	124
8.5	Counterexamples and Witnesses	125
8.6	Relational Product Computations	128

9 Propositional Satisfiability — 137

9.1	Conjunctive Normal Form	137
9.2	Encoding Propositional Logic into CNF	139
9.3	Propositional Satisfiability using Binary Search	140

	9.4	Boolean Constraint Propagation (BCP)	144
	9.5	Conflict-Driven Clause Learning	145
	9.6	Decision Heuristics	148
10	**SAT-Based Model Checking**		**153**
	10.1	Bounded Model Checking	153
	10.2	Verifying Reachability Properties with k-Induction	161
	10.3	Model Checking with Inductive Invariants	164
	10.4	Model Checking with Craig Interpolants	165
	10.5	Property-Directed Reachability	170
11	**Equivalences and Preorders between Structures**		**177**
	11.1	Bisimulation Equivalence	177
	11.2	Fair Bisimulation	182
	11.3	Preorders between Structures	182
	11.4	Games for Bisimulation and Simulation	185
	11.5	Equivalence and Preorder Algorithms	186
12	**Partial Order Reduction**		**189**
	12.1	Concurrency in Asynchronous Systems	190
	12.2	Independence and Invisibility	192
	12.3	Partial Order Reduction for LTL_{-X}	195
	12.4	An Example	199
	12.5	Calculating Ample Sets	202
	12.6	Correctness of the Algorithm	207
	12.7	Partial Order Reduction in SPIN	211
13	**Abstraction**		**219**
	13.1	Existential Abstraction	220
	13.2	Computation of Abstract Models	226
	13.3	Counterexample-Guided Abstraction Refinement (CEGAR)	231
14	**Software Model Checking**		**241**
	14.1	Representing Programs as Control-Flow Graphs	241
	14.2	Checking Assertions using Symbolic Execution	242
	14.3	Program Verification with Predicate Abstraction	244
	14.4	A Full Example	248
15	**Verification with Automata Learning**		**257**
	15.1	Angluin's L^* Learning Algorithm	257

15.2 Compositional Reasoning   260

15.3 Assume-Guarantee Reasoning for Communicating Components   262

15.4 Black Box Checking   270

16   Model Checking for the μ-Calculus   277

16.1 Introduction   277

16.2 The Propositional μ-Calculus   277

16.3 Evaluating Fixpoint Formulas   281

16.4 Representing μ-Calculus Formulas using OBDDs   284

16.5 Translating CTL into the μ-Calculus   287

17   Symmetry   291

17.1 Groups and Symmetry   291

17.2 Quotient Models   294

17.3 Model Checking with Symmetry   297

17.4 Complexity Issues   299

17.5 Empirical Results   303

18   Infinite Families of Finite-State Systems   307

18.1 Temporal Logic for Infinite Families   307

18.2 Invariants   308

18.3 Futurebus+ Example Reconsidered   310

18.4 Graph and Network Grammars   313

18.5 Undecidability Result for a Family of Token Rings   323

19   Discrete Real-Time and Quantitative Temporal Analysis   329

19.1 Real-Time Systems and Rate-Monotonic Scheduling   329

19.2 Model-Checking Real-Time Systems   330

19.3 RTCTL Model Checking   331

19.4 Quantitative Temporal Analysis: Minimum/Maximum Delay   332

19.5 Example: An Aircraft Controller   335

20   Continuous Real Time   341

20.1 Timed Automata   342

20.2 Parallel Composition   344

20.3 Modeling with Timed Automata   345

20.4 Clock Regions   346

20.5 Clock Zones   354

20.6 Difference-Bound Matrices   360

20.7 Complexity Considerations   364

Bibliography   367

Index   399

List of Figures

3.1   Synchronous modulo 8 counter   24

3.2   Reachable states of Kripke structure for mutual exclusion example   32

4.1   Computation trees   38

4.2   Illustration of temporal operators   39

4.3   A Kripke structure that satisfies neither $\mathbf{EX}\,p$ nor $\neg\,\mathbf{EX}\,p$ 42

4.4   The logic CTL* and its sublogics   43

4.5   Basic CTL operators   44

4.6   Counterexamples for LTL   50

5.1   Procedure for labeling the states satisfying $\mathbf{E}(f_1\,\mathbf{U}\,f_2)$ 54

5.2   Procedure for labeling the states satisfying $\mathbf{EG}\,f_1$ 56

5.3   Microwave oven example   57

5.4   Procedure for computing least fixpoints   62

5.5   Procedure for computing greatest fixpoints   63

5.6   Illustration of the computation of the set of reachable states using the post image   64

5.7   Procedure for reachability analysis for checking $\mathbf{AG}\,p$ 64

5.8   Sequence of approximations for $\mathbf{E}(p\,\mathbf{U}\,q)$ 66

6.1   Tableau for $(\neg heat)\,\mathbf{U}\,close$ 74

6.2   The product P of the microwave M and the tableau T 76

6.3   Procedure for computing the set of states satisfying the CTL* formula $g = \mathbf{E}\,g_1$ 82

7.1   A finite automaton   86

7.2   An automaton for words with finitely many a's   89

7.3 An automaton for an infinite number of a's and an automaton for an infinite number of b's   90

7.4 An automaton for words with an infinite number of a's and b's   90

7.5 The double DFS algorithm   93

7.6 Cases **2a** and **2b** in the proof of theorem 7.8   95

7.7 Transforming a Kripke structure into an automaton   96

7.8 A Büchi automaton specifying mutual exclusion   97

7.9 An eventuality property   97

7.10 A Büchi automaton constructed for the LTL formula $(\neg h) \mathbf{U} c$ 100

7.11 Splitting a node   103

7.12 Efficient translation of LTL to generalized Büchi automaton   103

7.13 Update the set *Closed*   105

7.14 Update and split   105

7.15 Split a node   105

7.16 Creating a successor   106

7.17 The Kripke structure resulting from algorithm *EfficientLTLBuchi* when given the formula $(\neg h) \mathbf{U} c$ 108

8.1 Binary decision tree for a two-bit comparator   114

8.2 OBDD for a two-bit comparator with ordering $a_1 < b_1 < a_2 < b_2$ 116

8.3 OBDD for a two-bit comparator with ordering $a_1 < a_2 < b_1 < b_2$ 117

8.4 Two-state Kripke structure   121

8.5 Witness is in the first strongly connected component   126

8.6 Witness spans three strongly connected components   127

8.7 Relational product algorithm   129

8.8 Algorithm for variable elimination   134

9.1 Procedure for binary search for a satisfying assignment for a given CNF C, implemented using a recursive call   141

9.2 Search tree for equation 9.6 with traversal using decisions $x_1 \mapsto 0$ and $x_2 \mapsto 1$ 142

9.3 Procedure for binary search for a satisfying assignment for a given CNF C, implemented using a trail   143

9.4 Algorithm for Boolean constraint propagation (BCP)   145

9.5 Implication graph for the clauses given as equation 9.8   146

9.6 Algorithm for computing a conflict clause   147

9.7 The resolution proof for justifying the conflict clause $\bar{x}_3\bar{x}_5$ generated by *Analyze-Conflict* for the implication graph given as figure 9.5 148

10.1 Application of bounded model checking (BMC) 154

10.2 Model with diameter 2 160

10.3 Model for illustration of the *k*-induction principle 161

10.4 A resolution proof for equation 10.10 167

10.5 Example for an application of McMillan's interpolation system 167

10.6 Procedure for reachability checking using overapproximating post-image computation with Craig interpolation 169

10.7 Illustration of frames $F_0, \ldots, F_k$, which are subsets of S, for $k = 2$ 171

10.8 Main loop of property-directed reachability (PDR) 172

10.9 Procedure for adding another frame in PDR 173

10.10 Procedure for removing counterexamples to induction in PDR 173

10.11 Propagation of clauses into other frames 173

10.12 Illustration of removal of counterexamples to induction, with $k = 2$ 174

11.1 Unwinding preserves bisimulation 178

11.2 Duplication preserves bisimulation 178

11.3 Two nonbisimilar structures 179

11.4 Simulation equivalent structures that are not bisimilar 185

12.1 Executing three independent transitions 191

12.2 Depth-first search with partial order reduction 192

12.3 Execution of independent transitions 193

12.4 Two stuttering-equivalent paths 194

12.5 Transition α commutes with $\beta_0\beta_1 \ldots \beta_m$ 197

12.6 Two concurrent processes 198

12.7 Full and reduced state graph 198

12.8 Diagram illustrating problem 2 199

12.9 Full and reduced (thick lines) state graph for a mutual exclusion program 201

12.10 Code for checking condition **C1** for the enabled transitions of a process P_i 206

12.11 Code for checking whether the transitions in the given set are invisible 206

12.12 Code for testing whether the execution of a transition in a given set is still on the search stack 206

12.13 *ample*(s) tries to find a process P_i such that $T_i(s)$ satisfies conditions **C0–C3** 207

12.14   Conditionals and loops in SPIN   212

12.15   The leader election protocol in PROMELA   216

12.16   The never claim for the specification   217

13.1   Existential abstraction   221

13.2   Two concrete states and a data abstraction   225

13.3   Netlist of original circuit with a cut and after localization reduction   232

13.4   Abstraction of a US traffic light   232

13.5   The abstract path in $\widehat{M}$ is spurious   233

13.6   An abstract counterexample   235

13.7   *SplitPATH* checks if an abstract path is spurious   236

14.1   A small program and its control-flow graph   242

14.2   Procedure for searching for a feasible path to the error location ℓ in the
           program given as CFG G using symbolic execution   244

14.3   A Boolean program with two Boolean variables b_1 and b_2 245

14.4   The two traces of the program in figure 14.3   246

14.5   Procedure for computing the initial predicate abstraction of a program given
           as a CFG   248

14.6   Procedure for checking assertions in a program given as a CFG using
           counterexample-guided abstraction refinement   249

14.7   Procedure for refining the abstraction during counterexample-guided
           abstraction refinement   249

14.8   Program fragment for processing incoming data   250

14.9   CFG of the running example   251

14.10 Program fragment after instrumenting the specification automaton   254

14.11 Predicate abstraction of the program in figure 14.10   255

15.1   The L^* algorithm   259

15.2   The initial table   260

15.3   The second table   260

15.4   The automaton derived from the second table   260

15.5   The third table   261

15.6   The fourth table   261

15.7   Minimal DFA for $L = a^*b^+$, derived from the fourth table   261

15.8   LTSs describing the *In* and *Out* components and the *Order* property   265

15.9   Incremental compositional verification during iteration i 267

15.10   The composed LTS   268

15.11   Table T_1 269

15.12   Table T_2 269

15.13   Assumption A_1, corresponding to table T_2 269

15.14   Table T_3 269

15.15   Table T_4 269

15.16   Assumption A_2, corresponding to table T_4 270

15.17   Procedure *unSeparated*   274

15.18   Algorithm for black box checking   275

16.1   A modified Kripke structure   280

16.2   Pseudocode for the naïve algorithm   282

16.3   Pseudocode for the Emerson and Lei algorithm   285

16.4   Pseudocode for the function *FIX*   286

17.1   A process component   293

17.2   The Kripke structure for $Q\|P$ 293

17.3   The quotient model for $Q\|P$ 295

17.4   Exploring state space in the presence of symmetry   298

17.5   Two isomorphic graphs   301

17.6   System structure   304

18.1   A process component   309

18.2   The Kripke structure for $Q\|P$ 310

18.3   The Kripke structure for $Q\|P\|P$ 311

18.4   Command part for the process P 312

18.5   Command part for the invariant P' 312

18.6   Rules for the graph grammar   314

18.7   Derivation of a ring of size 3   315

18.8   The network grammar G for binary trees   316

18.9   Internal node of the tree   318

18.10   The signals for process `inter`   318

18.11   Automaton for parity   319

18.12   Automaton for ready   320

18.13   Process P_i 324

18.14   Simulation program for process P_i for $i \geq 1$ 324

18.15   Counting program for process P_0 325

18.16   Counting program for process P_i for $i \geq 1$ 325

19.1   Minimum delay algorithm   333

19.2   Maximum delay algorithm   333

19.3   Timing requirements for the aircraft controller   336

19.4   Aircraft controller schedulability results   338

20.1   A simple timed automaton   342

20.2   A manufacturing example   345

20.3   Timed automaton for D-Robot   346

20.4   Timed automaton for G-Robot   347

20.5   Timed automaton for processing station   348

20.6   Timed automaton for box   349

20.7   Clock region example   350

20.8   The clock zones φ and $\varphi^{\Uparrow}$ 356

Foreword

It is widely agreed that the main obstacle to "help computers help us more" and relegate to these helpful partners even more complex and sensitive tasks is not inadequate speed and unsatisfactory raw computing power in the existing machines but, rather, our limited ability to design and implement complex systems with sufficiently high degree of confidence in their correctness under all circumstances.

This problem of *design validation*—ensuring the correctness of the design at the earliest stage possible—is a major challenge in any responsible system development process, and the activities intended for its solution occupy an ever increasing portions of the development cycle cost and time budgets.

The currently practiced methods for design validation in most sites are still the veteran techniques of *simulation* and *testing*. Although provably effective in the very early stages of debugging, when the design is still infested with multiple bugs, their effectiveness drops quickly as the design becomes cleaner, and they require an alarmingly increasing amount of time to uncover the more subtle bugs. A serious problem with these techniques is that one is never sure when they have reached their limits or even an estimate of how many bugs may still lurk in the design. As the complexity of designs drastically increases, say from having .5 million gates per chip to advanced designs with 5 million gates per chip, some far-seeing managers foresee the complete collapse of these conventional methods and their total inability to scale up.

A very attractive and increasingly appealing alternative to simulation and testing is the approach of *formal verification*, which is the main topic of this book. While simulation and testing explore *some* of the possible behaviors and scenarios of the system, leaving open the question of whether the unexplored trajectories may contain the fatal bug, formal verification conducts an *exhaustive exploration* of all possible behaviors. Thus, when a design is pronounced correct by a formal verification method, it implies that all behaviors have been explored, and the questions of adequate coverage or a missed behavior become irrelevant.

Several approaches to formal verification have been proposed over the years. This book concentrates on the method of *model checking* by which a desired behavioral property of a reactive system is verified over a given system (the model) through exhaustive enumeration (explicit or implicit) of all the states reachable by the system and the behaviors that traverse through them.

Compared to other approaches, the *model checking* method enjoys two remarkable advantages:

- It is fully automatic, and its application requires no user supervision or expertise in mathematical disciplines such as logic and theorem proving. Anyone who can run simulations of a design is fully qualified and capable of model-checking the same design. In the context of currently practiced techniques, model checking can be viewed as the ultimately superior simulation tool.
- When the design fails to satisfy a desired property, the process of model checking always produces a *counterexample* that demonstrates a behavior that falsifies the property. This faulty trace provides a priceless insight to understanding the real reason for the failure as well as important clues for fixing the problem.

These two significant advantages and the advent of *symbolic model checking*, which allows exhaustive implicit enumeration of an astronomic number of states, completely revolutionized the field of formal verification and transformed it from a purely academic discipline into a viable practical technique that can potentially be integrated as an additional valuable method for design validation within many industrial development processes.

An ample evidence of the wide industrial recognition of the great practical potential of model-checking is provided by the large number of researchers and developers who work on the development of in-house model checkers and their applications within most of the advanced semi-conductors and processor manufacturers big companies.

We are very fortunate that finally a definitive textbook on the principles and methods of model checking is available, written by authors who helped conceive the idea of model checking in the first place, and followed it through with impressive ingenuity and perseverance until it became the amazing success story it is.

I am fully confident that this textbook will provide an excellent reference and introduction to many readers, students, and practitioners who are interested in the exciting promising discipline of formal verification and its implementation by model checking.

Amir Pnueli

1 Introduction to the Second Edition

When the first edition of this book appeared in print in 1999, the history of model checking was half as long and the number of research papers and tools was an order of magnitude smaller than they are now. Although model checking had achieved significant breakthroughs by 1999, it was still considered new among more traditional approaches to verification, such as theorem proving and testing. A series of game-changing ideas, including symbolic model checking and partial order reduction, had made it possible, for the first time, to verify large finite-state systems and attracted significant interest from the hardware industry. The paradigmatic tools from this era, such as SMV and SPIN, are still in use, and their clean and simple concepts have been shaping the research agenda in model checking ever since. Although even the first edition of this book was not able to cover all research directions in model checking, we do believe it reflected the state of the art comprehensively and made a significant contribution to the unity of the field.

Today, almost two decades later, model checking has established itself as a mature research discipline with hundreds of research papers every year and an abundance of practical tools from academia and industry. Model checking has learned from and contributed to a large variety of foundational and applied disciplines, including software engineering, programming languages, abstract interpretation, SAT and SMT solvers, theorem proving, automata theory, hardware design, testing, cyberphysical systems, and even systems biology. It is impossible to cover model checking in a single volume, not to mention a one-semester course. This provides evidence for the enormous success of model checking but also makes it a challenge to select material for the second edition of this book. Model checking now has many facets and is frequently combined with other paradigms. It is thus more important than ever to have a common basis for new researchers to start their journey into model checking.

Our idea for the second edition, therefore, is to focus on the material that we consider the core of our research field, and that we are using as the syllabus for our own model-checking courses at advanced undergraduate and beginning graduate levels. Thus, the book retains its previous focus on the foundations of temporal logic model checking. However, chapters have been reorganized and extended according to our current view of the material. We have also added new chapters on topics that did not exist in 1999: propositional satisfiability, SAT-based model checking, counterexample-guided abstraction refinement, and software model checking. Chapters 16–20 remained unchanged. Each covers some basic background on a subject, which may be useful to newcomers to the area. However, their full update is beyond the scope of this book.

We hope that this collection of topics will enable the reader to acquire a thorough mastery of the foundations of model checking, and to navigate the current research landscape.

The authors would like to thank those who read and commented on earlier drafts of the second edition of this book: Parosh Abdulla, Armin Biere, Hana Chockler, Rance Cleaveland, Alain Finkel, Eugene Goldberg, Ganesh Gopalakrishnan, Matthias Güdemann, Arie Gurfinkel, Martin Lange, Daniel Le Berre, Sharad Malik, Ruben Martins, Thomas Melham, Kedar Namjoshi, Corina Pasareanu, Karem Sakallah, Ofer Strichman, Tom van Dijk, Yakir Vizel, Thomas Wahl, and Trish Watson.

2 Introduction to the First Edition

Model checking is an automatic technique for verifying finite state concurrent systems. It has a number of advantages over traditional approaches to this problem that are based on simulation, testing, and deductive reasoning. The method has been used successfully in practice to verify complex sequential circuit designs and communication protocols. The main challenge in model checking is dealing with the *state space explosion* problem. This problem occurs in systems with many components that can interact with each other or systems that have data structures that can assume many different values (for example, the data path of a circuit). In such cases the number of global states can be enormous. During the past ten years considerable progress has been made in dealing with this problem. In this chapter we compare model checking with other formal methods for verifying hardware and software designs. We describe how model checking is used to verify complex system designs. We also trace the development of different model checking algorithms and discuss various approaches that have been proposed for dealing with the state explosion problem.

2.1 The Need for Formal Methods

Today, hardware and software systems are widely used in applications where failure is unacceptable: electronic commerce, telephone switching networks, highway and air traffic control systems, medical instruments, and other examples too numerous to list. We frequently read of incidents where some failure is caused by an error in a hardware or software system. A recent example of such a failure is the Ariane 5 rocket, which exploded on June 4th, 1996, less than 40 seconds after it was launched. The committee that investigated the accident found that it was caused by a software error in the computer that was responsible for calculating the rocket's movement. During the launch, an exception occurred when a large 64 bit floating point number was converted to a 16 bit signed integer. This conversion was not protected by code for handling exceptions and caused the computer to fail. The same error also caused the backup computer to fail. As a result incorrect altitude data was transmitted to the on-board computer, which caused the destruction of the rocket. The team investigating the failure suggested that several measures be taken in order to prevent similar incidents in the future, including the verification of the Ariane 5 software.

Clearly, the need for reliable hardware and software systems is critical. As the involvement of such systems in our lives increases, so too does the burden for ensuring their correctness. Unfortunately, it is no longer feasible to shut down a malfunctioning system in order to restore safety. We are very much dependent on such systems for continuous operation; in fact, in some cases, devices are less safe when they are shut down. Even when failure is not life-threatening, the consequences of having to replace critical code or circuitry can be economically devastating.

Due to the success of the *Internet* and *embedded systems* in automobiles, airplanes, and other safety critical systems, we are likely to become even more dependent on the proper functioning of computing devices in the future. In fact, the pace of change will likely accelerate in coming years. Because of this rapid growth in technology, it will become even more important to develop methods that increase our confidence in the correctness of such systems.

2.2   Hardware and Software Verification

The principal validation methods for complex systems are simulation, testing, deductive verification, and model checking. Simulation and testing [389] both involve making experiments before deploying the system in the field. While simulation is performed on an abstraction or a model of the system, testing is performed on the actual product. In the case of circuits, simulation is performed on the design of the circuit, while testing is performed on the circuit itself. In both cases, these methods typically inject signals at certain points in the system and observe the resulting signals at other points. For software, simulation and testing usually involve providing certain inputs and observing the corresponding outputs. These methods can be a cost-efficient way to find many errors. However, checking *all* of the possible interactions and potential pitfalls using simulation and testing techniques is rarely possible.

The term *deductive verification* normally refers to the use of axioms and proof rules to prove the correctness of systems. In early research on deductive verification, the main focus was on guaranteeing the correctness of critical systems. It was assumed that the importance of their correct behavior was so great, that the developer, or a verification expert (usually a mathematician or a logician) would spend whatever time was required for verifying the system. Initially, such proofs were constructed entirely by hand. Eventually, researchers realized that software tools could be developed to enforce the correct use of axioms and proof rules. Such tools can also apply a systematic search to suggest various ways to progress from the current stage of the proof.

The importance of deductive verification is widely recognized by computer scientists. It has significantly influenced the area of software development (for example, the notion of an *invariant* originated in research on deductive verification). However, deductive verification is a time-consuming process that can only be performed by experts who are educated in logical reasoning and have considerable experience. The proof of a single protocol or circuit can last days or months. Consequently, use of deductive verification is rare. It is applied primarily to highly sensitive systems such as *security protocols*, where enough resources need to be invested to guarantee their safe usage.

Also, it is important to realize that some mathematical tasks cannot be performed by an algorithm. The theory of *computability* [276] provides limitations on what can be decided by an algorithm. In particular, it shows that there cannot be an algorithm that decides whether an arbitrary computer program (written in some programming language like C or Pascal) terminates. This immediately limits what can be verified automatically. In particular, correct termination of programs cannot be verified automatically in general. Thus, most proof systems cannot be completely automated.

An advantage of deductive verification is that it can be used for reasoning about infinite state systems. This task can be automated to a limited extent. However, even if the property to be verified is true, no limit can be placed on the amount of time or memory that may be needed in order to find a proof.

Model checking is a technique for verifying finite state concurrent systems. One benefit of this restriction is that verification can be performed automatically. The procedure normally uses an exhaustive search of the state space of the system to determine if some specification is true or not. Given sufficient resources, the procedure will always *terminate* with a **yes/no** answer. Moreover, it can be implemented by algorithms with reasonable efficiency, which can be run on moderate-sized machines.

Although the restriction to finite state systems may seem to be a major disadvantage, model checking is applicable to several very important classes of systems. Hardware controllers are finite state systems, and so are many communication protocols. In some cases, systems that are not finite state may be verified using model checking in combination with various abstraction and induction principles. Finally, in many cases errors can be found by restricting unbounded data structures to specific instances that are finite state. For example, programs with unbounded message queues can be debugged by restricting the size of the queues to a small number like two or three.

Since model checking can be performed automatically, it is preferable to deductive verification whenever it can be applied. However, there will always be some critical applications in which theorem proving is necessary for complete verification. An exciting research direction [420] attempts to integrate deductive verification and model checking, so that the finite state parts of a complex system can be verified automatically.

2.3   The Process of Model Checking

Applying model checking to a design consists of several tasks, each of which will be discussed in detail later in this book.

Modeling   The first task is to convert a design into a formalism accepted by a model checking tool. In many cases, this is simply a compilation task. In other cases, due to limitations on time and memory, the modeling of a design may require the use of abstraction to eliminate irrelevant or unimportant details.

Specification   Before verification, it is necessary to state the properties that the design must satisfy. The specification is usually given in some logical formalism. For hardware and software systems, it is common to use *temporal logic*, which can assert how the behavior of the system evolves over time.

An important issue in specification is *completeness*. While, model checking provides means for checking that a model of the design satisfies a given specification, it is impossible to determine whether the given specification covers all the properties that the system should satisfy.

Verification   Ideally the verification is completely automatic. However, in practice it often involves human assistance. One such manual activity is the analysis of the verification results. In case of a negative result, the user is often provided with an error trace. This can be used as a counterexample for the checked property and can help the designer in tracking down where the error occurred. In this case, analyzing the error trace may require a modification to the system and reapplication of the model checking algorithm.

An error trace can also result from incorrect modeling of the system or from an incorrect specification (often called a *false negative*). The error trace can be useful in identifying and fixing these two problems. A final possibility is that the verification task will fail to terminate normally, due to the size of the model, which is too large to fit into the computer memory. In this case, it may be necessary to redo the verification after changing some of the parameters of the model checker or by adjusting the model (for example, by using additional abstractions).

2.4   Temporal Logic and Model Checking

Temporal logics have proved to be useful for specifying concurrent systems, because they can describe the ordering of events in time without introducing time explicitly. They were originally developed by philosophers for investigating the way that time is used in natural language arguments [281]. Although a number of different temporal logics have been studied, most have an operator like $\mathbf{G}\, f$ that is true in the present if f is always true in the future (that is, if f is globally true). To assert that two events e_1 and e_2 never occur at the same time, one would write $\mathbf{G}(\neg e_1 \vee \neg e_2)$. Temporal logics are often classified according to whether time is assumed to have a *linear* or a *branching* structure. In this book the meaning of a temporal logic formula will always be determined with respect to a labeled state-transition graph; such structures are called *Kripke structures* [281].

Several people, including Burstall [95], Kröger [314] and Pnueli [410], all proposed using temporal logic for reasoning about computer programs. However, Pnueli [410] was the first to use temporal logic for reasoning about concurrency. His approach involved proving properties of the program under consideration from a set of axioms that described the behavior of the individual statements in the program. The method was extended to sequential circuits by Bochmann [67] and Malachi and Owicki [359]. Since proofs were constructed by hand, the technique was often difficult to use in practice.

The introduction of temporal logic model checking algorithms by Clarke and Emerson [121, 196] in the early 1980's allowed this type of reasoning to be automated. Since checking that a single model satisfies a formula is much easier than proving the validity of a formula for all models, it was possible to implement this technique very efficiently. The algorithm developed by Clarke and Emerson for the branching-time logic CTL was polynomial in both the size of the model determined by the program under consideration and in the length of its specification in temporal logic. They also showed how *fairness* [229] could be handled without changing the complexity of the algorithm. This was an important step since the correctness of many concurrent programs depends on some type of fairness assumption; for example, absence of starvation in a mutual exclusion algorithm may depend on the assumption that each process makes progress infinitely often.

At roughly the same time Queille and Sifakis [418] gave a model checking algorithm for a subset of CTL, but they did not analyze its complexity. Later Clarke, Emerson, and Sistla [123] devised an improved algorithm that was linear in the product of the length of the formula and the size of the state transition graph. The algorithm was implemented in the EMC model checker, which was widely distributed and used to check a number of network protocols and sequential circuits [79, 80, 81, 82, 123, 182, 385]. Early model checking systems were able to check state transition graphs with between 10^4 and 10^5 states at a rate of about 100 states per second for typical formulas. In spite of these limitations, model checking systems were used successfully to find previously unknown errors in several published circuit designs.

Sistla and Clarke [445, 446] analyzed the model checking problem for a variety of temporal logics and showed, in particular, that for linear temporal logic (LTL) the problem was PSPACE-complete. Pnueli and Lichtenstein [347] reanalyzed the complexity of checking linear-time formulas and discovered that although the complexity appears exponential in the length of the formula, it is linear in the size of the global state graph. Based on this observation, they argued that the high complexity of linear-time model checking might still be acceptable for short formulas. The same year, Fujita [228] implemented a tableau based verification system for LTL formulas and showed how it could be used for hardware verification.

CTL* is a very expressive logic that combines both branching-time and linear-time operators. The model checking problem for this logic was first considered in [122] where it was shown to be PSPACE-complete, establishing that it is in the same general complexity class as the model checking problem for LTL. This result can be sharpened to show that CTL* and LTL model checking are of the same algorithmic complexity (up to a constant factor) in both the size of the state graph and the size of the formula. Thus, for purposes of model checking, there is no practical complexity advantage to restricting oneself to a linear temporal logic [204].

Alternative techniques for verifying concurrent systems have been proposed by a number of other researchers. Many of these approaches use automata for specifications as well as for implementations. The implementation is checked to see whether its behavior conforms to that of the specification. Because the same type of model is used for both implementation and specification, an implementation at one level can also be used as a specification for the next level of refinement. The use of language containment is implicit in the work of Kurshan [11], which ultimately resulted in the development of a powerful verifier called COSPAN [259, 324, 257]. Vardi and Wolper [471] first proposed the use of ω-automata (automata over infinite words) for automated verification. They showed how the linear temporal logic model checking problem could be formulated in terms of language containment between ω-automata. Other notions of conformance between the automata have also been considered, including observational equivalence [146, 381, 426], and various refinement relations [146, 380, 425].

2.5   Symbolic Algorithms

In the original implementation of the model checking algorithm, transition relations were represented explicitly by adjacency lists. For concurrent systems with small numbers of processes, the number of states was usually fairly small, and the approach was often quite practical. In systems with many concurrent parts however, the number of states in the global state transition graph was too large to handle. In the fall of 1987, McMillan [94, 369], then a graduate student at Carnegie Mellon, realized that by using a symbolic representation for the state transition graphs, much larger systems could be verified. The new symbolic representation was based on Bryant's *ordered binary decision diagrams* (OBDDs) [85]. OBDDs provide a canonical form for Boolean formulas that is often substantially more compact than conjunctive or disjunctive normal form, and very efficient algorithms have been developed for manipulating them. Because the symbolic representation captures some of the regularity in the state space determined by circuits and protocols, it is possible to verify systems with an extremely large number of states—many orders of magnitude larger than could be handled by the explicit-state algorithms. By using the original CTL model checking algorithm [121] of Clarke and Emerson with the new representation for state transition graphs, it became possible to verify some examples that had more than 10^{20} states [94, 369]. Since then, various refinements of the OBDD-based techniques by other researchers have pushed the state count up to more than 10^{120} [92, 93].

The implicit representation is quite natural for modeling sequential circuits and protocols. Each state is encoded by an assignment of Boolean values to the set of state variables associated with the circuit or protocol. The transition relation can, therefore, be expressed as a Boolean formula in terms of two sets of variables, one set encoding the old state and the other encoding the new. This formula is then represented by a binary decision diagram. The model checking algorithm is based on computing fixpoints of *predicate transformers* that are obtained from the transition relation. The fixpoints are sets of states that represent various temporal properties of the concurrent system. In the new implementations, both the predicate transformers and the fixpoints are represented with OBDDs. Thus, it is possible to avoid explicitly constructing the state graph of the concurrent system.

The model checking system that McMillan developed is called SMV [369]. It is based on a language for describing hierarchical finite-state concurrent systems. Programs in the language can be annotated by specifications expressed in temporal logic. The model checker extracts a transition system represented as an OBDD from a program in the SMV language and uses an OBDD-based search algorithm to determine whether the system satisfies its specification. If the transition system does not satisfy some specification, the verifier will produce an execution trace that shows why the specification is false. The SMV system has been widely distributed, and a large number of examples have now been verified with it. These examples provide convincing evidence that SMV can be used to debug real industrial designs.

An impressive example that illustrates the power of symbolic model checking is the verification of the cache coherence protocol described in the IEEE Futurebus+ standard (IEEE Standard 896.1-1991). Although development of the Futurebus+ cache coherence protocol began in 1988, all previous attempts to validate the protocol were based entirely on informal techniques. In the summer of 1992 researchers at Carnegie Mellon [127, 354] constructed a precise model of the protocol in SMV language and then used SMV to show that the resulting transition system satisfied a formal specification of cache coherence. They were able to find a number of previously undetected errors and potential errors in the design of the protocol. This appears to be the first time that an automatic verification tool has been used to find errors in an IEEE standard.

One of the best indications of the power of the symbolic verification methods comes from studying how the CPU time required for verification grows asymptotically with larger and larger instances of the circuit or protocol. In many of the examples that have been considered by a variety of groups, this growth rate is a small polynomial in the number of components of the circuit [43, 92, 93].

A number of other researchers have independently discovered that OBDDs can be used to represent large state-transition systems. Coudert, Berthet, and Madre [156] have developed an algorithm for showing equivalence between two deterministic finite-state automata by performing a breadth first search of the state space of the product automata. They use OBDDs to represent the transition functions of the two automata in their algorithm. Similar algorithms have been developed by Pixley [407, 408, 409]. In addition, several groups including Bose and Fisher [71], Pixley [407], and Coudert et al. [157] have experimented with model checking algorithms that use OBDDs.

In related work Bryant, Seger and Beatty [43, 88] have developed an algorithm based on symbolic simulation for model checking in a restricted linear time logic. Specifications consist of precondition–postcondition pairs expressed in the logic. The precondition is used to restrict inputs and initial states of the circuit; the postcondition gives the property that the user wishes to check. Formulas in the logic have the form

$$p_0 \wedge \mathbf{X}p_1 \wedge \mathbf{X}^2 p_2 \wedge \cdots \wedge \mathbf{X}^{n-1} p_{n-1} \wedge \mathbf{X}^n p_n.$$

The syntax of the formulas is highly restricted compared to most other temporal logics used for specifying programs and circuits. In particular, the only logical operator that is allowed is conjunction, and the only temporal operator is *next time* (**X**). By limiting the class of formulas that can be handled, it is possible to check certain properties very efficiently.

2.6 Partial Order Reduction

Verifying software causes some problems for model checking. Software tends to be less structured than hardware. In addition, concurrent software is usually *asynchronous*, that is, most of the activities taken by different processes are performed independently, without a global synchronizing clock. For these reasons, the state explosion phenomenon is a particularly serious problem for software. Consequently, model checking has been used less frequently for software verification than for hardware verification. Recently, considerable progress has been made on the state explosion problem for software. The most successful techniques for dealing with this problem are based on the *partial order reduction* [244, 398, 465]. These techniques exploit the independence of concurrently executed events. Two events are *independent* of each other when executing them in either order results in the same global state.

A common model for representing concurrent software is the *interleaving model*, in which all of the events in a single execution are arranged in a linear order called an *interleaving sequence*. Concurrently executed events appear arbitrarily ordered with respect to each other. Most logics for specifying properties of concurrent systems can distinguish between interleaving sequences in which two independent events are executed in different orders. Because of this, all possible interleavings of such events are normally considered. This can result in an extremely large state space.

The partial order reduction techniques make it possible to decrease the number of interleaving sequences that must be considered. As a result, the number of states that are needed for model checking is reduced. When a specification cannot distinguish between two interleaving sequences that differ only by the order in which concurrently executed events are taken, it is sufficient to analyze only one of them. These methods are related to the *partial order model of program execution*. According to this model, concurrently executed events are not ordered. Each partially ordered execution can correspond to multiple interleaving sequences. If it is impossible to distinguish between such sequences, it is sufficient to select one interleaving sequence for each partial ordering of events.

The idea of reducing the state space by selecting only a subset of the ways one can interleave independently executed transitions has been studied by many researchers. One of the first researchers to propose such a reduction technique was Overman [392]. However, he only considered a restricted model of concurrency that did not include looping and nondeterministic choice. The proof system of Katz and Peled [300] suggests using an equivalence relation between interleaving sequences that correspond to the same partially ordered execution. Their system includes proof rules for reasoning about a selection of interleaved sequences rather than all of them. Model checking algorithms that incorporate the partial order reduction are described in several different papers. The *stubborn sets* of Valmari [465], the *persistent sets* of Godefroid [241] and the *ample sets* of Peled [398] differ on the actual details, but contain many similar ideas. In this book we will describe the ample set method. Other methods that exploit similar observations about the relation between the partial and total order models of execution are McMillan's *unfolding technique* [368] and Godefroid's *sleep sets* [241].

2.7   Other Approaches to the State Explosion Problem

While symbolic representations and the partial order reduction have greatly increased the size of the systems that can be verified, many realistic systems are still too large to be handled. Thus, it is important to find techniques that can be used in conjunction with the symbolic methods to extend the size of the systems that can be verified. Four such techniques are compositional reasoning, abstraction, symmetry, and induction.

The first technique exploits the *modular structure* of complex circuits and protocols [141, 247, 249, 289, 290, 336, 413, 443]. Many finite state systems are composed of multiple processes running in parallel. The specifications for such systems can often be decomposed into properties that describe the behavior of small parts of the system. An obvious strategy is to check each of the local properties using only the part of the system that it describes. If it is possible to show that the system satisfies each local property, and if the conjunction of the local properties implies the overall specification, then the complete system must satisfy this specification as well.

When this naive form of compositional reasoning is not feasible because of mutual dependencies between the components, a more complex strategy is necessary. In such cases, when verifying a property of one component we must make assumptions about the behavior of the other components. The assumptions must later be discharged when the correctness of the other components is established. This strategy is called *assume-guarantee reasoning* [249, 289, 290, 386, 413].

The second technique involves using *abstraction*. The symbolic methods make it possible to handle some systems that involve nontrivial data manipulation, but the complexity of verification is often high. The use of abstraction is based on the observation that the specifications of systems that include data elements usually involve fairly simple relationships among the data values in the system. For example, in verifying the addition operation of a microprocessor, we might require that the value in one register is eventually equal to the sum of the values in two other registers. In such situations *abstraction* can be used to reduce the complexity of model checking [47, 133, 163, 164, 323, 486]. The abstraction is usually specified by giving a mapping between the actual data values in the system and a small set of abstract data values. By extending the mapping to states and transitions, it is possible to produce an abstract version of the system under consideration. The abstract system is often much smaller than the actual system, and as a result, it is usually much simpler to verify properties at the abstract level.

Symmetry can also be used to reduce the state explosion problem [125, 211, 279, 283]. Finite state concurrent systems frequently contain replicated components. For example, a large number of protocols involve a network of identical processes communicating in some fashion. Hardware devices contain parts such as memories and register files that have many replicated elements. These facts can be used to obtain reduced models for the system. Having symmetry in a system implies the existence of a non-trivial permutation group that preserves the state transition graph. Such a group can be used to define an equivalence relation on the state space of the system, and to reduce the state space. The reduced model can be used to simplify the verification of properties of the original model expressed by a temporal logic formula.

Induction involves reasoning automatically about entire families of finite-state systems [84, 128, 303, 327, 364, 441, 488]. Such families arise frequently in the design of reactive systems in both hardware and software. Typically, circuit and protocol designs are parameterized, that is, they define an infinite family of systems. For example, a circuit designed to add two integers has the width of the integers n as a parameter; a bus protocol may be designed to accommodate an arbitrary number of processors, and a mutual exclusion protocol can be given for a parameterized number of processes. We would like to be able to check that every system in a given family satisfies some temporal logic property. In general the problem is undecidable [28, 455], but in many interesting cases, it is possible to provide a form of *invariant process* that represents the behavior of an arbitrary member of the family. Using this invariant, we can then check the property for all of the members of the family at once. An inductive argument is used to verify that the invariant is an appropriate representative.

3 Modeling Systems

The first step in verifying the correctness of a system is *requirements engineering*, that is, specifying the properties that the system should have and understanding at which abstraction level the truth or falsity of these properties can be assessed. Requirements engineering usually starts with informal specifications and models and progresses to formal models and specifications, which facilitate algorithmic verification. Correspondingly, this chapter deals with *formal models*, and the next chapter introduces formal specifications by temporal logic. Suppose, for example, that we want to assure the absence of deadlocks in a given concurrent program. Then we have to provide not only a precise specification for the absence of deadlocks but also a model that adequately represents the concurrent behavior of the system, including, for instance, a notion of atomic operations and assumptions about scheduling policies.

Thus, once we understand which properties are important, the first crucial step is to construct a formal model for the system. In order to be useful for automated verification, the model should capture those aspects of the system that affect the correctness of the properties. On the other hand, the model should abstract away those details that are irrelevant for the specified properties but make verification more complicated. Thus, the formal model should represent the real-life system at a level of abstraction that contains sufficient detail to verify the properties of interest but is simple enough to facilitate algorithmic verification. For example, when modeling synchronous digital circuits, it is useful to reason in terms of gates and Boolean values, rather than actual voltage levels. Likewise, when reasoning about a communication protocol, we may want to focus on the exchange of messages and ignore the textual contents of the messages or the implementation details in a specific operating system or device. Note that in modeling "ignoring" does not imply to forget details but, rather, to use restrictions under which a verification result is applicable to a given real-life system.

Many digital circuits and programs are examples of *reactive systems* [362]. Such systems typically exhibit frequent interactions with their environment and often do not terminate. Therefore, they cannot be understood and modeled adequately by their input–output behavior but, rather, by their internal state. Hence, the most important feature of a reactive system that we need to capture is its *state*. A state is a snapshot or instantaneous description of the system that captures the values of the variables of the system at a particular instant of time. To analyze system behavior we also need to know how the state of the system changes as the result of some action of the system. We can describe the change by associating the state before the action occurs with the system state acquired after the action. Such a pair of states determines a *transition* of the system. Consequently, the behaviors of a reactive system can be defined in terms of its transitions. A *path* is a (possibly infinite) sequence of states where each state is obtained from the previous state by some transition.

We use a type of state transition graph called a *Kripke structure* to capture this intuition about the behavior of reactive systems. A Kripke structure consists of a set of states, a set of transitions between states, and a function that labels each state with a set of properties that are true in this state. Paths in a Kripke structure correspond to behaviors of the system. Although Kripke structures are very simple models, they are sufficiently expressive to capture those aspects of temporal behavior that are most important for reasoning about reactive systems. We discuss ways to specify temporal behaviors of reactive systems in chapter 4.

Real-life system descriptions are usually given in a programming language such as C or Java or a hardware description language (HDL) such as Verilog or VHDL. Given the abundance of programming languages and broad variety of system types (including, for instance, synchronous and asynchronous circuits, programs with shared variables, and programs that communicate by message passing), we need a unifying formalism to model systems. We will use formulas of first-order logic for this purpose. We will argue that it is straightforward to translate a program into a first-order logic representation, and equally straightforward to construct a Kripke structure from a first-order formula.

In the following sections we formally define Kripke structures. We then show how to extract such structures from first-order formulas that represent system descriptions. Finally, we demonstrate how different programming constructs can be formalized with first-order formulas.

3.1   Transition Systems and Kripke Structures

We begin by formalizing *transition systems*. A transition system T is a triple (S, S_0, R) where

1. S is a set of states,
2. $S_0 \subseteq S$ is the set of initial states, and
3. $R \subseteq S \times S$ is a *transition relation*.

We require that the transition relation R must be left total; that is, for every state $s \in S$ there is a successor state $s' \in S$ such that $R(s, s')$.

A *finite path* from some state $s \in S$ is a sequence $s_0, s_1, \ldots, s_n$ such that $s_0 = s$ and $R(s_i, s_{i+1})$ for all $0 \leq i < n$. Similarly, an *infinite path* is an infinite sequence of states $s_0, s_1, \ldots$ such that $R(s_i, s_{i+1})$ for all $i \geq 0$. When we speak of *paths*, we mean both finite and infinite paths. Thus, the notion of paths in this book is the standard notion used in graph theory. Owing to the requirement that R is left total, each finite path can be extended into an infinite path; moreover, each finite path can also be obtained as a prefix of an infinite path.

Throughout most of the book, we will assume that S is finite. In chapters 13, 14, 18, and 20, we deal with infinite-state systems, but the characteristic approach in these chapters is a reduction to finite-state systems. We return to this question later in this chapter.

In order to make observations about particular states, we define a set of *state labels*. We refer to these labels as *atomic propositions* and use AP to denote the set of all atomic propositions. A transition system enriched with such a state-labeling is called a *Kripke structure*. A Kripke structure M is a five-tuple $M = (S, S_0, R, AP, L)$ where

1. S, S_0, and R are defined as above,
2. AP is the set of atomic propositions, and
3. $L : S \to 2^{AP}$ is a function that labels each state with the set of those atomic propositions that are true in that state.

Sometimes we will not be concerned with the set of initial states S_0. In such cases, we will omit this set of states from the definition.

Kripke structures are frequently visualized by means of directed graphs. The states of the Kripke structure form the nodes and the transitions between the states define the edges between the nodes. The state labels are usually annotated on or next to the nodes. As an example, a Kripke structure with $S = \{s_1, s_2, s_3\}$, $S_0 = \{s_1\}$, $R = \{(s_1, s_2), (s_2, s_1), (s_3, s_2)\}$, $AP = \{p, q\}$, and $L = \{s_1 \mapsto \{p\}, s_2 \mapsto \{p, q\}, s_3 \mapsto \emptyset\}$ can be drawn as follows:

Observe that the initial states are identified by an edge without source node.

Concerning the word *model*, a word of caution is in place: in the context of model checking, Kripke structures are often referred to as "models", because they are models of the system under analysis. In logic, however, a Kripke structure M is a model of a specification if M satisfies the specification. Indeed, this logical notion of models gave rise to the name *model checking*. The intended meaning of *model* is usually clear from the context.

3.2 Nondeterminism and Inputs

When modeling systems, we are frequently missing details or refrain from committing to a particular behavior among a range of possible behaviors of the system. The definition above permits transition systems (and thus Kripke structures) in which the transition taken from a given state is not fixed. Formally, this means that there exist two or more successor states for a given state. Similarly, the initial state of the system need not be unique. In either case, we say that the transition system contains *nondeterminism*. Nondeterminism is frequently used to model unknown details about the system itself or the environment the system operates in.

As an example of nondeterminism to model inputs from an environment, consider a model of a light switch as follows. Initially, the light is off. Once a button is pressed, the light is turned on. To turn the light off, the button has to be released and pressed again. We obtain a Kripke structure with four states:

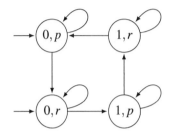

A state is labeled 1 if the light is on and 0 if the light is off. Similarly, we use the label r for states in which the button is released and p for those states in which the button is pressed. As we do not wish to model the person pressing (or releasing) the button, we use nondeterminism as follows:

1. The initial state is nondeterministic: initially, the button may either be pressed or released. This is modeled by means of two initial states.
2. There are nondeterministic transitions, as each of the four states has two successors. As an example, consider the state labeled with $0, r$: to model the case the button is pressed, there is a transition to the state labeled $1, p$. Otherwise, the system remains in state $0, r$ by means of a self-transition.

The use of nondeterminism is not limited to inputs from the environment. We give an example of nondeterminism arising from within the system in section 3.6.2.

3.3   First-Order Logic and Symbolic Representations

In order to abstract from the specific semantics of the programming language or hardware description language used to describe the system, we use first-order formulas to represent the set of initial states and the transition relation. We assume only a basic knowledge of first-order logic. The reader should be familiar with the logical connectives (*and* $\wedge$, *or* $\vee$, *not* $\neg$, *implies* $\rightarrow$, etc.) and should know how universal ($\forall$) and existential ($\exists$) quantification work.

In comparison to the literature in mathematical logic and in program semantics, our use of logic and semantics in this chapter is quite informal. In particular, we are concerned not with first-order theories and axiom systems but with the evaluation of first-order formulas over fixed mathematical structures. Usually, we use first-order logic to describe constraints between program variables. Thus, the program variables appear as first-order variables in the formulas, and the mathematical structures over which the variables are interpreted correspond to the data types of the program variables.

For instance, a program variable of integer type may be interpreted over the natural numbers $\mathbb{N}$ together with the associated operations, or by 32-bit bit-vectors. In the first case, we will obtain a Kripke structure with an infinite state space; in the second case, the state space will be large but finite. Both models are adequate in their own right: the infinite-state model corresponds to an idealized mathematical view as we would find it in an algorithms book, while the finite-state model can accurately represent a real-life C program. It is easy to construct cases where a program is correct in one of the two interpretations but not both.

Technically, we draw our formulas from multi-sorted first-order formulas that are interpreted over fixed first-order structures that correspond to the data types and value domains of the program variables in the natural way. In this chapter, we restrict our attention to simple variable types such as integers and Booleans. We introduce more notions of program semantics as needed.

Since states are instantaneous descriptions of a system, it is natural to identify states with valuations of the system variables. (As we shall see below, the program counter in imperative programs is a special case of such a variable.) To this end, let $V = \{v_1, \ldots, v_n\}$ be the set of system variables, and let D_v be the respective domain of variable v. A *valuation* for the variables V is a function that associates with each variable v in V a value in D_v. Thus, a state is a mapping $s : V \to \bigcup_{v \in V} D_v$.

Let us consider an example with a set $V = \{v_1, v_2, v_3\}$ of variables and domains $D_{v_i} = \mathbb{N}$ for all i. Then the set of states is

$$\mathbb{N} \times \mathbb{N} \times \mathbb{N}$$

or simply $\mathbb{N}^3$. For a given valuation, we can write a formula that is true for exactly that valuation. For instance, the valuation $\langle v_1 \mapsto 2, v_2 \mapsto 3, v_3 \mapsto 5 \rangle$ can be represented by the formula

$$(v_1 = 2) \wedge (v_2 = 3) \wedge (v_3 = 5).$$

In general, a formula may be true for many valuations. If we adopt the convention that a formula precisely represents the set of *all* valuations that make it true, then we can describe certain subsets of the set of states by means of first-order formulas. Thus, a first-order formula can be viewed as the *characteristic function* or *symbolic representation* of a set of states. In particular, the set of *initial states* of the system can be described by a first-order formula $\mathcal{S}_0$ over the variables in V.

Continuing the example from above we now consider the following subset of the set of states:

$$\{ \quad \langle v_1 \mapsto 2, v_2 \mapsto 3, v_3 \mapsto 1 \rangle,$$
$$\langle v_1 \mapsto 2, v_2 \mapsto 3, v_3 \mapsto 2 \rangle,$$
$$\langle v_1 \mapsto 2, v_2 \mapsto 3, v_3 \mapsto 3 \rangle \quad \}$$

This set can be represented by means of a first-order formula with disjunction:

$$((v_1 = 2) \wedge (v_2 = 3) \wedge (v_3 = 1)) \quad \vee$$
$$((v_1 = 2) \wedge (v_2 = 3) \wedge (v_3 = 2)) \quad \vee$$
$$((v_1 = 2) \wedge (v_2 = 3) \wedge (v_3 = 3))$$

Given a first-order formula ϕ with free variables in V, we will write $s \models \phi$ to indicate that s is in the set represented by ϕ.

The use of first-order formulas offers the opportunity to obtain a more compact representation of sets by simplifying the formula. In the example above, we can use the following formula that is logically equivalent to the one above and therefore represents the same set of states:

$$(v_1 = 2) \wedge (v_2 = 3) \wedge (v_3 \geq 1) \wedge (v_3 \leq 3)$$

When using first-order formulas to characterize sets, we can perform the usual set operations by appropriate transformations of the characteristic functions in first-order logic. Let A and B denote subsets of a set S, and let $\mathcal{A}(s)$ and $\mathcal{B}(s)$ over $s \in S$ denote the respective characteristic functions of A and B. Then

$$
\begin{array}{lll}
A \cup B & & \mathcal{A}(s) \vee \mathcal{B}(s) \\
A \cap B & \text{correspond to} & \mathcal{A}(s) \wedge \mathcal{B}(s) \\
S \setminus A & & \neg \mathcal{A}(s).
\end{array}
$$

Similar transformations apply in the case of relational operators over sets. As an instance, we can check $A \subseteq B$ by determining whether the formula $\mathcal{A}(s) \Rightarrow \mathcal{B}(s)$ evaluates to true for all s.

We now show that first-order logic can provide symbolic representations of transition relations, too. To do this, we extend the idea used for symbolic representation of sets of states above. This time, we use a formula to represent a *set of ordered pairs of states*. Since a pair of states refers to two valuations of the system variables, we cannot describe a pair using the variables in V only. Therefore, we create a second set of variables V'. We think of the variables in V as *present state* variables and the variables in V' as *next state* variables. Each variable v in V has a corresponding next state variable in V', which we denote by v'. A valuation for the variables in $V \cup V'$ can be viewed as designating an ordered pair of states or, equivalently, a transition. We can represent sets of these valuations using formulas as above. If $R \subseteq S \times S$ is a transition relation, then we write $\mathcal{R}(V, V')$ to denote a formula that represents it. For instance, the formula

$$(v_1' = v_1) \wedge (v_2' = v_2 + 1)$$

represents a transition relation where v_1 remains constant, v_2 is incremented in each step, and v_3 is unconstrained, that is, nondeterministic. Given a first-order formula ϕ with free variables in $V \cup V'$, we will write $s, s' \models \phi$ to indicate that the pair (s, s') is in the transition relation represented by ϕ.

We will use a similar mechanism to define the set of atomic propositions AP. Recall that AP is a fixed finite set of labels that contain information about the system states. For each label $l \in AP$, we write $s \models l$ to indicate that $l \in L(s)$, and we write $s \not\models l$ to indicate that $l \notin L(s)$. It is important to note, however, that AP can contain labels with a quite complex meaning: essentially, AP can contain arbitrary properties whose truth or falsity is uniquely determined by the state, that is, by the variable valuation. In particular, a label in AP can be a formula of the form $v = d$, where $v \in V$ and $d \in D_v$. A proposition $(v = d)$ will be true in a state s if $s(v) = d$. In this case, we have $(v = d) \in L(s)$; that is, $s \models (v = d)$. More generally, a proposition can be described by a first-order formula with free variables from V. For instance, a more complex proposition can be

$$v_1 > v_2 \wedge v_2 > v_3.$$

When v is a variable over the Boolean domain $\{true, false\}$, it is not necessary to include both $v = true$ and $v = false$ in AP. We will write $s \models v$ to indicate that $s(v) = true$ and $s \models \neg v$ to indicate that $s(v) = false$.

We now show how to derive a Kripke structure $M = (S, S_0, R, AP, L)$ from the first-order formulas S_0 and $\mathcal{R}$ that represent the concurrent system.

- The set of states S is the set of all valuations for V.
- The set of initial states S_0 is the set of all valuations s_0 for V that satisfy the formula S_0; that is, $s_0 \models S_0$.
- Let s and s' be two states; then $R(s, s')$ holds if and only if $s, s' \models \mathcal{R}$.
- The labeling function $L : S \to 2^{AP}$ is defined so that $L(s)$ is the set of all labels that hold true at s, that is, for which $s \models l$.

Since we require the transition relation of a Kripke structure to be total, we extend the relation R if some state s has no successor. By convention, we modify R so that $R(s, s)$ holds in this case.

Example 3.1 *To illustrate the notions defined in this section, we consider a simple system with two variables x and y that range over $D = \{0, 1\}$. Thus, a valuation for the variables x and y is just a pair $(d_1, d_2) \in D \times D$ where d_1 is the value for x and d_2 is the value for y. The system can perform one action, described by*

$$x := (x + y) \bmod 2.$$

The system starts from the state in which $x = 1$ and $y = 1$. This system will be described by two first-order formulas. The set of initial states of the system is represented by

$$\mathcal{S}_0(x,y) \equiv x = 1 \wedge y = 1,$$

and the set of transitions is represented by

$$\mathcal{R}(x,y,x',y') \equiv x' = (x+y) \bmod 2 \wedge y' = y.$$

The Kripke structure $M = (S, S_0, R, AP, L)$ extracted from these formulas is as follows:

- $S = D \times D$.
- $S_0 = \{(1,1)\}$.
- $R = \{((1,1),(0,1)),((0,1),(1,1)),((1,0),(1,0)),((0,0),(0,0))\}$.
- $AP = \{x = 0, x = 1, y = 0, y = 1\}$.
- $L((1,1)) = \{x = 1, y = 1\}$, $L((0,1)) = \{x = 0, y = 1\}$, $L((1,0)) = \{x = 1, y = 0\}$, and $L((0,0)) = \{x = 0, y = 0\}$.

The only path in the Kripke structure that starts in an initial state is

$$(1,1)\,(0,1)\,(1,1)\,(0,1)\ldots$$

3.4   Boolean Encoding

In propositional logic, formulas are restricted to propositional variables, which can be either *true* or *false*, and logical connectives such as *and*, *or*, and *not*. We will frequently write 1 for *true* and 0 for *false*. The Boolean encoding enables us to use reasoning techniques for propositional logic such as BDDs or propositional satisfiability, and we therefore need a way to transform the characteristic functions for $\mathcal{S}_0$ and $\mathcal{R}$ into propositional logic. This transformation is always possible if the set of states S is finite, and we will illustrate it with an example.

Example 3.2 *We will use the following Kripke structure with four states to explain the propositional encoding:*

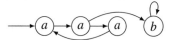

The states are labeled with labels a or b. We can encode the four states of the model with two Boolean variables, which we will denote v_0 and v_1. Their domains are $D_{v_0} = D_{v_1} = \{true, false\}$. We encode the left most state with $v_0 = false$ and $v_1 = false$, the second state with $v_0 = true$ and $v_1 = false$ and so on. Recall that we are using formulas to represent the set of all elements that correspond to the set of assignments that satisfy it. Using this encoding, we obtain the following formula that represents the set of initial states:

$$\mathcal{S}_0(v_0, v_1) = \neg v_0 \wedge \neg v_1$$

The transition relation is represented by

$$
\begin{aligned}
R(v_0, v_1, v'_0, v'_1) \quad = \quad & \neg v_0 \wedge \neg v_1 \wedge v'_0 \wedge \neg v'_1 \\
\vee \quad & v_0 \wedge \neg v_1 \wedge v'_1 \\
\vee \quad & \neg v_0 \wedge v_1 \wedge \neg v'_0 \wedge \neg v'_1 \\
\vee \quad & v_0 \wedge v_1 \wedge v'_0 \wedge v'_1 .
\end{aligned}
$$

Observe that the second clause of R represents two transitions.

3.5   Modeling Digital Circuits

3.5.1   State-holding Elements

In this section, we show how to describe digital circuits by formulas. Only specific elements in the circuit are used to store data; we refer to these as the *state-holding elements*. For simplicity, we assume that each of the state-holding elements can have only the value 0 or 1, and we use V to denote the set of state holding elements. For a synchronous circuit, the set V typically consists of the outputs of all the registers in the circuit together with the primary inputs. For asynchronous circuits, all wires in the circuit are usually considered to be state holding elements. If we create a Boolean variable for each element in V, then a state can be described by a valuation assigning either 0 or 1 to each variable. Given a valuation, we can write a Boolean expression that is true for exactly that valuation. For example, given $V = \{v_1, v_2\}$ and the valuation $\langle v_1 \mapsto 1, v_2 \mapsto 0 \rangle$, we derive the Boolean formula $v_1 \wedge \neg v_2$. As before, we adopt the convention that a formula represents the set of *all* valuations that make it true. Thus, for describing circuits the full expressive power of first-order logic is not needed; Boolean formulas are sufficient. The Boolean formulas $S_0(V)$ and $\mathcal{R}(V, V')$ will represent the set of initial states and the transition relation of the circuit, respectively.

3.5.2   Synchronous Circuits

The operation of a synchronous circuit consists of a sequence of steps. In each step, the inputs to the circuit change and the circuit is allowed to stabilize. Then a clock pulse occurs, and the state-holding elements change.

The method for deriving the transition relation of a synchronous circuit can be illustrated using a small example. The circuit in figure 3.1 is a modulo 8 counter. Let $V = \{v_0, v_1, v_2\}$ be the set of state variables for this circuit, and let $V' = \{v'_0, v'_1, v'_2\}$ be another copy of the state variables. The transitions of the modulo 8 counter are given by

$$
\begin{aligned}
v'_0 &= \neg v_0 \\
v'_1 &= v_0 \oplus v_1 \\
v'_2 &= (v_0 \wedge v_1) \oplus v_2,
\end{aligned}
$$

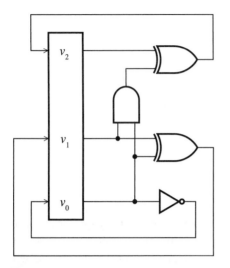

Figure 3.1
Synchronous modulo 8 counter.

where $\oplus$ is the *exclusive or* operator. The above equations can be used to define the relations

$$\mathcal{R}_0(V,V') \equiv (v_0' \Leftrightarrow \neg v_0)$$
$$\mathcal{R}_1(V,V') \equiv (v_1' \Leftrightarrow v_0 \oplus v_1)$$
$$\mathcal{R}_2(V,V') \equiv (v_2' \Leftrightarrow (v_0 \wedge v_1) \oplus v_2),$$

which describe the constraints each v_i' must satisfy in a legal transition. Since all of the changes in a synchronous circuit occur at the same time, the constraints are combined by taking their conjunction to construct a formula for the transition relation:

$$\mathcal{R}(V,V') \equiv \mathcal{R}_0(V,V') \wedge \mathcal{R}_1(V,V') \wedge \mathcal{R}_2(V,V')$$

In the general case of a synchronous circuit with n state-holding elements, we let $V = \{v_0, \ldots, v_{n-1}\}$ and $V' = \{v_0', \ldots, v_{n-1}'\}$. Analogous to the modulo 8 counter, for each state variable v_i' that corresponds to a register there is a Boolean function f_i such that

$$v_i' = f_i(V).$$

These equations are used to define the relations

$$\mathcal{R}_i(V,V') \equiv (v_i' \Leftrightarrow f_i(V)).$$

It is not necessary to define such a function for variables that correspond to the primary inputs of the circuit. These variables are usually left unconstrained by defining

$$\mathcal{R}_i(V, V') \equiv true.$$

Continuing the analogy with the modulo 8 counter, the conjunction of the formulas above forms the transition relation

$$\mathcal{R}(V, V') \equiv \mathcal{R}_0(V, V') \wedge \ldots \wedge \mathcal{R}_{n-1}(V, V').$$

Thus, the transition relation for a synchronous circuit can be expressed as the conjunction of the transition relations of the individual state-holding elements.

3.5.3   Asynchronous Circuits

We discuss only a very simplistic, untimed model for asynchronous circuits. The transition relation for an asynchronous circuit is most naturally expressed as a disjunction. To simplify the description of how the transition relations are obtained, we assume that all the components of the circuit have exactly one output and have no internal state variables. In this case, it is possible to describe each component by a function $f_i(V)$; given values for the present-state variables in V, the component drives its output to the value specified by $f_i(V)$. Extending the method to handle components with multiple outputs is straightforward.

Since the value of a component can change so rapidly, it is unlikely that two components will change at the same time. For this reason, it is customary to use an *interleaving semantics* in which exactly one component changes at a time. This results in a disjunction of the form:

$$\mathcal{R}(V, V') \equiv \mathcal{R}_0(V, V') \vee \ldots \vee \mathcal{R}_{n-1}(V, V'),$$

where

$$\mathcal{R}_i(V, V') \equiv \left(v_i' \Leftrightarrow f_i(V)\right) \wedge \bigwedge_{j \neq i} (v_j' \Leftrightarrow v_j).$$

Note that some component may change repeatedly, without another component ever making a step. In practice, this is extremely unlikely. It is possible to augment the model with an additional *fairness* constraint that will disallow such behaviors. This topic is discussed further in chapter 4.

Example 3.3 *To illustrate the difference between the synchronous and the asynchronous models, consider the following example. Let $V = \{v_0, v_1\}$, $v_0' = v_0 \oplus v_1$, and $v_1' = v_0 \oplus v_1$. Let s be a state with $v_0 = 1 \wedge v_1 = 1$. According to the synchronous model, the only successor of s is the state with $v_0 = 0 \wedge v_1 = 0$, since both assignments are executed simultaneously. According to the asynchronous model, the state s has two successors:*

1. *$v_0 = 0 \wedge v_1 = 1$ (the assignment to v_0 is taken first).*
2. *$v_0 = 1 \wedge v_1 = 0$ (the assignment to v_1 is taken first).*

3.6   Modeling Programs

3.6.1   Sequential Processes

We start by discussing the basic case of sequential programs, and then provide an extension to the case of concurrent programs with asynchronous interleaving semantics. The approach that we use is similar to the approach used by Manna and Pnueli [362]. We begin with a model for an idealized programming language. For a more detailed treatment of the issues related to industrial programming languages, see chapter 14.

A program consists of statements that are sequentially composed with each other. We describe a translation procedure C that takes the text of a sequential program P and transforms it into a first-order formula $\mathcal{R}$ that represents the set of transitions of the program. Without loss of generality, we assume that each statement has a unique *entry point* and a unique *exit point*. The translation procedure is simplified significantly if each entry and exit point of a statement in the program is uniquely labeled. Thus, we define a labeling transformation that given an unlabeled program P results in a program labeled $P^{\mathcal{L}}$. We refer to the labels as *program locations*.

The labeling transformation defined below attaches a single location with the entry point of each statement in P, except for P itself. No two attached labels are identical. In sequential programs, the exit point of a statement is identical to the entry point of the following statement. Thus, it is sufficient to label entry points. If we also provide labels for the entry and the exit points of P, then we get a unique labeling of the entry and exit points of all statements of the program.

Since we aim to abstract the details of any specific programming language, we define the labeling transformation for a number of common types of statements. It is easy to extend the definition to other statement types. Given a statement P, the *labeled statement $P^{\mathcal{L}}$* is defined as follows:

- If P is not a composite statement (for instance, P is $x := e$, **skip**, **wait**, **lock**, **unlock**, etc.), then $P^{\mathcal{L}} = P$.
- If $P = P_1; P_2$, then $P^{\mathcal{L}} = P_1^{\mathcal{L}}; l_1 : P_2^{\mathcal{L}}$, where l_1 is a new label.
- If $P = $ **if** b **then** P_1 **else** P_2 **end if**, then
  $P^{\mathcal{L}} = $ **if** b **then** $l_1 : P_1^{\mathcal{L}}$ **else** $l_2 : P_2^{\mathcal{L}}$ **end if**, where l_1 and l_2 are new labels.
- If $P = $ **while** b **do** P_1 **end while**, then
  $P^{\mathcal{L}} = $ **while** b **do** $l_1 : P_1^{\mathcal{L}}$ **end while**, where l_1 is a new label.

In the remainder of this section, we assume that P is a labeled statement and that the entry and exit points of P are labeled by m and m', respectively. Let pc be a special variable called the *program counter* that ranges over the set of program locations and an additional value **susp**, which is used to indicate that the program is *suspended*. This value is needed when concurrent programs are considered. In this case, $pc = $ **susp** indicates that the program is currently not active.

Let V denote the set of program variables. Let V' be the set of primed variables v' for each $v \in V$, and let pc' be the primed variable for pc. Recall that the unprimed copy refers to the value of the variables before a transition, while the primed copy refers to the value after the transition. Since each transition typically changes only a small number of the program variables, we will use $same(Y)$ as an abbreviation for the formula

$$\bigwedge_{y \in Y} (y' = y).$$

We first give the formula that describes the set of initial states of the program P. Given some condition $pre(V)$ on the initial values of the variables of P,

$$\mathcal{S}_0(V, pc) \equiv pre(V) \wedge pc = m.$$

The translation procedure $\mathcal{C}$ depends on three parameters: the entry label l, the labeled statement P, and the exit label l'. The procedure is defined recursively with one rule for each statement type in the language. $\mathcal{C}(l,\ P,\ l')$ describes the set of transitions in P as a disjunction of all the transitions in the set. For each disjunct, a condition on the program counter value guards the execution of the respective transition.

- **Assignment**
  $\mathcal{C}(l,\ v := e,\ l') \equiv pc = l \wedge pc' = l' \wedge v' = e \wedge same(V \setminus \{v\})$
- **Skip**
  $\mathcal{C}(l,\ skip,\ l') \equiv pc = l \wedge pc' = l' \wedge same(V)$
- **Sequential composition**
  $\mathcal{C}(l,\ P_1;\ l'' : P_2,\ l') \equiv \mathcal{C}(l,\ P_1,\ l'') \vee \mathcal{C}(l'',\ P_2,\ l')$
  Thus, the formula for the transitions of $P_1;\ l'' : P_2$ is a disjunction of the formulas for the transitions of P_1 and of P_2. The intermediate label l'' has the effect that statement P_2 can only be executed after l'' is reached, that is, after statement P_1.
- **Conditional**
  $\mathcal{C}(l,\ \textbf{if } b \textbf{ then } l_1 : P_1 \textbf{ else } l_2 : P_2 \textbf{ end if},\ l')$ is a disjunction of four formulas:

  $\quad (pc = l \wedge pc' = l_1 \wedge b = true \wedge same(V))$

  $\vee\ (pc = l \wedge pc' = l_2 \wedge b = false \wedge same(V))$

  $\vee\ \mathcal{C}(l_1,\ P_1,\ l')$

  $\vee\ \mathcal{C}(l_2,\ P_2,\ l')$

  The first disjunct corresponds to the case where condition b is true. In this case, statement P_1 will be executed next. The second disjunct corresponds to the case where condition b is false. In this case, statement P_2 will be executed next. Both disjuncts describe transitions that involve only a change of the program counter. The third and fourth disjuncts are formulas for the transitions of P_1 and P_2, respectively. Note that l' is the exit point for both P_1 and P_2. The translation for the **if** statement can easily be extended to handle nondeterministic choice between several alternatives, for example, by removing b from the formula.

- **While**

  $C(l, \textbf{while } b \textbf{ do } l_1 : P_1 \textbf{ end while}, l')$ is a disjunction of three formulas:

  $$(pc = l \wedge pc' = l_1 \wedge b \wedge same(V))$$

  $$\vee \ (pc = l \wedge pc' = l' \wedge \neg b \wedge same(V))$$

  $$\vee \ C(l_1, P_1, l)$$

  The first disjunct corresponds to the case where condition b is true. In this case, statement P_1 will be executed next. The second disjunct corresponds to the case where condition b is false, in which case the execution of the **while** statement terminates. The third disjunct is a formula for the set of transitions of P_1. Note that the exit point of P_1 is identical to the entry point of the while statement. Thus, once P_1 terminates, the execution of the while statement restarts.

In the next section, we first discuss various styles of modeling for a variety of concurrent systems, and then return to modeling software when describing models for concurrent programs.

3.6.2   Modeling Concurrent Processes

A concurrent system consists of a set of components that execute together. Normally, the components have some means of communicating with each other. The mode of execution and the mode of communication may differ from one system to another. We will consider two modes of execution: *asynchronous* or *interleaved execution*, in which only one component makes a step at a time, and *synchronous execution*, in which all of the components make a step at the same time. One can also distinguish different modes of communication. As an example, components can communicate either by changing the values of *shared variables* or by *exchanging messages* using queues or some type of handshaking protocol. Since modeling is not the main concern of this book, we only discuss communication by means of shared variables.

In the following we describe some important types of concurrent systems and show how they can be represented in terms of first-order formulas. From these formulas we can derive Kripke structures for the systems, as shown in section 3.3.

A *concurrent program* consists of a set of processes that can be executed in parallel. A *process* is a sequential statement as described in the previous section. In this section, we consider asynchronous programs in which exactly one process can make a transition at any time. We begin by introducing some terminology that will be used throughout the section. V_i is the set of variables that can be changed by process P_i. We do not require that these sets be disjoint. As before, V is the set of all program variables. The program counter of a process P_i is pc_i. PC is the set of all program counters.

A concurrent program P has the form

$$\mathbf{cobegin}\ P_1 \| P_2 \| \ldots \| P_n\ \mathbf{coend},$$

where $P_1, \ldots, P_n$ are processes. We extend the labeling transformation for sequential programs so that a concurrent program can occur as a statement in a sequential program. The transformation attaches a label to the entry point and to the exit point of each process. Unlike exit points in sequential programs, no exit point of a concurrent process is identical to an entry point. As a result, the exit points of processes must be explicitly labeled. As before, we assume that no two labels are identical and that the entry and exit points of P are labeled m and m', respectively.

- If $P = \mathbf{cobegin}\ P_1 \| P_2 \| \ldots \| P_n\ \mathbf{coend}$, then
  $P^{\mathcal{L}} = \mathbf{cobegin}\ l_1 : P_1^{\mathcal{L}}\ l_1' \| l_2 : P_2^{\mathcal{L}}\ l_2' \| \ldots \| l_n : P_n^{\mathcal{L}}\ l_n'\ \mathbf{coend}.$

The formula that describes the initial states of a concurrent program P is

$$\mathcal{S}_0(V, PC) \equiv pre(V) \wedge pc = m \wedge \bigwedge_{i=1}^{n} (pc_i = \mathbf{susp}),$$

where $pc_i = \mathbf{susp}$ indicates that process P_i has not been activated yet and therefore cannot be executed from the current state.

The translation procedure $\mathcal{C}$ is extended to concurrent programs as follows. The result of $\mathcal{C}(l,\ \mathbf{cobegin}\ l_1 : P_1\ l_1' \| \ldots \| l_n : P_n\ l_n'\ \mathbf{coend},\ l')$ is a disjunction of three formulas:

$$(pc = l\ \wedge\ pc_1' = l_1\ \wedge\ \ldots\ \wedge\ pc_n' = l_n\ \wedge pc' = \mathbf{susp})$$
$$\vee\ (pc = \mathbf{susp}\ \wedge pc_1 = l_1'\ \wedge\ \ldots\ \wedge\ pc_n = l_n'\ \wedge\ pc' = l'\ \wedge \bigwedge_{i=1}^{n} (pc_i' = \mathbf{susp}))$$
$$\vee\ \bigvee_{i=1}^{n} \left(\mathcal{C}(l_i, P_i, l_i')\ \wedge\ same(V \setminus V_i)\ \wedge\ same(PC \setminus \{\ pc_i\ \}) \right)$$

The first disjunct describes the initialization of the concurrent processes. A transition is made from the entry point of the **cobegin** statement to the entry points of the individual subprocesses. At the same time, the program that creates the subprocesses is suspended. The second disjunct describes the termination of the concurrent program. A transition is made from the exit points of the subprocesses to the exit of the **cobegin** statement. This transition will be executed only if all the processes terminate.

The third disjunct describes execution of concurrent processes. We use *interleaving semantics*; that is, only one of the processes makes a transition at any time. The formula for the transition relation of process P_i is conjuncted with

$$same(V \setminus V_i)\ \wedge\ same(PC \setminus \{\ pc_i\ \})).$$

This guarantees that a transition in process P_i can only change variables in V_i. It also ensures that only one of the processes can make a transition. The process that makes the transition is chosen nondeterministically.

Shared Variables   Recall that V_i is the set of variables that may be changed by process P_i. Concurrent programs for which the sets V_i overlap are called *shared variable* programs. We show how to extend the translation procedure $\mathcal{C}$ to some commonly used *process synchronization* statements. Such statements are frequently needed to provide processes with exclusive access to shared variables. These statements are atomic and treated by the labeling transformation accordingly. Assume that the statement belongs to the text of process P_i.

- **Wait**
  Since our primary interest is in finite state programs, we only describe how to implement this statement using *busy waiting*. In particular, we do not consider implementations that require complex data structures like process queues. The statement **wait**(b) repeatedly tests the value of the Boolean variable b until it determines that b is true. When b becomes true, a transition is made to the next program point.
  $\mathcal{C}(l,\ \mathbf{wait}(b),\ l')$ is a disjunction of two formulas:

  $$(pc_i = l \ \wedge \ pc_i' = l \ \wedge \ \neg b \ \wedge \ same(V_i))$$
  $$\vee \ (pc_i = l \ \wedge \ pc_i' = l' \ \wedge \ b \ \wedge \ same(V_i))$$

- **Lock**
  The statement **lock**(v) is similar to the statement **wait**$(v = 0)$, except that when $v = 0$ is true the transition changes the value of v to 1. This statement is often used to guarantee *mutual exclusion* by preventing more than one process from entering its critical region.
  $\mathcal{C}(l,\ \mathbf{lock}(v),\ l')$ is a disjunction of two formulas:

  $$(pc_i = l \ \wedge \ pc_i' = l \ \wedge \ v = 1 \ \wedge \ same(V_i))$$
  $$\vee \ (pc_i = l \ \wedge \ pc_i' = l' \ \wedge \ v = 0 \ \wedge \ v' = 1 \ \wedge same(V_i \setminus \{v\}))$$

- **Unlock**
  The statement **unlock**(v) assigns the value 0 to the variable v. Typically, this statement enables some other process to enter its critical region.

  $$\mathcal{C}(l,\ \mathbf{unlock}(v),\ l') \ \equiv \ pc_i = l \ \wedge \ pc_i' = l' \ \wedge \ v' = 0 \ \wedge \ same(V_i \setminus \{v\})$$

Example 3.4 *Consider a simple* mutual exclusion *program*

$$P = \ m : \mathbf{cobegin}\ P_0 \ \| \ P_1 \ \mathbf{coend}\ m'$$

with two processes P_0 and P_1, where

$P_0 ::\ \ l_0 :\ \mathbf{while}\ true\ \mathbf{do}$

$$NC_0 : \ \mathbf{wait}(turn = 0);$$
$$CR_0 : \ turn \ := 1$$
$$\mathbf{end\ while;}$$
$$l_0'$$

$P_1 :: \ \ l_1 : \ \mathbf{while}\ true\ \mathbf{do}$
$$NC_1 : \ \mathbf{wait}(turn = 1);$$
$$CR_1 : \ turn \ := 0$$
$$\mathbf{end\ while;}$$
$$l_1'.$$

The program counter pc of the program P only takes on three values: m, the label of the entry point of P; m', the label of the exit point of P; and **susp**, *the value of pc when P_1 and P_2 are active. Each process P_i has a program counter pc_i that ranges over the labels l_i, l_i', NC_i, CR_i, and* **susp**. *The two processes share a single variable turn. Thus, $V = V_0 = V_1 = \{turn\}$, and $PC = \{pc, pc_0, pc_1\}$. When the value of the program counter of a process P_i is CR_i, the process is in its* critical region. *Both processes are not allowed to be in their critical regions at the same time. When the value of the program counter is NC_i, the process is in its* noncritical region. *In this case it waits until $turn = i$ in order to gain exclusive entry into the critical region.*

The initial states of P are described by the formula

$$\mathcal{S}_0(V, PC) \ \equiv \ pc = m \ \wedge \ pc_0 = \mathbf{susp} \ \wedge \ pc_1 = \mathbf{susp}.$$

Note that no restriction is imposed on the value of turn. Thus, it may initially be either 0 or 1. Applying the translation procedure $\mathcal{C}$ we obtain the formula for the transition relation of P, $\mathcal{R}(V, PC, V', PC')$, which is a disjunction of four formulas:

$$(pc = m \ \wedge \ pc_0' = l_0 \ \wedge \ pc_1' = l_1 \ \wedge pc' = \mathbf{susp})$$
$$\vee \ (pc_0 = l_0' \ \wedge \ pc_1 = l_1' \ \wedge \ pc' = m' \ \wedge \ pc_0' = \mathbf{susp} \ \wedge \ pc_1' = \mathbf{susp})$$
$$\vee \ (\mathcal{C}(l_0, P_0, l_0') \ \wedge \ same(V \setminus V_0) \ \wedge \ same(PC \setminus \{\ pc_0\ \}))$$
$$(\text{which is equivalent to } \mathcal{C}(l_0, P_0, l_0') \ \wedge \ same(pc, pc_1))$$
$$\vee \ (\mathcal{C}(l_1, P_1, l_1') \ \wedge \ same(V \setminus V_1) \ \wedge \ same(PC \setminus \{\ pc_1\ \})$$
$$(\text{which is equivalent to } \mathcal{C}(l_1, P_1, l_1') \ \wedge \ same(pc, pc_0))$$

For each process P_i, $\mathcal{C}(l_i, P_i, l_i')$ is the disjunction of

$$(pc_i = l_i \ \wedge \ pc_i' = NC_i \ \wedge \ true \ \wedge \ same(turn))$$
$$\vee \ (pc_i = NC_i \ \wedge \ pc_i' = CR_i \ \wedge \ turn = i \ \wedge \ same(turn))$$
$$\vee \ (pc_i = CR_i \ \wedge \ pc_i' = l_i \ \wedge \ turn' = (i+1) \ \mathrm{mod}\ 2)$$
$$\vee \ (pc_i = NC_i \ \wedge \ pc_i' = NC_i \ \wedge \ turn \neq i \ \wedge \ same(turn))$$
$$\vee \ (pc_i = l_i \ \wedge \ pc_i' = l_i' \ \wedge \ false \ \wedge \ same(turn))$$

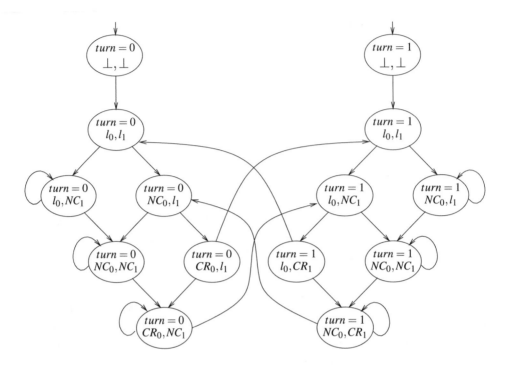

Figure 3.2
Reachable states of Kripke structure for mutual exclusion example.

The Kripke structure in figure 3.2 is derived from the formulas S_0 and $\mathcal{R}$ as described in section 3.3. Unreachable states are omitted. By examining the state space of the Kripke structure, it is easy to see that the processes will never be in their critical regions at the same time. Thus, the program guarantees the required mutual exclusion property. However, this program fails to guarantee absence of starvation, *since one of the processes may continuously try to enter its critical region without ever being able to do so, while the other process stays in its critical region forever. Later, we show how to formulate and model check such properties.*

Granularity of Transitions   A critical issue in modeling concurrent systems is determining the granularity of the transitions. It is important to identify transitions that are *atomic* in the sense that no observable state of the system can result from executing a transition only partially. A common mistake is to define transitions that are too coarse. In this case, the Kripke structure may not include some states that are observable. As a result, verification techniques like model checking may fail to find important errors. A problem can also arise when the granularity is too fine. In this case transitions can interact to create new states that are not reachable in the actual system. As a result, model checking may find spurious errors that will never occur in practice.

For an example in which the granularity is too coarse, consider a system with two variables x and y and two transitions α and β that can be executed concurrently:

$$\alpha: \quad x := x + y \quad \text{and}$$
$$\beta: \quad y := y + x,$$

with the initial state $x = 1 \wedge y = 2$. Also consider a finer-grained implementation of the same transitions. This implementation uses the assembly language instructions for loading, adding, and storing between a memory address and a register:

α_0 :	load R_1, x	β_0 :	load R_2, y
α_1 :	add R_1, y	β_1 :	add R_2, x
α_2 :	store R_1, x	β_2 :	store R_2, y

Executing α and then β results in the state $x = 3 \wedge y = 5$. When β is executed before α, we obtain $x = 4 \wedge y = 3$. If, on the other hand, the finer grained implementation is executed in the order $\alpha_0 \beta_0 \alpha_1 \beta_1 \alpha_2 \beta_2$, the result is $x = 3 \wedge y = 3$.

Suppose that $x = 3 \wedge y = 3$ violates some desired property of the system. Further, suppose that the system is implemented using the transitions α and β. Then, it is impossible to have $x = 3$ and $y = 3$ at the same time. However, if we model the system with the finer-grained transitions $\alpha_0, \alpha_1, \alpha_2, \beta_0, \beta_1,$ and β_2, we may erroneously conclude that the system is incorrect. Next, suppose that the system is implemented using $\alpha_0, \alpha_1, \alpha_2, \beta_0, \beta_1,$ and β_2. In this case it is possible to reach a state in which both $x = 3$ and $y = 3$. If we now model the system with α and β, we will erroneously conclude that the system is correct.

Extracting a first-order representation from the text of a program or a diagram of a circuit can be viewed as a compilation task. This task must take into account granularity considerations like the one described above.

3.7   Fairness

We have shown how to use nondeterminism to account for missing details in our models. As an example, recall the model of concurrent processes given in section 3.6.2 and consider a concurrent program P of the form

$$\textbf{cobegin } P_1 \parallel P_2 \parallel \ldots \parallel P_n \textbf{ coend}.$$

The interleavings observed on a real system may be governed by a *scheduler*, which imposes one particular, deterministic interleaving of the processes P_1 to P_n. We nevertheless refrain from modeling the scheduler. This may be owing to the complexity of the scheduler, or because we wish to validate the program P for a broad range of systems with different schedulers. Our model therefore permits *any* interleaving of the statements of the processes, thereby overapproximating the behavior of the real system. As a side effect of overapproximation, we sometimes add undesired behaviors to the model. Continuing the example, our model contains abnormal paths that are never observed on the real system. For instance, the model permits paths along which only one of the processes is executed while the other processes are suspended indefinitively. Our model therefore exhibits starvation of processes.

There are numerous ways to add constraints to Kripke structures in order to eliminate unwanted behaviors. We will focus on *fairness constraints*. Formally, a *fair Kripke structure M* is a six-tuple $M = (S, S_0, R, AP, L, F)$ where

1. S, S_0, R, AP, and L are defined as above, and
2. $F \subseteq 2^S$ is a set of *fairness constraints*.

Let $F = \{F_1, F_2, \ldots\}$, where each F_j is a subset of S. Let $s_0, s_1, \ldots$ denote the states that form a path π in M. Path π is called *fair* if along π there are infinitely many $s_i \in F_j$ for each fairness constraint $F_j \in F$. From now on, we consider only those paths in M that are fair.

Continuing the example above, we can prevent process starvation as follows. Let a state in which process P_i is chosen to perform a transition be labeled with σ_i. We now use the following fairness constraints:

$$\{s \in S \mid \sigma_1 \in L(s)\}, \ldots, \{s \in S \mid \sigma_n \in L(s)\}$$

In the resulting fair Kripke structure, every process is required to be scheduled infinitively often.

Bibliographic Notes

The formalization of programs using first-order formulas in section 3.6 is similar to the presentation in Manna and Pnueli's book [362].

Many additional aspects can be considered in system models. We defer the discussion of modeling aspects of timed systems to chapters 19 and 20. Numerous modeling formalisms have been devised for concurrent systems, for example, Communicating Sequential Processes (CSP), the Calculus of Communicating Systems (CCS), the π-calculus, and Petri-nets.

This chapter also does not cover hybrid systems or probabilistic models. These and many further aspects are discussed in the chapter on modeling in the Handbook of Model Checking [136]. Probabilistic models are covered in depth in Baier and Katoen [35].

Problems

Problem 3.1 (Characteristic functions). We are using characteristic functions to define transition relations and sets of states.

a. Write a concise characteristic function for the relation

$$T : \{1, \ldots, 10\}^2 = \{(1,2), (2,3), (3,4), (4,5), (5,6), (6,7), (7,8), (8,9), (9,5)\}.$$

b. Is T a left-total relation?

c. What is the reflexive transitive closure of the relation T?

Problem 3.2 (Modelling Verilog). The purpose of this exercise is to gain confidence in modelling transition systems. In this problem, we formalize the meaning of circuit descriptions given in the *Verilog hardware description language* (HDL). For this exercise, first read an informal description of the semantics of Verilog HDL.

a. The Verilog HDL distinguishes two types of assignment operators: the *blocking assignment* with the $=$ operator, and the *non-blocking assignment* with the $<=$ operator (not to be confused with the $\leq$ operator). Explain the difference informally.

b. Define a transition system for the following Verilog fragment:

input clk;
reg [31:0] A, B;

always @(**posedge** clk) **begin**
   A=B;
   B=A;
end

Assume that the clock is triggered in every transition.

c. Define a transition system for the Verilog fragment above if the $=$ operator is replaced by $<=$.

d. The **reg** keyword does not always result in a state variable in the model. Explain why, and give an example.

4 Temporal Logic

Temporal logic is a formalism to specify the dynamic behavior of systems, modeled as Kripke structures. In the temporal logics that we will consider, a formula might specify that a property holds in the *next time*, after one computation step; it can specify that *eventually* some designated state is reached, or that an error state is *never* entered. Properties like *next time*, *eventually*, and *never* are specified using special temporal operators. Temporal logic also contains path quantifiers to relate temporal properties to the paths of the Kripke structure. The operators and quantifiers can be nested and combined with Boolean connectives. We focus on the powerful logic CTL* [121, 123, 199] and its important fragments *computation tree logic* (CTL) [46, 121, 198], *universal CTL** (ACTL*) [249, 354] and *linear temporal logic* (LTL) [411, 412], whose specific properties can be exploited in model checking algorithms.

4.1 The Computation Tree Logic CTL*

The intuitive semantics of *computation tree logic* is based on the notion of computation trees. Given an initial state s_0 in a Kripke structure M, the tree is formed by unwinding the structure into a tree with root s_0, as illustrated in figure 4.1. The computation tree shows all of the possible executions starting from the initial state. We require the transition relation of M to be left-total; that is, each state has a successor. Thus, all branches of the tree are infinite.

The temporal logic CTL* defines properties of computation trees, and thus, of the underlying Kripke structures. CTL* formulas are composed of *path quantifiers* and *temporal operators*. CTL* has two path quantifiers:

A φ "all computation paths"
   This means that all paths from a given state have property φ.

E φ "there exists a computation path"
   This means that at least one path from a given state has property φ.

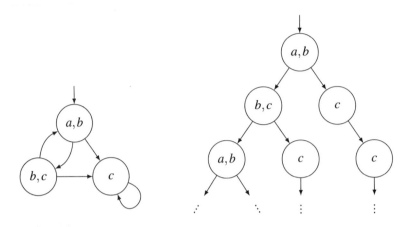

Figure 4.1
Computation trees: state transition graph or Kripke model (left), unwinding the state graph to obtain an infinite tree (right).

Path quantifiers are used in a particular state to specify that all of the paths or some of the paths starting at that state have property φ. As we show below, combinations of multiple **A** and **E** quantifiers can describe the branching structure in the computation tree. The temporal operators describe properties that hold *along a given infinite path* through the tree. There are five basic operators. Their intuitive meaning is presented below, assuming p and q are formulas describing state properties (see also figure 4.2):

X p "next time p"
  Intuitively, this requires that proposition p holds on the second state of the path.

F p "eventually p" or "in the future p"
  This is used to assert that property p holds at some state on the path.

G p "always p" or "globally p"
  This specifies that proposition p holds at every state on the path.

p **U** q "p until q"
  The **U** operator is a bit more complicated since it is used to combine two properties. It holds if there is a state on the path where the second property q holds, and at every preceding state on the path (if it exists), the first property p holds.

p **R** q "p release q"
  This is the logical dual of the **U** operator. It requires that the second property q holds along the path up to and including the first state where the first property p holds. However, the first property p is not required to eventually hold.

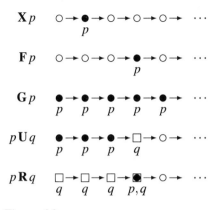

Figure 4.2
Illustration of temporal operators along (a prefix of) an infinite path. Circles and squares represent states along the path, and arrows represent transitions between states. Atomic propositions labeling the states explain why the paths satisfy the formulas.

Example 4.1 *Let us illustrate the CTL* semantics informally on the example of figure 4.1. Let π_1 and π_2 denote the leftmost and rightmost paths, respectively. On π_1, property b holds in every state, and thus $\mathbf{G}\,b$ holds true. Formally, we write $\pi_1 \models \mathbf{G}\,b$. By contrast, it is easy to see that $\pi_2 \not\models \mathbf{G}\,b$. Thus, one but not all paths from the initial state satisfy $\mathbf{G}\,b$, and hence, $s_0 \models \mathbf{EG}\,b$, but $s_0 \not\models \mathbf{AG}\,b$. Similarly, it is easy to see that $s_0 \models \mathbf{EXX}(a \wedge b)$, but $s_0 \not\models \mathbf{EXAX}(a \wedge b)$.*

From this informal introduction to CTL* we see an important difference between path quantifiers and temporal operators: while path quantifiers describe properties of a state (for example, "does a certain path start in this state?"), temporal operators describe properties of paths (for example, "can a certain state be reached along this path?"). In the following section this distinction will give rise to the notion of *path formulas* and *state formulas*.

4.2 Syntax and Semantics of CTL*

We now formally define the syntax and semantics of CTL*.

4.2.1 Syntax of CTL*

The syntax of propositional CTL* is the natural extension of propositional logic by the temporal operators and path quantifiers introduced above. There are two types of formulas in CTL*: *state formulas* (which are true in a specific state) and *path formulas* (which are true along a specific path). Let AP be the set of atomic propositions. The syntax of state formulas is given by the following rules:

A1 If $p \in AP$, then p is a state formula.

A2 If f and g are state formulas, then $\neg f$, $f \vee g$, and $f \wedge g$ are state formulas.

A3 If f is a path formula, then $\mathbf{E} f$ and $\mathbf{A} f$ are state formulas.

Two additional rules are needed to specify the syntax of path formulas:

A4 If f is a state formula, then f is also a path formula.

A5 If f and g are path formulas, then $\neg f$, $f \vee g$, $f \wedge g$, $\mathbf{X} f$, $\mathbf{F} f$, $\mathbf{G} f$, $f \mathbf{U} g$, and $f \mathbf{R} g$ are path formulas.

CTL* is the set of *state formulas* permitted by the above rules.

Thus, CTL* formulas are Boolean propositions, temporal formulas with a leading path quantifier, and Boolean combinations thereof.

4.2.2   Semantics of CTL*

Recall that a Kripke structure M is a 5-tuple (S, S_0, R, AP, L), where S is the set of states; $S_0 \subseteq S$ is the set of initial states; $R \subseteq S \times S$ is the transition relation, which must be *left-total* (that is, for all states $s \in S$ there exists a state $s' \in S$ such that $(s, s') \in R$); AP is the set of atomic propositions; and $L : S \rightarrow 2^{AP}$ is a function that labels each state with a set of atomic propositions true in that state. An *infinite path in M*, starting at state s, is an infinite sequence of states, $\pi = s_0, s_1, \ldots$, such that $s_0 = s$ and for every $i \geq 0$, $(s_i, s_{i+1}) \in R$. We use π^i to denote the *suffix* of π starting at s_i.

The modeling relation $\models$ is defined inductively over the formula structure. If f is a state formula, the notation $M, s \models f$ means that f holds at state s in the Kripke structure M. Similarly, if f is a path formula, $M, \pi \models f$ means that f holds along path π in the Kripke structure M. We will use the symbol $\equiv$ to denote logical equivalence. That is, if f and g are state formulas, then $f \equiv g$ holds if for all M, s, we have $M, s \models f$ if and only if $M, s \models g$. Similarly, if f and g are path formulas, then $f \equiv g$ holds if for all M, π, $M, \pi \models f$ if and only if $M, \pi \models g$. When the Kripke structure M is clear from the context, we will sometimes omit it.

In the following definition we assume that f_1, f_2 are state formulas and g_1, g_2 are path formulas. We further assume that all atomic propositions in the formula are included in AP. This guarantees that the base case of the definition is well defined.

Definition 4.2 *Let f_1, f_2 be state formulas, and let g_1, g_2 be path formulas. The notion of $\models$ is defined by induction on the structure of the formula.*

1. $M, s \models p$ $\qquad\qquad \Leftrightarrow \qquad$ *$p \in L(s)$, for $p \in AP$.*

2. $M, s \models \neg f_1$ $\qquad\quad \Leftrightarrow \qquad$ *$M, s \not\models f_1$.*

3. $M, s \models f_1 \vee f_2$ $\qquad \Leftrightarrow \qquad$ *$M, s \models f_1$ or $M, s \models f_2$.*

4. $M, s \models f_1 \wedge f_2$ $\qquad \Leftrightarrow \qquad$ *$M, s \models f_1$ and $M, s \models f_2$.*

5. $M, s \models \mathbf{E} g_1$ $\qquad\quad \Leftrightarrow \qquad$ *there is an infinite path π starting from s such that $M, \pi \models g_1$.*

6. $M, s \models \mathbf{A} g_1$ $\qquad\quad \Leftrightarrow \qquad$ *for every infinite path π starting from s we*

			have $M, \pi \models g_1$.
7.	$M, \pi \models f_1$	$\Leftrightarrow$	s *is the first state of* π, *and* $M, s \models f_1$.
8.	$M, \pi \models \neg g_1$	$\Leftrightarrow$	$M, \pi \not\models g_1$.
9.	$M, \pi \models g_1 \vee g_2$	$\Leftrightarrow$	$M, \pi \models g_1$ *or* $M, \pi \models g_2$.
10.	$M, \pi \models g_1 \wedge g_2$	$\Leftrightarrow$	$M, \pi \models g_1$ *and* $M, \pi \models g_2$.
11.	$M, \pi \models \mathbf{X} g_1$	$\Leftrightarrow$	$M, \pi^1 \models g_1$.
12.	$M, \pi \models \mathbf{F} g_1$	$\Leftrightarrow$	*there exists a* $k \geq 0$ *such that* $M, \pi^k \models g_1$.
13.	$M, \pi \models \mathbf{G} g_1$	$\Leftrightarrow$	*for all* $i \geq 0$, $M, \pi^i \models g_1$.
14.	$M, \pi \models g_1 \mathbf{U} g_2$	$\Leftrightarrow$	*there exists a* $k \geq 0$ *such that* $M, \pi^k \models g_2$ *and* *for all* $0 \leq j < k$, $M, \pi^j \models g_1$.
15.	$M, \pi \models g_1 \mathbf{R} g_2$	$\Leftrightarrow$	*for all* $j \geq 0$, *if for every* $i < j$ $M, \pi^i \not\models g_1$, *then* $M, \pi^j \models g_2$.

Finally, we define $\models$ *over Kripke structure M as follows:*

16.	$M \models f_1$	$\Leftrightarrow$	*for all* $s \in S_0$, $M, s \models f_1$.

We say that a CTL* formula f is *satisfiable* if $M \models f$ for some Kripke structure M. Formula f is *valid* if $M \models f$ for all M. Satisfiability and validity of formulas are classical problems, often discussed in logic. By contrast, the *model-checking* problem is defined for a formula f and a given Kripke structure M. Its goal is to determine whether M is a model for f, that is, whether $M \models f$. Note that while the notion of model checking is well defined for any Kripke structure, later on when we discuss *model-checking algorithms* we will restrict our attention to *finite* Kripke structures, that is, Kripke structures in which the set of states S is finite.

The semantics of CTL* has the following interesting and important properties:

- It is an easy exercise to see that the operators $\vee$, $\neg$, $\mathbf{X}$, $\mathbf{U}$, and $\mathbf{E}$ are sufficient to express any other CTL* formula:

$$f \wedge g \equiv \neg(\neg f \vee \neg g)$$
$$f \mathbf{R} g \equiv \neg(\neg f \mathbf{U} \neg g)$$
$$\mathbf{F} f \equiv true \mathbf{U} f$$
$$\mathbf{G} f \equiv \neg \mathbf{F} \neg f$$
$$\mathbf{A}(f) \equiv \neg \mathbf{E}(\neg f)$$

- Clause 16 of definition 4.2 has a somewhat unexpected effect when formulas are interpreted over structures with multiple initial states. Consider, for example, the structure of figure 4.3, where $S_0 = \{s_0, s_1\}$. Note that $M, s_0 \models \mathbf{EX} p$ and $M, s_1 \not\models \mathbf{EX} p$. Then by definition $M \not\models \mathbf{EX} p$ because only one initial state has property $\mathbf{EX} p$. On the other hand, the formula $\neg \mathbf{EX} p$ holds on s_1, but not on s_0, and thus $M \not\models \neg \mathbf{EX} p$. Consequently,

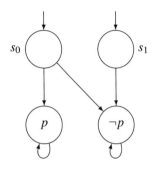

Figure 4.3
A Kripke structure that satisfies neither **EX** p nor $\neg$**EX** p.

neither **EX** p nor $\neg$**EX** p holds in M. Exercise 4.6 further elaborates on this point. Note that such a situation never happens in a structure with a single initial state.

4.2.3   Negation Normal Form (NNF)

Negation normal form (NNF) is a syntactic form of logical formulas, in which negations are applied only to atomic propositions. In subsequent chapters we show the usefulness of the NNF of CTL*. Here we show that every CTL* formula is equivalent to a formula in NNF. To see why this is true, notice that for every CTL* formula, negations can be pushed inward by repeated application of the following equivalences:

$$\neg \mathbf{A}\,\phi \;\equiv\; \mathbf{E}\neg\phi$$
$$\neg \mathbf{E}\,\phi \;\equiv\; \mathbf{A}\neg\phi$$
$$\neg \mathbf{G}\,\phi \;\equiv\; \mathbf{F}\neg\phi$$
$$\neg \mathbf{F}\,\phi \;\equiv\; \mathbf{G}\neg\phi$$
$$\neg \mathbf{X}\,\phi \;\equiv\; \mathbf{X}\neg\phi$$
$$\neg(\phi\,\mathbf{U}\,\psi) \;\equiv\; (\neg\psi\,\mathbf{R}\,\neg\psi)$$
$$\neg(\phi\,\mathbf{R}\,\psi) \;\equiv\; (\neg\psi\,\mathbf{U}\,\neg\psi)$$
$$\neg(\phi\wedge\psi) \;\equiv\; (\neg\phi)\vee(\neg\psi)$$
$$\neg(\phi\vee\psi) \;\equiv\; (\neg\phi)\wedge(\neg\psi)$$

Example 4.3 *Consider the formula $\neg((A\,\mathbf{U}\,B)\vee\mathbf{F}C)$. The formula can be transformed into NNF using the following equivalences:*

$$\neg((A\,\mathbf{U}\,B)\vee\mathbf{F}C) \;\equiv\; (\neg(A\,\mathbf{U}\,B)\wedge\neg\mathbf{F}C) \;\equiv\; ((\neg A)\,\mathbf{R}\,(\neg B))\wedge(\mathbf{G}\neg C)$$

It is important to note that the conversion of a CTL* formula to NNF is linear in the size of the formula. This is true for many fragments of CTL*. Note, however, that for the NNF

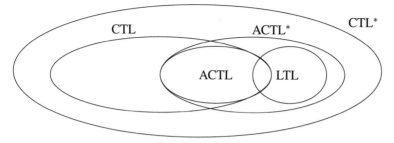

Figure 4.4
The logic CTL* and its sublogics.

of CTL*, we need to have $\wedge$, $\vee$, **E**, **A**, **X**, **U**, and **R**; a reduction to **E**, **X**, **U** like above is not possible.

4.3 Temporal Logics Based on CTL*

In this section, we consider several important sublogics of CTL*. The logics CTL, ACTL*, and ACTL are *branching-time* logics, while LTL is a *linear-time* logic. Syntactically and semantically, the logics are subsets of CTL*, as illustrated in figure 4.4.

The distinction between the two groups is in how they handle branching in the underlying computation tree. In branching-time temporal logic, path quantifiers can repeatedly quantify over the paths that can be reached from different states in the computation tree. In linear-time temporal logic, a single universal path quantifier quantifies over all paths starting at initial states.

Since all four logics are syntactic restrictions of CTL*, their semantics is predefined in accordance with the CTL* semantics, given above. However, it is sometimes simpler to define a direct (equivalent) semantics on the restricted syntax. The syntax of the four logics is described as follows.

4.3.1 The Branching-Time Logic CTL

Computation Tree Logic CTL [46, 121, 198] is the sublogic of CTL* where the path quantifiers and the temporal operators always occur in pairs. Thus, we can use the following syntax:

B1 If $p \in AP$, then p is a CTL formula.

B2 If f is a CTL formula, then $\neg f$, **AX**f, **EX**f, **AF**f, **EF**f, **AG**f, and **EG**f are CTL formulas.

B3 If f and g are CTL formulas, then $f \wedge g$, $f \vee g$, **A**$(f\,\mathbf{U}\,g)$, **E**$(f\,\mathbf{U}\,g)$, **A**$(f\,\mathbf{R}\,g)$, and **E**$(f\,\mathbf{R}\,g)$ are CTL formulas.

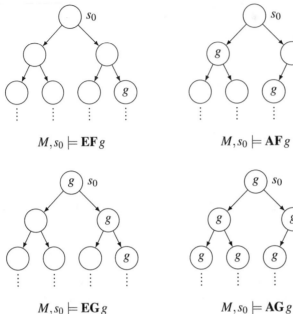

Figure 4.5
Basic CTL operators.

When we refer to a *subformula of a CTL formula*, we mean a subformula according to the CTL syntax given here. For example, the subformulas of **AX EX** p are **AX EX** p, **EX** p, and p. Note that all subformulas of CTL formulas are state formulas. If we view **AX EX** p as a CTL* formula, then it has the additional subformulas **X EX** p and **X** p, which are path formulas.

It is natural to view CTL as a logic that is based on the following 10 compound temporal operators: **AX, EX, AF, EF, AG, EG, AU, EU, AR**, and **ER**. Figure 4.5 illustrates the computation trees of formulas written with four of these operators. In fact, each of the 10 operators can be expressed in terms of the three operators **EX**, **EG**, and **EU**:

$$\mathbf{AX}\,f \equiv \neg\mathbf{EX}(\neg f)$$
$$\mathbf{EF}\,f \equiv \mathbf{E}(true\,\mathbf{U}\,f)$$
$$\mathbf{AG}\,f \equiv \neg\mathbf{EF}(\neg f)$$
$$\mathbf{AF}\,f \equiv \neg\mathbf{EG}(\neg f)$$
$$\mathbf{A}(f\,\mathbf{U}\,g) \equiv \neg\mathbf{E}(\neg g\,\mathbf{U}\,(\neg f \wedge \neg g)) \wedge \neg\mathbf{EG}\,\neg g$$
$$\mathbf{A}(f\,\mathbf{R}\,g) \equiv \neg\mathbf{E}(\neg f\,\mathbf{U}\,\neg g)$$
$$\mathbf{E}(f\,\mathbf{R}\,g) \equiv \neg\mathbf{A}(\neg f\,\mathbf{U}\,\neg g)$$

Consequently, CTL can also be defined as a logic based on just three operators $\mathbf{EX}, \mathbf{EG}, \mathbf{EU}$ with the following semantics:

1. $M, s \models p$, for $p \in AP$ $\quad\Leftrightarrow\quad$ $p \in L(s)$.
2. $M, s \models \neg f$ $\quad\Leftrightarrow\quad$ $M, s \not\models f$.
3. $M, s \models f_1 \vee f_2$ $\quad\Leftrightarrow\quad$ $M, s \models f_1$ or $M, s \models f_2$.
4. $M, s \models f_1 \wedge f_2$ $\quad\Leftrightarrow\quad$ $M, s \models f_1$ and $M, s \models f_2$.
5. $M, s \models \mathbf{EX} f$ $\quad\Leftrightarrow\quad$ there exists a state t such that $R(s,t)$ and $M, t \models f$.
6. $M, s \models \mathbf{EG} f$ $\quad\Leftrightarrow\quad$ there exists an infinite path π starting at s such that for all $i \geq 0$, $M, s_i \models f$.
7. $M, s \models \mathbf{E}(f_1 \mathbf{U} f_2)$ $\quad\Leftrightarrow\quad$ there exists an infinite path π starting at s and there exists a $k \geq 0$ such that $M, s_k \models f_2$ and for all $0 \leq j < k$, $M, s_j \models f_1$.

Finally, we define $\models$ for M as before:

8. $M \models f$ $\quad\Leftrightarrow\quad$ for all $s \in S_0$, $M, s \models f$.

The remaining seven CTL operators can then be introduced as abbreviations. It is easy to see that this definition of CTL semantics is equivalent to the semantics derived from CTL*.

4.3.2   The Universal Computation Tree Logics ACTL* and ACTL

ACTL* [249, 354] is the sublogic of CTL* where only the universal path quantification $\mathbf{A}$ is allowed. Since we saw above that $\mathbf{A}$ can be obtained from $\mathbf{E}$ by negation, we also need to require that ACTL* formulas are in NNF. Thus, we obtain the following syntax, using ACTL* state formulas and ACTL* path formulas:

C1   If $p \in AP$, then p and $\neg p$ are ACTL* state formulas.
C2   If f and g are ACTL* state formulas, then $f \vee g$ and $f \wedge g$ are ACTL* state formulas.
C3   If f is an ACTL* path formula, then $\mathbf{A} f$ is an ACTL* state formula.

Two additional rules are needed to specify the syntax of path formulas:

C4   If f is an ACTL* state formula, then f is also an ACTL* path formula.
C5   If f and g are ACTL* path formulas, then $f \vee g$, $f \wedge g$, $\mathbf{X} f$, $\mathbf{F} f$, $\mathbf{G} f$, $f \mathbf{U} g$, and $f \mathbf{R} g$ are ACTL* path formulas.

As for CTL*, ACTL* is the set of *state formulas* permitted by the rules above.

The logic ECTL* is defined analogously with $\mathbf{E}$ instead of $\mathbf{A}$. It is easy to see that the negation of each ACTL* formula is equivalent to an ECTL* formula and vice versa. Note that, for both ACTL* and ECTL*, the temporal operators $\mathbf{X}$, $\mathbf{U}$, and $\mathbf{R}$ are sufficient in order to represent every other temporal operator.

In chapter 11, we show that ACTL* has very useful preservation properties, which enable us to transfer specifications from one Kripke structure to another, simpler one.

The logic ACTL combines the syntactic restrictions of CTL and ACTL* in the natural way:

D1 If $p \in AP$, then p and $\neg p$ are ACTL formulas.

D2 If f is an ACTL formula, then $\mathbf{AX}\,f$, $\mathbf{AF}\,f$, and $\mathbf{AG}\,f$ are ACTL formulas.

D3 If f and g are ACTL formulas, then $f \wedge g$, $f \vee g$, $\mathbf{A}(f\,\mathbf{U}\,g)$, $\mathbf{A}(f\,\mathbf{R}\,g)$, are ACTL formulas.

Note that ACTL formulas can be translated into formulas that use $\mathbf{AX}$, $\mathbf{AU}$, and $\mathbf{AR}$.

4.3.3   Linear Temporal Logic LTL

The logic LTL [412] is a linear temporal logic. Rather than referring to the computation tree of a Kripke structure, LTL refers to the set of single computations of the tree. Its formulas are of the form $\mathbf{A}\,f$, where f is a CTL* path formula that does not include path quantifiers. This means that such a path formula may only contain atomic propositions as state subformulas.

To obtain LTL, we restrict CTL* to disallow path quantification in a path formula. Thus, LTL formulas are of the form $\mathbf{A}\,f$, where f is an LTL path formula and LTL path formulas are defined as follows:

E1 If $p \in AP$, then p is an LTL path formula.

E2 If f is an LTL path formula, then $\neg f$, $\mathbf{X}\,f$, $\mathbf{F}\,f$ and $\mathbf{G}\,f$ are LTL path formulas.

E3 If f and g are LTL path formulas, then $f \wedge g$, $f \vee g$, $f\,\mathbf{U}\,g$, and $f\,\mathbf{R}\,g$ are LTL path formulas.

Since we know from above that $f\,\mathbf{R}\,g \equiv \neg(\neg f\,\mathbf{U}\,\neg g)$, $\mathbf{F}\,f \equiv true\,\mathbf{U}\,f$, and $\mathbf{G}\,f \equiv \neg\mathbf{F}\neg f$, it follows that LTL can be defined from the operators $\mathbf{X}$ and $\mathbf{U}$.

In the literature (for instance, [412] and Piterman's temporal logic chapter in [136]), the single universal quantification in LTL formulas is sometimes omitted. In those cases, $M \models f$ for an LTL path formula f means $M \models \mathbf{A}\,f$.

4.3.4   Relationships between Fragments of CTL*

It can be shown [119, 199, 333] that the five logics that we have discussed have different expressive powers. That is, the inclusions of figure 4.4 are strict for both the syntax and the expressive power of the logics. For example, there is no CTL formula that is equivalent to the LTL formula $\mathbf{A}\,\mathbf{F}\mathbf{G}\,p$. This formula expresses the property that along every path, there is some state from which p will hold forever. Likewise, there is no LTL formula that is equivalent to the CTL formula $\mathbf{AG}(\mathbf{EF}\,p)$. The disjunction of these two formulas $\mathbf{A}(\mathbf{FG}\,p) \vee \mathbf{AG}(\mathbf{EF}\,p)$ is a CTL* formula that is not expressible in either CTL or LTL. The formulas $\mathbf{AF}\mathbf{AG}\,a$ and $\mathbf{AF}\mathbf{AX}\,a$ are examples of ACTL formulas. These formulas are not expressible in LTL [119]. Since ACTL is a subset of CTL, the logics ACTL and

LTL are incomparable. Moreover, ACTL* is more expressive than LTL. For example, the ACTL* formula **AG** $p \vee$ **AG** q is not expressible in LTL [119]. Finally, the CTL formulas **AG EF** p and **AG** $\neg$ **AF** p are not expressible in ACTL. Surprisingly, there are LTL properties expressible in CTL that are not expressible in ACTL [68].

4.4   Temporal Logic with Set Atomic Propositions and Set Semantics

It is common in logic to associate a formula with the set of assignments that satisfy it. In the context of temporal logics interpreted over a Kripke structure, this amounts to identifying a formula with the set of Kripke structure states in which the formula is true.

The semantics of a CTL* state formula f can thus be described in terms of the states that satisfy f. In later chapters, it will be useful to have notation for this property. Given a Kripke structure M, we thus define

$$\llbracket f \rrbracket_M := \{ s \in S \mid M, s \models f \}$$

to associate f with the set of states where it holds true. When M is clear from the context, we omit it from the notation.

We will extend the syntax and semantics of CTL* to directly refer to states of the Kripke structure, and not just to labels. To this end, we will allow the occurrence of sets of states as atomic CTL* formulas. Let $Q = \{s_1, \ldots, s_n\} \subseteq S$ be a set of states. Then, Q can be understood as a predicate. That is, it represents the property that holds exactly at the states in Q. We can reflect this in the syntax as follows:

If $\{s_1, \ldots, s_n\} \subseteq S$, then $\{s_1, \ldots, s_n\}$ is a CTL* state formula called *set atomic proposition*.

Extending the semantics in definition 4.2 is straightforward as well:

1a. $M, s \models \{s_1, \ldots, s_n\}$ $\Leftrightarrow$ $s \in \{s_1, \ldots, s_n\}$

For instance, the formula **EX**$\{s, t\}$ holds true in those states from which state s or t is reachable in one step.

4.5   Fairness

In chapter 3 we discussed the importance of fairness for system modeling. We can model a system with fairness constraints using a *fair Kripke structure*, defined as follows: $M = (S, S_0, R, L, AP, F)$, where S, S_0, R, L, and AP are defined as before. The set of *fairness constraints* is $F = \{P_1, \ldots, P_k\} \subseteq 2^S$, where $P_i \subseteq S$. A similar notion to F in automata is called generalized Büchi acceptance conditions (see chapter 7, section 7.6).

Let $\pi = s_0, s_1, \ldots$ be a path in M. Define

$$\inf(\pi) = \{ s \mid s = s_i \text{ for infinitely many } i \}.$$

We say that π is *fair* if and only if for every $P \in F$, $\inf(\pi) \cap P \neq \emptyset$.

In CTL* with set atomic propositions (section 4.4), we can explicitly express the fairness of a path by the formula

$$\text{fpath} :\equiv \bigwedge_{P \in F} \bigvee_{s \in P} \mathbf{GF}\{s\},$$

which states that each P must contain one state that appears infinitely often on the path. Thus, specifications of the form $\mathbf{E}\,\varphi$ and $\mathbf{A}\,\varphi$ can be adapted for fairness by writing

$$\mathbf{E}(\text{fpath} \wedge \varphi) \qquad \text{and} \qquad \mathbf{A}(\text{fpath} \rightarrow \varphi),$$

respectively. The left-hand side describes the case where there exists a path that is both fair and satisfies φ. The right-hand side describes the case where for every path, if it is fair, then it must satisfy φ.

Note that $\mathbf{GF}$ and, more generally, fairness properties cannot be expressed in CTL [119, 198, 199]. Thus, in order to deal with fairness in CTL we must modify its semantics slightly. We call the new semantics of the logic the *fair semantics*. For the sake of generality, we will define the fair semantics in terms of CTL*. We write $M, s \models_F f$ to indicate that the state formula f is true in state s of the fair Kripke structure M. Similarly, we write $M, \pi \models_F g$ to indicate that the path formula g is true along path π in the fair Kripke structure M. Only clauses 5 and 6 in definition 4.2 change:

5. $M, s \models_F \mathbf{E} g_1$ $\Leftrightarrow$ there exists a fair path π starting from s such that $\pi \models_F g_1$.
6. $M, s \models_F \mathbf{A} g_1$ $\Leftrightarrow$ for all fair paths π starting from s, $\pi \models_F g_1$.

We will sometimes write $\mathbf{E_f}$ and $\mathbf{A_f}$ instead of $\mathbf{E}$ and $\mathbf{A}$ to indicate that a fair interpretation of the formula is intended.

Note that by clause 6 if no fair path starts at a state s, then vacuously $M, s \models \mathbf{A_f}\,\varphi$ for every formula φ. Also note that, as opposed to the semantics without fairness where for $p \in AP$, the three formulas p, $\mathbf{E}p$, and $\mathbf{A}p$ are all equivalent, here p is not equivalent to either $\mathbf{E_f}\,p$ or $\mathbf{A_f}\,p$. In particular, $M, s \models p \wedge \neg \mathbf{E_f}\,p$ if $p \in L(s)$, but no fair path is starting at s, and $M, s \models \neg p \wedge \mathbf{A_f}\,p$, if $p \notin L(s)$, and no fair path is starting at s. This is in contrast with the regular semantics in which $p \wedge \neg \mathbf{E_f}\,p$ and $\neg p \wedge \mathbf{A_f}\,p$ would inherently be *false*.

Section 3.7 in chapter 3 presents an example that demonstrates the usefulness of fairness in modeling systems. In coming chapters we show how fairness can be incorporated into model-checking algorithms.

Sometimes it is convenient to represent a structure that does not have fairness constraints as a structure with fairness constraints, while preserving the set of paths considered as computations. This can be accomplished by letting $F = \{S\}$.

4.6   Counterexamples

Counterexample generation is a central feature of model checking, which distinguishes model checking from other approaches to verification such as theorem proving or abstract interpretation. In its simplest form, counterexamples are traces that demonstrate the violation of a specification. Thus, counterexamples provide valuable feedback to the engineers who developed the system.

Ideally, when a specification f is violated on a system model M, that is, $M \not\models f$, a counterexample C is an easy-to-understand description of the behavior of M that enables the user to systematically analyze and diagnose the problem. Note that the simplicity of the counterexample is crucial for human analysis. If simplicity were not important, even M itself would be an (entirely useless) counterexample.

Another essential requirement is a finite representation for C, so that it can be inspected and analyzed. In order to get a useful characterization of counterexamples in practice, we restrict the discussion to *finite Kripke structures*, that is, to Kripke structures whose set of states is finite.

Counterexamples not only are important for human readers, but also have algorithmic applications. In chapter 13 we introduce counterexample-guided abstraction refinement (CEGAR), where a counterexample obtained by a model checker is algorithmically analyzed to further guide the verification process. We will therefore discuss the structure of counterexamples in some detail.

For a simple specification $\mathbf{AX}\,p$, a counterexample is a path that leads from an initial state in a single step to a violation of p. Thus, a counterexample of $\mathbf{AX}\,p$ is a witness of $\mathbf{EX}\,\neg p$, which is the negation of the specification.

For the simplest nontrivial case, consider a counterexample for specification $\mathbf{AG}\,p$, which states that p is an invariant of the system model M. A counterexample C for $\mathbf{AG}\,p$ is a finite path (a program trace) that starts in an initial state and ends in a violation of p, that is, in a state s where $s \models \neg p$. As before, the counterexample is a witness for $\mathbf{EF}\,\neg p$, that is, the negated specification.

Consider now the more complex specification $\mathbf{AF}\,p$. A counterexample for $\mathbf{AF}\,p$ is an infinite path, all of its states satisfying $\neg p$. For finite Kripke structures, however, it can be shown that there always exists a counterexample π of the form $\pi = \pi_0(\pi_1)^\omega = \pi_0, \pi_1, \pi_1, \ldots$, where π_0 and π_1 are finite paths and the superscript ω refers to infinitely many repetitions. A path of that form is called a *lasso*. Figure 4.6 illustrates the form of counterexamples for the LTL formulas $\mathbf{AG}\,p$ and $\mathbf{AF}\,p$.

We prove the existence of a lasso-shape counterexample using a simple argument similar to the pumping lemma. Let the path $\pi = s_0, s_1, \ldots$ be a counterexample for $\mathbf{AF}\,p$. That is, for all s_i we have $M, s_i \models \neg p$. Since M has only a finite number of states, there must be two indices $1 \leq n < m$ such that $s_n = s_m$. We can now construct a lasso-shape counterexample by choosing $\pi_0 = s_0, \ldots, s_{n-1}$ and $\pi_1 = s_n, \ldots, s_{m-1}$. Note that the original counterexample may contain states that are not contained in the lasso counterexample.

The argument above can be extended to showing that every LTL formula has a lasso-shaped counterexample. However, for the general case fairness constraints should be

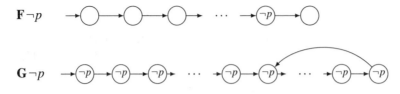

Figure 4.6
Counterexamples for LTL.

involved in the argument. A full discussion of this matter appears in the context of automata
in chapter 7, section 7.5, where an algorithm for checking emptiness is discussed.

More elaborate counterexamples are given for ACTL in [137] and for CTL in [440].

4.7   Safety and Liveness Properties

The notions of safety and liveness properties have been widely discussed [363, 362, 320].
Intuitively, a safety property guarantees that something wrong will never happen, whereas a
liveness property ensures that something good will eventually happen. The most typical
safety property is $\mathbf{AG}\,p$. Examples of typical liveness properties are $\mathbf{AF}\,p$ and $\mathbf{A}(p\,\mathbf{U}\,q)$.
These examples can be further complicated.

Counterexamples provide a natural way to distinguish between safety and liveness properties. Safety properties are those properties that can be disproved by finite loop-free
counterexamples, that is, finite paths. By contrast, since we are dealing with finite-state
structures, liveness properties will in general require lasso-shaped counterexamples.

The notions of safety and liveness were first introduced in [411] and then refined in [333]
and [16]. Piterman's temporal logic chapter in [136] gives a formal definition of these
notions.

Bibliographic Notes

The use of temporal logic as a specification language in computer science was proposed
by Pnueli [411]. This was recognized with the Turing award in 1996. Pnueli proposed
the linear temporal logic LTL. The Computation Tree Logic (CTL) has been introduced
in [45, 121], while CTL* has been defined in [199]. For an excellent survey on temporal
logics, see the chapter by Emerson in [197]. The book by Demri, Goranko and Lange [179],
the chapter by Clarke and Schlingloff in [142], the book by Baier and Katoen [35] and the
chapter by Piterman in [136] are also excellent sources for additional reading on temporal
logics.

Temporal logic is a branch of modal logic [280] and has found multiple applications in
formal methods as well as in artificial intelligence [255].

The operators of temporal logic can be extended and generalized in multiple ways. First, it is natural to introduce past operators [348, 298, 317]; somewhat surprisingly, past operators do not necessarily extend the expressive power of LTL [348]. However, they may be valuable in other respects, such as providing modular specification or shorter counterexamples [348, 335, 433]. Several logical systems are extending the operators of temporal logic by regular expressions [485, 131, 137]; the most prominent of these systems is *dynamic logic* [416, 258]. The most important practical extensions of temporal logic in this tradition are industrial specification logics such as PSL [192] and ForSpec [30].

The μ-calculus is another generalization of temporal logic, which we study in chapter 16.

Another possibility to enrich temporal logic is by quantification. Here, we distinguish propositional quantification—where the quantifier ranges over labelings of the Kripke structure or the computation tree [484]—and first-order temporal logic [362], where the states are logical structures and the first-order quantifiers range over domain elements in these structures.

Temporal logic can also be studied as a fragment of first- or second-order logic. For LTL these relations have been studied in [229] and for CTL* in [253].

In the research literature [362, 363], the syntax of temporal logic is sometimes based on graphical symbols rather than letters. In particular, $\bigcirc$ stands for **X**, $\square$ for **G**, and $\diamond$ for **F**. Moreover, $\forall$ and $\exists$ denote **A** and **E**, respectively. Note that this use of $\diamond$ and $\square$ is different from classical modal logic, where $\diamond$ is equivalent to the CTL* **EX**, and $\square$ to **AX**.

Problems

Problem 4.1 (Equivalence of CTL formulas, attributed to Alan Hu). A pair of CTL formulas is *equivalent* if they are true in exactly the same set of states in a given Kripke structure. Determine whether the following pairs of CTL formulas are equivalent. If so, give a proof. If they are not equivalent, give an example of a Kripke structure and a state in which one formula is *true* and one is *false*.

1. **EF** $p \wedge$ **EG** q and   **EF**$(p \wedge$ **EG** $q)$
2. **AF** $p \wedge$ **AG** q and   **AF**$(p \wedge$ **AG** $q)$
3. **AF** $p \wedge$ **AG** q and   **AG**(**AF** $p \wedge q)$
4. **AFAG** $p \wedge$ **AFAG** q and   **AF**(**AG** $p \wedge$ **AG** $q)$
5. **E**$(p\,\mathbf{U}\,q) \wedge$ **E**$(q\,\mathbf{U}\,r)$ and   **E**$(p\,\mathbf{U}\,r)$
6. **A**$(p\,\mathbf{U}\,q) \wedge$ **A**$(q\,\mathbf{U}\,r)$ and   **A**$(p\,\mathbf{U}\,r)$

Problem 4.2 (Expanding LTL operators). Give a proof for the following properties of LTL formulas:

$$f_1\,\mathbf{U}\,f_2 \Leftrightarrow f_2 \vee (f_1 \wedge \mathbf{X}(f_1\,\mathbf{U}\,f_2))$$
$$f_1\,\mathbf{R}\,f_2 \Leftrightarrow f_2 \wedge (f_1 \vee \mathbf{X}(f_1\,\mathbf{R}\,f_2))$$

Problem 4.3 (Temporal operator Weak Until). The *weak until* temporal operator is denoted **W** and has the following semantics:

$$\pi \models f_1 \mathbf{W} f_2 \;\Leftrightarrow\; \text{for all } i \geq 0, \text{ if } \pi^i \not\models f_2 \text{ then for all } 0 \leq j < i, \pi^j \models f_1.$$

Show that $f_1 \mathbf{W} f_2$ does not add expressive power to CTL*; that is, that it can be expressed by means of other CTL* operators.

Problem 4.4 (Expressiveness of CTL operators). Show that all the CTL operators listed in section 4.3.1 can be expressed with the three CTL operators **AX**, **A U**, and **A R**, together with any Boolean operators, including negations.

Problem 4.5 (CTL semantics). Prove that the direct semantics of CTL is identical to the semantics of CTL as a sublogic of CTL*. That is, show that for every CTL formula f and every M, s, the value of f in M, s is identical under the two semantics.

Problem 4.6 (Semantics over structures with multiple initial states). Let f be a CTL* formula that is satisfiable but not valid. Prove that there is a structure M such that $M \not\models f$ and $M \not\models \neg f$.

5 CTL Model Checking

The *model-checking problem for CTL* is defined as follows. Given a Kripke structure $M = (AP, S, R, S_0, L)$ that represents a finite-state system and a CTL formula f expressing some desired specification, determine whether M is a *model* for f, that is, $M \models f$. Alternatively, the model-checking problem can be defined as finding the set $[\![f]\!]_M$ of all states in M that satisfy f:

$$[\![f]\!]_M = \{\, s \in S \mid M, s \models f \,\}.$$

The set notation is introduced in chapter 4, section 4.4. Recall that M is omitted from the notation whenever M is clear from the context. Once the set $[\![f]\!]$ is computed, the original problem can be solved by checking whether $S_0 \subseteq [\![f]\!]$. Thus, S_0 is needed only when model checking is completed. Since AP is fixed throughout the chapter, we will omit both S_0 and AP from the definition of the Kripke structure.

In this chapter we present a model-checking algorithm for CTL that uses an *explicit* representation of the Kripke structure as a directed graph (S, R) with labeling L. We then extend the explicit algorithm to handle CTL with respect to the fairness semantics. Next, we define a fixpoint characterization to CTL operators according to the regular and the fair semantics and show how to use it for model checking. We describe model checking for LTL and CTL* in chapter 6.

5.1 Explicit-State CTL Model Checking

Let us fix a CTL specification f. To determine which states in S satisfy f, our algorithm will operate by labeling each state s with the set *label*(s) of subformulas of f that are true in s. Initially, *label*(s) is just $L(s)$. The algorithm then goes through a series of stages. During the i-th stage, subformulas with $i - 1$ nested CTL operators are processed. When a subformula is processed, it is added to the labeling of each state in which it is true. Once the algorithm terminates, we will have that $M, s \models f$ if and only if $f \in label(s)$.

Recall from section 4.3.1 that any CTL formula can be expressed in terms of $\neg$, $\vee$, **EX**, **EU**, and **EG**. Thus, for the intermediate stages of the algorithm it is sufficient to be able to

procedure *CheckEU*(f_1, f_2)
    $T := \{ s \mid f_2 \in label(s) \}$;
    for all $s \in T$ **do** $label(s) := label(s) \cup \{ \mathbf{E}(f_1 \mathbf{U} f_2) \}$;
    while $T \neq \emptyset$ **do**
        choose $s \in T$;
        $T := T \setminus \{s\}$;
        for all t **such that** $R(t,s)$ **do**
            if $\mathbf{E}(f_1 \mathbf{U} f_2) \notin label(t)$ **and** $f_1 \in label(t)$ **then**
                $label(t) := label(t) \cup \{ \mathbf{E}(f_1 \mathbf{U} f_2) \}$;
                $T := T \cup \{t\}$;
            end if
        end for all
    end while
end procedure

Figure 5.1
Procedure for labeling the states satisfying $\mathbf{E}(f_1 \mathbf{U} f_2)$.

handle six cases, depending on whether g is atomic or has one of the following forms: $\neg f_1$, $f_1 \vee f_2$, $\mathbf{EX} f_1$, $\mathbf{E}(f_1 \mathbf{U} f_2)$, or $\mathbf{EG} f_1$.

For formulas of the form $\neg f_1$, we label those states that are not labeled by f_1. For $f_1 \vee f_2$, we label any state that is labeled either by f_1 or by f_2. For $\mathbf{EX} f_1$, we label every state that has some successor labeled by f_1.

To handle formulas of the form $g = \mathbf{E}(f_1 \mathbf{U} f_2)$ we first find all states that are labeled with f_2. We then work backward using the converse of the transition relation R and find all states that can be reached by a path in which each state is labeled with f_1. All such states should be labeled with g.

In figure 5.1 we give a procedure *CheckEU*, which adds $\mathbf{E}(f_1 \mathbf{U} f_2)$ to *label*(s) for every s that satisfies $\mathbf{E}(f_1 \mathbf{U} f_2)$, assuming that f_1 and f_2 have already been processed correctly; that is, for every state s, $f_1 \in label(s)$ if and only if $s \models f_1$ and $f_2 \in label(s)$ if and only if $s \models f_2$. This procedure requires time $O(|S| + |R|)$.

The case in which $g = \mathbf{EG} f_1$ is slightly more complicated. It is based on the decomposition of the graph into nontrivial strongly connected components. A *strongly connected component* (SCC) C is a subgraph such that every node in C is reachable from every other node in C along a directed path entirely contained within C. An SCC C is also *maximal* (denoted MSCC) if there is no other SCC C' such that $C \subset C'$. A component C is *nontrivial* if and only if either it has more than one node or it contains one node with a self-loop.

Let M' be obtained from M by deleting from S all of those states at which f_1 does not hold and restricting R and L accordingly. Thus, $M' = (S', R', L')$, where $S' = \{ s \in S \mid M, s \models f_1 \}$, $R' = R|_{S' \times S'}$, and $L' = L|_{S'}$. Note that R' may not be left-total in this case. The states with no outgoing transitions may be eliminated, but this is not essential for the correctness of our algorithm. The algorithm depends on the following observation.

Lemma 5.1 $M,s \models \mathbf{EG}\,f_1$ *if and only if the following two conditions are satisfied:*

(1) $s \in S'$.

(2) *There exists a path in M' that leads from s to some node t in a nontrivial maximal strongly connected component C of the graph (S',R').*

Proof Assume that $M,s \models \mathbf{EG}\,f_1$. Clearly $s \in S'$. Let π be an infinite path starting at s such that f_1 holds at each state on π. Then π is contained in S'. Since M is finite, it must be possible to write π as $\pi = \pi_0\pi_1$, where π_0 is a finite initial segment and π_1 is an infinite suffix of π with the property that each state on π_1 occurs infinitely often. Let C be the set of states in π_1. We now show that there is a path within C between any pair of states in C. Let s_1 and s_2 be states in C. Pick some instance of s_1 on π_1. By the way in which π_1 was selected, we know that there is an instance of s_2 farther along π_1. The segment from s_1 to s_2 lies entirely within C. This segment is a finite path from s_1 to s_2 in C. Thus, C is a nontrivial SCC. Note that if C is not maximal then it is contained in an MSCC C' and π_0 leads to C' since it leads to C. Thus, both conditions (1) and (2) are satisfied.

Next, assume that conditions (1) and (2) are satisfied. Let π_0 be the path from s to t. Let π_1 be a finite path of length at least 1 that leads from t back to t. The existence of π_1 is guaranteed since t is a state in a nontrivial strongly connected component. All the states on the infinite path $\pi = \pi_0\pi_1^{\omega}$ satisfy f_1. Since π is a path starting at s in M, we see that $M,s \models \mathbf{EG}\,f_1$. $\square$

Lemma 5.1 suggests how to reduce the search for an infinite path to a search for an MSCC. The significance of searching for MSCCs rather than for SCCs lies in the fact that the set of all MSCCs can be found in time linear in the number of states and transitions of M. Finding all SCCs, on the other hand, is exponential as they might include all subsets of S.

The algorithm for the case of $g = \mathbf{EG}\,f_1$ follows directly from lemma 5.1. We construct the restricted Kripke structure $M' = (S',R',L')$ as described above. We partition the graph (S',R') into maximal strongly connected components using the algorithm of Tarjan [12, section 5.5]. This algorithm finds the set of all MSCCs, including the trivial ones, and has time complexity of $O(|S'| + |R'|)$. Next, we find those states that belong to nontrivial components. We then work backward using the converse of R' and find all of those states that can be reached by a path in which each state is labeled with f_1. The entire computation can be performed in time $O(|S| + |R|)$. In figure 5.2 we give a procedure *CheckEG* that adds $\mathbf{EG}\,f_1$ to *label(s)* for every s that satisfies $\mathbf{EG}\,f_1$, assuming that f_1 has already been processed correctly.

In order to handle an arbitrary CTL formula f, we decompose f into subformulas and successively apply the state-labeling algorithm to the subformulas of f. Starting with the shortest, most deeply nested, the algorithm works outward to include all of f. By proceeding

procedure *CheckEG*(f_1)
   $S' := \{ s \mid f_1 \in label(s) \}$;
   $MSCC := \{ C \mid C$ is a nontrivial maximal SCC of $S' \}$;
   $T := \bigcup_{C \in MSCC}\{ s \mid s \in C \}$;
   for all $s \in T$ **do** $label(s) := label(s) \cup \{$ **EG** $f_1 \}$;
   while $T \neq \emptyset$ **do**
      choose $s \in T$;
      $T := T \setminus \{s\}$;
      for all t **such that** $t \in S'$ **and** $R(t,s)$ **do**
         if EG $f_1 \notin label(t)$ **then**
            $label(t) := label(t) \cup \{$ **EG** $f_1 \}$;
            $T := T \cup \{t\}$;
         end if
      end for all
   end while
end procedure

Figure 5.2
Procedure for labeling the states satisfying **EG** f_1.

in this manner we guarantee that whenever we process a subformula g of f all subformulas of g have already been processed. Since each pass takes time $O(|S| + |R|)$ and since f has at most $|f|$ different subformulas, the entire algorithm requires time $O(|f| \cdot (|S| + |R|))$.

Theorem 5.2 *There is an algorithm for determining* $[\![f]\!]$ *that runs in time* $O(|f| \cdot (|S| + |R|))$.

It is straightforward to see that theorem 5.2 holds for every CTL formula over the temporal operators **EX**, **E(U)**, and **EG**. As explained in chapter 4, every other CTL formula can be expressed by means of these three operators. Thus, we can preprocess the CTL formula to obtain a formula that contains only these operators. Except for **A(U)**, all translations are linear in the size of the original formula. Thus, the theorem immediately follows for specifications without **A(U)**. In order to show that it holds for **A(U)** as well, recall that **A**(f **U** g) is equivalent to

$$\neg \mathbf{E}(\neg g \,\mathbf{U}\,(\neg f \wedge \neg g)) \wedge \neg \mathbf{EG} \,\neg g.$$

Note that this formula contains only eight different subformulas: f, g, $\neg f$, $\neg g$, $\mathbf{E}(\neg g \,\mathbf{U}\, (\neg f \wedge \neg g))$, $\mathbf{EG} \,\neg g$, the conjunction of the last two, and the formula itself. Although we have multiple occurrences of g in the subformulas, the state-labeling algorithm will do labeling for g only once. Thus, the overall time complexity is preserved.

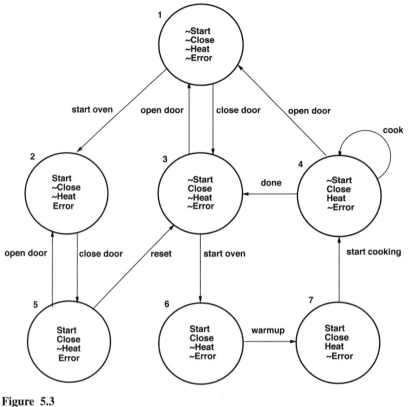

Figure 5.3
Microwave oven example.

We will illustrate the model-checking algorithm for CTL on a small example that describes the behavior of a microwave oven. Figure 5.3 gives the Kripke structure for the oven. For clarity, each state is labeled with both the atomic propositions that are true in the state and the negations of the propositions that are false in the state. The labels on the arcs indicate the actions that cause transitions and are not part of the Kripke structure.

We check the CTL formula **AG**(*Start* → **AF** *Heat*), which is equivalent to the formula ¬**EF**(*Start* ∧ **EG** ¬*Heat*) (here, we use **EF** *f* as an abbreviation for **E**(*true* **U** *f*)). We start by computing the set of states that satisfy the atomic formulas and proceed to more complicated subformulas. Let [[*g*]] denote the set of all states labeled by the subformula *g*. Note that, with a suitable data structure, the computation of [[*p*]] for all *p* ∈ *AP* requires time $O(|S| + |R|)$.

$$[[Start]] = \{2,5,6,7\}$$
$$[[Heat]] = \{1,2,3,5,6\}$$

In order to compute $[\![\mathbf{EG}\,\neg Heat]\!]$, we first find the set of nontrivial strongly connected components in $S' = [\![\neg Heat]\!]$. $MSCC = \{\{1,2,3,5\}\}$. We proceed by setting T, the set of all states that should be labeled by $\mathbf{EG}\,\neg Heat$, to be the union over the elements of $MSCC$, that is, initially $T = \{1,2,3,5\}$. No other state in S' can reach a state in T along a path in S'. Thus, the computation terminates with

$$[\![\mathbf{EG}\,\neg Heat]\!] = \{1,2,3,5\}.$$

Next we compute

$$[\![Start \wedge \mathbf{EG}\,\neg Heat]\!] = \{2,5\}.$$

When computing $[\![\mathbf{EF}(Start \wedge \mathbf{EG}\,\neg Heat)]\!]$, we start by setting

$$T = [\![Start \wedge \mathbf{EG}\,\neg Heat]\!]\,.$$

Next, we use the converse of the transition relation to label all states in which the formula holds. We get

$$[\![\mathbf{EF}(Start \wedge \mathbf{EG}\,\neg Heat)]\!] = \{1,2,3,4,5,6,7\}.$$

Finally, we compute that

$$[\![\neg\,\mathbf{EF}(Start \wedge \mathbf{EG}\,\neg Heat)]\!] = \emptyset.$$

Since the initial state 1 is not contained in this set, we conclude that the system described by the Kripke structure does not satisfy the given specification.

5.2   Model-Checking CTL with Fairness Constraints

In this subsection, we show how to extend the CTL model-checking algorithm to handle fairness constraints. Let $M = (S,R,L,F)$ be a fair Kripke structure. Let $F = \{P_1,\ldots,P_k\}$ be the set of fairness constraints. We will say that a strongly connected component C of the graph of M is *fair* with respect to F if and only if for each $P_i \in F$ there is a state $t_i \in (C \cap P_i)$. We first give an algorithm for checking $\mathbf{EG}\,f_1$ with respect to a fair structure. In order to establish the correctness of this algorithm, we need a lemma that is analogous to lemma 5.1. As before, let M' be obtained from M by deleting from S all of those states at which f_1 does not *fairly* hold. Thus, $M' = (S',R',L',F')$, where $S' = \{s \in S \mid M,s \models_F f_1\}$, $R' = R|_{S' \times S'}$, $L' = L|_{S'}$, and $F' = \{P_i \cap S' \mid P_i \in F\}$.

Lemma 5.3 $M,s \models_F \mathbf{E}_f\,\mathbf{G}\,f_1$ *if and only if the following two conditions are satisfied:*

1. *$s \in S'$.*
2. *There exists a path in S' that leads from s to some node t in a nontrivial* fair *maximal strongly connected component of the graph (S',R').*

The proof of this lemma is similar to the proof of lemma 5.1 and is not given. We can now describe the procedure *CheckFairEG*(f_1) that adds $\mathbf{E}_f\,\mathbf{G}\,f_1$ to the label of s for every s such that $M, s \models_F \mathbf{EG} f_1$. We assume that the states have been labeled correctly with f_1 using the fair semantics for the logic; that is, we assume $f_1 \in label(s)$ if and only if $M, s \models_F f_1$. The procedure *CheckFairEG* is identical to the procedure *CheckEG* given in figure 5.2. The only difference is that *MSCC* now consists of the set of nontrivial *fair* maximal strongly connected components. The complexity of this computation is $O((|S| + |R|) \cdot |F|)$ since it is necessary to determine which components are fair. This involves examining every component to see if it has a state from each fairness constraint.

In order to check other CTL formulas with respect to fair Kripke structures, we introduce an additional atomic proposition *fair*, which is true at a state if and only if there is a fair path starting from that state. Thus, we have that *fair* = $\mathbf{E}_f \mathbf{G}$ *true* according to the fair semantics for the logic. The procedure *CheckFairEG*(*true*) can be used to label states with the new atomic proposition. In order to determine if $M, s \models_F \mathbf{E}_f \mathbf{X} f_1$, we check $M, s \models \mathbf{EX}(f_1 \wedge fair)$. In order to determine if $M, s \models_F \mathbf{E}_f f_1 \mathbf{U} f_2$, we check $M, s \models \mathbf{E}(f_1 \mathbf{U} (f_2 \wedge fair))$ by calling the procedure *CheckEU*$(f_1, f_2 \wedge fair)$.

The complexity analysis is similar to the nonfair case. Each stage requires time $O((|S| + |R|) \cdot |F|)$. Since there are at most $|f|$ stages, the total time complexity is $O(|f| \cdot (|S| + |R|) \cdot |F|)$.

Theorem 5.4 *There is an algorithm for determining whether a CTL formula f is true with respect to the fair semantics in a state s of the structure $M = (S, R, L, F)$ that runs in time $O(|f| \cdot (|S| + |R|) \cdot |F|)$.*

To illustrate the use of fairness constraints, we check a formula similar to the one checked before:

$$\mathbf{A}_f \mathbf{G}(Start \rightarrow \mathbf{A}_f \mathbf{F} Heat),$$

which is again equivalent to

$$\neg \mathbf{E}_f \mathbf{F}(Start \wedge \mathbf{E}_f \mathbf{G} \neg Heat).$$

We check it on the model given in figure 5.3. However, this time we consider only paths along which the user operates the microwave oven correctly infinitely often. This means that infinitely often $Start \wedge Close \wedge \neg Error$ should hold. Thus, $F = \{P\}$, where $P = \{s \mid s \models Start \wedge Close \wedge \neg Error\}$. The sets $[[Start]]$ and $[[\neg Heat]]$ remain as before. When we compute the set of strongly connected components over $S' = [[\neg Heat]]$, we realize that $\{1, 2, 3, 5\}$ is not fair since it does not contain a state that satisfies $Start \wedge Close \wedge \neg Error$. Thus,

$$[[\mathbf{E}_f \mathbf{G} \neg Heat]] = \emptyset.$$

As a result we get

$$[[\mathbf{E}_f \mathbf{F}(Start \wedge \mathbf{E}_f \mathbf{G} \neg Heat)]] = \emptyset,$$

which implies that

$$[\![\neg(\mathbf{E_f}\,\mathbf{F}(Start \wedge \mathbf{E_f}\,\mathbf{G}\,\neg Heat))]\!] = \{1,2,3,4,5,6,7\}.$$

Thus, all states of the program satisfy the formula under the given fairness constraints.

5.3   CTL Model Checking via Fixpoint Computation

The explicit model-checking algorithm presented in section 5.1 manipulates individual states and transitions. In this section we present an alternative algorithm that manipulates entire sets. For this purpose, we use a *fixpoint* characterization of the temporal logic operators. In chapter 8, we will use ordered binary decision diagrams (OBDDs) [85] to represent sets of states and transitions. The symbolic CTL model-checking algorithm presented there is based on the fixpoint characterization and requires only standard OBDD operations on sets. While the run-time complexity of the explicit-model checking algorithm is linear in the size of the system, the new algorithm is quadratic. Nevertheless, its implementation with OBDDs significantly reduces space requirements and thus enables verifying systems that are orders of magnitude larger.

5.3.1   Background on Fixpoint Theory

In this section we present some basic background on fixpoint theory. Fixpoint theory is usually defined over a general domain with a complete partial order. Here, we restrict ourselves to the domain of the powerset of states with the inclusion order.

A set $S' \subseteq S$ is a fixpoint of a function $\tau\colon \mathcal{P}(S) \to \mathcal{P}(S)$ if $\tau(S') = S'$. We first show how the set of states satisfying a CTL formula can be characterized as a least or greatest fixpoint of an appropriate function. Iterative techniques based only on set operations are used to calculate these fixpoints. In the next section we show how to incorporate fairness constraints into the fixpoint characterization.

Let $M = (S,R,L)$ be a finite Kripke structure. The set $\mathcal{P}(S)$ of all subsets of S forms a lattice under the set inclusion ordering. In this section, we use $\mathcal{P}(S)$ to denote the lattice. Each element S' of the lattice can also be thought of as a *predicate* on S, where the predicate is viewed as being *true* for exactly the states in S'. The least element in the lattice is the empty set, which we also refer to as *false*, and the greatest element in the lattice is the set S, which we sometimes write as *true*. A function that maps $\mathcal{P}(S)$ to $\mathcal{P}(S)$ will be called a *predicate transformer*. Let $\tau\colon \mathcal{P}(S) \to \mathcal{P}(S)$ be such a function; then

1. τ is *monotonic* provided that $P \subseteq Q$ implies $\tau(P) \subseteq \tau(Q)$;
2. τ is $\cup$-*continuous* provided that $P_1 \subseteq P_2 \subseteq \ldots$ implies $\tau(\cup_i P_i) = \cup_i \tau(P_i)$;
3. τ is $\cap$-*continuous* provided that $P_1 \supseteq P_2 \supseteq \ldots$ implies $\tau(\cap_i P_i) = \cap_i \tau(P_i)$.

We write $\tau^i(Z)$ to denote i applications of τ to Z. More formally, $\tau^i(Z)$ is defined recursively by $\tau^0(Z) = Z$ and $\tau^{i+1}(Z) = \tau(\tau^i(Z))$.

Theorem 5.5 (Tarski–Knaster [459]) *Let τ be a predicate transformer on $\mathcal{P}(S)$. Then if τ is monotonic it has a greatest fixpoint, $\nu Z . \tau(Z)$, and a least fixpoint, $\mu Z . \tau(Z)$, defined as follows:*

- $\nu Z . \tau(Z) = \bigcup \{ Z \mid Z \subseteq \tau(Z) \}$
- $\mu Z . \tau(Z) = \bigcap \{ Z \mid Z \supseteq \tau(Z) \}$

Furthermore, if τ is $\bigcap$-continuous, then $\nu Z . \tau(Z) = \bigcap \tau^i(true)$, and if τ is $\bigcup$-continuous, then $\mu Z . \tau(Z) = \bigcup \tau^i(false)$.

Proof We will prove the case for the greatest fixpoint. The case for the least fixpoint follows by duality.

Let $\Gamma = \{ Z \mid Z \subseteq \tau(Z) \}$. Let $P = \bigcup \Gamma$. Then for each $Z \in \Gamma$, $Z \subseteq P$. Since τ is monotonic, then $\tau(Z) \subseteq \tau(P)$. Since for each $Z \in \Gamma$, $Z \subseteq \tau(Z)$, thus, $Z \subseteq \tau(P)$. Furthermore, by monotonicity, for each such Z, $\tau(Z) \subseteq \tau(\tau(Z))$, and hence also $\tau(Z) \in \Gamma$. Since for each $Z \in \Gamma$, $Z \subseteq \tau(Z) \subseteq \tau(P)$, taking the union over all sets Z in Γ, we obtain $\bigcup \Gamma = P \subseteq \tau(P)$. Hence, by definition of Γ, $P \in \Gamma$, and also $\tau(P) \in \Gamma$. Since P is the union of the sets in Γ, then $\tau(P) \subseteq P$. We established the inclusion between P and $\tau(P)$ in both directions. Hence $\tau(P) = P$; that is, P is a fixpoint of τ. Since $\subseteq$ is reflexive, then every fixpoint of τ is also in Γ. So P, which includes all the sets in Γ, in particular the fixpoints, must be the greatest fixpoint of τ.

For the second part of the theorem, observe that $S \supseteq \tau(S)$; S, which is denoted also as *true*, is the largest subset, including all the other subsets. By monotonicity, $\tau(S) \supseteq \tau(\tau(S))$, and by induction, $\tau^i(S) \supseteq \tau^{i+1}(S)$. By continuity, $\tau(\bigcap \tau^i(S)) = \bigcap \tau^{i+1}(S) \supseteq \bigcap \tau^i(S)$. Therefore, $\bigcap \tau^i(S) \in \Gamma$. Consequently, $P \supseteq \bigcap \tau^i(S)$. We need to show now the converse, that is, that $P \subseteq \bigcap \tau^i(S)$. Obviously, $P \subseteq S$. Thus, by monotonicity, $P = \tau(P) \subseteq \tau(S)$. By induction, $P \subseteq \tau^i(S)$ for each i, and thus $P \subseteq \bigcap \tau_i(S)$.   □

The Tarski–Knaster theorem implies that if τ is continuous then it can be computed by a (possibly infinite) sequence of τ applications. In the following lemmas we show that for $\tau \colon \mathcal{P}(S) \to \mathcal{P}(S)$, if S is finite, then whenever τ is monotonic, it is also continuous. We further show that in this case, only a finite number of τ applications are needed. Thus, we obtain an algorithm to compute the fixpoints.

Lemma 5.6 *If S is finite and τ is monotonic, then τ is also $\bigcup$-continuous and $\bigcap$-continuous.*

Proof Let $P_1 \subseteq P_2 \subseteq \ldots$ be a sequence of subsets of S. Since S is finite, there is j_0 such that for every $j \geq j_0$, $P_j = P_{j_0}$. For every $j < j_0$, $P_j \subseteq P_{j_0}$. Thus, $\bigcup_i P_i = P_{j_0}$, and as a result, $\tau(\bigcup_i P_i) = \tau(P_{j_0})$. On the other hand, since τ is monotonic, $\tau(P_1) \subseteq \tau(P_2) \subseteq \ldots$. Thus, for every $j < j_0$, $\tau(P_j) \subseteq \tau(P_{j_0})$, and for every $j \geq j_0$, $\tau(P_j) = \tau(P_{j_0})$. As a result, $\bigcup_i \tau(P_i) = \tau(P_{j_0})$, and τ is $\bigcup$-continuous. The proof that τ is $\bigcap$-continuous is similar.   □

Lemma 5.7 *If τ is monotonic, then for every i, $\tau^i(false) \subseteq \tau^{i+1}(false)$ and $\tau^i(true) \supseteq \tau^{i+1}(true)$.*

function *Lfp*(*Tau* : *PredicateTransformer*) : *Predicate*
   Q := *false*;
   Q' := *Tau*(*Q*);
   while *Q* ≠ *Q'* **do**
      Q := *Q'*;
      Q' := *Tau*(*Q'*);
   end while
   return *Q*;
end function

Figure 5.4
Procedure for computing least fixpoints.

Lemma 5.8 *If* τ *is monotonic and S is finite, then there is an integer* i_0 *such that for every* $j \geq i_0$, $\tau^j(\text{false}) = \tau^{i_0}(\text{false})$. *Similarly, there is some* j_0 *such that for every* $j \geq j_0$, $\tau^j(\text{true}) = \tau^{j_0}(\text{true})$.

Lemma 5.9 *If* τ *is monotonic and S is finite, then there is an integer* i_0 *such that* $\mu Z . \tau(Z) = \tau^{i_0}(\text{false})$. *Similarly, there is an integer* j_0 *such that* $\nu Z . \tau(Z) = \tau^{j_0}(\text{true})$.

As a consequence of the preceding lemmas, if τ is monotonic, its least fixpoint can be computed by the program in figure 5.4.

The invariant for the **while** loop in the body of the procedure is given by the assertion

$$(Q' = \tau(Q)) \wedge (Q' \subseteq \mu Z . \tau(Z)).$$

It is easy to see that at the beginning of the *i*-th iteration of the loop, $Q = \tau^{i-1}(\text{false})$ and $Q' = \tau^i(\text{false})$. Lemma 5.7 implies that

$$\text{false} \subseteq \tau(\text{false}) \subseteq \tau^2(\text{false}) \subseteq \ldots .$$

Consequently, the maximum number of iterations before the while loop terminates is bounded by the number of elements in the set *S*. When the loop does terminate, we will have that $Q = \tau(Q)$ and that $Q \subseteq \mu Z . \tau(Z)$. Since *Q* is also a fixpoint, $\mu Z . \tau(Z) \subseteq Q$, and hence $Q = \mu Z . \tau(Z)$. Thus, the value returned by the procedure is the required least fixpoint. The greatest fixpoint of τ may be computed in a similar manner by the program in figure 5.5. Essentially the same argument can be used to show that the procedure terminates and that the value it returns is $\nu Z . \tau(Z)$.

5.3.2   Fixpoint-Based Reachability Analysis

In model checking, one of the most frequently analyzed properties is reachability. Given a model *M*, *reachability analysis* computes the set of all states that are reachable from an initial state of *M*. Reachability analysis can be easily extended to checking whether

function *Gfp*(*Tau* : *PredicateTransformer*) : *Predicate*
    $Q :=$ *true*;
    $Q' := Tau(Q)$;
    while $Q \neq Q'$ **do**
        $Q := Q'$;
        $Q' := Tau(Q')$;
    end while
    return Q;
end function

Figure 5.5
Procedure for computing greatest fixpoints.

$M \models \mathbf{AG}\, p$, where p is a Boolean combination of atomic formulas. This can be done by checking that no reachable state violates p. Reachability analysis then also returns, in addition to the set of reachable states, "True" or "False", to indicate whether $M \models \mathbf{AG}\, p$ or not.

It is interesting to compare reachability analysis with CTL model checking, when applied to M and $\mathbf{AG}\, p$. The latter will return the set $[\![\mathbf{AG}p]\!]$, that is, the set of all states in M that satisfy $\mathbf{AG}\, p$. This set may contain unreachable states. Further, it will *not* contain those reachable states that do not satisfy $\mathbf{AG}\, p$. Note that once CTL model checking computes $[\![\mathbf{AG}p]\!]$, it can also check $S_0 \subseteq [\![\mathbf{AG}p]\!]$ and conclude $M \models \mathbf{AG}\, p$.

We now give a fixpoint-based algorithm for reachability analysis for checking $M \models \mathbf{AG}\, p$. The algorithm is based on *least fixpoint* computation. For the algorithm we need to define the following operator. Given a model M, the *post image* of a set of states Q is the set of states that are reachable from Q with one transition. This operation is often called just *image*. We write *post-image*(Q) for this set:

$$post\text{-}image(Q) = \{s' \mid \exists s \in Q.\, R(s, s')\}$$

Having *post-image*(Q) we can now define the predicate transformer *Tau*:

$$Tau(Q) = S_0 \cup post\text{-}image(Q)$$

Using this *Tau* in the function for computing least fixpoints, presented in figure 5.4, the function returns the set of reachable states. Figure 5.6 illustrates this computation.

Figure 5.7 presents the extension of reachability analysis for checking $M \models \mathbf{AG}\, p$. It is easy to see that *On-the-fly Reach* computes the set of states that are reachable in M. Note that the check of whether there is a reachable state that is not labeled with p is performed "on-the-fly" during the fixpoint iteration. This allows the procedure to terminate early in case there is such a state. If all reachable states satisfy p, we conclude that $M \models \mathbf{AG}\, p$.

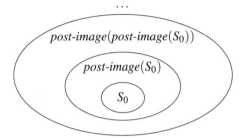

Figure 5.6
Illustration of the computation of the set of reachable states using the post image.

function *On-the-fly Reach*(model M, $p \in AP$)
    $Q := \emptyset$;
    $Q' := S_0$;
    while $Q' \neq Q$ **do**
        if $\exists s \in Q'.s \not\models p$ **then**
            return "Model does not satisfy **AG** p"
        end if
        $Q := Q'$;
        $Q' := Q' \cup post\text{-}image(Q')$;
    end while
    return ("Model satisfies **AG** p", Q);
end function

Figure 5.7
Procedure for reachability analysis for checking **AG** p.

5.3.3 Fixpoint-Based Model-Checking Algorithm for CTL

We now show how to use fixpoint theory to provide fixpoint algorithms for CTL model checking. To this end, we use CTL state formulas to describe mappings between sets of states. Let f be a CTL formula which contains Z as a placeholder for a set of states, that is, in the syntactic position of a propositional variable. Then f defines the following predicate transformer $f : \mathcal{P}(S) \to \mathcal{P}(S)$:

$$f(Q) = [\![f[Z/Q]]\!]_M = \{s \mid M, s \models f[Z/Q]\},$$

where $f[Z/Q]$ is the formula obtained from f by replacing Z by the set Q. For instance, **EX** Z is the mapping that takes a set of states Q and returns the set of predecessor states of Q.

Then each of the basic CTL operators can be characterized as a least or greatest fixpoint of an appropriate predicate transformer [198].

- $[\![\mathbf{AF}\,f_1]\!]_M = \mu Z.\, f_1 \vee \mathbf{AX}\, Z$
- $[\![\mathbf{EF}\,f_1]\!]_M = \mu Z.\, f_1 \vee \mathbf{EX}\, Z$
- $[\![\mathbf{AG}\,f_1]\!]_M = \nu Z.\, f_1 \wedge \mathbf{AX}\, Z$
- $[\![\mathbf{EG}\,f_1]\!]_M = \nu Z.\, f_1 \wedge \mathbf{EX}\, Z$
- $[\![\mathbf{A}(f_1\,\mathbf{U}\,f_2)]\!]_M = \mu Z.\, f_2 \vee (f_1 \wedge \mathbf{AX}\, Z)$
- $[\![\mathbf{E}(f_1\,\mathbf{U}\,f_2)]\!]_M = \mu Z.\, f_2 \vee (f_1 \wedge \mathbf{EX}\, Z)$
- $[\![\mathbf{A}(f_1\,\mathbf{R}\,f_2)]\!]_M = \nu Z.\, f_2 \wedge (f_1 \vee \mathbf{AX}\, Z)$
- $[\![\mathbf{E}(f_1\,\mathbf{R}\,f_2)]\!]_M = \nu Z.\, f_2 \wedge (f_1 \vee \mathbf{EX}\, Z)$

Intuitively, least fixpoints correspond to eventualities whereas greatest fixpoints correspond to properties that should hold forever. Thus, $\mathbf{AF}\,f_1$ has a least fixpoint characterization and $\mathbf{EG}\,f_1$ has a greatest fixpoint characterization.

We prove only the correctness of the fixpoint characterizations for **EG** and **EU**. The fixpoint characterizations of the remaining CTL operators can be established in a similar manner.

Lemma 5.10 $\mathbf{E}(f_1\,\mathbf{U}\,f_2)$ *is the least fixpoint of the function*

$$\tau(Z) = f_2 \vee (f_1 \wedge \mathbf{EX}\, Z).$$

Proof First we notice that $\tau(Z) = f_2 \vee (f_1 \wedge \mathbf{EX}\, Z)$ is monotonic. By lemma 5.6, τ is therefore $\cup$-continuous. It is also straightforward to show that $\mathbf{E}(f_1\,\mathbf{U}\,f_2)$ is a fixpoint of $\tau(Z)$. We still need to prove that $\mathbf{E}(f_1\,\mathbf{U}\,f_2)$ is the least fixpoint of $\tau(Z)$. For that, it is sufficient to show that $\mathbf{E}(f_1\,\mathbf{U}\,f_2) = \cup_i \tau^i(\textit{false})$. For the first direction, it is easy to prove by induction on i that for every i, $\tau^i(\textit{false}) \subseteq \mathbf{E}(f_1\,\mathbf{U}\,f_2)$. Consequently, we have that $\cup_i \tau^i(\textit{false}) \subseteq \mathbf{E}(f_1\,\mathbf{U}\,f_2)$.

The other direction, $\mathbf{E}(f_1\,\mathbf{U}\,f_2) \subseteq \cup_i \tau^i(\textit{false})$, is proved by induction on the length of the prefix of the path along which $f_1\,\mathbf{U}\,f_2$ is satisfied. More specifically, if $s \models \mathbf{E}(f_1\,\mathbf{U}\,f_2)$, then there is a path $\pi = s_1, s_2, \ldots$ with $s = s_1$ and $j \geq 1$ such that $s_j \models f_2$ and for all $l < j$, $s_l \models f_1$. We show that for every such state s, $s \in \tau^j(\textit{false})$. The basis case is trivial. If $j = 1$, $s \models f_2$ and therefore $s \in \tau(\textit{false}) = f_2 \vee (f_1 \wedge \mathbf{EX}(\textit{false}))$.

For the inductive step, assume that the above claim holds for every s and every $j \leq n$. Let s be the start of a path $\pi = s_1, s_2, \ldots$ such that $s_{n+1} \models f_2$ and for every $l < n+1$, $s_l \models f_1$. Consider the state s_2 on the path. It is the start of a prefix of length n along which $f_1\mathbf{U}f_2$ holds, and therefore, by the induction hypothesis, $s_2 \in \tau^n(\textit{false})$. Since $(s, s_2) \in R$ and $s \models f_1$, $s \in f_1 \wedge \mathbf{EX}(\tau^n(\textit{false}))$; thus, $s \in \tau^{n+1}(\textit{false})$. $\square$

Figure 5.8 shows how the set of states that satisfy $\mathbf{E}(p\,\mathbf{U}\,q)$ may be computed for a simple Kripke structure by using the procedure Lfp. In this case the predicate transformer τ is

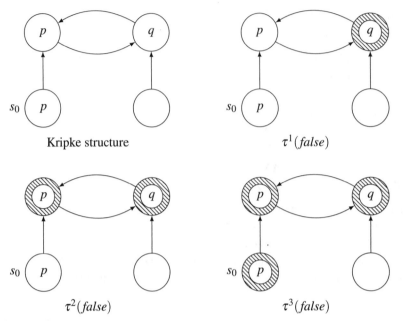

Figure 5.8
Sequence of approximations for $\mathbf{E}(p\,\mathbf{U}\,q)$.

given by
$$\tau(Z) = q \vee (p \wedge \mathbf{EX}\,Z).$$

The figure demonstrates how the sequence of approximations $\tau^i(\mathit{false})$ converges to $\mathbf{E}(p\,\mathbf{U}\,q)$. The states that constitute the current approximation to $\mathbf{E}(p\,\mathbf{U}\,q)$ are shaded. It is easy to see that $\tau^3(\mathit{false}) = \tau^4(\mathit{false})$. Hence, $\mathbf{E}(p\,\mathbf{U}\,q) = \tau^3(\mathit{false})$. Because s_0 is in $\tau^3(\mathit{false})$, we see that $M, s_0 \models \mathbf{E}(p\,\mathbf{U}\,q)$.

Lemmas 5.11–5.14 below show that $\mathbf{EG}\,f_1 = \nu Z \,.\, f_1 \wedge \mathbf{EX}\,Z$.

Lemma 5.11 $\tau(Z) = f_1 \wedge \mathbf{EX}\,Z$ *is monotonic.*

Proof Let $P_1 \subseteq P_2$. To show that $\tau(P_1) \subseteq \tau(P_2)$, consider some state $s \in \tau(P_1)$. Then $s \models f_1$ and there exists a state s' such that $(s, s') \in R$ and $s' \in P_1$. Since $P_1 \subseteq P_2$, $s' \in P_2$ as well. Thus, $s \in \tau(P_2)$. $\square$

Lemma 5.12 *Let* $\tau(Z) = f_1 \wedge \mathbf{EX}\,Z$, *and let* $\tau^{i_0}(\mathit{true})$ *be the limit of the sequence* $\mathit{true} \supseteq \tau(\mathit{true}) \supseteq \dots$. *For every* $s \in S$, *if* $s \in \tau^{i_0}(\mathit{true})$ *then* $s \models f_1$, *and there is a state* s' *such that* $(s, s') \in R$ *and* $s' \in \tau^{i_0}(\mathit{true})$.

Proof Let $s \in \tau^{i_0}(true)$; then, since $\tau^{i_0}(true)$ is a fixpoint of τ, $\tau^{i_0}(true) = \tau(\tau^{i_0}(true))$. Thus, $s \in \tau(\tau^{i_0}(true))$. By definition of τ we get that $s \models f_1$ and there is a state s' such that $(s, s') \in R$ and $s' \in \tau^{i_0}(true)$. $\square$

Lemma 5.13 $\mathbf{EG}\, f_1$ *is a fixpoint of the function* $\tau(Z) = f_1 \wedge \mathbf{EX}\, Z$.

Proof Suppose that $s_0 \models \mathbf{EG}\, f_1$. Then by the definition of $\models$, there is a path $s_0, s_1, \ldots$ in M such that for all k, $s_k \models f_1$. This implies that $s_0 \models f_1$ and $s_1 \models \mathbf{EG}\, f_1$. In other words, $s_0 \models f_1$ and $s_0 \models \mathbf{EX}\,\mathbf{EG}\, f_1$. Thus, $\mathbf{EG}\, f_1 \subseteq f_1 \wedge \mathbf{EX}\,\mathbf{EG}\, f_1$. Similarly, if $s_0 \models f_1 \wedge \mathbf{EX}\,\mathbf{EG}\, f_1$, then $s_0 \models \mathbf{EG}\, f_1$. Consequently, $\mathbf{EG}\, f_1 = f_1 \wedge \mathbf{EX}\,\mathbf{EG}\, f_1$. $\square$

Lemma 5.14 $\mathbf{EG}\, f_1$ *is the greatest fixpoint of the function*

$$\tau(Z) = f_1 \wedge \mathbf{EX}\, Z.$$

Proof Since τ is monotonic, by lemma 5.6 it is also $\cap$-continuous. Therefore, in order to show that $\mathbf{EG}\, f_1$ is the greatest fixpoint of τ, it is sufficient to prove that $\mathbf{EG}\, f_1 = \cap_i \tau^i(true)$.

We first show that $\mathbf{EG}\, f_1 \subseteq \cap_i \tau^i(true)$. We establish this claim by applying induction on i to show that, for every i, $\mathbf{EG}\, f_1 \subseteq \tau^i(true)$. Clearly, $\mathbf{EG}\, f_1 \subseteq true$. Assume that $\mathbf{EG}\, f_1 \subseteq \tau^n(true)$. Since τ is monotonic, $\tau(\mathbf{EG}\, f_1) \subseteq \tau^{n+1}(true)$. By lemma 5.13, $\tau(\mathbf{EG}\, f_1) = \mathbf{EG}\, f_1$. Hence, $\mathbf{EG}\, f_1 \subseteq \tau^{n+1}(true)$.

We now show that $\cap_i \tau^i(true)$ is a subset of $\mathbf{EG}\, f_1$. Consider some state $s \in \cap_i \tau^i(true)$. This state is included in every $\tau^i(true)$. Hence, the state s is also in the fixpoint $\tau^{i_0}(true)$. By lemma 5.12, s is the start of an infinite sequence of states in which each state is related to the previous one by the relation R. Furthermore, each state in the sequence satisfies f_1. Thus, $s \models \mathbf{EG}\, f_1$. $\square$

5.3.4   Characterizing Fairness with Fixpoints

Fairness constraints and their significance were discussed in chapter 4. In section 5.2, fairness constraints were added to the explicit-state model-checking algorithm for CTL. In this section we extend the fixpoint characterization of CTL temporal operators, given in the previous section, to include fairness constraints as well. We assume the fairness constraints are given by a set of CTL formulas $F = \{P_1, \ldots, P_n\}$.

Consider the formula $\mathbf{E}_f\,\mathbf{G}\, f$ given fairness constraints F. The formula means that there exists a path beginning with the current state on which f holds globally (invariantly) and each formula in F holds infinitely often on the path. The set of such states Z is the largest set with the following two properties:

1. All of the states in Z satisfy f.
2. For all fairness constraints $P_k \in F$ and all states $s \in Z$, there is a sequence of states of length 1 or greater from s to a state in Z satisfying P_k such that all states on the path satisfy f.

This characterization is somewhat different from the one given for the explicit state case in lemma 5.3. It is more appropriate for fixpoint characterization since it can be expressed by means of a fixpoint as follows:

$$\mathbf{E_f}\,\mathbf{G}\,f = \nu Z.\,f \wedge \bigwedge_{k=1}^{n} \mathbf{EX}\,\mathbf{E}(f\,\mathbf{U}\,(Z \wedge P_k)) \tag{5.1}$$

Notice that this formula uses both CTL and fixpoint operators. Using the fixpoint characterization of CTL operators given in the previous section, we can obtain a fixpoint characterization to $\mathbf{E_f}\,\mathbf{G}\,f$ with fairness constraints. Note that the resulting formula includes nesting of fixpoint operators.

It is possible to show that the formula in equation 5.1 is not directly expressible in CTL. In chapter 16 we describe a very expressive logic called the μ-calculus, which includes both the least and greatest fixpoint operators. The hybrid formula given above for the fair version of $\mathbf{EG}$ can be easily translated into the μ-calculus.

Below we prove the correctness of equation 5.1. We split the proof into two lemmas. The first lemma shows that $\mathbf{E_f}\,\mathbf{G}\,f$ is a fixpoint of the equation

$$Z = f \wedge \bigwedge_{k=1}^{n} \mathbf{EX}\,\mathbf{E}(f\,\mathbf{U}\,(Z \wedge P_k)). \tag{5.2}$$

Thus, it is included in the greatest fixpoint. The second shows that the greatest fixpoint of the equation is included in $\mathbf{E_f}\,\mathbf{G}\,f$. Combining the two parts of the proof, it follows that $\mathbf{E_f}\,\mathbf{G}\,f$ is the greatest fixpoint.

Lemma 5.15 $\mathbf{E_f}\,\mathbf{G}\,f$ *is a fixpoint of the formula in equation 5.2.*

Proof Let $s \in \mathbf{E_f}\,\mathbf{G}\,f$; then s is the start of a fair path all of whose states satisfy f. Let s_i be the first state on this path such that $s_i \in P_i$ and $s_i \neq s$. The state s_i is also a start of a fair path along which all states satisfy f. Thus, $s_i \in \mathbf{E_f}\,\mathbf{G}\,f$. It follows that, for every i,

$$s \models f \wedge \mathbf{EX}\,\mathbf{E}(f\,\mathbf{U}\,(\mathbf{E_f}\,\mathbf{G}\,f \wedge P_i)),$$

and therefore,

$$s \models f \wedge \bigwedge_{k=1}^{n} \mathbf{EX}\,\mathbf{E}(f\,\mathbf{U}\,(\mathbf{E_f}\,\mathbf{G}\,f \wedge P_k)).$$

Thus, we conclude that $\mathbf{E_f}\,\mathbf{G}\,f \subseteq f \wedge \bigwedge_{k=1}^{n} \mathbf{EX}\,\mathbf{E}(f\,\mathbf{U}\,(\mathbf{E_f}\,\mathbf{G}\,f \wedge P_k))$. To show that

$$f \wedge \bigwedge_{k=1}^{n} \mathbf{EX}\,\mathbf{E}(f\,\mathbf{U}\,(\mathbf{E_f}\,\mathbf{G}\,f \wedge P_k)) \subseteq \mathbf{E_f}\,\mathbf{G}\,f,$$

note that if $s \models f \wedge \bigwedge_{k=1}^{n} \mathbf{EX}\,\mathbf{E}(f\,\mathbf{U}\,(\mathbf{E_f}\,\mathbf{G}\,f \wedge P_k))$, then there is a finite path starting from s to a state s' such that $s' \models (\mathbf{E_f}\,\mathbf{G}\,f \wedge P_k)$. Moreover, every state on the path from s to s' satisfies f. Thus, $s \models \mathbf{E_f}\,\mathbf{G}\,f$, as required. It follows that $\mathbf{E_f}\,\mathbf{G}\,f$ is a fixpoint. $\square$

Lemma 5.16 *The greatest fixpoint of the formula in equation 5.2 is included in* $\mathbf{E_f\,G}\,f$.

Proof Let Z be an arbitrary fixpoint of the formula in equation 5.2. We show that Z is included in $\mathbf{E_f\,G}\,f$. Assume that $s \in Z$. Then, s satisfies f. Moreover, it has a successor s' that is a start of a path to a state s_1 such that all states on this path satisfy f and s_1 satisfies $Z \wedge P_1$. Since $s_1 \in Z$ we can conclude by the same argument that there is a path from s_1 to a state s_2 in P_2. Using this argument n times we conclude that s is the start of a path along which all the states satisfy f and that passes through $P_1, \ldots, P_n$. Moreover, the last state on this path is in Z. Thus, there is a path from this state back to some state in P_1, and the construction can be repeated.

Induction can be used to show formally that there exists a path starting at s such that f holds on every state on the path and each fairness constraint holds infinitely often. Thus, s is in $\mathbf{E_f\,G}\,f$. Since Z is an arbitrary fixpoint, it follows that the greatest fixpoint is contained in $\mathbf{E_f\,G}\,f$. $\square$

As in section 5.2, let *fair* denote the set of all states that satisfy $\mathbf{E_f\,G}\,true$ according to the fair semantics. Then, the formulas $\mathbf{E_f\,X}\,f_1$ and $\mathbf{E_f}\,f_1\,\mathbf{U}\,f_2$ according to the fairness semantics are expressible by the formulas $\mathbf{EX}(f_1 \wedge fair)$ and $\mathbf{E}(f_1\,\mathbf{U}\,(f_2 \wedge fair))$, respectively. The fixpoint characterization of these formulas can now be obtained by using the fixpoint characterizations of $\mathbf{EX}$, $\mathbf{E\,U}$, and *fair*.

5.3.5 Fixpoint Characterization over Finite Paths

We consistently assume Kripke structures with a left-total transition relation. Several notions significantly change if we relax this assumption. One of these notions is the fixpoint characterization of CTL formulas. We first define the semantics of temporal operators over finite paths:

$$M, \pi \models \mathbf{F}\,g_1 \quad \Leftrightarrow \quad \text{there exists a } 0 \le i \le length(\pi) \text{ such that } M, \pi^i \models g_1.$$
$$M, \pi \models \mathbf{G}\,g_1 \quad \Leftrightarrow \quad \text{for all } 0 \le i \le length(\pi), M, \pi^i \models g_1.$$

The fixpoint characterization of CTL formulas will be changed accordingly:

- $[\![\mathbf{AF}\,f_1]\!]_M = \mu Z . f_1 \vee (\mathbf{AX}\,Z \wedge \mathbf{EX}\,true)$
- $[\![\mathbf{EG}\,f_1]\!]_M = \nu Z . f_1 \wedge (\mathbf{EX}\,Z \vee \mathbf{AX}\,false)$

The fixpoint characterization for the other CTL formulas can be defined similarly. Note that for $\mathbf{AF}\,f_1$ (and similarly for $\mathbf{EF}\,f_1$), if f_1 does not hold at a state, we require that the state must have a successor. Such a requirement is unnecessary for Kripke structures with a left-total transition relation since all their paths are infinite. Dually, for $\mathbf{EG}\,f_1$, every state that has no successor satisfies the formula vacuously. This is reflected by adding $\mathbf{AX}\,false$, which holds at a state if and only if the state has no successors.

Note also that the duality between $\mathbf{AF}$ and $\mathbf{EG}$ as well as between $\mathbf{EF}$ and $\mathbf{AG}$ is preserved in the semantics and in the fixpoint characterization over finite paths.

Bibliographic Notes

In Chapter 4 we distinguished between safety and liveness properties based on their goal and the type of their counterexamples. Here we consider their model-checking algorithms. Safety properties have the advantage that they can easily be checked by, for instance, reachability analysis (see section 5.3.2). Hence, many efficient model-checking tools for safety properties exist. For liveness, on the other hand, more sophisticated algorithms are usually used. Biere, Artho, and Schuppan [56] present an efficient translation of liveness checking into safety checking. Their approach can handle fairness as well and thus extends to full LTL. This may lead to simpler and more uniform model checking of liveness properties, and it may help to find shortest counterexamples. Further, it allows adding liveness checking to model-checking tools that handle only safety, without changing their internal behavior. In [434], this approach is extended to a variety of infinite-state systems.

Safety, liveness, and CTL model checking are also discussed in [35].

Problems

Problem 5.1 (Disjointness of MSCCs). Let C_1 and C_2 be two MSCCs. Prove that they are disjoint. Conclude that the sum of states over all MSCCs of M is bounded by the size of S.

6 LTL and CTL* Model Checking

In this chapter and in the next we present model-checking algorithms for LTL. Recall from section 4.3.4 that CTL and LTL are both sublogics of CTL*, with incomparable expressive power. Thus, LTL can express properties that cannot be expressed in CTL. Further, some properties are more conveniently expressible in LTL. We are therefore motivated to develop a model-checking algorithm for LTL.

The algorithms for LTL are significantly different from the algorithms for CTL presented before. CTL model checking essentially computes a set of states for each of the subformulas of the checked formula. This is possible since all these subformulas are state formulas, which are interpreted over states. By contrast, an LTL formula is interpreted over a path, and all its subformulas should be checked along the same path. Thus, the algorithm for LTL handles the formula as a whole. Given an LTL formula φ, LTL model checking constructs a structure, called *tableau* or *automaton*, for the *negation* of φ, which represents the set of all paths that do not satisfy φ. It then uses this structure for checking whether the system model includes a path that does not satisfy the formula.

In this chapter we define a tableau for LTL and show how to use it for LTL model checking. We prove the correctness of the tableau-based model-checking algorithm. We next present a model checking algorithm for CTL*, which is constructed as a combination of the algorithms for CTL and LTL model checking. Chapter 7 defines finite automata on infinite words and discusses some of their properties. It then presents an automata-based model-checking algorithm, in which the specification automaton can be given directly or obtained by a translation from an LTL formula.

Let $M = (S, S_0, R, AP, L)$ be a Kripke structure, and let $\mathbf{A}g$ be an LTL formula. Thus, g is a *LTL path formula* in which the only state subformulas are atomic propositions. Given a state $s \in S$, we wish to determine if $M, s \models \mathbf{A}g$. Notice that $M, s \models \mathbf{A}g$ if and only if $M, s \models \neg \mathbf{E} \neg g$. Consequently, it is sufficient to be able to check the truth of formulas of the form $\mathbf{E}f$, where f is an LTL path formula. In general, this problem is PSPACE-complete [445, 446]. However, a more careful analysis by Lichtenstein and Pnueli [347] shows that, although the complexity is apparently exponential in the length of the formula, it is linear in the size of the global state graph, representing the system to be verified. The analysis in [347] is based on an algorithm that involves a *tableau construction*.

In the following section we present a simpler algorithm for LTL model checking that is based on a tableau construction, taken from [126]. We show that this algorithm can be implemented using CTL model checking.

6.1   The Tableau Construction

In this section we describe the tableau construction and its use for model checking. We give a formal proof of correctness of this technique. Some of the theorems and lemmas are quite technical. When reading this section for the first time, their proofs can be skipped.

We begin with an informal description of the model-checking algorithm. Recall that it is sufficient to be able to check the truth of formulas of the form $\mathbf{E}f$, where f is an LTL path formula. Given a formula $\mathbf{E}f$ and a Kripke structure M, we construct a *tableau* T for the path formula f. The tableau T is a Kripke structure and includes *every* path that satisfies f. By composing T with M, we find the set of paths that appear in both T and M. A state in M will satisfy $\mathbf{E}f$ if and only if it is the start of a path in the composition that satisfies f.

We now describe the construction of the tableau T in detail. Let AP_f be the set of atomic propositions in f. The tableau associated with f is a fair Kripke structure $T = (S_T, S_T^0, R_T, AP_f, L_T, F_T)$ (see section 4.5). Recall that the set of fairness constraints is $F = \{P_1, \ldots, P_n\}$, where each P_i is a set of states of which at least one state should repeat infinitely often. Unlike the algorithm of Lichtenstein and Pnueli, we do not use the full closure of the formula. Each state in the tableau is a set of *elementary* formulas obtained from f. We later see that this set is sufficient for determining the truth value of every subformula of f. The set of elementary subformulas of f is denoted by $el(f)$ and is defined recursively as follows:

- $el(p) = \{p\}$ for $p \in AP_f$
- $el(\neg g) = el(g)$
- $el(g \vee h) = el(g) \cup el(h)$
- $el(\mathbf{X}g) = \{\mathbf{X}g\} \cup el(g)$
- $el(g\,\mathbf{U}\,h) = \{\mathbf{X}(g\,\mathbf{U}\,h)\} \cup el(g) \cup el(h)$

The set $el(f)$ includes only atomic propositions and formulas of the form $\mathbf{X}g$, where g is a subformula of f. The set of states S_T of the tableau includes all subsets of $el(f)$. That is, $S_T = \mathcal{P}(el(f))$. The labeling function L_T is defined so that each state is labeled by the set of atomic propositions contained in the state. The idea is that atomic formulas in s determine the set of atomic propositions true in s; formulas of the form $\mathbf{X}g$ indicate that g should be true in each of the successors of s.

In order to construct the set of initial states S_T^0 and the transition relation R_T, we need an additional function *sat* that associates with each subformula g of f a set of states from S_T. Intuitively, $sat(g)$ will be the set of states that satisfy g.

- $sat(g) = \{ s \in S_T \mid g \in s \}$ where $g \in el(f)$
- $sat(\neg g) = \{ s \in S_T \mid s \notin sat(g) \}$
- $sat(g \lor h) = sat(g) \cup sat(h)$
- $sat(g \, \mathbf{U} \, h) = sat(h) \cup \big(sat(g) \cap sat(\mathbf{X}(g \, \mathbf{U} \, h)) \big)$

We define the initial states S_T^0 of the tableau to be $sat(f)$, which are the states that satisfy f. We want the transition relation to have the property that each elementary formula included in a state is true in all paths starting at this state. Clearly, if $\mathbf{X}g$ is in some state s, then all the successors of s should satisfy g. Furthermore, since we are dealing with LTL formulas, if $\mathbf{X}g$ is not included in s, then s should satisfy $\neg \mathbf{X}g$. Hence, no successor of s should satisfy g. Thus, we define R_T to be

$$R_T(s,s') = \bigwedge_{\mathbf{X}g \in el(f)} s \in sat(\mathbf{X}g) \Leftrightarrow s' \in sat(g).$$

Let $g = (\neg heat) \, \mathbf{U} \, close$ be a specification for the microwave oven example from chapter 5. Figure 6.1 gives the transition relation R_T for the tableau of the formula $\neg g$. To reduce the number of edges, we connect two states s and s' with a bidirectional arrow if there is an edge from s to s' and also from s' to s. Each subset of $el(g)$ is a state of T. When labeling the states in figure 6.1 we use h as an abbreviation for *heat* and c as an abbreviation for *close*. For clarity we also include negations of atomic propositions. Note that $sat(\mathbf{X}g) = \{1,2,3,5\}$, since each of these states contains the formula $\mathbf{X}g$. We have $sat(g) = \{1,2,3,4,6\}$, since each of these states either contains *close* or contains $\neg heat$ and $\mathbf{X}g$. We can now define the initial states as $S_T^0 = \{1,2,3,4,6\}$.

Furthermore, $sat(\neg g) = \{5,7,8\}$ is the complement of $sat(g)$. There is a transition from each state in $sat(\mathbf{X}g)$ to each state in $sat(g)$ and from each state in the complement of $sat(\mathbf{X}g)$ to each state in the complement of $sat(g)$. This is because the definition of R_T is a conjunction of "if and only if" conditions.

Unfortunately, the definition of R_T does not guarantee that *eventuality* properties are fulfilled. We can see this behavior in figure 6.1. Although state 3 belongs to $sat(g)$, the path that loops forever in state 3 does not satisfy the formula g since *close* never holds on that path. Consequently, an additional condition is necessary in order to identify those paths along which f holds. A path π that starts from a state $s \in sat(f)$ will satisfy f if and only if the following holds: For every subformula $g \, \mathbf{U} \, h$ of f and for every state s on π, if $s \in sat(g \, \mathbf{U} \, h)$, then either $s \in sat(h)$ or there is a later state t on π such that $t \in sat(h)$.

The additional condition is introduced into the tableau by adding the following fairness constraints:

$$F_T = \{ \, sat(\neg(g \, \mathbf{U} \, h) \lor h) \mid g \, \mathbf{U} \, h \text{ occurs in } f \, \} \tag{6.1}$$

This completes the construction of the tableau.

Consider again the example of figure 6.1. $F_T = sat(\neg((\neg heat) \, \mathbf{U} \, close)) \cup sat(close) = \{5,7,8\} \cup \{1,2,4,6\} = S_T \setminus \{3\}$.

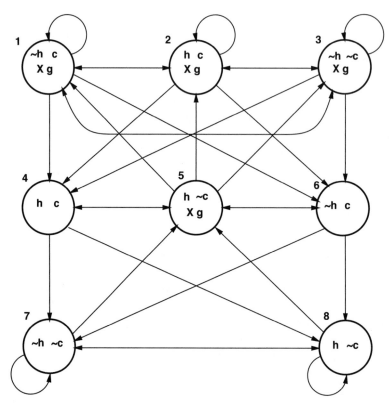

Figure 6.1
Tableau for $(\neg heat)\,\mathbf{U}\,close$.

Note that the tableau for $\neg g$ is identical to that of g except that the initial states in $T_{\neg g}$ are the complement of the initial states of T_g.

6.2   LTL Model Checking with Tableau

Next, we want to compute the product $P = (S, S_0, R, AP_f, L, F)$ of the tableau $T = (S_T, S_T^0, R_T, AP_f, L_T, F_T)$ and $M = (S_M, S_M^0, R_M, AP, L_M)$.

- $S = \{\, (s, s') \mid s \in S_T, s' \in S_M,\ \text{and}\ L_M(s')\,|_{AP_f} = L_T(s)\,\}$.
- $S_0 = \{\, (s, s') \mid s \in S_T^0, s' \in S_M^0,\ \text{and}\ (s, s') \in S\,\}$.
- $R((s, s'), (t, t'))$ if and only if $R_T(s, t)$ and $R_M(s', t')$.
- $L((s, s')) = L_T(s)$.
- $F = \{\, P_i \times S_M \mid P_i \in F_T\,\}$.

The transition relation of this product may fail to be total. If this happens, we iteratively remove from S all of those states that do not have successors and restrict the transition relation R to the remaining states.

Note that the product P contains exactly the composed sequences π'' for which there are paths π in T and π' in M that have the same labeling of propositions in AP_f.

We extend the function *sat* to be defined over the set of states of the product P by $(s, s') \in sat(g)$ if and only if $s \in sat(g)$. We next find the set of all states V in P such that $V \subseteq sat(f)$ and, in addition, every state in V is the start of an infinite path that satisfies all of the fairness constraints in F_T. These paths have the property that no subformula $g\,\mathbf{U}\,h$ holds almost always on the path while h remains false. Thus, every state in V satisfies $\mathbf{E}f$. From V we can extract the set of states in M which satisfy $\mathbf{A}\neg f$ (see definition in section 4.4).

$$[\![\mathbf{A}\neg f]\!]_M = S_M \setminus \{s' \mid \text{there exists } s \in S_T : (s, s') \in V\}.$$

Recall that our goal was to check LTL formulas of the form $\mathbf{A}g$, and for that we applied the algorithm for checking $\mathbf{E}\neg g$.

Note that all states in V thus satisfy $\mathbf{EG}\,true$ with the fairness constraints F_T. This implies that LTL model checking can in fact be reduced to model-checking CTL with fairness constraints. The CTL model checking algorithm will be applied to P and will compute the set of states V. An algorithm for checking CTL with fairness constraints is described in section 5.2.

The correctness of this algorithm is summarized by the following theorem (the theorem reappears as theorem 6.11 in the next section, where it is also proved).

Theorem 6.1 *$M, s' \models \mathbf{E}f$ if and only if there is a state s in T such that $(s, s') \in sat(f)$ and (s, s') is a start of a fair path in P.*

Example 6.2 *To illustrate the construction described above, we explain how to check the formula $\mathbf{A}((\neg heat)\,\mathbf{U}\,close)$ on the Kripke structure M in figure 5.3, describing the microwave oven. We construct a tableau for the formula*

$$\neg g = \neg((\neg heat)\,\mathbf{U}\,close).$$

The tableau T for this formula is given in figure 6.1. Note that, it is identical to the tableau for $(\neg heat)\,\mathbf{U}\,close$, except that now the set of initial states is $sat(\neg((\neg heat)\,\mathbf{U}\,close)) = \{5, 7, 8\}$. If we compute the product P as described above, we obtain the Kripke structure given in figure 6.2. Each state in the product is marked by a pair of states (s, s') where $s \in T$ and $s' \in M$. We have omitted the states $(4, 4)$, $(4, 7)$, $(6, 3)$, $(6, 5)$, $(6, 6)$, $(7, 1)$, and $(7, 2)$ from the diagram for the product structure since they are not the beginning of an infinite path. A transition in the product represents a pair of transitions in T and in M. For instance, there is a transition from state $(3, 1)$ to state $(3, 2)$ in P since there in a transition $(3, 3) \in R_T$ and a transition $(1, 2) \in R_M$.

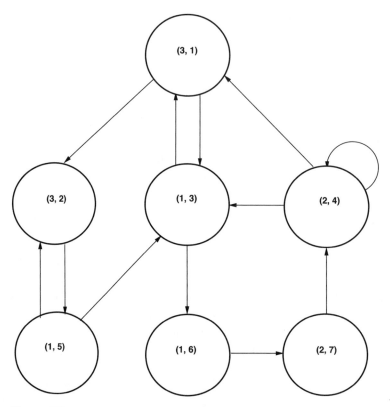

Figure 6.2
The product P of the microwave M and the tableau T.

We use the CTL model-checking algorithm to find the set V of states of P, which are in $sat(\neg g)$ and satisfy the formula $\mathbf{EG}$ true with the fairness constraint $sat(\neg((\neg heat)\,\mathbf{U}\,close)\vee close)$. Since $sat(\neg g) = \{(7,1),(7,2)\}$ but neither of these states is the beginning of an infinite path, $V = \emptyset$. We can therefore conclude that no state in M satisfies $\mathbf{E}\,\neg((\neg heat)\,\mathbf{U}\,close)$ and therefore that all states satisfy $\mathbf{A}((\neg heat)\,\mathbf{U}\,close)$.

6.3   Correctness Proof of the Tableau Construction

To state the key property of the tableau construction, we must introduce some new notation. Let $\pi' = s_0', s_1', \ldots$ be a path in a Kripke structure $M = (S, S_0, R, AP, L)$; then $label(\pi') = L(s_0'), L(s_1'), \ldots$. Let $l = l_0, l_1, \ldots$ be a sequence of subsets of the set AP, and let $AP' \subseteq AP$. The *restriction* of l to AP', denoted by $l \mid_{AP'}$, is the sequence $m_0, m_1, \ldots$ where $m_i = l_i \cap AP'$ for every $i \geq 0$. In addition, we use $sub(f)$ to denote the set of subformulas of f.

The following theorem makes precise the intuitive claim that T includes every path that satisfies f.

Theorem 6.3 *Let T be the tableau for the path formula f. Then, for every Kripke structure M and every path π' of M, if $M, \pi' \models f$ then there is a fair path π in T that starts in a state in $sat(f)$ such that $label(\pi') \mid_{AP_f} = label(\pi)$.*

Example 6.4 *Consider again the Kripke structure M of figure 5.3 and the tableau T of figure 6.1.*

Let $\pi' = 1, (2, 5)^\omega$ be an infinite path in M, such that $\pi' \models ((\neg heat) \mathbf{U} close)$. The path $\pi = 3(3, 1)^\omega$ in T satisfies the requirements of theorem 6.3: $label(\pi') \mid_{AP_f} = label(\pi)$ and state 3 is in $sat(g)$. Moreover, π is fair since state 1 is in $sat(heat)$ and therefore in F_T.

Note that here we implicitly assume that $AP_f \subseteq AP$. This necessarily holds since a formula is checked on a structure only if the atomic propositions of the formula are included in those of the structure.

In order to prove this theorem, we need the following two lemmas. In the remainder of this section, $\pi' = s'_0, s'_1, \ldots$ represents a path in M. We denote the suffix of π' starting from the state s'_i by π'_i; that is, $\pi'_i = s'_i, s'_{i+1}, \ldots$. For the path π'_i, we define

$$s_i = \{ \psi \mid \psi \in el(f) \text{ and } M, \pi'_i \models \psi \}. \tag{6.2}$$

Thus, s_i includes all elementary formulas satisfied by the suffix π'_i of π'. Note that s_i is a state in T.

Lemma 6.5 *Let $\pi' = s'_0, s'_1, \ldots$ be a path in M'. For all $i \geq 0$, let s_i be the tableau state defined by equation 6.2. Then, for all $g \in sub(f) \cup el(f)$, $M, \pi'_i \models g$ if and only if $s_i \in sat(g)$.*

Proof The proof proceeds by induction on the structure of the formula.

1. Let $g \in el(f)$. By the definition of s_i, it is easy to see that $M, \pi'_i \models g$ if and only if $g \in s_i$. By the definition of sat, $g \in s_i$ if and only if $s_i \in sat(g)$. Note that the base case includes all atomic formulas and all formulas of the form $\mathbf{X}g$ for any LTL path formula g.

2. Let $g = \neg g_1$ or $g = g_1 \vee g_2$. By the induction hypothesis and the definition of sat, it is easy to prove these cases.

3. Let $g = g_1 \mathbf{U} g_2$. By the definition of $\mathbf{U}$, $M, \pi'_i \models g_1 \mathbf{U} g_2$ if and only if $M, \pi'_i \models g_2$ or $(M, \pi'_i \models g_1$ and $M, \pi'_i \models \mathbf{X}(g_1 \mathbf{U} g_2))$. By the induction hypothesis and the definition of s_i, $M, \pi'_i \models g_2$ or $(M, \pi'_i \models g_1$ and $M, \pi'_i \models \mathbf{X}(g_1 \mathbf{U} g_2))$ if and only if $s_i \in sat(g_2) \vee (s_i \in sat(g_1) \wedge s_i \in sat(\mathbf{X}(g_1 \mathbf{U} g_2)))$. Note that $\mathbf{X}(g_1 \mathbf{U} g_2)$ is in $el(f)$ and therefore has already been handled in the base case. By the definition of sat, $s_i \in sat(g_2) \vee (s_i \in sat(g_1) \wedge s_i \in sat(\mathbf{X}(g_1 \mathbf{U} g_2)))$ if and only if $s_i \in sat(g_1 \mathbf{U} g_2)$. $\square$

Lemma 6.6 *Let $\pi' = s'_0, s'_1, \ldots$ be a path in M'. For all $i \geq 0$, let s_i be the tableau state defined by equation 6.2. Then $\pi = s_0, s_1, \ldots$ is a path in T.*

Proof Clearly, for all i, $s_i \in S_T$. By lemma 6.5 and the definition of $\mathbf{X}$, it is easy to see the following relation: $s_i \in sat(\mathbf{X}g)$ if and only if $M, \pi_i' \models \mathbf{X}g$ if and only if $M, \pi_{i+1}' \models g$ if and only if $s_{i+1} \in sat(g)$. By the definition of R_T, if $s_i \in sat(\mathbf{X}g) \Leftrightarrow s_{i+1} \in sat(g)$, then $(s_i, s_{i+1}) \in R_T$. Therefore $\pi = s_0, s_1, \ldots$ is a path in T. $\square$

Lemma 6.7 *Let $\pi' = s_0', s_1', \ldots$ be a path in M'. For all $i \geq 0$, let s_i be the tableau state defined by equation 6.2. The path $\pi = s_0, s_1, \ldots$ is a fair path of T.*

Proof In order to show that π is fair, we need to prove that, for every subformula $g \mathbf{U} h$ of f, there are infinitely many states s_i on π such that $s_i \in sat(\neg(g \mathbf{U} h) \vee h)$. Suppose this is not the case; then there exists i_0 such that, for all $i \geq i_0$, $s_i \notin sat(\neg(g \mathbf{U} h) \vee h)$. Thus, $s_i \in sat(g \mathbf{U} h)$ and $s_i \notin sat(h)$. By lemma 6.5, for all $i \geq i_0$, $\pi_i' \models g \mathbf{U} h$ and $\pi_i' \not\models h$. Since $\pi_i' \models g \mathbf{U} h$ means $\pi_j' \models h$ for some $j \geq i$, this leads to a contradiction. $\square$

We can now prove theorem 6.3.

Proof Suppose that, for a path π' in M, $\pi' \models f$. By lemma 6.6, we can find a path $\pi = s_0 s_1 \ldots$ in T. By lemma 6.7, this path is fair. Lemma 6.5 guarantees that $s_0 \in sat(f)$. By the definition of s_i given in equation 6.2, $L(s_i') \mid_{AP_f} = L_T(s_i)$, and thus $label(\pi') \mid_{AP_f} = label(\pi)$. This leads to theorem 6.3. $\square$

In section 6.2 we defined the product P of the tableau T and the Kripke structure M for the LTL model-checking algorithm. The next lemma states that P contains exactly the sequences π'' for which there are paths π in T and π' in M that have the same labeling of propositions in AP_f.

Lemma 6.8 $\pi'' = (s_0, s_0'), (s_1, s_1'), \ldots$ *is a path in P with $L_P((s_i, s_i')) = L_T(s_i)$ for all $i \geq 0$ if and only if there exist a path $\pi = s_0, s_1 \ldots$ in T, and a path $\pi' = s_0', s_1', \ldots$ in M with $L_T(s_i) = L_M(s_i') \mid_{AP_f}$ for all $i \geq 0$. Moreover, π'' is fair if and only if π is fair.*

Proof The proof of this lemma is straightforward. Given π'' in P, π and π' are obtained by projecting each state on the path onto the appropriate structure. For the other direction, since π and π' agree on the labeling restricted to AP_f, we see that (s_i, s_i') is a state in P for all $i \geq 0$. Moreover, there is a transition from (s_i, s_i') to (s_{i+1}, s_{i+1}').

By definition, π'' is fair if and only if for every $P_i \in F$ there are infinitely many j such that $(s_j, s_j') \in (P_i \times S_M)$ if and only if there are infinitely many j such that $s_j \in P_i$ if and only if π is fair. $\square$

In section 6.2 we also extend the function *sat* to be defined over the set of states of the product P. We then find the set of all states V in P, such that $V \subseteq sat(f)$ and, in addition, every state in V is the start of a fair path in P.

The following two lemmas describe properties of paths in the tableau T. Lemma 6.9 shows that if for some s on π, $s \in sat(g_1 \mathbf{U} g_2)$, then all of its successors on π will remain in $sat(g_1 \mathbf{U} g_2)$ until a successor in $sat(g_2)$ is reached. Lemma 6.10 proves that if π is fair then a necessary and sufficient condition for π to satisfy f is that its initial state is in $sat(f)$. Lemma 6.10 tells us that in order to find paths in the tableau that satisfy f, we should look for fair paths that start in $sat(f)$. This observation extends naturally to the product P.

Lemma 6.9 *Assume that, for all $k \geq j$, $s_k \in sat(g_1) \Leftrightarrow \pi_k \models g_1$ and $s_k \in sat(g_2) \Leftrightarrow \pi_k \models g_2$. If $\pi_j \not\models g_1 \mathbf{U} g_2$ and $s_j \in sat(g_1 \mathbf{U} g_2)$, then, for all $k \geq j$, $\pi_k \not\models g_1 \mathbf{U} g_2$ and $s_k \in sat(g_1 \mathbf{U} g_2)$.*

Proof First we prove that if $s_j \in sat(g_1 \mathbf{U} g_2)$ and $\pi_j \not\models g_1 \mathbf{U} g_2$, then $s_{j+1} \in sat(g_1 \mathbf{U} g_2)$ and $\pi_{j+1} \not\models g_1 \mathbf{U} g_2$. From the definition of sat, $s_j \in sat(g_1 \mathbf{U} g_2)$ implies that $s_j \in sat(g_2)$ or $(s_j \in sat(g_1)$ and $s_j \in sat(\mathbf{X}(g_1 \mathbf{U} g_2)))$. From the assumptions and the definition of R_T, it follows that

$$\pi_j \models g_2 \text{ or } (\pi_j \models g_1 \text{ and } s_{j+1} \in sat(g_1 \mathbf{U} g_2)). \tag{6.3}$$

Since $\pi_j \not\models g_1 \mathbf{U} g_2$ implies $\pi_j \not\models g_2$, (6.3) simplifies to

$$\pi_j \models g_1 \text{ and } s_{j+1} \in sat(g_1 \mathbf{U} g_2). \tag{6.4}$$

We know that $\pi_j \models g_1$ from equation 6.4 and that $\pi_j \not\models g_1 \mathbf{U} g_2$ from the assumption. If π_{j+1} satisfied $g_1 \mathbf{U} g_2$, then since $\pi_j \models g_1$ we could conclude that $\pi_j \models g_1 \mathbf{U} g_2$. But this is impossible, so it must be the case that $\pi_{j+1} \not\models g_1 \mathbf{U} g_2$.

Similarly, we can get, for all $k = j+2, j+3, j+4, \ldots$, that $s_k \in sat(g_1 \mathbf{U} g_2)$ and $\pi_k \not\models g_1 \mathbf{U} g_2$. □

Lemma 6.10 *Let $\pi = s_0, s_1, \ldots$ be a fair path in T; then $T, \pi \models f$ if and only if $s_0 \in sat(f)$.*

Proof By induction on the structure of the formula, we prove, for each $g \in sub(f) \cup el(f)$, that for all j, $T, \pi_j \models g$ if and only if $s_j \in sat(g)$.

1. Let $g = p \in AP_f$. By the definition of s_j and the definition of sat, it is easy to see the following relation: $\pi_j \models p$ if and only if $p \in L_T(s_j)$ if and only if $p \in s_j$ if and only if $s_j \in sat(p)$.

2. Let $g = \neg g_1$ or $g = g_1 \vee g_2$. By the induction hypothesis and the semantics of $\neg$ and $\vee$, it is easy to prove these cases.

3. Let $g = \mathbf{X} g_1$. By the definition of R_T and the induction hypothesis, we can see the following relation: $s_j \in sat(\mathbf{X} g_1)$ if and only if $s_{j+1} \in sat(g)$ if and only if $\pi_{j+1} \models g$ if and only if $\pi_j \models \mathbf{X} g$.

4. Let $g = g_1 \mathbf{U} g_2$. For the first direction, assume that $\pi_j \models g_1 \mathbf{U} g_2$; then for some $l \geq j$, $\pi_l \models g_2$, and for all $j \leq i < l$, $\pi_i \models g_1$. By the induction hypothesis, $s_l \in sat(g_2)$, and therefore $s_l \in sat(g_1 \mathbf{U} g_2)$. By the definition of R_T, it follows that $s_{l-1} \in sat(\mathbf{X}(g_1 \mathbf{U} g_2))$. But $\pi_{l-1} \models g_1$, so by induction $s_{l-1} \in sat(g_1)$ and therefore $s_{l-1} \in sat(g_1 \mathbf{U} g_2)$. By induction on $(l - j)$ we eventually get $s_j \in sat(g_1 \mathbf{U} g_2)$.
   For the other direction, suppose that $s_j \in sat(g_1 \mathbf{U} g_2)$ and $\pi_j \not\models g_1 \mathbf{U} g_2$. The inductive hypothesis guarantees that the conditions for lemma 6.9 hold. Thus, for all $k \geq j$, $s_k \in sat(g_1 \mathbf{U} g_2)$ and $\pi_k \not\models g_1 \mathbf{U} g_2$. This implies that $\pi_k \not\models g_2$, and thus $s_k \notin sat(g_2)$ from

the induction hypothesis. Consequently, $s_k \in sat(g_1 \mathbf{U} g_2)$ and $s_k \notin sat(g_2)$ for all $k \geq j$. This leads to a contradiction, because $\pi \models \mathbf{G} \, true$ guarantees that there are infinitely many states s_k such that $s_k \in sat(\neg(g_1 \mathbf{U} g_2) \vee g_2)$. Therefore, if $s_j \in sat(g_1 \mathbf{U} g_2)$, then $\pi_j \models g_1 \mathbf{U} g_2$. □

The correctness of our construction is summarized by the following theorem.

Theorem 6.11 $M, s' \models \mathbf{E} f$ if and only if there is a state s in T such that $(s, s') \in sat(f)$ and (s, s') is the start of a fair path in P.

Proof For the first direction, since $M, s'_0 \models \mathbf{E} f$, then there exists a path π' in M such that $\pi' \models f$. By theorem 6.3 and lemma 6.7, we conclude that there is a fair path π in T such that $label(\pi) = label(\pi') \mid_{AP_f}$. By lemma 6.8, there is a path π'' in P such that $label(\pi'') = label(\pi)$. Since $label(\pi) = label(\pi') \mid_{AP_f}$ and $\pi' \models f$, we can see that $\pi \models f$. Also, since π is fair, by lemma 6.10 $s_0 \in sat(f)$. Thus, $(s_0, s'_0) \in sat(f)$. Since π is fair, by definition π'' is also fair. Therefore, (s_0, s'_0) is a start of a fair path P.

For the other direction, assume that $(s_0, s'_0) \in sat(f)$ and (s_0, s'_0) is the start of a fair path π'' in P. By lemma 6.8, there exist paths $\pi \in T$ and $\pi' \in M$ such that $label(\pi'') = label(\pi) = label(\pi') \mid_{AP_f}$. Further, since π'' is fair, π is also fair. Moreover, since $(s_0, s'_0) \in sat(f)$, $s_0 \in sat(f)$. By lemma 6.10, $\pi \models f$. Since $label(\pi) = label(\pi') \mid_{AP_f}$, $\pi' \models f$ as well. Therefore, $M, s'_0 \models \mathbf{E} f$. □

6.4   CTL* Model Checking

One would expect that the complexity of the model-checking problem for CTL* should be greater than the complexity of the model-checking problems for both CTL and LTL. Surprisingly, this is not the case. In [122, 204] it is shown that the model-checking problem for CTL* has essentially the same complexity as the model-checking problem for LTL.

The basic idea is to combine the state-labeling technique from CTL model checking with LTL model checking. The original algorithm for LTL can handle formulas of the form $\mathbf{E} f$ where f is an LTL path formula in which the only state subformulas are atomic propositions. This algorithm can be extended to handle formulas in which f contains arbitrary state subformulas. Assume that the state subformulas of f have already been processed and that the state labels have been updated accordingly. Each state subformula will be replaced by a fresh atomic proposition in both the labeling of the model and the formula. Let the new formula be denoted by $\mathbf{E} f'$. If the formula is in CTL, then we apply the CTL model-checking procedure. Otherwise, f' is a pure LTL path formula, and the algorithm for LTL model checking is used. In both cases, the formula is added to the label of all of those states that satisfy it. If $\mathbf{E} f$ is a subformula of a more complex CTL* formula, then the procedure is repeated with $\mathbf{E} f$ replaced by a fresh atomic proposition. This is continued until the entire formula is processed.

Like the CTL algorithm, the algorithm for CTL* works in stages such that in stage i
formulas of level i are processed. Let f be a CTL* formula. The state subformulas of level i
are defined inductively as follows:

- Level 0 contains all atomic propositions.
- Level $i + 1$ contains all state subformulas g such that all state subformulas of g are of
  level i or less and g is not contained in any lower level.

To illustrate the levels of a CTL* formula, we return to the microwave oven example. The
following CTL* formula asserts that whenever an illegal sequence of steps occurs, then
either the oven will never heat or it will eventually be reset:

$$\mathbf{AG}((\neg Close \wedge Start) \rightarrow \mathbf{A}(\mathbf{G}\,\neg Heat \vee \mathbf{F}\,\neg Error))$$

The illegal sequence is described by $(\neg Close \wedge Start)$, which means that the start button
is pressed before the door is closed. The result of the reset step is indicated by $\neg Error$. This
property is not expressible in CTL.

In order to simplify the model checking, we work only with existential path quantifiers.
Thus, we first rewrite the above formula to

$$\neg \mathbf{EF}(\neg Close \wedge Start \wedge \mathbf{E}(\mathbf{F}\,Heat \wedge \mathbf{G}\,Error)).$$

The levels of the subformulas of this formula are as follows:

- Level 0 subformulas are *Close*, *Start*, *Heat*, and *Error*.
- Level 1 subformulas are $\mathbf{E}(\mathbf{F}\,Heat \wedge \mathbf{G}\,Error)$ and $\neg Close$.
- Level 2 subformula is $\mathbf{EF}(\neg Close \wedge Start \wedge \mathbf{E}(\mathbf{F}\,Heat \wedge \mathbf{G}\,Error))$.
- Level 3 contains the entire formula.

Let g be a CTL* formula; then a subformula $\mathbf{E}h_1$ of g is *maximal* if and only if $\mathbf{E}h_1$ is not a
strict subformula of any strict subformula $\mathbf{E}h$ of g. For example, consider the formula

$$\mathbf{E}(a \vee \mathbf{E}(b \wedge \mathbf{EF}c)).$$

Then, $\mathbf{EF}c$ is a maximal subformula of $\mathbf{E}(b \wedge \mathbf{EF}c)$ but not of $\mathbf{E}(a \vee \mathbf{E}(b \wedge \mathbf{EF}c))$.

Let $M = (S, S_0, R, AP, L)$ be a Kripke structure; let f be a CTL* formula, and let g be a
state subformula of f of level i. We assume that the states of M have already been labeled
correctly with all state subformulas of level smaller than i. In stage i of the algorithm for
CTL*, g is added to all states that make it true. Several cases are considered according to
the form of the formula g:

- If g is an atomic proposition, then g is in *label*(s) if and only if it is in $L(s)$.
- If $g = \neg g_1$, then g is added to *label*(s) if and only if g_1 is not in *label*(s).
- If $g = g_1 \vee g_2$, then g is added to *label*(s) if and only if either g_1 or g_2 are in *label*(s).

procedure *CheckE*(*g*)
    if *g* is a CTL formula **then**
        apply CTL model checking for *g*;
        return;
    end if
    $g' := g[a_1/\mathbf{E}h_1, \ldots, a_k/\mathbf{E}h_k]$;
    for all $s \in S$ **do**
        for $i = 1, \ldots, k$ **do**
            if $\mathbf{E}h_i \in label(s)$ **then** $label(s) := label(s) \cup \{a_i\}$;
    end for all
    apply LTL model checking for g';
    for all $s \in S$ **do**
        if $g' \in label(s)$ **then** $label(s) := label(s) \cup \{g\}$;
    end for all
end procedure

Figure 6.3
Procedure for computing the set of states satisfying the CTL* formula $g = \mathbf{E}g_1$.

- If $g = \mathbf{E}g_1$, then the procedure *CheckE*(*g*), given in figure 6.3, is applied to add *g* to the label of all states that satisfy the formula, where $\mathbf{E}h_1, \ldots, \mathbf{E}h_k$ are the maximal subformulas of *g*, and $a_1, \ldots, a_k$ are fresh atomic propositions. The formula g' in the procedure is obtained by replacing each subformula $\mathbf{E}h_i$ by the atomic proposition a_i. Note that the resulting formula is of the form $\mathbf{E}g_1'$, where g_1' is a pure LTL path formula. Here we assume that the LTL model checker updates $label(s)$ so that $M, s \models g'$ if and only if $label(s) := label(s) \cup \{g'\}$.

The complexity of this algorithm depends on the complexity of the model-checking algorithms for CTL and LTL that are used. As shown in chapter 5, the complexity of CTL model checking is linear in both the size of the structure *M* and the formula *f*. The best currently known time complexity for LTL model checking is $|M| \cdot 2^{O(|f|)}$.

Theorem 6.12 *There is a CTL* model-checking algorithm with complexity $|M| \cdot 2^{O(|f|)}$.*

Note that in an actual implementation there is no need to replace state subformulas by auxiliary atomic propositions. Once the labels of the states are updated with respect to a given subformula, this subformula can be referred to as an atomic proposition.

To demonstrate the CTL* model-checking algorithm, we consider again the CTL* formula

$$\neg \mathbf{EF}(\neg Close \wedge Start \wedge \mathbf{E}(\mathbf{F}\,Heat \wedge \mathbf{G}\,Error))$$

and check it on the microwave oven model given in figure 5.3.

At level 0 all atomic propositions are handled. At level 1, the formula ¬*Close* is first added to the labels of states 1 and 2. The other formula of level 1, $\mathbf{E}(\mathbf{F}\,Heat \wedge \mathbf{G}\,Error)$, is a pure LTL formula and therefore is handled by an LTL model-checking procedure. Since no state satisfies this formula, it is not added to any state label. At level 2, the formula $\mathbf{E}(\mathbf{F}\,Heat \wedge \mathbf{G}\,Error)$ is first replaced by the atomic proposition a. An LTL model-checking procedure is then applied to the pure LTL formula $\mathbf{EF}(\neg Close \wedge Start \wedge a)$. No state is labeled with this formula either, and therefore, at level 3 all states are labeled with

$$\neg\,\mathbf{EF}(\neg Close \wedge Start \wedge \mathbf{E}(\mathbf{F}\,Heat \wedge \mathbf{G}\,Error)).$$

Thus, this property always holds for the microwave oven.

Bibliographic Notes

The two main temporal logics that were used in model checking are CTL [198, 122] and LTL [410]. They differ in expressive power and the complexity of model checking; hence, they have given rise to a large number of works that support one of these logics or another, or try to reconcile them by providing a logic that inherits elements and properties from both of them. CTL was shown to be efficient for model checking in the size of the property in [198, 418] but using a a system model that is linear in the full state space explicitly. LTL was shown to be in PSPACE for both a compact (nonexplicit) representation of the state space and the size of the property in [446]. The PSPACE result is rather theoretical (using a binary search), and practical algorithms for LTL model checking are exponential in the size of the property and linear in the full state space [347]. Automata-theoretic algorithms for LTL model checking [471, 239] are presented in chapter 7.

Several extensions of CTL and their model-checking algorithms are suggested in [122, 204, 199], including the ability to reason about fair executions, and a full model checking algorithm for CTL*, as presented in this chapter.

CTL* model checking is PSPACE-complete both in the size of the formula when fixing the size of the property, and in the size of the representation of the checked system (based on the compact representation, as a collection of processes or as a digital circuit) when fixing the size of the formula. An algorithm that achieves this (hence shows the upper bound) is given in [321]. The lower bound follows from the same result for LTL [308, 446].

Problems

Problem 6.1 (Tableau for ACTL). Give a tableau construction for ACTL and prove its correctness.

7 Automata on Infinite Words and LTL Model Checking

In this chapter we present some basic facts from automata theory. We then demonstrate how automata can be used to represent system models and specifications. We also show how to check that a system satisfies a specification within the automata-theoretic approach. In particular, we present a translation from an LTL formula to a finite automaton on infinite words (to be defined later). This provides an alternative algorithm for LTL model checking to the one presented in chapter 6.

Similarly to the tableau-based algorithm of chapter 6, the automata-theoretic approach takes advantage of the fact that both the system and the specification are described using the same notation. There, Kripke structures are used to present both entities, while here they are presented by automata. Since Kripke structures can be translated to automata and vice versa (see section 7.7), the difference is not significant. Indeed, the general ideas underlying both methods are very similar.

Most of this chapter focuses on finite automata on infinite words. As a first step we give a short overview of the more standard notion of finite automata on finite words.

7.1 Finite Automata on Finite Words

A finite automaton is a mathematical model of a device that has a constant amount of memory, independent of the size of its input. We will consider finite automata over finite words (also called *regular automata*) and finite automata over infinite words (also called *ω-regular automata*).

Formally, a finite automaton (over finite words) $\mathcal{A}$ is a 5-tuple $(\Sigma, Q, \Delta, Q^0, F)$ such that

- Σ is the finite *alphabet*,
- Q is the finite set of *states*,
- $\Delta \subseteq Q \times \Sigma \times Q$ is the *transition relation*,
- $Q^0 \subseteq Q$ is the set of *initial states*, and
- $F \subseteq Q$ is the set of *accepting states*.

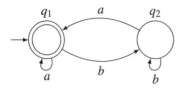

Figure 7.1
A finite automaton.

An automaton can be represented as a graph with labeled transitions, in which the set of nodes is Q and the edges are given by Δ. An example of an automaton is given in figure 7.1. There, $\Sigma = \{a, b\}$, $Q = \{q_1, q_2\}$, $Q^0 = \{q_1\}$ (initial states are marked with an incoming arrow), and $F = \{q_1\}$ (accepting states are marked with a double circle).

Let v be a word (string, sequence) in Σ^* of length $|v|$. A *run* of $\mathcal{A}$ over v is a mapping $\rho : \{1, \ldots, |v| + 1\} \mapsto Q$ such that the following hold:

- The first state is an initial state, that is, $\rho(1) \in Q^0$.
- Moving from the i-th state $\rho(i)$ to the $(i+1)$-th state $\rho(i+1)$ upon reading the i-th input letter $v(i)$ is consistent with the transition relation. That is, for $1 \leq i \leq |v|$ $(\rho(i), v(i), \rho(i+1)) \in \Delta$.

A run ρ of $\mathcal{A}$ on v corresponds to a path in the automaton graph from an initial state $\rho(1)$ to a state $\rho(|v| + 1)$, where the edges on this path are labeled according to the letters in v. We say that v is an *input* to the automaton $\mathcal{A}$ or that $\mathcal{A}$ *reads* v. A run ρ over v is *accepting* if it ends in an accepting state, that is, if $\rho(|v| + 1) \in F$. An automaton $\mathcal{A}$ *accepts* a word v if and only if there exists an accepting run of $\mathcal{A}$ on v. For example, the automaton in figure 7.1 accepts the word *aabba* because there is a run that traverses the states $q_1 q_1 q_1 q_2 q_2 q_1$.

The *language* of $\mathcal{A}$, denoted by $\mathcal{L}(\mathcal{A}) \subseteq \Sigma^*$, consists of all the words accepted by $\mathcal{A}$. Languages accepted by finite automata on finite words are called *regular languages*.

The automaton in figure 7.1 accepts the regular language described by the regular expression $\varepsilon + (a + b)^* a$, that is, either the empty word ε, or words that consist of any number of a's or b's and end with an a. The operator $+$ indicates a choice, and the $*$ operator indicates a finite, possibly zero number of repetitions.

7.1.1   Determinization and Complementation

For regular automata we allow the transition relation Δ to be nondeterministic. That is, there can be transitions $(q, a, l), (q, a, l') \in \Delta$, where $l \neq l'$. An automaton is called *deterministic* if no such transition exists and, in addition, $|Q^0| = 1$.

Any nondeterministic finite automaton on *finite words* can be translated into an equivalent deterministic automaton, that is, one that accepts the same language. This is done using the *subset construction* [419]. For a nondeterministic automaton $\mathcal{A} = (\Sigma, Q, \Delta, Q^0, F)$, we construct an equivalent deterministic automaton $\mathcal{A}' = (\Sigma, \mathcal{P}(Q), \Delta', \{Q^0\}, F')$ such that

$\Delta' \subseteq \mathcal{P}(Q) \times \Sigma \times \mathcal{P}(Q)$, where $(Q_1, a, Q_2) \in \Delta'$ if

$$Q_2 = \bigcup_{q \in Q_1} \{q' \mid (q, a, q') \in \Delta\}.$$

The set F' is defined as $\{Q' \mid Q' \cap F \neq \emptyset\}$. Since $\mathcal{A}'$ is deterministic, Δ' can be represented as a function $\Delta' : \mathcal{P}(Q) \times \Sigma \to \mathcal{P}(Q)$. Each state of $\mathcal{A}'$ corresponds to the set of states that $\mathcal{A}$ can reach after reading some given input sequence.

Complementation of a nondeterministic automaton over finite words can be performed by first determinizing it and then interchanging the accepting and the nonaccepting states.

7.2 Automata on Infinite Words

Frequently we are interested in reactive systems, which are designed not to halt during normal execution. For such systems, computations should be modeled as *infinite* sequences of states. Thus, this chapter focuses on finite automata over infinite words. These automata have the same structure as finite automata over finite words. However, they recognize words from Σ^{ω}, where the superscript ω indicates an infinite number of repetitions. The acceptance or rejection of an infinite word will be determined along an infinite run of the automaton. The acceptance condition should thus be adjusted to infinite runs.

The simplest automata over infinite words are Büchi [90] automata. A Büchi automaton has the same components as an automaton over finite words. A run of a Büchi automaton $\mathcal{A}$ over an infinite word $v \in \Sigma^{\omega}$ is defined in almost the same way as a run of a finite automaton over a finite word, except that now $|v| = \infty$. Thus, the domain of a run is the set of all natural numbers. Again, a run corresponds to a path in the graph of the automaton, but the path is now an infinite one.

Let $inf(\rho)$ be the set of states that appear infinitely often in the run ρ (when treating the run as an infinite path). Since the set of states Q is finite and ρ is infinite, $inf(\rho)$ is guaranteed not to be empty. A run ρ of a Büchi automaton $\mathcal{A}$ over an infinite word is *accepting* if and only if $inf(\rho) \cap F \neq \emptyset$, that is, when some accepting state appears in ρ infinitely often.

The *language* of $\mathcal{A}$, $\mathcal{L}(\mathcal{A}) \subseteq \Sigma^{\omega}$ consists of all the infinite words accepted by $\mathcal{A}$. Languages accepted by finite automata on infinite words are called *ω-regular languages*.

The structure shown in figure 7.1 can be interpreted as a Büchi automaton. In this case, one of the words it accepts is $(ab)^{\omega}$, that is, an infinite sequence of alternating a's and b's, starting with an a. The infinite run on $(ab)^{\omega}$ is $q_1(q_1q_2)^{\omega}$, which is accepting since it visits the accepting state q_1 infinitely often. The language accepted by the Büchi automaton of figure 7.1 is the set of words with *infinitely* many a's, which can be written as the ω-regular expression $(b^*a)^{\omega}$.

7.3   Deterministic versus Nondeterministic Büchi Automata

Unlike automata on finite words, deterministic Büchi automata are strictly less expressive than nondeterministic Büchi automata. This means that not every nondeterministic Büchi automaton has an equivalent deterministic Büchi automaton.

Lemma 7.1 *Let $\mathcal{B}$ be a deterministic Büchi automaton. Then for every word $v \in \Sigma^{\omega}$, v is in the language of $\mathcal{B}$ if and only if there are infinitely many finite prefixes of v on which $\mathcal{B}$ reaches an accepting state.*

Proof A deterministic automaton $\mathcal{B}$ can have at most one run (path) from its initial state for any finite or infinite input. If infinitely many prefixes of v reach an accepting state, then at least one accepting state $q \in F$ will be reached infinitely many times by prefixes of v, because there are only finitely many accepting states. Because of determinism, if v' and v'' are finite prefixes of v, where v'' is longer than v', then the path for v'' extends the path for v'. Hence, the unique path that agrees with all the finite paths for prefixes of v that reach q is accepting. Conversely, if v is accepted by $\mathcal{B}$, then there is a run on v that reaches an accepting state q of $\mathcal{B}$ infinitely many times. Each time that q occurs in this path corresponds to a finite prefix of the path labeled with a prefix of v. □

Theorem 7.2 *Nondeterministic Büchi automata are more expressive than deterministic Büchi automata. That is, there is a nondeterministic Büchi automaton that has no equivalent deterministic Büchi automaton.*

Proof Consider the language of the nondeterministic Büchi automaton $\mathcal{B}$ in figure 7.2. It consists of the infinite words over $\Sigma = \{a, b\}$ that have only finitely many a's. We show that there is no deterministic automaton that can recognize this language.

By way of contradiction, suppose that $\mathcal{C}$ is such an automaton. Observe that for each finite word σ we have that σa^{ω} is in $L(\mathcal{B})$. Now, we construct a sequence of infinite words $v_0, v_1, v_2, \ldots$ as follows. We start with $v_0 = \varepsilon$. Then we set $v_{i+1} = vba^n$ with the smallest n such that v_{i+1} reaches an accepting state. That is, we append to v_i a single b and then add a sequence of a's until the unique run of $\mathcal{C}$ on v_{i+1} reaches an accepting state. We know that v_{n+1} exists since $v_i ba^{\omega} \in L(\mathcal{B})$, as noted before. Now, each v_i is a prefix of v_{i+1}. Hence, there is an infinite sequence v that includes all the above sequences v_i as prefixes. By lemma 7.1, the automaton $\mathcal{C}$ accepts v. However, v includes infinitely many b's and hence is not in $L(\mathcal{B})$, a contradiction. □

It is interesting to note that the complement of the language of $\mathcal{B}$, that is, the language of infinite words with infinitely many a's, can be recognized by a deterministic Büchi automaton (see the automaton presented in figure 7.1). This results in the following lemma.

Lemma 7.3 *The set of languages accepted by deterministic Büchi automata is not closed under complementation.*

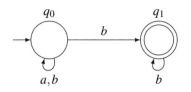

Figure 7.2
An automaton for words with finitely many a's.

In contrast to deterministic Büchi automata, nondeterministic Büchi automata are closed under complementation [90]. This means that there exists an automaton that recognizes exactly the complement of the language of a given automaton. The details of computing the complement of a non-deterministic Büchi automaton are rather involved. Constructions for this purpose can be found in [396, 447, 428, 306, 461, 318, 224].

In the following two sections we show how to compute the intersection of two Büchi automata, and how to check for emptiness. We later describe an automata-based model checking algorithm, based on these operations.

7.4   Intersection of Büchi Automata

Let $\mathcal{B}_1 = (\Sigma, Q_1, Q_1^0, \Delta_1, F_1)$ and $\mathcal{B}_2 = (\Sigma, Q_2, Q_2^0, \Delta_2, F_2)$ be two Büchi automata. We can construct an automaton $\mathcal{B}_1 \cap \mathcal{B}_2$ that accepts $\mathcal{L}(\mathcal{B}_1) \cap \mathcal{L}(\mathcal{B}_2)$ as follows:

$$\mathcal{B}_1 \cap \mathcal{B}_2 = (\Sigma, Q_1 \times Q_2 \times \{0,1,2\}, Q_1^0 \times Q_2^0 \times \{0\}, \Delta, Q_1 \times Q_2 \times \{2\})$$

We have $((r_i, q_j, x), a, (r_m, q_n, y)) \in \Delta$ if and only if the following conditions hold:

- $(r_i, a, r_m) \in \Delta_1$ and $(q_j, a, q_n) \in \Delta_2$; that is, the local components agree with the transitions of $\mathcal{B}_1$ and $\mathcal{B}_2$.
- The third component is affected by the accepting conditions of $\mathcal{B}_1$ and $\mathcal{B}_2$:
  - If $x = 0$ and $r_m \in F_1$, then $y = 1$.
  - If $x = 1$ and $q_n \in F_2$, then $y = 2$.
  - If $x = 2$, then $y = 0$.
  - Otherwise, $y = x$.

The third component is responsible for guaranteeing that accepting states from both $\mathcal{B}_1$ and $\mathcal{B}_2$ appear infinitely often. Note that accepting states from both automata may appear together only finitely many times even if they appear individually infinitely often. Hence, setting $F = F_1 \times F_2$ does not work. The third component is initially 0. It changes from 0 to 1 when an accepting state of the first automaton is seen. It changes from 1 to 2 when an accepting state of the second automaton is seen and, in the next state, returns back to 0. The constructed automaton accepts exactly when infinitely many states from F_1 and

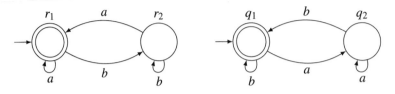

Figure 7.3
An automaton for an infinite number of a's (left) and an automaton for an infinite number of b's (right).

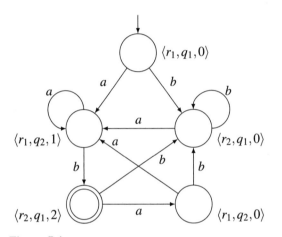

Figure 7.4
An automaton for words with an infinite number of a's and b's, obtained as intersection of the automata in figure 7.3.

infinitely many states from F_2 occur. The intersection of the automata in figure 7.3 appears in figure 7.4. Only nodes reachable from the initial state are given.

A simpler intersection is obtained when all of the states of one of the automata are accepting. Such an intersection is used, for instance, in section 7.8, since all the states of the automaton for the modeled system are accepting. Assume that all of the states of B_1 are accepting and that the acceptance set of B_2 is F_2. Their intersection will be defined as follows:

$$B_1 \cap B_2 = (\Sigma, Q_1 \times Q_2, \Delta', Q_1^0 \times Q_2^0, Q_1 \times F_2)$$

The accepting states are pairs from $Q_1 \times F_2$ in which the second component is an accepting state. Moreover, $((r_i, q_j), a, (r_m, q_n)) \in \Delta'$ if and only if $(r_i, a, r_m) \in \Delta_1$ and $(q_j, a, q_n) \in \Delta_2$.

The general algorithm for computing intersection is useful for verifying systems with fairness constraints. In this case, some of the states of the system automaton B_1 may not be accepting.

7.5   Checking Emptiness

In this section we show how to check for emptiness of a Büchi automaton, that is, to check whether the language of the automaton is empty. Let ρ be an accepting run of a Büchi automaton $B = (\Sigma, Q, \Delta, Q^0, F)$. Then, ρ contains infinitely many accepting states from F. Since Q is finite, there is some suffix ρ' of ρ such that every state on it appears infinitely many times. This implies that, for any two states s and s' in ρ, s is reachable from s' along ρ and s' is reachable from s. Hence, the states in ρ' are included in a nontrivial strongly connected component of the graph (Q, Δ), induced by B. This component is reachable from an initial state and contains an accepting state. Conversely, any nontrivial strongly connected component that is reachable from an initial state and contains an accepting state generates an accepting run of the automaton.

Thus, checking nonemptiness of $\mathcal{L}(B)$ is equivalent to finding a strongly connected component that is reachable from an initial state and contains an accepting state. This also implies that the language $\mathcal{L}(B)$ is nonempty if and only if there is a reachable accepting state with a cycle back to itself. Clearly, the nodes in such a cycle must belong to some strongly connected component. Conversely, given a strongly connected component with an accepting state, it is always possible to find a cycle through the accepting state. The significance of this observation is that if the language $\mathcal{L}(B)$ is nonempty, then there is a counterexample that can be represented in a *finite* manner. The counterexample is a run constructed from a finite prefix and a periodic sequence of states. A run of this form is sometimes referred to as *ultimately periodic* [460]. We say that such a run has a *lasso shape*.

The discussion above can be summarized by the following lemma.

Lemma 7.4 *Let $B = (\Sigma, Q, \Delta, Q^0, F)$ be a Büchi automaton. The following conditions are equivalent:*

- *$\mathcal{L}(B)$ is nonempty.*
- *The graph induced by B contains a strongly connected component C, which includes an accepting state. Moreover, C is reachable from an initial state of B.*
- *The graph induced by B contains a path from an initial state of B to a state $t \in F$. Moreover, it contains a path from t back to itself.*

Example 7.5 *The following example demonstrates the three equivalent conditions in the lemma. Consider the automaton of figure 7.4. First note that its language is not empty. For instance, the run $12(352)^\omega$ visits state 3 infinitely often and thus accepts the word $a(bba)^\omega$.*

Note also that the graph of the automaton includes the strongly connected component $\{2, 3, 4, 5\}$, which contains the accepting state 3 and is reachable from the initial state 1.

*Furthermore, the graph includes a path from 1 to 3 (via 2) and has also a path from 3 back
to itself (via 5 and 2). Thus, all three conditions of the lemma are fulfilled.*

Checking emptiness is particularly useful in automata-based model checking where the
checked automaton is the intersection of the automaton representing the system and the
automaton representing the complement of the specification, as described in section 7.8.

Taking advantage of the second condition of lemma 7.4, Tarjan's *depth-first search*
(DFS) algorithm [458] for finding strongly connected components can be used for deciding
emptiness of Büchi automata in time $O(|S| + |R|)$. An alternative algorithm, based on [158,
274], follows the third condition of the lemma. We describe it in the next section.

7.5.1   Checking Emptiness with Double DFS

We describe here the algorithm *double DFS* [158, 274], also called *nested DFS* [270], for
checking emptiness of Büchi automata. The algorithm is often more efficient in practice than
calculating first the strongly connected components and then analyzing them. In particular,
it is more suitable for on-the-fly model checking, as explained in section 7.11.

The double DFS algorithm uses two DFSs for finding a cycle from a reachable accepting
state back to itself. The two searches are interleaved. The first one can activate the second,
while the second search may terminate the entire algorithm or resume the first search from
where it has last stopped.

The first DFS activates the second DFS when it is ready to backtrack from an accepting
state q, after completing the search of all successors of q. The second search then looks for a
cycle through q. If it fails to do so, the first search resumes from the point it was interrupted.

A high-level description of the double DFS algorithm is given in figure 7.5. In the
algorithm we store a node in a hash table when it is discovered by the first DFS and say that
the node is *hashed*. A Boolean flag is used to indicate whether a node has been encountered
by *some* invocation of the second DFS. If this is the case, then we say that the node is
flagged. The use of flagged nodes in the second DFS is a subtle part of the algorithm. This
guarantees that the second DFS, which is called several times by the first DFS, does not
explore the same edges on subsequent calls. We prove the correctness of the algorithm in
theorem 7.8. For an efficient implementation, each node in the hash table includes two
bits that indicate whether the node is on the search stack of the first or the second DFS
(corresponding to *hashed* and *flagged*, respectively).

The algorithm uses the command **terminate** to stop the execution of the entire program
and return a value. When the algorithm terminates with *true*, a cycle through a reachable
accepting state is reported as a counterexample for emptiness. Let q_1 be the accepting state
with which the second DFS is started. Note that q_1 is at the top of the first DFS stack. Then
the first DFS stack contains a path from an initial state to q_1. This path is the finite prefix of
the counterexample. Let q_2 be the state that terminates the second DFS. The periodic part is
constructed as follows. The second DFS stack contains a path from q_1 to q_2. The node q_2

procedure *emptiness*
    for all $q_0 \in Q^0$ **do**
        dfs1(q_0);
    terminate(*false*);
end procedure

procedure *dfs1*(q)
    local q';
    hash(q);
    for all successors q' of q **do**
        if q' not in the hash table **then** *dfs1*(q');
    if *accept*(q) **then** *dfs2*(q);
end procedure

procedure *dfs2*(q)
    local q';
    flag(q);
    for all successors q' of q **do**
        if q' on dfs1 stack **then terminate**(*true*);
        else if q' not flagged **then** *dfs2*(q');
    end if
end procedure

Figure 7.5
The double DFS algorithm.

appears on the search stack of the first DFS as well, and the states that were inserted on the first DFS stack after q_2 was inserted complete a cycle back to q_1.

Example 7.6 *Consider a run of the double DFS algorithm on the automaton in figure 7.4. The first DFS may progress along the path* $1 \to 2 \to 3 \to 5 \to 2$. *Then it backtracks from 2 to 5 (then discovering the self loop at 5) and from 5 to 3. Then it tries progressing from 3 to 4, then to 5 again, followed by backtracking to 4 and then to 3. At this point, all the successors of 3 (namely, 4 and 5) were explored, and since 3 is an accepting state, we are ready to call the second DFS. At this point we have* $(1, 2, 3)$ *on the search stack of the first DFS. The second DFS may progress through 5 to 2, with its stack containing* $(5, 2)$. *Since 2 is already on the first DFS stack, we terminate. The returned counterexample consists of the prefix* $(1, 2, 3)$ *taken from the first stack, and a cycle* $(5, 2, 3)$, *where* $(5, 2)$ *is on the second stack and* $(2, 3)$ *is on the first one.*

7.5.2   Correctness of the Double DFS Algorithm

The following well-known property of DFS is essential for proving the correctness of the algorithm.

Lemma 7.7 *Let q be a node that does not appear on any cycle. Then the DFS algorithm will backtrack from q only after all the nodes that are reachable from q have been explored and backtracked from.*

It is easy to see that this lemma still holds for the first DFS in the double DFS algorithm, which simply follows the DFS search order.

Theorem 7.8 *The double DFS algorithm returns a counterexample for the emptiness of the checked automaton $\mathcal{B}$ exactly when the language $\mathcal{L}(\mathcal{B})$ is not empty.*

Proof When the double DFS returns a path to an accepting state and a cycle through that state, it has found a counterexample for emptiness of the checked automaton. The difficult case is showing that, when the algorithm reports emptiness of $\mathcal{L}(\mathcal{B})$, this is indeed the case.

Note that the second DFS flags the states it has reached when started from previous states by the first DFS. Suppose a second DFS is started from a state q and there is a path from q to some state p on the search stack of the first DFS. Then the path from q to p can be completed to a cycle through q, by including the states that appear after p on that stack. Consider the following two cases:

1. There exists a path from q to a state on the search stack of the first DFS that contains only unflagged nodes when the second DFS is started from q. In this case, the second DFS will find a cycle as expected.

2. On every path from q to a state on the search stack of the first DFS there exists a state r that is already flagged. In this case, the algorithm would not discover a cycle through q.

We show that the second case is impossible. Suppose the contrary. Then there is an accepting state from which a second DFS starts but fails to find a cycle even though one exists. Let q be the first such state. Let r be the first flagged state that is reached from q during the second DFS and is on a cycle through q. Finally, let q' be the accepting state that starts the second DFS in which r was first encountered. Thus, according to our assumptions, a second DFS was started from q' before a second DFS was started from q. There are two cases (see figure 7.6):

2a. *The state q' is reachable from q.* Then there is a cycle $q' \to \ldots \to r \to \ldots \to q \to \ldots \to q'$. This cycle could not have been found previously. Otherwise, the algorithm would already have terminated. However, this contradicts our assumption that q is the first accepting state from which the second DFS missed a cycle.

2b. *The state q' is not reachable from q.* If q' appears on a cycle, then a cycle was missed before starting the second DFS from q, contrary to our assumption. According to our assumption, q is reachable from r. Hence, q is reachable from q'. Thus, if q' does not occur on a cycle, then by lemma 7.7 we must have discovered and backtracked from q in the first DFS before backtracking from q'. Hence, according to the double DFS

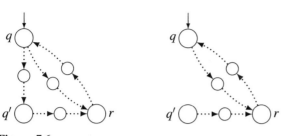

Figure 7.6
Cases **2a** and **2b** in the proof of theorem 7.8.

algorithm, we must have started a second DFS from q before starting it from q'. This contradicts our assumption about the order of doing the second DFS. □

7.6 Generalized Büchi Automata

Sometimes it is convenient to work with Büchi automata with several sets of accepting sets, even though this type of automaton does not extend the set of languages that can be accepted. In particular, we will subsequently describe a translation from an LTL specification into a generalized Büchi automaton. A *generalized Büchi automaton* has an acceptance component of the form $F \subseteq \mathcal{P}(Q)$. That is, $F = \{P_1, \ldots, P_k\}$, where for every $1 \leq i \leq k$, $P_i \subseteq Q$. A run ρ of a generalized Büchi automaton is accepting if for each $P_i \in F$, $inf(\rho) \cap P_i \neq \emptyset$. Note that the use of multiple fairness constraints with Kripke structures in section 4.5 corresponds to the notion of acceptance used in generalized Büchi automata.

There is a simple translation from a generalized Büchi automaton $\mathcal{B} = (\Sigma, Q, Q^0, \Delta, F)$ to a Büchi automaton. Let $F = \{P_1, \ldots, P_k\}$. Construct

$$\mathcal{B}' = (\Sigma, Q \times \{0, \ldots, k\}, Q^0 \times \{0\}, \Delta', Q \times \{k\}).$$

The transition relation Δ' is constructed such that $((q,x), a, (q',y)) \in \Delta'$ when $(q,a,q') \in \Delta$ and x and y are defined according to the following rules:

- If $q' \in P_i$ and $x = i$, then $y = i + 1$.
- If $x = k$, then $y = 0$.
- Otherwise, $x = y$.

Intuitively, a state (q,i) is reached if, in this round, we visited already states from $P_1, \ldots, P_i$. A state (q,k) is reached when $P_1, \ldots, P_k$ were all visited in this round, and a new round begins.

The translation expands the size of the automaton by a factor of $k + 1$. Note that, if the set F of the generalized Büchi automaton is empty, all infinite words over Σ are accepted.

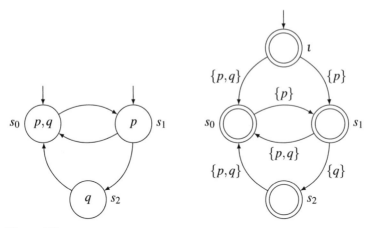

Figure 7.7
Transforming a Kripke structure (left) into an automaton (right).

7.7   Automata and Kripke Structures

Finite automata can be used to model concurrent and reactive systems. Either the states Q or the alphabet Σ can then represent the states of the modeled system. One of the main advantages of using automata for modeling is that both the modeled system and the specification can be represented in the same way. We now show that a Büchi automaton can be easily constructed from a Kripke structure.

A Kripke structure $M = (S, S_0, R, AP, L)$ can be translated into a (generalized) Büchi automaton $\mathcal{A}_M = (\Sigma, S \cup \{\iota\}, \{\iota\}, \Delta, S \cup \{\iota\})$, where $\Sigma = \mathcal{P}(AP)$. We have $(s, \alpha, s') \in \Delta$ for $s, s' \in S$ if and only if $(s, s') \in R$ and $\alpha = L(s')$. In addition, $(\iota, \alpha, s) \in \Delta$ if and only if $s \in S_0$ and $\alpha = L(s)$. Intuitively, the translation "pushes backwards" the labeling on states to the transitions entering those states. Note that all states of the automaton are accepting. This agrees with the convention that in a Kripke structure with no fairness constraints all paths are fair. Figure 7.7 shows a Kripke structure and its corresponding automaton.

Assume now that M is a fair Kripke structure with a set F of fairness constraints. Then, the set of accepting sets of states in the generalized Büchi automaton is identical to the set of fairness sets in the Kripke structure.

Theorem 7.9 *For the translations described above, $\mathcal{L}(M) = \mathcal{L}(\mathcal{A}_M)$.*

The proof of the theorem is straightforward and is left as a problem.

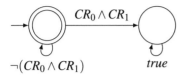

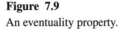

Figure 7.8

A Büchi automaton specifying mutual exclusion.

Figure 7.9

An eventuality property.

7.8   Model Checking using Automata

If our system is modeled by an automaton $\mathcal{A}$, then a natural way to provide a specification for $\mathcal{A}$ is by means of an automaton $\mathcal{S}$, over the same alphabet as $\mathcal{A}$. In this case, $\mathcal{L}(\mathcal{S})$ is the set of allowed behaviors for $\mathcal{A}$.

We first present several examples of properties expressed using Büchi automata. The properties refer to the mutual exclusion example in figure 3.2. In these examples, we annotate edges with Boolean expressions rather than a subset of the propositions in AP. Each edge may represent several transitions, where each transition corresponds to a truth assignment for AP that satisfies the Boolean expression. For example, when $AP = \{X,Y,Z\}$, an edge labeled $X \wedge \neg Y$ matches the transitions labeled with $\{X,Z\}$ and $\{X\}$ (that is, the sets of propositions that include X and do not include Y but may or may not include Z).

The set of atomic propositions AP in the following examples corresponds to the labels CR_0 and CR_1 of the mutual exclusion example. For instance, the proposition CR_0 holds in the states where the program counter of process P_0 is CR_0. Figure 7.8 gives an automaton that specifies the property that the two processes cannot enter their critical section at the same time. This specification is given by the LTL path formula $\mathbf{G} \neg (CR_0 \wedge CR_1)$. The property obviously holds for the mutual exclusion example.

Figure 7.9 shows an automaton that specifies the property that the process P_0 will eventually enter its critical section, and is given by the LTL path formula $\mathbf{F}\, CR_0$. This property does not hold in our example system since it is possible that P_0 never attempts to enter its critical section.

Next, we consider the model-checking problem for cases where both the system and the specification are given as an automaton. The system $\mathcal{A}$ satisfies the specification $\mathcal{S}$ when

$$\mathcal{L}(\mathcal{A}) \subseteq \mathcal{L}(\mathcal{S}). \tag{7.1}$$

That is, each behavior of the modeled system is among the behaviors that are allowed by the specification. Let $\overline{\mathcal{L}(\mathcal{S})}$ be the language $\Sigma^\omega - \mathcal{L}(\mathcal{S})$. Then equation 7.1 can be rewritten as

$$\mathcal{L}(\mathcal{A}) \cap \overline{\mathcal{L}(\mathcal{S})} = \emptyset. \tag{7.2}$$

This means that there is no behavior of $\mathcal{A}$ that is disallowed by $\mathcal{S}$. If the intersection is not empty, any behavior in it corresponds to a counterexample.

The formulation of the correctness criterion in equation 7.2 suggests the following automata-based model checking procedure:

1. Complement the automaton S; that is, construct an automaton $\overline{S}$ that recognizes the language $\overline{\mathcal{L}(S)}$.
2. Construct the automaton that accepts the intersection of the languages $\mathcal{L}(\mathcal{A})$ and $\overline{\mathcal{L}(S)}$.
3. Check emptiness of the intersection automaton.
4. If the intersection is empty, announce that the specification S holds for $\mathcal{A}$. Otherwise, provide a counterexample.

As shown in section 7.5, in this case we are guaranteed to have an infinite word in the intersection that can be represented in a finite way. Specifically, there is a counterexample of the form uv^{ω} where u and v are finite words.

Since complementing a Büchi automaton is expensive, several ways to avoid it have been suggested in practice. In some implementations such as SPIN [270, 273], the user can provide the automaton for the complement of S directly instead of providing the automaton for S. In this approach, the user specifies the bad behaviors rather than the good ones. Another possibility [324] is to use a different type of ω-regular automata, for which complementation is easy.

Finally, the automaton S may be obtained using a translation from some specification language such as LTL. In this case, instead of translating a property φ into S and then complementing S, we can simply translate $\neg\varphi$, which immediately provides an automaton for the complement language, as required in equation 7.2. In the next section, we provide a translation from LTL to Büchi automata.

Note that the automata-based model-checking algorithm suggested here is very similar to the tableau-based algorithm presented in chapter 6. The product structure P, defined there, directly corresponds to the intersection between the system and specification automata, described here. Checking if a state in P satisfies **EG** *true* under fairness constraints corresponds to checking emptiness of the intersection.

7.9   From LTL to Büchi Automata

Given an LTL path formula φ, we construct a generalized Büchi automaton $\mathcal{A}_{\varphi}$ such that $\mathcal{A}_{\varphi}$ accepts exactly all the computations that satisfy φ. Such a construction was first suggested by Vardi and Wolper in 1986 [471]. We present this construction here but replace its involved construction for Büchi accepting states with the one from [239], which uses generalized Büchi acceptance. The latter construction is described in more detail in the next section.

For an LTL path formula φ, the *closure* of φ, denoted $cl(\varphi)$, is the set of φ's subformulas and their negation ($\neg\neg g$ is identified with g). Formally, $cl(\varphi)$ is the smallest set of formulas that satisfies the following:

- $\varphi \in cl(\varphi)$.
- If $\varphi_1 \in cl(\varphi)$, then $\neg\varphi_1 \in cl(\varphi)$.
- If $\neg\varphi_1 \in cl(\varphi)$, then $\varphi_1 \in cl(\varphi)$.
- If $\varphi_1 \vee \varphi_2 \in cl(\varphi)$, then $\varphi_1 \in cl(\varphi)$ and $\varphi_2 \in cl(\varphi)$.
- If $\mathbf{X}\varphi_1 \in cl(\varphi)$, then $\varphi_1 \in cl(\varphi)$.
- If $\varphi_1 \mathbf{U} \varphi_2 \in cl(\varphi)$, then $\varphi_1 \in cl(\varphi)$ and $\varphi_2 \in cl(\varphi)$.

For example,

$$cl((\neg p\,\mathbf{U}\,((\mathbf{X}q)\vee r))) = \{(\neg p\,\mathbf{U}\,((\mathbf{X}q)\vee r)),\ \neg(\neg p\,\mathbf{U}\,((\mathbf{X}q)\vee r)),\ \neg p,\ p,$$
$$((\mathbf{X}q)\vee r),\ \neg((\mathbf{X}q)\vee r),\ (\mathbf{X}q),\ \neg(\mathbf{X}q),\ r,\ \neg r\}.$$

In the construction of a Büchi automaton for φ we will use subsets of $cl(\varphi)$ as automata states with the goal that exactly those formulas appearing in a state will be satisfied by any word accepted from this state. We therefore consider only consistent subsets, which we call *good*.

We say that a set $S \subseteq cl(\varphi)$ is *good in* $cl(\varphi)$ if S is a maximal set of formulas in $cl(\varphi)$ that satisfies the following conditions:

1. For all $\varphi_1 \in cl(\varphi)$, we have $\varphi_1 \in S$ if and only if $\neg\varphi_1 \notin S$, and
2. for all $\varphi_1 \vee \varphi_2 \in cl(\varphi)$, we have $\varphi_1 \vee \varphi_2 \in S$ if and only if at least one of φ_1, φ_2 is in S.

Given an LTL path formula φ over a set AP of atomic propositions, we define $\mathcal{A}_\varphi = (\mathcal{P}(AP), Q, \Delta, Q^0, F)$, where

- the set of states $Q \subseteq \mathcal{P}(cl(\varphi))$ is the set of all the good sets in $cl(\varphi)$.
- Let q and q' be two states (that is, good sets in $cl(\varphi)$), and let $\sigma \subseteq AP$ be a letter. Then $(q, \sigma, q') \in \Delta$ if the following hold:

  1. $\sigma = q \cap AP$;

  2. for all $\mathbf{X}\varphi_1 \in cl(\varphi)$, we have $\mathbf{X}\varphi_1 \in q$ if and only if $\varphi_1 \in q'$; and

  3. for all $\varphi_1 \mathbf{U} \varphi_2 \in cl(\varphi)$, we have $\varphi_1 \mathbf{U} \varphi_2 \in q$ iff either $\varphi_2 \in q$ or both $\varphi_1 \in q$ and $\varphi_1 \mathbf{U} \varphi_2 \in q'$.

  Note that the last condition also means that, for all $\neg(\varphi_1 U \varphi_2) \in cl(\varphi)$, we have that $\neg(\varphi_1 \mathbf{U} \varphi_2) \in q$ if and only if $\neg\varphi_2 \in q$ and either $\neg\varphi_1 \in q$ or $\neg(\varphi_1 \mathbf{U} \varphi_2) \in q'$.

- $Q^0 \subseteq Q$ is the set of all states $q \in Q$ for which $\varphi \in q$.
- For every formula $(\varphi_1 \mathbf{U} \varphi_2) \in cl(\varphi)$, F includes the set $P_{\varphi_1 \mathbf{U} \varphi_2} = \{q \in Q \mid \varphi_2 \in q$ or $\neg(\varphi_1 \mathbf{U} \varphi_2) \in q\}$.

It is easy to see the similarity between the tableau, presented in chapter 6, and the automaton defined here. The main differences stem from the fact that the tableau is based on the set of *elementary formulas* of φ, while here the good subsets of the *closure* of φ are used.

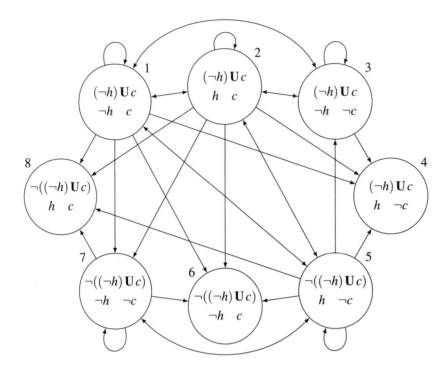

Figure 7.10
A Büchi automaton constructed for the LTL formula $(\neg h)\,\mathbf{U}\,c$.

Example 7.10 *Figure 7.10 gives the Büchi automaton constructed by the definition given in this section for the LTL formula $((\neg h)\,\mathbf{U}\,c)$. States $1,2,3,4$ are the initial states. The set F includes just one set, $F = \{\{1,2,5,6,7,8\}\}$. Note that the states $4,6,8$ have no outgoing edges since they do not satisfy the third condition in the definition of Δ.*

7.10   Efficient Translation of LTL into Automata

7.10.1   Overview of the Algorithm

The translation algorithm by Vardi and Wolper is simple and serves as a tool to demonstrate the possibility of performing model checking of LTL properties within the automata-theoretic framework. However, the size of the automaton produced is always exponential in the size of the specification, as each subformula appears in each node, either negated or nonnegated. Indeed, there are cases where the exponential explosion of the translation from an LTL formula to a Büchi automaton is unavoidable. However, the exponential explosion is not uniformly inherent over all LTL formulas.

In this section we present an algorithm by Gerth, Peled, Vardi, and Wolper [239] for translating an LTL (path) formula φ into a generalized Büchi automaton. While this translation still has exponential worst-case complexity, it often results in a smaller automaton (see, for instance, example 7.13).

As in previous constructions, states here correspond to subsets of φ's subformulas. However, in this construction each state includes only those subformulas that are required to be true for this state. Subformulas that do not appear in a state have an implicit *don't care* value. Thus, the number of states is reduced.

Example 7.11 *Consider an automaton for the LTL formula $\varphi = \mathbf{X}\mathbf{X}p$. The set of subformulas of φ consists of $\{\mathbf{X}\mathbf{X}p, \mathbf{X}p, p\}$. Thus, the number of states used in the translation of section 7.9 is 8. We may, however, notice that in the initial state s_0 we need to require only that the subformula $\mathbf{X}\mathbf{X}p$ holds. We actually do not care whether $\mathbf{X}p$ and p are true or false in this state. Its successor s_1 must satisfy only $\mathbf{X}p$. Again, we do not care whether it satisfies $\mathbf{X}\mathbf{X}p$ or p. Finally, the successor of s_1, s_2, must satisfy p. An additional empty state will indicate that the formula is satisfied with no further requirement. Thus, only four states are needed with this approach.*

The algorithm presented in this section assumes that LTL formulas are given in *negation normal form (NNF)*, in which negations are applied only to atomic propositions (see definition and conversion in section 4.2.3).

Similarly to the construction of section 7.9, the algorithm here is based on the fact that the temporal operators *until* ($\mathbf{U}$) and *release* ($\mathbf{R}$) can be written as fixpoints (also see discussion on fixpoints in section 5.3). That is,

$$\mu \mathbf{U} \eta \equiv \eta \vee (\mu \wedge \mathbf{X}(\mu \mathbf{U} \eta)), \text{ and} \tag{7.3}$$

$$\mu \mathbf{R} \eta \equiv \eta \wedge (\mu \vee \mathbf{X}(\mu \mathbf{R} \eta)) \equiv (\eta \wedge \mu) \vee (\eta \wedge \mathbf{X}(\mu \mathbf{R} \eta)). \tag{7.4}$$

This suggests two observations:

1. The requirements can be split.
   For instance, the requirement for $\mu \mathbf{U} \eta$ can be split to either η holds starting from the current state, or both μ holds starting now, and $\mu \mathbf{U} \eta$ holds starting at the subsequent states.

2. Requirements may refer to *current* and *next* states.
   For instance, in the second split for $\mu \mathbf{U} \eta$, μ is required to hold from the current state while $\mu \mathbf{U} \eta$ should hold from the *successor* states.

These observations suggest the following data structure for holding and manipulating potential automaton states.

7.10.2   Data structure

The basic data structure used in the algorithm is called a *node*. The states of the resulting automaton, as well as some intermediate representations, are kept as nodes. A node q contains the following fields, where *New*, *Now*, and *Next* are sets of subformulas of the translated formula φ.

- *ID* is a unique identifier for the node.
- *Incoming* is a set of predecessor nodes of q. Each node r in this set represents an edge from r to q. A special value *init* in this field represents the case where q is (or will become) an initial state.
- *New* is a set of subformulas of φ that need to be processed. These subformulas need to hold from the current state q.
- *Now* is a set of subformulas of φ that have been processed and need to hold from the current state q.
- *Next* is a set of subformulas of φ that have been processed and need to hold from the successor states of q.

We hold two sets of nodes called *Open* and *Closed*. *Closed* contains the nodes whose processing has been completed. In particular, their *New* field is empty. Only their set of incoming edges may still be augmented. The nodes in *Closed* will serve as the states of the constructed automaton.

The nodes in *Open* are temporary representations of states that are still being processed. While processing them the values of their fields might be changed. The goal of the construction is to guarantee that for every node q, the *node requirement*

$$Prop(q) \ = \ \bigwedge q.New \wedge \bigwedge q.Now \wedge \mathbf{X} \bigwedge q.Next \tag{7.5}$$

will hold along every path starting at q.

We say that two nodes q_1 and q_2 are *equivalent* if $Prop(q_1) = Prop(q_2)$. Figure 7.11 contains several nodes that are processed by the algorithm when translating the property $(A \mathbf{U} (B \mathbf{U} C))$. The details of this step are explained later.

7.10.3   A Detailed Description of the Algorithm

The algorithm is implemented in the procedure *EfficientLTLBuchi* (figure 7.12).

Initialization   Our algorithm starts with an empty set *Closed* and a single node q in the set *Open*, where q is defined as follows:

- *q.Incoming* is initialized with $\{init\}$, indicating that the nodes that evolve from q are the initial states of the automaton.
- *q.New* is initialized with the property φ that is being translated. Recall that for model checking we usually translate $\neg\varphi$, as explained above.

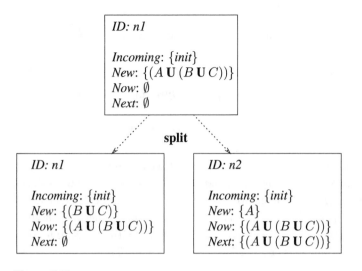

Figure 7.11
Splitting a node.

procedure *EfficientLTLBuchi*(φ)
    Closed := $\emptyset$;
    Open := ((n_0, {*init*}, {φ}, $\emptyset$, $\emptyset$)) ; // Initialization
    while *Open* $\neq \emptyset$ **do**
        Choose $q \in$ *Open*;
        if *q.New* = $\emptyset$ **then**   // Node q is fully processed
            Remove q from *Open*;
            Update_Closed(q);
        else
            Choose $\psi \in$ *q.New*;
            Move ψ from *q.New* to *q.Now*;
            Update_Split(q, ψ);
        end if
    end while
    define F;   // Generalized Büchi acceptance constraints
    $\mathcal{A}$:= *Build_Automaton*(*Closed*, F);
    return $\mathcal{A}$;
end procedure

Figure 7.12
Efficient translation of LTL to generalized Büchi automaton.

- *q.Now* and *q.Next* are initialized to the empty set.

Processing the set *Open*   The algorithm proceeds by iterating the following actions on the nodes in *Open* as long as *Open* is nonempty:

1. Let *q* be a node in *Open*.
2. If the field *q.New* is empty, then remove *q* from *Open* and apply the procedure *Update_Closed*(*q*), described in figure 7.13.
3. Otherwise (*q.New* is not empty), choose a subformula *ψ* from *q.New* and move it to *q.Now*.
4. Apply procedure *Update_Split* (figure 7.14) to *q* and *ψ*, as described below. If a split is needed, then apply *Split*(*q*) (figure 7.15) and obtain a new node *q'* with fresh *ID*, where all fields except *ID* are identical to those of *q*. *Update_Split* updates the fields *New* and *Next* of both *q* and *q'*, according to the processed formula. Then *q'* is inserted into the set *Open* (*q* is already in *Open*). For **U** and **R** formulas, *Update_Split* follows their fixpoint characterization, as described in equations 7.3 and 7.4.

Update the set *Closed*   *Update_Closed*(*q*) (figure 7.13) is applied when *q.New* is empty and *q* has been removed from *Open*. There are two cases:

1. A node *q'* with the same values in *Now* and *Next* as *q* already exists in *Closed*. In this case, the elements in *q.Incoming* are added to *q'.Incoming*.
   Note that in this case $Prop(q) = Prop(q')$ (see equation 7.5) and therefore we keep just one copy of such a node. However, we need to keep track of the predecessors of both nodes. We therefore add the predecessors of *q* to the set of predecessors of *q'*. Note also that such updates to *Close* may form loops in the resulting automaton.
2. If no such node exists in *Closed*, then *q* is inserted to *Closed*. In addition, a new node *q'* is created and inserted to *Open* as a candidate successor to *q*. Node *q'* is defined as follows: *q'.Now* and *q'.Next* are initialized to the empty sets. The set *q'.New* inherits its value from *q.Next*. Thus, it will fulfil the requirements that the successors of *q* should fulfil. The set *q'.Incoming* is equal to $\{q\}$, to indicate that the nodes evolved from *q'* will be successors of *q*.
   Here as well we avoid adding a node more than once. Thus, if there is already a node *q''* in *Open* with $Prop(q'') = Prop(q')$, then *q'* is not inserted. Instead, *q* is added to *q''.Incoming*.

Example 7.12   *Consider the nodes in figure 7.11, which describes a few initial steps of our construction for the formula* $A \mathbf{U} (B \mathbf{U} C)$. *The construction starts by inserting node q with* $q.ID = n1$ *to Open with* $q.Incoming = \{init\}$. *The formula* $A \mathbf{U} (B \mathbf{U} C)$ *is put into q.New, while q.Now and q.Next are empty.*

Next, Procedure Update_Split moves $A \mathbf{U} (B \mathbf{U} C)$ *to q.Now and then splits q according to the until case in Procedure Update_Split, by adding a new node q' with* $q'.ID = n2$.

procedure *Update_Closed*(q)
    if there is $q' \in Closed$ **such that** $q.Now = q'.Now$ **and** $q.Next = q'.Next$ **then**
        $q'.Incoming := q'.Incoming \cup q.Incoming;$
    else
        add q **to** *Closed*;
        create $q' = (freshID, \{q\}, q.Next, \emptyset, \emptyset);$
        // Node q' is a candidate successor of q
        add q' **to** *Open*
    end if
end procedure

Figure 7.13
Update the set *Closed*.

procedure *Update_Split*(q, ψ)
    case of
        $\psi = p$ **or** $\psi = \neg p$: **skip**; // $p \in AP$
        $\varphi = \mathbf{X}\mu$: **add** μ **to** $q.Next$;
        $\varphi = \mu \vee \eta$: $q' := Split(q)$; **add** μ **to** $q.New$; **add** η **to** $q'.New$;
        $\varphi = \mu \wedge \eta$: **add** $\{\mu, \eta\}$ **to** $q.New$;
        $\varphi = \mu \mathbf{U} \eta$: $q' := Split(q)$; **add** η **to** $q.New$; **add** $\{\mu, \mathbf{X}(\mu \mathbf{U} \eta)\}$ **to** $q'.New$;
        $\varphi = \mu \mathbf{R} \eta$: $q' := Split(q)$; **add** $\{\mu, \eta\}$ **to** $q.New$; **add** $\{\eta, \mathbf{X}(\mu \mathbf{R} \eta)\}$ **to** $q'.New$;
    end case;
end procedure

Figure 7.14
Update and split.

procedure *Split*(q)
    create $q' = (freshID, q.Incoming, q.New, q.Now, q.Next);$
    // q' identical to q except for ID
    return q';
end procedure

Figure 7.15
Split a node.

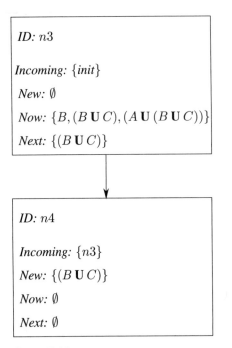

Figure 7.16
Creating a successor.

Procedure Update_Split then adds $(B\,\mathbf{U}\,C)$ to q.New. It also adds A and $\mathbf{X}(A\,\mathbf{U}\,(B\,\mathbf{U}\,C))$ to q'.New.

Next, $\mathbf{X}(A\,\mathbf{U}\,(B\,\mathbf{U}\,C))$ is removed from q'.New and $A\,\mathbf{U}\,(B\,\mathbf{U}\,C)$ is added to q'.Next. The updated node n2 is split again and the processing proceeds.

The edges in figure 7.11 are dotted since they indicate evolution of nodes in Open and not transition between automaton states.

At some point, a node q_3 with $q_3.ID = n3$, as shown in figure 7.16, is obtained. Since $q_3.New = \emptyset$, q_3 is moved to Closed. A new node q_4 is inserted into Open, with $q_4.Incoming = n3$, indicating that q_3 is a predecessor of q_4. The set $q_4.New$ then gets the value of $q_3.Next = \{(B\,\mathbf{U}\,C)\}$.

Enforcing eventualities   The construction of the nodes and the edges between them guarantees that the constraints along an automaton run are propagated correctly from each node to its successors, starting with the constraint φ in the initial node. In particular, every property of the form $\mathbf{X}\mu$ is propagated in the state from *New* to *Next* and subsequently to the successors of the state.

However, this is not sufficient. For properties of the form $\mu \,\mathbf{U}\, \eta$ (including properties of the form $\mathbf{F}\, \eta$, which are translated to $true\, \mathbf{U}\, \eta$), nothing guarantees that η will indeed eventually hold. The requirement that it eventually holds (while meanwhile μ holds) is just postponed from one node to another. Our goal is thus to force η to eventually hold in any accepting run of the automaton that passes through a node where $\mu \,\mathbf{U}\, \eta$ needs to hold. For that, we will use acceptance conditions.

The generalized Büchi automaton allows us several acceptance sets of states. Recall that an accepting run needs to pass through at least one state from each such set infinitely often. We assign an acceptance set for each subformula of the form $\mu \,\mathbf{U}\, \eta$. The accepting states are those nodes in *Closed* in which either,

1. η is in *Now*, or
2. $\mu \,\mathbf{U}\, \eta$ is not in *Now*.

This guarantees that, if $\mu \,\mathbf{U}\, \eta$ is required at some state on a run, then the run cannot be accepting unless η holds at some later state on that run. This is because, according to our construction, the property $\mu \,\mathbf{U}\, \eta$ in *Now* propagates to the next state, unless η itself is also in *Now*. If this persists forever without η being in *Now*, the run will not be accepting. Conversely, on an accepting run, the property $\mu \,\mathbf{U}\, \eta$ cannot be in *Now* for all states from a certain point on, while η is not in *Now* anymore.

Note the similarity between the acceptance conditions defined here and the fairness constraints used in the tableau construction for LTL (section 6.1).

Automaton construction   Once *Open* is empty, a fair Kripke structure can be constructed as follows:

- The set of states S is the set of nodes in *Closed*.
- The set of initial states is $S_0 = \{\, q \in S \,|\, init \in q.Incoming \,\}$.
- The transition relation $R \subseteq S \times S$ is defined as follows: $(q, q') \in R$ if and only if $q \in q'.Incoming$.
- AP is the set of atomic propositions in φ. That is, $AP = \{\, p \,|\, p \in AP_\varphi \,\}$. Let $\overline{AP} = \{\neg p \,|\, p \in AP\}$.
- The labeling of states is $L(q) = q.Now \cap (AP \cup \overline{AP})$.
- The generalized Büchi acceptance sets F includes, for every subformula of φ of the form $\mu \,\mathbf{U}\, \eta$, a set $P_{\mu \mathbf{U} \eta} = \{\, q \,|\, \eta \in q.Now$ or $(\mu \,\mathbf{U}\, \eta) \notin q.Now \,\}$.

By the method described in section 7.6, this Kripke structure can be transformed to a generalized Büchi automaton and then to a simple (nongeneralized) Büchi automaton. Further, by the method described in section 7.7, the labeling on the nodes is transferred to their incoming edges (while a new initial node is added).

The automaton constructed by the *EfficientLTLBuchi* algorithm can be seen as a "*3-valued automaton*" in the sense that each proposition p from AP can appear either positive (as p),

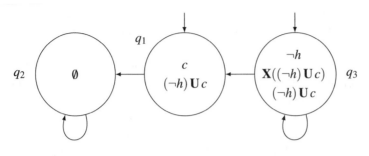

Figure 7.17
The Kripke structure resulting from algorithm *EfficientLTLBuchi* when given the formula $(\neg h)\,\mathbf{U}\,c$.

negative (as $\neg p$), or not at all. The latter corresponds to "don't care". In contrast, in the translation presented in section 7.9 each edge is labled by a subset of the propositions in *AP* that are considered to be positive, and the rest are considered to be negative. As mentioned above, this is an important feature of the translation, which often results in significantly smaller Büchi automata. We can thus consider every edge (q, α, q') of the efficient construction, labeled by α, as a compact representation of the set of edges from q to q' agreeing with the positive and negative propositions in α.

Example 7.13 *Figure 7.17 presents the Kripke structure resulting from applying algorithm EfficientLTLBuch for the formula $(\neg h)\,\mathbf{U}\,c$. The Kripke structure consists of three states. Transforming it to a Büchi automaton will add another state, making it four. This should be compared with other constructions for the same formula: the tableau in figure 6.1 and the automaton in figure 7.10. Both consist of eight states and many more transitions. This demonstrates the efficiency of the EfficientLTLBuch algorithm.*

7.11   On-the-Fly Model Checking

In the previous sections, we decribed various algorithms that can be combined for checking whether a system satisfies a property φ. The modeled system is converted into a corresponding Büchi automaton $\mathcal{A}$, and the negation of the specification φ is translated into another automaton $\mathcal{S}$. Then, the emptiness of the intersection of $\mathcal{A}$ and $\mathcal{S}$ is checked. If the intersection is not empty, a counterexample is reported. We now show how to exploit the machinery developed so far in order to perform the model checking in an efficient way. Instead of constructing the automata for both $\mathcal{A}$ and $\mathcal{S}$, we construct only the property automaton $\mathcal{S}$. We then use it to guide the construction of the system automaton $\mathcal{A}$ while computing the intersection. In this way, we may frequently construct only a small portion of the state space before we find a counterexample to the property being checked. Once a counterexample has been found and reported, there is no need to complete the construction. Furthermore, when computing the intersection of $\mathcal{A}$ and $\mathcal{S}$, some states of $\mathcal{A}$ may never be generated at all because they do not have a counterpart state in S. This tactic is called *on-the-fly* model checking.

Specifically, suppose that the double DFS of section 7.5 is used to check the emptiness of the intersection of $\mathcal{A}$ and S. Recall that the states used in constructing the automaton for the intersection are pairs consisting of a state from $\mathcal{A}$ and a state from S. Note that all the states of $\mathcal{A}$ are accepting. Hence, a state of the automaton for the intersection is accepting if and only if its S component is accepting.

In on-the-fly model checking, the states of the automaton for the intersection are computed as they are needed by the double DFS algorithm. Assume that the automaton S has already been constructed from $\neg\varphi$. Assume also that part of the automaton $\mathcal{A}$ used in the search so far has already been constructed.

Let $s = (r, q)$ be the current state of the search, where r is a state of $\mathcal{A}$ and q a state of S. To continue the search we compute the successors of s one at a time. Since S is already constructed, the successors $q_1, q_2, \ldots, q_n$ of q in S have already been computed. Let r' be the successor of r that is calculated next. Then, a successor $s_i = (r', q_i)$, where $1 \leq i \leq n$, exists exactly if the labelings of the transition from r to r' and from q to q_i with propositions from AP are the same. The two ways of reducing the state space using on-the-fly model checking can now be described.

1. The labeling of r' does not agree with any of the successors q_i of q. Then the search algorithm does not continue to explore the successors of r'.

2. A cycle is detected before the search algorithm backtracks to s. The search then terminates before additional successors of s, which may involve other successors of r, are explored.

In both cases, we obtain a reduction in the number of states by guiding the construction of $\mathcal{A}$ with the checked property using the automaton S.

Note that the specification automaton S can also be constructed on the fly, where successor states in S are developed only when a corresponding successor in the system exists.

The double DFS algorithm [158, 274], presented in section 7.5, is particularly suitable for finding counterexamples in LTL model checking in an on-the-fly manner.

On-the-fly algorithms, while highly efficient for explicit-state model checking, will not be useful for symbolic model checking algorithms, based on BDDs and SAT, to be introduced in chapters 8 and 10. This is because on-the-fly algorithms handle successors one at a time (using depth-first search (DFS) or breadth-first search (BFS)), whereas both BDD-based and SAT-based algorithms are most efficient when they handle the set of all successors at once.

Bibliographic Notes

Automata-based algorithms for model checking have been implemented in both academic and industrial tools. They include, for instance, COSPAN [257], FormalCheck [325], SPIN [269], NuSMV [114], NuSMV 2 [113], ForSpec [30], and EBMC [388].

The explicit-state model-checking tool SPIN [270] applies the double DFS algorithm [158, 274], described in section 7.5. Double DFS fits nicely with other features that make SPIN highly efficient. SPIN also implements the efficient translation of LTL to Büchi automata, described in section 7.10.

Section 7.11 discusses on-the-fly model checking, sometimes referred to as *local* model checking. Tableau-based local approaches for μ-calculus have been developed, for instance, by Stirling and Walker [453, 454], Cleaveland [144], and Winskel [482]. Mader [357] has proposed improvements to the tableau-based method of Stirling and Walker. Andersen [26] and Larsen [337] have developed efficient local methods for a subset of the μ-calculus. On-the-fly algorithms in other contexts were suggested, for instance, in [53, 158, 220].

Translations from temporal logics to automata are discussed in depth in [179]. Additional translation is described in [178]. Translations from LTL to Büchi automata, which use intermediate alternating automata appear, for example, in [233]. Other constructions appear in [363, 299].

Other types of automata on infinite words appear in the relevant literature. Essentially, they are of the same expressive power (can accept the same languages) as nondeterministic Büchi automata. However, the translation between the different types might increase their size. Nevertheless, it is sometimes useful to obtain determinization by translating to automata with different accepting conditions [428, 406, 431]. See [136] for more details.

As mentioned in section 7.3, algorithms for determinization (into an automaton with a different acceptance condition) and complementation of nondeterministic Büchi automata are complicated and of high complexity. A lot of research has been invested in these problems, searching for tighter analysis as well as more efficient algorithms. In [90, 111, 322, 447, 428] complementation via determinization has been investigated. Later, complementation that avoids determinization has been suggested (for example, [306, 318]).

The work in [120] suggests an interesting application of model-checking techniques to decide language containment between ω-automata of six different types: Büchi, Muller, Rabin, Streett, the L-automata of Kurshan, and the $\forall$-automata of Manna and Pnueli. For two ω-automata A and A', the techniques can determine $\mathcal{L}(\mathcal{A}) \subseteq \mathcal{L}(\mathcal{A}')$ provided A' is deterministic. The paper provides a 6×6 matrix in which each row and column is associated with one of these types of automata.

Automata theory was applied also to model checking of branching time logics, such as CTL and CTL*, using tree automata [316, 321].

Problems

Problem 7.1 (Infinite counterexamples for LTL properties). Show that if an LTL property is falsified by an infinite counterexample, then it also has a counterexample that is lasso shaped.

Problem 7.2 (Intersection of Büchi automata). Consider the intersection definition in section 7.4. Let $\mathcal{B}_1 = (\Sigma, Q_1, Q_1^0, \Delta_1, F_1)$ and $\mathcal{B}_2 = (\Sigma, Q_2, Q_2^0, \Delta_2, F_2)$ be two Büchi automata. Suggest an alternative definition for intersection of Büchi automata in which the states of the resulting automaton are $Q_1 \times Q_2 \times \{1, 2\}$. Pay special attention to the definition of the accepting states.

Problem 7.3 (Generalized Büchi condition). Define a translation from generalized Büchi condition to simple Büchi that requires only k copies of the states rather than $k + 1$ copies.

Problem 7.4 (LTL translation). Translate the following properties into generalized Büchi automata: $\mathbf{G}\,\mathbf{F}\,p$, $\mathbf{F}\,\mathbf{G}\,p$. Then, translate these automata into simple Büchi automata.

Problem 7.5 (Checking emptiness). Prove lemma 7.4.

Problem 7.6 (Checking emptiness). Prove that regular DFS may miss accepting cycles. Conclude that it therefore cannot be used instead of double DFS in nonemptiness checking.

8 Binary Decision Diagrams and Symbolic Model Checking

In this chapter we describe how to represent finite state reactive systems symbolically using binary decision diagrams [85, 94, 369]. We first discuss how binary decision diagrams can be used to represent Boolean functions. The Boolean functions are defined over 0 and 1, where 0 represents *false* and 1 represents *true*. We show that the size of the binary decision diagrams depends strongly on the ordering selected for the variables and briefly discuss some heuristics that can be used for selecting good orderings. We also describe how various logical operations can be efficiently implemented using this representation. Next, we explain how to encode Kripke structures using binary decision diagrams, thus enabling both synchronous and asynchronous systems to be represented concisely. Realizing that binary decision diagrams are useful for model checking has revolutionized computer-aided verification. It made symbolic model checking possible and permitted systems with 10^{20} states and more to be handled routinely [94, 369]. This revolution attracted the attention of the hardware industry and thus transformed model checking from an academic toy into an industrial-strength technique. Even though model checking is now mostly performed using SAT-based methods, there are still many use-cases where BDD-based tools work best.

8.1 Representing Boolean Formulas

Ordered binary decision diagrams (OBDDs) are a canonical representation for Boolean formulas [85]. They are often substantially more compact than traditional normal forms such as conjunctive normal form and disjunctive normal form, and they can be manipulated very efficiently. Hence, they have become widely used for a variety of applications in computer-aided design, including symbolic simulation, verification of combinational logic, and verification of finite-state systems. The latter is discussed in detail in the following sections.

To motivate our discussion of binary decision diagrams, we first consider *binary decision trees*. A binary decision tree is a rooted, directed tree that consists of two types of vertices, *terminal* vertices and *nonterminal* vertices. Each nonterminal vertex v is labeled by a variable $var(v)$ and has two successors: $low(v)$, corresponding to the case where the

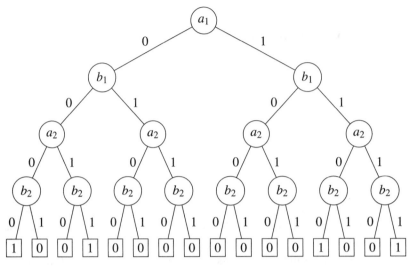

Figure 8.1
Binary decision tree for a two-bit comparator.

variable v is assigned 0, and *high*(v), corresponding to the case where v is assigned 1. Each terminal vertex v is labeled by *value*(v), which is either 0 or 1. A binary decision tree for the two-bit comparator, given by the formula $f(a_1, a_2, b_1, b_2) = (a_1 \leftrightarrow b_1) \wedge (a_2 \leftrightarrow b_2)$, is shown in figure 8.1.

One can decide whether a particular truth assignment to the variables makes the formula *true* or not by traversing the tree from the root to a terminal vertex. If the variable v is assigned 0, then the next vertex on the path from the root to the terminal vertex will be *low*(v). If v is assigned 1, then the next vertex on the path will be *high*(v). The value that labels the terminal vertex will be the value of the function for this assignment. For example, the assignment $\{a_1 \mapsto 1, a_2 \mapsto 0, b_1 \mapsto 1, b_2 \mapsto 1\}$ leads to a leaf vertex labeled 0; hence, the formula is *false* for this assignment.

Binary decision trees do not provide a very concise representation for Boolean functions. In fact, they are essentially the same size as truth tables. Fortunately, there is usually a lot of redundancy in such trees. For example, the tree of figure 8.1 has eight subtrees with roots labeled by b_2, but only three are distinct. Thus, we can obtain a more concise representation for the Boolean function by merging isomorphic subtrees. This results in a directed acyclic graph (DAG) called a *binary decision diagram*. More precisely, a binary decision diagram is a rooted, directed acyclic graph with two types of vertices, *terminal* vertices and *nonterminal* vertices. As in the case of binary decision trees, each nonterminal vertex v is labeled by a variable *var*(v) and has two successors, *low*(v) and *high*(v). Each terminal vertex is labeled by either 0 or 1. Every binary decision diagram B with root v determines a Boolean function $f_v(x_1, \ldots, x_n)$ in the following manner:

1. If v is a terminal vertex:

    (a) If $value(v) = 1$, then $f_v(x_1, \ldots, x_n) = 1$.

    (b) If $value(v) = 0$, then $f_v(x_1, \ldots, x_n) = 0$.

2. If v is a nonterminal vertex with $var(v) = x_i$, then f_v is the function

$$f_v(x_1, \ldots, x_n) = (\neg x_i \wedge f_{low(v)}(x_1, \ldots, x_n)) \vee (x_i \wedge f_{high(v)}(x_1, \ldots, x_n)).$$

In practical applications it is desirable to have a *canonical representation* for Boolean functions. Such a representation must have the property that two Boolean functions are logically equivalent if and only if they have isomorphic representations. This property simplifies tasks like checking equivalence of two formulas and deciding if a given formula is satisfiable or not. Two binary decision diagrams are *isomorphic* if there exists a one-to-one and onto function h that maps terminals of one to terminals of the other and nonterminals of one to nonterminals of the other, such that for every terminal vertex v, $value(v) = value(h(v))$, and for every nonterminal vertex v, $var(v) = var(h(v))$, $h(low(v)) = low(h(v))$, and $h(high(v)) = high(h(v))$.

Bryant [85] showed how to obtain a canonical representation for Boolean functions by placing two restrictions on binary decision diagrams. First, the variables should appear in the same order along each path from the root to a terminal. Second, there should be no isomorphic subtrees or redundant vertices in the diagram. The first requirement is achieved by imposing a total ordering $<$ on the variables that label the vertices in the binary decision diagram and requiring that, for any vertex u in the diagram, if u has a nonterminal successor v, then $var(u) < var(v)$. The second requirement is achieved by repeatedly applying three transformation rules that do not alter the function represented by the diagram:

1. **Remove duplicate terminals:** Eliminate all but one terminal vertex with a given label and redirect all arcs to the eliminated vertices to the remaining one.

2. **Remove duplicate nonterminals:** If two nonterminals u and v have $var(u) = var(v)$, $low(u) = low(v)$, and $high(u) = high(v)$, then eliminate u or v and redirect all incoming arcs to the other vertex.

3. **Remove redundant tests:** If nonterminal v has $low(v) = high(v)$, then eliminate v and redirect all incoming arcs to $low(v)$.

Starting with a binary decision diagram satisfying the ordering property, the canonical form is obtained by applying the transformation rules until the size of the diagram can no longer be reduced. Bryant shows how this can be done in a bottom-up manner by a procedure called *Reduce* in time that is linear in the size of the original binary decision diagram [85]. The term *ordered binary decision diagram* (OBDD) will be used to refer to

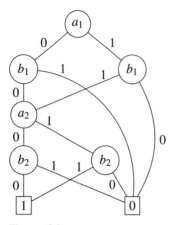

Figure 8.2
OBDD for a two-bit comparator with ordering $a_1 < b_1 < a_2 < b_2$.

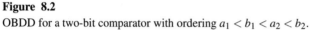

the graph obtained in this manner. For example, if we use the ordering $a_1 < b_1 < a_2 < b_2$ for the two-bit comparator function, we obtain the OBDD given in figure 8.2.

If OBDDs are used as a canonical form for Boolean functions, then checking equivalence is reduced to checking isomorphism between binary decision diagrams. Similarly, satisfiability can be determined by checking equivalence to the trivial OBDD that consists of only one terminal labeled by 0.

The size of an OBDD can depend critically on the variable ordering. For example, if we use the variable ordering $a_1 < a_2 < b_1 < b_2$ for the bit-comparator function, we get the OBDD shown in figure 8.3. Note that this OBDD has 11 vertices, whereas the OBDD shown in figure 8.2 has only 8 vertices. For an n-bit comparator, if we choose the ordering $a_1 < b_1 < \ldots < a_n < b_n$, then the number of OBDD vertices will be $3n + 2$. On the other hand, if we choose the ordering $a_1 < \ldots < a_n < b_1 \ldots < b_n$, then the number of OBDD vertices is $3 \cdot 2^n - 1$. In general, finding an optimal ordering for the variables is computationally hard; in fact, it can be shown that even checking that a particular ordering is optimal is NP-complete [87, 444]. Moreover, there are Boolean functions that have exponential size OBDDs for any variable ordering. One example is the Boolean function for the middle output (or n-th output) of a combinational circuit to multiply two n-bit integers [86, 87].

Several heuristics have been developed for finding a good variable ordering when such an ordering exists. If the Boolean function is given by a combinational circuit, then heuristics based on a depth-first traversal of the circuit diagram generally give good results [227, 360]. The intuition for these heuristics comes from the observation that OBDDs tend to be small when related variables are close together in the ordering. The variables appearing in a subcircuit are related in that they determine the subcircuit's output. Hence, these variables

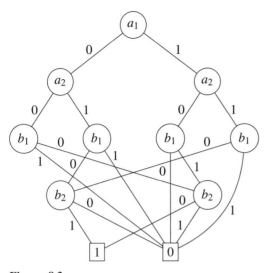

Figure 8.3
OBDD for a two-bit comparator with ordering $a_1 < a_2 < b_1 < b_2$.

should usually be grouped together in the ordering. This may be accomplished by placing the variables in the order in which they are encountered during a depth-first traversal of the circuit diagram. Another approach to variable ordering, implemented in the FORCE tool [14], analyzes the structure of the Boolean formula in order to find a good ordering.

A technique called *dynamic reordering* [427] is useful in those situations where no obvious ordering heuristics apply. When this technique is used, the OBDD package internally reorders the variables periodically to reduce the total number of vertices in use. The reordering method is designed to save memory rather than to find an optimal ordering.

We next explain how to implement various important logical operations using OBDDs. We begin with the function that *restricts* some argument x_i of the Boolean function f to a constant value b. This function is denoted by $f|_{x_i \leftarrow b}$ and satisfies the identity

$$f|_{x_i \leftarrow b}(x_1, \ldots, x_n) = f(x_1, \ldots, x_{i-1}, b, x_{i+1}, \ldots, x_n).$$

Note that the restricted function depends on $n-1$ variables only. If f is represented as an OBDD, then the OBDD for the restriction $f|_{x_i \leftarrow b}$ can be easily computed by a depth-first traversal of the OBDD. For any vertex v that has a pointer to a vertex w such that $var(w) = x_i$, we replace the pointer by $low(w)$ if b is 0 and by $high(w)$ if b is 1. The resulting graph may not be in canonical form, so we apply the *Reduce* function to obtain the OBDD representation for $f|_{x_i \leftarrow b}$. Note that the resulting OBDD does not depend on x_i.

All 16 two-argument logical operations can be implemented efficiently on Boolean functions that are represented as OBDDs. In fact, the complexity of these operations is linear in the product of the sizes of the argument OBDDs. The key idea for efficient implementation of these operations is the *Shannon expansion*

$$f = (\neg x \wedge f|_{x \leftarrow 0}) \vee (x \wedge f|_{x \leftarrow 1}).$$

Bryant [85] gives a uniform algorithm called *Apply* for computing all 16 logical operations. Below we briefly explain how *Apply* works. Let $\star$ be an arbitrary two argument logical operation, and let f and f' be two Boolean functions. To simplify the explanation of the algorithm, we introduce the following notation:

- v and v' are the roots of the OBDDs for f and f', and
- $x = var(v)$ and $x' = var(v')$.

We consider several cases depending on the relationship between v and v':

- If v and v' are both terminal vertices, then $f \star f' = value(v) \star value(v')$.
- If $x = x'$, then we use the Shannon expansion

$$f \star f' = (\neg x \wedge (f|_{x \leftarrow 0} \star f'|_{x \leftarrow 0})) \vee (x \wedge (f|_{x \leftarrow 1} \star f'|_{x \leftarrow 1}))$$

  to break the problem into two subproblems, each depending on less variables. The subproblems are solved recursively. The root of the resulting OBDD will be a new node w with $var(w) = x$, $low(w)$ will be the OBDD for $(f|_{x \leftarrow 0} \star f'|_{x \leftarrow 0})$, and $high(w)$ will be the OBDD for $(f|_{x \leftarrow 1} \star f'|_{x \leftarrow 1})$.
- If $x < x'$, then $f'|_{x \leftarrow 0} = f'|_{x \leftarrow 1} = f'$ since f' does not depend on x. In this case the Shannon expansion simplifies to

$$f \star f' = (\neg x \wedge (f|_{x \leftarrow 0} \star f')) \vee (x \wedge (f|_{x \leftarrow 1} \star f'))$$

  and the OBDD for $f \star f'$ is computed recursively as in the second case.
- If $x' < x$, then the required computation is similar to the previous case.

Since each subproblem can generate two subproblems, care must be used to prevent the algorithm from being exponential. By using dynamic programming, it is possible to keep the algorithm polynomial. Each subproblem corresponds to a pair of OBDDs that are subgraphs of the original OBDDs for f and f'. Since each subgraph is uniquely determined by its root, the number of subgraphs in the OBDD for f is bounded by the size of the OBDD for f. A similar bound holds for f'. Thus, the number of subproblems is bounded by the product of the size of the OBDDs for f and f'. A hash table, called a *result cache*, is used to record previously computed subproblems. Before any recursive call, the cache is checked to see if the subproblem has been solved. If it has, the result is obtained from the cache; otherwise, the recursive call is performed. The result must be reduced to ensure that it is in canonical form. It is then stored in the result cache.

Boolean negation is one of the 16 two-argument logical operations that can be implemented using *Apply*. That is, $\neg f \equiv f \rightarrow false$.

It should be noted that an OBDD for a Boolean function is never constructed by reducing the decision tree for that function. This is because the decision tree might often be too large to be held in memory. Instead, the OBDD is constructed by starting with OBDDs for each of the individual variables, applying Boolean operators, and reducing intermediate results whenever they include redundancies. Reordering may also be applied during the construction.

Several extensions have been developed to decrease the space requirements of Bryant's original OBDD representation for Boolean functions [75]. A single multi-rooted graph can be used to represent a collection of Boolean functions that share subgraphs. The same variable ordering is used for all of the formulas in the collection. As in the case of standard OBDDs, the graph contains no isomorphic subgraphs or redundant vertices. If this extension is used then two functions in the collection are identical if and only if they have the same root. Consequently, checking whether two functions are equal can be implemented in constant time. Another useful extension is adding labels to the arcs in the graph to denote Boolean negation. This makes it unnecessary to use different subgraphs to represent a formula and its negation. OBDD packages have been shown to permit graphs with millions of vertices.

OBDDs can also be viewed as a form of deterministic finite automata [456]. An n-argument Boolean function can be identified with the set of strings in $\{0,1\}^n$ that evaluate to 1. Since this is a finite language and all finite languages are regular, there is a minimal finite automaton that accepts this set. This automaton provides a canonical representation for the original Boolean function. Logical operations on Boolean functions can be implemented by set operations on the languages accepted by the finite automata. For example, AND corresponds to set intersection. Standard constructions from elementary automata theory can be used to compute these operations on languages. The standard OBDD operations can be viewed as analogs of these constructions.

8.2 Representing Kripke Structures with OBDDs

OBDDs are extremely useful for obtaining concise representations of relations over finite domains [94, 369]. We will see later how to use such representations to describe Kripke structures and to analyze them. If Q is an n-ary relation over $\{0,1\}$, then Q can be represented by the OBDD for its *characteristic function*

$$f_Q(x_1,\ldots,x_n) = 1 \ \text{ iff } \ Q(x_1,\ldots,x_n).$$

Otherwise, let Q be an n-ary relation over the finite domain D. Without loss of generality we assume that D has 2^m elements for some $m > 1$. In order to represent Q as an OBDD, we encode elements of D, using a bijection $\phi : \{0,1\}^m \to D$ that maps each Boolean vector of length m to an element of D. Using the encoding ϕ, we construct a Boolean relation $\hat{Q}$ of arity $m \times n$ according to the following rule:

$$\hat{Q}(\bar{x}_1, \ldots, \bar{x}_n) = Q(\phi(\bar{x}_1), \ldots, \phi(\bar{x}_n))$$

where $\bar{x}_i$ is a vector of m Boolean variables that encodes the variable x_i that takes values in D. The relation Q can now be represented as the OBDD determined by the characteristic function $f_{\hat{Q}}$ of $\hat{Q}$. This technique can be easily extended to relations over different domains $D_1, \ldots, D_n$. Moreover, since sets can be viewed as unary relations, the same technique can be used to represent sets as OBDDs.

Consider now the Kripke structure $M = (S, R, L)$. To represent this structure, we must describe the set S, the relation R, and the mapping L. For the set S, we first need to encode the states; for simplicity, we assume that there are exactly 2^m states. As above, we let $\phi : \{0, 1\}^m \to S$ be a function mapping Boolean vectors to states. Since each assignment is the encoding of a state in S, the characteristic function representing S is the OBDD for 1. For the transition relation R, we use the same encoding for the states. As in chapter 3, we will need two sets of Boolean variables, one to represent the starting state and another to represent the final state of a transition. If the transition relation R is encoded by the Boolean relation $\hat{R}(\bar{x}, \bar{x}')$, then R is represented by the characteristic function $f_{\hat{R}}$. Finally we consider the mapping L. While L is defined as a mapping from states to subsets of atomic propositions, it will be more convenient to consider it as a mapping from atomic propositions to subsets of states. The atomic proposition p is mapped to the set of states that satisfy it: $\{ s \mid p \in L(s) \}$. Call this set of states L_p; it can be represented using the encoding ϕ as above. We represent each atomic proposition separately in this way.

In order to illustrate how OBDDs can be used to represent a Kripke structure, consider the two-state structure given in figure 8.4. There are two state variables, a and b. We introduce two additional state variables, a' and b', to encode successor states. Thus, we will represent the transition from state s_1 to state s_2 by the conjunction

$$(a \wedge b \wedge a' \wedge \neg b').$$

The Boolean formula for the entire transition relation is given by

$$(a \wedge b \wedge a' \wedge \neg b') \vee (a \wedge \neg b \wedge a' \wedge \neg b') \vee (a \wedge \neg b \wedge a' \wedge b').$$

There are three disjuncts in the formula because the Kripke structure has three transitions. This formula is now converted to an OBDD to obtain a concise representation for the transition relation.

Sometimes we also want to describe sets of possible initial states or fair Kripke structures. The set of initial states is represented in the same way as any other set. For the fairness constraint $F = \{P_1, \ldots, P_n\}$, we simply represent each P_i separately. From now on, we will generally use the same name for a relation, such as R, and for the encoded version of the relation, $\hat{R}$.

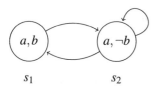

Figure 8.4
Two-state Kripke structure.

In many cases, building an explicit representation of the Kripke structure M and then encoding it as above is not feasible because the structure is too large, even when the final symbolic representation would be concise. Thus, in practice we construct the OBDDs in the representation directly from some concise high-level description of the system. The translation procedure given in chapter 3 converts systems into formulas. If the domain is encoded as described above, this procedure can be used to construct an OBDD for the transition relation directly from a high-level description of the system.

8.3   Symbolic Model Checking for CTL

The explicit-state model-checking algorithm for CTL, presented in chapter 5, is linear in the size of the graph and in the length of the formula. At the time of its development, the algorithm was shown to be fast in practice [121, 123]. However, an explosion in the size of the model may occur when the state transition graph is extracted from a finite-state concurrent system that has many processes or components.

In this section, we describe an algorithm that uses the OBDD representation for Kripke structures to perform model checking. This model-checking algorithm is called *symbolic* since it is based on the manipulation of Boolean formulas. Since the OBDDs represent sets of states and transitions, we need to operate on entire sets rather than on individual states and transitions. For this purpose, we use a *fixpoint* characterization of the temporal logic operators. Recall that a set $S' \subseteq S$ is a fixpoint of a function $\tau \colon \mathcal{P}(S) \to \mathcal{P}(S)$ if $\tau(S') = S'$. In section 5.3, we show how the set of states satisfying a CTL formula can be characterized as a least or greatest fixpoint of an appropriate function. Iterative techniques based only on set operations are used to calculate these fixpoints.

Based on the fixpoint characterization of CTL formulas given in section 5.3, we next give a CTL model checking algorithm that requires only standard OBDD operations. The incorporation of fairness constraints and the generation of counterexamples are then presented in sections 8.4 and 8.5. Section 8.6 discusses some efficiency issues in symbolic model checking.

In order to present the symbolic model checking algorithm, it is convenient to have a more succinct notation for complex operations on Boolean formulas. For this, we will use the logic of quantified Boolean formulas (QBF) [12, 232].

8.3.1   Quantified Boolean Formulas

Given a set $V = \{v_0, \ldots, v_{n-1}\}$ of propositional variables, QBF(V) is the smallest set of formulas such that

- every variable in V is a formula;
- if f and g are formulas, then $\neg f$, $f \vee g$, and $f \wedge g$ are formulas; and
- if f is a formula and $v \in V$, then $\exists v.f$ and $\forall v.f$ are formulas.

A *truth assignment* for QBF(V) is a function $\sigma : V \to \{0, 1\}$. If $a \in \{0, 1\}$, then we will use the notation $\sigma[v \leftarrow a]$ for the truth assignment defined by

$$\sigma[v \leftarrow a](w) = \begin{cases} a & \text{if } v = w, \\ \sigma(w) & \text{otherwise.} \end{cases}$$

If f is a formula in QBF(V) and σ is a truth assignment, we will write $\sigma \models f$ to denote that f is true under the assignment σ. The relation $\models$ is defined inductively in the obvious manner:

- $\sigma \models v$ iff $\sigma(v) = 1$,
- $\sigma \models \neg f$ iff $\sigma \not\models f$,
- $\sigma \models f \vee g$ iff $\sigma \models f$ or $\sigma \models g$,
- $\sigma \models f \wedge g$ iff $\sigma \models f$ and $\sigma \models g$,
- $\sigma \models \exists v.f$ iff $\sigma[v \leftarrow 0] \models f$ or $\sigma[v \leftarrow 1] \models f$, and
- $\sigma \models \forall v.f$ iff $\sigma[v \leftarrow 0] \models f$ and $\sigma[v \leftarrow 1] \models f$.

QBF formulas have the same expressive power as ordinary propositional formulas; however, they are sometimes much more succinct. Every QBF formula determines an n-ary Boolean relation on the set V which consists of those truth assignments for the variables in V that make the formula true. We will identify each QBF formula with the Boolean relation that it determines. Earlier, we showed how to associate an OBDD with each formula of propositional logic. The quantification operators in QBF can be implemented as combinations of the restrict and apply operators described previously:

- $\exists x.f = f|_{x \leftarrow 0} \vee f|_{x \leftarrow 1}$
- $\forall x.f = f|_{x \leftarrow 0} \wedge f|_{x \leftarrow 1}$

We will use quantifiers most frequently in *relational product* operations, which have the form

$$\exists \bar{v} [f(\bar{v}, \bar{w}) \wedge g(\bar{v}, \bar{x})].$$

8.3.2   The Symbolic Model-Checking Algorithm

The symbolic model-checking algorithm is implemented by a procedure *Check* that takes the CTL formula to be checked as its argument and returns an OBDD that represents exactly those states of the system that satisfy the formula. Of course, the output of *Check* depends on the OBDD representation of the transition relation of the system being checked; this parameter is implicit in the discussion below. We define *Check* inductively over the structure of CTL formulas. If f is an atomic proposition a, then $Check(f)$ is the OBDD representing the set of states satisfying a. If $f = f_1 \wedge f_2$ or $f = \neg f_1$, then $Check(f)$ is obtained by using the function *Apply* described in section 8.1, with the arguments $Check(f_1)$ and $Check(f_2)$. Formulas of the form $\mathbf{EX}\, f$, $\mathbf{E}(f\, \mathbf{U}\, g)$, and $\mathbf{EG}\, f$ are handled by the following procedures:

$$Check(\mathbf{EX}\, f) = bddCheckEX(Check(f))$$
$$Check(\mathbf{E}(f\, \mathbf{U}\, g)) = bddCheckEU(Check(f), Check(g))$$
$$Check(\mathbf{EG}\, f) = bddCheckEG(Check(f))$$

Notice that these intermediate procedures take OBDDs as their arguments, while *Check* takes a CTL formula as its argument. Since the other temporal operators can all be rewritten using just the ones above, this definition of *Check* covers all CTL formulas.

The procedure for *bddCheckEX* is straightforward since the formula $\mathbf{EX}\, f$ is true in a state if the state has a successor in which f is true:

$$bddCheckEX(f(\bar{v})) = \exists \bar{v}' \left[f(\bar{v}') \wedge R(\bar{v}, \bar{v}') \right],$$

where $R(\bar{v}, \bar{v}')$ is the OBDD representation of the transition relation. If we have OBDDs for f and R, then we can compute an OBDD for

$$\exists \bar{v}' \left[f(\bar{v}') \wedge R(\bar{v}, \bar{v}') \right]$$

by using the operations of QBF.

The procedure for *bddCheckEU* is based on the least fixpoint characterization for the CTL operator $\mathbf{EU}$ given in section 5.3:

$$\mathbf{E}(f_1\, \mathbf{U}\, f_2) = \mu Z . f_2 \vee (f_1 \wedge \mathbf{EX}\, Z).$$

We use the function *Lfp* (figure 5.4) to compute a sequence of approximations

$$Q_0, Q_1, \ldots, Q_i, \ldots$$

that converges to $\mathbf{E}(f\, \mathbf{U}\, g)$ in a finite number of steps. If we have OBDDs for f, g, and the current approximation Q_i, then we can compute an OBDD for the next approximation Q_{i+1}. Since OBDDs provide a canonical form of Boolean functions, it is easy to test for convergence by comparing consecutive approximations. When $Q_i = Q_{i+1}$, the function *Lfp* terminates. The set of states corresponding to $\mathbf{E}(f\, \mathbf{U}\, g)$ will be represented by the OBDD for Q_i.

The procedure for *bddCheckEG* is similar. It is based on the greatest fixpoint characterization for the CTL operator **EG** that is given in section 5.3:

$$\mathbf{EG}\, f_1 = \nu Z. f_1 \wedge \mathbf{EX}\, Z$$

If we have an OBDD for f, then the function *Gfp* (figure 5.5) can be used to compute an OBDD representation for the set of states that satisfy **EG** f.

8.4   Fairness in Symbolic Model Checking

Fairness constraints and their significance are discussed in chapter 4. In section 5.2 fairness constraints were added to the explicit-state model-checking algorithm for CTL. In this section we extend the symbolic model checking for CTL, given in the previous section, to include fairness constraints as well. We assume the fairness constraints are given by a set of CTL formulas $F = \{P_1, \ldots, P_n\}$. We define a new procedure *bddDCheckFair* for checking CTL formulas relative to the fairness constraints in F. We do this by defining new intermediate procedures *bddCheckFairEX*, *bddCheckFairEU*, and *bddCheckFairEG*, which correspond to the intermediate procedures used to define *Check*.

Recall the fixpoint characterization of the set of states satisfying **EG** f under the fairness constraints $F = \{P_1, \ldots, P_n\}$:

$$\mathbf{EG}\, f = \nu Z. f \wedge \bigwedge_{k=1}^{n} \mathbf{EX}\, \mathbf{E}(f\, \mathbf{U}\, (Z \wedge P_k)). \tag{8.1}$$

Based on this characterization, the set of states can be computed by the procedure *bddCheckFairEG*$(f(\bar{v}))$ as follows:

$$\nu Z(\bar{v}). f(\bar{v}) \wedge \bigwedge_{k=1}^{n} bddCheckEX\big(bddCheckEU(f(\bar{v}), Z(\bar{v}) \wedge Check(P_k))\big)$$

The fixpoint can be evaluated in the same manner as before. The main difference is that each time the above expression is evaluated, several nested fixpoint computations are performed (inside *bddCheckEU*).

Checking **EX** f and $\mathbf{E}(f\, \mathbf{U}\, g)$ under fairness constraints is similar to the explicit state case. The set of all states that are the start of some fair computation is

$$fair(\bar{v}) = bddDCheckFair(\mathbf{EG}\, true).$$

The formula **EX** f is true under fairness constraints in a state s if and only if there is a successor state s' such that s' satisfies f and s' is at the beginning of some fair computation path. It follows that the formula **EX** f (under fairness constraints) is equivalent to the formula $\mathbf{EX}(f \wedge fair)$ (without fairness constraints). Therefore, we define

$$bddCheckFairEX(f(\bar{v})) = bddCheckEX(f(\bar{v}) \wedge fair(\bar{v})).$$

Similarly, the formula $\mathbf{E}(f \mathbf{U} g)$ (under fairness constraints) is equivalent to the formula $\mathbf{E}(f \mathbf{U} (g \wedge fair))$ (without fairness constraints). Hence, we define

$$bddCheckFairEU(f(\bar{v}), g(\bar{v})) = bddCheckEU(f(\bar{v}), g(\bar{v}) \wedge fair(\bar{v})).$$

8.5 Counterexamples and Witnesses

One of the most important features of CTL model-checking algorithms is the ability to find *counterexamples* and *witnesses*. When this feature is enabled and the model checker determines that a formula with a universal path quantifier is false, it will find a computation path that demonstrates that the negation of the formula is true. Likewise, when the model checker determines that a formula with an existential path quantifier is true, it will find a computation path that demonstrates why the formula is true. For example, if the model checker discovers that the formula $\mathbf{AG}\,f$ is false, it will produce a path to a state in which $\neg f$ holds. Similarly, if it discovers that the formula $\mathbf{EF}\,f$ is true, it will produce a path to a state in which f holds. Note that the counterexample for a universally quantified formula is the witness for the dual existentially quantified formula. By exploiting this observation we can restrict our discussion of this feature to finding witnesses for the three basic CTL operators $\mathbf{EX}$, $\mathbf{EG}$, and $\mathbf{EU}$.

In order to explain the procedure for finding a witness for some CTL formula, we will consider the strongly connected components of the transition graph determined by the Kripke structure. Conceptually, we form a new graph in which the nodes are the strongly connected components and there is an edge from one strongly connected component to another if and only if there is an edge from a state in one to a state in the other. It is easy to see that the new graph does not contain any proper cycles; that is, each cycle in the graph is contained in one of the strongly connected components. Moreover, since we consider only finite Kripke structures, each infinite path must have a suffix that is entirely contained within a strongly connected component of the transition graph.

We start by considering the problem of how to find a witness for the formula $\mathbf{EG}\,f$ under the set of fairness constraints $F = \{P_1, \ldots, P_n\}$. We will identify each P_i with the set of states that make it true. Recall that the set of states that satisfy the formula $\mathbf{EG}\,f$ with the fairness constraints F is given by the formula

$$\nu Z . f \wedge \bigwedge_{k=1}^{n} \mathbf{EX} \big(\mathbf{E}(f \mathbf{U} (Z \wedge P_k)) \big). \tag{8.2}$$

As in the previous section, we will use $\mathbf{EG}\,f$ to denote the set of states that satisfy $\mathbf{EG}\,f$ under the fairness constraints F. Given a state s in $\mathbf{EG}\,f$, we would like to exhibit a path π starting with s that satisfies f in every state and visits every set $P \in F$ infinitely often. We can always find such a path that consists of a finite prefix followed by a repeating cycle. We construct the path incrementally by giving a sequence of prefixes of the path of increasing length until a cycle is found. At each step in the construction we must ensure

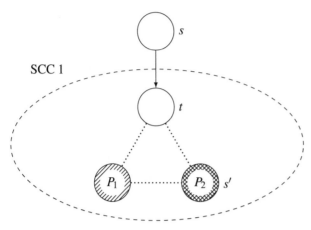

Figure 8.5
Witness is in the first strongly connected component.

that the current prefix can be extended to a fair path along which each state satisfies f. This invariant is guaranteed by making sure that each time we add a state to the current prefix, the state satisfies $\mathbf{EG}\,f$.

First, we evaluate the above fixpoint formula. In every iteration of the outer fixpoint computation, we compute a collection of least fixpoints associated with the formulas $\mathbf{E}(f\,\mathbf{U}\,(Z \wedge P))$, for each fairness constraint $P \in F$. For every constraint P, we obtain an increasing sequence of approximations $Q_0^P \subseteq Q_1^P \subseteq Q_2^P \subseteq \ldots$, where Q_i^P is the set of states from which a state in $Z \wedge P$ can be reached in i or fewer steps, while satisfying f. In the last iteration of the outer fixpoint when $Z = \mathbf{EG}\,f$, we save the sequence of approximations Q_i^P for each P in F.

Now, suppose we are given an initial state s satisfying $\mathbf{EG}\,f$. Then s belongs to the set of states computed in equation (8.2), so it must have a successor in $\mathbf{E}(f\,\mathbf{U}\,(\mathbf{EG}\,f \wedge P))$ for each $P \in F$. In order to minimize the length of the witness path, we choose the first fairness constraint that can be reached from s. This is accomplished by looking for a successor t of s in the saved sets Q_0^P for all $P \in F$. If no such t is found, we search the sets Q_1^P for all $P \in F$. If we still do not find a suitable t, we search the sets Q_2^P, and so forth. Since s is in $\mathbf{EG}\,f$, we must eventually find a successor t such that $t \in Q_i^P$. Note that t has a path of length i to a state in $(\mathbf{EG}\,f) \wedge P$ and therefore that t is in $\mathbf{EG}\,f$. If $i > 0$, we find a successor of t in Q_{i-1}^P. This is done by finding the set of successors of t, intersecting it with Q_{i-1}^P, and then choosing an arbitrary element of the resulting set. Continuing until $i = 0$, we obtain a path from the initial state s to some state u in $(\mathbf{EG}\,f) \wedge P$. We then eliminate P from further consideration, and repeat the above procedure from u until all of the fairness constraints have been visited. Let s' be the final state of the path obtained thus far.

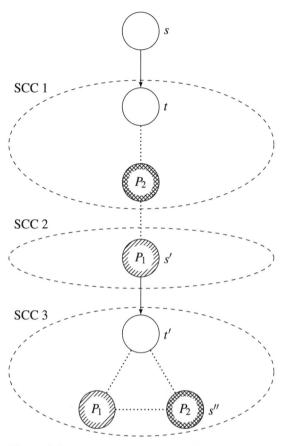

Figure 8.6
Witness spans three strongly connected components.

To complete a cycle, we need a non-trivial path from s' to the state t along which each state satisfies f. In other words, we need a witness for the formula $\{s'\} \wedge \mathbf{EX}\mathbf{E}(f\,\mathbf{U}\,\{t\})$. If this formula is true, we have found the witness path for s. This case is illustrated in figure 8.5. If the formula is false, there are several possible strategies. The simplest is to restart the procedure from the final state s' using the entire set of fairness constraints F. Since $\{s'\} \wedge \mathbf{EX}\mathbf{E}(f\,\mathbf{U}\,\{t\})$ is false, we know that s' is not in the strongly connected component of f containing t; however, s' is in $\mathbf{EG}\,f$. Thus, if we continue this strategy, we must descend in the directed acyclic graph of strongly connected components, eventually either finding a cycle π, or reaching a terminal strongly connected component of f. In the latter case, we are guaranteed to find a cycle, since we cannot exit a terminal strongly connected component. This case is illustrated in figure 8.6.

A slightly more sophisticated approach would be to precompute $\mathbf{E}(f \, \mathbf{U} \, \{t\})$. The first time we exit this set, we know the cycle cannot be completed, so we restart from that state. Heuristically, these approaches tend to find short counterexamples (probably because the number of strongly connected components tends to be small), so no attempt is made to find the shortest cycle.

Finally, we explain how to find witnesses for $\mathbf{E}(f \, \mathbf{U} \, g)$ and $\mathbf{EX} f$ in the presence of fairness constraints. Recall that *fair* is the set of states that satisfy $\mathbf{EG} \, true$ under the fairness constraints F. It is possible to compute $\mathbf{E}(f \, \mathbf{U} \, g)$ under F by using the standard CTL model-checking algorithm (without fairness constraints) to compute $\mathbf{E}(f \, \mathbf{U} \, (g \wedge fair))$. Similarly, we can compute $\mathbf{EX} f$ by using the standard CTL model-checking algorithm to compute $\mathbf{EX}(f \wedge fair)$. The witness procedure for $\mathbf{EG} \, true$ under fairness constraints F can be used to extend witnesses for $\mathbf{E}(f \, \mathbf{U} \, g)$ and $\mathbf{EX} f$ to infinite fair paths.

8.6   Relational Product Computations

Most of the operations used in the symbolic model-checking algorithm are linear in the product of the sizes of the operand OBDDs. The main exception is the relational product operation used to compute $\mathbf{EX} h$:

$$\exists \vec{v}' [h(\vec{v}') \wedge R(\vec{v}, \vec{v}')]$$

While it is possible to implement this operation with one conjunction and a series of existential quantifications, in practice this would be fairly slow. In addition, the OBDD for $h(\vec{v}') \wedge R(\vec{v}, \vec{v}')$ is often much larger than the OBDD for the final result, and we would like to avoid constructing it if possible. For these reasons, we use a special algorithm to compute the OBDD for the relational product in one step from the OBDDs for h and R. Figure 8.7 gives this algorithm for two arbitrary OBDDs f and g. Like many OBDD algorithms, *RelProd* uses a result cache. In this case, entries in the cache are of the form (f, g, E, r), where E is a set of variables that are quantified out and f, g, and r are OBDDs. If such an entry is in the cache, it means that a previous call to $RelProd(f, g, E)$ returned r as its result.

Although the above algorithm works well in practice, it has exponential complexity in the worst case. Most of the situations where this complexity is observed are cases in which the OBDD for the result is exponentially larger than the OBDDs for the arguments $f(\vec{v})$ and $g(\vec{v})$. In such situations, any method of computing the relational product must have exponential complexity.

8.6.1   Partitioned Transition Relations

The relational product algorithm described previously requires having $R(\vec{v}, \vec{v}')$ as a *monolithic transition relation*, consisting of a single OBDD. We showed in section 8.2 how to construct this OBDD when the system is given as a Kripke structure. Unfortunately, for many practical examples, this OBDD is very large. *Partitioned transition relations* can

function $RelProd(f, g : OBDD, E : \text{set of variables}) : OBDD$

    if $f = 0 \vee g = 0$ **then**
        return 0;
    else if $f = 1 \wedge g = 1$ **then**
        return 1;
    else if (f, g, E, r) is in the result cache **then**
        return r;
    else
        let x be the top variable of f;
        let y be the top variable of g;
        let z be the topmost of x and y;
        $r_0 := RelProd(f|_{z \leftarrow 0}, g|_{z \leftarrow 0}, E)$;
        $r_1 := RelProd(f|_{z \leftarrow 1}, g|_{z \leftarrow 1}, E)$;
        if $z \in E$ **then**
            $r := Or(r_0, r_1)$;
            /* OBDD for $r_0 \vee r_1$ */
        else
            $r := IfThenElse(z, r_1, r_0)$;
            /* OBDD for $(z \wedge r_1) \vee (\neg z \wedge r_0)$ */
        end if
        insert (f, g, E, r) in the result cache;
        return r;
    end if

end function

Figure 8.7
Relational product algorithm.

provide a much more concise representation, but they cannot be used with the relational product algorithm given in figure 8.7. In chapter 3 the transition relations for synchronous and asynchronous circuits are described in the form of conjunctions or disjunctions of a number of pieces, $R_i(\vec{v}, \vec{v}')$. Each of these pieces can typically be represented by a small OBDD. Instead of forming the conjunction or disjunction of the $R_i(\vec{v}, \vec{v}')$ to get $R(\vec{v}, \vec{v}')$, we can represent the models by a list of these OBDDs, which are implicitly conjuncted or disjuncted. We call such a list a *partitioned transition relation* [91, 92].

For synchronous circuits, the R_i are of the form

$$R_i(\vec{v}, \vec{v}') = (v_i' \equiv f_i(\vec{v})),$$

where f_i is the function computed by the combinational logic that determines the value of variable v_i. R is the conjunction of the R_i. If the transition relation is instead represented by a list of the R_i, with an implicit conjunction, then we call this a *conjunctive partitioned transition relation*.

For asynchronous circuits, the R_i are of the form:

$$R_i(\bar{v}, \bar{v}') = \left(v_i' \equiv f_i(\bar{v})\right) \wedge \bigwedge_{j \neq i} (v_j' \equiv v_j).$$

The OBDD for R is the disjunction of the R_i. We call the list of the R_i with an implicit disjunction a *disjunctive partitioned transition relation*. In this case the OBDD for R_i can be much larger than the OBDD for f_i (up to a factor of n larger, where n is the number of variables used to encode the state of the circuit). However, there is an additional technique for efficiently representing relations of this form. Let

$$N_i(\bar{v}, v_i') = v_i' \equiv f_i(\bar{v}).$$

We use the pair $(N_i(\bar{v}, v_i'), i)$ to represent $R_i(\bar{v}, \bar{v}')$ with the interpretation that v_i' is constrained by N_i, and that if $j \neq i$, then v_j' is constrained to be equal to v_j. We exploit this representation during the relational product computation by replacing

$$\exists \bar{v}' \left[h(\bar{v}') \wedge R_i(\bar{v}, \bar{v}') \right]$$
$$= \exists \bar{v}' \left[h(\bar{v}') \wedge (N_i(\bar{v}, v_i') \wedge \bigwedge_{j \neq i} (v_j' \equiv v_j)) \right]$$

with the equivalent expression

$$\exists v_i' \left[h(v_1, \ldots, v_{i-1}, v_i', v_{i+1}, \ldots, v_n) \wedge N_i(\bar{v}, v_i') \right].$$

While a partitioned transition relation with one OBDD for each state variable is often more efficient than constructing a monolithic transition relation, it may not be the best choice. As long as the OBDDs do not become too large, it is better to combine some of the R_i into one OBDD by forming their conjunction or disjunction, as appropriate. Fewer OBDD nodes may be needed in this representation if the R_i that are combined have similar structure near the root of their OBDDs. Combining some of the OBDDs in a partitioned transition can also speed up the relational product computations. Next, we show how to extend the basic algorithm to compute relational products for partitioned transition relations.

8.6.1.1 Disjunctive partitioning   For a disjunctive partitioned transition relation, the relational product computed is of the form

$$\exists \bar{v}' \left[h(\bar{v}') \wedge (R_0(\bar{v}, \bar{v}') \vee \ldots \vee R_{n-1}(\bar{v}, \bar{v}')) \right].$$

This relational product can be computed without ever constructing the OBDD for the full transition relation by distributing the existential quantification over the disjunctions:

$$\exists \vec{v}' \left[h(\vec{v}') \wedge R_0(\vec{v}, \vec{v}') \right] \vee \ldots \vee \exists \vec{v}' \left[h(\vec{v}') \wedge R_{n-1}(\vec{v}, \vec{v}') \right].$$

Thus, we are able to reduce the problem of computing the relational product to a series of relational products involving relatively small OBDDs. Much larger asynchronous circuits can be verified using this representation than with a monolithic transition relation.

8.6.1.2   Conjunctive Partitioning   When using a conjunctive partitioned transition relation, the relational product computed is of the form

$$\exists \vec{v}' \left[h(\vec{v}') \wedge (R_0(\vec{v}, \vec{v}') \wedge \ldots \wedge R_{n-1}(\vec{v}, \vec{v}')) \right]. \tag{8.3}$$

The main difficulty in computing this relational product without building the conjunction is that existential quantification does not distribute over conjunction. The method we now describe overcomes this difficulty.

The technique in [91, 92] is based on two observations. First, circuits exhibit locality, so many of the R_i will depend on only a small number of the variables in $\vec{v}$ and $\vec{v}'$. (In the earlier discussion on extracting transition relations from circuits, there was only one primed variable per R_i, but in section 8.6.2, we show that it is sometimes advantageous to combine some of the pieces, giving a dependence on multiple primed variables.) Second, although existential quantification does not distribute over conjunction, subformulas can be moved out of the scope of existential quantification if they do not depend on any of the variables being quantified. We will take advantage of these observations by conjuncting the $R_i(\vec{v}, \vec{v}')$ with $h(\vec{v}')$ one at a time and using "early quantification" to eliminate each variable v'_j when none of the remaining $R_i(\vec{v}, \vec{v}')$ depends on v'_j.

Consider the modulo 8 counter described in section 3.5.2. Recall that

$$R_0(\vec{v}, v'_0) = (v'_0 \Leftrightarrow \neg v_0)$$
$$R_1(\vec{v}, v'_1) = (v'_1 \Leftrightarrow v_0 \oplus v_1)$$
$$R_2(\vec{v}, v'_2) = (v'_2 \Leftrightarrow (v_0 \wedge v_1) \oplus v_2).$$

In this case, the relational product for **EX** h is

$$\exists v'_0 \exists v'_1 \exists v'_2 \left[h(\vec{v}') \wedge (R_0(\vec{v}, v'_0) \wedge R_1(\vec{v}, v'_1) \wedge R_2(\vec{v}, v'_2)) \right].$$

We can rewrite this as

$$\exists v'_2 \exists v'_1 \exists v'_0 \left[((h(\vec{v}') \wedge R_0(\vec{v}, v'_0)) \wedge R_1(\vec{v}, v'_1)) \wedge R_2(\vec{v}, v'_2) \right]. \tag{8.4}$$

The reasons for doing the conjunctions and quantifications in this particular order will become clear shortly. As mentioned above, subformulas can be moved out of the scope of existential quantification if they do not depend on any of the variables being quantified.

Since $R_2(\bar{v}, v_2')$ does not depend on v_0' or v_1', we can re-express the relational product as:

$$\exists v_2' \left[\exists v_1' \, \exists v_0' \left[(h(\bar{v}') \wedge R_0(\bar{v}, v_0')) \wedge R_1(\bar{v}, v_1') \right] \wedge R_2(\bar{v}, v_2') \right].$$

Now since $R_1(\bar{v}, v_1')$ does not depend on v_0', we obtain

$$\exists v_2' \left[\exists v_1' \left[\exists v_0' \left[(h(\bar{v}') \wedge R_0(\bar{v}, v_0') \right] \wedge R_1(\bar{v}, v_1') \right] \wedge R_2(\bar{v}, v_2') \right].$$

We can compute this relational product by starting with $h(\bar{v}')$ and at each step combining the previous result with an $R_i(\bar{v}, \bar{v}')$ and quantifying out the appropriate variables. Thus, we have reduced the problem of computing the full relational product to one of performing a series of smaller relational product-like steps. Notice that the intermediate results may depend both on variables in $\bar{v}$ and on variables in $\bar{v}'$.

Now we can explain why we chose the ordering of conjuncts given in equation 8.4. We wish to order the $R_i(\bar{v}, \bar{v}')$ so that the variables in $\bar{v}'$ can be quantified out as soon as possible and the variables in $\bar{v}$ are added as slowly as possible. This is desirable since it reduces the number of variables that the intermediate OBDDs depend on and hence can greatly reduce the size of these OBDDs. In this particular example, the variables in $\bar{v}'$ are eliminated one at a time, independent of the ordering of the $R_i(\bar{v}, \bar{v}')$. Thus, the optimum ordering for the $R_i(\bar{v}, \bar{v}')$ is determined by how quickly the variables in $\bar{v}$ are added. For each of the variables v_i in $\bar{v}$, consider the number of R_j that depend on v_i: all three depend on v_0, while two depend on v_1, and one depends on v_2. Thus, by dealing with R_0 first, we introduce only one new variable, v_0, while at the same time eliminating v_0'. This explains why we chose to combine $h(\bar{v}')$ and $R_0(\bar{v}, \bar{v}')$ as the first step in the computation. Similarly, $R_1(\bar{v}, \bar{v}')$ was chosen next because it introduces only one new variable, v_1, while v_1' is eliminated. In [235], a heuristic algorithm for ordering partitions is described, which is independent of the model details and can be run prior to symbolic model checking.

The above example involved computing the relational product for **EX**h, that is, we computed the predecessors of a set of states. We also sometimes need to compute the successors of a state set. The relational product in this case is quite similar to that described above. However, instead of quantifying out the next state variables when performing the relational product, we quantify out the present state variables. This change may affect the optimal ordering of the $R_i(\bar{v}, \bar{v}')$ when using conjunctive partitioning. To illustrate this, we consider the modulo 8 counter again. The relational product for a successor computation has the form:

$$\exists v_0 \, \exists v_1 \, \exists v_2 \left[h(\bar{v}) \wedge (R_0(v_0, \bar{v}') \wedge R_1(v_0, v_1, \bar{v}') \wedge R_2(v_0, v_1, v_2, \bar{v}')) \right].$$

In this case we write the unprimed variables explicitly and leave the primed variables implicit in the relations R_i. Since conjunction is commutative and associative, we can rewrite this as

$$\exists v_0 \, \exists v_1 \, \exists v_2 \left[((h(\bar{v}) \wedge R_2(v_0, v_1, v_2, \bar{v}')) \wedge R_1(v_0, v_1, \bar{v}')) \wedge R_0(v_0, \bar{v}') \right].$$

Since $R_0(v_0, \vec{v}')$ does not depend on v_1 or v_2, we get

$$\exists v_0 \left[\exists v_1 \, \exists v_2 \left[(h(\vec{v}) \wedge R_2(v_0, v_1, v_2, \vec{v}')) \wedge R_1(v_0, v_1, \vec{v}') \right] \wedge R_0(v_0, \vec{v}') \right].$$

Now $R_1(v_0, v_1, \vec{v}')$ does not depend on v_2, so we obtain

$$\exists v_0 \left[\exists v_1 \left[\exists v_2 \left[(h(\vec{v}) \wedge R_2(v_0, v_1, v_2, \vec{v}')) \right] \wedge R_1(v_0, v_1, \vec{v}') \right] \wedge R_0(v_0, \vec{v}') \right].$$

In this particular example, the number of new state variables v_i' in the intermediate OBDDs is independent of the ordering of the $R_i(\vec{v}, \vec{v}')$. However, the number of old state variables v_i remaining at each stage depends on the ordering, and is minimized by the ordering given. Note that this ordering is different from the one in equation 8.4.

The method described above for computing the relational product for the modulo 8 counter can be generalized to an arbitrary conjunctive partitioned transition relation with n state variables, as follows. The user must choose a permutation ρ of $\{0, \ldots, n-1\}$. This permutation determines the order in which the partitions $R_i(\vec{v}, \vec{v}')$ are combined. For each i, let D_i be the set of variables v_i' that $R_i(\vec{v}, \vec{v}')$ depends on. Also, let

$$E_i = D_{\rho(i)} - \bigcup_{k=i+1}^{n-1} D_{\rho(k)}.$$

Thus, E_i is the set of variables contained in $D_{\rho(i)}$ that are not contained in $D_{\rho(k)}$ for any k larger than i. The E_i are pairwise disjoint, and their union contains all the variables. The relational product for **EX** h can be computed as

$$h_1(\vec{v}, \vec{v}') = \underset{v_j' \in E_0}{\exists} \left[h(\vec{v}') \wedge R_{\rho(0)}(\vec{v}, \vec{v}') \right]$$

$$h_2(\vec{v}, \vec{v}') = \underset{v_j' \in E_1}{\exists} \left[h_1(\vec{v}, \vec{v}') \wedge R_{\rho(1)}(\vec{v}, \vec{v}') \right]$$

$$\vdots$$

$$h_n(\vec{v}) = \underset{v_j' \in E_{n-1}}{\exists} \left[h_{n-1}(\vec{v}, \vec{v}') \wedge R_{\rho(n-1)}(\vec{v}, \vec{v}') \right].$$

The result of the relational product is h_n. Note that if some E_i is empty, then

$$h_{i+1}(\vec{v}, \vec{v}') = \left[h_i(\vec{v}, \vec{v}') \wedge R_{\rho(i)}(\vec{v}, \vec{v}') \right]$$

and no existential quantification will be used at this stage. The ordering ρ has a significant impact on how early in the computation state variables can be quantified out. This affects the size of the OBDDs constructed and the efficiency of the verification procedure. Thus, it is important to choose ρ carefully, just as with the OBDD variable ordering.

while $V \neq \phi$ **do**

    For each $v \in V$ compute the cost of eliminating v;

    Eliminate variable with lowest cost by updating C and V;

end while

Figure 8.8
Algorithm for variable elimination.

We search for a good ordering ρ by using a greedy algorithm to find a good ordering on the variables v_i to be eliminated. For each ordering on the variables, there is an obvious ordering on the relations R_i such that when this relation ordering is used, the variables can be eliminated in the order given by the greedy algorithm.

The algorithm in figure 8.8 gives the basic greedy technique. We start with the set of variables V to be eliminated and a collection C of sets where every $D_i \in C$ is the set of variables on which R_i depends. We then eliminate the variables one at a time by always choosing the variable with the least cost and then updating V and C appropriately.

All that remains is to determine the cost metric to use. We will consider three different cost measures. To simplify our discussion, we will use R_v to refer to the relation created when eliminating variable v by taking the conjunction of all the R_i that depend on v and then quantifying out v. We will use D_v to refer to the set of variables on which this R_v depends.

1. **Minimum size:** The cost of eliminating a variable v is simply $|D_v|$. With this cost function, we always try to ensure that the new relation we create depends on the fewest number of variables.

2. **Minimum increase:** The cost of eliminating variable v is

$$|D_v| - \max_{A \in C, v \in A} |A|,$$

which is the difference between the size of D_v and the size of the largest D_i containing v. The intuition here is to try to avoid eliminating variables that would create a large relation from many small relations. In other words, we prefer to make a small increase in the size of an already large relation than to create a new large relation.

3. **Minimum sum:** The cost of eliminating variable v is

$$\sum_{A \in C, v \in A} |A|,$$

which is simply the sum of the sizes of all the D_i containing v. Since the cost of conjunction depends on the sizes of the arguments, we approximate this cost by the number of variables on which each of the argument R_i depends.

The overall goal is to minimize the size of the largest BDD created during the elimination process. In our abstraction, this translates to finding an ordering that minimizes the size of the largest set D_v created during the process. Always making a locally optimal choice does not guarantee an optimal solution, and there are counterexamples for each of the three cost functions. In fact, the problem of finding an optimal ordering can be shown to be NP-complete. However, the minimum sum cost function seems to provide the best approximation of the cost of the actual BDD operations and in practice has the best performance.

8.6.2   Recombining Partitions

Earlier, we described how a synchronous circuit could be represented by a set of transition relations $R_i(\vec{v}, \vec{v}')$, each depending on exactly one variable in $\vec{v}'$. We also pointed out that combining some of the R_i together into one OBDD can result in a smaller representation. Combining parts of a transition relation in this way can also significantly speed up the computation of relational products.

For example, consider the case of an n-bit counter. With the usual variable ordering, the number of OBDD nodes needed to represent the transition relation is linear in n in both the monolithic and fully partitioned cases. Suppose that $h(\vec{v}')$ represents a single state of the counter. Computing the relational product with the fully partitioned representation requires n OBDD operations, each of which has complexity $O(n)$, for a total complexity of $O(n^2)$. On the other hand, if we use the monolithic relation, we perform one operation of complexity $O(n)$, a savings in time of a factor of n. In practice, we can often get a speed-up by combining all of the OBDDs for any given register, without significantly increasing the number of OBDD nodes in the transition relation.

Bibliographic Notes

BDDs were first suggested for symbolic simulation of hardware designs by Bryant [85, 86, 87]. In [85], Bryant presents Ordered BDDs (OBDDs) as a new data structure for representing Boolean functions. Functions are represented by directed, acyclic graphs in a manner similar to the representation introduced by Lee [342] and Akers [13] but with further restrictions on the ordering of the decision variables in the graph, which guarantee a canonical representation. The work also shows how operations on Boolean functions can be applied efficiently with OBDDs.

McMillan [369] and Clarke et al. [94] then suggested using BDDs for symbolic model checking. SMV [369] was the first BDD-based symbolic model checker. Its success in handling circuits with several hundreds of state variables attracted the attention of the hardware industry. SMV has strongly influenced the industrial model-checking tools, including RuleBase [44] at IBM. The Forte [435] tool at Intel uses BDDs for symbolic simulation of circuits and is based on the Voss tool [292]. Centaur Technology maintains a verification tool for circuit verification that, among others, includes a BDD engine [449].

In academia, NuSMV [114] and NuSMV2 [113] reimplement SMV but also extend it with further model-checking techniques, described in other chapters. PRISM [329] is a BDD-based model checker for probabilistic systems. In [54], BDD-based model checking for the μ-calculus is described. EBMC [388] is a recent model checker for hardware designs given in the Verilog hardware description language and implements multiple engines, including one that uses BDDs. A multi-core implementation of BDD operations has been developed in Sylvan [470, 468].

Some of the tools provide their own BDD library, which includes efficient implementations of commonly used operations on OBDDs. However, the Colorado University Decision Diagram (CUDD) package [450] is the library that is most widely used. The Sylvan library offers a scalable multi-threaded implementation [469].

The *Handbook of Model Checking* [136] has a chapter on BDDs, written by Randy Bryant. The survey [382] presents the history of and more recent research activity related to BDDs.

Problems

Problem 8.1 (BDD basics). Draw a BDD for $x \vee (y \wedge z)$ with variable ordering $x < y < z$. Give the BDD after reordering the variables to $y < x < z$.

Problem 8.2 (Restrict). Let f be $(x_1 \wedge x_2) \vee (x_3 \wedge x_4)$. Draw the BDD for ordering $x_1 < x_2 < x_3 < x_4$. Draw the BDD for $f|_{x_2 \leftarrow 0}$ for the same ordering.

Problem 8.3 (Apply). Let f be $a \Rightarrow b$, and let f' be $\neg b$. Draw BDDs for f and f' with the variable ordering $a < b$. Then show how *Apply* generates the BDD for $f \leftrightarrow f'$.

9 Propositional Satisfiability

Given a quantifier-free first-order formula, a satisfiability (SAT) solver determines whether there is an assignment to the variables in the formula that satisfies the formula. Modern satisfiability solvers have numerous applications in formal verification and model checking. In this chapter, we focus on the specific case of propositional formulas, that is, quantifier-free formulas that use only Boolean variables and Boolean connectives. Despite their apparent simplicity, propositional formulas can be used to model a very broad range of problems.

The scalability of algorithms for determining satisfiability of propositional formulas has made tremendous progress. The best-performing implementations of propositional SAT are based on the Davis–Putnam–Logemann–Loveland (DPLL) algorithm [166] with conflict-driven clause learning (CDCL) [365]. In this chapter, we formalize the propositional satisfiability problem and illustrate how to generate formulas in conjunctive normal form. We then explain the details of the DPLL algorithm and CDCL.

9.1 Conjunctive Normal Form

In this chapter, we use ϕ to denote a propositional formula and assume that ϕ is defined over Boolean variables $x_1, \ldots, x_n$. For ease of implementation, most SAT solvers operate on formulas given in conjunctive normal form (CNF). We refer the reader to the bibliographic notes of this chapter for an overview of nonclausal SAT solvers.

We introduce the following symbols and terminology to define CNF. The set of Boolean truth values is $\{true, false\}$, and we use 1 and 0 as shorthands for $true$ and $false$, respectively. We write V for the set of variables $x_1, \ldots, x_n$.

CNF is defined as follows:

- A *literal* is one of the variables $x_i \in V$ or the negation of a variable in V, denoted by $\bar{x}_i$. A literal is called *positive* if it is just a variable. A literal is called *negative* if it is the negation of a variable.

- A *clause* is a (possibly empty) disjunction of literals. We write $\emptyset$ for the empty clause, which is equivalent to *false*.

- A formula in CNF is a conjunction of clauses $c_1, \ldots, c_m$. A CNF formula that does not contain any clause is equivalent to *true*.

We frequently write the clauses in CNF as sequences of literals, that is, we write

$$x_1 x_2 \bar{x}_3 \tag{9.1}$$

to mean

$$x_1 \vee x_2 \vee \bar{x}_3. \tag{9.2}$$

Similarly, we use a set of clauses as a shorthand for a formula in CNF. For instance, we write

$$\{x_1 x_2 \bar{x}_3, \, \bar{x}_1 x_2\} \tag{9.3}$$

to mean

$$(x_1 \vee x_2 \vee \bar{x}_3) \wedge (\bar{x}_1 \vee x_2). \tag{9.4}$$

A *truth assignment* σ is a (possibly partial) function that maps variables to truth values, that is, $\sigma : V \to \{0, 1\}$. Truth assignments are typically written as sets of pairs of variables and truth values. For example, we write

$$\{x_1 \mapsto 1, \, x_2 \mapsto 1, \, x_3 \mapsto 0\}$$

for the assignment that gives the value 1 to x_1 and x_2 and the value 0 to x_3. We introduce the following terminology for truth assignments:

- The assignment is *complete* if all variables have a value.
- An assignment may not assign a value for some variable $x_i \in V$. In this case, we write $\sigma(x_i) = \bot$.
- We say that a clause c is *satisfied* by the assignment σ if there is a positive literal $x_i \in c$ with $\sigma(x_i) = 1$ or if there is a negative literal $\bar{x}_i \in c$ with $\sigma(x_i) = 0$. We then write $\sigma \models c$.
- We say that the formula ϕ is satisfied by σ if all clauses in ϕ are satisfied. We then write $\sigma \models \phi$.
- We say that a clause c is *conflicting* with σ if c is not satisfied and all variables in c are given a value by σ. We then write $\sigma \not\models c$.

Finally, we say that ϕ is *satisfiable* if there exists some assignment σ that satisfies ϕ.

Example 9.1 *Equation 9.4 is satisfiable, as its clauses are satisfied by the (partial) assignment $\{x_2 \mapsto 1\}$.*

Example 9.2 *The following formula is unsatisfiable:*

$$\{x_1, \bar{x}_1 x_2, \bar{x}_1 \bar{x}_2\} \tag{9.5}$$

To see why, observe that any satisfying assignment would need to assign 1 *to* x_1 *because of the first clause. Hence, to satisfy the second clause,* x_2 *must be* 1 *as well. This implies that the third clause cannot be satisfied.*

9.2   Encoding Propositional Logic into CNF

Formulas in conjunctive normal form are conjunctions of disjunctions of literals. Applications in model checking frequently require solving satisfiability problems that are given as a propositional formula without any restriction of the Boolean connectives. These formulas need to be converted into CNF before they can be given to the SAT solver. It is always possible to transform a Boolean formula into CNF that is equivalent. However, there are propositional formulas whose equivalent representation in CNF is necessarily exponential (problem 9.1 gives an example). We therefore refrain from generating CNF that is equivalent but instead perform a transformation that only preserves satisfiability. One way to perform this conversion is *Tseitin's method* [462].

We will explain Tseitin's method for formulas that are restricted to the Boolean connectives $\wedge$ and $\neg$. It is well known that these connectives are sufficient to represent any Boolean formula.

Tseitin's method takes the syntax tree for the formula ϕ as input. An internal node in this tree is a Boolean connective, while a leaf is a Boolean variable. The algorithm traverses the tree, beginning with the leaves. It associates a labeling ℓ_v with each node v. It also collects a set of clauses.

1. If the node v is a leaf, it is a Boolean variable x_i. Set $\ell_v = x_i$.
2. If v is $\neg$, it has one child node a. Set $\ell_v = \neg \ell_a$.
3. If v is $\wedge$, it has two child nodes. Let a and b denote the child nodes, which are labeled with ℓ_a and ℓ_b, respectively. Let ℓ_v be a new propositional variable. We associate the following three clauses with the node:

$$\neg \ell_a \vee \neg \ell_b \vee \ell_v$$
$$\ell_a \vee \neg \ell_v$$
$$\ell_b \vee \neg \ell_v$$

We briefly justify the three clauses that are generated for $\wedge$ nodes. The first clause ensures that ℓ_v is 1 when both ℓ_a and ℓ_b are 1. The second clause ensures that ℓ_v is 0 when ℓ_a is 0. The third clause ensures that ℓ_v is 0 when ℓ_b is 0. We can obtain a formal proof of the correctness of this encoding by showing that

$$(\neg \ell_a \vee \neg \ell_b \vee \ell_v) \wedge (\ell_a \vee \neg \ell_v) \wedge (\ell_b \vee \neg \ell_v) \Leftrightarrow (\ell_a \wedge \ell_b \Leftrightarrow \ell_v)$$

holds.

Let C denote the set of clauses that is generated by the procedure. We make two observations about C:

1. The number of variables and clauses in C is linear in the size of ϕ. We have thus avoided the exponential blowup we would have observed when constructing equivalent CNF.

2. The CNF C has a satisfying assignment if and only if there is a satisfying assignment for ϕ. For the first direction, observe that we obtain a satisfying assignment for ϕ from the satisfying assignment for C by simply dropping the additional variables that the algorithm has introduced. We leave the other direction of the proof of correctness to problem 9.3.

The encoding can easily be extended to support further Boolean connectives. In particular, problem 9.2 considers the constraints for the XOR operator.

9.3   Propositional Satisfiability using Binary Search

9.3.1   Binary Search using Recursion

Here we discuss a first, very simplistic procedure based on the DPLL algorithm for determining satisfiability of a propositional formula given in CNF. The basic idea of the DPLL algorithm is a *backtracking search*. Any backtracking search begins with an empty assignment. The search space is split into parts, which are then searched recursively. If the search in one of the parts fails, the algorithm *backtracks* and proceeds with a different part of the search space.

In the context of propositional SAT, the partitioning of the search space is performed by assigning a particular truth value to one of the variables. As there are two possible choices for every variable, the search algorithm is said to perform a *binary search*.

Before describing our first procedure for checking satisfiability, we introduce notation for updating a variable assignment σ. We write $\sigma[x_i \leftarrow d]$ for the assignment in which x_i is assigned to d and is equal to σ otherwise.

The recursive implementation of binary search for a satisfying assignment is given as procedure *Binary-Search* in figure 9.1. The procedure is called with the CNF C as argument. The procedure starts the recursion, performed by *Binary-Search-Recursion*, with the empty assignment. In each recursion, the procedure *Binary-Search-Recursion* first checks whether there is a clause that is conflicting with the assignment σ. If so, no extension of σ will satisfy C, and the procedure returns. If not, we check whether σ is total. In this case, we have a total assignment that satisfies C, and report that C is satisfiable. The procedure also provides the satisfying assignment σ.

If σ is not total, then there is at least one variable that is not yet assigned. The algorithm then invokes the *decision heuristic*, which is implemented in the sub-procedure *Decision-Heuristic*. The decision heuristic picks one of these unassigned variables, that is, some x_i such that $\sigma(x_i) = \bot$, and chooses a truth value for it. The choice of the variable and the truth value is immaterial for the correctness of the algorithm and can thus be a heuristic choice. We discuss the most important decision heuristics in section 9.6.

procedure *Binary-Search*(C)
   Binary-Search-Recursion$(C, \emptyset)$;
   return "UNSAT";
end procedure

procedure *Binary-Search-Recursion*(C, σ)
   if there is $c \in C$ with $\sigma \not\models c$ **then**
      return;
   else if σ is total **then**
      abort "SAT", σ;
   else
      $(x_i, d) := $ *Decision-Heuristic*(C, σ);
      Binary-Search-Recursion$(C, \sigma[x_i \leftarrow d])$;
      Binary-Search-Recursion$(C, \sigma[x_i \leftarrow \neg d])$;
      return;
   end if
end procedure

Figure 9.1
Procedure for binary search for a satisfying assignment for a given CNF C, implemented using a recursive call.

Once the choice is made, we update the assignment σ accordingly and then perform the recursive call to *Binary-Search-Recursion* with that new assignment. The recursive call may have one of two outcomes. It may succeed in finding a satisfying assignment, in which case the recursion is aborted. If the recursive call returns, we have thus failed to find a satisfying assignment in the part of the search space given by the assignment σ. The binary search algorithm then flips the truth value of the decision that the decision heuristic has made, and performs a second recursive call in order to search the other half of the search space. Note that the decision heuristic may choose a different sequence of variables as we traverse the tree this time.

The search with the flipped assignment may fail as well, in which case *Binary-Search-Recursion* backtracks. If we return to the top level of the recursion, and return to procedure *Binary-Search*, we have exhausted the search tree without finding a satisfying assignment. We can then conclude that the formula is unsatisfiable.

Example 9.3 *We recall the three clauses given as equation 9.5 to illustrate the search performed by the binary search procedure:*

$$\{x_1, \bar{x}_1 x_2, \bar{x}_1 \bar{x}_2\} \tag{9.6}$$

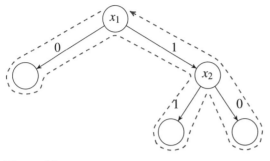

Figure 9.2
Search tree for equation 9.6 with traversal using decisions $x_1 \mapsto 0$ and $x_2 \mapsto 1$.

We suppose that the decision heuristic first picks value 0 for variable x_1. The search backtracks immediately, as the first clause is conflicting. We then flip the value of x_1. Then suppose that the decision heuristic picks 1 for x_2. This conflicts with the third clause, and we backtrack again. We flip the value of x_2. The resulting assignment conflicts with the second clause. We backtrack, after which the search tree is exhausted. The search tree and the traversal that we have just described are given in figure 9.2.

9.3.2   Binary Search with a Trail

Figure 9.3 gives a nonrecursive version of the binary backtracking search algorithm. Procedure *Binary-Search-with-Trail* maintains the assignment σ as a procedure-local variable instead of passing it as a parameter. The procedure initializes σ to be the empty assignment. In addition, the procedure maintains a variable named *trail*, which tracks the position of the search in the binary search tree. The variable *trail* holds an ordered sequence of pairs (b, x_i), where $b \in \{\mathsf{L}, \mathsf{R}\}$ denotes whether we are in the left-hand or right-hand branch, and x_i is the variable chosen by the decision heuristic.

The procedure iterates until either a satisfying assignment is found or the search tree has been exhausted. The three cases in the body of the loop correspond to the three cases in *Binary-Search-Recursive*. In the first case, σ is conflicting with one of the clauses. In the second, σ is not conflicting and is total, and thus, we have found a satisfying assignment. Finally, if neither case applies, the procedure invokes the decision heuristic.

We first discuss the third case, in which σ is neither conflicting nor total. As in the recursive variant, we call the decision heuristic and obtain a pair (x_i, d) of a variable and a truth value. We now record on the trail that we are in the left-hand branch of the search tree, and that we have made a decision on variable x_i by appending (L, x_i) to *trail*. Note that we use $\beta \cdot \gamma$ to denote the concatenation of the sequences β and γ. We update the value of x_i in σ to d to reflect the decision. The loop then re-iterates, which means that we will check whether this new decision is causing any conflicts.

procedure *Binary-Search-with-Trail*(C)

    Initialize σ such that $\sigma(x_i) = \bot$ for all $x_i \in V$;
    Initialize *trail* = ();
    while *true* **do**
        if there is $c \in C$ with $\sigma \not\models c$ **then**
            while *trail* ends on (R, x_i) **do**
                $\sigma := \sigma[x_i \leftarrow \bot]$;
                Remove last element of *trail*;
            end while
            if *trail* = () **then return** "UNSAT";
            Let (L, x_i) be the last element of *trail*;
            Let *trail'* be the prefix of *trail*;
            $trail := trail' \cdot (R, x_i)$;
            $\sigma := \sigma[x_i \leftarrow \neg\sigma(x_i)]$;   /* Flip assignment to x_i */
        else if σ is total **then**
            abort "SAT", σ;
        else
            $(x_i, d) := Decision\text{-}Heuristic(C, \sigma)$;
            $trail := trail \cdot (L, x_i)$;
            $\sigma := \sigma[x_i \leftarrow d]$;
        end if
        end while

end procedure

Figure 9.3
Procedure for binary search for a satisfying assignment for a given CNF C, implemented using a trail.

We now discuss the first case in *Binary-Search-with-Trail*, that is, there is a clause that is conflicting with σ. We now have to consider which branch of the search tree we are in. We obtain this information by examining the end of the trail. If we are in the left-hand branch (case $b = L$), we need to flip the decision by inverting the value of $\sigma(x_i)$. We then switch into the right-hand side of the search tree, which we record by changing the end of *trail* to (R, x_i), and the search continues. If we are already in the right-hand side of the search tree, we need to backtrack. If this happens at the root node of the tree, the trail is empty, and we know that the search tree has been exhausted. The formula is thus unsatisfiable. At any other node, we remove the last element of the trail, record that the value of x_i is now again unassigned ($\bot$), and resume the search.

9.4   Boolean Constraint Propagation (BCP)

We now discuss a series of improvements over the basic binary search algorithm. A very important improvement is called *Boolean constraint propagation* (BCP). This optimization was introduced as part of the DPLL procedure. To motivate BCP, we introduce the concept of a *unit clause*. A clause c is said to be unit under some assignment σ if the following two conditions hold:

1. The clause c is not satisfied by σ.
2. All *but one* of the variables in c are given a value by σ. Consequently, there is precisely one variable x_i in c with $\sigma(x_i) = \bot$.

The key observation is that, in order to extend σ to a satisfying assignment for any formula that contains a unit clause c, we must make the following decision:

- If $x_i \in c$, then x_i must be assigned 1.
- If $\bar{x}_i \in c$, then x_i must be assigned 0.

The above is called the *unit rule*, and we say that the assignment to x_i is an *implication* of σ and c. If we choose an assignment that violates the unit rule, then c becomes conflicting, and our search will have to backtrack, which is wasted effort.

Example 9.4 *Consider the partial assignment* $\{x_2 \mapsto 0\}$ *and the formula*

$$(x_1 \vee x_2 \vee \bar{x}_3) \wedge (\bar{x}_1 \vee x_2). \tag{9.7}$$

Under this assignment, the second clause of the formula is unit. The first clause is not unit, as it contains two unassigned variables. The unit rule requires us to assign 0 to x_1.

   Now note that the assignment we do because of the unit rule may cause further clauses to become unit. In our example, assigning 0 to x_1 makes the first clause unit under the new assignment. This requires us to apply the unit rule again, and we assign 0 to x_3.

   BCP is a procedure that applies the unit rule repeatedly. A possible implementation is given in figure 9.4. We pass the set of clauses and the current assignment as arguments. BCP then returns the new assignment after the unit rule has been applied exhaustively. We discuss a data structure that is specialized to the detection of unit clauses in problem 9.4. We call BCP in our binary search algorithm directly after doing a decision using the decision heuristic. Furthermore, we call BCP at the beginning of the search, as the original set of clauses may contain clauses that have only a single literal.

   We remark that we have to revert the assignments that BCP performs once the search algorithm backtracks. This is straight-forward in the recursive variant, as we construct a new assignment σ for every recursive call. This assignment is discarded when the procedure backtracks. The variant with trail given as *Binary-Search-with-Trail*, however, only maintains one assignment, which is more efficient. It thus reverts the changes to the

procedure *Boolean-Constraint-Propagation*(C, σ)
    while there is unit clause $c \in C$ under σ **do**
        Let x_i be the unassigned variable in c;
        if $x_i \in c$ **then**
            $\sigma := \sigma[x_i \leftarrow 1]$;
        else
            $\sigma := \sigma[x_i \leftarrow 0]$;
        end if
    end while
    return σ;
end procedure

Figure 9.4
Algorithm for Boolean constraint propagation (BCP).

assignment explicitly. The most common approach to revert the assignments made by BCP when using a trail is to record them on the trail together with the decisions.

9.5 Conflict-Driven Clause Learning

9.5.1 Implication Graphs

Let us assume that we are given a formula in CNF as a set of clauses C, and suppose that this set contains, among others, the following clauses:

$$\bar{x}_3 x_4, \ \bar{x}_5 x_6, \ \bar{x}_4 \bar{x}_5 \bar{x}_6 \tag{9.8}$$

We now discuss how our binary search algorithm performs on this example. Suppose that our decision heuristic chooses $x_1 \mapsto 1$, and suppose that this causes no BCP to happen. Suppose that the decision heuristic then chooses $x_3 \mapsto 1$. Under this assignment, the clause $\bar{x}_3 x_4$ becomes unit, and BCP assigns x_4 to 1. Suppose we then proceed with the decision $x_5 \mapsto 1$. Under this new assignment, the last two clauses become unit. Suppose we first process clause $\bar{x}_5 x_6$, which implies $x_6 \mapsto 1$. The clause $\bar{x}_4 \bar{x}_5 \bar{x}_6$ is then conflicting, and thus, we have a conflict. We therefore have to revert our last decision, and flip x_5 to 0. The three clauses in our subset of C are then satisfied.

Assume, then, that we proceed in the search, but find that we have to backtrack to the decision on x_1, that is, we will assign x_1 to 0 after backtracking. Our partial assignment is now $\{x_1 \mapsto 0\}$, and suppose that we repeat the decisions $x_3 \mapsto 1$ and $x_5 \mapsto 1$. Note that we will redo all steps outlined above. This effort is clearly wasted: we run into the same conflict that we have seen before and will eventually flip the assignment to x_5.

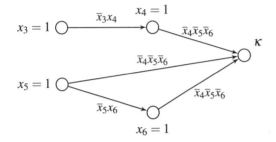

Figure 9.5
Implication graph for the clauses given as equation 9.8.

The key insight of *conflict-driven clause learning* (CDCL) is not to repeat steps that lead to a conflict [365]. The data structure that CDCL maintains for this is the *implication graph*. The implication graph is a directed graph with labeled nodes. It is constructed as follows:

1. For every decision, create a new node that is labeled with that decision.
2. For every implication detected by BCP, create a new node that is labeled with that implication. Every implication detected by BCP is triggered by a unit clause. Create an edge from the nodes that correspond to the literals in the unit clause to the new node. We label the edge with the unit clause.
3. In case of a conflict, add a node labeled with κ, and add edges from the nodes that correspond to the assignments in the conflicting clause. The edges are labeled with the conflicting clause. The node is called the *conflict node*.

Figure 9.5 gives the state of the implication graph for our example when the first conflict is reached. The root nodes of the graph are the decisions on x_1, x_3, and x_5. The node on the right-hand side labeled with κ is the node for the conflict. The two inner nodes, labeled with values for x_4 and x_6, were created for the implications detected by BCP.

9.5.2   Clause Learning

CDCL generates new clauses from the existing set of clauses by traversing the implication graph. The new clauses are implied by the existing clauses, which is proven using the *resolution rule*, given in the following theorem.

Theorem 9.5 (Resolution rule) *Let $c_1 = (A \vee x_i)$ and $c_2 = (B \vee \bar{x}_i)$ be two clauses, where A and B denote disjunctions of arbitrary literals. Then the clause $A \vee B$ is implied by $c_1 \wedge c_2$.*

The proof of the resolution rule is easily done with a case-split over the truth value of x_i. We introduce some standard terminology and notation used when we apply the resolution

procedure *Analyze-Conflict*(clause c, implication graph G)
   while ¬*termination-criterion*(c) **do**
       Let x_i be the variable that was last implied in c;
       Let v be node in G generated for x_i;
       Let c_l be the clause that labels the edges that lead to v;
       $c := Res(c, c_l, x_i)$;
   end while
   return c;
end procedure

Figure 9.6
Algorithm for computing a conflict clause.

rule. The variable x_i is called the *pivot* or *resolution variable*. The clause $A \vee B$ is called the *resolvent*, and we write $Res(c_1, c_2, x_i)$ for the clause that we obtain by resolution of c_1 and c_2 using pivot x_i.

We now explain how the resolution rule is applied. Once we reach a conflict, we call procedure *Analyze-Conflict* (figure 9.6). It takes the conflicting clause and the implication graph as arguments. The procedure contains a **while** loop, which is terminated heuristically. The loop processes a clause c, beginning with the conflicting clause. In every iteration, we perform the following steps:

1. We identify the variable x_i in c that was most recently implied.
2. We find the node labeled with x_i in the implication graph, and note the clause on the incoming edges. We let c_l be that clause.
3. We compute a new clause by resolving the clauses c and c_l using pivot x_i.

We then add the clause returned by procedure *Analyze-Conflict* to our clause set. The clause we have built is called a *conflict clause* (this term is not to be confused with a conflicting clause for a given σ). We remark that we can always obtain at least one clause that is false under σ and in addition has exactly one literal left from the current decision level.

We continue our example. Recall that we have reached a conflict after assignments $x_3 \mapsto 1$ and $x_5 \mapsto 1$ with $\bar{x}_4 \bar{x}_5 \bar{x}_6$ as the conflicting clause. We follow the steps above and iterate until we have removed all variables from the clause whose value was set by BCP. In the first iteration, we resolve on x_6, which was assigned last, and obtain the clause $\bar{x}_4 \bar{x}_5$. In the second iteration, we resolve on x_4 and obtain the conflict clause $\bar{x}_3 \bar{x}_5$. We can add this clause to our formula just before we backtrack. We say that we have *learned* the clause.

Now observe that, once we make the decision $x_3 \mapsto 1$ the second time, the learned clause becomes unit, and BCP detects that x_5 must be 0. Thus, we have successfully avoided the repetition of the conflict.

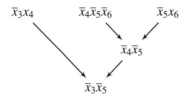

Figure 9.7
The resolution proof for justifying the conflict clause $\bar{x}_3\bar{x}_5$ generated by *Analyze-Conflict* for the implication graph given as figure 9.5.

9.5.3   Generating Resolution Proofs with CDCL

We have seen that CDCL generates new clauses using resolution. The resolvent can then be used to perform further resolution steps. The dependencies between these proof steps are captured by a *resolution proof*, defined next.

Definition 9.6 (Resolution proof) *A resolution proof $\mathcal{R}$ is a DAG $(V_\mathcal{R}, E_\mathcal{R}, piv_\mathcal{R}, \ell_\mathcal{R})$, where $V_\mathcal{R}$ is a set of nodes, $E_\mathcal{R}$ is a set of edges, $piv_\mathcal{R}$ labels nodes with the pivot, and $\ell_\mathcal{R}$ labels nodes with clauses. For an internal node v and edges $(v_1, v), (v_2, v) \in E_\mathcal{R}$, we require that v is labeled with the resolvent of the parent nodes with pivot $piv_\mathcal{R}(v)$, that is,*

$$\ell_\mathcal{R}(v) = Res(\ell_\mathcal{R}(v_1), \ell_\mathcal{R}(v_2), piv_\mathcal{R}(v)).$$

Nodes with in-degree 0 correspond to clauses that are part of the original formula. All other nodes have in-degree 2 and correspond to clauses that have been obtained by resolution from other clauses.

Solvers that implement conflict-driven clause learning implicitly generate resolution proofs. The resolution proofs are rooted in the set of clauses C that are given as input to the solver. The inner nodes of the proof are the clauses that are generated by procedure *Analyze-Conflict*. The resolution proof for our example for the run of *Analyze-Conflict* is given in figure 9.7.

In the case of a formula that is determined to be unsatisfiable, the solver ultimately generates a proof for the empty clause; that is, the proof shows that C implies *false*.

9.6   Decision Heuristics

SAT solvers that implement DPLL or CDCL make heuristic choices when they need to pick a variable and a value for a decision. We have denoted the procedure that performs this decision by *Decision-Heuristic*. We now discuss commonly used methods for making such decisions.

A very basic way of performing decisions is to pick the decision that satisfies the largest number of clauses. This is a greedy heuristic, and is called the *Dynamic Largest Individual Sum* (DLIS) heuristic.

We illustrate the benefit of DLIS using the set of clauses we have given as equation 9.8:

$$\bar{x}_3 x_4, \ \bar{x}_5 x_6, \ \bar{x}_4 \bar{x}_5 \bar{x}_6. \tag{9.9}$$

An assignment to x_3, x_4, or x_6 satisfies only one of the clauses. By contrast, assigning 0 to x_5 satisfies two clauses and thus is the decision chosen by DLIS. Subsequently, assigning 0 to x_3 or 1 to x_4 satisfies the remaining clause. This sequence of assignments has avoided the conflict we have seen in section 9.5.

It is known that this heuristic can be further improved. A common way of obtaining decisions that result in better runtimes is to bias the decision heuristic towards variables that have recently participated in a conflict. To this end, many solvers maintain an *activity score* for every variable. This score is increased whenever a variable participates in a conflict. Periodically, all variable scores are divided by a constant, which means that variables that have recently participated in a conflict retain larger scores. We discuss further decision heuristics in the bibliographic notes.

Bibliographic Notes

A history of satisfiability is presented in [60, chap. 1]. Foundations of modern algorithms for solving propositional satisfiability problems can be found in the Davis–Putnam procedure [167], which checks validity of first-order logic using the resolution principle explained in section 9.5.3. The Davis–Putnam–Logemann–Loveland (DPLL) algorithm [166] is specialized to propositional logic and extends the Davis–Putnam procedure with pure literal elimination, which eagerly sets any variable that is used either only positively or only negatively in the unsatisfied clauses. This rule is not implemented in modern solvers. The DPLL algorithm has introduced Boolean constraint propagation (BCP), which is standard in modern solvers and is explained in section 9.4. The two-watched literal scheme (problem 9.4), which improves the performance of BCP significantly, was introduced in the Chaff SAT solver [387].

Conflict-driven clause learning (CDCL), explained in section 9.5.2, has resulted in major improvements in the performance of solvers for propositional SAT. It was first implemented in the GRASP SAT solver [365]. GRASP also implements nonchronological backtracking by jumping back to the most recent decision in the learned clause. A comparison of different learning strategies is given in [492].

The Chaff SAT solver has introduced the Variable State Independent Decaying Sum (VSIDS) decision heuristic, which was the first conflict-driven decision heuristic [387]. In VSIDS, higher scores are given to those variables that have recently been used in a learned clause, which biases the search towards variables that participate in conflicts. Similar to that, the Berkmin SAT solver gives absolute priority to unresolved conflicts by maintaining a stack of unsatisfied conflict clauses [245]. A full discussion of branching heuristics is in Kullmann's chapter in [315]. The chapter by Heule and van Maaren in [267] provides an extensive list of heuristics. An experimental comparison of scoring heuristics is given in [59].

Modern solvers contain many further optimizations that we do not cover in this chapter. It is possible to learn a variety of clauses from a given implication graph by choosing different separating cuts through the graph. Numerous heuristics exist for choosing particularly useful conflict clauses. Clauses that are learned consume memory and computational effort. Modern SAT solvers, notably Glucose [32], therefore remove most of the learned clauses, retaining only few according to heuristic criteria. Further refinements of nonchronological backtracking exist. For instance, Chaff backtracks to the decision that is the second most recent in the learned clause.

Modern SAT solvers furthermore include *preprocessors*, which, among other transformations, eliminate variables before DPLL commences [34, 188]. They also implement periodic *restarts*, which aim to explore different parts of the search space [55]. Modern SAT solvers are able to solve instances *incrementally*, which means that the SAT instance can be changed after it has been solved [275, 479]. Removal of constraints from the input formula is now typically performed by means of *assumptions* [189], which was made popular by the MiniSat solver [191]. Further details on CDCL can be found in [60, chapt. 4]. An in-depth presentation is given by Knuth in [307].

While all best-performing propositional SAT solvers operate on a clausal CNF representation, nonclausal SAT solvers have been investigated. The argument in favor of nonclausal algorithms is that the Tseitin transformation destroys the structure of the formula. A very early nonclausal solver for propositional logic is Stålmarck's proof procedure [439]. In [285], a solver that uses general matings and implements learning and nonchronological backtracking is presented. Given the importance of verification in hardware designs, SAT solvers have been proposed that operate directly on circuits [230].

There are numerous variants of the SAT problem. For instance, there are algorithms that solve various optimization problems in addition to the satisfiability problem. Optimization goals can be given directly, for example, as linear polynomials over problem variables [15]. Other methods aim to identify a particularly small or minimal unsatisfiable core [390]. Techniques such as conflict-driven learning have also been applied to Boolean formulas with quantifiers (QBF) [493].

The technology in CDCL-based solvers for propositional logic has been extended to richer fragments of first-order logic. Early instances of encodings of such fragments include [414], where equality logic is encoded eagerly into propositional logic. The integration of a solver for a conjunction of constraints in difference logic and a propositional SAT solver was proposed in [29]. Modern solvers for satisfiability modulo theories (SMT) such as Z3 [170] support a broad range of theories, including bit-vectors and arrays.

Problems

Transformation into CNF

Problem 9.1 (Parity). Given variables $x_1, \ldots, x_n$, we say that the *parity bit* for these variables is true if and only if the number of x_i that are true is odd:

$$p = x_1 \oplus \ldots \oplus x_n$$

Give equivalent CNF over $x_1, \ldots, x_n$ for the parity bit p. How large is your formula for n variables?

Problem 9.2 (Tseitin's transformation for XOR). Give the clauses required for a constraint that encodes $\ell_v = \ell_a \oplus \ell_b$ into CNF.

Problem 9.3 (Correctness of Tseitin's method). Let C be the CNF generated by Tseitin's method for a propositional formula ϕ.

(a) Prove that any satisfying assignment for ϕ can be transformed into a satisfying assignment for C.

(b) Prove that any satisfying assignment for C can be transformed into a satisfying assignment for ϕ.

Boolean Constraint Propagation

Problem 9.4 (Two watched literal scheme). Recall the procedure *Boolean-Constraint-Propagation*. It identifies unsatisfied clauses in which precisely one variable is unassigned. A naïve implementation of this procedure iterates over all clauses and checks whether they are unit under the current assignment. In this problem we discuss a data structure that enables efficient identification of unit clauses.

We maintain two additional data structures:

1. For each variable and for positive and negative use, build a list of the clauses that contain the corresponding literal.

2. For each clause that is not yet satisfied, maintain indices of *two literals* (called the *watched literals*): the first index is the number of the first literal in the clause that is unassigned under the current assignment, and the second index is the number of the last literal in the clause that is unassigned.

To see an example of the data structure, recall the clauses given as equation 9.8. Under the partial assignment $x_4 \mapsto 0$, we obtain the following data structure:

$\overline{x}_3$	x_4

$\overline{x}_5$	x_6

$\overline{x}_4$	$\overline{x}_5$	$\overline{x}_6$

The key insight is that a clause is unit if and only if the two indices are identical.

Give a procedure that updates the two indices whenever a variable is assigned. Then give a new implementation of *Boolean-Constraint-Propagation* that uses the data structures above. What needs to be done when the search algorithm backtracks?

Problem 9.5 (Horn satisfiability). We say that a clause that contains at most one positive literal is a *Horn clause*. A formula that only contains Horn clauses is a Horn formula. Now consider the following algorithm, which is given a Horn formula as a set of clauses C:

1. Run BCP on C.
2. Update σ such that all x_i with $\sigma(x_i) = \bot$ are assigned to 0.
3. If there is $c \in C$ such that $\sigma \not\models c$, then return "UNSAT". Otherwise, return "SAT".

Prove that the procedure above determines satisfiability of the formula. What is the runtime complexity of this procedure in the size of C?

Conflict Analysis

Problem 9.6 (Ordering in BCP). The outcome of BCP depends on the ordering in which unit clauses are processed. This, in turn, can affect the resolution steps performed by CDCL. In the example in section 9.5.1 we have identified two unit clauses after the assignment to x_5. We have processed the clause $\bar{x}_5 x_6$ first, which implies the assignment $x_6 \mapsto 1$.

Give the resolution proof for the alternative ordering, that is, assume that BCP processes clause $\bar{x}_4 \bar{x}_5 \bar{x}_6$ first.

10 SAT-Based Model Checking

The performance and scalability of propositional satisfiability (SAT) and satisfiability modulo theories (SMT) solvers have improved tremendously. We discuss here several techniques that exploit these improvements in model checking. The first technique, called *bounded model checking* (BMC) [58, 57], generates a formula that corresponds to an unwinding of a model M and a property φ for a given depth bound k. This formula is satisfiable if and only if φ can be refuted on M by means of a counterexample of length k. BMC is therefore primarily used for identifying errors in designs.

The second technique, *k-induction* [438], uses BMC to check whether φ can be proven by induction. Only particular properties are suitable for *k*-induction, and writing inductive properties is difficult. The third and fourth techniques, *model checking with Craig interpolation* [374] and *property-directed reachability* (PDR) [76], aim to compute a new inductive invariant that implies φ. All of these techniques employ a propositional SAT solver as their main reasoning engine, and therefore benefit from any improvements in propositional SAT solving.

The details of modern DPLL-based propositional SAT solvers are covered in chapter 9. For this chapter, we will recall only two important concepts from chapter 9: satisfying assignments and resolution proofs. The SAT or SMT solver is otherwise treated as a blackbox.

10.1 Bounded Model Checking

10.1.1 Overview of Bounded Model Checking

We focus the presentation on properties that belong to the class of linear temporal logic (LTL), as described in chapter 4. As argued there, an LTL formula is of the form $\mathbf{A}\,\varphi$, where φ is an LTL path formula. Any counterexample for $\mathbf{A}\,\varphi$ is thus a witness for $\mathbf{E}\,\neg\varphi$. As LTL path formulas are closed under negation, the counterexample always has the form of a path. A counterexample to a given LTL property is therefore a sequence of states $s_0, s_1, \ldots$, which is potentially infinite. The key idea of BMC is to restrict the search for a counterexample to paths that have at most k transitions, for some $k \in \mathbb{N}$. We refer to k as the *bound*.

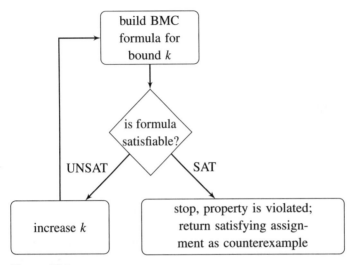

Figure 10.1
Application of bounded model checking (BMC).

   BMC is typically applied in the following fashion (figure 10.1). The process begins with
a small bound. The model and the negation of φ are then unwound to this bound, and
encoded by means of a propositional formula, which is passed to the solver. If the solver
determines that the formula is satisfiable, we conclude that φ is refuted on M. Otherwise,
the bound is increased to search for a longer counterexample. As we show in section 10.1.5,
we can often calculate an upper bound on the length of the execution paths that have to be
considered. If k exceeds this bound, we can conclude that the property holds. Such a bound
is called a *completeness threshold*. As the completeness threshold is frequently large, the
solver may run out of computational resources before it is reached.

10.1.2   Reachability Properties

We now describe methods to encode the unwinding of the model and the property with a
propositional formula. We first consider the special case of a property of the form **AG** p,
where p is an atomic proposition. This property holds if all states of all paths in M are
labeled with p. A counterexample to the LTL property **AG** p is a witness for **EF** $\neg p$ and
therefore is a path in M that contains a state in which p does not hold. In the following path,
the state s_{k-1} is labeled with $\neg p$; the path is therefore a witness for **EF** $\neg p$:

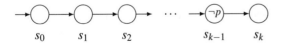

As BMC is a symbolic model-checking technique, it relies on a symbolic representation of the Kripke structure M, as introduced in section 3.3. Let $M = (S, S_0, R, AP, L)$. Recall that we have first-order predicates that serve as *characteristic functions* for S_0, R, and any $p \in AP$. For example, we write $S_0(s)$ to denote that state s is an initial state of M. As described in chapter 3, we can obtain purely propositional formulas for R, S_0, and p for finite-state models.

Following the propositional encoding, we may assume that any state s of M is a valuation of a set of Boolean variables $V = \{v_1, \ldots, v_n\}$. Thus, the state s is a valuation of a vector $(v_1, \ldots, v_n)$. The first step in BMC is to introduce $k+1$ copies of the variables, denoted by $V_0, \ldots, V_k$. We will use the variables in V_0 to encode the initial state, and the variables in V_i for the state that the system reaches after i transitions. We will use s_i as a shorthand for the vector of the variables in V_i. By abuse of notation, we will also write s_i for the state that corresponds to the values that are assigned to the variables in V_i.

We now construct a formula $path_k$ over the vectors $s_0, \ldots, s_k$ that has a satisfying assignment if and only if $\pi = s_0, \ldots, s_k$ is a sequence of states in M that begins in an initial state and conforms to the transition relation R:

$$path_k(s_0, \ldots, s_k) \Leftrightarrow S_0(s_0) \wedge \bigwedge_{i=0}^{k-1} R(s_i, s_{i+1}) \qquad (10.1)$$

The first conjunct of $path_k$ enforces s_0 to be an initial state, whereas the second conjunct enforces that there is a transition from any s_i to s_{i+1}. Observe that this formula contains a total of k copies of the transition relation R. The size of the formula $path_k$ is therefore linear in k and linear in the size of the transition relation.

In order to obtain a path that contains at least one state that is labeled with $\neg p$, we add one further conjunct as follows:

$$path_k(s_0, \ldots, s_k) \wedge \bigvee_{i=0}^{k} \neg p(s_i) \qquad (10.2)$$

Equation 10.2 can subsequently be transformed into a formula f in conjunctive normal form (CNF) using the techniques described in section 9.2. The formula f is satisfiable if and only if equation 10.2 is satisfiable, and we therefore say that they are *equisatisfiable*. The formula f is then passed to a propositional SAT solver. If f is found to be satisfiable, then so is equation 10.2.

Theorem 10.1 *Equation 10.2 is satisfiable if and only if there is a counterexample of length k or less.*

Proof If equation 10.2 is satisfiable, we obtain an assignment for all variables in $V_0, \ldots, V_k$. We can then extract a sequence of states from the satisfying assignment provided by the solver. By abuse of notation, we will write $s_0, \ldots, s_k$ for this sequence of states. It is easy to see that this sequence is a counterexample path for $\mathbf{G}\, p$. The other direction of the claim is shown as follows. If there is a counterexample to $\mathbf{G}\,p$ with length k or less, then there is a path π of length l with $l \leq k$ from an initial state to a state that is labeled with $\neg p$. To obtain a satisfying assignment for equation 10.2, use the states on π for $s_0, \ldots, s_l$, and note that $path_l(s_0, \ldots, s_l)$ and $\neg p(s_l)$ hold. Recall that we assume that R is left-total; that is, every state has at least one successor. Thus, there exist some $s_{l+1}, \ldots, s_k$ with $R(s_i, s_{i+1})$ for all i with $l \leq i < k$, which implies that $path_k(s_0, \ldots, s_k)$ is also satisfied. $\square$

Note that if equation 10.2 is unsatisfiable there might still exist a counterexample that is longer than k. However, there cannot be any counterexample of length k or less.

Example 10.2 *We recall the Kripke structure we have used in section 3.4. It has four states, which are labeled with a or b:*

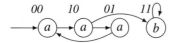

We also recall that we have encoded the four states of the model with two Boolean variables, which we have denoted v_0 and v_1. The picture above gives the valuations of v_0 and v_1 above the state that is encoded. Recall that we use a formula to represent sets. The formula represents the set that contains those elements that correspond to a satisfying assignment. We obtain the following formula over v_0 and v_1 that represents the set of initial states:

$$S_0(v_0, v_1) = \neg v_0 \wedge \neg v_1$$

Note that $\{v_0 \mapsto 0, v_1 \mapsto 0\}$ corresponds exactly to the single initial state of the example. The transition relation is represented by

$$
\begin{aligned}
R(v_0, v_1, v_0', v_1') \quad = \quad & \neg v_0 \wedge \neg v_1 \wedge v_0' \wedge \neg v_1' \\
\vee \quad & v_0 \wedge \neg v_1 \wedge v_1' \\
\vee \quad & \neg v_0 \wedge v_1 \wedge \neg v_0' \wedge \neg v_1' \\
\vee \quad & v_0 \wedge v_1 \wedge v_0' \wedge v_1'.
\end{aligned}
$$

Recall that the second clause of R represents two transitions, as it allows the transitions $10 \to 01$ and $10 \to 11$.

We use the property $\mathbf{AG}\,a$ for this example. The atomic predicate a can be encoded as

$$p(v_0, v_1) = \neg v_0 \vee \neg v_1.$$

We will use $k = 2$. We will thus have three different copies of the state variables. The first copy for s_0 is $\{v_{0,0}, v_{1,0}\}$, the second copy for s_1 is $\{v_{0,1}, v_{1,1}\}$, and the third copy for s_2 is $\{v_{0,2}, v_{1,2}\}$.

We will now present the two conjuncts of equation 10.2. We obtain the following formula for $path_2(s_0, s_1, s_2)$, which contains two copies of the transition relation R:

$$
\begin{aligned}
path_2(s_0, s_1, s_2) \;=\; & S_0(s_0) \wedge R(s_0, s_1) \wedge R(s_1, s_2) \\[4pt]
=\; & \neg v_{0,0} \wedge \neg v_{1,0} \wedge \\
& \left(
\begin{array}{l}
\quad\; \neg v_{0,0} \wedge \neg v_{1,0} \wedge v_{0,1} \wedge \neg v_{1,1} \\
\vee \;\; v_{0,0} \wedge \neg v_{1,0} \wedge v_{1,1} \\
\vee \;\; \neg v_{0,0} \wedge v_{1,0} \wedge \neg v_{0,1} \wedge \neg v_{1,1} \\
\vee \;\; v_{0,0} \wedge v_{1,0} \wedge v_{0,1} \wedge v_{1,1}
\end{array}
\right) \wedge \\
& \left(
\begin{array}{l}
\quad\; \neg v_{0,1} \wedge \neg v_{1,1} \wedge v_{0,2} \wedge \neg v_{1,2} \\
\vee \;\; v_{0,1} \wedge \neg v_{1,1} \wedge v_{1,2} \\
\vee \;\; \neg v_{0,1} \wedge v_{1,1} \wedge \neg v_{0,2} \wedge \neg v_{1,2} \\
\vee \;\; v_{0,1} \wedge v_{1,1} \wedge v_{0,2} \wedge v_{1,2}
\end{array}
\right)
\end{aligned}
$$

The second conjunct of equation 10.2 is as follows:

$$
\bigvee_{i=0}^{2} \neg p(s_i) = \neg(\neg v_{0,0} \vee \neg v_{1,0}) \vee \neg(\neg v_{0,1} \vee \neg v_{1,1}) \vee \neg(\neg v_{0,2} \vee \neg v_{1,2})
$$

Both conjuncts are propositional formulas and can be converted into CNF using the technique described in section 9.2. They can then be passed to a SAT solver, which will determine that the formula is satisfiable. We obtain a satisfying assignment as follows:

$$
v_{0,0} = 0, \; v_{1,0} = 0, \; v_{0,1} = 1, \; v_{1,1} = 0, \; v_{0,2} = 1, \; v_{1,2} = 1
$$

This satisfying assignment corresponds to the sequence of states in a path from an initial state to a state that is not labeled with a. We can therefore conclude that the model does not satisfy $\mathbf{AG}\, a$.

10.1.3   Eventuality Properties

We now consider properties of the form $\mathbf{AF}\, p$. Such a property holds if every path in M includes a state in which p is true. A counterexample to $\mathbf{AF}\, p$ is thus an infinite path in which all states satisfy $\neg p$; that is, the path satisfies $\mathbf{G}\, \neg p$. In section 4.6, we argue that if an $\mathbf{AF}\, p$ property is falsified, then there exists an infinite path that has a finite representation in the form of a lasso:

In the above, the part π_0 is called the *stem* and the part π_1 is called the *loop* of the lasso.

For $k \geq 1$, we observe that $s_0, \ldots, s_k$ is a path of length k of the form of a lasso if s_k is equal to one of the previous states. We capture the lasso property by means of the predicate

$lasso_k$:

$$lasso_k(s_0,\ldots,s_k) \Leftrightarrow path_k(s_0,\ldots,s_k) \wedge \bigvee_{i=0}^{k-1} s_i = s_k \qquad (10.3)$$

In order to obtain a lasso-shaped path of length k on which all states satisfy $\neg p$, we add one further conjunct as follows:

$$lasso_k(s_0,\ldots,s_k) \wedge \bigwedge_{i=0}^{k-1} \neg p(s_i) \qquad (10.4)$$

Observe that there is no need to constrain s_k, since s_k is equal to one of the s_i, which are already required to satisfy $\neg p$. A path that satisfies the constraint above can be illustrated as follows:

Equation 10.4 is satisfiable if and only if there is a lasso that has k transitions or fewer. To see why the formula is satisfied by lassos with fewer than k transitions, observe that the loop of the lasso can be unfolded in order to obtain a longer lasso.

The satisfiability of equation 10.4 can be determined using a propositional SAT solver as described above. If equation 10.4 is satisfiable, a counterexample path for the property **AF** p can be extracted from the satisfying assignment provided by the solver. Now consider the case that equation 10.4 is unsatisfiable. It is clear that there might still exist a counterexample that has more than k transitions. However, we know that there is no counterexample that has k or fewer transitions.

10.1.4   BMC for Full LTL

In chapter 6, we show how to translate an LTL formula φ into a Kripke structure with fairness, called *tableau*. This Kripke structure can be used for the construction of a BMC encoding for φ. We recall the definition of finite-state Kripke structures with fairness. A finite-state Kripke structure with fairness is a 6-tuple (S, S_0, R, AP, L, F), where

- S is a finite set of states,
- $S_0 \subseteq S$ is the set of initial states,
- $R \subseteq (S \times S)$ is the transition relation,
- AP is the set of atomic propositions,
- L is the labeling function that maps a state to the set of atomic propositions that are true at the state, and
- $F = \{P_1,\ldots,P_n\}$ with $P_j \subseteq S$ is the set of fairness constraints.

A path in the Kripke structure is *fair* if and only if the path visits each of the sets P_i an infinite number of times.

The idea of the BMC translation using the Kripke structure with fairness follows the model checking algorithm introduced in chapter 6. We are given an LTL property $\mathbf{A}\,\varphi$. In order to check whether $M \models \mathbf{A}\,\varphi$, we compute a Kripke structure with fairness $T_{\neg\varphi}$ for the negation of φ, and then form the product of M and $T_{\neg\varphi}$. Let $\Psi = (S^{\Psi}, S_0^{\Psi}, R^{\Psi}, AP^{\Psi}, L^{\Psi}, F^{\Psi})$ denote the resulting model. The fair paths in the model Ψ are counterexamples to φ in M and thus Ψ does not include a fair path if and only if $M \models \mathbf{A}\,\varphi$.

Recall that we can build propositional formulas that represent infinite paths by means of the lasso construction described in section 10.1.3. We now show how to encode fair paths that are lassos of length k. The following formula is satisfiable if there exists a fair, lasso-shaped path of length k:

$$S_0^{\Psi}(s_0) \wedge \bigwedge_{i=0}^{k-1} R^{\Psi}(s_i, s_{i+1}) \wedge \bigvee_{i=0}^{k-1} \left(s_i = s_k \wedge \bigwedge_{P \in F^{\Psi}} Fair_i^P \right) \tag{10.5}$$

The first conjunct enforces that the state s_0 is an initial state of Ψ. The second ensures that two adjacent states s_i and s_{i+1} are connected by a transition. The final conjunct ensures that the path is a lasso and that the states in the loop of the lasso satisfy all fairness constraints $P \in F$. The fairness condition $Fair_i^P$ for a loop that begins in state s_i and one of the $P \in F^{\Psi}$ is defined as follows:

$$Fair_i^P \Leftrightarrow \bigvee_{j=i}^{k-1} P(s_j)$$

Note that we do not need to check state s_k, as s_k is equal to s_i. When reusing common subformulas, the size of the resulting formula is linear in the bound k.

As before, if equation 10.5 is unsatisfiable, then there is no counterexample of length k or less. However, there might be a counterexample that is longer.

10.1.5   Completeness Thresholds

In BMC, the model and the property φ are jointly unwound up to some depth k to form a propositional formula. If this formula is unsatisfiable, there is no counterexample of length k or less. If the bound k is large enough, then we can conclude that φ holds for paths of arbitrary length. But how large is "large enough"?

We write $M \models_k \varphi$ if no computation of M of length k or less violates φ. A completeness threshold is any natural number $\mathcal{CT}$ that guarantees that

$$M \models_{\mathcal{CT}} \varphi \implies M \models \varphi.$$

The benefit of a completeness threshold $\mathcal{CT}$ is that we can stop the BMC process as soon as we have determined that any BMC instance with $k \geq \mathcal{CT}$ is unsatisfiable.

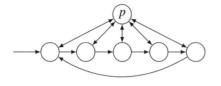

Figure 10.2
Model with diameter 2.

It is easy to see that determining a tight (the smallest possible) completeness threshold is as difficult as the model-checking problem itself. If $M \models \varphi$, then the smallest possible completeness threshold is zero, as the implication above is trivially satisfied. Otherwise, the smallest completeness threshold is equal to the length of the shortest counterexample. It is also easy to see that the completeness threshold depends on both the model and the property (we leave the proof to problems 10.1 and 10.2).

We now give a very simple completeness threshold for properties of the form **AG** p, where p is a propositional formula.

Lemma 10.3 *Given a model M, the number of states $|S|$ is a completeness threshold for any property of the form **AG** p.*

Proof Consider the case that the property does not hold. Counterexamples to **AG** p properties have the form of a path from an initial state to a state that satisfies $\neg p$. We need to show that there exists a counterexample with up to $|S|$ states. Suppose this is not so; that is, suppose that the shortest counterexample π is longer than $|S|$. It follows that at least one state must occur twice in π; that is, π contains a loop. We can then construct a new path π' by removing the loop, which is also a counterexample to **AG** p, which contradicts that π is the shortest counterexample.   □

The completeness threshold given above, while correct, is not very useful: the number of states is typically too large, and the satisfiability problem constructed when using this number as bound is too complex.

To obtain a tighter completeness threshold, we recall that we can view the model as a directed graph, where the nodes are the states and the edges are the transitions between the states. The *diameter* of a graph is the length of the longest shortest path that exists between any two different nodes in the graph.

Lemma 10.4 *Given a model M, the diameter of the graph $G = (S, R)$ is a completeness threshold for any property of the form **AG** p.*

The proof uses the argument that any counterexample for **AG** p is a path between two states (an initial state and a state that satisfies $\neg p$).

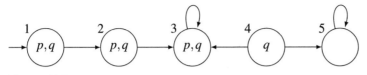

Figure 10.3
Model for illustration of the k-induction principle.

Observe that the diameter is not a completeness threshold for arbitrary properties. As an example, consider the property **AF** p on the model given in figure 10.2. It is easy to see that the diameter of the graph is 2 (counting transitions) but that the shortest counterexample for **AF** p requires five transitions. We consider a completeness threshold for properties of the form **AF** p as part of problem 10.3.

10.2   Verifying Reachability Properties with k-Induction

10.2.1   Induction with Propositional SAT

BMC, as described above, when aimed at verification relies on unwinding the model M and the property φ up to a bound k that exceeds a completeness threshold for M and φ. However, the completeness threshold that we can determine is often impractically large. In this section, we discuss a technique that uses unwinding as a building block and is frequently able to prove the property φ with only a few unwindings.

We illustrate the technique with the Kripke structure M with states $S = \{1,2,3,4,5\}$, given as figure 10.3. The state 1 is the only initial state. We label states 1, 2, and 3 with p and q, and state 4 with $\neg p$ and q. State 5 is labeled with $\neg p$ and $\neg q$.

We observe that the Kripke structure above satisfies both **AG** p and **AG** q, since states 4 and 5 are unreachable. It is easy to see that the diameter of the graph is two, and thus, two is a completeness threshold for this model for properties of the form **AG** φ, where φ is any Boolean combination of atomic predicates. We can therefore use BMC with $k = 2$ to establish the properties **AG** p and **AG** q.

An alternative way to see that **AG** p holds is to use the *induction principle*. To prove a claim $Q(n)$ for all values of some parameter $n \in \mathbb{N}$, we show validity of the two following statements:

$$Q(0) \qquad \text{called the } \textit{base case}$$
$$Q(n-1) \Rightarrow Q(n) \quad \text{called the } \textit{step case}$$

This principle can be used to prove our properties. Consider any path π of M. We denote the i-th state on path π by $\pi(i)$. To prove **AG** p, we prove that $p(\pi(n))$ holds for all n.

To show $p(\pi(n))$, the two steps of the induction principle are performed as follows:

- For the base case, note that the only initial state is labeled with p.

- For the step case, we assume that $p(\pi(n-1))$ holds; that is, we only consider those states in figure 10.3 that are labeled with p. These are $\{1,2,3\}$. The state $p(n)$ must thus be a successor of $\{1,2,3\}$. This set of successors is $\{2,3\}$, which satisfy p.

The two observations above establish the inductive argument that p holds on all reachable states. How can we use propositional SAT to check the validity of the base case and step case? Note that in order to prove *validity* of a statement f it is sufficient to prove that $\neg f$ is *not satisfiable*. If $\neg f$ is satisfiable, the satisfying assignment is a counterexample to the validity of f.

We can thus use propositional SAT to perform the two steps above as follows. The base case corresponds to the claim that all initial states satisfy p. This can be done by checking the satisfiability of

$$S_0(s_0) \wedge \neg p(s_0). \tag{10.6}$$

If the formula above is unsatisfiable, all initial states satisfy p.

We continue with the step case. To prove that $p(\pi(n-1))$ implies $p(\pi(n))$, we first observe that the states $\pi(n-1)$ and $\pi(n)$ are connected by a transition; that is, that $R(\pi(n-1),\pi(n))$ holds. Let us write s for the state $\pi(n-1)$ and s' for the state $\pi(n)$. We then check the validity of $(p(s) \wedge R(s,s')) \Rightarrow p(s')$, which corresponds to checking the satisfiability of

$$p(s) \wedge R(s,s') \wedge \neg p(s'). \tag{10.7}$$

If this formula is unsatisfiable, then p holds for any reachable state in the model M. Note that the formula passed to the satisfiability solver requires only a single copy of the transition relation R.

However, not all true properties are inductive. Recall that the model above also satisfies $\mathbf{AG}\,q$. The base case succeeds, as state 1 is labeled with q. However, the step case fails: equation 10.7 is satisfiable with $s = 4$ and $s' = 5$. The problem arises from the fact that the assumption $p(\pi(n-1))$ refers also to states that are not reachable.

10.2.2   Generalization to k-Induction

The step case of the induction principle applied above corresponds to checking that the successors of all states labeled with p are also labeled with p.

The induction principle can be generalized in order to improve its applicability. One such generalization is called k-*induction*. In k-induction, we *strengthen* the criterion for the base case and we *weaken* the criterion for the step case as follows:

$$Q(0) \wedge \ldots \wedge Q(k-1) \qquad\qquad \text{called the } k\text{-induction } base\ case$$
$$(Q(n-k) \wedge \ldots \wedge Q(n-1)) \Rightarrow Q(n) \quad \text{called the } k\text{-induction } step\ case$$

Thus, we need to prove that any path with k states labeled with p is followed by states labeled with p.

Reconsider the property **AG** q in the example above. We will attempt to apply the k-induction principle for $k = 2$ to prove that for all n, $\pi(n) \models q$ for all paths.

- To establish the base case, we need to check all states on every path with two states from an initial state. The only such path is $(1,2)$. Both states on this path are labeled with q.
- To establish the step case, we consider all paths with two states that are labeled with q:

  - $\pi_1 = (1,2)$

  - $\pi_2 = (2,3)$

  - $\pi_3 = (3,3)$

  - $\pi_4 = (4,3)$

Note that the path $(4,5)$ is not considered, since state 5 is not labeled with q. The set of successor states of the last state of the paths above is the singleton $\{3\}$, and this state is labeled with q. This establishes the step case for 2-induction.

We can apply propositional SAT in order to establish that a property **AG** p is k-inductive as follows. First observe that the base case for k-induction corresponds exactly to the BMC problem for **AG** p with bound $k - 1$. The step case for k-induction can be established in a very similar fashion. First observe that a counterexample for the step case has the following form:

The following formula is satisfiable if and only if such a path exists:

$$\bigwedge_{i=0}^{k-1} R(s_i, s_{i+1}) \wedge \bigwedge_{i=0}^{k-1} p(s_i) \wedge \neg p(s_k) \tag{10.8}$$

If the formula is unsatisfiable, the step case for k-induction is established. Note that s_0 is not required to be an initial state, which is a key difference to a BMC instance for bound k. In practice, the k-induction check is often successful with values of k that are smaller than the diameter of the model. If equation 10.8 is satisfiable, no conclusion about the property can be made. The next step is then to perform both base case and step case for a larger value of k. This is in contrast to BMC, where a satisfiable instance provides a genuine counterexample, which lets us conclude that the property is refuted.

10.2.3 Completeness

The k-induction principle, when applied as described above, is incomplete; that is, there are properties that cannot be proven with the technique. To see an instance, add the following states 6 and 7 with the given transitions and labels to the model given as figure 10.3:

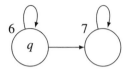

Neither of the two states is an initial state, nor are they reachable from an initial state. Thus, the property **AG** q still holds. However, the step case for k-induction now fails irrespectively of the value of k: equation 10.8 is satisfied with the assignment $s_0 \mapsto 6, \ldots, s_{k-1} \mapsto 6$ and $s_k \mapsto 7$.

To obtain a complete variant of k-induction for **AG** p properties, we add the conjunct

$$\bigwedge_{i=0}^{k-1} \bigwedge_{j=i+1}^{k} s_i \neq s_j \tag{10.9}$$

to equation 10.8. This conjunct enforces that all states on any counterexample to the step case are pairwise different. As a consequence, the step case is guaranteed to succeed with any value of k that exceeds the diameter of M. In the example above, the step case for **AG** q succeeds with $k = 2$. One can show that adding the conjunct does not cause counterexamples to be missed. A formal proof uses the argument that if there exists a counterexample for a property of the type **AG** φ, then there also exists a loop-free one in which no state is repeated.

10.3   Model Checking with Inductive Invariants

We have seen in the previous section that inductive reasoning can be applied to prove properties of the form **AG** p. However, we have also seen that not every true property is also 1-inductive, and that k-induction sometimes requires a very large value for k. The remainder of this chapter presents SAT-based techniques that aim at automatically generating a predicate I that is an inductive invariant and implies p.

In order to give a formal definition of an inductive invariant for a transition system, we first recall *image computation* and *fixedpoints*, which are introduced in section 5.3.2. We are given a model M. Recall the *post image* of a set of states Q is the set of states that are reachable from Q with one transition. We write *post-image*(Q) for this set:

$$post\text{-}image(Q) = \{s' \mid \exists s \in Q. R(s, s')\}$$

In section 5.3.2, we show that the post-image operator can be applied iteratively to compute the set of reachable states. This method is called *reachability analysis*. In reachability analysis, we maintain a set of states Q, which contains the states we know to be reachable from an initial state. We begin with the set of initial states, and apply the post-image operator until no new states are added to Q. That is, a fixpoint is reached. We can use reachability analysis to decide properties of the form **AG** p by checking whether the states in Q are labeled with p. If all states in Q satisfy p, we can conclude that $M \models$ **AG** p.

We can now capture formally what an inductive invariant is.

Definition 10.5 (Inductive invariant) *Let M be a model. We say that the set $I \subseteq S$ is an inductive invariant for the property **AG** p when the following conditions hold:*

1. *The set I must include the set of initial states; that is, $S_0 \subseteq I$.*
2. *The set I must not include a state that is labeled with $\neg p$; that is, $\forall s \in I.s \models p$.*
3. *The set I must be closed under the transition relation; that is, post-image$(I) \subseteq I$ holds.*

It is trivial to see that the existence of an inductive invariant for **AG** p implies that **AG** p holds on M. In the next section, we discuss the use of Craig interpolants to obtain an inductive invariant algorithmically.

10.4   Model Checking with Craig Interpolants

10.4.1   Craig Interpolation

Model checking with *Craig interpolants* is a technique that uses a logical notion called interpolation, suggested by Craig in 1957 [161].

Let A and B be two first-order formulas. An interpolant I for A and B is a first-order formula such that

$$A \Rightarrow I \quad \text{and} \quad I \Rightarrow \neg B,$$

and all the symbols in I occur in both A and B. A pair of formulas A and B where $A \wedge B$ is unsatisfiable is called *inconsistent*. Craig's theorem states that interpolants exist for any two inconsistent first-order formulas A and B. In the context of algorithmic verification, the theorem is usually stated in the following equivalent form.

Theorem 10.6 (Craig's interpolation theorem) *Given an inconsistent pair of first-order formulas A and B, there exists an interpolant I such that*

1. *A implies I,*
2. *I is inconsistent with B, and*
3. *I only uses symbols that are both in A and B.*

Algorithmic techniques for computing Craig interpolants from a proof of unsatisfiability of $A \wedge B$ exist for many fragments of first-order logic. We now give a technique for computing Craig interpolants for the special case of resolution proofs and propositional logic.

10.4.2   Craig Interpolants from Resolution Proofs

We describe here a procedure that computes an interpolant for an inconsistent pair of formulas A and B. We focus on the case that A and B are propositional formulas. Recall that DPLL-based SAT solvers for propositional logic implement conflict-driven clause learning

and are therefore able to generate a resolution proof for unsatisfiable formulas. The details
of how to compute resolution proofs are in section 9.5.

Recall that the DPLL-based SAT solvers operate on propositional formulas that are given
in conjunctive normal form (CNF). Let X be a set of propositional variables. A literal
is a variable $x_i \in X$ or its negation $\bar{x}_i$. A clause C is a disjunction of literals, which we
represent as a set of literals. The empty clause $\emptyset$ contains no literals. A formula in CNF is a
conjunction of clauses, and can also be represented as a set of clauses.

Recall the principle of *resolution* between two clauses $A \vee x$ and $B \vee \bar{x}$: any assignment
that satisfies both $A \vee x$ and $B \vee \bar{x}$ also satisfies $A \vee B$:

$$\frac{A \vee x \qquad B \vee \bar{x}}{A \vee B}$$

The variable x is called the *pivot*. We write $Res(A, B, x)$ for the *resolvent* of the clauses $A \vee x$
and $B \vee \bar{x}$ using the pivot x.

We now recall the definition of a *resolution proof* from chapter 9 (definition 9.6). A res-
olution proof $\mathcal{R}$ is a DAG $(V_\mathcal{R}, E_\mathcal{R}, piv_\mathcal{R}, \ell_\mathcal{R})$, where $V_\mathcal{R}$ is a set of nodes, $E_\mathcal{R}$ is a set of
edges, $piv_\mathcal{R}$ labels nodes with the pivot, and $\ell_\mathcal{R}$ labels nodes with clauses. Initial nodes
have in-degree 0, and correspond to clauses that are part of the formula. All other vertices
are internal and have in-degree 2. They correspond to clauses that have been obtained by
resolution from other clauses. For an internal vertex v and edges $(v_1, v), (v_2, v) \in E_\mathcal{R}$, we
require that v is labeled with the resolvent; that is,

$$\ell_\mathcal{R}(v) = Res(\ell_\mathcal{R}(v_1), \ell_\mathcal{R}(v_2), piv_\mathcal{R}(v)).$$

In this case, we say that nodes v_1 and v_2 are the *parents* of v. The sink node has out-degree 0,
and is labeled with the empty clause. We write v^+ for the parent of v for which $piv_\mathcal{R}(v)$ is
in $\ell_\mathcal{R}(v^+)$ and v^- for the parent for which $\neg piv_\mathcal{R}(v)$ is in $\ell_\mathcal{R}(v^-)$.

Example 10.7 *Consider the formula*

$$(a_1 \vee \bar{a}_2) \wedge (\bar{a}_1 \vee \bar{a}_3) \wedge a_2 \wedge (\bar{a}_2 \vee a_3) \wedge (a_2 \vee a_4) \wedge \bar{a}_4. \qquad (10.10)$$

The formula is unsatisfiable. A resolution proof is given in figure 10.4.

We now consider a partitioning of the set of clauses into sets A and B. An (A, B)-refutation
$\mathcal{R}$ of an unsatisfiable CNF pair (A, B) is one in which $\ell_\mathcal{R}(v)$ is an element of either A or
B for each initial vertex $v \in V_\mathcal{R}$. An *interpolation system* is a procedure that takes an
(A, B)-refutation as input and constructs an interpolant from it.

Definition 10.8 (McMillan's interpolation system) *McMillan's interpolation system Itp
maps the nodes in an (A, B)-refutation $\mathcal{R}$ to a formula, as follows:*

1. *An initial node v with $\ell_\mathcal{R}(v) = C$ and $C \in A$ is mapped to $C|_B$; that is, only the literals
   that occur in B are kept.*

2. *An initial node v with $\ell_\mathcal{R}(v) = C$ and $C \in B$ is mapped to true.*

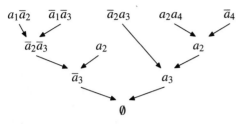

Figure 10.4
A resolution proof for equation 10.10.

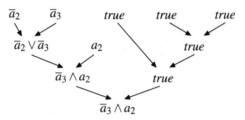

Figure 10.5
Example for an application of McMillan's interpolation system.

3. *Consider an internal node v with pivot variable x. If variable x occurs in B, then*

$$Itp(v) = Itp(v^+) \wedge Itp(v^-).$$

If variable x does not occur in B, then

$$Itp(v) = Itp(v^+) \vee Itp(v^-).$$

The formula Itp(v) is called the partial interpolant *for v. The interpolant generated by the interpolation system is the partial interpolant for the sink node.*

Example 10.9 *We will partition equation 10.10 as follows. Let A be the formula $(a_1 \vee \overline{a}_2) \wedge (\overline{a}_1 \vee \overline{a}_3) \wedge a_2$, and let B be the formula $(\overline{a}_2 \vee a_3) \wedge (a_2 \vee a_4) \wedge \overline{a}_4$. The partial interpolants generated by McMillan's system are given in figure 10.5. The final interpolant is $\overline{a}_3 \wedge a_2$.*

Further interpolation systems are discussed in the bibliographic notes for this chapter. We also discuss interpolation procedures for other fragments of first-order logic in the bibliographic notes.

10.4.3 Reachability Checking with Craig Interpolation

Model checking with Craig interpolation uses an unwinding in the style of bounded model checking (BMC) as a starting point. Recall the translation performed by BMC for properties of the form **AG** p for a given bound k (equation 10.2):

$$S_0(s_0) \wedge \bigwedge_{i=0}^{k-1} R(s_i, s_{i+1}) \wedge \bigvee_{i=0}^{k} \neg p(s_i) \tag{10.11}$$

We will now consider three changes to the formula above. First, let us assume that we have already checked that all states in the set of initial states S_0 are labeled with p. We can thus omit the disjunct $p(s_0)$ from the formula, as it is redundant. Furthermore, we will consider an arbitrary set Q as the set of initial states. Finally, we split the conjunction in equation 10.11 into two parts, which we call A and B. We then obtain

$$\underbrace{Q(s_0) \wedge R(s_0, s_1)}_{A} \quad \text{and} \quad \underbrace{\bigwedge_{i=1}^{k-1} R(s_i, s_{i+1}) \wedge \bigvee_{i=1}^{k} \neg p(s_i)}_{B}. \tag{10.12}$$

Now suppose that $A \wedge B$ is unsatisfiable. Then A and B are inconsistent, and Craig's theorem implies that there is an interpolant I. Observe that the only variables common to A and B are those in the vector s_1, and thus, I is a predicate over s_1 only. We record the following lemma.

Lemma 10.10 *Given an inconsistent pair A, B as defined above, and an interpolant I for A and B, the following hold:*

1. *I does not contain any states that are labeled with $\neg p$.*
2. *I overapproximates the post image of Q; that is, post-image$(Q) \subseteq I$.*

Proof To see the first claim, recall that Craig's theorem states that I is inconsistent with B. For sake of contradiction, assume that there exists a state s_1 with $\neg p(s_1)$ and $I(s_1)$. Then the right-hand side conjunct in B will be satisfied. The left-hand side conjunct can be satisfied since R is left-total.

To see the second claim, suppose that there is a state s_1 that is in *post-image*(Q) but does not satisfy I for sake of contradiction. As A implies I, one cannot obtain a satisfying assignment to A that includes state s_1. Thus, there must not be a transition from any state in Q to s_1, which contradicts $s_1 \in$ *post-image*(Q). $\square$

We remark that the set I is not necessarily *equal* to *post-image*(Q); it may contain additional states, and thus the computation of the post image is overapproximating.

The procedure *CraigReachability* (figure 10.6) is an application of Craig interpolation for reachability checking. Recall that we first have to check whether there is an initial state that is labeled with $\neg p$. If so, the property is known to be false, and the procedure terminates.

Otherwise, the procedure begins with a small value of k. The set of states Q is initialized to the set of initial states. It then builds equation 10.12 using the set Q as the starting point and for the bound k. If the instance is unsatisfiable, the Craig interpolant I is computed, and

procedure *CraigReachability*(model M, $p \in AP$)

    if $S_0 \wedge \neg p$ is SAT **return** "$M \not\models \mathbf{AG}\, p$";

    $k := 1$;

    $Q := S_0$;

    while *true* **do**

        $A := Q(s_0) \wedge R(s_0, s_1)$;

        $B := \bigwedge_{i=1}^{k-1} R(s_i, s_{i+1}) \wedge \bigvee_{i=1}^{k} \neg p(s_i)$;

        if $A \wedge B$ is SAT **then**

            if $Q = S_0$ **then return** "$M \not\models \mathbf{AG}\, p$";

            Increase k

            $Q := S_0$

        else

            compute interpolant I for A and B

            if $I \subseteq Q$ **then return** "$M \models \mathbf{AG}\, p$";

            $Q := Q \cup I$

        end if

    end while

end procedure

Figure 10.6
Procedure for reachability checking using overapproximating post-image computation with Craig interpolation.

it is an overapproximating post image of Q according to lemma 10.10. If that interpolant is contained in Q, then Q is closed under the post image and is thus an inductive invariant. As Q does not contain $\neg p$ states, we can conclude that the property holds. Otherwise, the procedure *CraigReachability* continues with the next iteration, where a post image of $Q \cup I$ is computed.

We now discuss what happens if equation 10.12 is satisfiable. Then, one of two cases applies:

- If $Q = S_0$, the algorithm performs the first iteration after setting a new value of k. Thus, Q has not yet been overapproximated, and thus, the formula we have checked is a BMC instance. The satisfying assignment to $A \wedge B$ is thus a genuine counterexample to $\mathbf{AG}\, p$. The procedure reports this and terminates.

- Otherwise, nothing can be concluded about the property, as Q may contain unreachable states. The procedure then resets Q to the set of initial states and increases k.

10.4.4   Correctness

The procedure is sound; that is, when it detects that $Q \subseteq I$ we indeed have an inductive invariant for $\mathbf{AG}\,p$. This is shown by induction on the number of iterations and lemma 10.10. The argument that any counterexample returned by the procedure is indeed genuine is the same we use to argue that BMC returns genuine counterexamples.

It is left to show that the procedure is complete; that is, it will terminate eventually. For sake of contradiction, suppose that it does not terminate. We first show that k must eventually increase. To this end, observe that otherwise, the sequence of the set Q is increasing monotonically, and that each iteration adds at least one state to Q. This cannot repeat infinitely often as Q is chosen from a finite set.

Thus, k is increasing. Recall the properties that the interpolant I has according to theorem 10.6. The theorem states that I is inconsistent with B. Consequently, I does not contain a state labeled with $\neg p$, and furthermore, no state in I can reach a $\neg p$ state with $k - 1$ transitions or fewer.

First consider the case $M \not\models \mathbf{AG}\,p$. The value of k is eventually increased to the length of the shortest counterexample for the property. The following SAT instance will be satisfiable, and the procedure terminates.

For the case $M \models \mathbf{AG}\,p$, first recall the definition of the diameter of M. The diameter is the longest shortest path between any two states in the Kripke structure. Eventually, k will reach the diameter of M. At this point, the interpolant is precisely the set of reachable states that do not reach a $\neg p$ state. This set is closed under the post image, and the procedure terminates.

10.5   Property-Directed Reachability

10.5.1   Overview

We observe that the approaches we have discussed so far in this chapter rely on an unwinding of the transition relation; that is, the formula that is given to the solver consists of multiple copies of the transition relation. The resulting memory consumption can be prohibitive. We now present *property-directed reachability* (PDR) [76], which is a technique that performs SAT-based reachability checking without making copies of the transition relation. PDR is therefore usually more memory efficient. PDR is called IC3 in [76].

Similarly to reachability checking with Craig interpolants, PDR computes overapproximations of the post image of the set of initial states. It is therefore an instance of overapproximating reachability checking, and aims to compute an inductive invariant I that satisfies the conditions of definition 10.5.

Reachability checking with Craig interpolants uses precisely one such candidate invariant. A key difference between reachability checking with Craig interpolants and PDR is that PDR uses *multiple* candidate invariants. The candidate invariants are called *frames* and are

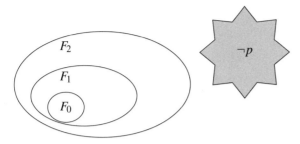

Figure 10.7
Illustration of frames $F_0, \ldots, F_k$, which are subsets of S, for $k = 2$.

denoted by $F_0, \ldots, F_k$. Each F_i is a subset of S. The algorithm maintains the following four invariants:

(Inv1) Frame F_0 contains the set of initial states; that is, $S_0 \subseteq F_0$.

(Inv2) The series of frames F_i is monotone; that is, $F_i \subseteq F_{i+1}$.

(Inv3) None of the frames contains a $\neg p$ state.

(Inv4) Frame F_{i+1} is an overapproximation of the post image of frame F_i; that is,

$$post\text{-}image(F_i) \subseteq F_{i+1}.$$

We illustrate the partitioning of S that is given by the frames $F_0, \ldots, F_k$ in figure 10.7.

We now recall the conditions that a set of states has to satisfy in order to be an inductive invariant (definition 10.5). It follows from the PDR invariants (Inv1) and (Inv2) that all F_i contain the set of initial states. Furthermore, they do not contain $\neg p$ states (Inv3). Now observe that, once we obtain any F_i with $F_i = F_{i+1}$, we have $post\text{-}image(F_i) \subseteq F_i$ (Inv4). Thus, when $F_i = F_{i+1}$, then F_i is an inductive invariant for **AG** p.

New frames are initialized to contain the set of all states labeled with p, which is the largest candidate invariant that could possibly prove **AG** p. The key operation of PDR is then to remove states from the frames that are counterexamples to $F_i = F_{i+1}$. Since we always have $F_i \subseteq F_{i+1}$, these must be states that are in F_{i+1} but not in F_i. PDR does this until it either finds a counterexample path from an initial state to a $\neg p$ state or until it obtains a frame that satisfies $F_i = F_{i+1}$.

10.5.2   Main Procedure

The main loop of the algorithm is given in pseudo-code in figure 10.8. As first step, it checks whether there is an initial state labeled $\neg p$, in which case **AG** p is refuted and the procedure terminates. Otherwise, the algorithm proceeds and can assume that the initial states are all labeled with p.

function *PDR*(model M, $p \in AP$)

    if $S_0 \wedge \neg p$ is SAT **return** "$M \not\models \textbf{AG}\, p$";

    $F_0 := S_0$; $k := 0$;

    while *true* **do**

        extendFrontier(M, k)

        propagateClauses(M, k)

        if $F_i = F_{i+1}$ for some i **then return** "$M \models \textbf{AG}\, p$";

        $k := k + 1$

    end while

end function

Figure 10.8

Main loop of property-directed reachability (PDR).

We then set k to zero and construct frame F_0. It is initialized to be the set of initial states. It is trivial to establish that (Inv1)–(Inv4) hold after this setup phase. The main loop performs four actions:

1. A new frame F_{k+1} is set up by calling *extendFrontier* (figure 10.9).
2. Clauses are forward-propagated by calling *propagateClauses* (figure 10.11).
3. We check whether we have obtained an inductive invariant that proves **AG** p, in which case we terminate.
4. Otherwise, k is increased by one, and the procedure proceeds with the first step.

We now discuss each of the subprocedures in turn.

10.5.3   Extending the Frontier

Procedure *extendFrontier* adds a new frame F_{k+1}. The frame is initialized to be the set of states that are labeled with p, which is the largest possible inductive invariant that can be used to prove **AG** p. Observe that the new frame then satisfies (Inv1)–(Inv3). However, it might violate (Inv4); that is, there might be a state $s \in F_k$ such that there is a transition from s to an s' that is not in F_{k+1}. The loop in procedure *extendFrontier* uses a satisfiability check to identify these transitions, and calls *removeCTI* in order to remove the states s that are sources of such transitions from F_k. After they have been removed, all invariants are reestablished.

We illustrate the steps taken by procedure *removeCTI* using figure 10.12. The procedure is given a state s and the index of the frame F_i in which the state was found as parameters. We furthermore ensure that we only pass states to this procedure that can reach a $\neg p$ state. Procedure *removeCTI* aims to determine whether the state s can be reached from an initial state with i or fewer steps.

Procedure *removeCTI* distinguishes three cases:

procedure *extendFrontier*(model M, $k : \mathbb{N}$)
    $F_{k+1} := \{s \mid p \in L(s)\};$
    while $F_k \wedge R \wedge \neg p'$ is SAT **do**
        $s' :=$ state labeled with $\neg p$ extracted from satisfying assignment
        $s :=$ predecessor of s' extracted from satisfying assignment
        removeCTI(M, s, k)
    end while
end procedure

Figure 10.9
Procedure for adding another frame in PDR.

procedure *removeCTI*(model M, $s : S$, $i : \mathbb{N}$)
    if $S_0 \wedge s$ is SAT **then abort** "$M \not\models \mathbf{AG}\,p$";
    while $F_i \wedge R \wedge \neg s \wedge s'$ is SAT **do**
        for l **from** 0 **to** i
            $F_l := F_l \wedge \neg s$
        end for
        $t :=$ predecessor of s, extracted from SAT witness
        removeCTI$(M, t, i-1)$
    end while
end procedure

Figure 10.10
Procedure for removing counterexamples to induction in PDR.

procedure *propagateClauses*($k : \mathbb{N}$)
    for i **from** 1 **to** k
        for every clause $c \in F_i$
            if $F_i \wedge R \wedge \neg c'$ is UNSAT **then**
                $F_{i+1} := F_{i+1} \wedge c$
            end if
        end for
    end for
end procedure

Figure 10.11
Propagation of clauses into other frames.

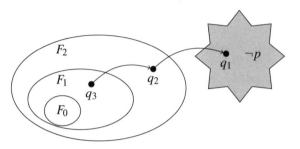

Figure 10.12
Illustration of removal of counterexamples to induction, with $k = 2$.

1. It first checks whether s is an initial state. If this is the case, we know that there is a path from an initial state to a $\neg p$ state, which implies that **AG** p is refuted. The procedure aborts.

2. Otherwise, the procedure checks whether there is a transition from F_i to s using the satisfiability solver. If not so, we have shown that state s cannot be reached from an initial state with i or fewer steps. The procedure returns.

3. If there is a transition from t in F_i to s, we cannot conclude anything, as the set of states F_i is an overapproximation of the states that are reachable with i steps. Thus, state t might itself not be reachable in i steps. In order to decide whether this is the case or not, the procedure calls itself recursively, this time with state t as the argument and $i - 1$ as the frame in order to determine whether t is reachable from F_{i-1}. Before doing so, we remove the state s from the frames F_0 to F_i.

10.5.4   Correctness

We first show soundness and then termination.

Soundness   We have already argued the correctness of the case when PDR returns "$M \models$ **AG** p" in section 10.5.1. Consider the case when PDR returns "$M \not\models$ **AG** p" in *removeCTI*. It is easy to see that the parameter s to *removeCTI* is a state that can reach a state labeled with $\neg p$. Thus, there is an initial state from which a state labeled with $\neg p$ can be reached, and thus, M does not satisfy **AG** p.

Termination   We first argue termination of *removeCTI*. The **while** loop stops eventually as state s only has a finite number of predecessors, and each iteration removes the predecessor found by the solver. The recursion stops eventually as i decreases with every recursive call. The loop in *extendFrontier* terminates eventually as there are only finitely many states that have $\neg p$ successors, and *removeCTI* removes s from F_k.

The key argument to termination of *PDR* is that every iteration of the loop in *PDR* increases k. Recall that the F_i are a sequence that is taken from a finite set and that is strictly increasing. Thus, for large enough k, there will be $F_i = F_{i+1}$ for some i, and the procedure terminates.

Bibliographic Notes

The bounded model checking technique with propositional SAT was introduced in 1999 by Biere et al. [58, 57]. There has been a substantial body of work on bounded encodings for temporal logic formulas. We remark that the bound k is sometimes interpreted as the number of *states* in the counterexample and sometimes (as in this chapter) as the number of *transitions*. In [58] a syntactic method for unwinding arbitrary LTL properties is included, but the size of the resulting formulas is at least quadratic [340]. An encoding for ACTL* is given in [405] and an encoding for CTL* in [457].

The term completeness threshold was introduced in [312]. In [58] the theorem that the recurrence diameter of M is a completeness thresholds for **EF** p witnesses is stated. Since LTL model checking is known to be PSPACE-complete in the size of the property [446], the paper also conjectures that there is no completeness threshold for LTL properties that is polynomial in the size of the model. This conjecture is shown in [311] using simple examples of LTL properties that require exponential bounds.

BMC was initially applied to models of digital circuits. An implementation of BMC for circuits given in the Verilog HDL can be found in the EBMC [388] tool. A variant of BMC for software programs was presented in [162, 138]; it is discussed in chapter 14.

The k-induction technique using a SAT solver was proposed by Sheeran et al. [438] and independently by Bjesse and Claessen [64]. Several optimizations and extensions to the technique have been proposed, including property strengthening to reduce induction depth [473], improving performance via incremental SAT solving [190], and the verification of temporal properties [31]. Initial applications of k-induction have focused on hardware designs [64, 349, 438]. The application to software programs followed later [186, 184].

A model-checking technique based on all-SAT was presented by McMillan in 2002 [373]. In 2003, McMillan introduced unbounded reachability checking with propositional SAT and Craig interpolation [374]. Methods for computing Craig interpolants from resolution proofs pre-date this paper. The first systems were proposed by Huang [278], Krajíček [310], and Pudlák [417]. McMillan has proposed a different system in [374], which generates stronger interpolants. Stronger interpolants result in more precise approximations but may result in slower convergence. The relationship between the different interpolation systems with respect to logical strength of the interpolants generated is discussed in [187]. The style of presenting interpolation systems using annotations with partial interpolants has been introduced by McMillan [375].

A precursor to PDR was given in [78], where individual inductive clauses are computed. Property-directed reachability (PDR) was proposed by Bradley [76]. Refinements and clarifications for the algorithm were presented in [77], and an extension to CTL in [260].

An improvement to the generalization procedure was given in [261]. A combination of PDR with k-induction was presented in [291]. A combination of PDR with interpolation was given in [476].

Problems

Problem 10.1 (Completeness threshold depends on the model). Show that there is no completeness threshold that is independent of the model.

Problem 10.2 (Completeness threshold depends on the property). Show that there is no completeness threshold that is independent of the property.

Problem 10.3 (Completeness threshold for AF p). The *recurrence diameter* of a graph is the length of the longest path in the graph that is loop-free. Show that the recurrence diameter is a completeness threshold for properties of the form **AF** p.

11 Equivalences and Preorders between Structures

In this chapter we discuss logical and structural relations between Kripke structures. We say that two structures are *logically equivalent* with respect to a logic $\mathcal{L}$ if they satisfy exactly the same set of formulas of $\mathcal{L}$. We will exploit this notion of equivalence in fighting the state explosion problem: instead of checking the truth value of a formula on the full model of a system, we will check it on a logically equivalent structure that is smaller in size (number of states and transitions). In later chapters we discuss several ways to extract and exploit such small models in making model checking more tractable.

In order for logical equivalence to be useful in practice, we accompany it with a corresponding notion of *structural equivalence*, which is defined over the states and transitions of the Kripke structures and can be checked efficiently. We first consider the logic CTL* and *bisimulation equivalence* [394].

11.1 Bisimulation Equivalence

Let $M = (S, S_0, R, AP, L)$ and $M = (S', S'_0, R', AP, L')$ be two structures with the same set of atomic propositions AP. A relation $B \subseteq S \times S'$ is a *bisimulation relation* between M and M' if and only if for all s and s', if $B(s, s')$ then the following conditions hold:

1. $L(s) = L'(s')$.
2. For every state s_1 such that $R(s, s_1)$ there is s'_1 such that $R'(s', s'_1)$ and $B(s_1, s'_1)$.
3. For every state s'_1 such that $R'(s', s'_1)$ there is s_1 such that $R(s, s_1)$ and $B(s_1, s'_1)$.

The structures M and M' are *bisimulation equivalent* (denoted $M \equiv M'$) if there exists a bisimulation relation B such that for every initial state $s_0 \in S_0$ in M there is an initial state $s'_0 \in S'_0$ in M' such that $B(s_0, s'_0)$. In addition, for every initial state $s'_0 \in S'_0$ in M' there is an initial state $s_0 \in S_0$ in M such that $B(s_0, s'_0)$.

Figures 11.1 and 11.2 demonstrate simple examples of bisimulation equivalent structures. The figures show that unwinding a structure or duplicating some part of a structure may result in a bisimulation equivalent structure. Figure 11.3, on the other hand, shows two structures that are not bisimulation equivalent. In order to see this, note that the state labeled

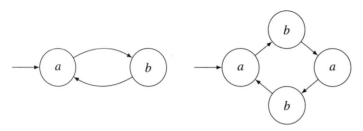

Figure 11.1
Unwinding preserves bisimulation.

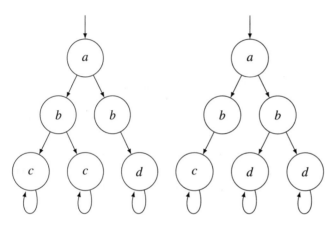

Figure 11.2
Duplication preserves bisimulation.

with b in M' does not correspond to any of the states labeled with b in M since none of these states has both a successor labeled by c and a successor labeled by d.

Next we establish the connection between CTL* equivalence and bisimulation equivalence. We start with the following lemma. We say that two paths $\pi = s_0 s_1 \ldots$ in M and $\pi' = s'_0 s'_1 \ldots$ in M' *correspond* if and only if for every $i \geq 0$, $B(s_i, s'_i)$.

Lemma 11.1 *Let s and s' be two states such that $B(s, s')$. Then for every path starting from s there is a corresponding path starting from s', and for every path starting from s' there is a corresponding path starting from s.*

Proof Let $B(s, s')$, and let $\pi = s_0 s_1 \ldots$ be a path from $s = s_0$. We construct a corresponding path $\pi' = s'_0 s'_1 \ldots$ from $s' = s'_0$ by induction. It is clear that $B(s_0, s'_0)$. Assume that $B(s_i, s'_i)$ for some i. We will show how to choose s'_{i+1}. Since $B(s_i, s'_i)$ and $R(s_i, s_{i+1})$, there must be a successor t' of s'_i such that $B(s_{i+1}, t')$. We choose s'_{i+1} to be t'.

Given a path π' from s', the construction of a path π from s is similar. $\square$

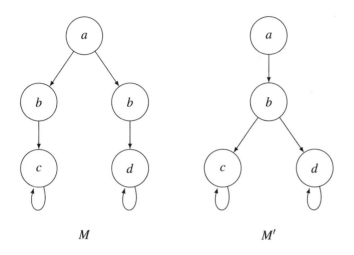

Figure 11.3
Two nonbisimilar structures.

The next lemma shows that if two states are bisimilar, then they satisfy the same set of CTL* state formulas. Furthermore, if two paths correspond, then they satisfy the same set of path formulas.

Lemma 11.2 *Let f be either a state formula or a path formula. Assume that s and s' are bisimilar states and that π and π' are corresponding paths. Then,*

- *if f is a state formula, then $s \models f \Leftrightarrow s' \models f$, and*
- *if f is a path formula, then $\pi \models f \Leftrightarrow \pi' \models f$.*

Proof We prove the lemma by induction on the structure of f.
Base: $f = p$ for $p \in AP$. Since $B(s, s')$, we know that $L(s) = L'(s')$. Thus, $s \models p$ if and only if $s' \models p$.
Induction: Consider the following cases.

1. $f = \neg f_1$, a state formula:

$$s \models f \Leftrightarrow s \not\models f_1$$
$$\Leftrightarrow s' \not\models f_1 \quad \text{(induction hypothesis)}$$
$$\Leftrightarrow s' \models f$$

The same reasoning holds if f is a path formula.

2. $f = f_1 \vee f_2$, a state formula:

$$s \models f \Leftrightarrow s \models f_1 \text{ or } s \models f_2$$
$$\Leftrightarrow s' \models f_1 \text{ or } s' \models f_2 \quad \text{(induction hypothesis)}$$
$$\Leftrightarrow s' \models f$$

We can also use this argument if f is a path formula.

3. $f = f_1 \wedge f_2$, a state formula: This case is similar to the previous case. Furthermore, the same argument can be used if f is a path formula.

4. $f = \mathbf{E} f_1$, a state formula: Suppose that $s \models f$. Then there is a path π_1 starting from s such that $\pi_1 \models f_1$. By lemma 11.1, there is a corresponding path π'_1 in M' starting from s'. So by the induction hypothesis, $\pi_1 \models f_1$ if and only if $\pi'_1 \models f_1$. Therefore, $s' \models \mathbf{E} f_1$. The same argument can be used to prove that if $s' \models f$ then $s \models f$.

5. $f = \mathbf{A} f_1$, a state formula: The argument for this case is similar to the argument for $f = \mathbf{E} f_1$.

6. $f = f_1$, where f is a path formula and f_1 is a state formula: Although the lengths of f and f_1 are the same, we can imagine that $f = \mathbf{path}(f_1)$, where **path** is a special operator that converts a state formula into a path formula. Therefore, we are simplifying f by dropping this **path** operator. If s_0 and s'_0 are the first states of π and π', respectively, then

$$\pi \models f \Leftrightarrow s_0 \models f_1$$
$$\Leftrightarrow s'_0 \models f_1 \quad \text{(induction hypothesis)}$$
$$\Leftrightarrow \pi' \models f.$$

7. $f = \mathbf{X} f_1$, a path formula: Suppose that $\pi \models f$. By the definition of the next time operator, $\pi^1 \models f_1$. Since π and π' correspond, so do π^1 and π'^1. Therefore, by the induction hypothesis, $\pi'^1 \models f_1$, and so $\pi' \models f$. The same argument can be used to prove that if $\pi' \models f$ then $\pi \models f$.

8. $f = f_1 \mathbf{U} f_2$, a path formula: Suppose that $\pi \models f_1 \mathbf{U} f_2$. By the definition of the until operator, there is a k such that $\pi^k \models f_2$ and for all $0 \leq j < k$, $\pi^j \models f_1$. Since π and π' correspond, so do π^j and π'^j for any j. Therefore, by the induction hypothesis, $\pi'^k \models f_2$ and for all $0 \leq j < k$, $\pi'^j \models f_1$. Therefore, $\pi' \models f$. The same argument can be used to prove that if $\pi' \models f$ then $\pi \models f$.

9. $f = f_1 \mathbf{R} f_2$, a path formula: The argument in this case is similar to the argument for $f = f_1 \mathbf{U} f_2$. $\square$

The next theorem is a consequence of the preceding lemma.

Theorem 11.3 *If $B(s, s')$, then for every CTL* formula f, $s \models f \Leftrightarrow s' \models f$.*

If two structures are bisimulation equivalent, then every initial state of one is bisimilar to some initial state of the other. Since a structure satisfies a formula if and only if each of its initial states satisfies the formula, both structures will satisfy the same set of CTL* formulas.

Theorem 11.4 *If $M \equiv M'$, then for every CTL* formula f, $M \models f \Leftrightarrow M' \models f$.*

The converse of this theorem is also true. If two structures satisfy the same set of CTL* formulas, then they are bisimulation equivalent. In fact, we can show that if two structures satisfy the same CTL formulas, then they are bisimulation equivalent. Next, we give a simple proof of this statement for Kripke structures with single initial states. A different proof, which can easily be extended to structures with multiple initial states, can be found in [83].

Theorem 11.5 *Let M and M' be two Kripke structures with $S_0 = \{s_0\}$ and $S'_0 = \{s'_0\}$. If for every CTL formula f, $M \models f \Leftrightarrow M' \models f$, then $M \equiv M'$.*

Proof We define a relation $B \subseteq S \times S'$ as follows: $B(s, s')$ if and only if for every CTL formula f, $s \models f \Leftrightarrow s' \models f$. We show that B is a bisimulation relation. Note first that $B(s_0, s'_0)$ holds. Let s and s' be states such that $B(s, s')$.

1. For every $p \in AP$, $s \models p \Leftrightarrow s' \models p$. Thus, $L(s) = L'(s')$.
2. Let $R(s, s_1)$, and let $s'_1, \ldots, s'_k$ be the successors of s' in M'. Since M' is finite, the set of successors is finite. Assume by way of contradiction that for every $1 \leq j \leq k$, $B(s_1, s'_j)$ does not hold. Then, for every $1 \leq j \leq k$, there is a CTL formula f_j that is false in s_1 but true in s'_j. Note that if the formula is true in s_1 and false in s'_j, then we choose the negation of the formula as f_j. Consequently, the formula $\mathbf{AX}(f_1 \vee \ldots \vee f_k)$ is true in s' but not in s. This is in contradiction to $B(s, s')$. Thus, there is s'_j so that $R'(s', s'_j)$ and $B(s_1, s'_j)$.
3. The proof that every successor of s' has a corresponding successor of s is similar. □

The proof implies that theorem 11.5 holds also in the case where M and M' agree on the subset of CTL formulas that includes only the **AX** and **EX** operators.

Theorem 11.5 implies that if two structures can be *distinguished* by a formula of CTL* (that is, there is a CTL* formula that is true of one structure and not of the other), then they can also be distinguished by a formula of CTL. Note that this result does not imply that CTL* and CTL have the same expressive power. For comparing the expressiveness of two logics, we view a formula as defining the set of models where the formula is true. For CTL to have the same expressiveness as CTL*, it would be necessary for every formula of CTL* to have a corresponding formula of CTL that defines the same set of models. This, however, is known not to be true [199]. Instead, the above result implies that for every model, there exists a CTL formula that is true in that model but not in any other, inequivalent model.

11.2   Fair Bisimulation

The notion of bisimulation equivalence can be extended to structures with *fairness constraints*. Let M and M' be two structures with fairness constraints. Assume that both have the same set of atomic propositions AP. A relation $B \subseteq S \times S'$ is a *fair bisimulation relation* between M and M' if and only if for all s and s', if $B(s, s')$, then the following conditions hold:

1. $L(s) = L'(s')$.
2. For every *fair* path $\pi = s_0 s_1 \ldots$ from $s = s_0$ in M there is a *fair* path $\pi' = s'_0 s'_1 \ldots$ from $s' = s'_0$ in M' such that for all $i \geq 0$, $B(s_i, s'_i)$.
3. For every *fair* path $\pi' = s'_0 s'_1 \ldots$ from $s' = s'_0$ in M' there is a *fair* path $\pi = s_0 s_1 \ldots$ from $s = s_0$ in M such that for all $i \geq 0$, $B(s_i, s'_i)$.

In this case, two structures M and M' are *fair bisimulation equivalent* (denoted $M \equiv_F M'$) if there exists a fair bisimulation relation B such that for every initial state $s_0 \in S_0$ in M there is an initial state $s'_0 \in S'_0$ in M' such that $B(s_0, s'_0)$. In addition, for every initial state $s'_0 \in S'_0$ in M' there is an initial state $s_0 \in S_0$ in M such that $B(s_0, s'_0)$. If the semantics of CTL* is given with respect to fair paths, then we can prove an analog of theorem 11.4 for fair structures.

Theorem 11.6 *If* $M \equiv_F M'$, *then for every CTL* formula f interpreted over fair paths,* $M \models_F f \Leftrightarrow M' \models_F f$.

The proof of this theorem is similar to the proof of theorem 11.4 and is omitted.

11.3   Preorders between Structures

Sometimes bisimulation equivalence does not result in a significant reduction in the number of states. By restricting the logic and relaxing the requirement that the structures should satisfy exactly the same formulas, a greater reduction can be obtained. In order to achieve this goal we introduce the notion of a *simulation relation*. Simulation is closely related to bisimulation. Bisimulation guarantees that two structures have the same behaviors. Simulation, on the other hand, relates a structure to another structure that is an *over-approximation* of the original one in the sense that it has all its behaviors, but possibly more. Such a relation holds, for example, between a structure and its *abstraction*. An abstraction can hide some of the details of the original structure; thus, it might have a smaller set of atomic propositions. An over-approximating abstraction guarantees that every behavior of a structure is also a behavior of its abstraction. However, the abstraction might have behaviors that are not possible in the original structure. For example, in an actual implementation some event always occurs within twenty execution steps, but in an abstraction this event may occur after any number of execution steps. We discuss abstraction and other use of the simulation relation in later chapters.

Given two structures M and M' with $AP \supseteq AP'$, a relation $H \subseteq S \times S'$ is a *simulation relation* [380] between M and M' if and only if for all s and s', if $H(s,s')$ then the following conditions hold:

1. $L(s) \cap AP' = L'(s')$.
2. For every state s_1 such that $R(s,s_1)$, there is a state s_1' with the property that $R'(s',s_1')$ and $H(s_1,s_1')$.

We say that M' *simulates* M (denoted by $M \preceq M'$) if there exists a simulation relation H such that for every initial state s_0 in M there is an initial state s_0' in M' for which $H(s_0,s_0')$.

Consider again the structures in figure 11.3. We showed previously that they were not bisimulation equivalent. We will now show that the structure M is smaller in the simulation preorder than the structure M'. We choose a simulation relation $\preceq$ that associates with each state in M the state in M' that has the same label. The relation $\preceq$ has the property that if it associates a state s with a state s', then every successor of s has a corresponding successor of s'. On the other hand, M does not simulate M', since the state in M' labeled with b does not have a corresponding state in M.

Now, we show that simulation is a preorder, that is, a reflexive and transitive relation.

Lemma 11.7 *The relation $\preceq$ is a preorder on the set of structures.*

Proof The relation $H = \{ (s,s) \mid s \in S \}$ is a simulation between M and M, so $\preceq$ is reflexive. Thus, it only remains to show that $\preceq$ is transitive. Assume that $M \preceq M'$ and $M' \preceq M''$. Let H_0 be a simulation between M and M', and let H_1 be a simulation between M' to M''. Define H_2 as the relational product of H_0 and H_1; that is,

$$H_2 = \{ (s,s'') \mid \exists s'. [H_0(s,s') \wedge H_1(s',s'')] \}.$$

If $s_0 \in S_0$, then by the definition of simulation, there exists $s_0' \in S_0'$ such that $H_0(s_0,s_0')$. Similarly, there exists $s_0'' \in S_0''$ such that $H_1(s_0',s_0'')$, and hence $H_2(s_0,s_0'')$.

Suppose that $H_2(s,s'')$, and let s' be such that $H_0(s,s')$ and $H_1(s',s'')$. By the definition of simulation, $L(s) \cap AP' = L'(s')$ and $L'(s') \cap AP'' = L''(s'')$. Then since $AP' \supseteq AP''$, we have $L(s) \cap AP'' = L''(s'')$. Let $R(s,s_1)$ be a transition in M from s. Then there exists a transition $R(s',s_1')$ in M' such that $H_0(s_1,s_1')$. Since H_1 is a simulation, there exists a transition $R''(s'',s_1'')$ in M'' such that $H_1(s_1',s_1'')$. Hence, $H_2(s,s_1'')$, and H_2 is a simulation between M and M''. Thus, $M \preceq M''$. $\square$

The following lemma is the analog of lemma 11.1 for simulation relations. In this case, we also say that paths $\pi = s_0 s_1 \ldots$ in M and $\pi' = s_0' s_1' \ldots$ in M' *correspond* if and only if for every i, $H(s_i,s_i')$.

Lemma 11.8 *Assume that s and s' are states such that $H(s,s')$. Then for every path π starting from s there is a corresponding path π' starting from s'.*

Theorem 11.9 *Suppose that $M \preceq M'$. Then for every ACTL* formula f (with atomic propositions in AP'), $M' \models f$ implies $M \models f$.*

Intuitively, this theorem is true because formulas in ACTL* describe properties that are quantified over all possible behaviors of a structure. Since every behavior of M is a behavior of M', every formula of ACTL* that is true in M' must also be true in M. A formal proof can be obtained from lemma 11.8 by using an argument similar to the one used to establish theorem 11.4. This theorem is very useful for model checking when M is much more complicated than M'. If it is possible to establish an ACTL* property f for M', then f will also be true of the more complex model M. On the other hand, if f does not hold for M', then f may or may not hold for M. Thus, if a counterexample is obtained when checking f on M', it is still necessary to check whether the counterexample actually corresponds to an error in M. This theorem will be used frequently in subsequent chapters.

The following is a straightforward consequence of theorem 11.9, since every ECTL* formula is equivalent to the negation of an ACTL* formula.

Corollary 11.9.1 *Suppose that $M \preceq M'$. Then for every ECTL* formula f (with atomic propositions in AP'), $M \models f$ implies $M' \models f$.*

Figure 11.4 illustrates the difference between simulation and bisimulation. The two structures in the figure are not bisimulation equivalent, but each simulates the other. In order to show that M simulates M' we choose a simulation relation that associates both states 3 and 4 in M' with the state 1 in M. Each of the other states in M' is associated with all of the states in M that have the same label.

To see that M' simulates M, we choose the relation that associates both states 1 and 2 in M with state 3 in M'. All of the other states of M are associated with states in M' as in the previous case.

M and M' are not bisimulation equivalent since no state in M can be associated with state 4 in M'. Another way to see why this is true is to use theorem 11.3, which states that two bisimulation-equivalent structures satisfy the same CTL formulas. It is easy to see that the CTL formula $\mathbf{AG}(b \to \mathbf{EX}c)$ it true in M but false in M'. However, because of theorem 11.9, the two structures do satisfy the same ACTL* formulas. This shows that equivalence with respect to ACTL* is different from equivalence with respect to CTL*.

Simulation can be extended to fair structures in the same way that bisimulation is extended to fair structures. Let M and M' be two structures with fairness constraints. Assume that $AP \supseteq AP'$. The relation $H \subseteq S \times S'$ is a *fair simulation relation* between M and M' if and only if for all s and s', if $H(s,s')$, then the following conditions hold:

1. $L(s) \cap AP' = L'(s')$.
2. For every *fair* path $\pi = s_0 s_1 \ldots$ from $s = s_0$ in M, there is a *fair* path $\pi' = s'_0 s'_1 \ldots$ from $s' = s'_0$ in M' such that for all $i \geq 0$, $H(s_i, s'_i)$.

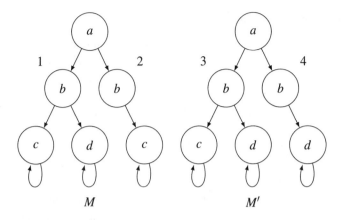

Figure 11.4
Simulation equivalent structures that are not bisimilar.

We write $M \preceq_F M'$ if there exists a fair simulation relation H such that for every initial state $s_0 \in S_0$ in M there is an initial state $s_0' \in S_0'$ in M' such that $H(s_0, s_0')$. It is easy to show that $\preceq_F$ determines a preorder on fair structures. When it is clear from the context that we are dealing with fair simulation, we will sometimes use $\preceq$.

Every fair behavior of M is a fair behavior of M'. Thus, if the semantics of ACTL* is given with respect to fair paths then we can prove the following theorem.

Theorem 11.10 *If $M \preceq_F M'$, then for every ACTL* formula f interpreted over fair paths, $M' \models_F f$ implies $M \models_F f$.*

11.4 Games for Bisimulation and Simulation

Simulation and bisimulation can also be defined in terms of combinatorial games. In this game, two players—the Spoiler and the Duplicator—are moving two pebbles along the transition relations of M and M'. For the bisimulation game, the Spoiler chooses an initial state of either M or M' and places the pebble there. The Duplicator has to reply by placing a pebble on an initial state of the other structure such that the two pebble-carrying states have the same labeling. In the following rounds, the Spoiler challenges the Duplicator by moving one of the pebbles, and the Duplicator has to reply by moving the other pebble to an equivalently labeled state. If the Duplicator has a strategy to match all moves of the Spoiler, it can be shown that the structures M and M' are bisimilar.

The simulation game is very similar. The only difference is that the Spoiler always plays on the simulated structure M, and the Duplicator on the simulating structure M'.

For a detailed exposition of games, we refer to [451, 452].

11.5   Equivalence and Preorder Algorithms

We next consider algorithms that determine whether two structures are bisimulation equivalent or whether one structure precedes another in the simulation preorder. Bisimulation equivalence is easy to check if both structures are *deterministic*; that is, if each has a single initial state, and if $R(s,t)$ and $R(s,u)$, then $L(t) \neq L(u)$. The *language of a structure* is the set of sequences of labelings that occur along paths that start from initial states. It can be shown that two deterministic structures are bisimulation equivalent if and only if they have the same language. Efficient algorithms are known for checking language equivalence for deterministic structures [120]. These algorithms can be used to check bisimulation equivalence for deterministic structures.

We now present a general algorithm that handles both deterministic and nondeterministic structures that do not include fairness constraints. Let M and M' be two structures with the same set of atomic propositions AP. We define a sequence of relations $B_0^*, B_1^*, \ldots$ on $S \times S'$ as follows:

1. $B_0^*(s,s')$ if and only if $L(s) = L'(s')$.
2. $B_{n+1}^*(s,s')$ if and only if
   - $B_n^*(s,s')$, and
   - $\forall s_1.[R(s,s_1) \implies \exists s_1'.[R'(s',s_1') \wedge B_n^*(s_1,s_1')]]$, and
   - $\forall s_1'.[R'(s',s_1') \implies \exists s_1.[R(s,s_1) \wedge B_n^*(s_1,s_1')]]$.

We write $B^*(s,s')$ if and only if $B_i^*(s,s')$ for all $i \geq 0$. Note that, by definition $B_i^* \supseteq B_{i+1}^*$ for all $i \geq 0$. Thus, since M and M' are finite, there is an n such that $B_n^* = B_{n+1}^*$. It is easy to see that B_n^* is exactly B^*.

Two structures M and M' are B^*-*equivalent* if for every initial state $s_0 \in S_0$ in M there is an initial state $s_0' \in S_0'$ in M' such that $B^*(s_0, s_0')$. In addition, for every initial state $s_0' \in S_0'$ in M' there is an initial state $s_0 \in S_0$ in M such that $B^*(s_0, s_0')$. It is easy to see that B^* is a bisimulation between M and M'. In fact, we will show that B^* is the *largest* such bisimulation; that is, every bisimulation between M and M' is included in B^*. (Inclusion between bisimulation relations is interpreted as set inclusion.) Thus, M and M' are bisimulation equivalent if and only if they are B^*-equivalent.

Lemma 11.11 B^* *is the largest bisimulation between M and M' (in terms of set inclusion).*

Proof   It is sufficient to prove that if B is a bisimulation between M and M', then B is contained in B_i^* for every $i \geq 0$. We show this by induction on i. Clearly, B is contained in B_0^*, since any pair of states in B have the same labeling. Assume that B is contained in B_n^* and that $B(s,s')$. Let $R(s,s_1)$ be a transition in M. Since B is a bisimulation, there exists a state s_1' such that $R'(s',s_1')$ is a transition in M' and $B(s_1,s_1')$. Since B is contained in B_n^*, we have that $B_n^*(s_1,s_1')$. The third requirement can be proved in a similar manner. Thus, $B_{n+1}^*(s,s')$. □

As explained above, the finiteness of the structures guarantees that there exists some n such that $B^* = B_n^*$. Thus, the definition gives an algorithm for computing the largest bisimulation between two structures. If an explicit state representation is used for the transition relations, then the algorithm has polynomial time complexity in the size of the two structures. A more efficient polynomial algorithm for this case is given in [393]. If OBDDs are used to represent the transition relations, then the definition can be used directly to compute the largest bisimulation—it just describes the computation of the greatest fixpoint of an appropriate function.

Algorithms for checking fair bisimulation have not been widely investigated. If the structures are deterministic, then an efficient algorithm, based on language equivalence, can also be given in this case. The only change that is necessary is to restrict the language of a structure to fair paths. With this change it is possible to prove that two structures are fair bisimulation equivalent if and only if they are language equivalent with respect to fair paths. Thus, algorithms that check language equivalence for fair structures [120] can be used to handle this case. A general procedure that also handles nondeterministic structures is given in [33]. This problem is PSPACE-complete in the size of the structures [319].

Each of the algorithms mentioned above can be adapted to check the simulation preorder between two structures M and M'. Language inclusion replaces language equivalence in the deterministic case. For the general case without fairness, we define a sequence of relations $H_0^*, H_1^*, \ldots$ on $S \times S'$ as follows:

1. $H_0^*(s, s')$ if and only if $L(s) \cap AP' = L'(s')$;
2. $H_{n+1}^*(s, s')$ if and only if

   - $H_n^*(s, s')$, and
   - $\forall s_1. [R(s, s_1) \implies \exists s_1'. [R'(s', s_1') \wedge H_n^*(s_1, s_1')]]$.

The procedure is guaranteed to terminate since the structures are finite. We write $H^*(s, s')$ if and only if $H_i^*(s, s')$ for all $i \geq 0$. As in the previous case, H^* is the largest simulation relation between the two structures M and M'. Thus, M' simulates M if and only if for every $s_0 \in S_0$ in M there is a state $s_0' \in S_0'$ in M' such that $H^*(s_0, s_0')$.

Bibliographic Notes

Bisimulation and simulation were originally introduced in the context of process algebra [380, 381, 268, 262]. Many notions of equivalence and preorder relations are defined in the relevant literature. The chapter by Cleaveland, Roscoe, and Smolka in [136] gives a thorough survey of these relations for different notions of process algebras, and discusses their logic preservation. More information can be found in [48] and in [171]. Games for bisimulation are described in [451].

A somewhat surprising result is presented in [33], where the authors extend the notion of bisimulation to Kripke structures with fairness and obtain the coarsest equivalence that preserves fair CTL*. They also define a relation that is the weakest equivalence preserving fair CTL. They show that in the presence of fairness, two Kripke structures that are distinguished by a CTL* formula, may become indistinguishable by any CTL formula. This is in contrast to the results presented in [83] for structures with no fairness. Additional reading can be found in [35].

Problems

Problem 11.1 (CTL* preservation under bisimulation). Complete the missing cases in the proof of lemma 11.2. In particular, prove the cases for the state formula $f = \mathbf{A} f_1$ and the path formula $f = f_1 \mathbf{R} f_2$.

Problem 11.2 (From CTL to bisimulation). Make sure you understand why the proof of theorem 11.5 cannot be extended to structures with more than one initial state.

12 Partial Order Reduction

Partial order reduction is aimed at reducing the size of the state space that needs to be searched by model-checking algorithms. It exploits the commutativity of concurrently executed transitions, which result in the same state when executed in different orders. Thus, this reduction technique is best suited for asynchronous systems (in synchronous systems, concurrent transitions are executed simultaneously rather than being interleaved).

The method consists of constructing a reduced state graph. The full state graph, which may be too large to fit in memory, is never constructed. The behaviors of the reduced graph are a subset of the behaviors of the full state graph. The justification of the reduction method shows that the behaviors that are not present do not add any information. More precisely, it is possible to define an equivalence relation among behaviors such that the checked property cannot distinguish between equivalent behaviors. If a behavior is not present in the reduced state graph, then an equivalent behavior must be included.

The name *partial order reduction* has its justification in early versions of the algorithms that were based on the partial order model of program execution [244, 300, 465]. However, the method can be described better as *model-checking using representatives* [399, 401], since the verification is performed using representatives from the equivalence classes of behaviors.

In this chapter the *transitions* of a system play a significant role. Partial order reduction is based on the *dependency relation* that exists between the transitions of a system. Furthermore, this reduction method specifies which transitions should be included in the reduced model and which should not. As in chapter 16, we want to distinguish between different transitions in a system. Thus, we modify the definition of a Kripke structure slightly. Instead of having one transition relation R, we will now have a *set* of transition relations T. For simplicity, we will refer to each element α in T as a *transition*, instead of a transition relation.

A *state transition system* is a quadruple (S, T, S_0, L) where the set of states S, the set of initial states S_0, and the labeling function L are defined as for Kripke structures, and T is a set of transitions such that for each $\alpha \in T$, $\alpha \subseteq S \times S$. A Kripke structure $M = (S, R, S_0, L)$

may be obtained by defining R so that $R(s,s')$ holds when there exists a transition $\alpha \in T$ such that $\alpha(s,s')$.

For a transition $\alpha \in T$, we say that α is *enabled* in a state s if there is a state s' such that $\alpha(s,s')$ holds. Otherwise, α is *disabled* in s. The set of transitions enabled in s is *enabled*(s). A transition α is *deterministic* if for every state s there is at most one state s' such that $\alpha(s,s')$. When α is deterministic we often write $s' = \alpha(s)$ instead of $\alpha(s,s')$. Henceforth, we will consider only deterministic transitions.

A *path* from a state s in a state transition system is a finite or infinite sequence defined as follows: $\pi = s_0 \xrightarrow{\alpha_0} s_1 \xrightarrow{\alpha_1} \ldots$ such that $s = s_0$ and for every i, $\alpha_i(s_i,s_{i+1})$ holds. Here, we do not require paths to be infinite. Moreover, any prefix of a path is also a path. If π is finite, then the *length* of π is the number of transitions in π and will be denoted by $|\pi|$.

12.1   Concurrency in Asynchronous Systems

A common observation about concurrent asynchronous systems is that the interleaving model imposes an arbitrary ordering between concurrent events. To avoid discriminating against any particular ordering, the events are interleaved in all possible ways. The ordering between independent transitions is largely meaningless. However, common specification languages, including many temporal logics, can distinguish between behaviors that differ only in this manner. Our aim is to take advantage of the cases where the specifications do not distinguish between such behaviors. In these cases, partial order reduction checks only a subset of the behaviors. However, it checks sufficiently many of them to guarantee the soundness of the verification.

Putting concurrent events in various possible orderings is a potential cause of the state explosion problem. To see this, consider n transitions that can be executed concurrently. In this case, there are $n!$ different orderings and 2^n different states (one state for each subset of the transitions). If the specification does not distinguish between these sequences, it is clearly beneficial to consider only one sequence, with $n + 1$ states. This is demonstrated in figure 12.1 with $n = 3$.

Our aim is to reduce the number of states that are considered in the model-checking process, while preserving the correctness of the checked property. We will assume for simplicity of presentation that a *reduced state graph* is first generated explicitly using DFS. The model-checking algorithm is then applied to the resulting state graph. The reduction constructs a graph with fewer states and edges. This speeds up the construction of the graph and uses less memory, thus resulting in a more efficient model-checking algorithm. The DFS can also be replaced by breadth-first search [110] and combined with symbolic model-checking [18, 326].

The reduction is performed by modifying the DFS used to construct the state graph, as in figure 12.2. The search starts with an initial state s_0 (line 1) and proceeds recursively. For each state s it selects only a subset *ample*(s) of the enabled transitions *enabled*(s) (in line 5),

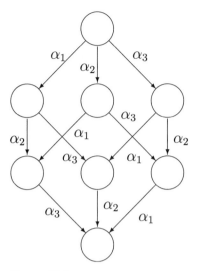

Figure 12.1
Executing three independent transitions.

rather than the full set of enabled transitions, as in the full state space construction. The DFS explores only successors generated by these transitions (lines 6–16). In the DFS algorithm in figure 12.2, a state is added to the hash table (lines 1, 11) when it is first encountered and is labeled there as *on_stack* (lines 2, 12). When all of its successors have been searched, it is relabeled as *completed* (line 17). Thus, a state is marked *on_stack* when it is on the DFS search stack. This information is useful for computing the function *ample*.

When the model-checking algorithm is applied to the reduced state graph, it terminates with a positive answer when the property holds for the original full state graph. Otherwise, it produces a counterexample. Since the reduced state graph contains fewer behaviors, the counterexample can differ from the one that would have resulted from using the full state graph.

Notice that the algorithm in figure 12.2 constructs the reduced state graph *directly*. Constructing the full state graph and later reducing it would defy the purpose of the reduction.

In order to implement the algorithm, we must find a systematic way of calculating $ample(s)$ for any given state s. The calculation of $ample(s)$ needs to satisfy three goals:

1. When $ample(s)$ is used instead of $enabled(s)$, sufficiently many behaviors must be present in the reduced state graph to guarantee that the model-checking algorithm gives correct result.
2. Using $ample(s)$ instead of $enabled(s)$ should result in a significantly smaller state graph.
3. The overhead in calculating $ample(s)$ must be reasonably small.

```
 1  hash(s₀);
 2  set on_stack(s₀);
 3  expand_state(s₀);
 4  procedure expand_state(s)
 5      work_set(s) := ample(s);
 6      while work_set(s) is not empty do
 7          let α ∈ work_set(s);
 8          work_set(s) := work_set(s) \ {α};
 9          s' := α(s);
10          if new(s') then
11              hash(s');
12              set on_stack(s');
13              expand_state(s');
14          end if
15          create_edge(s, α, s');
16      end while
17      set completed(s);
18  end procedure
```

Figure 12.2
Depth-first search with partial order reduction.

12.2   Independence and Invisibility

In this section, we define two concepts that can assist in reducing the state graph. As noted above, in the interleaving model for concurrent systems, transitions that can be executed concurrently from some state are interleaved in either order. This can be formulated by defining an independence relation on pairs of transitions that can execute concurrently. An *independence* relation $I \subseteq T \times T$ is a symmetric, antireflexive relation, satisfying the following two conditions for each state $s \in S$ and for each $(\alpha, \beta) \in I$:

Enabledness If $\alpha, \beta \in enabled(s)$, then $\alpha \in enabled(\beta(s))$.
Commutativity If $\alpha, \beta \in enabled(s)$, then $\alpha(\beta(s)) = \beta(\alpha(s))$.

The *dependency* relation D is the complement of I, namely,

$$D = (T \times T) \setminus I.$$

The enabledness condition states that a pair of independent transitions do not *disable* one another. Note, however, that it is possible for one to *enable* another. Note also that the definition makes use of the fact that I is symmetric. The commutativity condition, which is

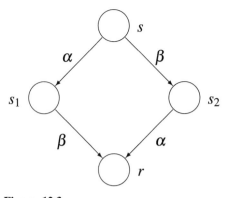

Figure 12.3
Execution of independent transitions.

well defined due to the enabledness condition, states that executing independent transitions
in either order results in the same state. These conditions are illustrated in figure 12.3.
When it is hard to check whether two transitions α and β are independent or not, assuming
that they are dependent always preserves the correctness of the reductions described in this
chapter.

The definition of independence can be used for the reduction even when two independent
transitions cannot actually be executed in parallel. For example, when two transitions of
different processes increment a shared variable, they satisfy the independence conditions,
although some type of physical arbitration must be used to prevent them from executing
simultaneously.

The commutativity condition, illustrated in figure 12.3 suggests a potential reduction to
the state graph, since it does not matter whether α is executed before β or vice versa in
order to reach the state r from s. Thus, it is tempting to select only one of the transitions
originating from s. This is not appropriate for the following reasons:

PROBLEM 1:   The checked property might be sensitive to the choice between the states s_1
and s_2, not only the states s and r.

PROBLEM 2:   The states s_1 and s_2 may have other successors in addition to r, which may
not be explored if either is eliminated.

We return to these problems at the end of section 12.3. The first step in solving them is to
define what it means for a transition to be invisible.

Let $L : S \to 2^{AP}$ be the function that labels each state with a set of atomic propositions.
A transition $\alpha \in T$ is *invisible* with respect to a set of propositions $AP' \subseteq AP$ if for each pair
of states $s, s' \in S$ such that $s' = \alpha(s)$, $L(s) \cap AP' = L(s') \cap AP'$. In other words, a transition
is invisible when its execution from any state does not change the value of the propositional
variables in AP'. A transition is *visible* if it is not invisible.

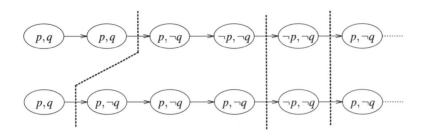

Figure 12.4
Two stuttering-equivalent paths.

A closely related concept is that of *stuttering* [334], which refers to a sequence of identically labeled states along a path in a Kripke structure. Two infinite paths $\sigma = s_0 \xrightarrow{\alpha_0} s_1 \xrightarrow{\alpha_1} \ldots$ and $\rho = r_0 \xrightarrow{\beta_0} r_1 \xrightarrow{\beta_1} \ldots$ are *stuttering equivalent*, denoted $\sigma \sim_{st} \rho$ if there are two infinite sequences of positive integers $0 = i_0 < i_1 < i_2 < \ldots$ and $0 = j_0 < j_1 < j_2 < \ldots$ such that for every $k \geq 0$,

$$L(s_{i_k}) = L(s_{i_k+1}) = \ldots = L(s_{i_{k+1}-1}) = L(r_{j_k}) = L(r_{j_k+1}) = \ldots = L(r_{j_{k+1}-1}).$$

We call a finite sequence of identically labeled states a *block*. Intuitively, two paths are stuttering equivalent when they can be partitioned into infinitely many blocks, such that the states in the kth block of one are labeled the same as the states in the kth block of the other (see figure 12.4). Note that corresponding blocks may have different lengths. Stuttering equivalence can be defined in a similar way for finite paths using finite sequences of indexes $0 = i_0 < i_1 < i_2 < \ldots i_n$ and $0 = j_0 < j_1 < j_2 < \ldots j_n$. Stuttering is a particularly important concept for asynchronous systems since there is no correlation between the time separating two events and the number of transitions occurring between them.

An LTL path formula f is *invariant under stuttering* if and only if, for each pair of paths π and π' such that $\pi \sim_{st} \pi'$,

$$\pi \models f \text{ if and only if } \pi' \models f.$$

We denote the subset of the logic LTL without the next time operator by LTL_{-X}.

Theorem 12.1 *Any* LTL_{-X} *path property is invariant under stuttering.*

The theorem is proved using a simple induction on the size of the LTL path formula. It is interesting to note that the converse of theorem 12.1 also holds [400]:

Theorem 12.2 *Every LTL path property that is stuttering closed can be expressed in* LTL_{-X}.

We now extend the notion of stuttering equivalence to structures. Two structures M and M' are *stuttering equivalent* if and only if

- M and M' have the same set of initial states;
- for each path σ of M that starts from an initial state s of M there exists a path σ' of M' from the same initial state s such that $\sigma \sim_{st} \sigma'$;
- for each path σ' of M' that starts from an initial state s of M' there exists a path σ of M from the same initial state s such that $\sigma' \sim_{st} \sigma$.

The following corollary is useful for showing that an LTL$_{-X}$ formula does not distinguish between structures that are stuttering equivalent. It is exploited later, since partial order reduction generates a structure that is stuttering equivalent to the full state graph.

Corollary 12.2.1 *Let M and M' be two stuttering-equivalent structures. Then, for every* LTL$_{-X}$ *property* $\mathbf{A} f$, *and every initial state* $s \in S_0$, $M, s \models \mathbf{A} f$ *if and only if* $M', s \models \mathbf{A} f$.

Returning to figure 12.3, suppose that at least one transition, say α, is invisible; then $L(s) = L(s_1)$ and $L(s_2) = L(r)$. Consequently,

$$s\, s_1\, r \sim_{st} s\, s_2\, r.$$

12.3   Partial Order Reduction for LTL$_{-X}$

When the specification is invariant under stuttering, commutativity and invisibility allow us to avoid generating some of the states. Based on this observation, we suggest a systematic way of selecting an ample set of transitions for any given state. The ample sets will be used by the DFS algorithm to construct a reduced state graph so that for every path not considered by the DFS algorithm there is a stuttering-equivalent path that is considered. This guarantees that the reduced state graph is stuttering equivalent to the full state graph.

We say that state s is *fully expanded* when $ample(s) = enabled(s)$. In this case, all of the successors of that state will be explored by the DFS algorithm.

Instead of giving a specific algorithm for constructing ample sets, we first provide four conditions for selecting $ample(s) \subseteq enabled(s)$ such that the satisfaction of the LTL$_{-X}$ specification is preserved. The reduction will depend on the set of propositions AP' that appear in the LTL$_{-X}$ formula.

Condition **C0** guarantees that, if the state has at least one successor, then the reduced state graph also contains a successor for this state:

C0 $ample(s) = \emptyset$ if and only if $enabled(s) = \emptyset$.

Condition **C1** is the most complicated among the constraints on $ample(s)$:

C1 [244, 300, 397, 465] Along every path in the full state graph that starts at s, the following condition holds: a transition that is dependent on a transition in $ample(s)$ cannot be executed without a transition in $ample(s)$ occurring first.

Note that Condition **C1** refers to paths in the *full* state graph. We need a way of checking that **C1** holds without actually constructing the full state graph. Later, we show how to restrict **C1** so that *ample*(s) can be calculated based on the current state s.

Lemma 12.3 *The transitions in enabled*(s) \ *ample*(s) *are all independent of those in* *ample*(s).

Proof Let $\gamma \in$ *enabled*(s) \ *ample*(s). Suppose that $(\gamma, \delta) \in D$, where $\delta \in$ *ample*(s). Since γ is enabled in s, in the full graph there is a path starting with γ. But then a transition dependent on some transition in *ample*(s) is executed before a transition in *ample*(s), contradicting condition **C1**.   □

In order to guarantee the correctness of the DFS reduction algorithm, we need to know that, if we always choose the next transition to explore from *ample*(s), we do not omit any paths that are essential for checking the correctness of the state graph. Condition **C1** implies that such a path will have one of two forms:

- The path has a prefix $\beta_0 \beta_1 \ldots \beta_m \alpha$, where $\alpha \in$ *ample*(s) and each β_i is independent of all transitions in *ample*(s) including α.
- The path is an infinite sequence of transitions $\beta_0 \beta_1 \ldots$, where each β_i is independent of all transitions in *ample*(s).

Condition **C1** also implies that, if along a finite sequence of transitions $\beta_0 \beta_1 \ldots \beta_m$ executed from s, none of the transitions in *ample*(s) have occurred, then all the transitions in *ample*(s) remain enabled. This is because each β_i is independent of the transitions in *ample*(s) and, therefore, cannot disable them.

In the first case, assume that the sequence of transitions $\beta_0 \beta_1 \ldots \beta_m \alpha$ reaches a state r. This sequence will not be considered by the DFS algorithm. However, by applying the enabledness and commutativity conditions m times, we can construct a finite sequence $\alpha \beta_0 \beta_1 \ldots \beta_m$ that also reaches r. This is illustrated in figure 12.5. In other words, even if the reduced state graph does not contain the sequence $\beta_0 \beta_1 \ldots \beta_m \alpha$ that reaches the state r, we can still construct from s another sequence that reaches the same state r.

Consider the two sequences of states $\sigma = s_0 s_1 \ldots s_m r$ and $\rho = s r_0 r_1 \ldots r_m$ in figure 12.5, generated by $\beta_0 \beta_1 \ldots \beta_m \alpha$ and $\alpha \beta_0 \beta_1 \ldots \beta_m$, respectively. In order to discard σ, we want σ and ρ to be stuttering equivalent. This is guaranteed if α is invisible, since then $L(s_i) = L(r_i)$ for $0 \le i \le m$. Thus, the checked property will not be able to distinguish between the two sequences above. This can be achieved by condition **C2**:

C2 [*Invisibility* [398]] If s is not fully expanded, then every $\alpha \in$ *ample*(s) is invisible.

Consider now the second case, in which an infinite path $\beta_0 \beta_1 \beta_2 \ldots$ that starts at s does not include any transition from *ample*(s). By condition **C2** all transitions in *ample*(s) are invisible. Let α be such a transition in *ample*(s). Then the path generated by the infinite sequence of transitions $\alpha \beta_0 \beta_1 \beta_2 \ldots$ is stuttering equivalent to the one generated

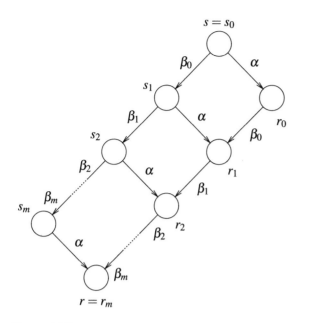

Figure 12.5
Transition α commutes with $\beta_0 \beta_1 \ldots \beta_m$.

by $\beta_0 \beta_1 \beta_2 \ldots$. Again, even though the path $\beta_0 \beta_1 \beta_2 \ldots$ is not included in the reduced state graph, there is a stuttering-equivalent path that is included.

Conditions **C1** and **C2** are not yet sufficient to guarantee that the reduced state graph is stuttering equivalent to the full state graph. In fact, there is a possibility that some transition will actually be delayed forever because of a cycle in the constructed state graph. As an example, consider the processes in figure 12.6. Assume that the transition β is independent of the transitions α_1, α_2, and α_3. The transitions α_1, α_2, and α_3 are interdependent. The process on the left can execute the visible transition β exactly once. Assume that there is one proposition p, which is changed from *true* to *false* by β, so that β is visible. The process on the right performs the invisible transitions α_1, α_2, and α_3 repeatedly in a loop.

The full state graph of the system in figure 12.6 is shown on the left in figure 12.7. The right side of the figure shows the first stages of constructing the reduced state graph, where α_1, α_2 and α_3 are invisible. Starting with the initial state s_1, we can select $ample(s_1) = \{\alpha_1\}$. Conditions **C0**, **C1**, and **C2** are satisfied. Thus, we generate $s_2 = \alpha_1(s_1)$. Similarly, we can select $ample(s_2) = \{\alpha_2\}$, generating $s_3 = \alpha_2(s_2)$. Finally, reaching s_3, conditions **C0**, **C1** and **C2** allow selecting $ample(s_3) = \{\alpha_3\}$. But, the reduced state graph generated in this way does not contain any sequences where p is changed from *true* to *false*. The problem is

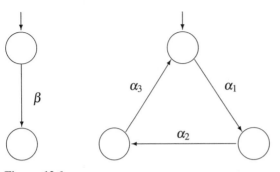

Figure 12.6
Two concurrent processes.

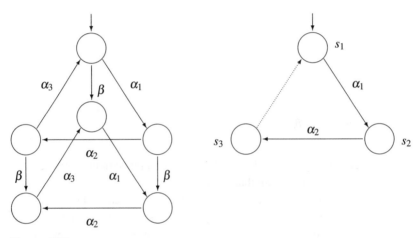

Figure 12.7
Full and reduced state graph.

that each state along the cycle s_1, s_2, s_3, s_1 has deferred β to a possible future state. When the cycle is closed, the construction terminates, and transition β is ignored.

To remedy this problem, we add the following condition:

C3 [*Cycle condition* [397, 110]] A cycle is not allowed if it contains a state in which some transition α is enabled, but is never included in *ample(s)* for any state s on the cycle.

We are now able to address problems 1 and 2 described in the previous section. Consider figure 12.3 again. Assume that the DFS reduction algorithm chooses β as *ample(s)* and does not include state s_1 in the reduced graph.

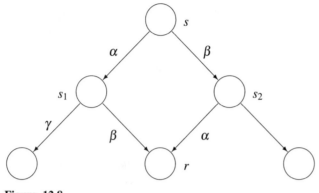

Figure 12.8
Diagram illustrating problem 2.

We consider problem 1 first. By condition **C2**, β must be invisible; thus s, s_2, r and s, s_1, r are stuttering equivalent. In this chapter we are interested only in properties that are invariant under stuttering. Such properties will not be able to distinguish between the two sequences.

We next consider problem 2. Assume that there is a transition γ enabled from s_1, as in figure 12.8. We show that γ is still enabled at state r. Moreover, the transition sequences α, γ and β, α, γ lead to stuttering equivalent state sequences. We first note that γ cannot be dependent on β. Otherwise, the sequence α, γ violates condition **C1**, since a transition dependent on β is executed before β. Thus, γ is independent of β. Since it is enabled in s_1, it must also be enabled in state r. Assume that γ, when executed from r, results in state r', and when executed from s_1, results in state s_1'. Since β is invisible, the two state sequences s, s_1, s_1' and s, s_2, r, r' are stuttering equivalent. Therefore, properties that are invariant under stuttering will not distinguish between the two.

12.4 An Example

Consider the mutual exclusion program P, presented in chapter 3. The state graph for P is given in figure 12.9. The states of the program are labeled with $AP = \{NC_i, CR_i, l_i, turn = i, \bot \mid i = 0, 1\}$, where $CR_i \in L(s)$ if $pc_i = CR_i$ in the state s, and $CR_i \notin L(s)$ if $pc_i \neq CR_i$ in s. The labeling $L(s)$ is defined similarly for all other atomic propositions in AP.

Let $f = \mathbf{G} \neg (CR_0 \wedge CR_1)$ be an LTL$_{-X}$ formula describing the mutual exclusion property. We will show how the DFS algorithm of figure 12.2 can be used to construct a reduced state graph that is stuttering equivalent to the full state graph with respect to a subset AP' of the atomic propositions. Since we are interested in checking whether P satisfies f, we choose $AP' = \{CR_0, CR_1\}$.

Following is a list of the transitions of the program P that are enabled in some reachable state of P, where $i = 0, 1$. For brevity we omitted $same(pc_j)$ for $j \neq i$ from each of the transitions.

$$\alpha : \quad pc = m \,\wedge\, pc'_0 = l_0 \,\wedge\, pc'_1 = l_1 \,\wedge\, pc' = \bot \,\wedge\, same(turn)$$

$$\beta_i : \quad pc_i = l_i \,\wedge\, pc'_i = NC_i \,\wedge\, true \,\wedge\, same(turn)$$

$$\gamma_i : \quad pc_i = NC_i \,\wedge\, pc'_i = CR_i \,\wedge\, turn = i \,\wedge\, same(turn)$$

$$\delta_i : \quad pc_i = CR_i \,\wedge\, pc'_i = l_i \,\wedge\, turn' = (i+1) \bmod 2$$

$$\varepsilon_i : \quad pc_i = NC_i \,\wedge\, pc'_i = NC_i \,\wedge\, turn \neq i \,\wedge\, same(turn)$$

The visible transitions with respect to AP' are those in which CR_0 or CR_1 has different values before and after the transition. Thus, $\{\gamma_0, \gamma_1, \delta_0, \delta_1\}$ are visible.

Each transition is dependent on itself since the dependency relation is reflexive. All of the transitions are dependent on α since it must be executed before any other transition in the program. The dependency relation for the remaining transitions is calculated using the following two rules:

- Two transitions that change the same variable (including the program counters) are dependent.
- If one transition sets a variable and the other checks that variable, then the transitions are dependent.

Thus, all of the transitions in the same process are interdependent. Also, (γ_1, δ_0), (γ_0, δ_1), $(\varepsilon_1, \delta_0)$, $(\varepsilon_0, \delta_1)$, (δ_0, δ_1) are in D since δ_i changes the variable *turn*, while γ_i and ε_i check its value. Finally, we complete the relation D to be symmetric.

Figure 12.9 shows the full state graph. The states and edges included in the reduced state graph are shown using thick lines. The states of the reduced state graph in the order they are visited by the DFS algorithm follow: $s_0, s_1, s_3, s_4, s_6, s_{10}, s_{11}, s_{13}, s_7, s_8$.

The DFS algorithm starts with s_0 which is one of the two initial states. For this state, $ample(s_0) = enabled(s_0) = \{\alpha\}$. For s_1, it is possible to select as $ample(s_1)$ either $\{\beta_0\}$, $\{\beta_1\}$, or $\{\beta_0, \beta_1\}$. The latter choice usually results in a smaller reduction and therefore is not considered. The first choice corresponds to selecting the enabled transitions of P_0, while the second choice corresponds to selecting P_1. Condition **C0** is trivially satisfied. In both cases, **C1** is satisfied. For example, suppose that $ample(s_1) = \{\beta_0\}$; then along all paths leaving s_1, either β_0 is immediately executed or β_1 is executed before β_0. However, β_1 is independent of β_0.

Condition **C2** is also satisfied, since β_0 and β_1 are invisible. Finally, **C3** is satisfied since no cycle is yet formed. The choice between the two sets is arbitrary, although one may provide a better reduction in a later stages of the algorithm. We select $ample(s_1) = \{\beta_0\}$.

Executing β_0 from s_1 results in the state s_3. By using a similar argument, we select as $ample(s_3)$, the transitions of P_1 that are enabled in s_3, namely $\{\beta_1\}$. Next, we select $ample(s_4) = \{\gamma_0, \varepsilon_1\}$. We cannot select for s_4 the set $\{\gamma_0\}$, since γ_0 is visible. We also

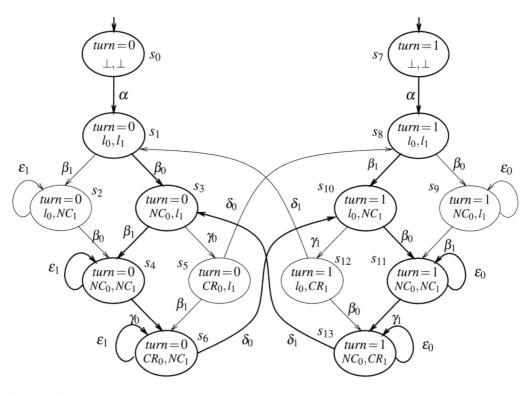

Figure 12.9
Full and reduced (thick lines) state graph for a mutual exclusion program.

cannot select the singleton $\{\varepsilon_1\}$, since this will construct a self loop on which the transition γ_0 is enabled but never included in an ample set, thus violating condition **C3**.

We can now select, $ample(s_6) = \{\varepsilon_1, \delta_0\}$. Since they are dependent we have to choose both in order not to violate condition **C1**. For states s_{10} and s_{11} we choose $ample(s_{10}) = \{\beta_0\}$ and $ample(s_{11}) = \{\gamma_1, \varepsilon_0\}$. The arguments are similar to the ones for states s_3 and s_4, respectively. We next select $ample(s_{13}) = \{\delta_1, \varepsilon_0\}$. The transition δ_1 taken from s_{13} closes the cycle $s_3 s_4 s_6 s_{10} s_{11} s_{13}$. By examining figure 12.9 it is easy to check that condition **C3** is satisfied for this cycle.

The DFS algorithm continues the search from the other initial state s_7. We select $ample(s_7) = \{\alpha\}$. Based on arguments similar to those for s_1, we also select $ample(s_8) = \{\beta_1\}$. By executing β_1 from s_8, we reach only the state s_{10} that has already been visited. Thus, the algorithm terminates.

A model-checking algorithm for LTL can now be applied to check if the reduced state graph constructed by the algorithm satisfies the formula $\mathbf{A} f$ since $\mathbf{A} f \in \text{LTL}_{-X}$. The full state graph satisfies the formula if and only if the reduced state graph does.

12.5   Calculating Ample Sets

12.5.1   The Complexity of Checking the Conditions

In order to make partial order reduction efficient, we need to be able to calculate the ample sets for the states in the reduced graph with minimal overhead. We will consider the related problem of checking conditions **C0** to **C3** for a set of enabled transitions at a given state. Condition **C0** for a particular state can be checked in constant time. Condition **C2** is also simple to check, by examining the transitions in the set.

Condition **C1** is a constraint that is not immediately checkable by examining the current state of the search, since it refers to future states (some of which need not even be in the reduced state graph). The next theorem shows that, in general, checking **C1** is at least as hard as searching the full state space.

Theorem 12.4   *Checking condition* **C1** *for a state s and a set of transitions* $T \subseteq enabled(s)$ *is at least as hard as checking reachability for the full state space.*

Proof   Consider checking whether a state r is reachable in a transition system $\mathcal{T}$ from an initial state s_0. We will reduce this problem to deciding condition **C1**. First, let α and β be new transitions. Let the transition α be only enabled at the state r. Let the transition β be enabled from the initial state and independent of all the transitions of $\mathcal{T}$. We construct β and α so that they are dependent (for example, they both change the value of the same variable).

Consider $\{\beta\}$ as a candidate for being an ample set from s_0. First assume that **C1** is violated. Then there is a path in the new state graph along which α is performed before β. Since α is enabled only in r, this path leads from s_0 to r. The sequence of transitions on the path from s_0 to r also exists in the original state graph, since it does not include the added transitions α or β. Thus, r is reachable from s_0 in the original system.

For the other direction, assume that r is reachable in the original state graph from s_0. Then, there is a sequence from s_0 to r, which does not include β. This sequence also appears in the new state graph, and now can be extended by the transition α taken from r. The resulting sequence violates **C1**.   □

In view of the previous theorem, we will avoid checking condition **C1** for an arbitrary subset of enabled transitions. In section 12.5.2 we give a procedure to compute a set of transitions that is guaranteed by construction to satisfy **C1**. Although the procedure may not lead to ample sets that achieve the greatest possible reduction, it is quite efficient. There is evidently a trade-off between efficiency of computation and the amount of reduction.

Condition **C3** is also defined in global terms. However, it refers to the reduced state graph, whereas **C1** refers to the full state graph. A possible way of implementing this constraint is to first generate a reduced state graph and then to *correct* it by adding additional transitions until it satisfies **C3** [464]. On the other hand, the approach we take replaces **C3** by a stronger condition that can be checked directly on the current state.

Lemma 12.5 *A sufficient condition for* **C3** *is that at least one state along each cycle is fully expanded.*

Proof   Assume there is a cycle with a fully expanded state, but the cycle does not satisfy condition **C3**. Thus, we have some transition α that is enabled in some state s of the cycle but is never included in an ample set along the cycle. By lemma 12.3, if α is not included in an ample set then it is independent of all the transitions in it. Thus, α is independent of all transitions in the ample sets selected along the cycle. Consequently, it remains enabled in all the states along the cycle. However, if one of the states s' is fully expanded, meaning that $ample(s') = enabled(s')$, α is necessarily included in $ample(s')$. This contradicts the assumption that α is never selected. $\square$

Efficient ways of enforcing **C3** are based on the specific search strategy that is used to generate the reduced state space. For depth-first search, we can use the fact that every cycle includes an edge that goes back to a node on the search stack. Such an edge is also called a *back edge*. Thus, we strengthen **C3** in the following manner.

C3′ If s is not fully expanded, then no transition in $ample(s)$ may reach a state that is on the search stack.

We thus always try to select an ample set that does not include a back edge. If we do not succeed, the current state is fully expanded.

In breadth-first search, the search progresses in levels, where level k consists of a set of states reachable from the initial state using k transitions. A necessary condition for closing a cycle during breadth-first search is the following: a transition applied to a state s in the current level either results in s itself, in which case there is a self loop, or results in a state s' at a previous level of the breadth-first search. This condition is not sufficient, however, since s' may not be an ancestor of the current state. Consequently, using this condition to detect when a cycle is closed may cause more states than necessary to be fully expanded.

12.5.2   Heuristics for Calculating Ample Sets

In view of the complexity results in section 12.5.1, we give some heuristics for calculating ample sets. The algorithm depends on the model of computation. We will consider shared variables and message passing with handshaking and with queues.

Common to all of these models of computation is the notion of a *program counter*, which is part of the state. We will denote the program counter of a process P_i in a state s by $pc_i(s)$.

In order to present the algorithm, we will use the following notation:

- $pre(\alpha)$ is a set of transitions that includes the transitions whose execution may enable α. More formally, $pre(\alpha)$ includes all the transitions β such that there exists a state s for which $\alpha \notin enabled(s)$, $\beta \in enabled(s)$, and $\alpha \in enabled(\beta(s))$.
- $dep(\alpha)$ is the set of transitions that are dependent on α; that is,

$$\{\beta \mid (\beta, \alpha) \in D\}.$$

- T_i is the set of transitions of process P_i. $T_i(s) = T_i \cap enabled(s)$ denotes the set of transitions of P_i that are enabled in the state s.
- $current_i(s)$ is the set of transitions of P_i that are enabled in some state s' such that $pc_i(s') = pc_i(s)$. The set $current_i(s)$ always contains $T_i(s)$. In addition, it may include transitions whose program counter has the value $pc_i(s)$, but are not enabled in s.

Note that, on any path starting from s, some transition in $current_i(s)$ must be executed before other transitions of T_i can execute. The definitions of $pre(\alpha)$ and the dependency relation D (which directly effects $dep(\alpha)$) may not be exact: The set $pre(\alpha)$ may contain transitions that do not enable α. Likewise, the dependency relation D may also include pairs of transitions that are actually independent. This freedom makes it possible to calculate ample sets efficiently while still preserving the correctness of the reduction.

The above definitions are extended to sets in the natural way. For instance, $dep(T) = \bigcup_{\alpha \in T} dep(\alpha)$.

Next, we specialize $pre(\alpha)$ for various models of computation. Recall that $pre(\alpha)$ includes all transitions whose execution from some state can enable α. We construct $pre(\alpha)$ as follows:

- The set $pre(\alpha)$ includes the transitions of the processes that contain α and that can change the program counter to a value from which α can execute.
- If the enabling condition for α involves shared variables then $pre(\alpha)$ includes all other transitions that can change these shared variables.
- If α involves message passing with queues, that is, α sends or receives data on some queue q, then $pre(\alpha)$ includes the transitions of other processes that receive or send data, respectively, through q.

We now describe the dependency relation for the different models of computation.

1. Pairs of transitions that share a variable, which is changed by at least one of them, are dependent.
2. Pairs of transitions belonging to the same process are dependent. This includes in particular pairs of transitions in $current_i(s)$ for any given state s and process P_i. Note that a transition that involves handshaking or rendezvous communication as in CSP or ADA can be treated as a joint transition of both processes. Therefore, it depends on all of the transitions of both processes.

3. Two send transitions that use the same message queue are dependent. This is because executing one may cause the message queue to fill, disabling the other. Also, the contents of the queue depends on their order of execution. Similarly, two receive transitions are dependent.

Note that a pair of send and receive transitions in different processes that use the same message queue are independent. This is because any one of these transitions can potentially enable the other but cannot disable it.

An obvious candidate for *ample*(s) is the set $T_i(s)$ of transitions enabled in s for some process P_i. Since the transitions in $T_i(s)$ are interdependent, an ample set for s must include either all of the transitions or none of them. To construct an ample set for the current state s, we start with some process P_i such that $T_i(s) \neq \emptyset$. We want to check whether *ample*(s) = $T_i(s)$ satisfies condition **C1**. There are two cases in which this selection might violate **C1**. In both of these cases, some transitions independent of those in $T_i(s)$ are executed, eventually enabling a transition α that is dependent on $T_i(s)$. The independent transitions in the sequence cannot be in T_i, since all the transitions of P_i are interdependent.

1. In the first case, α belongs to some other process P_j. A necessary condition for this to happen is that $dep(T_i(s))$ includes a transition of process P_j. By examining the dependency relation, this condition can be checked effectively.

2. In the second case, α belongs to P_i. Suppose that the transition $\alpha \in T_i$ that violates **C1** is executed from a state s'. The transitions executed on the path from s to s' are independent of $T_i(s)$ and hence, are from other processes. Therefore, $pc_i(s') = pc_i(s)$, so α must be in *current*$_i(s)$. In addition, $\alpha \notin T_i(s)$, otherwise it does not violate **C1**. Thus, $\alpha \in current_i(s) \setminus T_i(s)$.

   Since α is not in $T_i(s)$, it is disabled in s. Therefore, a transition in $pre(\alpha)$ must be included in the sequence from s to s'. A necessary condition for this case is that $pre(current_i(s) \setminus T_i(s))$ includes transitions of processes other than P_i. This condition can also be checked effectively.

In both cases we discard $T_i(s)$ as an ample set, and can try the transitions $T_j(s)$ of another process j as a candidate for *ample*(s). Note that we take a conservative approach discarding some ample sets even though at run time it might be that condition **C1** would actually not be violated.

The code in figure 12.10 checks condition **C1** for the enabled transitions of a process P_i, as explained above.

The function *check_C2* (figure 12.11) is given a set of transitions and returns *true* if all of the transitions in the set are invisible. Otherwise, it returns *false*.

The procedure *check_C3'* (figure 12.12) tests whether the execution of a transition in a given set $X \subseteq enabled(s)$ is still on the search stack. For that, we can use our marking of

function $check\_C1(s, P_i)$
   for all $P_j \neq P_i$ **do**
      if $dep(T_i(s)) \cap T_j \neq \emptyset$ **or** $pre(current_i(s) \setminus T_i(s)) \cap T_j \neq \emptyset$ **then**
         return *false*;
      end if
   end for all
   return *true*;
end function

Figure 12.10
Code for checking condition **C1** for the enabled transitions of a process P_i.

function $check\_C2(X)$
   for all $\alpha \in X$ **do**
      if $visible(\alpha)$ **then return** *false*;
   end for all
   return *true*;
end function

Figure 12.11
Code for checking whether the transitions in the given set are invisible.

function $check\_C3'(s, X)$
   for all $\alpha \in X$ **do**
      if $on\_stack(\alpha(s))$ **then return** *false*;
   end for all
   return *true*;
end function

Figure 12.12
Code for testing whether the execution of a transition in a given set is still on the search stack.

function *ample*(*s*)
    for all P_i **such that** $T_i(s) \neq \emptyset$ **do**
        if *check_C1*(*s*, P_i) **and** *check_C2*($T_i(s)$) **and** *check_C3*(*s*, $T_i(s)$) **then**
            return $T_i(s)$;
        end if
    end for all
    return *enabled*(*s*);
end function

Figure 12.13
ample(*s*) tries to find a process P_i such that $T_i(s)$ satisfies conditions **C0–C3**.

the states as *on_stack* or *completed* in figure 12.2. Recall that a state is *on_stack* when the state is on the search stack.

The algorithm for *ample*(*s*) (figure 12.13) tries to find a process P_i such that $T_i(s)$ satisfies all the conditions **C0** to **C3**. If no such process can be found, *ample* returns the set *enabled*(*s*).

The SPIN [270, 273] system includes an implementation [272] of partial order reduction. The heuristics used for selecting ample sets are similar to the ones described in this section. However, in SPIN, for many of the states, conditions **C0**, **C1**, and **C2** are precomputed when the system being verified is translated into its internal representation.

12.6   Correctness of the Algorithm

Let M be the full state graph of some system. Let M' be a reduced state graph constructed using the partial order reduction algorithm described in section 12.1.

A *string* is a sequence of transitions from T. Denote by *vis*(*v*), where *v* is either a finite or infinite string, the projection of *v* onto the visible transitions. Thus, if *a* and *b* are visible and *c* and *d* are not, then *vis*(*abddbcbaac*) = *abbbaa*. Let $tr(\sigma)$ be the sequence of transitions on a path σ. Let *v*, *w* be two finite strings. We write $v \sqsubset w$ if *v* can be obtained from *w* by erasing one or more transitions. For example *abbcd* $\sqsubset$ *aabcbccde*. We denote $v \sqsubseteq w$ if either $v = w$ or $v \sqsubset w$.

Let $\sigma \circ \eta$ denote the concatenation of the paths σ and η of M, where σ is finite, and the last state $last(\sigma)$ of σ is the same as the first state $first(\eta)$ of η. The *length* of a path σ, denoted $|\sigma|$, is the number of edges of σ.

Let σ be some infinite path of the full state graph M, starting with some initial state. We will construct an infinite sequence of paths $\pi_0, \pi_1, \ldots$, where $\pi_0 = \sigma$. Each path π_i will be decomposed into $\eta_i \circ \theta_i$, where η_i is of length i. Assuming that we have constructed the paths $\pi_0, \ldots, \pi_i$, we describe how to construct $\pi_{i+1} = \eta_{i+1} \circ \theta_{i+1}$. Let $s_0 = last(\eta_i) = first(\theta_i)$, and let α the transition labeling the first edge of θ_i. Denote $\theta_i = s_0 \xrightarrow{\alpha_0 = \alpha} s_1 \xrightarrow{\alpha_1} s_2 \xrightarrow{\alpha_2} \dots$. There are two cases:

A $\alpha \in ample(s_0)$. Then select $\eta_{i+1} = \eta_i \circ (s_0 \xrightarrow{\alpha} \alpha(s_0))$. θ_{i+1} is $s_1 \xrightarrow{\alpha_1} s_2 \xrightarrow{\alpha_2} \dots$; that is, θ_i without its first edge.

B $\alpha \notin ample(s_0)$. By **C2**, all of the transitions in $ample(s_0)$ must be invisible since s_0 is not fully expanded. Here again, there are two cases, **B1** and **B2**:

> **B1.** Some $\beta \in ample(s_0)$ appears on θ_i after some sequence of independent transitions $\alpha_0 \alpha_1 \alpha_2 \dots \alpha_{k-1}$; that is, $\beta = \alpha_k$. Then there is a path $\xi = s_0 \xrightarrow{\beta} \beta(s_0) \xrightarrow{\alpha_0 = \alpha} \beta(s_1) \xrightarrow{\alpha_1} \dots \xrightarrow{\alpha_{k-1}} \beta(s_k) \xrightarrow{\alpha_{k+1}} s_{k+2} \xrightarrow{\alpha_{k+2}} \dots$ in M. That is, β is moved to appear before $\alpha_0 \alpha_1 \alpha_2 \dots \alpha_{k-1}$. Note that $\beta(s_k) = s_{k+1}$. Therefore, $\beta(s_k) \xrightarrow{\alpha_{k+1}} s_{k+2}$ is the same as $s_{k+1} \xrightarrow{\alpha_{k+1}} s_{k+2}$.
>
> **B2.** Some $\beta \in ample(s_0)$ is independent of all the transitions that appear on θ_i. Then there is a path $\xi = s_0 \xrightarrow{\beta} \beta(s_0) \xrightarrow{\alpha_0 = \alpha} \beta(s_1) \xrightarrow{\alpha_1} \beta(s_2) \xrightarrow{\alpha_2} \dots$ in M. That is, β is executed from s_0 and then applied to each state of θ_i.

In both cases, $\eta_{i+1} = \eta_i \circ (s_0 \xrightarrow{\beta} \beta(s_0))$, and θ_{i+1} is the path that is obtained from ξ by removing the first transition $s_0 \xrightarrow{\beta} \beta(s_0)$.

Let η be the path such that the prefix of length i is η_i. The path η is well defined since η_i is constructed from η_{i-1} by appending a single transition.

Lemma 12.6 *The following hold for all i, j such that $j \geq i \geq 0$:*

1. $\pi_i \sim_{st} \pi_j$.
2. $vis(tr(\pi_i)) = vis(tr(\pi_j))$.
3. *Let ξ_i be a prefix of π_i, and ξ_j be a prefix of π_j, such that $vis(tr(\xi_i)) = vis(tr(\xi_j))$. Then $L(last(\xi_i)) = L(last(\xi_j))$.*

Proof It is sufficient to consider the case where $j = i + 1$. Consider the three ways of constructing π_{i+1} from π_i. In case **A**, $\pi_i = \pi_{i+1}$, and all three parts of the lemma hold trivially.

Next, consider case **B1** of the construction, in which π_{i+1} is obtained from π_i by executing some invisible transition β in π_{i+1} earlier than it is executed in π_i. In this case, we replace the sequence $s_0 \xrightarrow{\alpha_0} s_1 \xrightarrow{\alpha_1} \dots \xrightarrow{\alpha_{k-2}} s_{k-1} \xrightarrow{\beta} s_k$ by $s_0 \xrightarrow{\beta} \beta(s_0) \xrightarrow{\alpha_0} \beta(s_1) \xrightarrow{\alpha_1} \dots \xrightarrow{\alpha_{k-1}} \beta(s_k)$. Since β is invisible, corresponding states have the same label; that is, for each $0 < l \leq k$, $L(s_l) = L(\beta(s_l))$. Also, the order of the visible transitions remains unchanged. Parts 1, 2, and 3 follow immediately.

Finally, in case **B2** of the construction, the difference between π_i and π_{i+1} is that π_{i+1} includes an additional invisible transition β. Thus, we replace some suffix $s_0 \xrightarrow{\alpha_0} s_1 \xrightarrow{\alpha_1} \dots$ of π_i by $s_0 \xrightarrow{\beta} \beta(s_0) \xrightarrow{\alpha_0 = \alpha} \beta(s_1) \xrightarrow{\alpha_1} \beta(s_2) \xrightarrow{\alpha_2} \dots$. So, $L(s_l) = L(\beta(s_l))$ for $l \geq 0$. Again, the order of the visible transitions remains unchanged. As in the previous case, parts 1, 2, and 3 follow immediately. □

Lemma 12.7 *Let η be the path constructed as the limit of the finite paths η_i. Then, η belongs to the reduced state graph M'.*

Proof The proof is by induction on the length of the prefixes η_i of η. The base case is that η_0 is a single node, which is an initial state in S. According to the reduction algorithms, all the initial states are included in S' as well. For the inductive step, assume that η_i is in M'. Then notice that η_{i+1} is obtained from η_i by appending a transition from $ample(last(\eta_i))$. □

The following three lemmas will be used to show that the path η that is constructed as the limit of the finite paths η_i contains all of the visible transitions of σ, and in the same order.

Lemma 12.8 *Let α be the first transition on θ_i. Then there exists $j > i$ such that α is the last transition of η_j, and for $i \leq k < j$, α is the first transition of θ_k.*

Proof According to the above construction, if α is the first transition of θ_k, then either it is the first transition of θ_{k+1} (case **B**), or it will become the last transition of η_{k+1} (case **A**). We need to show that the first case cannot hold for every $k \geq i$. Suppose, on the contrary, that this is the case. Let $s_k = first(\theta_k)$. Consider the infinite sequence $s_i, s_{i+1}, \ldots$. According to the above construction, $s_{k+1} = \gamma_k(s_k)$ for some $\gamma_k \in ample(s_k)$. Moreover, since α is the first transition of θ_k and was not selected in case **A** to be moved to η_{k+1}, α must be in $enabled(s_k) \setminus ample(s_k)$. Since the number of states in S is finite, there is some state s_k that is the first to repeat on the sequence $s_i, s_{i+1}, \ldots$. Thus, there is a cycle $s_k, s_{k+1}, \ldots, s_r$, with $s_r = s_k$, where α does not appear in any of the ample sets. This violates condition **C3**. □

Lemma 12.9 *Let γ be the first visible transition on θ_i, and let $\text{prefix}_\gamma(\theta_i)$ be the maximal prefix of $tr(\theta_i)$ that does not contain γ. Then one of the following holds:*

- *γ is the first transition of θ_i and the last transition of η_{i+1}, or*
- *γ is the first visible transition of θ_{i+1}, the last transition of η_{i+1} is invisible, and $\text{prefix}_\gamma(\theta_{i+1}) \sqsubseteq \text{prefix}_\gamma(\theta_i)$.*

Proof The first case of the lemma holds when γ is selected from $ample(s_i)$ and becomes the last transition of η_{i+1}, according to case **A** of the construction. If this does not happen, there exists another transition β that is appended to η_i to form η_{i+1}. The transition β cannot be visible. Otherwise, according to condition **C2**, $ample(s_i) = enabled(s_i)$. By case **B1** of the construction, β must be the first transition of θ_i. But then β is a visible transition that precedes γ in θ_i, a contradiction.

There are three possibilities:

1. β appears on θ_i before γ (case **B1** in the construction),
2. β appears on θ_i after γ (case **B1** in the construction), or

3. β is independent of all the transitions of θ_i (case **B2** in the construction).

According to the above construction, in possibility 1, $prefix_\gamma(\theta_{i+1}) \sqsubset prefix_\gamma(\theta_i)$, since β is removed from the prefix of θ_i before γ when constructing θ_{i+1}. In possibilities 2 and 3, $prefix_\gamma(\theta_{i+1}) = prefix_\gamma(\theta_i)$ since the prefix of θ_{i+1} that precedes the transition γ has the same transitions as the corresponding prefix of θ_i. $\square$

Lemma 12.10 *Let v be a prefix of $vis(tr(\sigma))$. Then there exists a path η_i such that $v = vis(tr(\eta_i))$.*

Proof   The proof is by induction on the length of v. The base holds trivially for $|v| = 0$. In the inductive step we must prove that if $v\gamma$ is a prefix of $vis(tr(\sigma))$ and there is a path η_i such that $vis(tr(\eta_i)) = v$, then there is a path η_j with $j > i$ such that $vis(tr(\eta_j)) = v\gamma$. Thus, we need to show that γ will be eventually added to η_j for some $j > i$, and that no other visible transition will be added to η_k for $i < k < j$. According to case **A** in the construction, we may add a visible transition to the end of η_k to form η_{k+1} only if it appears as the first transition of θ_k. Lemma 12.9 shows that γ remains the first visible transition in successive paths θ_k after θ_i unless it is being added to some η_j. Moreover, the sequence of transitions before γ can only shrink. Lemma 12.8 shows that the first transition in each θ_k is eventually removed and added to the end of some η_l for $l > k$. Thus, γ as well is eventually added to some sequence η_j. $\square$

Theorem 12.11   *The structures M and M' are stuttering equivalent.*

Proof   Each infinite path of M' that begins from an initial state must also be a path of M, since it is constructed by repeatedly applying transitions from the initial state. We need to show that for each path $\sigma = s_0 \xrightarrow{\alpha_0} s_1 \xrightarrow{\alpha_1} \dots$ in M, where s_0 is an initial state, there exists a path $\eta = r_0 \xrightarrow{\beta_0} r_1 \xrightarrow{\beta_1} \dots$ in M' such that $\sigma \sim_{st} \eta$. We will show that the path η that is constructed above for σ is indeed stuttering equivalent to σ.

First, we show that σ and η have the same sequence of visible transitions; that is,

$$vis(tr(\sigma)) = vis(tr(\eta)).$$

According to lemma 12.10, η contains the visible transitions of σ in the same order, since for any prefix of σ with m visible transitions, there is a prefix η_i of η with the same m visible transitions. On the other hand, σ must contain the visible transitions of η in the same order. Take any prefix η_i of η. According to lemma 12.6, $\pi_i = \eta_i \circ \theta_i$ has the same visible transitions as $\pi_0 = \sigma$. Thus, σ has a prefix with the same sequence of visible transitions as η_i.

We now construct two infinite sequences of indexes $0 = i_0 < i_1 < \dots$ and $0 = j_0 < j_1 < \dots$ that define corresponding stuttering blocks of σ and η, as required in the definition of stuttering. Assume that both $\sigma = \pi_0$ and η have at least n visible transitions. Let i_n be the length of the smallest prefix ξ_{i_n} of σ that contains exactly n visible transitions. Let j_n be the length of the smallest prefix η_{j_n} of η that contains the same sequence of visible transitions as ξ_{i_n}. Recall that η_{j_n} is a prefix of π_{j_n}. Then by part 3 of lemma 12.6, $L(s_{i_n}) = L(r_{j_n})$. By the definition of visible transitions we also know that if $n > 0$, for $i_{n-1} \leq k < i_n - 1$, $L(s_k) = L(s_{i_{n-1}})$. This is because i_{n-1} is the length of the smallest prefix $\xi_{i_{n-1}}$ of σ that contains exactly $n - 1$ visible transitions. Thus, there is no visible transition between i_{n-1} and $i_n - 1$. Similarly, for $j_{n-1} \leq l < j_n - 1$, $L(r_l) = L(r_{j_{n-1}})$.

If both σ and η have infinitely many visible transitions, then this process will construct two infinite sequences of indexes. In the case where σ and η contain only a finite number of visible transitions m, we have that, for $k > i_m$, $L(s_k) = L(s_{i_m})$, and for $l > j_m$, $L(r_l) = L(r_{j_m})$. We then set for $k \geq m$, $i_{k+1} = i_k + 1$, and $j_{k+1} = j_k + 1$. By the above, for $k \geq 0$, the blocks of states $s_{i_k}, s_{i_k+1}, \ldots, s_{i_{k+1}-1}$ and $r_{j_k}, r_{j_k+1}, \ldots, r_{j_{k+1}-1}$ are corresponding stuttering blocks that have the same labeling. Thus, $\sigma \sim_{st} \eta$. $\square$

12.7 Partial Order Reduction in SPIN

SPIN [270, 273] is an on the fly LTL model checker that uses explicit state enumeration and partial order reduction. It was developed at Bell Laboratories by Gerard Holzmann and Doron Peled. The tool is used primarily for verifying asynchronous software systems, in particular communication protocols. It can check a model of a program for deadlocks or unreachable code or determine if it satisfies an LTL specification, based on the translation algorithm [239] described in section 7.10. The tool uses partial order reduction [272, 398] to limit the state space that is searched.

The input language for SPIN, called PROMELA, was developed by Gerard Holzmann. This language uses syntactic constructs from several different programming languages. PROMELA expressions are inherited from the language C [302]. Thus, the language has the operators == (equals), ! = (not equals), || (logical or), && (logical and), and % (reminder modulo an integer). Assignment is denoted by a single = symbol. Negation is denoted by prefixing a Boolean expression by the operator !.

The syntax for communication commands is inherited from CSP [268]. Sending a message that contains the tag tg and the values $val_1, val_2, \ldots, val_n$ over channel ch is denoted by

$$ch!tg(val_1, val_2, \ldots, val_n)$$

in the sending process. Receiving a message with tag tg over channel ch is denoted by

$$ch?tg(var_1, var_2, \ldots, var_n)$$

in the receiving process. The message consists of n values that are stored in the variables $var_1, var_2, \ldots, var_n$. SPIN also allows untagged message passing. The language implements both message passing with queues and message passing using handshaking. In message passing with queues, a channel of some fixed length temporarily stores the values sent, so that the sending process can proceed to its next command, even if the receiving process

if   **do**
:: $guard_1 -> S_1$ :: $guard_1 -> S_1$
:: $guard_2 -> S_2$ :: $guard_2 -> S_2$

    $\vdots$ $\vdots$

:: $guard_n -> S_n$ :: $guard_n -> S_n$
fi   **od**

Figure 12.14
Conditionals and loops in SPIN.

is not yet ready to process the incoming data. In message passing with handshaking, a channel is defined in SPIN to be of length 0. Then, a send and a receive command with the same channel and tag (if a tag is present) are executed simultaneously. This results in the assignment of val_i to var_i, for $1 \leq i \leq n$.

The conditional constructs and loops are based on Dijkstra's *guarded commands* [180] and use the syntax in figure 12.14.

Each guard consists of a condition, a communication command, or both. In order for a guard to be *passable*, its condition must hold, and its communication command must not be blocked. In message passing with queues, a send command is blocked when the queue is full, and a receive command is blocked when the queue is empty. In message passing based on handshaking, communication is blocked when only one of the communicating processes is ready to send or to receive.

When executing the if construct and at each iteration of the do loop, one of the passable guards $guard_i$ is selected nondeterministically and then the corresponding command S_i is executed. A do loop repeats until either a goto command forces a branch to a particular label outside its scope, or a break command forces a skip to the first command after the do loop.

The reduction obtained by using the ample set technique described in section 12.3 is demonstrated using the *leader election* algorithm, which was developed by Dolev, Klawe, and Rodeh [183]. This algorithm operates on a ring of N processes. Each process initially has a unique number. The purpose of this algorithm is to find the largest number assigned to a process. The ring of processes is unidirectional; hence, each process can receive messages from its left and send messages to its right.

Initially, each process P_i is *active* and holds some integer value in its local variable my_val. As long as P_i is active, it is *responsible* for some value. This value may change during the execution of the algorithm. The current value of P_i is held in the variable max. A process becomes *passive* when it finds out that it does not hold a value that can be the maximum one. A passive process can pass messages only from left to right. Each active process P_i sends its own value to the right and then waits to receive the value of the closest active process P_j on its left. This value is received using a communication command tagged with one.

If the value received by P_i is the same as the value it sent, then P_i can conclude that it is the only active process and, hence, its value is the maximum. Then process P_i sends this value to the right with the tag winner. Every other process receives this value and sends it to the right exactly once, so that all the processes can learn the winning number.

If the value received by P_i is not the same as the value it sent, then P_i waits for a second message, tagged with two, that includes the value of the second closest active process on its left P_k. Then, P_i compares its own value with the two values it received from P_j and P_k. If the value received from P_j is the largest among the three, then P_i keeps this value. That is, P_i becomes responsible for the role of the closest active process P_j. Otherwise, P_i becomes passive.

The execution of the algorithm can be divided into phases. In each *phase*, except the last, all of the active processes receive messages tagged with one and two. In the last phase, the surviving process receives its own value via a message tagged with one and then this value is propagated around the ring.

The protocol guarantees low message complexity $O(N \times \log(N))$. This complexity bound holds because at least half of the active processes become passive in each phase. To see this, consider the case where P_i remains active. Then the value of P_j must be bigger than the values of P_i and P_k. If P_j also survives, then the value of P_k must be larger than the value of P_j. This is a contradiction. Thus, in each phase except for the last, if a process remains active, the first active process to its left must become passive. In each phase, the number of messages passed is limited to $2 \times N$, since each process receives two messages from its left neighbor.

The PROMELA code for the leader election algorithm appears in figure 12.15. We omit the code for initializing the processes. This includes assigning a distinct number to each process and starting the execution of that process. The channel $q[(i+1)\%N]$ is used to send messages from process P_i to process $P_{(i+1)\%N}$, where $\%N$ denotes the reminder modulo N.

The property that we checked is given by the LTL formula

$$noLeader \, \mathbf{U} \, \mathbf{G} \, oneLeader.$$

This formula asserts that in each execution there is no leader until some time in the future when a leader is selected. From that point onward, there is exactly one leader. The predicates *noLeader* and *oneLeader* in the property are defined as number_leaders == 0 and number_leaders == 1, respectively.

The negation of the checked property is automatically translated into a Büchi automaton, based on the algorithm described in section 7.10. An additional minimization stage combines nodes with the same branching structure. The automaton is described using a special syntactical construct of PROMELA called the *never claim*. The reason for this name is that the automaton, obtained by translating the negation of the checked property, represents the computations that should never happen. The never claim for the above property is shown in figure 12.16. The label of each initial node contains the word `init` and the label of each accepting node contains the word `accept`. SPIN intersects the automaton extracted from the program and the never claim automaton. This intersection is done on-the-fly, using the double DFS algorithm presented in section 7.5 and partial order reduction. If the intersection is not empty, an error trace is reported.

Bibliographic Notes

Exploiting commutativity between concurrent events, which stands in the basis of partial order reduction, was used in program verification in three ways: exploiting commutativity for reasoning due to partial order semantics [367] on representative sequences, obtaining a simpler and more intuitive proof [300], and verifying properties that are specific to the partial order semantics rather than the interleaving semantics [402].

The use of commutativity to reduce the space and time needed during model-checking was introduced in a series of papers by Godefroid, Peled, Valmari, and Wolper. One can partition these methods into two main groups: *prediction methods*, called *ample* sets [397], *persistent* sets [487] or *stubborn sets* [465], and *history-based elimination*, called *sleep sets* [241]. The prediction methods look at the current state, reached during the reduced state space search, and the independence between program transitions, and then choose a subset of the enabled transitions that is sufficient to explore enough executions to verify the system. The history based elimination methods aim at reducing the number of transitions used, but reaching *all* of the possible states.

Several subtle differences are used to tune partial order methods to become more efficient and cover a wider class of applications. First, a subtle point was raised with respect to repeatedly deferring some independent transition forever. Condition **C3** [398] in this chapter is provided to preserve LTL properties. A different condition was suggested in [271]. In [464] this problem was tackled using the analysis of strongly connected components, which leads to modifying the reduction. For history based elimination reduction, guaranteeing that every state is found in the presence of cycles, the algorithm in [72] presents a more moderate reduction than the one in [241], but also shows an example where the algorithm in [241] would fail to reach some states when cycles are possible in the state space. The independence between transitions used by partial order reduction is refined, to be state dependent in [301, 244]. Partial order reduction for branching temporal logic (CTL, CTL*) and process algebra is presented in [238, 466, 480].

A different approach for partial order reduction, called *unfolding*, was suggested by McMillan [368]. The idea was to keep a partial order structure representation [481] directly, rather than to reduce the number of interleavings that relate to the partial order structure.

Then, global states can be obtained as consistent combination of local states. This idea was further refined in [219].

Work on improving and expanding the use of partial order reduction is still active, with different ideas how to optimize the reduction (see, for instance, [403, 467, 223]). There is also a renewed interest in the technique coming from AI planning research [478]. Additional reading can be found in [35, 136].

```
#define noLeader        (number_leaders == 0)
#define oneLeader       (number_leaders == 1)

byte number_leaders = 0;

#define N      6        /* number of processes in the ring */
#define L      12       /* 2xN */
byte I;

mtype = { one, two, winner };
chan q[N] = [L] of { mtype, byte };

proctype P (chan in, out; byte my_val)
{       bit Active = 1, know_winner = 0;
        byte number, max = my_val, neighbor;

        out!one(my_val);
        do
        :: in?one(number) ->  /*Get left active neighbor value*/
           if
           :: Active ->
              if
              :: number != max ->
                 out!two(number); neighbor = number
              :: else ->
                 know_winner = 1; out!winner(number);
              fi
           :: else ->
              out!one(number)
           fi

        :: in?two(number) ->  /*Get second left active neighbor value*/
           if
           :: Active ->
              if
              :: neighbor > number && neighbor > max ->
                 max = neighbor; out!one(neighbor)
              :: else ->
                 Active = 0 /* Becomes passive */
              fi
           :: else ->
              out!two(number)
           fi
        :: in?winner(number) ->
           if
           :: know_winner
           :: else -> out!winner(number)
           fi;
           break
        od
```

Figure 12.15

The leader election protocol in PROMELA.

```
never {      /* !(noLeader U [] oneLeader) */
T0_init:
    if
    :: (! ((noLeader))) -> goto T0_S28
    :: (! ((noLeader)) && ! ((oneLeader))) -> goto accept_all
    :: (1) -> goto T0_S9
    :: (! ((oneLeader))) -> goto accept_S1
    fi;
accept_S1:
    if
    :: (! ((noLeader))) -> goto T0_S28
    :: (! ((noLeader)) && ! ((oneLeader))) -> goto accept_all
    :: (1) -> goto T0_S9
    :: (! ((oneLeader))) -> goto T0_init
    fi;
accept_S9:
    if
    :: (! ((noLeader))) -> goto T0_S28
    :: (! ((noLeader)) && ! ((oneLeader))) -> goto accept_all
    :: (1) -> goto T0_S9
    :: (! ((oneLeader))) -> goto T0_init
    fi;
accept_S28:
    if
    :: (1) -> goto T0_S28
    :: (! ((oneLeader))) -> goto accept_all
    fi;
T0_S9:
    if
    :: (! ((noLeader))) -> goto T0_S28
    :: (! ((noLeader)) && ! ((oneLeader))) -> goto accept_S28
    :: (! ((noLeader)) && ! ((oneLeader))) -> goto accept_all
    :: (! ((oneLeader))) -> goto accept_S9
    :: (1) -> goto T0_S9
    :: (! ((oneLeader))) -> goto accept_S1
    fi;
T0_S28:
    if
    :: (1) -> goto T0_S28
    :: (! ((oneLeader))) -> goto accept_all
    fi;
accept_all:
    skip
}
```

Figure 12.16
The never claim for the specification.

13 Abstraction

Abstraction is one of the most important techniques for reducing the state explosion problem. An abstract model is obtained by hiding some details of the system that appear to be irrelevant for the property of interest, and is usually much smaller than the full model. Because of the reduction in the size of the model, it is frequently easier to verify the abstract model than the original model.

The model of the system before abstraction is applied is called the *concrete model*. Abstractions are usually chosen to be *conservative* for the property of interest: whenever the property holds on the abstract model, then it holds on the concrete model as well. We consider only abstractions that produce finite-state models, so that we can apply model checking to them. In this chapter we focus on abstractions that are *overapproximations*. Such abstractions include a representative for each of the behaviors of the concrete model. They may also include additional behaviors that have no corresponding behaviors in the concrete model. Nevertheless, they are usually smaller in terms of number of states and transitions. Consequently, such abstractions are easier to model check. Further, they are guaranteed to be conservative for properties in LTL and ACTL*, that is, properties with universal path quantification.

The most natural way to construct an overapproximating abstraction is to define a mapping from the states of the concrete model to the states of the abstract model, and to extend this mapping to the transitions. Thus, it is possible to obtain an abstract model that simulates the original system and is usually much smaller. This abstraction technique is called *existential abstraction*.

In the next sections we survey three implementations of methods based on existential abstraction that are widely used and feasible in practice. *Localization reduction* [324] is particularly suitable for hardware models. It abstracts the circuit by identifying variables that are irrelevant for the property and removing them from the model. In *data abstraction* [132, 354], the domain of the individual state variables is abstracted. *Predicate abstraction* [246] identifies a set of predicates and merges the concrete states that agree on the valuation of these predicates. Predicate and data abstraction are most suitable for software models.

Overapproximating abstractions are conclusive only if the property is true in the abstract model. If the property fails, however, we cannot deduce that it is false in the concrete model. This is because the counterexample for the property in the overapproximated abstract model might not have a corresponding one in the concrete model. Such counterexamples are called *spurious* or "false negatives". We therefore have to check whether there is a corresponding concrete counterexample, which demonstrates that the property is indeed refuted in the concrete model. If the abstract counterexample is found to be spurious, we have to identify the shortcomings in the abstraction and *refine* it. This method is called *counterexample-guided abstraction refinement* (CEGAR) [130].

13.1   Existential Abstraction

We begin with a formal definition of existential abstraction that relies on an explicitly given concrete model. This definition is used to prove that the abstraction is conservative. In practice, however, abstraction is needed in situations where the full concrete model is too large to fit into memory. We will therefore construct the abstract models directly from some high-level description of the system. This is explained in section 13.2.

Recall that we write $M = (S, S_0, R, AP, L)$ for the Kripke structure of the concrete model. The abstract model is defined as a Kripke structure $\widehat{M} = (\widehat{S}, \widehat{S_0}, \widehat{R}, \widehat{AP}, \widehat{L})$. We choose $\widehat{AP}$ to be identical to AP. As usual, AP (and therefore $\widehat{AP}$) includes all atomic propositions that appear in the checked property φ.

In order to define $\widehat{M}$, we need to provide a set of abstract states $\widehat{S}$. Each of the abstract states in $\widehat{S}$ represents a set of concrete states in S. We assume that every concrete state is represented by a unique abstract state. Thus, the sets of states represented by two distinct abstract states are disjoint, and we can define an *abstraction function* (rather than an abstraction relation) that maps a concrete state to its abstract representative:

$$\alpha : S \to \widehat{S}$$

We require that each concrete state be represented by some abstract state, which makes α a total function. We furthermore require that the abstraction group together states only if they agree on the valuation of the propositions in $\widehat{AP}$. This requirement, called the *appropriateness* of α, is defined formally as follows.

Definition 13.1 *An abstraction function α is* appropriate for $\widehat{AP}$ *if and only if $L(s) = L(s')$ holds for every pair of concrete states s and s' with $\alpha(s) = \alpha(s')$.*

The appropriateness of α for $\widehat{AP}$ allows us to define the labeling of the abstract states in a straightforward way: an abstract state $\widehat{s}$ is labeled with an atomic proposition in $\widehat{AP}$ if the concrete states it represents are labeled with that proposition.

Figure 13.1 gives a concrete model M and its abstraction $\widehat{M}$. The dashed lines in M indicate the partitioning of S into abstract states. We must still define the transitions and the

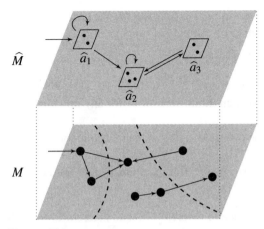

$\widehat{M}$

M

Figure 13.1

Existential abstraction. M is the original Kripke structure, and is $\widehat{M}$ the abstracted one. The dashed lines in M indicate how the states of M are clustered into abstract states. The concrete states and the abstract states are labeled by $AP = \widehat{AP} = \{p,q\}$.

set of initial states of the abstract model. Since we want an overapproximation, we ensure that every concrete transition and every concrete initial state has an abstract counterpart. Existential abstraction defines an abstract state to be an initial state if it represents an initial concrete state. Similarly, there is a transition from abstract state $\widehat{s}$ to abstract state $\widehat{s}'$ if there is a transition from a state represented by $\widehat{s}$ to a state represented by $\widehat{s}'$. This is formally defined as follows.

Definition 13.2 Let $M = (S, S_0, R, AP, L)$ be a (concrete) Kripke structure, let $\widehat{S}$ be a set of abstract states, and let $\widehat{AP} = AP$ be a set of (abstract) atomic propositions. Further, let $\alpha : S \to \widehat{S}$ be an abstraction function that is appropriate for $\widehat{AP}$. The Kripke structure $\widehat{M} = (\widehat{S}, \widehat{S_0}, \widehat{R}, \widehat{AP}, \widehat{L})$ is an (existential) abstraction of M with respect to α if the following holds:

1. $\widehat{s} \in \widehat{S_0}$ if $\exists s\,(\alpha(s) = \widehat{s} \land s \in S_0)$;
2. $(\widehat{s_1}, \widehat{s_2}) \in \widehat{R}$ if $\exists s_1, s_2\,(\alpha(s_1) = \widehat{s_1} \land \alpha(s_2) = \widehat{s_2} \land (s_1, s_2) \in R\,)$; and
3. $\widehat{L}(\widehat{s}) = L(s)$ for some s with $\alpha(s) = \widehat{s}$.

Informally, an abstraction $\widehat{M}$ has more behaviors than M. This is formalized by the following theorem, which states that $\widehat{M}$ is greater in the simulation preorder than M. By theorem 11.9, every ACTL* formula that holds for $\widehat{M}$ holds for M as well.

Theorem 13.3 Let M be a Kripke structure, and let $\widehat{M}$ be an abstraction of M. Then $M \preceq \widehat{M}$.

Proof Let α be the abstraction function that was used to construct $\widehat{M}$. We give a relation H between M and $\widehat{M}$ and show that it is a simulation relation. For every $s \in S, \widehat{s} \in \widehat{S}$, we define

$$(s, \widehat{s}) \in H \text{ iff } \alpha(s) = \widehat{s}.$$

We first show that for every $s_0 \in S_0$ there exists an $\widehat{s_0} \in \widehat{S_0}$ such that $(s_0, \widehat{s_0}) \in H$. By the definition of existential abstraction, $\alpha(s_0)$ is an initial state of $\widehat{M}$ for any initial state s_0. By definition of H, $(s_0, \alpha(s_0)) \in H$.

Assume that $(s, \widehat{s}) \in H$. Note first that the two states agree on their labeling for $\widehat{AP}$. Thus, $L(s) \cap \widehat{AP} = \widehat{L}(\widehat{s})$.

Let $(s, t) \in R$. We must show that $(\alpha(s), \alpha(t)) \in \widehat{R}$. But this immediately follows from the definition of existential abstraction. $\square$

The following corollary is a direct consequence of theorem 13.3 and theorem 11.9 and is the key property of our abstraction:

Corollary 13.3.1 *For every ACTL* formula φ over $\widehat{AP}$, $\widehat{M} \models \varphi$ implies $M \models \varphi$.*

Corollary 13.3.1 provides information about M only in those cases where $\widehat{M} \models \varphi$, that is, where property φ holds true on the abstract model. If $\widehat{M} \not\models \varphi$, no information about M can be inferred. (It is not possible to instantiate the corollary with $\widehat{M} \models \neg\varphi$, because the corollary assumes that the verified property is in ACTL*.) Thus, M allows us to prove more ACTL* properties than $\widehat{M}$, and it depends on the choice of the abstraction function α if we are able to verify property φ by abstraction: if the abstraction is too coarse, that is, if we have abstracted away too many details of the model, then the model checker may (very quickly) reply that $\widehat{M} \not\models \varphi$. If, on the other hand, the abstraction is too fine (in the extreme case, α may just be the identity function), then the abstract model is too large to be verified. In section 13.3.2, we will demonstrate the CEGAR approach, which enables us to gradually add more details into the abstraction.

Consider again definition 13.2 and note that in we used *if* in items 1 and 2. As a consequence, the abstraction $\widehat{M}$ is not uniquely determined, as we allow an abstract model to have initial states and transitions that do not have a concrete counterpart. Replacing *if* by *if and only if* in the definition above results in the *most precise* abstract model of M, with respect to α. We write $\widehat{M}_p$ for this abstract model. Any abstract model $\widehat{M}$ simulates the most precise abstract model $\widehat{M}_p$. Thus, we have the following theorem.

Theorem 13.4 *Given a model M and an abstraction function α, let $\widehat{M}$ be an abstract model of M, and let $\widehat{M}_p$ be the most precise abstraction, both with respect to α. Then $M \preceq \widehat{M}_p \preceq \widehat{M}$.*

Proof Clearly, $M \preceq \widehat{M}_p$ holds as a special case of theorem 13.3. To show that $\widehat{M}_p \preceq \widehat{M}$ we choose H to be the identity function on $\widehat{S}$. By definition, $\widehat{M}$ and $\widehat{M}_p$ are defined over the same set of abstract states. Further, $\widehat{M}$ has more initial states and more transitions than $\widehat{M}_p$. Thus, H is a simulation relation between $\widehat{M}_p$ and $\widehat{M}$. $\square$

The most precise abstraction will generally allow us to prove more properties about the concrete model, but is also more expensive to compute.

In the next section, we describe several common ways to define abstractions. They are all instances of existential abstraction. They differ from one another in their choice of abstract states $\widehat{S}$, their set of atomic propositions $\widehat{AP} = AP$, and the definition of the abstraction function α. This is sufficient as definition 13.2 provides $\widehat{S_0}$, $\widehat{R}$, and $\widehat{L}$.

13.1.1   Localization Reduction

We use the symbolic representation of systems, as defined in chapter 3, to describe the concrete model. Let $\mathcal{P}$ be a system over a set of variables $V = \{v_1, \ldots, v_n\}$, and let D_v be the domain of $v \in V$. Let M be a concrete model for $\mathcal{P}$ with $S = D_{v_1} \times \ldots \times D_{v_n}$. *Localization reduction* [324] is an abstraction technique that is based on a partitioning of the variables into *visible* and *invisible* variables. It is widely used in model checking of hardware.

The visible variables, denoted $\mathcal{V}$, are considered to be important for the checked property φ and hence are retained in the abstract model. The rest of the variables, called *invisible*, are considered irrelevant for checking φ. Ideally, only a small subset of the variables will be visible. The set of visible variables always includes the variables that appear in the atomic propositions $\widehat{AP}$.

Recall that a concrete state is a valuation of all variables in V. We now define an abstract state $\widehat{s} \in \widehat{S}$ to be a valuation of the visible variables. Let $\mathcal{V} = \{u_1, \ldots, u_q\} \subseteq V$ be the set of visible variables. The set of abstract states is then $\widehat{S} = D_{u_1} \times \ldots \times D_{u_q}$.

Given a concrete state s, the corresponding abstract state $\alpha(s)$ is the projection of s onto the variables in $\mathcal{V}$:

$$\alpha(s) = (s(u_1), s(u_2), \ldots, s(u_q)).$$

The abstract state represents all those concrete states that agree with it on the values of the visible variables.

Since $\mathcal{V}$ includes all variables that appear in $\widehat{AP}$, the valuation of $\widehat{AP}$ is the same on all concrete states that are mapped to the same abstract state. Thus, α is appropriate for $\widehat{AP}$. Once α is defined, the remaining components of $\widehat{M}$ follow from definition 13.2.

Cone of Influence Reduction   Next we present a conservative choice of the set of visible variables. We repeat here some definitions of chapter 3, section 3.3 for hardware modeling. Assume that each variable $v \in V$ is associated with a next state function $f_v(V)$. Typically, f_v depends only on a subset of V. The cone of influence (COI) [134] of a formula φ is defined inductively as follows. It includes all the variables in φ. In addition, if v is in COI, then all variables on which f_v depends are also in COI.

Taking the COI of φ to be the set of visible variables results in an abstract model that is *equivalent* to the concrete model with respect to φ. That is, the abstract model satisfies φ if and only if the concrete model satisfies it. As a result, refutation of φ on the abstract model implies refutation on the concrete model. This choice, however, is often not practical, since COI is often too large.

Example 13.10 in section 13.2.2 demonstrates why localization reduction is most suitable for hardware. When only Boolean variables are considered, it is often useful to leave the behavior of some of the variables completely unspecified (meaning they behave like inputs) while including in full the behavior of others. For software, including the full behavior of a variable might not be feasible if the domain of the variable is very large or even infinite.

Localization reduction can, in principle, be used to abstract an infinite-state model to a finite-state abstract model by making all variables with infinite domains invisible. However, the resulting abstraction cannot be used to prove any property about these variables. In the next section we present an abstraction that can map infinite domains to finite domains, and is thus able to reason about infinite-domain variables.

13.1.2   Data Abstraction

We assume that the concrete model is given as in the previous section. We describe a special kind of data abstraction [132, 354] in which an abstract domain is chosen separately for each variable of the system. The abstract domain is typically finite and significantly smaller than the original domain of the variable. We define one abstraction function α_v for each variable v, which maps the concrete domain of v to the abstract domain of v. The abstraction function for concrete states is composed of the abstraction functions for the individual variables.

Recall that D_v denotes the concrete domain of variable v. Let $\widehat{D}_v$ be the abstract domain of v, and $\alpha_v : D_v \to \widehat{D}_v$ be the abstraction function for v. The abstract state space is then defined by

$$\widehat{S} = \widehat{D}_{v_1} \times \ldots \times \widehat{D}_{v_n}.$$

For a concrete state $s = (d_1, \ldots, d_n)$, the abstraction function α is defined as

$$\alpha((d_1, \ldots, d_n)) = (\alpha_{v_1}(d_1), \ldots, \alpha_{v_n}(d_n)).$$

Data abstraction is often easier to compute than abstractions that are defined over the full concrete state, as the variables are abstracted separately.

Example 13.5 *Let $\mathcal{P}$ be a program with variables x and y over the integers. Let $AP = \widehat{AP} = \{ x < 0,\ x = 0,\ even(y) \}$. We may choose*

$$\widehat{D}_x = \{a_-, a_0, a_+\} \quad and$$

$$\alpha_x(d) = \begin{cases} a_+ & \text{if } d > 0 \\ a_0 & \text{if } d = 0 \\ a_- & \text{if } d < 0 \end{cases}$$

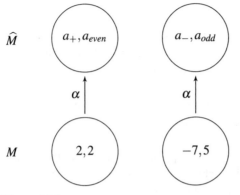

$\widehat{M}$

Figure 13.2
Two concrete states and a data abstraction.

and

$$\widehat{D}_y = \{a_{even}, a_{odd}\} \quad and$$

$$\alpha_y(d) = \begin{cases} a_{even} & \text{if } even(|d|) \\ a_{odd} & \text{if } odd(|d|). \end{cases}$$

Let s, s' be two program states such that $s(x) = s(y) = 2$, $s'(x) = -7$, and $s'(y) = 5$. Then $\alpha(s) = (a_+, a_{even})$ and $\alpha(s') = (a_-, a_{odd})$. The concrete and abstract states are illustrated in figure 13.2. Note that the resulting α is appropriate for $\widehat{AP}$.

It is not always easy to satisfy the appropriateness requirement for data abstraction if each variable is abstracted in isolation. If each of the atomic propositions in $\widehat{AP}$ refers to one variable only, it is always possible to define a suitable abstract domain for the variables. The abstract domain $\widehat{D}_v$ can be defined by using the partitioning induced by the atomic propositions referring to v. This results in an appropriate abstraction function α as shown, for instance, in example 13.5.

On the other hand, if there is an atomic proposition in AP that refers to two or more variables, it may be impossible to find abstract domains for the individual variables that yield an appropriate abstraction function. This can be addressed by using an abstraction that abstracts several variables together. Such an abstraction is called *relational abstraction* [383, 130]. Abstractions such as data abstraction are referred to as *non-relational*. A well-known example of a relational abstraction is the *octagon abstract domain* [384], which permits the representation of constraints of the form $\pm x \pm y \leq c$, where x and y are variables and c is constant. Another widely used relational abstraction is the predicate abstraction, which is discussed next.

13.1.3   Predicate Abstraction

Predicate abstraction [246] is based on a set of predicates $\{P_1, \ldots, P_k\}$, where each P_i is a subset of the concrete states. Predicates are typically given by means of atomic first-order formulas over the variables of the system. We will identify a formula with the set of states that satisfy it.

Each predicate P_j is associated with a Boolean state variable B_j. These Boolean variables define the abstract state space, that is, an abstract state $\widehat{s} \in \{0,1\}^k$ is a valuation of $\{B_1, \ldots, B_k\}$.

The predicates define the abstraction function α, mapping the concrete to the abstract state space. The concrete state s is mapped to the abstract state in which the values of the B_i match the values of the predicates P_i when evaluated in the state s:

$$\alpha(s) = (P_1(s), \ldots, P_k(s))$$

We write $\widehat{s}(B_i)$ to denote the truth value of B_i in an abstract state $\widehat{s}$.

In order to satisfy the appropriateness requirement, we require that all atomic propositions in $\widehat{AP}$ (and thus all atomic propositions in the property ϕ) be included in the set of predicates. Observe that an abstract state $\widehat{s}$ is then labeled with $P_i \in \widehat{AP}$ if and only if $\widehat{s}(B_i)$.

Predicate abstraction is frequently applied to programs. We elaborate on optimizations for this case in chapter 14.

Example 13.6 *We will illustrate some of the notions defined above on a simple example. Consider a program $\mathcal{P}$ with variables x and y over the natural numbers and a single transition $x := x + 1$. Let $AP = \widehat{AP} = \{P_1, P_2, P_3\}$, where $P_1 \Leftrightarrow (x \le 1)$, $P_2 \Leftrightarrow (x > y)$, and $P_3 \Leftrightarrow (y = 2)$.*

Let s and t be two concrete states such that $s(x) = s(y) = 0$, $t(x) = 1$, and $t(y) = 2$. Then, $L(s) = \{P_1\}$ and $L(t) = \{P_1, P_3\}$.

The abstract states are defined over valuations of the Boolean variables B_1, B_2, B_3. Thus, $\widehat{S} = \{0,1\}^3$. The abstraction function α maps s and t to the following abstract states:

$$\alpha(s) = (1,0,0) \text{ and } \alpha(t) = (1,0,1)$$

Note that $\widehat{L}((1,0,0)) = L(s) = \{P_1\}$, where $\widehat{L}((1,0,1)) = L(t) = \{P_1, P_3\}$.

13.2   Computation of Abstract Models

In chapter 3 we demonstrate how a concrete model can be derived from a high-level description of the system. In this section we explain how an abstract model can be derived directly from the high-level system description such as a program or a circuit description. We build the abstract model without even constructing the concrete model. As in chapter 3, to avoid the details of a specific programming language or hardware description language, we assume that the system is described by means of first-order formulas. For the sake of completeness of presentation, we repeat part of the example used in chapter 3.

13.2.1   Abstracting Software Programs

Let $\mathcal{P}$ be a program, and let s, s' be program states representing current and next states. We assume that the concrete model of the program is given by two first-order formulas, $\mathcal{S}_0(s)$ and $\mathcal{R}(s,s')$, describing the set of initial states and the set of transitions, respectively. We furthermore assume that the transition relation is constructed as described in chapter 3, and therefore uses a program counter pc, which enables a compositional construction of $\mathcal{R}$.

Below are several simple examples that illustrate the construction of the first-order formulas that represent the concrete model. Each statement in the program starts and ends with labels that uniquely define the corresponding locations in the program. The variable pc represents the program counter, and ranges over the set of program labels.

Example 13.7 *Let $\mathcal{P}$ be a program with one variable x that starts at label l_0 in any state in which x is even. Then, the set of its initial states is described by the formula:*

$$\mathcal{S}_0(pc,x) \equiv pc = l_0 \wedge even(x).$$

Let $l : x := e \; l'$ be some assignment statement in $\mathcal{P}$. The transition relation associated with this statement is given by the formula:

$$\mathcal{R}(pc,x,pc',x') \equiv pc = l \wedge x' = e \wedge pc' = l'.$$

Given the statement

$$l_0 : \textbf{if } x = 0 \textbf{ then } l_1 : x := 1 \textbf{ else } l_2 : x := x+1 \textbf{ end if } l_3 \, ,$$

the transition relation associated with it is represented by the formula:

$$\begin{aligned}
\mathcal{R}(pc,x,pc',x') \equiv \; & (pc = l_0 \wedge x = 0 \wedge x' = x \wedge pc' = l_1) \\
& \vee (pc = l_0 \wedge x \neq 0 \wedge x' = x \wedge pc' = l_2) \\
& \vee (pc = l_1 \wedge x' = 1 \wedge pc' = l_3) \\
& \vee (pc = l_2 \wedge x' = x+1 \wedge pc' = l_3).
\end{aligned}$$

*The formula above describes a model in which checking the condition of an **if** statement takes one transition, along which the value of the program variable is checked but not changed. The formula also models the two assignment statements that are labeled with l_1 and l_2, respectively.*

Let $\mathcal{S}_0$ and $\mathcal{R}$ be the formulas describing a concrete model M. We would like to have a similar description for an abstract model $\widehat{M}$, defined according to definition 13.2 for M and α. We can obtain formulas $\widehat{\mathcal{S}}_0$ and $\widehat{\mathcal{R}}$ that represent $\widehat{\mathcal{S}}_0$ and $\widehat{\mathcal{R}}$ by means of an existential quantification over concrete current and next states:

$$\widehat{\mathcal{S}}_0(\widehat{s}) = \exists s.(\alpha(s) = \widehat{s} \wedge \mathcal{S}_0(s)), \text{ and}$$

$$\widehat{\mathcal{R}}(\widehat{s}, \widehat{s}') = \exists s \exists s'.(\mathcal{R}(s, s') \wedge \alpha(s) = \widehat{s} \wedge \alpha(s') = \widehat{s}') .$$

The following lemma asserts that the model represented by these formulas is the most precise existential abstraction with respect to α.

Lemma 13.8 *Let $\mathcal{S}_0$ and $\mathcal{R}$ be the formulas describing a model M. Then the formulas $\widehat{\mathcal{S}}_0$ and $\widehat{\mathcal{R}}$ describe $\widehat{M}_p$, which is the most precise abstract model for M and α.*

As mentioned before, the abstract model is sometimes expensive to compute. In particular, its computation involves applying existential quantification to the formula that describes the transition relation of the entire program. Depending on the particular fragment of first-order logic that is used, this formula might be either very difficult to compute or very large.

We will present a method that simplifies the computation of the abstract model for software programs. An important property of this abstract model is that it replicates the control-flow skeleton of the concrete program; that is, it uses the same set of labels, branches, and looping constructs. We introduce a program counter for the abstract model that ranges over the same set of labels as the program counter for the concrete model. Furthermore, any state s with $s(pc) = l$ will be abstracted to an abstract state for which $\widehat{s}(pc) = l$.

Before giving the method for constructing $\widehat{\mathcal{R}}$, we make an observation on the shape of $\mathcal{R}$. To illustrate this point, we will continue the example from above. First, note that we can rewrite the encoding for the **if** statement by factoring out the term $pc = l$ using DeMorgan's laws.

$$\mathcal{R}(pc, x, pc', x') \equiv$$
$$\begin{aligned} &\left(pc = l_0 \wedge ((x = 0 \wedge x' = x \wedge pc' = l_1) \vee (x \neq 0 \wedge x' = x \wedge pc' = l_2))) \right) \vee \\ &(pc = l_1 \wedge x' = 1 \wedge pc' = l_3) \vee \\ &(pc = l_2 \wedge x' = x + 1 \wedge pc' = l_3) \end{aligned}$$

Recall that the labels of the statements are unique. Consequently, $\mathcal{R}(s, s')$ has the form

$$\mathcal{R}(s, s') \Leftrightarrow \bigvee_l (s(pc) = l \wedge conjunct_l(s, s')), \tag{13.1}$$

where l in the disjunction ranges over all program locations, and $conjunct_l$ denotes an arbitrary conjunct that depends on the instruction at location l only. For our example above, we obtain

$$
conjunct_{l_0}(pc,x,pc',x') \equiv (x = 0 \ \land x' = x \land pc' = l_1) \lor
$$
$$
(x \neq 0 \ \land x' = x \land pc' = l_2)
$$
$$
conjunct_{l_1}(pc,x,pc',x') \equiv x' = 1 \land pc' = l_3
$$
$$
conjunct_{l_2}(pc,x,pc',x') \equiv x' = x+1 \land pc' = l_3.
$$

We remark that this is an equivalence-preserving transformation of $\mathcal{R}$. Furthermore, recall that pushing existential quantification into disjunctions is equivalence preserving. This is the key property that is exploited by the following lemma.

Lemma 13.9 *Let $\mathcal{R}(s,s')$ be a transition relation of the form*

$$
\bigvee_{l} (s(pc) = l \land conjunct_l(s,s')).
$$

Then, pushing the existential quantification over s and s' into the disjunction yields the most precise existential abstraction:

$$
\widehat{\mathcal{R}}(\widehat{s},\widehat{s}') \equiv \bigvee_{l} \left(\widehat{s}(pc) = l \land \exists s \exists s'.(conjunct_l(s,s') \land \alpha(s) = \widehat{s} \land \alpha(s') = \widehat{s}') \right) \quad (13.2)
$$

Proof We obtain

$$
\widehat{\mathcal{R}}(\widehat{s},\widehat{s}') \equiv \bigvee_{l} \exists s \exists s'. (\widehat{s}(pc) = l \land conjunct_l(s,s') \land \alpha(s) = \widehat{s} \land \alpha(s') = \widehat{s}') \quad (13.3)
$$

by pushing the existential quantification into the disjunction. We can further simplify equation 13.3 to obtain equation 13.2 by observing that the two conjuncts in Equation 13.3 use a disjoint set of variables, as $conjunct_l$ does not depend on the program counter. This allows us to push the quantification into the conjunction. Furthermore, recall that $\widehat{s}(pc) = s(pc)$ for any pair of s and $\widehat{s}$ with $\alpha(s) = \widehat{s}$. $\square$

What is the benefit of this lemma? Observe that the existential quantification is now performed over individual pieces of the transition relation, where the size of the pieces does not depend on the size of the program. The computation of $\widehat{\mathcal{R}}$ therefore becomes linear in the size of $\mathcal{P}$, measured in the number of labels.

We continue our running example. For the first statement of our program, we need to perform the following quantification:

$$
\exists s \exists s'.\alpha(s) = \widehat{s} \land \alpha(s') = \widehat{s}' \land \left((s(x) = 0 \ \land s'(x) = s(x) \land s'(pc) = l_1) \lor \right.
$$
$$
\left. (s(x) \neq 0 \ \land s'(x) = s(x) \land s'(pc) = l_2) \right)
$$

We will leave the computation of this existential for particular abstraction functions α as an exercise.

13.2.2   Abstracting Synchronous Circuits with Localization Reduction

As in the case of software, we aim to derive the abstract model directly from a high-level description of the circuit to avoid existential quantification for the computation of the set of initial states and the transition relation.

We first recall the high-level description of circuits given in chapter 3. A circuit has a set of variables $V = \{v_1, \ldots, v_n\}$, which are the registers and the primary inputs. We are given a propositional formula $\mathcal{R}(V, V')$, which is the characteristic function for the transition relation R of the model. We have defined $\mathcal{R}$ using a conjunction as follows:

$$\mathcal{R}(V, V') \equiv \bigwedge_{i=1}^{n} \mathcal{R}_i(V, V')$$

The definition of the $\mathcal{R}_i$ depends on whether v_i is a register or a primary input. In case v_i is a register, we are given a Boolean expression f_i, which computes the next state for v_i as a function of the current values of the variables. $\mathcal{R}_i$ is then defined as follows:

$$\mathcal{R}_i(V, V') \equiv (v_i' \Leftrightarrow f_i(V))$$

We leave v_i' unconstrained if v_i is a primary input; that is, we define $\mathcal{R}_i$ to be true:

$$\mathcal{R}_i(V, V') \equiv true$$

We recall the condition $\widehat{R}$ has to satisfy:

$$(\widehat{s}, \widehat{s'}) \in \widehat{R} \equiv \exists s, s'.(\alpha(s) = \widehat{s} \wedge \alpha(s') = \widehat{s'} \wedge (s, s') \in R)$$

In localization reduction, the set of variables is partitioned into a set of visible and a set of invisible variables. We use $\mathcal{V} \subseteq V$ to denote the set of visible variables. The variables not in $\mathcal{V}$ are invisible. We write $\mathcal{U}$ for the set of invisible variables. A concrete state s is thus a valuation of the variables $\mathcal{V}$ and $\mathcal{U}$, whereas an abstract state $\widehat{s}$ is a valuation of the variables $\mathcal{V}$ only. The abstraction function α is thus written as follows in terms of the visible and invisible variables:

$$\alpha(\mathcal{V}, \mathcal{U}) = \mathcal{V}$$

We now define our abstract transition relation $\widehat{\mathcal{R}}$ as a relation between the variables $\mathcal{V}$ and their next-state version $\mathcal{V}'$.

$$\widehat{\mathcal{R}}(\widehat{\mathcal{V}}, \widehat{\mathcal{V}'}) \equiv \exists \mathcal{V}, \mathcal{U}, \mathcal{V}', \mathcal{U}'.(\ \alpha(\mathcal{V}, \mathcal{U}) = \widehat{\mathcal{V}}$$
$$\wedge \alpha(\mathcal{V}', \mathcal{U}') = \widehat{\mathcal{V}'}$$
$$\wedge \mathcal{R}(\mathcal{V}, \mathcal{U}, \mathcal{V}', \mathcal{U}'))$$

In the definition, we quantify existentially over the values of the invisible variables, which implies that they behave as if they are primary inputs. Using the definition of α, the above simplifies as follows:

$$\widehat{\mathcal{R}}(\widehat{\mathcal{V}}, \widehat{\mathcal{V}'}) \equiv \exists \mathcal{U}, \mathcal{U}'.\mathcal{R}(\widehat{\mathcal{V}}, \mathcal{U}, \widehat{\mathcal{V}'}, \mathcal{U}')$$

Using the definition of $\mathcal{R}$, we get

$$\widehat{\mathcal{R}}(\widehat{\mathcal{V}},\widehat{\mathcal{V}}') \equiv \exists \mathcal{U},\mathcal{U}'. \bigwedge_{i=1}^{n} \mathcal{R}_i(\widehat{\mathcal{V}},\mathcal{U},\widehat{\mathcal{V}}',\mathcal{U}').$$

We split up the conjunction to distinguish the cases of visible and invisible variables:

$$\widehat{\mathcal{R}}(\widehat{\mathcal{V}},\widehat{\mathcal{V}}') \equiv \exists \mathcal{U},\mathcal{U}'. \bigwedge_{v_i \in \mathcal{V}} \mathcal{R}_i(\widehat{\mathcal{V}},\mathcal{U},\widehat{\mathcal{V}}') \wedge \bigwedge_{v_i \in \mathcal{U}} \mathcal{R}_i(\widehat{\mathcal{V}},\mathcal{U},\mathcal{U}').$$

The only part of the formula in which $\widehat{\mathcal{U}}'$ is used is the conjunction on the right. The formula is thus equivalent to

$$\widehat{\mathcal{R}}(\widehat{\mathcal{V}},\widehat{\mathcal{V}}') \equiv \exists \mathcal{U}. \bigwedge_{v_i \in \mathcal{V}} \mathcal{R}_i(\widehat{\mathcal{V}},\mathcal{U},\widehat{\mathcal{V}}') \wedge \exists \mathcal{U}'. \bigwedge_{v_i \in \mathcal{U}} \mathcal{R}_i(\widehat{\mathcal{V}},\mathcal{U},\mathcal{U}').$$

There always exists a valuation of the invisible variables in the next state, as the value of v_i is given by $f_i(\widehat{\mathcal{V}},\mathcal{U})$. We thus simplify the formula to

$$\widehat{\mathcal{R}}(\widehat{\mathcal{V}},\widehat{\mathcal{V}}') \equiv \exists \mathcal{U}. \bigwedge_{v_i \in \mathcal{V}} \mathcal{R}_i(\widehat{\mathcal{V}},\mathcal{U},\widehat{\mathcal{V}}').$$

It is thus sufficient to retain the next-state functions for the visible registers in $\widehat{R}$; the conjuncts for the invisible registers can simply be removed. Observe that we have used only equivalence-preserving transformations. The abstraction is therefore the most precise existential abstraction.

Example 13.10 *As an example, consider a sequential circuit given as a netlist (figure 13.3). A netlist is a directed graph in which the nodes are gates that compute Boolean functions, and the edges correspond to Boolean variables. The netlist contains two registers, which are named x and y. The inputs in the netlist are marked with i_1 and i_2. The dashed line defines a cut through the graph, separating the visible from the invisible variables. Figure 13.3 gives the abstract netlist on the right, where the variables removed by the cut are now inputs and the parts of the netlist that drive them have been removed. The abstract model is derived directly from the abstract netlist.*

13.3 Counterexample-Guided Abstraction Refinement (CEGAR)

13.3.1 Spurious Counterexamples

It is easy to see that, regardless of the type of abstraction we use, the abstract model $\widehat{M}$ contains less information than the concrete model M. Thus, model-checking $\widehat{M}$ potentially produces incorrect results. Theorem 13.3 guarantees that if an ACTL* specification is true in $\widehat{M}$, then it is also true in M. On the other hand, the following example shows that if the abstract model invalidates an ACTL* specification, *the actual model may still satisfy the specification.*

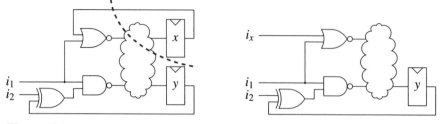

Figure 13.3
Netlist of original circuit with a cut (left) and netlist after localization reduction (right) with visible
register y and invisible register x.

Figure 13.4
Abstraction of a US traffic light.

Example 13.11 *The US traffic light controller presented in figure 13.4, is defined over the
set of states $S = \{red, green, yellow\}$ and the set of atomic propositions $AP = \{state = red\}$,
where state $= red$ is true in state red, but false in states green and yellow. We would like to
prove the formula $\psi = \mathbf{AG\,AF}(state = red)$. For that we choose $\widehat{AP} = AP$ and $\widehat{S} = \{\widehat{red}, \widehat{go}\}$.
We use the abstraction mapping $\alpha(red) = \widehat{red}$ and $\alpha(green) = \alpha(yellow) = \widehat{go}$. The transitions in the abstract model are defined by the existential abstraction (definition 13.2). For
instance, there is a transition from $\widehat{red}$ to $\widehat{go}$ since there is a transition from red to green;
there is a transition from $\widehat{go}$ to $\widehat{go}$ since there is a transition from green to yellow.*

*It is easy to see that $M \models \psi$ while $\widehat{M} \not\models \psi$. There exists an infinite abstract trace
$\langle \widehat{red}, \widehat{go}, \widehat{go}, \ldots \rangle$ that invalidates the specification. However, no corresponding concrete
trace exists.*

When an abstract counterexample does not correspond to some concrete counterexample,
we call it *spurious*. For example, $\langle \widehat{red}, \widehat{go}, \widehat{go}, \ldots \rangle$ in the above example is a spurious
counterexample.

Let us consider the situation outlined in figure 13.5. We see that the abstract path
$\langle \widehat{a_1}, \widehat{a_2}, \widehat{a_3} \rangle$ does not have a corresponding concrete path. Every concrete path from the
initial state ends up in state D, from which we cannot go further. Therefore, D is called a
dead-end state. On the other hand, B is a *bad state* because it made us believe that there is
an outgoing transition. Finally, state I is an *irrelevant state* since it is neither dead-end nor

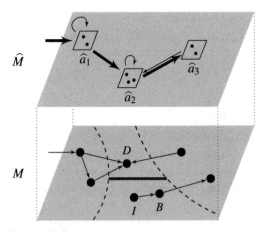

Figure 13.5
The abstract path in $\widehat{M}$ (indicated by the thick arrows) is spurious. To eliminate the spurious path, the
abstraction has to be refined as indicated by the thick line in M.

bad. To eliminate the spurious path, the abstraction can be refined, for instance, as indicated
by the thick line in figure 13.5 separating dead-end states from bad states.

13.3.2   The Abstraction-Refinement Framework for ACTL*

In this section we present the framework of *CounterExample-Guided Abstraction-Refinement* (CEGAR) [130], for the logic ACTL* and existential abstraction. The main steps of
the CEGAR framework are as follows:

1. *Generate the initial abstraction:* Given a model M and an ACTL* formula φ, generate
   an initial abstract model $\widehat{M}$, as discussed in the previous sections.
2. *Model-check the abstract structure:* Model-check $\widehat{M}$ with respect to φ. Most existing
   model-checking tools can handle ACTL or LTL; both are subsets of ACTL*. If φ is
   true, then conclude that the concrete model satisfies the formula and stop.
3. *Identify spurious counterexamples:* If a counterexample $\widehat{T}$ is found, check whether
   it corresponds to a counterexample in the concrete model. This part is described in
   section 13.3.3. If it is, conclude that the concrete model does not satisfy the formula and
   stop. Otherwise, the counterexample is spurious and refinement is required; proceed to
   step 4.
4. *Refine the abstraction:* Refine the abstract model, so that $\widehat{T}$ will not be included in the
   new, refined abstract model. Refinement is usually obtained by partitioning an abstract
   state along $\widehat{T}$ and updating α accordingly. This part is described in section 13.3.4.
   Build the new, refined abstract model and go back to step 2.

Suggesting an initial abstraction and refinements manually requires great ingenuity and considerable acquaintance with the verified system. We have already discussed how an (initial) abstract model can be constructed automatically from the program text. Below we follow [130] in showing how refinements can be automatically determined using spurious counterexamples.

13.3.3   Identifying Spurious Counterexamples

We use model checking to determine whether $\widehat{M}$ satisfies the specification φ. Assume that $\widehat{M}$ does not satisfy φ and that the model checker produces a counterexample $\widehat{T}$. We focus here on counterexamples for safety properties that are *finite paths*. At the end of this section we also briefly discuss counterexamples for liveness properties that consist of a finite path followed by a loop.

Assume that the counterexample $\widehat{T}$ is a path $\langle \widehat{s_1}, \ldots, \widehat{s_n} \rangle$. Given an abstract state $\widehat{s}$, the set of concrete states s such that $\alpha(s) = \widehat{s}$ is denoted by $\alpha^{-1}(\widehat{s})$. That is,

$$\alpha^{-1}(\widehat{s}) = \{s \mid \alpha(s) = \widehat{s}\}.$$

We extend α^{-1} to sequences in the following way: $\alpha^{-1}(\widehat{T})$ is the set of concrete paths defined by

$$\alpha^{-1}(\widehat{T}) = \left\{ \langle s_1, \ldots, s_n \rangle \mid \bigwedge_{i=1}^{n} \alpha(s_i) = \widehat{s_i} \wedge S_0(s_1) \wedge \bigwedge_{i=1}^{n-1} R(s_i, s_{i+1}) \right\}.$$

Notice that $\widehat{T}$ is spurious if and only if $\alpha^{-1}(\widehat{T})$ is empty. Next, we define a sequence of sets of concrete states $\langle T_1, \ldots, T_n \rangle$ that can be used to determine if $\alpha^{-1}(\widehat{T})$ is empty:

- $T_1 = \alpha^{-1}(\widehat{s_1}) \cap S_0$
- $T_i = Image(T_{i-1}) \cap \alpha^{-1}(\widehat{s_i})$ for $1 < i \leq n$

Recall that $Image(T_{i-1})$ is the set of all successors of states in T_{i-1}. The next lemma will be used to determine if $\alpha^{-1}(\widehat{T})$ is empty.

Lemma 13.12 *The following are equivalent:*

1. *The set of concrete paths $\alpha^{-1}(\widehat{T})$ is non-empty.*
2. *For all $1 \leq i \leq n$, $T_i \neq \emptyset$.*

Proof $(1 \rightarrow 2)$ Assume that $\alpha^{-1}(\widehat{T})$ is not empty. Then there exists a path $\langle s_1, \ldots, s_n \rangle$ where $\alpha(s_i) = \widehat{s_i}$ and $s_1 \in S_0$. Therefore, we have $s_1 \in T_1$. Let us assume that $s_i \in T_i$. By the definition of $\alpha^{-1}(\widehat{T})$, $s_{i+1} \in Image(s_i)$ and $s_{i+1} \in \alpha^{-1}(\widehat{s_{i+1}})$. Thus, $s_{i+1} \in Image(T_i) \cap \alpha^{-1}(\widehat{s_{i+1}}) = T_{i+1}$. By induction, $T_i \neq \emptyset$, for $i \leq n$.

$(2 \rightarrow 1)$ Assume that $T_i \neq \emptyset$ for $1 \leq i \leq n$. We choose a state $s_n \in T_n$ and inductively construct a trace backward. Assume that $s_i \in T_i$. From the definition of T_i, it follows that $s_i \in Image(T_{i-1}) \cap \alpha^{-1}(\widehat{s_i})$ and that T_{i-1} is not empty. Select s_{i-1} from T_{i-1} such that $R(s_{i-1}, s_i)$.

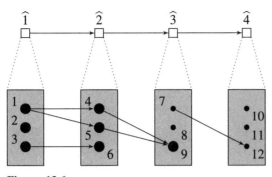

Figure 13.6
An abstract counterexample.

By the definition of T_{i-1}, $T_{i-1} \subseteq \alpha^{-1}(\widehat{s_{i-1}})$. Hence, $s_{i-1} \in \alpha^{-1}(\widehat{s_{i-1}})$. By induction, $s_1 \in T_1 = \alpha^{-1}(\widehat{s_1}) \cap S_0$. Therefore, the trace $\langle s_1, \ldots, s_n \rangle$ that we have constructed satisfies the definition of $\alpha^{-1}(\widehat{T})$. Thus, $\alpha^{-1}(\widehat{T})$ is not empty. $\square$

If condition 2 of lemma 13.12 holds, then the proof of the lemma provides an algorithm to construct a concrete counterexample.

Suppose now that condition 2 is violated, and let j be the largest index such that $T_j \neq \emptyset$. Then $\widehat{s_j}$ is called the *failure state* of the spurious counterexample $\widehat{T}$. It follows from lemma 13.12 that if $\alpha^{-1}(\widehat{T})$ is empty (that is, if the counterexample $\widehat{T}$ is spurious), then there exists a minimal i, $1 \le i \le n$, such that $T_i = \emptyset$.

In the following example we investigate an abstract counterexample and its concrete counterpart, as described in figure 13.6. The abstraction used is data abstraction.

Example 13.13 *Consider a program with only one variable with domain $D = \{1, \ldots, 12\}$. Thus, the concrete states are just $S = \{1, \ldots, 12\}$. Let $S_0 = \{1, 2, 3\}$. Assume that the abstract domain is $\widehat{D} = \{\widehat{1}, \widehat{2}, \widehat{3}, \widehat{4}\}$ and that the abstraction function α maps $d \in D$ to $\lfloor (d-1)/3 \rfloor + 1$. There are four abstract states, $\widehat{1}$, $\widehat{2}$, $\widehat{3}$, and $\widehat{4}$ that represent the four sets of concrete states $\{1, 2, 3\}$, $\{4, 5, 6\}$, $\{7, 8, 9\}$, and $\{10, 11, 12\}$. The transitions between states in the concrete model are indicated by the arrows in figure 13.6; small dots denote non-reachable states.*

Suppose we obtain an abstract counterexample $\widehat{T} = \langle \widehat{1}, \widehat{2}, \widehat{3}, \widehat{4} \rangle$. It is easy to see that $\widehat{T}$ is spurious. Using the terminology of lemma 13.12, we have $T_1 = \{1, 2, 3\}$, $T_2 = \{4, 5, 6\}$, $T_3 = \{9\}$, and $T_4 = \emptyset$. Since T_4 is empty, the abstract state $\widehat{3}$ is the failure state.

Based on lemma 13.12, the algorithm *SplitPATH* in figure 13.7 determines whether an abstract counterexample $\widehat{T}$ is spurious. Given $\widehat{T} = \langle \widehat{s_1}, \ldots, \widehat{s_n} \rangle$, *SplitPATH* computes the index $j - 1$ of the failure state and the set of states T_{j-1}; the states in T_{j-1} are *dead-end*

procedure *SplitPATH*$(\widehat{T})$

$\quad T_1 := \alpha^{-1}(\widehat{s_1}) \cap S_0;$

$\quad j := 1;$

$\quad$**if** $T_1 = \emptyset$ **then output** "spurious initial state";

$\quad$**while** $T_j \neq \emptyset$ and $j < n$ **do**

$\quad\quad j := j+1;$

$\quad\quad T_j := Image(T_{j-1}) \cap \alpha^{-1}(\widehat{s_j});$

$\quad$**end while**

$\quad$**if** $T_j \neq \emptyset$ **then**

$\quad\quad$**output** "counterexample exists";

$\quad$**else**

$\quad\quad$**output** $j-1$, T_{j-1};

$\quad$**end if**

end procedure

Figure 13.7
SplitPATH checks if an abstract path is spurious.

states. If no T_i is empty, then *SplitPATH* will report a "real" counterexample and we can stop.

A similar analysis can be applied if the counterexample returned by the model checking consists of a finite path followed by a loop. In that case, the analysis provides a bound on the number of loop unwindings that are needed to apply lemma 13.12. Algorithm *SplitPATH*, described in figure 13.7, can then be used with the unwound counterexample in order to determine if it is spurious or not. More details can be found in [130].

After the detection of the dead-end states, we proceed to the refinement step, as described in the next section.

13.3.4   Refining Abstract Models

In this section we explain how to refine an abstraction in order to eliminate the spurious counterexample. To simplify the presentation, we first assume that the abstract model is the most precise one for M and α (see the discussion following definition 13.2). We then explain how to handle abstract models that are not necessarily the most precise and prove that if the concrete model is finite then there are at most a finite number of refinement steps.

Let $\widehat{T}$ be a spurious counterexample, and let $\widehat{s_i}$ be the failure state on $\widehat{T}$. We define three subsets of $\alpha^{-1}(\widehat{s_i})$:

- The set of *dead-end states* S_D is the set of all states in $\alpha^{-1}(\widehat{s_i})$ that are reachable along paths in $\alpha^{-1}(\widehat{T})$ but have no outgoing transition to $\alpha^{-1}(\widehat{s_{i+1}})$.

- The set of *bad states* S_B is the set of all states in $\alpha^{-1}(\widehat{s_i})$ that are not reachable along paths in $\alpha^{-1}(\widehat{T})$ but have an outgoing transition to $\alpha^{-1}(\widehat{s_{i+1}})$.
- The set of *irrelevant states* S_I is the set of all states in $\alpha^{-1}(\widehat{s_i})$ that are not in $S_D \cup S_B$.

The refinement suggests a partitioning of the failure state, so that the set of dead-end states S_D is separated from the set of bad states S_B.

We already have the dead-end states. S_D is exactly the set T_{j-1}, returned by the algorithm *SplitPATH*. The algorithm also returns $j-1$, the index in the counterexample where a failure state is encountered. We use the *PreImage* operator, which given a set of states returns the set of predecessors of the states in that set. We can now compute the bad states as follows:

$$S_B = PreImage(\alpha^{-1}(\widehat{s_{j+1}})) \cap \alpha^{-1}(\widehat{s_j})$$

The state $\widehat{s_j}$ should now be partitioned to separate S_D from S_B. With slight abuse of notation we refer to partitioning $\widehat{s_j}$ while the actual partitioning is applied to $\alpha^{-1}(\widehat{s_j})$. Such a partition can be done in different ways. For example, we can add a new abstract state $\widehat{s}'_j$ to $\widehat{S}$ and update α so that states in S_D are now mapped to the new state $\widehat{s}'_j$. Alternatively, we can obtain a *criterion* for partitioning the failure state, for instance, in the form of a new predicate. We can then choose to apply this criterion to partitioning all abstract states. Doing so accelerates convergence of the refinement process. Thus, there is a trade-off between the number of refinement iterations and the size of the abstract models. We call a refinement that splits abstract states a *splitting-refinement*. Once the new $\widehat{S}$ and α are determined, $\widehat{R}$, $\widehat{S_0}$, and $\widehat{L}$ should be updated.

Next, we extend the discussion to the case where an abstract model of M may not be the most precise one. In this case, there are two additional reasons for a counterexample $\widehat{T} = \langle \widehat{s_1}, \ldots, \widehat{s_n} \rangle$ to be spurious:

- The initial state $\widehat{s_1}$ of $\widehat{T}$ does not represent an initial concrete state. Thus, $T_1 = \alpha^{-1}(\widehat{s_1}) \cap S_0$ is empty. We refer to $\widehat{s_1}$ as a *spurious initial state*. In this case, the refinement will eliminate $\widehat{s_1}$ from the set of abstract initial states $\widehat{S_0}$.
- The abstract transition from $\widehat{s_i}$ to $\widehat{s_{i+1}}$ has no corresponding transition in the concrete model. That is, there is no transition from state in $\alpha^{-1}(\widehat{s_i})$ to state in $\alpha^{-1}(\widehat{s_{i+1}})$. We refer to such a transition as a *spurious transition*. In this case, the refinement eliminates the pair $(\widehat{s_i}, \widehat{s_{i+1}})$ from $\widehat{R}$.

Example 13.14 *Consider again the abstract counterexample in figure 13.6 and a somewhat different concrete model than the one described in example 13.13.*

- *If states 1, 2, and 3 are not concrete initial states, then $\widehat{1}$ is a spurious initial state and will be removed from $\widehat{S_0}$.*
- *If there is no concrete transition from state 7 to state 12, then the abstract transition $(\widehat{3}, \widehat{4})$ is spurious and will be removed from $\widehat{R}$.*

Given a model M and a formula φ, the refinement step in the CEGAR algorithm (step 4; see section 13.3.2) can now be described in more detail as follows:

4a. If *SplitPATH* returns "spurious initial state," then eliminate $\widehat{s_1}$ from $\widehat{S_0}$ and go to step 2.

4b. Let $\widehat{s_i}$ be the failure state. If the set of bad states S_B is empty, then the transition $(\widehat{s_i}, \widehat{s_{i+1}})$ is spurious. Remove it from $\widehat{R}$ and go to step 2.

4c. Otherwise, apply a splitting-refinement. Let α be the resulting abstraction function. Construct an abstract model for M and α (not necessarily the most precise one). Go to step 2.

Note that α does not change in the first two cases. However, it is guaranteed to change in step 4c since this step is applied only when S_D and S_B are not empty.

In general, if the concrete model is infinite state, then termination of CEGAR is not guaranteed. The following definitions are used in proving that, if M is finite state, then CEGAR involves only finitely many refinement steps. We first observe that an abstraction function $\alpha : S \to \widehat{S}$ induces a *partition* P_α on the set of concrete states S:

$$P_\alpha = \{\, \alpha^{-1}(\widehat{s}) \mid \widehat{s} \in \widehat{S} \text{ and } \alpha^{-1}(\widehat{s}) \neq \emptyset \,\}.$$

These sets form a partition: they are disjoint. Further, since α is total, every concrete state belongs to some set. We now define an order on abstraction functions based on the partitions they induce.

Definition 13.15 *Let $\alpha_1 : S \to \widehat{S_1}$ and $\alpha_2 : S \to \widehat{S_2}$ be two abstraction functions on M. The abstraction α_2 is smaller than α_1, denoted $\alpha_2 < \alpha_1$, if the following hold:*

- *For every $S_2 \in P_{\alpha_2}$ there is $S_1 \in P_{\alpha_1}$ such that $S_2 \subseteq S_1$.*
- *There exists some $S_2 \in P_{\alpha_2}$ and $S_1 \in P_{\alpha_1}$ such that $S_2 \subset S_1$.*

In our setting we will use the order $\alpha_2 < \alpha_1$ when α_2 is obtained by a refinement step that splits partitions in P_{α_1}.

The following theorem states the conditions under which CEGAR is guaranteed to terminate.

Theorem 13.16 *Given a finite-state model M and an ACTL or LTL specification φ whose counterexample is either path or loop, CEGAR will find a model $\widehat{M}$ such that $\widehat{M} \models \varphi \Leftrightarrow M \models \varphi$.*

Proof Let $\widehat{M_1}, \widehat{M_2}, \ldots$ be a series of abstract models of M, obtained in CEGAR via a series of refinement steps. If for some $\widehat{M_i}$ the specification φ holds or a counterexample is found to be non-spurious, then the algorithm stops and we are done.

Otherwise, we show that within a finite number of refinement steps we will obtain an abstract model that is isomorphic to M. Hence, the theorem holds.

First note that any $\widehat{M_i}$ is finite and therefore contains only a finite number of spurious initial states and spurious transitions. Thus, only a finite number of refinement steps of type 4a and 4b can be applied before we obtain a model $\widehat{M_j}$ that is most precise for some α_j.

We show that if $\widehat{M_j}$ is most precise, then the refinement step will necessarily lead to $\alpha_{j+1} < \alpha_j$.

Since $\widehat{M_j}$ is most precise, an abstract state $\hat{s}$ with $\alpha^{-1}(\hat{s}) = \emptyset$ is not reachable in $\widehat{M_j}$ and therefore cannot be part of the counterexample. Thus, algorithm *SplitPATH* returns a non-empty failure state, which is refined in step 4c. The refinement partitions the failure state and possibly additional abstract states. Thus, every partition in $P_{\alpha_{j+1}}$ is a subset of some partition in P_{α_j}, and at least one partition in $P_{\alpha_{j+1}}$ is a proper subset of a partition in P_{α_j}. Consequently, $\alpha_{j+1} < \alpha_j$.

Clearly, only a finite number of steps 4c can be applied before the resulting model $\widehat{M_i}$ is defined over $\hat{S}_i$ in which every abstract state represents a single concrete state. Further, only a finite number of steps 4a and 4b are needed to make $\widehat{M_i}$ most precise. At this stage, the abstract model is isomorphic to the concrete model and the theorem holds. $\square$

Bibliographic Notes

A survey on abstraction can be found in the chapter by Dams and Grumberg in [136].

The topic of constructing abstractions is also one of the core topics of the theory of *abstract interpretation* [160, 159, 164, 353], which is not treated in this chapter.

Two of the most widely used abstractions are localization reduction [324], which is mostly used for hardware [42], and predicate abstraction [246], which is more suitable for software. Extensions, improvements, and applications of predicate abstraction in software verification are widely investigated [41, 39, 139, 51, 140, 52, 117]. They are also applied in hardware verification [287] and in the verification of concurrent [483] and sequential [376, 361] Linux device drivers. An early classification of different types of abstraction in hardware verification is given in [378].

Bisimulation and simulation   Many notions of equivalence relations over models and their related logic preservation have been defined; see, for example, [262, 171, 172, 452]. The relationship between the simulation relation and preservation of the μ-calculus has been established in [353].

An algorithm for computing the quotient structure with respect to bisimulation is suggested in [343]. Other symbolic algorithms for bisimulation minimization are proposed in [73, 74]. A notion of *simulation equivalence* and its related quotient structure has been introduced in [96]. An efficient algorithm for computing the quotient structure with respect to simulation is presented in [263].

Predicate abstraction   An important question is how to compute the needed predicates. This can be done, for instance, using theorem provers [430, 429], symbolic decision procedures [330], interpolation [288], and interpolation sequences [264, 474].

Some works try to avoid the increase in size of abstract models cased by refinement. Lazy abstraction, for instance, adds new predicates to the model only when needed and where needed [265, 264, 376, 313, 475, 477].

CEGAR   Depending on the type of α and the size of M, the initial abstract model (that is, abstract initial states and abstract transitions) can be built using BDDs, SAT solvers, or theorem provers. Similarly, the partitioning of abstract states, performed in the refinement, can be done using BDDs (for example, as in [130] and [40]), SAT solvers (for example, as in [105, 346, 286]), or linear programming and machine learning (for example, as in [135]).

We focus here on counterexamples that are *finite paths*. In [137] and in [440] counterexamples for all of ACTL and CTL, respectively, are handled.

An iterative abstraction-based verification method for hardware that is not based on counterexamples is presented in [377].

Three-valued model checking   This chapter does not cover many other approaches to abstraction. Those are usually based on more elaborate abstract models. Such models allow, for instance, for abstract states to represent non-disjoint sets of concrete states. Others allow two types of transitions that over- or under-approximate the concrete transition relation and thus preserve the truth of full branching-time logics. Others allow to interpret formulas over three-valued semantics and can preserve both truth and falsity of full branching-time logics. A survey of these approaches can be found in the chapter by Dams and Grumberg in [136].

Tools   We list here just a few of the tools which implement the CEGAR loop and predicate abstraction: SLAM [41], BLAST [51], SATABS [140], KRATOS [116], and Wolverine [313].

14 Software Model Checking

The techniques described in the previous chapters can be applied directly to models of software given as Kripke structures. In this chapter, by contrast, we consider alternative methods that yield better performance. The first technique considers only bounded executions. It is therefore aimed primarily at bug detection rather than at proving correctness. The second technique we consider addresses this gap. It is based on the principle of abstraction, which is introduced in chapter 13. Finally, we give a fully worked example.

Both methods presented in this chapter build on the symbolic representations for modeling software programs that are introduced in chapter 3. In order to simplify the presentation of the algorithms, we will restrict ourselves to programs that do not use multiple threads of execution and that do not have recursive procedure calls. The bibliographic notes discuss techniques that lift these restrictions.

14.1 Representing Programs as Control-Flow Graphs

In chapter 3, we give a procedure that labels the statements in a given program text with a set of program locations. In this section, we extract the *control-flow graph* (CFG) from this labeled program text, which represents all executions of the program. The structure of the graph will be used by the model-checking algorithms we discuss in the remainder of this chapter.

We furthermore introduce another statement type, called *assertion*. Assertions are means to specify properties of programs. Much like an **if** statement, assertion statements take a Boolean expression b as argument. If b evaluates to *false* when the statement is executed, then the flow of control is diverted to a designated *error label*, which we denote as $\frac{1}{2}$. In this case, we say that the program violates the assertion. If b evaluates to *true*, the assertion behaves like **skip**.

Example 14.1 *Figure 14.1 gives the text of a small program on the left-hand side. The program uses l_1 as the entry label and l_7 as the exit label. The statement at location l_6 is an assertion.*

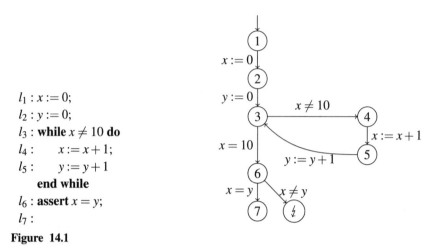

$l_1 : x := 0;$

$l_2 : y := 0;$

$l_3 : \textbf{while } x \neq 10 \textbf{ do}$

$l_4 : \quad x := x + 1;$

$l_5 : \quad y := y + 1$

$\quad \textbf{end while}$

$l_6 : \textbf{assert } x = y;$

$l_7 :$

Figure 14.1
A small program and its control-flow graph.

We now give a formal definition of the CFG.

Definition 14.2 (Control-flow graph) *The* control-flow graph *(CFG) of a program is a graph $G = (\mathcal{L}, E, I)$, where the nodes $\mathcal{L}$ are the program locations, $E \subseteq \mathcal{L} \times \mathcal{L}$ is a set of edges, and I is a labeling of the edges. The graph has an edge $(l, l') \in E$ if the statement at location l' is a successor of the statement at location l. If the statement at location l is an assignment, then the edge (l, l') is labeled with this assignment. If the statement at location l is an* **if** *or* **while** *or* **assert** *statement, then there are two edges (l, l') and (l, l''). One of the edges is labeled with the loop or branching condition or the assertion and the other is labeled with the negation. One of the nodes in $\mathcal{L}$ is the designated entry point, where the execution of the program begins, and one is the exit point.*

The CFG for our example program is given on the right-hand side of figure 14.1.

A path through the CFG that begins with the entry node is called a *program path*. We say that a program path is *feasible* if and only if there exists an execution of the program that follows this path. If we can identify a feasible program path that ends in the error location $\frac{1}{7}$, then we have shown that an assertion can be violated. We call these program paths *error paths*. We say that a program that does not have an error path is a *safe program*. We now discuss methods to determine whether there is such an error path.

14.2   Checking Assertions using Symbolic Execution

We begin by studying a very basic technique for symbolically checking whether an assertion can be violated. The technique performs a bounded analysis only, and is therefore restricted to refutation. The technique uses a satisfiability solver, which is discussed in chapter 9, as a sub-procedure. The method is effective because it constructs symbolic formulas that are very small, and checking their satisfiability is inexpensive.

The technique takes the CFG of the program as input. It constructs a symbolic formula that represents the set of states that can be reached by following a given program path.

We begin by giving the definition of the *strongest postcondition* of a program statement P and a state predicate X. The strongest postcondition gives a precise characterization of the set of states that can be reached by executing P in a state represented by X.

Definition 14.3 (Strongest postcondition)   *Given a statement P and a state predicate X, the strongest postcondition $sp(P,X)$ of P and X is the strongest state predicate that represents all states that can be reached by any execution of P from a state that satisfies X.*

Thus, $sp(P,X)$ implies any other state predicate that represents all states that are reachable by executing P from X.

We now give the strongest postcondition for common statements. The strongest postcondition for an assignment $v := e$ can be computed as follows:

$$sp(v := e, X) = \exists w. \ (v = e[v/w] \wedge X[v/w])$$

In the definition above, w denotes a new variable that ranges over the same domain as v. We write $e[v/w]$ for the expression e in which v has been replaced by w. The symbol w represents the value of the variable before the assignment and v represents the value of the variable after the assignment.

The strongest postcondition for a condition c can be computed as follows:

$$sp(c, X) = c \wedge X$$

The strongest postcondition for a sequence of statements is defined recursively as follows:

$$sp(P_1; \ldots; P_n, X) = sp(P_n, sp(P_1, \ldots, P_{n-1}, X))$$

The strongest postcondition for a sequence of statements can be used to define the strongest postcondition for a program paths. Let π be a path that traverses $n + 1$ program locations; that is, n statements are executed. Let $P_1; \ldots; P_n$ denote the sequence of program statements on this path. The strongest postcondition for the path π is defined to be the strongest postcondition of the sequence of statements on the path:

$$sp(\pi, X) = sp(P_1; \ldots; P_n, X)$$

When applying sp to a program path π, we say that we have performed *symbolic execution* of π.

Using the strongest postcondition for program paths, we can now give an algorithm that performs a heuristic search for error states using symbolic execution (figure 14.2).

The first step of procedure *Symbolic-Search*(G) is a heuristic choice of a path π in G. There are numerous heuristic techniques for picking program paths π that are likely error

procedure *Symbolic-Search*(G)
    while *true* **do**
        Pick some path π in G that ends with $\notin$;
        $C := sp(\pi, true)$;
        if *satisfiable*(C) **then**
            return "error is reachable via path π";
        end if
    end while
end procedure

Figure 14.2
Procedure for searching for a feasible path to the error location $\notin$ in the program given as CFG G using symbolic execution.

paths, and we discuss some of these in the bibliographic notes. The second step in the algorithm is to compute the strongest postcondition of the chosen path. We let C denote this condition. The algorithm then checks whether this condition is satisfiable. This check is performed using the techniques described in chapter 9. If so, π is an error path, and the search aborts. We remark that the techniques in chapter 9 provide satisfying assignments in case C is satisfiable. From this satisfying assignment, we can construct a sequence of states for the program that serves as witness that the assertion can be violated.

We note that the algorithm is not guaranteed to terminate, as programs in general may have an infinite number of paths.

14.3   Program Verification with Predicate Abstraction

In this section we discuss the application of *predicate abstraction* to software programs. Predicate abstraction is described in detail in section 13.1.3, but we will recall the basic principles. The key benefit of using predicate abstraction is that we will be able to obtain a proof that our specification holds for executions of the full program.

The basic idea of predicate abstraction is to transform the program into a *Boolean program* that abstracts the original program such that it overapproximates its behaviors. That is, any program path that is feasible in the original program is also feasible in the abstract program, but the other direction is not guaranteed. In chapter 13 we show that every ACTL* formula that is true in the abstract model is also true in the original program.

We begin by introducing Boolean programs and explain how they can be verified automatically using the methods based on ordered binary decision diagrams (OBDDs) given in chapter 8. In section 14.3.2 we show how to derive Boolean programs from general programs.

```
         procedure main()
l₁          b₁ := *;
l₂          b₂ := false;

l₃          while b₁ do
l₄              if ¬b₂ then
l₅                  b₁ = false;
                end if;
l₆              assert ¬b₁;
            end while;

l₇
         end procedure
```

Figure 14.3
A Boolean program with two Boolean variables b_1 and b_2.

14.3.1   Boolean Programs

Boolean programs are programs in which all variables are Boolean. The state space of such programs is smaller than that of programs with variables with bigger domains. The verification of assertions in such programs can be done with the help of OBDDs, which we study in chapter 8. We refrain from providing a full, formal definition of syntax and semantics and instead introduce Boolean programs informally by means of an example.

The program given in figure 14.3 is a Boolean program with two Boolean variables using our usual syntax. Note that the program is annotated with program locations. By convention, all variables in Boolean programs are initialized to *false*, and the control begins with the first statement in the main procedure. At location l_2, the symbol $*$ denotes a *nondeterministic choice*, which means that the value of b_1 can be either *true* or *false*. Such nondeterminism is commonly used for abstracting more complicated behavior. It is the role of the verification algorithm to verify the program under every possible choice at that statement.

The assertion at location l_6 specifies a desired behavior of the program, namely, that b_1 always evaluates to false at this location. We remark that the set of states of the Boolean program is defined as usual; that is, a state is a valuation of the program counter and the Boolean variables. We write $\mathbb{B}$ for the set of Booleans. For our example program with two variables and seven program locations, the set of states is thus

$$\{l_1, \ldots, l_7\} \times \mathbb{B} \times \mathbb{B}. \tag{14.1}$$

The first part of the cross product is the set of possible values of the program counter, and the other two parts define the set of values of the two Boolean variables.

Time frame	0	1	2	3
PC (line)	l_1	l_2	l_3	l_7
b_1	F	F	F	F
b_2	F	F	F	F

Time frame	0	1	2	3	4	5	6	7
PC (line)	l_1	l_2	l_3	l_4	l_5	l_6	l_3	l_7
b_1	F	T	T	T	T	F	F	F
b_2	F	F	F	F	F	F	F	F

Figure 14.4
The two traces of the program in figure 14.3.

Recall that a trace is a sequence of states. The behaviors of the program can be described as a set of traces. The set of traces that the program can exhibit appears in the table in the figure 14.4. Owing to the nondeterministic choice at location l_1, the program has two traces: one in which b_1 is chosen to be *true*, and one in which it is chosen to be *false*. We furthermore observe that b_1 is *false* whenever the control reaches location l_6, and thus, the assertion holds.

We have already given the set of states of our example program, and it is easy to see that the set of initial states is the singleton $\{(l_1, F, F)\}$. We refrain from giving the full transition relation R, as this set is already large:

$$R \;=\; \{ \quad \langle (l_1, F, F), (l_2, F, F) \rangle,$$
$$\langle (l_1, F, F), (l_2, T, F) \rangle,$$
$$\cdots \qquad\qquad \}$$

We can now pass our model to an algorithm for checking reachability properties. Any implementation of reachability checking with explicitly represented sets will suffer from the fact that these sets grow exponentially with the number of variables that the Boolean program declares. This problem can be partially addressed by representing S_0 and R *symbolically*. This means that, for a given set, we find a propositional formula that its solutions correspond exactly to the elements of the set; that is, we use the characteristic function of the set. As an example, recall the set of initial states S_0 of our example program. Explicitly given, this set is $\{(l_1, F, F)\}$. We can write the following characteristic function for it:

$$S_0(s) \Leftrightarrow s.PC = l_1 \land \neg s.b_1 \land \neg s.b_2 \tag{14.2}$$

We can use the same approach to represent the transition relation R symbolically. We also note that the formulas we obtain for Boolean programs are almost Boolean formulas; the only exception is the program counter component of the state, which uses a finite sub-range of the integers. This finite range, however, can be trivially re-encoded with Boolean variables only, using a binary or unary encoding, as described in section 3.4. We can now apply our symbolic methods for checking reachability, including the algorithms based on OBDDs given in chapter 8 or the SAT-based algorithms for full verification in chapter 10. They determine whether the Boolean program has an error trace or not without explicitly enumerating its states.

14.3.2 From Programs to Boolean Programs with Lazy Abstraction

We now show how to derive Boolean programs from general programs in an automated way. Most of this process is described in chapter 13. We assume here that the abstraction is given; that is, we are already given a set of predicates $\{P_1, \ldots, P_k\}$, where each P_i is a subset of the concrete states. We are furthermore assuming that the predicates are given by means of atomic first-order formulas over the variables of the program.

We recall from section 13.2.1 that the computation of the most precise existential abstraction is performed by quantifying over the concrete states. This operation can be very expensive. We therefore begin with a very inexpensive and coarse abstraction, and rely on the abstraction refinement procedure given in section 13.3.2 to refine it as required.

Procedure *abstract-CFG* in figure 14.5 produces the initial abstraction. It is given the CFG $G = (\mathcal{L}, E, I)$ of the concrete program. It generates a CFG for the abstract program as follows:

- The set of nodes and the edges of the CFG of the concrete program are replicated precisely.
- If the concrete instruction $I(l)$ associated with node l is an assignment, then the abstract instruction $\widehat{I}(l)$ sets all Boolean variables to a nondeterministic choice.
- If the concrete instruction $I(l)$ is a conditional, then the abstract instruction $\widehat{I}(l)$ is the nondeterministic conditional.

Now consider procedure *predicate-abstraction-CEGAR*(CFG) (figure 14.6). It implements CEGAR as described in section 13.3.2. We recall the basic steps of the procedure:

1. An initial abstraction $\widehat{M}$ is generated. We perform this step using procedure *initial-abstraction-CFG*.
2. If the abstraction satisfies the property, that is, if no error path exists in $\widehat{G}$, then the concrete program is safe and the procedure stops. This step can be performed using the technique explained in section 14.3.1.
3. If the abstraction has an error path, then attempt to simulate the error path on M. If this succeeds, the concrete program has an error path and the procedure stops. This step can be performed using the technique we have explained in section 14.2.
4. Otherwise, refine $\widehat{M}$ and resume with step 2.

procedure *initial-abstraction-CFG*(CFG $G = (\mathcal{L}, E, I)$)

    for all $l \in G$ **do**
        if $I(l)$ is assignment **then**
            $\widehat{I}(l) := "b_1, \ldots, b_k := *, \ldots, *";$
        else if $I(l)$ is conditional **then**
            $\widehat{I}(l) := " * ";$
        end if
    end for
    $\widehat{G} := (\mathcal{L}, E, \widehat{I});$
    return G;

end procedure

Figure 14.5
Procedure for computing the initial predicate abstraction of a program given as a CFG.

It remains to explain the refinement procedure, given as procedure *refinement* in figure 14.7. It is given the concrete CFG, the current abstract CFG, and the spurious abstract counterexample. We recall from chapter 13 that there are two potential reasons that the counterexample cannot be concretized:

1. We do not use the most precise existential abstraction. In this case, we have to refine the transitions in $\widehat{G}$; that is, we have to perform transformer refinement.
2. We do not have a sufficient set of predicates. In this case, we have to refine the set of predicates; that is, we have to perform domain refinement.

There are numerous techniques for both cases. Procedure *refinement* in figure 14.7 uses a basic approach. If we find that an abstract transition does not have a corresponding concrete transition, we simply remove this particular transition from the abstract program.

If none of the abstract transitions is spurious, we must refine our set of predicates. An option to perform this refinement is to compute the strongest postcondition, as described in section 14.2. In each step, we add the current predicate to our set of predicates. This guarantees that the same counterexample path will not be repeated again. We discuss more elaborate techniques for domain and transformer refinement in the bibliographic notes.

14.4   A Full Example

14.4.1   A Program

We use the program fragment in figure 14.8, taken with minor modifications from [41], as a running example. The program accesses some incoming data. To access these data it is necessary to open an external resource (such as a file or a network socket). This is achieved

procedure *predicate-abstraction-CEGAR*(CFG G)

$\widehat{G} := \textit{initial-abstraction-CEGAR}(G)$;

while $\widehat{G}$ has error path **do**

Let $\widehat{\pi}$ be a counterexample in $\widehat{G}$;

$\pi := \widehat{\pi}(0).PC, \widehat{\pi}(1).PC, \ldots$;

if $sp(\pi, true)$ is satisfiable **then**

return "G is unsafe";

end if

$\widehat{G} := \textit{refinement}(G, \widehat{G}, \widehat{\pi})$;

end while

return "G is safe";

end procedure

Figure 14.6
Procedure for checking assertions in a program given as a CFG using counterexample-guided abstraction refinement.

procedure *refinement*(CFGs $G, \widehat{G}$, path $\widehat{\pi}$)

Let $\widehat{\pi}$ be $\widehat{s}_0 \ldots, \widehat{s}_n$

for $i := 0$ **to** $n - 1$ **do**

if $(\widehat{s}_i, \widehat{s}_{i+1})$ is spurious in G **then**

$l := \widehat{s}_i.PC$;

Remove transition $(\widehat{s}_i, \widehat{s}_{i+1})$ from $\widehat{I}(l)$;

return;

end if

end for

$P := true$;

for $i := 0$ **to** $n - 1$ **do**

$P := sp(I(\pi(i)), P)$;

Add P to set of predicates

end for

end procedure

Figure 14.7
Procedure for refining the abstraction during counterexample-guided abstraction refinement.

```
          do
1 :           open();
2 :           old_count := count;
3 :           if data_available() then
4 :               process_data();
5 :               close();
6 :               count := count + 1
7 :           end if
8 :       while old_count ≠ count;
9 :       close();
```

Figure 14.8
Program fragment for processing incoming data using a resource that needs to be opened and closed [41].

by calling a function named *open*. The resource also needs to be closed, which is performed by calling the function *close*.

The program furthermore calls the function *data_available*, which returns *true* if there is data available for processing and *false* otherwise. The processing of the data is performed by the function *process_data*. We do not elaborate on either of the functions, as their workings is immaterial to the property we want to check.

The program contains a loop, and the loop body operates as follows. The program first opens the resource and checks if data is available. If so, the data is processed and the resource is closed. If no data is available, no action is taken.

Figure 14.9 is the CFG for our running example. Observe that the nodes for the **if** statements have two successors: we label the edge that leads to the *true* branch of the statement with the conditional *c*, and label the edge that leads to the *false* branch of the statement with ¬*c*.

14.4.2 A Specification

For correct operation, the program needs to obey a strict discipline when opening and closing the resource. Intuitively, the program must alternate strictly between opening and closing. More precisely, we say that the resource is in one of two states: it is either "closed" or "opened." The following rules must be followed:

- Initially, the resource is in the state "closed."
- In the "closed" state, the resource can be opened by calling the function *open*, which changes the state of the resource to "opened". In the "closed" state, the *close* function must not be called.

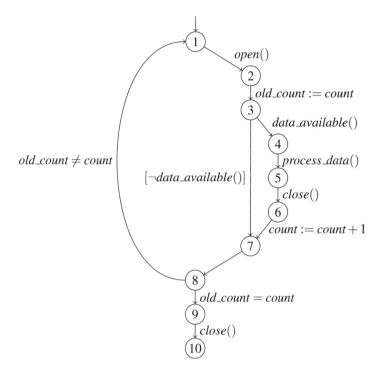

Figure 14.9
CFG of the running example.

- In the "opened" state, the resource can be closed by calling the function *close*, which changes the state of the resource back to "closed". In the "opened" state, the *open* function must not be called.

Any violation of these rules is considered an error, and the program contains two integer variables *count* and *old_count*, which are used to implement the rules. We aim to apply model checking to determine whether such an error can occur in our program. We use an automaton to formally capture the set of rules above. The automaton accepts words over an alphabet Σ whose elements are the actions *open* and *close*.

Recall that we build automata that accept the *negation* of the property we want to check. The rules above can be translated into the following automaton with three states:

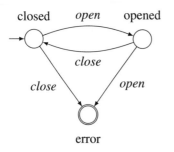

The error state is the only accepting state. All erroneous behaviors reach the error state and are therefore accepted by the automaton.

We now explain how to form a joint model from an arbitrary specification automaton and a program. In principle, we can build the product of the automaton of the program and the automaton of the specification. We can then check whether the language of this product automaton is empty. For a full description of how to check that a model satisfies a specification given as an automaton we refer the reader to chapter 7. Any run that is accepted by the product is a counterexample to our property. Conversely, if the product is empty, we have a proof that the property holds.

However, constructing the product is non-trivial. In particular, note that the program may have variables with an infinite domain, in which case the set of states of the program is infinite. Even if we assume that the variables have a finite machine-defined bit width, we still obtain a very large state space. We therefore need to apply methods that do not rely on enumeration of the states of the product automaton.

As a first step, we perform a syntactic construction of the product automaton by merging the program text with the specification automaton. This step is called the *instrumentation* of the program with the specification automaton. Recall that the automaton has a set of states Q. In order to track the state of the specification automaton in our program, we add a new program variable called *state* that ranges over Q. We also add a program statement that initializes this variable with an initial state of the specification automaton.

Also recall that the automaton has a set Δ of *transitions*, which are triplets (q, a, q') where q and q' are states and $a \in \Sigma$ is an element of the alphabet. We furthermore assume that we can identify syntactically which program statements perform which action, if any. For each program statement P in the program, we then perform the following two steps:

1. We determine whether the statement P performs any action from Σ. If no action is performed by P, the statement is not modified.

2. Otherwise, let $a \in \Sigma$ denote the action that statement P performs. Let $\{(q_1, a, q'_1), \ldots, (q_n, a, q'_n)\}$ be the set of transitions that perform the action a. We insert the following

new program statement just before *P*:

$$\textbf{if } state = q_1 \textbf{ then}$$
$$state := q_1'$$
$$\textbf{else if } state = q_2 \textbf{ then}$$
$$state := q_2'$$
$$\cdots$$
$$\textbf{else if } state = q_n \textbf{ then}$$
$$state := q_n'$$
$$\textbf{end if}$$

3. We also add the assertion

$$\textbf{assert } state \notin F$$

after any location that changes the state. It checks whether the automaton has transitioned into an accepting state. Recall that *F* is the set of accepting states of our specification automaton. If $state \in F$, the assertion fails.

Example 14.4 *We resume our running example. The result of instrumenting the program given in figure 14.8 with our specification automaton is given in figure 14.10.*

If we now build an automation for the instrumented program, the language it accepts is identical to the language accepted by the product of the automaton of the original program and the specification. The emptiness of the language can be verified directly on the instrumented program by checking whether it is safe. We remark that we do not build the product explicitly.

14.4.3   Abstracting the Program

The program has a very large number of states since the value of *count* can grow arbitrarily. However, as we only care to check the assertions, the actual values of *count* and *old_count* are not important; what matters is the *relationship* between *count* and *old_count*. Figure 14.11 gives a finite-state abstraction of the same locking program. The Boolean variable b_1 encodes the predicate $state = opened$, and b_2 encodes the predicate $count = old\_count$. In general, a predicate abstraction may use many predicates to capture the behaviors of a program that are relevant to checking a specification. In this example, two predicates suffice.

The finite-state abstraction provided in figure 14.11 can be constructed from the program in figure 14.10 automatically. In order to derive this abstraction, we need to abstract each statement in the program individually. For example, let us consider the statement

$$count := count + 1$$

```
state := closed;
do
    if state = closed then state := opened
    else if state = opened then state := error end if;
    assert state ≠ error;
    open();
    old_count := count;
    if data_available() then
        process_data();
        if state = closed then state := error
        else if state = opened then state := closed end if;
        assert state ≠ error;
        close();
        count := count + 1;
    end if;
while old_count ≠ count;
if state = closed then state := error
else if state = opened then state := closed end if;
assert state ≠ error;
close();
```

Figure 14.10
Program fragment after instrumenting the specification automaton. The parts in gray have been added.

in figure 14.10. We need to examine the effect of this assignment on the predicate b_2: $count = old\_count$. Let b_2' denote the value of b_2 after a statement. Hence, in the case of the statement above, the variable b_2' stands for $count + 1 = old\_count$. What relationships are there between b_2 and b_2'? We can find these relationships by enumerating formulas using b_2 and b_2' and checking each formula for validity. For example, in order to check if $b_2 \Rightarrow \neg b_2'$, we need to check whether the implication

$$(count = old\_count) \Rightarrow \neg(count + 1 = old\_count) \tag{14.3}$$

is valid. Equation 14.3 states that if the current value of b_2 is *true*, then after executing the statement $count := count + 1$ it will be *false*. Note that if b_2 is *false*, then neither of the following implications is valid:

$$\neg(count = old\_count) \Rightarrow (count + 1 = old\_count)$$
$$\neg(count = old\_count) \Rightarrow \neg(count + 1 = old\_count) \tag{14.4}$$

$b_1 := false;$
do
    assert $\neg b_1;$
    $b_1 := true;$
    $b_2 := true;$
    if $*$ **then**
        assert $b_1;$
    end if
    $b_1 := false;$
    if b_2 **then**
        $b_2 := false;$
    else
        $b_2 := *;$
    end if
while $\neg b_2;$
assert $b_1;$
$b_1 := false;$

Figure 14.11
Predicate abstraction of the program in figure 14.10; the variable b_1 represents *state = opened*, and b_2 represents *count = old_count*.

In both cases, a decision procedure produces a counterexample. Thus, when the current value of b_2 is *false*, nothing can be said about its value after the execution of the statement. The result of these three proof attempts is then used to replace the statement *count = count + 1;* with

$$\textbf{if } b_2 \textbf{ then } b_2 := \textit{false}; \textbf{ else } b_2 := *;$$

as shown in figure 14.11.

    Similarly, we abstract the assignment *old_count := count* with the assignment $b_2 := true$ because b_2', which summarizes the effect of the assignment, is equivalent to the valid equality *count = count*. The loop test *count $\neq$ old_count* is simply replaced by $\neg b_2$. Finally, the calls to the functions *open*, *close*, and *process_data* can be abstracted. The only property that is relevant with respect to the locking property is the test *data_available()*, which we can replace by a non-deterministic branch.

    This analysis allows the automatic construction of figure 14.11, which is a Boolean program, and hence can be verified as explained in section 14.3.1. In our example, the algorithm determines that the assertions hold, and hence we conclude that the program does not violate the locking policy.

The example used just two predicates b_1 and b_2, and the analysis used logical formulas over b_1, b_1', b_2, and b_2'. In general, with n predicates, there are 2^{2^n} nonequivalent logical formulas. It is therefore impractical to first enumerate these formulas and then check for validity. Many optimizations and heuristics are therefore used in tools that implement predicate abstraction.

Bibliographic Notes

Path-based symbolic simulation, as briefly discussed in section 14.2, has been used for a variety of applications, including automated testing [305]. The Java Path Finder (JPF) is a model checker for multi-threaded Java bytecode. The original version of JPF explores the program explicitly but has been extended with a symbolic variant that builds path constraints [304]. It uses a decision procedure to prune infeasible paths. Further tools that implement path-based symbolic simulation include PET [250, 251], DART [243], CUTE [436], SAGE [242], KLEE [97], and Pex [242].

The bounded model-checking (BMC) technique, described in chapter 10 for the case of hardware models, has also been specialized to the verification of software programs in CBMC [138]. Similarly, there are attempts to extend property-directed reachability (PDR; see chapter 10) to software [115].

Predicate abstraction (section 14.3.2) was introduced by Graf and Saïdi [246]. An automatic implementation of it was pioneered by Ball and Rajamani in Microsoft's SLAM tool [41, 39] with an application to Windows device drivers [37]. Magic [102] and SatAbs [139] reimplement this method but also verify concurrent programs. With the Windows 8.1 release, Microsoft's Static Driver Verifier uses Corral as verifier [331, 332].

Finally, in this chapter we have focussed on assertion checking, but there are tools that check a broader range of properties. In particular, there is a broad body of work on termination checking [154, 153, 165, 106].

15 Verification with Automata Learning

Automata learning is a technique for an automatic learning of an unknown regular language. This technique has proven useful in several applications. In this chapter we present two such applications. One is *compositional verification* with assume-guarantee reasoning, where learning is used for automatic construction of assumptions. The other is *black-box checking*, in which the correctness of a system given as a black box is proved. The algorithm that we use for learning is the L^* algorithm by Angluin [27], which we describe in the next section.

15.1 Angluin's L^* Learning Algorithm

The L^* algorithm learns a deterministic finite automaton (DFA) for an unknown regular language U over the alphabet Σ. The algorithm assumes the existence of a "teacher" that answers two types of queries about the regular language U. The first type of query, called a *membership query*, asks whether a given word is a member of U. The second, called an *equivalence query*, asks whether a candidate DFA C accepts the language U. If $\mathcal{L}(C)$ is different from U, the teacher returns a word in the symmetric difference of the two languages. In applications of the learning algorithm, the teacher can be implemented as a procedure that algorithmically provides answers to such queries.

The L^* algorithm uses two finite sets of finite strings S and E over the alphabet Σ, and a table T. The set S is prefix closed (so, in particular, it contains the empty string ε). The rows of the table T are the strings in $S \cup (S \cdot \Sigma)$, while the columns are the strings in E. The table T is defined so that $T(s, e) = 1$ if $s \cdot e$ is in U and $T(s, e) = 0$ otherwise. Intuitively, the strings in S correspond to states in the candidate automaton, and the strings in $S \cdot \Sigma$ correspond to their successors. It is convenient to think of the table as consisting of two parts: the top part corresponding to the states S, and the bottom part corresponding to the successors $S \cdot \Sigma$. The strings in E serve to distinguish different states from one another. The learning algorithm fills the table by posing membership queries to the teacher. Additional elements are added to the sets S and E in an incremental manner as the algorithm executes.

Since we want to learn the smallest automaton for U, we define an equivalence relation $\equiv mod(E)$ over strings in S as follows: $s_1 \equiv s_2 \; mod(E)$ if for each $e \in E$, $T(s_1, e) = T(s_2, e)$.

This means that $s_1 \cdot e \in U$ if and only if $s_2 \cdot e \in U$ for every $e \in E$. It is easy to check that $\equiv mod(E)$ is indeed an equivalence relation. Let $[s]$ denote the equivalence class that includes s. When the learning algorithm suggests a candidate automaton, these equivalence classes become the states of the automaton.

Note that the equivalence classes over S are defined in a manner that is similar to the way the states of a quotient automaton are defined. The only difference is that in the quotient automaton the equivalence is defined with respect to Σ^*, while here it is defined with respect to the subset E of Σ^*.

The table is supposed to represent a candidate automaton that can be checked for equivalence with U. In order for that to make sense, the table needs to be *closed* and *consistent*. Thus, we first explain these two notions.

Definition 15.1 *A table T is* closed *if for each $s \cdot a \in S \cdot \Sigma$ there is some $s' \in S$ such that $s \cdot a \equiv s' \, mod(E)$.*

Intuitively, if a table is not closed, then the set of successors includes a new state $s \cdot a$, that is not yet in S. We add it to S and add the row $s \cdot a$ to the top part of the table. We update the bottom part as well by adding rows of the form $s \cdot a \cdot b$ for every $b \in \Sigma$. We update the table entries $T(s \cdot a \cdot b, e)$, for every $e \in E$, by checking the membership query for $(s \cdot a \cdot b \cdot e)$.

Definition 15.2 *A table is* consistent *if for all $s_1, s_2 \in S$ such that $s_1 \equiv s_2 \, mod(E)$, for each $a \in \Sigma$, we have that $s_1 \cdot a \equiv s_2 \cdot a \, mod(E)$.*

Intuitively, a table is consistent if, whenever two states are equivalent, so are all their successors. If the table is not consistent, then there are $s_1, s_2 \in S$, $a \in \Sigma$, and $e \in E$ such that $s_1 \equiv s_2 \, mod(E)$, and $s_1 \cdot a \cdot e \in U$ but $s_2 \cdot a \cdot e \notin U$ or vice versa. In order to distinguish between s_1 and s_2, we add $a \cdot e$ to E and update the table T by checking the membership queries for every row in $S \cup (S \cdot \Sigma)$ and $a \cdot e$.

Definition 15.3 *Given a closed and consistent table T over the sets S and E, the* candidate automaton $M_T = (Q, q_0, \Sigma, \delta, F)$ *is constructed as follows:*

- *The set of states Q is $\{ [s] \mid s \in S \}$.*
- *The initial state q_0 is $[\varepsilon]$ (where ε is the empty string).*
- *The transition relation δ is defined as follows: for $s \in S, a \in \Sigma$, $\delta([s], a) = [s \cdot a]$.*
- *$F = \{ [s] \mid T(s, \varepsilon) = 1 \}$ (thus, for every $[s] \in F, s' \in [s]$, the string s' is accepted by U).*

Two basic steps are used in the learning algorithms for extending the table T:

add_rows(s): Add s to S. Update the table by moving the row s to the top part of T and adding $s \cdot a$ to the bottom part of T for each $a \in \Sigma$ (if not already present). Update $T(s \cdot a, e)$ for each $e \in E$ according to the membership query for $(s \cdot a \cdot e)$.

add_column(e): Add e to E. Update the table T by adding the column e. Set $T(s, e)$ for each $s \in S \cup (S \cdot \Sigma)$, according to the membership query for $(s \cdot e)$.

Initialize S and E to $\{\varepsilon\}$
Ask membership queries for ε and each $a \in \Sigma$
Construct the initial table (S, E, T)
repeat
    if (S, E, T) is not consistent or not closed **then**
        if (S, E, T) is not consistent **then**
            find $s_1, s_2 \in S$, $a \in \Sigma$, $e \in E$ such that
                $s_1 \equiv s_2 \bmod(E)$ and $T(s_1 \cdot a, e) \neq T(s_2 \cdot a, e)$;
            add_column$(a \cdot e)$;
        else /* (S, E, T) is not closed */
            find $s \in S$, $a \in \Sigma$ such that $s \cdot a \notin [s']$ for any $s' \in S$;
            add_rows$(s \cdot a)$;
        end if
    else /* (S, E, T) is closed and consistent */
        Construct the candidate automaton M_T (see Definition 15.3)
        Send M_T to Teacher
        if Teacher returns a counterexample c **then**
            add *pref*(c) to S;
            extend T to $(S \cup (S \cdot \Sigma)) \times E$ using membership queries
        else /* the teacher returns "yes" to the candidate M_T */
            return M_T
        end if
    end if
end repeat

Figure 15.1
The L^* algorithm.

Using *add_rows* and *add_column*, we give pseudo-code for the L^* algorithm in figure 15.1. It iteratively constructs a candidate automaton until one that is equivalent to U is found. The algorithm updates the sets S and E and the table T to a consistent and closed table. It then constructs the corresponding candidate automaton M_T, and generates an equivalence query for the teacher. If M_T is not equivalent to U, then a counterexample c in the symmetric difference of $\mathcal{L}(M_T)$ and U is returned. The algorithm then extends the top part of the table with rows corresponding to all the prefixes of the counterexample c, denoted *pref*(c), and extends the lower part of the table accordingly. The algorithm repeats until an automaton is obtained that is equivalent to U.

Theorem 15.4 ([27]) *The L^* algorithm terminates and returns the smallest DFA that accepts the unknown regular language U.*

	ε
ε	0
a	0
b	1

Figure 15.2
The initial table.

	ε
ε	0
b	1
a	0
ba	0
bb	1

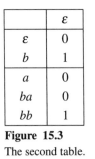

Figure 15.3
The second table.

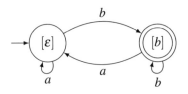

Figure 15.4
The automaton derived from the second table.

The algorithm is polynomial in n, the number of states in the smallest DFA for U, and in m, the length of the longest counterexample returned by the teacher. Note that while n depends on U, m may vary from one teacher to another.

15.1.1   Example

As an example we consider the regular language $U = a^*b^+$ over $\Sigma = \{a,b\}$. Initially, $S = E = \{\varepsilon\}$. The initial table, constructed by L^*, is presented in figure 15.2.

A line separates the top part of the table with rows in S from the bottom part with rows in $S \cdot \Sigma$. The table is consistent but not closed: ε, the only element in S, is not equivalent to b. We add b to S and add ba and bb to the set of successors.

The constructed table is presented in figure 15.3. The table is closed and consistent, and therefore we construct a conjecture automaton M_1, where $S_1 = \{[\varepsilon],[b]\}$, $q_0^1 = [\varepsilon]$, and $F_1 = \{[b]\}$, $\delta_1([\varepsilon],a) = [\varepsilon]$, $\delta_1([\varepsilon],b) = [b]$, $\delta_1([b],a) = [\varepsilon]$, and $\delta_1([b],b) = [b]$. The automaton is given in figure 15.4.

Since $\mathcal{L}(M_1) \neq U$, a counterexample in their symmetric difference is returned. Assume the counterexample is bab. Then, bab and all its prefixes are added to S and the set $S \cdot \Sigma$ is extended accordingly. This is demonstrated in the table in figure 15.5.

The table in figure 15.5 is closed but not consistent. For instance, $\varepsilon \equiv ba \bmod(E)$, but $b \not\equiv bab \bmod(E)$. This means that the states $[\varepsilon]$ and $[ba]$ should be distinguished, since the word b differentiates between them. We thus add b to E and extend the table in figure 15.5 with another column. The table in figure 15.6 is the result of this extension.

The table in 15.6 is closed and consistent. The candidate automaton M_2, given in figure 15.7, is the desired automaton: it is a minimal DFA that recognizes $U = a^*b^+$.

15.2   Compositional Reasoning

Efficient algorithms for compositional verification can extend the applicability of formal verification methods to much larger and more interesting systems. Many systems have a natural decomposition into components, for instance, multiple processes running in parallel in a software system, or modules composed synchronously in a hardware design.

	ε
ε	0
b	1
ba	0
bab	0
a	0
bb	1
baa	0
$baba$	0
$babb$	0

Figure 15.5
The third table.

	ε	b
ε	0	1
b	1	1
ba	0	0
bab	0	0
a	0	1
bb	1	1
baa	0	0
$baba$	0	0
$babb$	0	0

Figure 15.6
The fourth table.

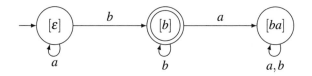

Figure 15.7
Minimal DFA for $L = a^* b^+$, derived from the fourth table.

An obvious strategy would be to decompose the specification of such a system into properties that describe the behavior of small parts of the system and check each of the local properties using only the part of the system that it describes. If we can deduce that the system satisfies each local property, and if we know that the conjunction of the local properties implies the overall specification, then we can conclude that the complete system satisfies this specification as well.

Unfortunately, this strategy is often not applicable. Specification may not be decomposable into local properties. Further, a component may satisfy its specification only under an assumption on the environment it interacts with (that is, the rest of the system).

In this chapter we focus on the *assume-guarantee paradigm* [225, 289, 386, 413] for compositional reasoning. Suppose that the system comprises two processes M and M'. Since the behavior of process M depends on the behavior of process M', the user specifies a set of assumptions that must be satisfied by M' in order to guarantee the correctness of process M. Since the behavior of process M' also depends on the behavior of process M, the user specifies a set of assumptions that must be satisfied by M in order to guarantee the correctness of process M'. By combining the set of assumed and guaranteed properties of M and M' in an appropriate manner, it is possible to establish correctness of the entire system $M \parallel M'$ without constructing the global state-transition graph.

Typically, a formula in the assume-guarantee paradigm is a triple $\langle g \rangle M \langle f \rangle$, where g represents the assumption on M's environment and f describes the specification to be proved on the system. The specification f and the assumption g can be given as temporal formulas or models such as Kripke structures or automata. While the formula looks like a Hoare triple, it is actually quite different. The formula is true if, whenever M is part of a system satisfying the assumption g, then the system must also guarantee the specification f. A typical proof shows that $\langle g \rangle M \langle f \rangle$ and $\langle true \rangle M' \langle g \rangle$ hold and concludes that $\langle true \rangle M \parallel M' \langle f \rangle$ is true. This proof strategy can also be expressed as an inference rule:

$$\frac{\begin{array}{c} \langle g \rangle M \langle f \rangle \\ \langle true \rangle M' \langle g \rangle \end{array}}{\langle true \rangle M \parallel M' \langle f \rangle} \quad (\text{ASYM})$$

The proof rule above, denoted ASYM, is asymmetric. It refers differently to M and M'. ASYM is a simple rule, yet it proved to be useful in many cases.

It is important to avoid circularity in assume-guarantee arguments. Consider the following inference rule:

$$\frac{\begin{array}{c} \langle f \rangle M \langle g \rangle \\ \langle g \rangle M' \langle f \rangle \end{array}}{M \parallel M' \models f \wedge g}$$

This rule is easily seen to be unsound. For instance, let M be $\textbf{wait}(x = 1); y := 1$, and let M' be $\textbf{wait}(y = 1); x := 1$. Let $g = \textbf{AF}(y = 1)$, and let $f = \textbf{AF}(x = 1)$. Then, the hypotheses for the proof rule hold while the conclusion does not. Sound "circular" rules break the circularity with some type of induction. They are discussed in the bibliographic notes.

15.3   Assume-Guarantee Reasoning for Communicating Components

As mentioned above, assume-guarantee reasoning provides solutions to the problem of decomposing the verification of a large system into local verification steps of the system components. The most challenging part of applying assume-guarantee reasoning is the creation of appropriate assumptions to use in the application of assume-guarantee rules.

In this section we describe a *fully automated* framework for the assume-guarantee rule ASYM. The presentation closely follows the presentation in [151]. In this framework the checked system is modeled as a composition of two communicating components in a concurrent system and the checked property is a safety property. Extensions to systems with many components and to more expressive properties are available and discussed in the bibliographic notes.

15.3.1   The System Model

We use *labeled transition systems (LTSs)* to model the communicating components. The components communicate with each other by synchronizing on their common actions.

Their executions otherwise interleave on their non-common actions. Formally, let *Act* be a universal set of observable actions, and let τ denote a local action, unobservable to a component's environment.

Definition 15.5 *A* Labeled Transition System (LTS) *M is a quadruple $M = (Q, \alpha M, \delta, q_0)$ where:*

- *Q is a finite set of states;*
- *$\alpha M \subseteq Act$ is a finite set of observable actions called* the alphabet *of M;*
- *$\delta \subseteq Q \times (\alpha M \cup \{\tau\}) \times Q$ is the transition relation;*
- *$q_0 \in Q$ is the initial state.*

LTSs are defined similarly to automata, except that every state is considered accepting. An LTS *M* is *nondeterministic* if it contains a τ transition or if there exist $(q, a, q') \in \delta$ and $(q, a, q'') \in \delta$ such that $q' \neq q''$. Otherwise, *M* is *deterministic*. For a deterministic LTS, we write $\delta(q, a) = q'$ instead of $(q, a, q') \in \delta$. Just like automata, every nondeterministic LTS can be transformed into a deterministic LTS.

A *trace* σ is a finite sequence of observable actions. We use σ_i to denote the prefix of σ of length *i*. A *path* in an LTS *M* is a finite sequence $p = q_0, a_0, q_1, a_1, \ldots, a_{n-1}, q_n$ of alternating states and observable or unobservable actions of *M*, such that for every $k \in \{0, \ldots, n-1\}$ we have $(q_k, a_k, q_{k+1}) \in \delta$. The *trace* of *p*, denoted $\sigma(p)$ is the sequence $b_0 b_1 \ldots b_l$ of actions along *p*, obtained by removing from $a_0 \cdots a_{n-1}$ all occurrences of τ. The set of all traces of paths in *M* is called the *language of M*, denoted $\mathcal{L}(M)$. A trace σ is *accepted* by *M* if $\sigma \in \mathcal{L}(M)$. Note that $\mathcal{L}(M)$ is prefix closed and that the empty trace, denoted ε, is accepted by any LTS.

For $\Sigma \subseteq Act$, the *projection of trace* σ on Σ, denoted $\sigma\downarrow_\Sigma$, is the trace obtained by removing from σ all occurrences of actions $a \notin \Sigma$. The *projection of an LTS M* on Σ, denoted $M\downarrow_\Sigma$, is the LTS over alphabet Σ obtained by renaming to τ all the transitions labeled with actions that are not in Σ. Note that $\mathcal{L}(M\downarrow_\Sigma) = \{\sigma\downarrow_\Sigma \mid \sigma \in \mathcal{L}(M)\}$.

Next, we define the parallel composition operator, which enables us to explicitly construct a system from its components. In other chapters of this book we are usually given a full system, while ignoring its lower-level building blocks. In this chapter, however, we need to know the lower-level structure of the system, in order to exploit it in compositional verification.

Definition 15.6 *Given two LTSs M_1 and M_2 over alphabet αM_1 and αM_2, respectively, their* interface alphabet *αI consists of their common alphabet. That is, $\alpha I = \alpha M_1 \cap \alpha M_2$. The* parallel composition *operator* $\|$ *is a commutative and associative operator that combines the behavior of two components by synchronizing on the actions in their interface and interleaving the remaining actions.*

Let $M_1 = (Q_1, \alpha M_1, \delta_1, q_{0_1})$ and $M_2 = (Q_2, \alpha M_2, \delta_2, q_{0_2})$ be two LTSs. Then $M_1 \| M_2$ is an LTS $M = (Q, \alpha M, \delta, q_0)$, where $Q = Q_1 \times Q_2$, $q_0 = (q_{0_1}, q_{0_2})$, $\alpha M = \alpha M_1 \cup \alpha M_2$, and δ is defined as follows where $a \in \alpha M \cup \{\tau\}$:

- *if $(q_1, a, q_1') \in \delta_1$ for $a \notin \alpha M_2$, then $((q_1, q_2), a, (q_1', q_2)) \in \delta$ for every $q_2 \in Q_2$;*
- *if $(q_2, a, q_2') \in \delta_2$ for $a \notin \alpha M_1$, then $((q_1, q_2), a, (q_1, q_2')) \in \delta$ for every $q_1 \in Q_1$;*
- *if $(q_1, a, q_1') \in \delta_1$ and $(q_2, a, q_2') \in \delta_2$ for $a \neq \tau$, then $((q_1, q_2), a, (q_1', q_2')) \in \delta$.*

The following lemma formally describes the intuition that each trace in the parallel composition corresponds to a pair of traces, one in each of its components. Note that if $\alpha M_1 = \alpha M_2$, then the language of M is the intersection of the languages of its components.

Lemma 15.7 ([395]) *For every $t \in (\alpha M_1 \cup \alpha M_2)^*$, it holds that $t \in \mathcal{L}(M_1 \| M_2)$ if and only if $t{\downarrow}_{\alpha M_1} \in \mathcal{L}(M_1)$ and $t{\downarrow}_{\alpha M_2} \in \mathcal{L}(M_2)$.*

15.3.2   Properties and Satisfiability

A safety property is given by a deterministic LTS P, whose language $\mathcal{L}(P)$ defines the set of acceptable behaviors over the alphabet αP of P (note that P can be determinized, if it is not originally so). An LTS M over $\alpha M \supseteq \alpha P$ satisfies P, denoted $M \models P$, if for every $\sigma \in \mathcal{L}(M)$, $\sigma{\downarrow}_{\alpha P} \in \mathcal{L}(P)$. In order to check a safety property P, an *error LTS* P_{err} is constructed. P_{err} includes a new error state π with no outgoing edges. Further, for every state q in P and every action $a \in \alpha P$, if there is no transition from q on a, then a new transition (q, a, π) is added to P_{err}. Note that P_{err} is *complete*. That is, except for π, every state has an outgoing edge on every action in αP.

P_{err} represents the negation of the property represented by P. Note that P_{err} is not a standard LTS. Its language is not prefix closed. Only traces reaching the error state π belong to $\mathcal{L}(P_{err})$. These are exactly those traces that do not belong to $\mathcal{L}(P)$. If we refer to P_{err} as an automaton, the only accepting state is π.

Checking that $M \models P$ can now be done by checking that π is not reachable in $M \| P_{err}$. A trace $\sigma \in \alpha M^*$ is a *counterexample* for $M \models P$ if $\sigma \in \mathcal{L}(M)$ but $\sigma{\downarrow}_{\alpha P} \notin \mathcal{L}(P)$.

Example 15.8 *Figure 15.8 presents three LTSs, In, Out, and Order, where Order, when ignoring the dotted edges, presents a safety property satisfied by the LTS In$\|$Out. Note that neither In nor Out satisfies this property individually. For example, the trace $\langle in, send, ack, ack \rangle$ of In is a counterexample for In $\models$ Order.*

15.3.3   Instantiation of the Assume-Guarantee Paradigm with LTSs

Recall that the assume-guarantee paradigm uses formulas of the form $\langle A \rangle M \langle P \rangle$, where M is a system component, A is an assumption on the environment of M, and P is a property. Such a formula is true if the following holds: for every system that contains M as a component, if the system satisfies A, then it also guarantees P.

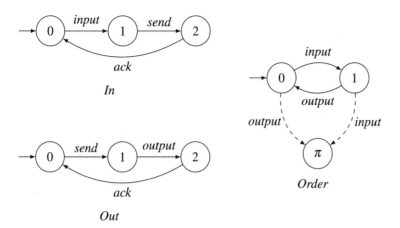

Figure 15.8
LTSs describing the *In* and *Out* components and the *Order* property (with error state).

When instantiating such a formula within the LTS framework, all of its components are LTSs. However, *A* and *P* are chosen to be *deterministic* LTSs. In this framework, checking $\langle A \rangle M \langle P \rangle$ can be reduced to checking if π is reachable in $A \| M \| P_{err}$. If it is, then the property is violated. Otherwise, it is satisfied.

Since assumptions and properties are presented by deterministic LTSs, an LTS *A* can serve both as an assumption and as a property. To serve as an assumption on the environment of *M*, *A* is composed with *M*. To check whether $M \models A$, A_{err} is composed with *M* and the reachability of π is checked. This enables a straightforward implementation of the assume-guarantee reasoning within this framework. Recall that the assume-guarantee rule ASYM has the following form:

> **Step 1** $\langle A \rangle M_1 \langle P \rangle$
> **Step 2** $\langle true \rangle M_2 \langle A \rangle$ (ASYM)
> ───────────────────
> $\langle true \rangle M_1 \| M_2 \langle P \rangle$.

Then, ASYM can be implemented as follows:

> **Step 1** $A \| M_1 \models P$
> **Step 2** $M_2 \models A$
> ─────────────
> $M_1 \| M_2 \models P$.

For a successful implementation of an assume-guarantee rule, the assumption *A* should be significantly smaller (in terms of states and transitions) than the component M_2 it abstracts. Yet, it should reflect the behavior of M_2 to the extent it is relevant to proving property *P* for M_1. In the next section we show how the automata learning algorithm L^*, presented in section 15.1, can be used to construct such an assumption.

15.3.4   Assume-Guarantee with Learning

In order to use L^*, we first define the unknown language U that will be learned. Our goal is to learn the *weakest assumption A_w* under which M_1 satisfies P. Formally, we have the following:

Definition 15.9 ([240]) *An LTS A_w is the* weakest assumption *for component M_1 and property P if for every LTS M_E the following holds:*

$$\langle true \rangle M_1 \| M_E \langle P \rangle \quad \text{if and only if} \quad \langle true \rangle M_E \langle A_w \rangle.$$

The weakest assumption A_w is defined over the *interface alphabet Σ_I* of M_2 with respect to M_1 and P, $\Sigma_I = (\alpha M_1 \cup \alpha P) \cap \alpha M_2$. This alphabet includes all actions in αM_2 that may restrict the behavior of M_1 and are relevant to verifying P. The language of A_w, $\mathcal{L}(A_w)$, contains all traces of M_2 (abstracted to Σ_I) that prevent M_1 from violating P. In addition, it may contain traces that are not abstraction of traces in M_2.

Algorithm L^* learns the traces of A_w through an iterative process, as described in section 15.1. The process terminates as soon as compositional verification returns conclusive results, which is often before the weakest assumption A_w is computed by L^*. For L^* to learn A_w, we need to provide a teacher that can answer the two types of queries asked by L^*. Our framework uses model checking to implement such a Teacher.

To answer a *membership query* for $\sigma = (a_1, a_2, \ldots, a_n)$ in Σ_I^* the teacher needs to determine whether σ can lead to π in $M_1 \| P_{err}$. This can be done by simulating σ on $M \| P_{err}$. An alternative, more unified way, constructs an LTS A_σ, which accepts σ (and all of its prefixes). It is defined as follows: $A_\sigma = (Q, \alpha A_\sigma, \delta, q_0)$, where $Q = q^0, q^1, \ldots, q^n$, $\alpha A_\sigma = \Sigma_I$, $\delta = \{(q^i, a_{i+1}, q^{i+1}) | 0 \leq i < n\}$, and $q_0 = q^0$. The teacher then model-checks $\langle A_\sigma \rangle M_1 \langle P \rangle$. If *true* is returned, it means that $\sigma \in \mathcal{L}(A_w)$, because M_1 does not violate P in the context of σ, so the teacher returns *true*. Otherwise, the answer to the membership query is *false*.

Note that in both implementations of the membership query, if a prefix $\sigma' = (a_1, \ldots, a_k)$ of σ reaches π, then for all $k \leq i \leq n$, the trace $(a_1, a_2, \ldots, a_i)$ is not in A_w. The teacher then returns *false* for all of these traces. On the other hand, for $1 \leq j < k$, the trace $(a_1, a_2, \ldots, a_j)$ should be checked independently for membership.

Equivalence queries should identify whether a candidate LTS, when used as an assumption in the ASYM rule, can result in a conclusive answer.

Because in our case the learned language $\mathcal{L}(A_w)$ is prefix closed, all conjectures returned by L^* are also prefix closed. Our framework transforms these conjectures into safety LTSs, which constitute the intermediate assumptions A_i (called *candidate automata* in section 15.1). In our framework, the first priority is to guide L^* towards a conjecture that is strong enough to make step 1 of the compositional rule returning true. Once this is accomplished, the resulting conjecture may be too strong, in which case our framework guides L^* towards a conjecture that is weak enough to make step 2 return conclusive results

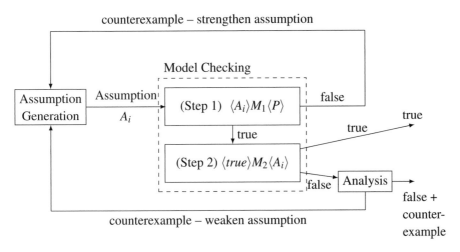

Figure 15.9
Incremental compositional verification during iteration *i*.

about whether the system satisfies P. Our teacher is thus implemented using two oracles and counterexample analysis to answer conjectures as follows.

Oracle 1   performs step 1 in figure 15.9. That is, it checks $\langle A_i \rangle M_1 \langle P \rangle$. If this does not hold, the model checker returns a counterexample c. The teacher informs L^* that its conjecture A_i is not correct and provides $c\,|_{\Sigma_I}$ to witness this fact. If, instead, $\langle A_i \rangle M_1 \langle P \rangle$ holds, the teacher forwards A_i to oracle 2.

Oracle 2   performs step 2 in figure 15.9 by checking $\langle true \rangle M_2 \langle A_i \rangle$. If the result of model checking is true, the teacher returns true. Our framework then terminates the verification because, according to the compositional rule, P has been proved on $M_1 \| M_2$. If model checking returns a counterexample c, the teacher performs some analysis to determine the underlying reason.

Counterexample analysis   is performed by the teacher in a way similar to that used for answering membership queries. Let c be the counterexample returned by oracle 2. The teacher computes $A_c\,|_{\Sigma_I}$ and checks $\langle A_c\,|_{\Sigma_I} \rangle M_1 \langle P \rangle$. If true, it means that A_i is too strong since M_1 does not violate P in the context of c, and therefore $c\,|_{\Sigma_I}$ should be added to A_w. The algorithm then returns $c\,|_{\Sigma_I}$ as a counterexample for conjecture A_i. If the model checker returns *false* with some counterexample c', it means that P is violated in $M_1 \| M_2$. To generate a counterexample for $\langle true \rangle M_1 \| M_2 \langle P \rangle$, our framework composes c and c' in a way similar to parallel composition of LTSs. That is, common actions in c and c' are synchronized, and some interleaving instance of the remaining actions is selected.

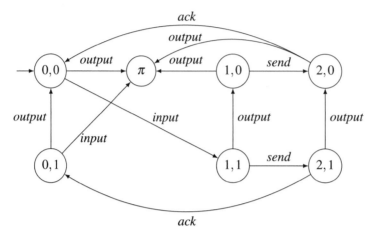

Figure 15.10
The composed LTS $In \| Order_{err}$ with alphabet $\{input, send, ack, output\}$.

15.3.5   Example of the Learning Algorithm for the Assume-Guarantee Rule

The example is taken from [151]. Our goal is to prove $In \| Out \models Order$, where LTSs *In* and *Out* are the system components and are shown in figure 15.8. $Order_{err}$, also presented in figure 15.8, is a safety LTS representing the negation of the property to be checked. In our application of the proof rule *In* plays the role of M_1 and *Out* plays the role of M_2. The learning algorithm will use the LTS $In \| Order_{err}$, given in figure 15.10.

Our goal is to learn an assumption A that will satisfy the two premises of the assume-guarantee Rule. The alphabet of A is $\Sigma_I = (\alpha In \cup \alpha Order) \cap \alpha Out = \{send, ack, output\}$.

We apply the L^* learning algorithm, gradually building a table. Recall that the entry $T(s,e)$ in the table is determined by the membership query for $s \cdot e$. In our case, $T(s,e) = 0$ if $s \cdot e$ or any of its prefixes reach the error state π in $Input \| Order_{err}$, and $T(s,e) = 1$, otherwise. In particular, if the run on $s \cdot e$ "gets stuck" without reaching π, then $T(s,e) = 1$. For instance, $T(ack, \varepsilon) = 1$. The first table T_1 is presented in figure 15.11.

Since T_1 is not closed, the table T_2 is constructed (figure 15.12). Table T_2 is closed and consistent. Thus, we build the assumption A_1, shown in figure 15.13, and send it as an equivalence query.

Figure 15.13 does not show the sink state corresponding to the *output* row in the table, from which no string is accepted.

We check whether $\langle A_1 \rangle Input \langle Order \rangle$ holds by checking if the language $\mathcal{L}(A_1 \| In \| Order_{err})$ is empty. The latter does not hold. The string $t = (input \cdot send \cdot ack \cdot input)$ is in $\mathcal{L}(A_1 \| M_1 \| Order_{err})$ and is returned as a counterexample. The string $t|\Sigma = (send \cdot ack)$ and its prefix *ack* are added to S, and the table is updated accordingly, resulting in table T_3 (figure 15.14):

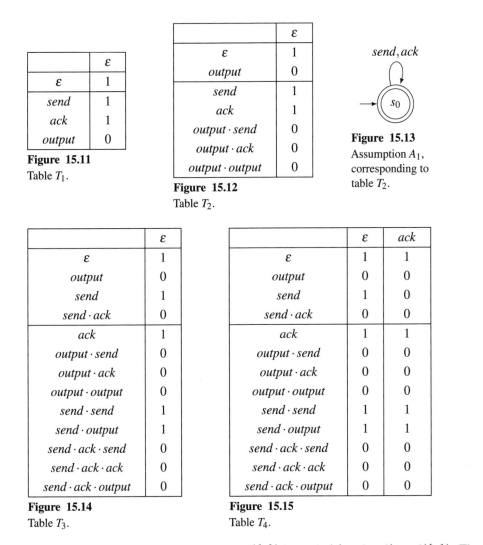

	ε
ε	1
send	1
ack	1
output	0

Figure 15.11
Table T_1.

	ε
ε	1
output	0
send	1
ack	1
output · send	0
output · ack	0
output · output	0

Figure 15.12
Table T_2.

send, ack

Figure 15.13
Assumption A_1,
corresponding to
table T_2.

	ε
ε	1
output	0
send	1
send · ack	0
ack	1
output · send	0
output · ack	0
output · output	0
send · send	1
send · output	1
send · ack · send	0
send · ack · ack	0
send · ack · output	0

Figure 15.14
Table T_3.

	ε	ack
ε	1	1
output	0	0
send	1	0
send · ack	0	0
ack	1	1
output · send	0	0
output · ack	0	0
output · output	0	0
send · send	1	1
send · output	1	1
send · ack · send	0	0
send · ack · ack	0	0
send · ack · output	0	0

Figure 15.15
Table T_4.

Table T_3 is not consistent: $\varepsilon \equiv send \bmod(\{\varepsilon\})$ but $ack \not\equiv (send \cdot ack) \bmod(\{\varepsilon\})$. Thus, ack is added to E and the table is extended with a new column, resulting in table T_4 (figure 15.15). Table T_4 is closed and consistent. The assumption A_2 built based on table T_4 is shown in figure 15.16 (not including the sink state).

An equivalence query with A_2 is sent to the teacher. Since both oracle 1 and oracle 2 return *true*, we conclude that $In \| Out \models Order$. A more elaborated example can be found in [151].

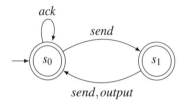

Figure 15.16
Assumption A_2, corresponding to table T_4.

15.4   Black Box Checking

Model checking provides efficient techniques for searching errors in the state space of a system or prove their absence. Most model-checking techniques assume that the set of states and the transitions between them are provided, either implicitly, for example, as a transition system (see section 3.1 of chapter 3), or explicitly, as a state graph. Testing techniques [389] are less comprehensive than model checking. They provide ways of sampling the executions of the system and are usually applied only to the input-output interface. Testing techniques thus present a practical compromise for checking reliability, especially when the system under test is a "black box," where the internal structure, and in particular the states of the system, is unknown.

In this section we describe *black box checking*, a technique for model-checking black box systems, based on experiments that interface with them. The technique is inspired by both worlds: it performs checks directly on the system itself, without having to build a model, yet it is as reliable and comprehensive as model checking. This comes with the price of high complexity.

The method we present is a combination of Angluin's learning algorithm and standard model checking. The algorithm presented here was first introduced in [404].

15.4.1   The Execution Model

In order to perform black box checking, several assumptions on the checked system are needed. First, we assume that we have a bound n on the number of states in the system. Without this assumption, no matter how many checks are made, the system may still deviate from the specification. Consider, for example, the simple specification $\mathbf{G}\, p$. For any length m of experiments (measured, for instance, by the sum of the lengths of the checked sequences), the system may consist of a single cycle that manifests p at the first m states, but $\neg p$ at the $m + 1^{st}$ state.

Since the system's states are unknown, we assume that the checked property is defined over a finite set Σ of alphabet, referring to the system's *inputs*. The property identifies the set of allowed sequences over the inputs. We use LTL formulas over Σ to express such properties.

Given a current state and an input from Σ, the system also produces an *output*. For simplicity, we assume that the output is either "0" or "1," where a "0" means that the current input is not allowed in the current state and there is no change of state, and a "1" means that the system may make a change of state on this input.

In order to be able to check different executions, we allow to reset the system to its initial state. For simplicity, we assume that the initial state is unique (otherwise, we would have needed to identify the initial state the system was reset to). We further assume that the transition relation is *deterministic*. Otherwise, any number of experiments might be insufficient: the system may consistently make one choice during testing, and another when deployed.

Formally, we model a black box system by a *black box automaton*, $\mathcal{S} = \langle S, \iota, \Sigma, \delta \rangle$, where S is a finite set of states, $\iota \in S$ is the unique initial state, Σ is the set of inputs, and $\delta \subseteq S \times \Sigma \times S$ is the transition relation, which satisfies the following:

- For every $s \in S$, there exists some $\sigma \in \Sigma$ and $s' \in S$ such that $(s, \sigma, s') \in \delta$. This means that for every s, the executions starting at s are infinite.
- If $(s, \sigma, s_1), (s, \sigma, s_2)$ are both in δ, then $s_1 = s_2$. This means that the transition relation is deterministic.

An *execution* of $\mathcal{S}$ from state s is an infinite sequence of alternating states and inputs $s_0, \sigma_0, s_1, \sigma_1, \ldots$, where for every $i \in \mathbb{N}$, $(s_i, \sigma_i, s_{i+1}) \in \delta$. We say that an input sequence $\pi = \sigma_0, \sigma_1, \ldots$ is *admitted* by $\mathcal{S}$ if there is $s_0, s_1, \ldots$, such that $s_0, \sigma_0, s_1, \sigma_1, \ldots$ is an execution of $\mathcal{S}$. The *language* of $\mathcal{S}$, $\mathcal{L}(\mathcal{S})$, is the set of input sequences admitted by $\mathcal{S}$.

In the algorithms presented below, we will need to test $\mathcal{S}$ on *finite* sequences of inputs. For that, we extend the notions defined above to finite sequences as well. We say that a finite sequence of inputs $\sigma_0, \sigma_1, \ldots, \sigma_n$ is *admitted* by $\mathcal{S}$ if there is $s_0, \sigma_0, s_1, \sigma_1, \ldots, \sigma_n, s_{n+1}$, which is a prefix of an execution of $\mathcal{S}$.

Recall, that for checking whether a system $\mathcal{S}$ satisfies an LTL formula φ, we can apply the automata-based algorithm (see section 7.8 of chapter 7). To do so, we first construct a Büchi automaton $\mathcal{A}_{\neg\varphi}$ such that $\mathcal{L}(\mathcal{A}_{\neg\varphi})$ consists of exactly all sequences that satisfy $\neg\varphi$. Checking whether $\mathcal{S} \models \varphi$ amounts to checking whether $\mathcal{L}(\mathcal{S}) \cap \mathcal{L}(\mathcal{A}_{\neg\varphi}) = \emptyset$. If the intersection is not empty, a lasso-shaped sequence exists in the intersection and can be returned as a counterexample.

In our case, the challenge is to check emptiness (or provide a counterexample) while the state space of $\mathcal{S}$ is unknown. In other words, we want to check the emptiness of the intersection of two automata, where one of them is a black box. The problem becomes somewhat easier since $\mathcal{S}$ does not include accepting states. Thus, the intersection is not empty if and only if there is an input sequence π that is *accepted* by $\mathcal{A}_{\neg\varphi}$ and, in addition, π is *admitted* by $\mathcal{S}$ (that is, $\mathcal{S}$ can run on it). By lemma 7.4, the former condition can be checked by searching in $\mathcal{A}_{\neg\varphi}$ a path from an initial state s to an accepting state t and a path from t back to itself. In the next section we present a simple, not highly efficient algorithm, that exploits this observation.

15.4.2   A Simple Solution

Assume that we are given a path π in $\mathcal{A}_{\neg\varphi}$ from an initial state s to an accepting state t and from t back to itself. Let ρ_1 be the input sequence that leads from s to t, and let ρ_2 be the input sequence that leads from t to t. Then $\rho_1\rho_2{}^\omega$ is accepted by $\mathcal{A}_{\neg\varphi}$. We next need to check whether $\rho_1\rho_2{}^\omega$ is also admitted by $\mathcal{S}$. Recall that the only way to check whether a certain input sequence is admitted by $\mathcal{S}$ is to run $\mathcal{S}$ on the sequence and see that at no point along the run the output 0 is returned. Also recall that the number of states in $\mathcal{S}$ is bound by n.

Our solution is based on the pigeon hole principle. According to this principle, if we have $n+1$ parcels that we want to deliver into n pigeon holes, then at least one pigeon hole will end up with more than one parcel.

The following algorithm checks whether $\rho_1\rho_2{}^\omega$ is admitted by $\mathcal{S}$ or not: reset the automaton $\mathcal{S}$ to its initial state, and run ρ_1. If ρ_1 was admitted, continue running ρ_2 for n times. If this was successful, that is, if no 0 has been returned, we know that $\rho_1\rho_2{}^\omega$ is in the intersection. This is because the number of occurrences of states in which the execution of ρ_2 either begins or ends is $n+1$, implying, according to the pigeon hole principle, that at least two of them are the same. Due to determinism of the black box, it implies that we can run ρ_2 infinitely many times. Otherwise, if $\rho_1\rho_2{}^\omega$ has some prefix that is not admitted by the black box, then $\rho_1\rho_2{}^\omega$ is not in the intersection.

The algorithm above can be extended to checking *all* lasso-shaped words accepted by $\mathcal{A}_{\neg\varphi}$. This is done by systematically generating sequences ρ_1 and ρ_2 as above, whose size is bounded by the product of the number of states in $\mathcal{S}$ and $\mathcal{A}_{\neg\varphi}$. For each such ρ_1, ρ_2 then check, using the pigeon hole principle, whether $\rho_1\rho_2{}^\omega$ is in the intersection. If so, a counterexample for whether $\mathcal{S}$ satisfies φ is found. Otherwise, $\mathcal{S}$ satisfies φ.

15.4.3   An Algorithm Based on Learning

The algorithm presented above has a very high complexity: it is always exponential in the assumed bound n on the size of the black box, even if the actual size of $\mathcal{S}$ is much smaller, or there is a very short counterexample. In order to provide a better algorithm, we use Angluin's learning algorithm L^*, described in section 15.1. L^* is used to learn the unknown language of $\mathcal{L}(\mathcal{S})$.

Recall that for L^* we need to implement a teacher that can answer two types of queries: membership queries and equivalence queries. Answering membership queries is straightforward. A word w is in $\mathcal{L}(\mathcal{S})$ if and only if when $\mathcal{S}$ runs on w, starting at its initial state, the output is always 1.

For equivalence queries, assume that the teacher returns a candidate automaton M as a conjecture. We apply the automata-theoretic model-checking algorithm to check whether

$M \models \varphi$. If the algorithm returns a counterexample c in the intersection of M and $\mathcal{A}_{\neg \varphi}$, then we check whether c is admitted by $\mathcal{S}$ using the pigeon hole principle, explained above. If it is, then we are done: $\mathcal{S} \not\models \varphi$.

Otherwise, $c \notin \mathcal{L}(\mathcal{S})$. Thus, it is in the symmetric difference of $\mathcal{L}(M)$ and the unknown language $\mathcal{L}(\mathcal{S})$. The shortest prefix of c, which is not admitted by $\mathcal{S}$, is returned to the learning algorithm and the learning proceeds.

Assume now that $M \models \varphi$. This gives are no indication of how to proceed with our analysis. In this case, we therefore take another approach and use the Vasilevskii–Chow algorithm described below.

15.4.4   Vasilevskii–Chow Algorithm

In this section we show how to exploit the Vasilevskii–Chow algorithm [112, 472], denoted VC, to check whether a candidate automaton M, constructed by L^*, is equivalent to the black box automaton $\mathcal{S}$. If M and $\mathcal{S}$ are not equivalent, then VC returns a sequence in the symmetric difference of their languages.

Recall that M is a DFA. It is constructed based on a closed and consistent table T with rows $(S \cup S \cdot \Sigma)$ and columns E, where S and E are strings over Σ (see section 15.1). Recall also that the set of states Q of M consists of the equivalence classes of S with respect to E. Each state $q \in Q$, where $q = [w_q]$, is identified by a string w_q that accesses q from the initial state of M. We exploit these facts in the algorithm described below.

Assume first that M and $\mathcal{S}$ have the same number of states n, where n is the assumed bound on the number of states of $\mathcal{S}$. In this case, VC uses two sets of sequences:

- *Accessing sequences*: For each state q in M there is an accessing sequence over Σ, which leads from the initial state of M to q.
  For M constructed by L^*, w_q can be used as the accessing sequence for $q = [w_q]$.
- *Separating sequences*: For any two distinct states q and q' of M, there is at least one separating sequence that is admitted from q and not admitted from q', or vice versa.
  For M constructed by L^*, the columns E of the table T can be used as the set of separating sequences.

Let V_S, V_E be the sets of accessing sequences and separating sequences, respectively, used by VC. We say that two states $q \in M$ and $s \in \mathcal{S}$ are *unseparated* by V_S and V_E if q and s are accessed by the same accessing sequence w_q. Moreover, they are not separated by any separating sequence in V_E. That is, for every $e \in V_E$, either both q and s admit e or both do not admit e.

Given $q \in M$ and $s \in \mathcal{S}$, the following algorithm checks if they are unseparated (figure 15.17). Let w_q be the accessing sequence in V_S that reaches q in M from the initial state. We reset $\mathcal{S}$ and run w_q from the initial state of $\mathcal{S}$. We then check that the reached state s in $\mathcal{S}$ admits exactly the same separating sequences as q in M. This is done as follows: for each

procedure *unSeparated*(q,s)
    Let q be accessed by w_q;
    reset $\mathcal{S}$;
    Run w_q on $\mathcal{S}$;
    if w_q is not admitted by $\mathcal{S}$ **then**
        return shortest prefix ρ' of w_q, not admitted by $\mathcal{S}$;
    end if
    for all $e \in V_E$ **do**
        reset $\mathcal{S}$;
        run $w_q \cdot e$ on $\mathcal{S}$;
        if M and $\mathcal{S}$ do not agree **then**
            return shortest separating prefix ρ' of $w_q \cdot e$;
        end if
    end for all
    return *true*;
end procedure

Figure 15.17
Procedure *unSeparated*.

separating sequence $e \in V_E$, we reset $\mathcal{S}$ and then run $w_q \cdot e$ on $\mathcal{S}$; q and s are unseparated if, for all e, $\mathcal{S}$ admits $w_q \cdot e$ from its initial state if and only if M admits e from q.

Next we check that for every transition (q, a, q') of M there is a transition (s, a, s') of $\mathcal{S}$ such that s' and q' are unseparated. We check it as above, accept that $w'_q = w_q \cdot a$ is used instead of w_q.

So far we assumed that M and $\mathcal{S}$ are both of size n. Consider now the case where n is larger than the number of states in M. Let $k = n - |Q|$. Assume that we show for some q and s that they are unseparated. Then instead of showing that their immediate successors are unseparated, we show, for every sequence $w \in \Sigma^k$, that if s' is accessed from s by w and q' is accessed from q by w, then s' and q' are unseparated. As before, since $\mathcal{S}$ is a black box automaton, we cannot obtain s' by running w from s. Instead, we reset $\mathcal{S}$ and then run $w_q \cdot w$ from the initial state of $\mathcal{S}$.

The algorithm given in figure 15.18 summarizes the presented technique for black box checking.

Bibliographic Notes

Compositional Verification

In [249, 354] a semiautomatic assume-guarantee reasoning is developed. The method handles synchronous systems and therefore is suitable for compositional verification of

procedure *BlackBoxChecking*$(\mathcal{S}, \varphi)$
    let M be a candidate automaton returned by L^* as a conjecture;
    while *true* **do**
        $X = M \cap \mathcal{A}_\varphi$;
        if $\mathcal{L}(X) \neq \emptyset$ **then**
            Let $\rho = \rho_1 \rho_2^\omega \in \mathcal{L}(X)$.
            if $\rho \in \mathcal{L}(\mathcal{S})$ (use the pigeon hole principle) **then**
                return "ρ is a counterexample for $\mathcal{S} \models \varphi$".
            else
                ρ' = the shortest prefix of ρ that is not in $\mathcal{L}(\mathcal{S})$
                comment ρ' is a separating sequence between $\mathcal{S}$ and M;
            end if
        else
            if $VC\,(M, \mathcal{S}) = true$ **then**
                return "$\mathcal{S} \models \varphi$";
            else
                $\rho' = VC\,(M, \mathcal{S})$
                comment ρ' is a separating sequence between $\mathcal{S}$ and M;
            end if
        end if
        Use ρ' to learn a new candidate M for $\mathcal{S}$.
    end while
end procedure

Figure 15.18
Algorithm for black box checking.

hardware designs. The specification is written in ACTL. Assumptions are given by the user as ACTL formulas, which are automatically transformed into a Kripke structure, using a tableau construction (see problem 6.1 for a tableau construction for ACTL). Several more involved assume-guarantee rules are presented there. Examples of the application of the technique to hardware designs are given in [354].

Automatic compositional verification has been the subject of intensive research. A special issue of the journal *Formal Methods in System Design* has been devoted to it [395]. Compositional verification is described in the chapter by Giannakopoulou, Namjoshi, and Pasareanu in [136].

Learning based automated compositional verification are proposed in [151]. In [395] it has been extended to systems with multiple components. It also proposed to use alphabet abstraction-refinement. The combination of the two significantly enhanced the applicability of learning-based compositional verification. In [66] abstraction-refinement techniques for automating the generation of assumptions has been proposed. Other learning-based approaches for automating assumption generation have been proposed (for example, in [103, 24, 252, 108, 108, 107]).

There is a large body of work on non-automated assume-guarantee reasoning using circular rules [386, 22, 370, 371]. In order to guarantee soundness, some type of inductive arguments, over time, formulas to be checked, or both, have been applied. While soundness for such rules is a prerequisite for using them, completeness has been less studied, sometimes leading to contradictory results (see [391] vs. [358]). An interesting result in [391] makes the connection between circular and non-circular rules, using complex (auxiliary) assumptions that use induction over time. Automated circular assume-guarantee reasoning has been proposed in [193, 194].

Black Box Checking

The problem of verifying a "black box" system whose model is unknown appears in the relevant literature with different types of model to be learned, different learning algorithms, and applications of other tools, such as abstraction and approximation.

An extentsion to black box checking includes using learning to update an already known (or learned) model, to which unknown small changes have been applied [248]. The verification of a model combined of known parts with black box parts is also studied in [195].

In [1], a method is suggested for learning infinite state space (with data) using abstraction for verifying and testing black box communication protocols. Practical experience with learning models and with applying verification appear, for example, in [277, 284]. In [442], a method similar to black box checking is used to check implementation of a security protocol. A verification method that is based on approximate learning is suggested in [109], where heuristic learning is used for increased coverage of Android applications.

16 Model Checking for the μ-Calculus

16.1 Introduction

The propositional μ-calculus is a powerful language for expressing properties of transition systems by using least and greatest fixpoint operators. The μ-calculus has generated much interest among researchers in computer-aided verification. This interest stems from the fact that many temporal and program logics can be encoded into the μ-calculus. This chapter describes the propositional μ-calculus [309] and general algorithms for evaluating μ-calculus formulas. Examples of verification problems that can be encoded within the language of the μ-calculus are also provided.

16.2 The Propositional μ-Calculus

Formulas in the μ-calculus are interpreted relative to a transition system. In order to be able to distinguish between different transitions in a system, we modify the definition of a Kripke structure slightly. Instead of having one transition relation R, we will now have a *set* of transition relations T. For simplicity, we will refer to each element a in T as a *transition*, instead of a transition relation. Formally, a modified Kripke structure $M = (S, T, L)$ consists of

- a nonempty set of states S;
- a set of transitions T, such that for each transition $a \in T$, $a \subseteq S \times S$; and
- a mapping $L : S \to 2^{AP}$ that gives the set of atomic propositions true in a state.

Let $VAR = \{Q, Q_1, Q_2, \dots\}$ be a set of *relational variables*. Each relational variable $Q \in VAR$ can be assigned a subset of S. The μ-calculus formulas are constructed as follows:

- If $p \in AP$, then p is a formula.
- A relational variable is a formula.
- If f and g are formulas, then $\neg f$, $f \wedge g$ and $f \vee g$ are formulas.
- If f is a formula, and $a \in T$, then $[a]f$ and $\langle a \rangle f$ are formulas.

- If $Q \in VAR$ and f is a formula, then $\mu Q.f$ and $\nu Q.f$ are formulas, provided that f is *syntactically monotone* in Q, that is, that all occurrences of Q within f fall under an even number of negations in f.

Variables in the µ-calculus can be either *free* or *bound* by a fixpoint operator. *Closed formulas* are the formulas without free variables. To emphasize that a µ-calculus formula f contains free relational variables $Q_1, \ldots, Q_n$, we sometimes write $f(Q_1, \ldots, Q_n)$.

The intuitive meaning of the formula $\langle a \rangle f$ is "it is possible to make an a-transition to a state where f holds." Similarly, $[a]f$ means that "f holds in all states reachable (in one step) by making an a-transition." The μ and ν operators are used to express least and greatest fixpoints, respectively. The empty set of states is denoted by *false*, and the set of all states S is denoted by *true*. Also, in the rest of this chapter, we will use the more intuitive notation $s \xrightarrow{a} s'$ to mean $(s, s') \in a$.

Formally, a formula f is interpreted as the set of states in which f is true. We denote such a set of states as $[\![f]\!]_M e$, where M is a transition system and $e : VAR \rightarrow 2^S$ is an *environment*. We denote by $e[Q \leftarrow W]$ a new environment that is the same as e except that $e[Q \leftarrow W](Q) = W$. The set $[\![f]\!]_M e$ is defined recursively as follows.

- $[\![p]\!]_M e = \{s \mid p \in L(s)\}$
- $[\![Q]\!]_M e = e(Q)$
- $[\![\neg f]\!]_M e = S \setminus [\![f]\!]_M e$
- $[\![f \wedge g]\!]_M e = [\![f]\!]_M e \cap [\![g]\!]_M e$
- $[\![f \vee g]\!]_M e = [\![f]\!]_M e \cup [\![g]\!]_M e$
- $[\![\langle a \rangle f]\!]_M e = \{s \mid \exists t [s \xrightarrow{a} t \text{ and } t \in [\![f]\!]_M e] \}$
  $[\![[a]f]\!]_M e = \{s \mid \forall t [s \xrightarrow{a} t \text{ implies } t \in [\![f]\!]_M e] \}$
- $[\![\mu Q.f]\!]_M e$ is the least fixpoint of the predicate transformer $\tau \colon 2^S \rightarrow 2^S$ defined by

$$\tau(W) = [\![f]\!]_M e[Q \leftarrow W].$$

- $[\![\nu Q.f]\!]_M e$ is the greatest fixpoint of the predicate transformer $\tau \colon 2^S \rightarrow 2^S$ defined by

$$\tau(W) = [\![f]\!]_M e[Q \leftarrow W].$$

Within formulas, the negation is restricted in use. Thus, monotonicity is guaranteed and the fixpoints are well defined. Formally, every logical connective except negation is monotonic ($f \rightarrow f'$ implies $f \wedge g \rightarrow f' \wedge g$, $f \vee g \rightarrow f' \vee g$, $\langle a \rangle f \rightarrow \langle a \rangle f'$, and $[a]f \rightarrow [a]f'$), and all the negations can be pushed down to the atomic propositions using De Morgan's laws and the dualities $\neg[a]f \equiv \langle a \rangle \neg f$, $\neg \langle a \rangle f \equiv [a] \neg f$, $\neg \mu Q.f(Q) \equiv \nu Q. \neg f(\neg Q)$, $\neg \nu Q.f(Q) \equiv \mu Q. \neg f(\neg Q)$. Since bound variables are under an even number of negations, they will be negation-free after this process. Thus, each possible formula in a fixpoint operator is monotonic, and hence each possible τ is also monotonic ($S \subseteq S'$ implies $\tau(S) \subseteq \tau(S')$). This is enough to ensure the existence of the fixpoints [459]. Furthermore, since we are evaluating formulas over finite transition systems, monotonicity of τ implies that τ is also $\cup$-continuous and $\cap$-continuous (see lemma 5.6 in chapter 5). Hence, the least and greatest fixpoints can be computed by iterative evaluation:

$$\llbracket \mu Q.f \rrbracket_M e = \bigcup_i \tau^i(\textit{false}) \qquad \llbracket \nu Q.f \rrbracket_M e = \bigcap_i \tau^i(\textit{true})$$

where $\tau^i(Q)$ is defined recursively by $\tau^0(Q) = Q$ and $\tau^{i+1}(Q) = \tau(\tau^i(Q))$. Since the domain S is finite, the iteration must stop after a finite number of steps (see lemma 5.8 in chapter 5). More precisely, for some $i, j \leq |S|$, the least fixpoint is equal to $\tau^i(\textit{false})$, and the greatest fixpoint is equal to $\tau^j(\textit{true})$. To find these fixpoints, we repeatedly apply τ starting from either *false* or *true* until the result does not change.

For example, let us work out the semantics of the formulas $\nu Q_1.(p \vee \langle b \rangle Q_1)$ and $\mu Q_2.(p \vee \langle b \rangle Q_2)$, interpreted over the Kripke structure M defined in figure 16.1. Given an environment e, we defined $\llbracket \nu Q_1.(p \vee \langle b \rangle Q_1) \rrbracket_M e$ as the greatest fixpoint of the predicate transformer $\tau \colon 2^S \to 2^S$ defined by

$$\tau(W) = \llbracket p \vee \langle b \rangle Q_1 \rrbracket_M e[Q_1 \leftarrow W].$$

From figure 16.1 we see that $\llbracket p \rrbracket_M e = \{s_2\}$. To find the greatest fixpoint of τ, we start iterating τ from *true*, as follows:

$$\begin{aligned}
\tau^1(\textit{true}) &= \llbracket p \vee \langle b \rangle Q_1 \rrbracket_M e[Q_1 \leftarrow \textit{true}] \\
&= \llbracket p \rrbracket_M e[Q_1 \leftarrow \textit{true}] \cup \llbracket \langle b \rangle Q_1 \rrbracket_M e[Q_1 \leftarrow \textit{true}] \\
&= \{s_2\} \cup \{ s \mid \exists t \ [s \xrightarrow{b} t \text{ and } t \in \llbracket Q_1 \rrbracket_M e[Q_1 \leftarrow \textit{true}]] \} \\
&= \{s_2\} \cup \{ s \mid \exists t \ [s \xrightarrow{b} t \text{ and } t \in \textit{true}] \} \\
&= \{s_2\} \cup \{s_1, s_3\} = \{s_1, s_2, s_3\} \\
\tau^2(\textit{true}) &= \tau(\tau(\textit{true})) = \tau(\{s_1, s_2, s_3\}) \\
&= \{s_2\} \cup \{s_1, s_2, s_3\} = \{s_1, s_2, s_3\}
\end{aligned}$$

Hence, the semantics of $\nu Q_1.(p \vee \langle b \rangle Q_1)$ is the set of states $\{s_1, s_2, s_3\}$. Analogously, the semantics of $\mu Q_2.(p \vee \langle b \rangle Q_2)$ is the least fixpoint of τ, which is computed by iterating τ

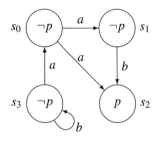

Figure 16.1
A modified Kripke structure.

from *false*:

$$\tau^1(\textit{false}) = [\![p \vee \langle b \rangle Q_2]\!]_M \, e\,[Q_2 \leftarrow \textit{false}]$$
$$= [\![p]\!]_M \, e\,[Q_2 \leftarrow \textit{false}] \cup [\![\langle b \rangle Q_2]\!]_M \, e\,[Q_2 \leftarrow \textit{false}]$$
$$= \{s_2\} \cup \textit{false} = \{s_2\}$$

$$\tau^2(\textit{false}) = \tau(\{s_2\})$$
$$= \{s_2\} \cup [\![\langle b \rangle Q_2]\!]_M \, e\,[Q_2 \leftarrow \{s_2\}]$$
$$= \{s_2\} \cup \{s_1\} = \{s_1, s_2\}$$

$$\tau^3(\textit{false}) = \tau(\{s_1, s_2\})$$
$$= \{s_2\} \cup [\![\langle b \rangle Q_2]\!]_M \, e\,[Q_2 \leftarrow \{s_1, s_2\}]$$
$$= \{s_2\} \cup \{s \mid \exists t \, [s \xrightarrow{b} t \text{ and } t \in \{s_1, s_2\}]\}$$
$$= \{s_2\} \cup \{s_1\} = \{s_1, s_2\}$$

Hence, $[\![\mu Q_2.(p \vee \langle b \rangle Q_2)]\!]_M = \{s_1, s_2\}$.

The *alternation depth* [205] of a formula is the number of alternations in the nesting of least and greatest fixpoints, when all negations are applied only to propositions. In order to make this definition formal, we need to define the top-level ν and μ-subformulas of a μ-calculus formula. A *top-level* ν-*subformula* of f is a subformula $\nu Q'.g$ of f that is not contained within any other greatest fixpoint subformula of f. For example, the top-level ν-subformulas of $f = \mu Q'.(\nu Q_1.g_1 \vee \nu Q_2.g_2)$ are $\nu Q_1.g_1$ and $\nu Q_2.g_2$. A *top-level* μ-*subformula* of f is defined in a similar manner. Formally, the *alternation depth* is defined as follows:

- The alternation depth of an atomic proposition or a relational variable is 0.
- The alternation depth for formulas like $f \wedge g$, $f \vee g$, $\langle a \rangle f$, and $[a]f$ is the maximum alternation depth of the subformulas f and g.
- The alternation depth of $\mu Q.f$ is the maximum of

1. the alternation depth of f,

2. one plus the maximum alternation depth of any top-level ν-subformulas of f if there is a top-level ν-subformula in f, and one otherwise.

- The alternation depth of $\nu Q . f$ is defined symmetrically.

For example, consider a transition system in which $T = \{a\}$. Recall that **EG** f with fairness constraint h holds at a state if there exists a path from the state along which f holds continuously, and h holds infinitely often on this path. This property is expressed using the fixpoint formula (see equation 5.1)

$$\mathbf{EG}\, f = \nu Z . f \wedge \mathbf{EX}(\mathbf{E}(f\, \mathbf{U}\, (Z \wedge h))). \tag{16.1}$$

Using the fixpoint characterization of **EU**, we obtain

$$\mathbf{E}(f\, \mathbf{U}\, (Z \wedge h)) = \mu Y . (Z \wedge h) \vee (f \wedge \mathbf{EX}Y). \tag{16.2}$$

Substituting the right-hand side of equation 16.2 in equation 16.1 gives

$$\nu Z . (f \wedge \mathbf{EX}(\mu Y . (Z \wedge h) \vee (f \wedge \mathbf{EX}Y))).$$

Finally, replacing **EX** by $\langle a \rangle$, we obtain the μ-calculus formula

$$\nu Z . (f \wedge \langle a \rangle (\mu Y . (Z \wedge h) \vee (f \wedge \langle a \rangle Y))). \tag{16.3}$$

This formula has an alternation depth of 2.

Because of the duality

$$\nu Q . f(\ldots, Q, \ldots) = \neg \mu Q . \neg f(\ldots, \neg Q, \ldots),$$

we could have defined the propositional μ-calculus with just the least fixpoint operator and negation. In order to give a succinct description of certain constructions, we sometimes use the dual formulation. However, the concept of alternation depth is easier to define using the formulation given earlier.

16.3   Evaluating Fixpoint Formulas

In this section we give a model-checking algorithm for the μ-calculus. This algorithm finds the set of states in a model that satisfy a formula of this logic. Figure 16.2 presents the naïve, straightforward, recursive algorithm for evaluating μ-calculus formulas. The time complexity of the algorithm in figure 16.2 is exponential in the length of the formula. To see this, we analyze the behavior of the algorithm when computing nested fixpoints. The algorithm computes fixpoints by iteratively computing approximations. These successive approximations form a chain of sets ordered by inclusion. Since the number of strict inclusions in such a chain is limited by the number of possible states, it follows that the loop (either in lines 14–17 for a least fixpoint or in lines 22–25 for a greatest fixpoint) will

function eval(f, e)

    if $f = p$ **then return** $\{s \mid p \in L(s)\}$;
    if $f = Q$ **then return** $e(Q)$;
    if $f = g_1 \wedge g_2$ **then return** eval$(g_1, e) \cap$ eval(g_2, e);
    if $f = g_1 \vee g_2$ **then return** eval$(g_1, e) \cup$ eval(g_2, e);
    if $f = \langle a \rangle g$ **then return** $\{s \mid \exists t \, [s \xrightarrow{a} t$ and $t \in$ eval$(g, e)]\}$;
    if $f = [a]g$ **then return** $\{s \mid \forall t \, [s \xrightarrow{a} t$ implies $t \in$ eval$(g, e)]\}$;

    if $f = \mu Q.g(Q)$ **then**
        $Q_{\text{val}} := \textit{false}$;
        repeat
            $Q_{\text{old}} := Q_{\text{val}}$;
            $Q_{\text{val}} :=$ eval$(g, e \, [Q \leftarrow Q_{\text{val}}])$;
        until $Q_{\text{val}} = Q_{\text{old}}$;
        return Q_{val};
    end if

    if $f = \nu Q.g(Q)$ **then**
        $Q_{\text{val}} := \textit{true}$;
        repeat
            $Q_{\text{old}} := Q_{\text{val}}$;
            $Q_{\text{val}} :=$ eval$(g, e \, [Q \leftarrow Q_{\text{val}}])$;
        until $Q_{\text{val}} = Q_{\text{old}}$;
        return Q_{val};
    end if

end function

Figure 16.2
Pseudocode for the naïve algorithm.

execute at most $n+1$ times, where $n = |S|$. Each iteration of the loop involves a recursive call to evaluate the body of the fixpoint with a different value for the fixpoint variable. If in turn, the subformula being evaluated contains a fixpoint, the evaluation of its body will also involve a loop containing up to $n+1$ recursive calls with a shorter subformula. In general, the body of the innermost fixpoint will be evaluated $O(n^k)$ times, where k is the maximum nesting depth of fixpoint operators in the formula.

    Note that we have considered only the number of iterations required when evaluating fixpoints and not the number of steps required to evaluate a μ-calculus formula. While each fixpoint may only take $O(n)$ iterations, each individual iteration can take up to $O(|M| \cdot |f|)$ steps, where $M = (S, T, L)$ is the model and $|M| = |S| + \sum_{a \in T} |a|$. In general, then, this algorithm has time complexity $O(|M| \cdot |f| \cdot n^k)$.

A result by Emerson and Lei [205] demonstrates that the value of a fixpoint formula can be computed with $O((|f| \cdot n)^d)$ iterations, where d is the alternation depth of f. Their algorithm is similar to the straightforward one described above, except when a fixpoint is nested directly within the scope of another fixpoint of the same type. In this case, the fixpoints are computed differently. The basic idea exploits sequences of fixpoints that have the same type to reduce the complexity of the algorithm. Then, it is unnecessary to reinitialize computations of inner fixpoints with *false* (for least fixpoint) or *true* (for greatest fixpoint) when calculating new approximations for the outer fixpoints.

A simple example will suffice to demonstrate the idea. When discussing the evaluation of fixpoint formulas, we will use $Q_1, \ldots, Q_k$ as the fixpoint variables, with Q_1 being the outermost fixpoint variable and Q_k being the innermost. We will use the notation $Q_j^{i_1 \ldots i_j}$ to denote the value of the i_j-th approximation for Q_j after having computed the i_l-th approximation for Q_l for $1 \leq l < j$. We use $i_j = \omega$ to indicate that we are considering the final approximation (the actual fixpoint value) for Q_j. For example, Q_1^ω is the value of the fixpoint for Q_1, and Q_2^{30} is the initial approximation for Q_2 after having computed the third approximation for Q_1. Consider the formula

$$\mu Q_1 . g_1(Q_1, \mu Q_2 . g_2(Q_1, Q_2)).$$

The subformula $\mu Q_2 . g_2(Q_1, Q_2)$ defines a monotonic predicate transformer τ taking one set (the value of Q_1) to another set (the value of the least fixpoint of Q_2); that is,

$$\tau(Q_1) = \mu Q_2 . g_2(Q_1, Q_2).$$

When evaluating the outer fixpoint, we start with the initial approximation $Q_1^0 = \textit{false}$ and then compute $\tau(Q_1^0)$. This is done by iteratively computing approximations for the inner fixpoint also starting from $Q_2^{00} = \textit{false}$ until we reach a fixpoint $Q_2^{0\omega}$. Now Q_1 is increased to Q_1^1, the result of evaluating $g_1(Q_1^0, Q_2^{0\omega})$:

$$Q_1^1 = g_1(Q_1^0, Q_2^{0\omega})$$

We next compute the least fixpoint $\tau(Q_1^1)$. Since $Q_1^0 \subseteq Q_1^1$, by monotonicity we know that $\tau(Q_1^0) \subseteq \tau(Q_1^1)$. Note that because τ is monotonic and S is finite, τ is $\bigcup$-continuous. Thus, it is easy to prove by induction that the following lemma holds.

Lemma 16.1 *If $W \subseteq \bigcup_i \tau^i(\textit{false})$, then $\bigcup_i \tau^i(W) = \bigcup_i \tau^i(\textit{false})$.*

In other words, to compute a least fixpoint, it is enough to start iterating with any approximation known to be below the fixpoint.

Thus, we can start iterating with $Q_2^{10} = Q_2^{0\omega} = \tau(Q_1^0)$ instead of $Q_2^{10} = \textit{false}$. When we compute the fixpoint $Q_2^{1\omega}$, we next compute the new approximation to Q_1, which is Q_1^2, the result of evaluating $g_1(Q_1^1, Q_2^{1\omega})$:

$$Q_1^2 = g_1(Q_1^1, Q_2^{1\omega}).$$

Again, we know that $Q_1^1 \subseteq Q_1^2$, which implies that $\tau(Q_1^1) \subseteq \tau(Q_1^2)$. But $\tau(Q_1^1) = Q_2^{1\omega}$, the value of the last inner fixpoint computed, and $\tau(Q_1^2) = Q_2^{2\omega}$, the fixpoint to be computed next. Again, we can start iterating with any approximation below the fixpoint. So to compute $Q_2^{2\omega}$ we begin with $Q_2^{20} = Q_2^{1\omega} = \tau(Q_1^1)$. In general, when computing $Q_2^{i\omega}$ we always begin with $Q_2^{i0} = Q_2^{(i-1)\omega}$. Since we never restart the inner fixpoint computation, we can have at most n increases in the value of the inner fixpoint variable. Overall, we need only $O(n)$ iterations to evaluate this expression, instead of $O(n^2)$. In general, this type of simplification leads to an algorithm that computes fixpoint formulas in time exponential in the alternation depth of the formula since we reset an inner fixpoint computation only when there is an alternation in fixpoints in the formula.

Assume that the formula f has N fixpoint subformulas. The algorithm uses an array $A[1 \ldots N]$ to store the approximations to the fixpoints. Initially, $A[i]$ is set to *false* if the i-th fixpoint formula is a least fixpoint and to *true* otherwise. The pseudocode for this algorithm is given in figure 16.3. When the main operator of the subformula is not a least or greatest fixpoint, the algorithm is the same as the naïve algorithm. Unlike the naïve algorithm, the approximation values $A[i]$ are not reset when evaluating the subformula $\mu Q_i . g(Q_i)$ ($\nu Q_i . g(Q_i)$). Instead, we reset all top-level greatest (least) fixpoint variables contained in g to *true* (*false*). This guarantees that when we evaluate a top-level fixpoint subformula of the same type, we start the computation not from *false* or *true* but from the previously computed value, as in our example.

In order to understand why the number of iterations of this algorithm is $O((|f| \cdot n)^d)$, note first that the size of the formula $|f|$ is an upper bound on the number of consecutive fixpoints of the same type in f. Since we never reinitialize the computation of inner fixpoints when calculating new approximations for outer fixpoints of the same type, the number of iterations for each such sequence is $O(|f| \cdot n)$ instead of $n^{|f|}$ as in the naïve case. The computation is reinitialized at the boundary between two sequences of different types. Thus, with d alternating sequences we have $O((|f| \cdot n)^d)$ iterations altogether.

16.4   Representing μ-Calculus Formulas using OBDDs

In this section we describe how to use OBDDs in the model checking algorithms described earlier. First, we show how to encode a transition system $M = (S, T, L)$ into OBDDs. This encoding is similar to the encoding of Kripke structures presented in section 8.2. The domain S is encoded by the set of values of the n Boolean variables $x_1, \ldots, x_n$; that is, S is now the space of Boolean vectors of length n. Each variable x_i has a corresponding primed variable x_i'. Instead of writing $x_1, \ldots, x_n$, we sometimes use the vector notation $\vec{x}$. Given an interpretation, we build the OBDDs corresponding to closed μ-calculus formulas in the following manner:

function eval(f, e)

    if $f = p$ **then return** $\{s \mid p \in L(s)\}$;

    if $f = Q$ **then return** $e(Q)$;

    if $f = g_1 \wedge g_2$ **then return** eval(g_1, e) $\cap$ eval(g_2, e);

    if $f = g_1 \vee g_2$ **then return** eval(g_1, e) $\cup$ eval(g_2, e);

    if $f = \langle a \rangle g$ **then return** $\{s \mid \exists t\, [s \xrightarrow{a} t \text{ and } t \in \text{eval}(g,e)]\}$;

    if $f = [a]g$ **then return** $\{s \mid \forall t\, [s \xrightarrow{a} t \text{ implies } t \in \text{eval}(g,e)]\}$;

    if $f = \mu Q_i.g(Q_i)$ **then**

        forall top-level greatest fixpoint subformulas $\nu Q_j.g'(Q_j)$ of g

            do $A[j] := \textit{true}$;

        repeat

            $Q_{\text{old}} := A[i]$;

            $A[i] := \text{eval}(g, e\,[Q_i \leftarrow A[i]])$;

        until $A[i] = Q_{\text{old}}$;

        return $A[i]$;

    end if

    if $f = \nu Q_i.g(Q_i)$ **then**

        forall top-level least fixpoint subformulas $\mu Q_j.g'(Q_j)$ of g

            do $A[j] := \textit{false}$;

        repeat

            $Q_{\text{old}} := A[i]$;

            $A[i] := \text{eval}(g, e\,[Q_i \leftarrow A[i]])$;

        until $A[i] = Q_{\text{old}}$;

        return $A[i]$;

    end if

end function

Figure 16.3
Pseudocode for the Emerson and Lei algorithm.

- Each atomic proposition p has an OBDD associated with it. We will denote this OBDD by $\text{OBDD}_p(\vec{x})$. $\text{OBDD}_p(\vec{x})$ has the property that $\vec{y} \in \{0,1\}^n$ satisfies OBDD_p if and only if $\vec{y} \in L(p)$.
- Each transition a has an ordered binary decision diagram $\text{OBDD}_a(\vec{x}, \vec{x}')$ associated with it. A Boolean vector $(\vec{y}, \vec{z}) \in \{0,1\}^{2n}$ satisfies OBDD_a if and only if $(\vec{y}, \vec{z}) \in a$.

Now we describe the translation of formulas into OBDDs. Assume that we are given a μ-calculus formula f with free relational variables $Q_1, \ldots, Q_k$. The function **assoc**$[Q_i]$ gives the OBDD corresponding to the set of states associated with the relational variable Q_i. The function **assoc**$\langle Q \leftarrow B_Q \rangle$ creates a new association by adding a relational variable Q

function $FIX(f, \mathbf{assoc}, B_Q)$

    result-bdd := B_Q;

    repeat

        old-bdd := result-bdd;

        result-bdd := $B(f, \mathbf{assoc}\langle Q \leftarrow \text{old-bdd}\rangle)$;

    until equal(old-bdd, result-bdd);

    return result-bdd;

end function

Figure 16.4
Pseudocode for the function *FIX*.

and associating an OBDD B_Q with Q. In other words, **assoc** can be considered as an environment with OBDD representation. The procedure B given below takes a μ-calculus formula f and an association list **assoc** (**assoc** assigns an OBDD to each free relational variable occurring in f) and returns an OBDD corresponding to the semantics of f:

- $B(p, \mathbf{assoc}) = \text{OBDD}_p(\vec{x})$
- $B(Q_i, \mathbf{assoc}) = \mathbf{assoc}[Q_i]$
- $B(\neg f, \mathbf{assoc}) = \neg B(f, \mathbf{assoc})$
- $B(f \wedge g, \mathbf{assoc}) = B(f, \mathbf{assoc}) \wedge B(g, \mathbf{assoc})$
- $B(f \vee g, \mathbf{assoc}) = B(f, \mathbf{assoc}) \vee B(g, \mathbf{assoc})$
- $B(\langle a \rangle f, \mathbf{assoc}) = \exists \vec{x}'(\text{OBDD}_a(\vec{x}, \vec{x}') \wedge B(f, \mathbf{assoc})(\vec{x}'))$, where we write $B(f, \mathbf{assoc})(\vec{x}')$ for the OBDD in which each Boolean variable x_i is replaced by its primed version x_i'.
- $B([a]f, \mathbf{assoc}) = B(\neg\langle a \rangle \neg f, \mathbf{assoc})$. The equality uses the dual formulation for $[a]$.
- $B(\mu Q.f, \mathbf{assoc}) = FIX(f, \mathbf{assoc}, \text{FALSE-BDD})$
- $B(\nu Q.f, \mathbf{assoc}) = FIX(f, \mathbf{assoc}, \text{TRUE-BDD})$

The OBDDs for the Boolean functions *false* and *true* are denoted by FALSE-BDD and TRUE-BDD, respectively. Notice that f has an extra free relational variable Q. The function *FIX* is described in figure 16.4. This procedure is similar to *Lfp* and *Gfp*, described in section 5.3.

    We now give a short example to illustrate our point. Let the state space S be encoded by n Boolean variables $x_1, \ldots, x_n$. Consider the following formula:

$$f = \mu Z.((q \wedge Y) \vee \langle a \rangle Z)$$

Notice that the variable Y is free in f. Let $\text{OBDD}_q(\vec{x})$ be the interpretation for q. Similarly, the OBDD corresponding to the transition a is $\text{OBDD}_a(\vec{x}, \vec{x}')$. Assume that we are given an association list **assoc** that pairs the OBDD $B_Y(\vec{x})$ with Y. In the routine *FIX* the OBDD result-bdd is initially set to

$$N^0(\vec{x}) = \text{FALSE-BDD}.$$

Let N^i be the value of result-bdd at the i-th iteration in the loop of the function *FIX*. At the end of the iteration the value of result-bdd is given by:

$$N^{i+1}(\vec{x}) = (\text{OBDD}_q(\vec{x}) \wedge B_Y(\vec{x})) \vee \exists \vec{x}'(\text{OBDD}_a(\vec{x}, \vec{x}') \wedge N^i(\vec{x}')).$$

The iteration stops when $N^i(\vec{x}) = N^{i+1}(\vec{x})$.

16.5   Translating CTL into the μ-Calculus

In this section we give a translation of *CTL* into the propositional μ-calculus. The algorithm *Tr* takes as its input a *CTL* formula and outputs an equivalent μ-calculus formula with only one transition a:

- $Tr(p) = p$.
- $Tr(\neg f) = \neg Tr(f)$.
- $Tr(f \wedge g) = Tr(f) \wedge Tr(g)$.
- $Tr(\mathbf{EX}\, f) = \langle a \rangle Tr(f)$.
- $Tr(\mathbf{E}(f\,\mathbf{U}\,g)) = \mu Y.(Tr(g) \vee (Tr(f) \wedge \langle a \rangle Y))$.
- $Tr(\mathbf{EG}\, f) = \nu Y.(Tr(f) \wedge \langle a \rangle Y)$.

Note that any resulting μ-calculus formula is closed. Thus, we can omit the environment e from the translation. For example, $Tr(\mathbf{EG}(\mathbf{E}(p\,\mathbf{U}\,q)))$ is given by the μ-calculus formula

$$\nu Y.(\mu Z.(q \vee (p \wedge \langle a \rangle Z)) \wedge \langle a \rangle Y).$$

We denote the states satisfying f by $[\![f]\!]_M$. Using the techniques described in section 5.3, it is easy to prove the following theorem.

Theorem 16.2 *Let $M = (S, T, L)$ be a Kripke structure with a total transition relation. Assume that the transition a in the translation algorithm Tr is the relation T of the Kripke structure. Let f be a CTL formula. Then, for all $s \in S$,*

$$M, s \models f \Leftrightarrow s \in [\![Tr(f)]\!]_M.$$

Bibliographic Notes

Several versions of the propositional μ-calculus have been described in the literature, and the algorithms in this chapter will work with any of them. For the sake of concreteness, this chapter uses the propositional μ-calculus of Kozen [309]. A considerable amount of research has focused on finding techniques for evaluating μ-calculus formulas efficiently, and many algorithms have been proposed for this purpose. These algorithms generally fall into two categories, local and global.

Local procedures   Local procedures are designed for proving that a specific state of the transition system satisfies the given formula. Because of this, it is not always necessary to examine all the states in the transition system. These algorithms are not suitable for implementation with BDDs. Tableau-based local approaches for μ-calculus have been developed, for instance, by Stirling and Walker [453, 454], Cleaveland [144], and Winskel [482]. Andersen [26] and Larsen [337] have developed efficient local methods for a subset of the μ-calculus. Mader [357] has also proposed improvements to the tableau-based method of Stirling and Walker that seem to increase its efficiency.

Global procedures   In this chapter, we have only considered global model checking procedures. Global procedures, based on BDDs, have been shown to be efficient in practice. For instance, the tools μcke [54] and Toupie [422] have implemented μ-calculus model-checking with BDDs. These procedures generally work bottom-up through the formula, evaluating each subformula based on the values of its subformulas. Iteration is used to compute the fixpoints. Because of fixpoint nesting, a naïve global algorithm may require $O(n^k)$ iterations to evaluate a formula, where n is the number of states in the transition system and k is the depth of nesting of the fixpoints. Emerson and Lei [205] improve on this by observing that successively nested fixpoints of the same type do not increase the complexity of the computation (section 16.3). They formalize this observation using the notion of *alternation depth* (section 16.2). Their procedure has complexity $O((|f| \cdot n)^d)$ iterations, where $|f|$ is the size of the formula f and d is the alternation depth. Subsequent work by Andersen, Cleaveland, Klein and Steffen [26, 145, 147] has reduced the complexity, but the overall number of iterations has remained $O(n^d)$. In [355] this result is improved by giving an algorithm that uses only $O(n^{d/2})$ iterations to evaluate a formula with alternation depth d. Thus, this algorithm requires only about the square root of the time needed by earlier algorithms.

Complexity   An important open question concerns the complexity of μ-calculus model checking. The most efficient algorithms currently known for this problem are exponential in the square-root of the alternation depth of the formula [355]. In [355] formulas with strict alternation of least and greatest fixpoint operators are considered. It is shown there that by storing even more intermediate values, the time complexity for evaluating fixpoint formulas can be reduced to $O(n^{\lfloor d/2 \rfloor + 1})$ where d is again the alternation depth of the formula and $|f|$ is replaced by 1. The model checking problem of the modal μ-calculus is polynomial time equivalent to the problem of solving parity games, and Jurdziński, Paterson and Zwick give a deterministic subexponential algorithm for this problem [293].

   We conjecture that there is no polynomial-time algorithm for the μ-calculus model checking problem. It is possible to show that the problem is in NP ∩ co-NP [49, 201, 355]. If the problem was NP-complete, then NP would be equal to co-NP, which is believed to be unlikely. This suggests that it would be very difficult to prove our conjecture.

In order to see that the μ-calculus model checking problem is in NP∩co-NP, consider the following nondeterministic algorithm that guesses the greatest fixpoints and computes the least fixpoints by iteration, starting with the most deeply nested fixpoint. The guess for a greatest fixpoint can be easily checked to see that it is a fixpoint. Furthermore, while we cannot verify that it is the *greatest* fixpoint, we know that the greatest fixpoint must contain any verified guess. By monotonicity, the final value computed by this nondeterministic algorithm will be a subset of the real interpretation of the formula. Moreover, there is a run of the algorithm which calculates the set of states satisfying the μ-calculus formula. Thus, a state s satisfies the formula if and only if s is in the set computed by some run of the algorithm. Consequently, the model checking problem for the μ-calculus formula is in NP. Note that we can negate formulas, so the complexity of determining if a state satisfies a formula is the same as the complexity of determining if a state does not satisfy the formula. Hence, the problem is in the intersection of NP and co-NP.

17 Symmetry

Finite-state concurrent systems frequently exhibit symmetry. It is possible to find symmetry in memories, caches, register files, bus protocols, network protocols—anything that has a lot of replicated structure. The use of symmetry in model checking has been investigated by several authors [124, 211, 279, 283]. These reduction techniques are based on the observation that having symmetry in the system implies the existence of non-trivial permutation groups that preserve both the state labeling and the transition relation. Such groups can be used to define an equivalence relation on the state space of the system. The quotient model induced by this relation is often smaller than the original model. Moreover, it is bisimulation equivalent to that model. Thus, it can be used to verify any property of the original model expressed by a CTL* formula.

17.1 Groups and Symmetry

We start by introducing some notions of group theory. Let G be a set. A *group* is a set G together with a binary operation on G, called the *group multiplication*, such that

- multiplication is associative, that is, $a \circ (b \circ c) = (a \circ b) \circ c$;
- there is an element $e \in G$, called the *identity*, such that for all elements $a \in G$, $e \circ a = a = a \circ e$; and
- for each element $a \in G$ there is an element a^{-1}, called the *inverse* of a, such that $a \circ a^{-1} = a^{-1} \circ a = e$.

We usually use G to denote the group and concatenation to denote the multiplication operator. H is a *subgroup* of G if $H \subseteq G$ and H is a group under the multiplication operation of G.

Let G be a group, and let $g_1, \ldots, g_k$ be designated elements of G. Define $\langle g_1, \ldots, g_k \rangle$ to be the smallest subgroup of G containing $g_1, \ldots, g_k$. If $H = \langle g_1, \ldots, g_k \rangle$, then we say that the group H is *generated* by the set $\{g_1, \ldots, g_k\}$. Note that H is the *closure* of the set $\{g_1, \ldots, g_k\}$ under the multiplication and inverse operations of G.

A *permutation* σ on a finite set of objects A is a bijection (that is, a function that is one-to-one and onto) $\sigma : A \longrightarrow A$. The set of all permutations on A, denoted by *Sym A*, forms a group under functional composition. To see this, note that the identity permutation e is in *Sym A*; if $\sigma \in$ *Sym A*, then its inverse, σ^{-1}, is in *Sym A*; and if $\sigma', \sigma'' \in$ *Sym A*, then $\sigma = \sigma'' \circ \sigma' \in$ *Sym A*. (In the expression $\sigma'' \circ \sigma'$, we apply σ' first and then apply σ''.) *Sym A* is called the *full symmetric group*. A subgroup G of *Sym A* is called a *permutation group* on A.

Two permutations σ_1, σ_2 are *disjoint* if and only if

$$\{i|\sigma_1(i) \neq i\} \cap \{j|\sigma_2(j) \neq j\} = \emptyset.$$

A permutation that maps

$$i_1 \mapsto i_2, \ i_2 \mapsto i_3, \ \ldots, \ i_{k-1} \mapsto i_k, \ i_k \mapsto i_1$$

is called a *cycle* and is denoted by $(i_1 \ i_2 \ \ldots \ i_k)$. A cycle of length 2 is called *transposition*. It is possible to show that every finite permutation can be written as a composition of disjoint cycles. Moreover, every permutation can be written as a composition of transpositions that are not necessarily disjoint [356].

For example, consider the permutation σ on $A = \{1, 2, 3, 4, 5\}$ given by

$$1 \mapsto 3, \ 2 \mapsto 4, \ 3 \mapsto 1, \ 4 \mapsto 5, \ 5 \mapsto 2.$$

The permutation σ can be written as a composition of disjoint cycles by $(1 \ 3) \circ (2 \ 4 \ 5)$ and also as a composition of transpositions $(1 \ 3) \circ (2 \ 5) \circ (2 \ 4)$. The subgroup of *Sym A* generated by the two permutations $(1 \ 3)$ and $(2 \ 4 \ 5)$ is a set with six elements:

$$\{e, \ (1 \ 3), \ (2 \ 4 \ 5), \ (2 \ 5 \ 4), \ (1 \ 3)(2 \ 4 \ 5), \ (1 \ 3)(2 \ 5 \ 4) \}$$

Let $M = (S, R, L)$ be a Kripke structure. Let G be a permutation group on the state space S of the structure M. A permutation $\sigma \in G$ is said to be a *automorphism* of M if and only if it preserves the transition relation R. More formally, σ should satisfy the following condition:

$$\forall s_1 \in S, \ \forall s_2 \in S, \ ((s_1, s_2) \in R \Rightarrow (\sigma(s_1), \sigma(s_2)) \in R)$$

G is an *automorphism group* for the Kripke structure M if and only if every permutation $\sigma \in G$ is an *automorphism* of M. Notice that our definition of an automorphism group does not refer to the labeling function L. Further note that since every $\sigma \in G$ has an inverse, which is also an automorphism, it can be proved that a permutation $\sigma \in G$ is an automorphism for a Kripke structure if and only if σ satisfies the following condition:

$$(\forall s_1 \in S)(\forall s_2 \in S)((s_1, s_2) \in R \Leftrightarrow (\sigma(s_1), \sigma(s_2)) \in R)$$

It is easy to see that if every generator of the group G is an automorphism of M, then the group G is an automorphism group for M.

As an example, consider a simple token ring algorithm with one component process Q and many component processes P. Both P and Q have the structure shown in figure 17.1.

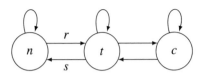

Figure 17.1
A process component.

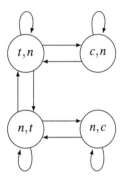

Figure 17.2
The Kripke structure for $Q\|P$.

Each component process has three states: n (non-critical section), t (has the token), and c (critical section). There are two visible actions in the process: s (send token), and r (receive token). We also have a silent, internal action denoted by τ. For simplicity, this action is not shown in the figures. Process Q is initially in the state t, and process P is initially in the state n. Composition of processes is synchronous. In the composition $Q\|P$, P and Q can either synchronize on the s action of Q and the r action of P or synchronize on the r action of Q and the s action of P. In both cases this results in an internal action τ. In addition, they can each perform an internal action τ. The Kripke structure corresponding to $Q\|P$ is shown in figure 17.2. Let P^i be the composition of the process P, i times. In the token ring $Q\|P^i$, the s action of each process is synchronized with the r action of its right neighbor and its r action is synchronized with the s action of its left neighbor.

Let σ be a permutation acting on the state set of $Q\|P$, which exchanges (n,t) with (t,n) and (n,c) with (c,n). To see that σ is an automorphism for $Q\|P$, we examine the transition from (t,n) to (c,n) and observe that there is also a transition from $\sigma((t,n)) = (n,t)$ to $\sigma((c,n)) = (n,c)$. Every other transition of $Q\|P$ is examined in a similar manner. Since each one of the transitions is preserved by σ, σ is an automorphism of $Q\|P$.

More generally, the behavior of a finite-state system is frequently determined by the values of a set of state variables $x_1, x_2, \ldots, x_n$, whose values are taken from some finite data domain D. For instance, a state of $Q\|P^i$ is an $(i+1)$-tuple of state variables, each of which ranges over the data domain $\{n,t,c\}$.

When we extract a Kripke structure from a system, the values of the state variables determine the atomic propositions. The resulting Kripke model $M = (S,R,L)$ will have the following components:

- $S \subseteq D^n$, where each state can be thought of as an assignment of values to the n state variables.
- $R \subseteq S \times S$, where R is determined by the behavior of the system.
- The labeling function L is defined so that $d_i \in L(s)$ if and only if $x_i = d$.

It is often the case that the automorphism group is given as a group acting on the indices of the state variables. For example, the permutation σ, defined on the state set of $Q\|P$, may be also described by the transposition $(1\ 2)$, which switches the state components corresponding to the first and the second processes.

A permutation σ, acting on the set of indices $\{1,2,\ldots,n\}$, defines a new permutation σ', acting on states in D^n, in the following manner:

$$\sigma'((x_1,x_2,\ldots,x_n)) = (x_{\sigma(1)},x_{\sigma(2)},\ldots,x_{\sigma(n)})$$

Given two states x and y in D^n, it is easy to see that $x \neq y$ implies $\sigma'(x) \neq \sigma'(y)$. Thus, σ' is a permutation on D^n. It is easy to show that a group G acting on the set $\{1,2,\ldots,n\}$ induces a permutation group G_1 acting on the set D^n. Consequently, an automorphism on the structure of a circuit induces an automorphism on the state space of the circuit.

17.2   Quotient Models

Let G be a permutation group acting on the set S, and let s be an element of S; then the *orbit* of s is the set $\theta(s) = \{t \mid \exists \sigma \in G(\sigma(s)=t)\}$. From each orbit $\theta(s)$ we pick a representative, which we call $rep(\theta(s))$. Intuitively, the quotient model is obtained by collapsing all the states in one orbit to a single representative state.

Formally, let $M = (S,R,L)$ be a Kripke Structure, and let G be an automorphism group acting on S. The *quotient structure* $M_G = (S_G,R_G,L_G)$ is defined as follows:

- The state set is $S_G = \{\theta(s) \mid s \in S\}$, the set of orbits of the states in S.
- The transition relation R_G is given by

$$R_G = \{(\theta(s_1),\theta(s_2)) \mid (s_1,s_2) \in R\}. \tag{17.1}$$

- The labeling function L_G is given by $L_G(\theta(s)) = L(rep(\theta(s)))$.

Note that, since G is an automorphism group, R_G is well defined and is independent of the chosen representatives. The definition of L_G, on the other hand, is not independent of the chosen representatives. To avoid this problem, we restrict our attention to symmetry groups that are also *invariance groups*.

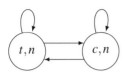

Figure 17.3
The quotient model for $Q \| P$.

G is an invariance group for an atomic proposition p if and only if the set of states labeled by p is closed under the application of all the permutations of G. More formally, an automorphism group G of a Kripke structure $M = (S, R, L)$ is an invariance group for an atomic proposition p if and only if the following condition holds:

$$\forall \sigma \in G. \forall s \in S. (p \in L(s) \Leftrightarrow p \in L(\sigma(s)))$$

We then say that p is an *invariant* under G. The notions of invariance group and invariant are extended to Boolean formulas in a straightforward way.

To illustrate some of the notions defined above, consider again the Kripke structure $Q \| P$ in figure 17.2. Let $G = \langle (1\ 2) \rangle$ be the group generated by $(1\ 2)$. Note that G is an automorphism group of $Q \| P$. In order to define the quotient model of $Q \| P$, induced by G, we first note that the orbits induced by G are

$$\{(t,n),(n,t)\} \ \text{ and } \ \{(c,n),(n,c)\}.$$

If we pick the states (t,n) and (c,n) as representatives, the resulting quotient model is shown in figure 17.3.

The Kripke structure corresponding to $Q \| P^i$ has $2(i+1)$ reachable states. The permutation group $G = \langle (1\ 2\ \ldots\ i+1) \rangle$ is an automorphism group for $Q \| P^i$. As in the case of $Q \| P$, the group G induces only two orbits,

$$\{(t,n^i),(n,t,n^{i-1}),\ldots,(n^i,t)\} \ \text{ and } \ \{(c,n^i),(n,c,n^{i-1}),\ldots,(n^i,c)\}.$$

Thus, the quotient model for $Q \| P^i$ is identical to that of $Q \| P$, as shown in figure 17.3. This example clearly demonstrates how exploiting symmetry can result in considerable savings.

Let c_i denote the Boolean variable c for the i-th component; that is, if c_i is true, then the i-th process is in the critical section. Observe that G is an invariance group for the Boolean formula *me* (for mutual exclusion) defined as follows:

$$me = (c_1 \rightarrow \neg c_2) \wedge (c_2 \rightarrow \neg c_1)$$

The theorem below states that if a temporal specification f has only invariant propositions, then f can be safely checked in the quotient model. We first present the following lemma, needed for the proof of the theorem.

Lemma 17.1 *Let $M = (S, R, L)$ be a Kripke structure with AP as the set of atomic proposi-tions, let G be an invariance group for all propositions in AP, and let M_G be the quotient model for M. Moreover, let $B \subseteq S \times S_G$ be a relation defined by*

$$\text{for every } s \in S, \quad B(s, \theta(s)).$$

Then, B is a bisimulation relation between M and M_G.

Proof To prove that B is a bisimulation, we first show that $L(s) = L_G(\theta(s))$. By the definition of M_G, we have $L_G(\theta(s)) = L(rep(\theta(s)))$. Since $rep(\theta(s)) \in \theta(s)$, there must be a permutation $\sigma \in G$ such that $\sigma(s) = rep(\theta(s))$. Since G is an invariance group for all $p \in AP$, we have that

$$\text{for all } p \in AP, \ p \in L(rep(\theta(s))) \ \Leftrightarrow \ p \in L(s).$$

Thus, $L(s) = L(rep(\theta(s))) = L_G(\theta(s))$.

Consider a transition $(s, t) \in R$. Then, by the definition of R_G, $(\theta(s), \theta(t)) \in R_G$. More-over, by the definition of the relation B we have that $B(t, \theta(t))$.

Now let ϑ be a state in S_G such that $(\theta(s), \vartheta) \in R_G$. The state ϑ contains at least one element, namely, $rep(\vartheta)$. Let t be equal to $rep(\vartheta)$. Then, $\vartheta = \theta(t)$, and $(\theta(s), \vartheta) \in R_G$ can be rewritten as $(\theta(s), \theta(t)) \in R_G$. By the definition of R_G, this means there exist two states s_1 and t_1 such that $(s_1, t_1) \in R$, $s_1 \in \theta(s)$, and $t_1 \in \theta(t)$. Since s_1 and s belong to the same orbit, there exists a permutation $\sigma_1 \in G$ such that $\sigma(s_1) = s$. By definition of a symmetry group, $(\sigma(s_1), \sigma(t)) \in R$ or, in other words, $(s, \sigma(t)) \in R$. Notice that t and $\sigma(t)$ belong in the same orbit. Hence, $\sigma(t) \in \vartheta$, and by definition of B, $B(\sigma(t), \vartheta)$. $\square$

By theorem 11.3, the previous lemma immediately implies the following corollary.

Corollary 17.1.1 *Let M be a structure defined over AP, and let G be an invariance group for AP. Then, for every $s \in S$ and every CTL* formula defined over AP,*

$$M, s \models f \ \Leftrightarrow \ M_G, \theta(s) \models f.$$

Theorem 17.2 *Let $M = (S, R, L)$ be a Kripke structure, let G be an automorphism group of M, and let f be a CTL* formula. If G is an invariance group for all the atomic propositions p occurring in f, then*

$$M, s \models f \ \Leftrightarrow \ M_G, \theta(s) \models f, \tag{17.2}$$

where M_G is the quotient structure corresponding to M.

Proof Assume that M is defined over AP and that f is defined over $AP' \subseteq AP$. The *restriction* of M to AP' is the structure $M' = (S, R, L')$ that is identical to M, except that for every $s \in S$, $L'(s) = L(s) \cap AP'$. Clearly, for every CTL* formula defined over AP', and for every $s \in S$,

$$M, s \models f \ \Leftrightarrow \ M', s \models f.$$

Let M'_G be the quotient model of M', induced by G. By the definition of quotient model, M'_G is the restriction of M_G to AP'. Thus, for every $\vartheta \in S_G$,

$$M_G, \vartheta \models f \;\Leftrightarrow\; M'_G, \vartheta \models f.$$

Since G is an invariance group for AP', corollary 17.1.1 applies and we have:

$$M', s \models f \;\Leftrightarrow\; M'_G, \theta(s) \models f.$$

Altogether, we conclude that

$$M, s \models f \;\Leftrightarrow\; M_G, \theta(s) \models f. \quad \square$$

17.3 Model Checking with Symmetry

In this section, we describe how to perform model checking in the presence of symmetry. First, we discuss how to find the set of states in a Kripke structure that are reachable from a given set of initial states using an explicit state representation. In the explicit state case, a breadth-first or depth-first search starting from the set of initial states is performed. Typically, two lists, a list of reached states and a list of unexplored states, are maintained. At the beginning of the algorithm, the initial states are put on both the lists. In the exploration step, a state is removed from the list of unexplored states, and all its successors are processed. An algorithm for exploring the state space of a Kripke structure in the presence of symmetry is discussed in [283]. The authors introduce a function $\xi(q)$, which maps a state q to the unique state representing the orbit of that state. While exploring the state space, only the unique representatives from the orbits are put on the list of reached and unexplored states. An outline of the algorithm is shown in figure 17.4. This simple reachability algorithm can be extended to a full CTL model-checking algorithm by using the technique described in [123]. In order to construct the function $\xi(q)$, it is important to compute the orbit relation efficiently.

When ordered binary decision diagrams (OBDDs) are used as the underlying representation, the construction of the quotient model is more complex. First note that, if R is represented by the OBDD $R(v_1, \ldots, v_k, v'_1, \ldots, v'_k)$ and σ is a permutation on the state variables, it is straightforward to check that σ is an automorphism of M. This is done by checking that $R(v_1, \ldots, v_k, v'_1, \ldots, v'_k)$ is identical to $R(v_{\sigma(1)}, \ldots, v_{\sigma(k)}, v'_{\sigma(1)}, \ldots, v'_{\sigma(k)})$, which is the OBDD representing the transition relation of the permuted structure.

Our method of computing the quotient model uses the OBDD for the *orbit relation* $\Theta(x, y) \Leftrightarrow (x \in \theta(y))$. Given a Kripke structure $M = (S, R, L)$ and an automorphism group G on M with r generators $g_1, g_2, \ldots, g_r$, the orbit relation Θ is the least fixpoint of the following equation:

$$Y(x, y) = \left(x = y \vee \exists z \left(Y(x, z) \wedge \bigvee_i y = g_i(z) \right) \right) \tag{17.3}$$

reached $:= \emptyset$;
unexplored $:= \emptyset$;

for all initial states s **do**
    append $\xi(s)$ to *reach*;
    append $\xi(s)$ to *unexplored*;
end for all

while *unexplored* $\neq \emptyset$ **do**
    remove a state s from *unexplored*;
    for all successor states q of s **do**
        if $\xi(q)$ is not in *reached* **then**
            append $\xi(q)$ to *reached*;
            append $\xi(q)$ to *unexplored*;
        end if
    end for all
end while

Figure 17.4
Exploring state space in the presence of symmetry.

This result is proved in the next lemma.

Lemma 17.3 *The least fixpoint of equation 17.3 is the orbit relation Θ induced by the group G generated by $g_1, g_2, \dots, g_r$.*

Proof First, we prove that Θ is a fixpoint of equation 17.3. It is obvious by the transitivity and reflexivity of the orbit relation Θ that

$$\Theta(x,y) \supseteq \left(x = y \vee \exists z\, (\Theta(x,z) \wedge \bigvee_i y = g_i(z))\right).$$

Suppose $\Theta(x,y)$, then $\Theta(y,x)$ holds as well. Thus, by the definition of the orbit relation there exists $\sigma \in G$ such that $y = \sigma(x)$. Let us assume that $x \neq y$ (if $x = y$, the result is immediate). This means there exists a generator $g_k, k \leq r$ such that $y = g_k(\sigma_1(x))$. Setting $z = \sigma_1(x)$, we see that $\Theta(x,z)$ and $y = g_k(z)$. Since x and y are arbitrary Boolean vectors, we get the following inclusion:

$$\Theta(x,y) \subseteq \left(x = y \vee \exists z\, (\Theta(x,z) \wedge \bigvee_i y = g_i(z))\right)$$

Hence, Θ is a fixpoint of equation 17.3.

    Next, we prove that if T is any fixpoint of equation 17.3, then $\Theta \subseteq T$. We prove that $\Theta(x,y) \Rightarrow T(x,y)$. The definition of the orbit relation $\Theta(x,y)$ implies that there exists a $\sigma = g_{i_m} \cdots g_{i_2} g_{i_1},\, 1 \leq i_j \leq r$, such that $\sigma(x) = y$. Since T is a fixpoint of equation 17.3, it can be proved by induction that for all $1 \leq l \leq m$, $T(x, g_{i_l} \ldots g_{i_1}(x))$ holds. Using this result for $l = m$, we see that $T(x, y)$ holds. Since $\Theta(x, y) \Rightarrow T(x, y)$, we obtain that $\Theta \subseteq T$. Hence, Θ is the least fixpoint. $\square$

If a suitable state encoding is available, this fixpoint equation can be computed using OBDDs [94]. Once we have the orbit relation Θ, we need to compute a function $\xi : S \rightarrow S$, which maps each state s to the unique representative in its orbit. If we view states as vectors of values associated with the state variables, it is possible to choose the lexicographically smallest state to be the unique representative of the orbit. Since Θ is an equivalence relation, these unique representatives can be computed using OBDDs by the method of Lin and Newton [350].

Assuming that we have the OBDD representation of the mapping function ξ, the transition relation R_G of the quotient structure can be expressed as follows:

$$R_G(x, y) = \exists x_1 \exists y_1 (R(x_1, y_1) \wedge \xi(x_1) = x \wedge \xi(y_1) = y)$$

17.4   Complexity Issues

In this section we consider complexity issues that arise in exploiting symmetry for model checking. We show that the orbit problem is at least as hard as the graph isomorphism problem, which is in NP, but not known to be NP complete. We also prove bounds on the size of the OBDD for the orbit relation.

17.4.1   The Orbit Problem and Graph Isomorphism

The most basic step in performing model checking with symmetry is to decide whether two states are in the same orbit. We now discuss the complexity of this problem.

Let G be a group acting on the set $\{1, 2, \ldots, n\}$. Assume that G is represented in terms of a finite set of generators. Given two vectors $x \in B^n$ and $y \in B^n$, the *orbit problem* asks whether there exists a permutation $\sigma \in G$ such that $y = \sigma(x)$.

Given two graphs $\Gamma_1 = (V_1, E_1)$ and $\Gamma_2 = (V_2, E_2)$ such that $|V_1| = |V_2|$, the *graph isomorphism problem* asks whether there exists a bijection $f : V_1 \rightarrow V_2$ such that the following condition holds:

$$(i, j) \in E_1 \Leftrightarrow (f(i), f(j)) \in E_2$$

Theorem 17.4 *The orbit problem is as hard as the graph isomorphism problem.*

Proof Given two graphs $\Gamma_1 = (V_1, E_1)$ and $\Gamma_2 = (V_2, E_2)$, we construct a group G and two $0 - 1$ vectors x and y such that x and y are in the same orbit under the action of the group G if and only if Γ_1 and Γ_2 are isomorphic. We assume that $|V_1| = |V_2| = n$. Let $A = \{a_{ij}\}$ and $B = \{b_{ij}\}$ be the adjacency matrices of the graph Γ_1 and Γ_2, respectively. Let $x \in \{0, 1\}^{n^2}$ be defined as follows:

$$x_{n(i-1)+j} = a_{ij}, 1 \leq i \leq n, 1 \leq j \leq n$$

The vector $x \in \{0,1\}^{n^2}$ is a list of the elements of the matrix A in row order. The vector $y \in \{0,1\}^{n^2}$ is defined in a similar fashion using the adjacency matrix B. Let $(i\ j)$ be a transposition acting on the set $\{1,2,\ldots,n\}$. Intuitively, we can think of this transposition as exchanging the vertices i and j in the graph Γ_1. This corresponds to exchanging the rows i and j and columns i and j in the adjacency matrix and has exactly the same effect as applying the following permutation σ to the vector x:

$$\sigma_{row} = (n(i-1)+1, n(j-1)+1)\ldots(n(i-1)+n, n(j-1)+n)$$
$$\sigma_{col} = (i,j)\ldots((n-1)n+i, (n-1)n+j)$$
$$\sigma = \sigma_{row}\sigma_{col}$$

Each permutation acting on the set of size $n = |V_1|$ corresponds to a bijection $f : V_1 \mapsto V_2$. We assume that the vertices are labeled by integers. If the bijection corresponding to the permutation $(i\ j)$ is an isomorphism between Γ_1 and Γ_2, then exchanging rows i and j and columns i and j in the adjacency matrix A gives B. This implies that $y = \sigma(x)$ because x and y are just encodings of the adjacency matrix A and B, respectively. Similarly, if $y = \sigma(x)$, then the bijection corresponding to the permutation $(i\ j)$ is an isomorphism between the graph Γ_1 and Γ_2. Therefore, $y = \sigma(x)$ if and only if the bijection corresponding to the permutation $(i\ j)$ is an isomorphism between Γ_1 and Γ_2. Every bijection $f : V_1 \mapsto V_2$ corresponds to some permutation in the full symmetric group S_n. Since the group S_n acting on the set $\{1,2,\ldots,n\}$ is generated by the transpositions $(1\ 2),(1\ 3), \ldots$ and $(1\ n)$, we have the result. We just have to code all these transpositions in the context of the $0-1$ vectors x and y. $\square$

As an example, consider the two graphs Γ_1 and Γ_2 given in the figure 17.5. The vectors x and y given below encode the adjacency matrices of the graphs Γ_1 and Γ_2, respectively:

$$x = (011\ 100\ 100)$$
$$y = (010\ 101\ 010)$$

The permutations σ_{row} and σ_{col} below exchange rows 1 and 2 and column 1 and 2, respectively, in the matrix described by x. Their composition corresponds to exchanging vertices 1 and 2 in graph Γ_1:

$$\sigma_{row} = (1\ 4)(2\ 5)(3\ 6)$$
$$\sigma_{col} = (1\ 2)(4\ 5)(7\ 8)$$
$$\sigma = \sigma_{row} \circ \sigma_{col}$$

Notice that $y = \sigma(x)$ and the bijection corresponding to the permutation $(1\ 2)$ is an isomorphism between Γ_1 and Γ_2.

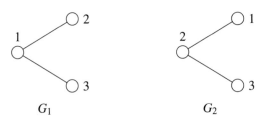

Figure 17.5
Two isomorphic graphs.

17.4.2   The Orbit Relation and OBDDs

Circuits are typically built from components, and the state bits are grouped according to the hierarchical structure of the system. In practice two types of symmetry groups occur frequently:

- *Rotation groups*, when equivalent components are ordered cyclically and can be rotated any number of steps. For example, the token ring protocol used in the solution to the distributed mutual exclusion problem exhibits rotational symmetry. A permutation group G acting on $\{1, 2, \ldots, n\}$ is a *rotation group* if it is generated by the cycle $(1\ 2\ \ldots\ n)$.
- *Full symmetric groups*, when equivalent components are unordered and can be exchanged arbitrarily. Such groups occur, for example, in systems where components communicate via a common bus (such as multiprocessor systems) or in systems where broadcasting is used.

We will prove only a lower bound on the size of the OBDD for the orbit relation of rotation groups. The proof for full symmetric groups is similar and is given in [124].

For simplicity we consider a system built by the composition of N instances of one component, for example, a ring or bus with N equivalent components. One component i is represented by a vector $\vec{x}_i$ of k state variables $x_{i,1}, \ldots, x_{i,k}$. We will refer to such a vector as a *block*. The state of the system is represented by $\langle \vec{x}_1, \ldots, \vec{x}_N \rangle$. A permutation σ acting on the components $\{1, \ldots, N\}$ induces a permutation on the state variables and hence also a permutation on the set of states: $\sigma(\langle \vec{x}_1, \ldots, \vec{x}_N \rangle) = \langle \vec{x}_{\sigma(1)}, \ldots, \vec{x}_{\sigma(N)} \rangle$.

The OBDD for the orbit relation Θ of a group G ranges over the variables $\vec{x}_1, \ldots, \vec{x}_N$, $\vec{x}'_1, \ldots, \vec{x}'_N$ and is defined by

$$\Theta(\vec{x}_1, \ldots, \vec{x}_N, \vec{x}'_1, \ldots, \vec{x}'_N) = 1$$

if and only if

$$\exists \sigma \in G : \sigma(\langle \vec{x}_1, \ldots, \vec{x}_N \rangle) = \langle \vec{x}'_1, \ldots, \vec{x}'_N \rangle.$$

The size of the OBDD representing Θ is denoted by $|\Theta|$.

Lemma 17.5 Let $f(x_1, \ldots, x_n, x_1', \ldots, x_n')$ be the following Boolean function:

$$\bigwedge_{i=1}^{n} (x_i = x_i')$$

Let F be the OBDD for f such that all the unprimed variables are ordered before all the primed variables. In this case $|F| \geq 2^n$.

Proof Consider two distinct assignments $(b_1, \ldots, b_n)$ and $(c_1, \ldots, c_n)$ to the Boolean vector $(x_1, \ldots, x_n)$. These two assignments can be distinguished because of the following equation:

$$f(b_1, \ldots, b_n, b_1, \ldots, b_n) \neq f(c_1, \ldots, c_n, b_1, \ldots, b_n)$$

Let v_1 and v_2 be the nodes reached after following the path $(b_1, \ldots, b_n)$ and $(c_1, \ldots, c_n)$ from the top node. Since these two assignments can be distinguished, we must have $v_1 \neq v_2$. There are 2^n different assignments to the Boolean vector $(x_1, \ldots, x_n)$, and each of them corresponds to a different node (at level n) in the OBDD F. Therefore, the number of nodes at level n in the OBDD F is $\geq 2^n$. $\square$

Theorem 17.6 *Let the state of a system be composed of N equivalent components each with k state variables. For a rotation group G acting on the set $\{1, \ldots, N\}$ we have the following lower bound for the OBDD representing the induced orbit relation Θ:*

$$|\Theta| > 2^K \text{ with } K = min(\sqrt{N}, 2^{k-1})$$

Proof Let Θ be the OBDD for the orbit relation. For the proof we consider the first variable of each block. From the top of the OBDD Θ we go down until we have K variables $x_{i,1}$ or K variables $x_{i,1}'$. We will cut the OBDD Θ at this level. Without loss of generality, we assume that we have K unprimed variables with indices $I = \{i_1, \ldots, i_K\}$ above the cut. Let J be the set of indices of primed variables of the form $x_{j,1}'$ above the cut. The set J must contain less than K elements.

Let T be the following set:

$$T = \{\sigma \in G \mid \sigma(I) \cap J \neq \emptyset\}$$

For each permutation $\sigma \in T$ there exists $i \in I, j \in J$ such that the permutation σ rotates the i-th block to the j-th block. Since σ is a rotation, knowing that it maps i to j determines it. The number of ways of choosing $i \in I$ and $j \in J$ is less than K^2. It follows from the definition of K that $K^2 \leq N$, and therefore, $|T| < N$ and $G - T$ is nonempty.

Any rotation $r \in G - T$ has the property that $r(I) \cap J = \emptyset$. In other words, each such rotation maps an unprimed variable $x_{i,1}$ that occurs above the cut to a primed variable $x_{j,1}'$ that occurs below the cut.

Our goal is to use lemma 17.5 to bound the size of the OBDD Θ. In order to accomplish this, we construct an OBDD Θ' that is smaller than Θ and has the property that all of the unprimed variables occur before all of the primed variables.

Choose a rotation $r \in G - T$. Instantiate the variables $\langle x_{i_j,2}, \ldots, x_{i_j,k} \rangle$ and $\langle x'_{i_j+r,2}, \ldots, x'_{i_j+r,k} \rangle$ for $i_j \in I$ with the binary encoding of the number j. (Since $1 \leq j \leq K$, we need $K \leq 2^{k-1}$.) The variables $x_{i,j}$ and $x'_{i+r,j}$ are instantiated with 0 for $i \notin I$.

The resulting OBDD Θ' has free variables $x_{i,1}, x'_{i+r,1}$, $i \in I$, where all the unprimed variables are above the cut and all primed variables are below, and is smaller than the OBDD Θ. The instantiation was chosen in such a way that for the rotation r the primed and unprimed variables must be equal. Thus, Θ' is the OBDD for the Boolean formula

$$\bigwedge_{i \in I} (x_{i,1} = x'_{i+r,1}).$$

Since the variables $x_{i,1}$ are ordered before the variables $x'_{i+r,1}$, it follows from lemma 17.5 that the size of the OBDD Θ' is greater than 2^K. Since the OBDD for Θ' is smaller than the OBDD for Θ, the desired result follows. $\square$

The OBDD of the orbit relation induced by a full symmetric or rotation group on the components is exponential in the minimum of the number of components and the number of states in one component. Consequently, using the orbit relation to exploit symmetries of that kind in symbolic model checking is restricted to examples with a small number of components or where each component has only a few states. An approach that avoids the computation of the orbit relation is described in [125]. Given a Kripke structure $M = (S, R, L)$ and a set of representatives $Rep \subseteq S$, their approach builds a model M_{Rep} whose state set is Rep. The set Rep can have more than one state from each orbit. This approach does not need the OBDD for the orbit relation.

17.5 Empirical Results

To illustrate these ideas, consider a simple cache coherence protocol for a single-bus multiprocessor system based on the Futurebus+ IEEE standard [282]. The system has a bus over which the processors and the global memory communicate. Each processor contains a local cache, which consists of a fixed number of cache lines (figure 17.6).

In each bus cycle the bus arbiter chooses one processor to be the master. The master processor selects a cache line address and a command it wants to put on the bus. The other processors and the memory respond to the bus command and change their local context. The reaction of the components is described in the protocol standard, which enforces the coherence of the cache lines among the different processors; that is, only valid data values are read by the processors, and no writes are lost. For the verification task, the protocol is formalized, and cache coherence and other important system properties are expressed in temporal logic.

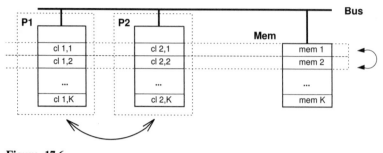

Figure 17.6
System structure.

The behavior of the processors, the bus, and the memory can be described by finite-state machines. The state of the processor P_i is a combination of the states of each cache line in the processor cache and the state of the bus interface. The global bus is represented by the command on the bus, the active cache line address, and other bus control signals, such as those for bus snooping and arbitration.

There are two obvious symmetries in the system. First, processors are symmetric; that is, we can exchange the context of any two processors in the system. Second, cache lines are symmetric; that is, any two cache lines can be exchanged simultaneously in all processors and the memory. To maintain consistency, along with applying the symmetries mentioned above all the cache lines and processor addresses in the system must be renamed. Both symmetries are indicated in figure 17.6 by arrows.

The complete system is the synchronous composition of all the components and is described by a Kripke structure $M = (S, R, L)$. Since domains can be encoded in binary, a state is just a binary vector, and the transition relation R can be represented by an OBDD.

When we use only processor symmetry, we choose as the set of representatives the states where processor 1 is the master. When we use only cache symmetry, we choose as the set of representatives the states where cache line 1 is active. When we use both symmetries we choose the set of states where processor 1 is the master and cache line 1 is active as the set of representatives.

Consider the following properties, each of which can be represented by a propositional formula:

Property p: For all cache lines it is true that if one processor is in *exclusive-modified* state, then all other processors are in the *invalid* state.

Property q: For all cache lines it is the case that if memory has valid data, then either all processors are in *shared-unmodified* or *invalid* state, or one processor is in *exclusive-unmodified* state.

Property m: All cache lines in memory are valid.

Property c: The command on the bus is either *read-modified* or *invalidate*.

Some important properties of the protocol are as follows:

- **AG** p and **AG** q — the properties p and q always hold.
- **AG**$(m \rightarrow$ **A**$(m$ **U** $c))$ — if the memory has valid data, then it remains valid until an appropriate command is issued.
- **AG**(**EF** m) — from all the reachable states it is possible to get to a state where the memory has valid data for all the cache lines,

In [125] symmetry is exploited in order to check these properties for a model of the cache consistency protocol, represented by OBDDs. For some configurations the OBDD sizes are reduced by a factor of 15.

Bibliographic Notes

Early research on symmetry reduction appears in the works of Clarke, Filkorn, and Jha [125], Emerson and Sistla [211], and Ip and Dill [283]. The method was extended to handle real time [213], for probabilistic model checking in [328]. Dealing with nearly symmetric systems is shown in [214]. Dealing with symmetry under fairness is described in [212]. Combining symmetry reduction with partial order reduction is studied in [200]. Symmetry reduction was used for the automatic verification of distributed protocols in [69].

18 Infinite Families of Finite-State Systems

The ability to reason automatically about entire families of finite-state systems is an important goal. Such families arise frequently in the design of reactive systems in both hardware and software. Typically, circuit and protocol designs are parameterized; that is, they define an infinite family of systems. For example, a circuit design to multiply two integers has the width of the integers n as a parameter; the design of a bus has the number of processors and caches on the bus parameterized, and in the design of a token-ring algorithm the number of processes on the ring is parameterized.

Most of the research done in the area of model checking focuses on verifying single finite-state systems. In this chapter we describe methods to verify parameterized designs, viewed as infinite families of finite-state systems. This problem can also be thought of as solving the state explosion problem because in this case the state set is unbounded. Formally, the problem can be stated as follows:

> Given an infinite family of systems $\mathcal{F} = \{M_i\}_{i=1}^{\infty}$ and a temporal formula f, verify that all the systems in $\mathcal{F}$ satisfy f, that is, that $\forall i \, [M_i \models f]$.

In general the problem is undecidable [28, 36, 455]. We give a formal proof of this result at the end of the chapter in section 18.5. It is not necessary to understand the details of this proof in order to read the remainder of this chapter.

18.1 Temporal Logic for Infinite Families

Traditionally, temporal logics specify properties of a single Kripke structure. These logics can be extended to specify properties of infinite families of Kripke structures. Two such logics are discussed below.

Browne, Clarke, and Grumberg [84] introduce a version of CTL* called *indexed* CTL* or ICTL*. The propositions in ICTL* are indexed by the natural numbers. Intuitively, if a proposition is indexed by i, it applies to the i-th component process. Let f be an arbitrary CTL* formula. Let $f(i)$ be the formula f where all the propositions have been indexed by i. The indexed logic ICTL* permits formulas of the form $\wedge_i f(i)$ (the formula f is true in all components) and $\vee_i f(i)$ (the formula f is true in some component). One can also have formulas like $\wedge_{j\neq i} f(j)$ (every component but the i-th component satisfies f) or $\vee_{j\neq i} f(j)$ (some component other than the i-component satisfies f). For example, consider the infinite family of token rings $\mathcal{F} = \{Q\|P^i\}_{i=1}^{\infty}$. The following ICTL* formula expresses the *mutual exclusion* property for the family $\mathcal{F}$:

$$\bigwedge_i \mathbf{AG}(c_i \Rightarrow \bigwedge_{i\neq j} \neg c_j)$$

In [129], another version of CTL* is proposed that replaces atomic propositions by regular expressions. Consider again the family $\mathcal{F} = \{Q\|P^i\}_{i=1}^{\infty}$, and let $S = \{n,t,c\}$. The states in any Kripke structure in $\mathcal{F}$ can be vectors of arbitrary size whose components are in S. In other words, the states of Kripke structures in $\mathcal{F}$ are strings over the alphabet S, and therefore belongs to S^*. Notice that the regular expression $\{n,t\}^* c\{n,t\}^*$ represents the mutual exclusion property for a state in some structure in $\mathcal{F}$. The advantage of regular expressions is that they apply to arbitrary sized vectors over S and can characterize states in any Kripke structure belonging to the infinite family $\mathcal{F}$. The following formula states the mutual exclusion property:

$$\mathbf{AG}(\{n,t\}^* c\{n,t\}^*)$$

18.2   Invariants

Most techniques for verifying families of finite-state structures rely on finding an *invariant*. Formally, an invariant can be defined as follows. Given a family $\mathcal{F} = \{M_1, M_2, \ldots\}$ and a reflexive, transitive relation $\geq$ on structures, an *invariant* $\mathcal{I}$ is a structure such that for all M in $\mathcal{F}, \mathcal{I} \geq M$.

The relation $\geq$ determines what kind of temporal property can be checked. The most widely used relations are the *bisimulation* equivalence ($M \equiv \mathcal{I}$) and the *simulation* preorder ($M \preceq \mathcal{I}$) that preserve the logics CTL* and ACTL*, and language equivalence ($M \cong \mathcal{I}$) and language inclusion ($M \subseteq \mathcal{I}$) that preserve the logic LTL. Both the bisimulation equivalence and the language equivalence provide *strong preservation*; that is, for all M in $\mathcal{F}$,

$$\mathcal{I} \models f \Longrightarrow M \models f, \text{ and}$$
$$\mathcal{I} \not\models f \Longrightarrow M \not\models f.$$

The simulation preorder and language inclusion, on the other hand, provide only *weak preservation*; that is, for all M in $\mathcal{F}$,

$$\mathcal{I} \models f \Longrightarrow M \models f.$$

However, if $\mathcal{I} \not\models f$, then nothing can be concluded about the truth of f in the family and a new invariant has to be suggested. The counterexample generated while checking whether f is true in $\mathcal{I}$ can be a useful aid in guessing a new invariant.

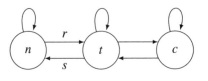

Figure 18.1
A process component.

In [84], a family of token rings is considered. It is shown that a ring of size n ($n \geq 2$) is bisimilar to a ring of size 2. In this case the token ring of size 2 is the invariant $\mathcal{I}$. Let f be an arbitrary CTL* formula. Using theorem 11.4, we have that $\mathcal{I} \models f$ if and only if f is true in the entire family of token rings. Unfortunately, the bisimulation has to be constructed manually. Moreover, since the bisimulation equivalence $\equiv$ is more stringent than the simulation preorder $\preceq$, it is harder to devise an invariant for $\equiv$. Alternative techniques for reasoning about families of finite state structures are given in [207, 208, 237].

Kurshan and McMillan [327] and Wolper and Lovinfosse [488] suggest an *invariant rule* as a more systematic way for establishing an invariant. Assume that each member M_i in the family $\mathcal{F}$, is a composition of some number of basic structures. Further assume that the composition operator $\|$ is *monotonic* with respect to the relation $\geq$; that is, for all structures P_1, P_1', P_2, P_2', if $P_1 \geq P_1'$ and $P_2 \geq P_2'$, then $P_1\|P_2 \geq P_1'\|P_2'$.

The *invariant rule* in its simplest form is given for the family $\mathcal{F} = \{P^i\}_{i=1}^{\infty}$. The following lemma states the invariant rule and proves its correctness.

Lemma 18.1 *Let $\geq$ be a reflexive, transitive relation and, let $\|$ be a composition operator that is monotonic with respect to $\geq$. If $\mathcal{I} \geq P$ and $\mathcal{I} \geq \mathcal{I}\|P$, then $\mathcal{I} \geq P^i$, for all $i \geq 1$.*

Proof We prove the result by induction on i. Using the hypothesis, the result is true for $i = 1$. Let $i \geq 2$, and assume that the result is true for $i - 1$. The first equation given below is the induction hypothesis. The second equation follows from the first by composing with process P and using the monotonicity of composition with respect to $\geq$.

$$\mathcal{I} \geq P^{i-1}$$
$$\mathcal{I}\|P \geq P^i$$

Now using the fact that $\mathcal{I} \geq \mathcal{I}\|P$ and the transitivity of $\geq$, we get that $\mathcal{I} \geq P^i$. □

This rule can easily be extended to families of the form $\{Q\|P^i\}_{i=1}^{\infty}$ for any structures Q and P. If $\mathcal{I}'$ satisfies the conditions above, then $\mathcal{I} = Q\|\mathcal{I}'$ is an invariant for this family. This rule is still valid if other operations on processes (such as renaming and hiding) are allowed, provided that they are monotonic with respect to $\geq$.

Sometimes it is difficult or even impossible to find an invariant $\mathcal{I}$ such that $\mathcal{I} \geq P^i$. However, if we consider the environment in which the P^is are running (for instance, Q in

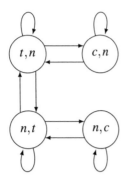

Figure 18.2
The Kripke structure for $Q\|P$.

the above example), then such an invariant exists. We show how this technique can be used
to verify the token ring example given in chapter 17. The processes P and Q from this
example are reproduced in figure 18.1. They are identical except that the initial state of Q
is t while the initial state of P is n. Figure 18.2 gives the structure $Q\|P$ corresponding to
the composition of Q and P. The composition operator $\|$ is defined in a similar manner to
the composition operator in chapter 15, and is monotonic with respect to the simulation
preorder.

We claim that $Q\|P$ is an invariant for the family $\{Q\|P^i\}_{i=1}^{\infty}$ with respect to the simulation
preorder ($\succeq$). To prove this, we only need to show that $Q\|P \succeq Q\|P\|P$. By monotonicity of
$\|$ with respect to $\succeq$ and the transitivity of $\succeq$, we conclude that $Q\|P \succeq Q\|P^i$, for every i.

$Q\|P\|P$ is given in figure 18.3. The simulation relation associates the initial state (t,n,n)
of $Q\|P\|P$ with the initial state (t,n) of $Q\|P$. It also associates (c,n,n) with (c,n). States
(n,t,n) and (n,n,t) are associated with (n,t), and states (n,c,n) and (n,n,c) are associated
with (n,c). It is easy to check that this relation is a simulation preorder.

In [327] and [488], extensions of the invariant rule are applied in the context of specific
models of computation with specific preorders.

18.3   Futurebus+ Example Reconsidered

In this section we apply the induction principle to a non-trivial example. We consider the
Futurebus+ cache-coherence protocol discussed in chapter 17 for the case of a single bus.
This example is described by the infinite family of Kripke structures $\mathcal{F} = \{P^1, P^2, \ldots\}$,
where P^i represents a bus with i processes on it. Each component structure P is given by an
SMV program. The portion of the program describing how the next command is generated
for process P is given in figure 18.4. We abbreviate the state values to be I for *invalid*,
EM for *exclusive-modified*, EU for *exclusive-unmodified*, and SU for *shared-unmodified*.

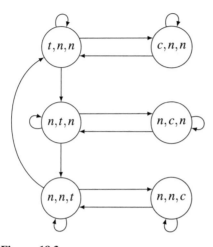

Figure 18.3
The Kripke structure for $Q\|P\|P$.

Each processor has a Boolean variable `master` that is true when the processor has write permission to the bus. Exactly one processor has its `master` variable set to 1 at any time.

Our first approximation for the invariant is the process P. By the induction principle, for P to be an invariant it should satisfy

$$P \succeq P\|P$$

that is, P should "mimic" the behavior of $P\|P$. Unfortunately, this does not hold. For instance, when $P\|P$ is in the state (*exclusive-modified*, *invalid*), it can issue the commands *copy-back* and *read-shared*. No state in P can issue both of these commands. To solve this problem, we guess a modification, called P', as the new invariant. P and P' differ mainly in the way they issue the next command. The portion of the modified program for P' is given in figure 18.5.

To prove that P' is an invariant, we have to check the following conditions:

$$P' \succeq P$$
$$P' \succeq P'\|P$$

The first requirement holds because P' is derived from P by adding more transitions. To prove that the second requirement holds, we establish a correspondence between reachable states in P' and $P'\|P$ and show that this correspondence is a simulation relation. A state s' in P' corresponds to a state (s_1, s_2) in $P'\|P$ if and only if the following conditions hold:

1. The cache states match; that is

```
ASSIGN
init(cmd) := idle;
next(cmd) :=
  case
    state = I & !master : {read_shared, read_modified, idle};
    state = EM & !master : {copy_back, idle};
    state = EU & !master : {copy_back, idle};
    state = SU & !master : {invalidate, copy_back, idle};
    master : cmd;
    1 : idle;
  esac;
```

Figure 18.4
Command part for the process *P*.

```
ASSIGN
init(cmd) := idle;
next(cmd) :=
  case
    state = I & !master :
        {copyback, read_shared, read_modified, idle};
    state = EM & !master :
        {copy_back, read_modified, read_shared, idle};
    state = EU & !master :
        {copy_back, read_modified, read_shared, idle};
    state = SU & !master :
        {invalidate, copy_back, idle};
    master : cmd;
    1 : idle;
  esac;
```

Figure 18.5
Command part for the invariant *P′* .

(a) if *s′* is in *invalid* state, then s_1 and s_2 are in *invalid* state;

(b) if *s′* is in *shared-unmodified* state, then at least one state s_1 or s_2 is in *shared-unmodified* state and the other one is in *invalid* or *shared-unmodified*;

(c) if *s′* is in *exclusive-modified* state, then exactly one of the components is in *exclusive-modified* state and the other one is in *invalid*; and

(d) if *s′* is in *exclusive-unmodified* state, then exactly one of the components is in *exclusive-unmodified* state and the other one is in *invalid*.

2. *s* has the master bit set to 1 if and only if exactly one of the states s_1 or s_2 has its master bit set to 1.

3. The value of the command variable cmd in the state s is the same as the value of the variable cmd in the state that has its master bit set to 1. Thus, if master $= 1$ in s_1, then the value cmd in s_1 should match the value of cmd in s. Similarly, if master $= 1$ in s_2, then the value cmd in s_2 should match the value of cmd in s.

It is straightforward to check that the initial states correspond and that for every pair of corresponding states s and (s_1, s_2), every possible transition from (s_1, s_2) is also possible from s. We check this fact for a specific pair of states. For other cases the analysis is similar. Consider the case where s is in the *exclusive-modified* state, s_1 is in the *exclusive-modified* state, and s_2 is in the *invalid* state. Thus, $s_1 \in P'$ can issue either call-back or read-modified or read-shared commands while $s_2 \in P$ can issue either a read-shared or a read-modified command. We will consider some of the transitions from the state (s_1, s_2) and show that there are corresponding transitions from the state s.

- Let master $= 1$ and cmd $=$ read-shared in the state s_2. Recall that by issuing a read-shared command the processor gets a readable copy of the cache line. This happens when the second processor issues a read-shared command. Let (s_1', s_2') be the next state in $P' \| P$. In s_2' the state of the cache is *shared-unmodified*, and in s_1' the state is *shared-unmodified* or *invalid*. Since the states s and (s_1, s_2) correspond, the cmd in the state s is also read-shared. Let s' be the successor state of s in P'. Thus, in s' the state of the cache is *shared-unmodified*. Hence, the states s' and (s_1', s_2') correspond.

- Let master $= 1$, and let cmd $=$ read-modified in s_2. Recall that by issuing the command read-modified the processor gets an exclusive copy of the cache line. Let (s_1', s_2') be the successor state of (s_1, s_2) in $P' \| P$. The state of the cache in s_1' is *invalid* and the state in s_2' is *exclusive-modified* or *exclusive-unmodified*. In the invariant process P' it is possible to issue a read-modified command and move to the *exclusive-modified* or *exclusive-unmodified* state. Therefore, the next state of s corresponds to (s_1', s_2').

- The cases when state s_1 has master $= 1$ and issues either a copy-back command, a read-shared command, or a read-modified command are similar to the preceding cases.

18.4 Graph and Network Grammars

An important question in the study of families of Kripke structures is, how does one generate the infinite family? Most authors consider standard topologies like rings or stars. We present a formalism based on graph grammars that lets us generate many interesting topologies.

Our treatment is based on the material in [173]. A graph over Σ (the *node alphabet*) and Δ (the *edge alphabet*) is a triple (N, ϕ, ψ), where N is a finite nonempty *set of nodes*, $\phi : N \to \Sigma$ is the *node labeling function*, and $\psi \subseteq N \times \Delta \times N$ is the *edge labeling function*. Let $\mathcal{G} = \{D \mid D$ is a graph over Σ and $\Delta\}$; a *graph language* $\mathcal{D}$ over Σ and Δ is a subset of $\mathcal{G}$. A *context-free graph grammar* (CFGG) is a 5-tuple $G = (\Sigma_n, \Sigma_t, \Delta, \mathcal{S}, \mathcal{R})$, where the

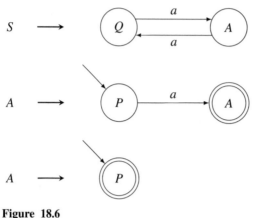

Figure 18.6
Rules for the graph grammar.

nonterminal node alphabet (Σ_n), the *terminal node alphabet* (Σ_t), and the *edge alphabet* (Δ) are finite nonempty mutually disjoint sets, $S \in \Sigma_n$ is the *start label*, and $\mathcal{R}$ is a finite nonempty set of *production rules*. Each element in $\mathcal{R}$ is a quadruple $r = (A, D, I, O)$, where

1. $A \in \Sigma_n$;
2. $D = (N, \phi, \psi)$ is a connected graph over $\Sigma = \Sigma_n \cup \Sigma_t$ and Δ; the set Σ is the *entire node alphabet*;
3. $I \in N$ is the *input node*; and
4. $O \in N$ is the *output node*.

Given a graph whose nodes are labeled, a new graph is derived using one of the rules of the grammar. We start with a graph with a single node whose label is the start symbol S. During a derivation, a node with label A is replaced by the graph D in some derivation rule (A, D, I, O). Every arc originally entering (exiting) the node labeled by A becomes an arc entering (exiting) the input node I (output node O).

Example 18.2 *Consider the grammar* $G = (\Sigma_n, \Sigma_t, \Delta, \mathcal{S}, R)$ *with* $\Sigma_n = \{\mathcal{S}, A\}$, $\Sigma_t = \{P, Q\}$, *and* $\Delta = \{\mathtt{a}\}$. *The rules are shown in figure 18.6. The grammar generates all rings of the form* $Q P^i$. *The input nodes are indicated by an arrow, and the output nodes are indicated by double circles.*

Derivation of ring of size 3 is illustrated in figure 18.7. Consider the second step. Since the node labeled with P is the input node, the arc from Q enters P. Similarly, the node labeled A has an arc going out to Q because it is the output node.

A *network grammar* is like a graph grammar except that the nodes in the graphs derived using the network grammar correspond to Kripke structures. The semantics of a derived graph is the Kripke structure obtained by composing the structures in all of its nodes.

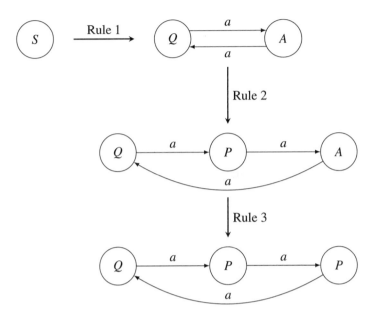

Figure 18.7
Derivation of a ring of size 3.

For example, if in the example given in figure 18.6 we interpret P, Q as the processes in figure 17.1 and the edges as composition operators, we can generate the infinite family $\mathcal{F} = \{Q \| P^i\}_{i=1}^{\infty}$ of token rings. Network grammars have been used to perform induction on the topological structure of the network [441, 364, 129].

In [441, 364, 129], the family $\mathcal{F}$ is defined by means of a network grammar. The rules of the grammar define inductively the legal configurations in the family, where a configuration is given as a communication graph with an assignment of basic processes (Kripke structures) to nodes of the graph. Based on the rules of the network grammar, induction on the topological structure of the network is performed to establish an invariant for the entire family. We will explain these techniques by an example. Consider the network grammar G in figure 18.8 that generates an infinite family of binary trees of depth ≥ 2. The symbols `root`, `inter`, `leaf` are the terminal processes. A system that checks parity based on this grammar is discussed later in the chapter.

For simplicity, we use a linear representation of the network grammars in the remainder of this chapter. For example, the second rule for SUB in figure 18.8 will be written as

$$\text{SUB} \quad \longrightarrow \quad \texttt{inter} \| \texttt{leaf} \| \texttt{leaf}.$$

In order to verify a family of Kripke structure derived by a network grammar, we extend the invariant rule presented in section 18.2. With each of the nonterminals in the network

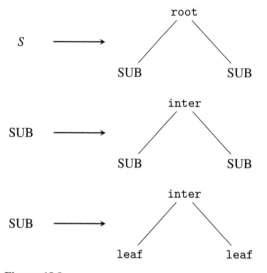

Figure 18.8
The network grammar G for binary trees.

grammar we associate an invariant that will be greater than any of the Kripke structures derived from this nonterminal. As before, we will assume that $\|$ is monotonic with respect to $\geq$.

To illustrate our idea, let $inv(\text{SUB})$ be the invariant associated with the non-terminal SUB in the network grammar for binary trees. This invariant must satisfy the following *monotonicity* conditions:

$$inv(\text{SUB}) \geq \texttt{inter}\|inv(\text{SUB})\|inv(\text{SUB}) \tag{18.1}$$

$$inv(\text{SUB}) \geq \texttt{inter}\|\texttt{leaf}\|\texttt{leaf} \tag{18.2}$$

Notice that the two equations correspond to the last two rules in the grammar. Now we prove that $inv(\text{SUB})$ is larger than any process derived by the non-terminal SUB in the ordering $\geq$. Our proof uses induction on the number of steps in a derivation. We use the symbol $\text{SUB} \stackrel{k}{\Rightarrow} w$ to denote that w is derived from SUB using k steps. The result is true for $k = 1$ because of equation 18.2. Let w be derived from SUB using $k > 1$ derivations. The process w has the following form:

$$w = \texttt{inter}\|w_1\|w_2$$

The processes w_1 and w_2 are derived using less than k derivations, so by the induction hypothesis we have the following equations:

$$inv(\text{SUB}) \geq w_1$$
$$inv(\text{SUB}) \geq w_2$$
$$\texttt{inter}\|inv(\text{SUB})\|inv(\text{SUB}) \geq \texttt{inter}\|w_1\|w_2$$

The third equation follows from the first two using monotonicity of the composition operator with respect to $\geq$. Using equation 18.1 and the equation given above, we get that $inv(\text{SUB}) \geq w$. Therefore, the process $\mathcal{I}$ given below is an invariant (using the partial order $\geq$) for the infinite family generated by the grammar.

$$\mathcal{I} = \texttt{root}\|inv(\text{SUB})\|inv(\text{SUB})$$

In Shtadler and Grumberg [441], a specific process generated by the non-terminal SUB is used as an invariant. This invariant is required to be equivalent to all other Kripke structures that can be derived from SUB. An abstraction based on the specification is used in [129] to construct an invariant. Next, we describe the method to derive invariants presented in [129].

We consider a family of binary trees, in which each leaf has a bit value. We verify an algorithm that computes the parity of the values at the leaves. The algorithm is taken from [463] and works as follows. The root process initiates a wave by sending the *readydown* signal to its children. Every internal node that gets the signal sends it to its children. When the signal *readydown* reaches a leaf process, the leaf sends the *readyup* signal and its *value* to its parent. An internal node that receives the *readyup* and *value* from both its children, sends the *readyup* signal and the $\oplus$ of the values received from the children to its parent. When the *readyup* signal reaches the root, one wave of the computation is terminated and the root can initiate another wave. The structure of the network derived from the grammar G is given schematically in figure 18.9. For example, the inputs *readyup_l* and *value_l* of an internal node are identified with the outputs *readyup* and *value* of its left child.

Next, we describe the various processes and their signals in detail. First, we describe the process `inter`. The process `inter` is the process corresponding to an internal node of the tree. The various signals for the process are shown in the table in figure 18.10. The state variables are internal variables that are used to preserve the value of the input variables. The input and the output variables provide the interface with the environment.

The following equations are invariants for the state variables:

$$root\_or\_leaf = 0$$
$$readyup = readyup\_l \wedge readyup\_r$$

Note that $root\_or\_leaf = 0$ since this is an internal node. The output variables have the same value in each state as the corresponding state variable; for example, the output variable *readydown* has the same value as the state variable *readydown*. The equations given below

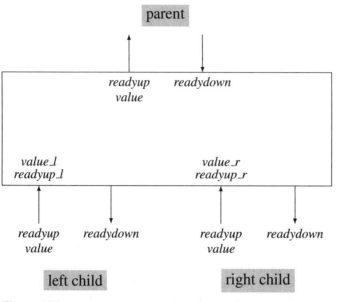

Figure 18.9
Internal node of the tree.

state variables	output variables	input variables
root_or_leaf	*readydown*	*readydown*
readydown	*readyup*	*readyup_l*
readyup_l	*value*	*readyup_r*
readyup_r		*value_l*
value		*value_r*
readyup		

Figure 18.10
The signals for process `inter`.

show how the input variables affect the state variables. In these equations, the primed variables on the left-hand side refer to the next state variables and the right-hand side refers to the input variables.

$$readydown' = readydown$$
$$readyup\_l' = readyup\_l$$
$$readyup\_r' = readyup\_r$$
$$value' = (readyup\_l \wedge value\_l) \oplus (readyup\_r \wedge value\_r)$$

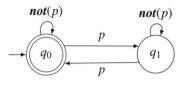

Figure 18.11
Automaton for parity.

Since the `root` process does not have a parent, it does not have the input variable *readydown*. The invariant *root_or_leaf* $= 1$ is maintained for the root and the leaf process. Since the leaf process does not have a child, the output variable *readydown* is absent. The leaf variable has only one input variable *readydown*, and the following equation between the next state variables and input variables is maintained:

$$readyup' = readydown$$

This equation holds for leaf nodes because they send a *readyup* signal immediately after they get the *readydown* signal. For each `leaf` process the assignment for the state variable *value* is decided non-deterministically in the initial state and then kept the same throughout the computation.

A state in the basic processes (`root`, `leaf`, `inter`) is a specific assignment to the state variables. We call the set of such states Σ. Notice that the state set is $\Sigma \cong \{0, 1\}^6$ because there are six state variables. Let $value_1, \ldots, value_n$ be the values in the n leaves. Let *value* be the value calculated at the root. Since at the end of the computation the root process should have the parity of the bits $value_i$ ($1 \leq i \leq n$), the following equation should hold at the end of the computation:

$$value \oplus \bigoplus_{i=1}^{n} value_i = 0. \tag{18.3}$$

Let p be a new proposition that is true of all states in Σ that satisfy *root_or_leaf* $\wedge$ *value*. The proposition p will be true at any root or leaf node that has bit value 1. The proposition **not**(p) is the complement of p and is true in states of internal nodes and in states of root or leaf nodes with value bit 0. Notice that the state set of `inter||leaf||leaf` is Σ^3. In general, a tree consisting of n processes (the processes are from the set $\{$`root`, `inter`, `leaf`$\}$) has the state set Σ^n. Therefore, the state set of the entire family of parity trees is $\bigcup_{i=1}^{\infty} \Sigma^i$, which is a subset of $\Sigma^\star$. In order to reason about the entire family of parity trees, we need to have a formalism that accepts states from the set $\Sigma^\star$. In section 18.1 we show how this can be done using regular expressions. For efficiency concerns we use instead deterministic finite-state automata over the alphabet Σ. The finite-state automata will perform the role of atomic propositions in the logic ACTL.

Figure 18.12
Automaton for ready.

The automaton given in figure 18.11 accepts the strings in Σ^* that satisfy equation 18.3. Since *root_or_leaf* $= 0$ for internal nodes, the automaton essentially ignores the values at the internal nodes. Unlike the notation for graph grammars, here an arrow indicates an initial state and a double circle indicates an accepting state. This notation is standard for finite automata. We also want to assert that every process is finished with its computation. This is signaled by the fact that *readyup* $= 1$ for each process. The automaton given in figure 18.12 accepts a string $w \in \Sigma^*$ if and only if *readyup* is true in each letter of w (notice that each letter in $w \in \Sigma^*$ corresponds to a state in a component), that is, if all processes have finished their computation. We use the product of these two automata as our atomic formula. We use $\mathcal{P}$ to denote the product automaton. Let Q be the set of states of the product automaton, let $\delta : Q \times \Sigma \to Q$ be the next state function, and let $s_0 = (m_0, q_0)$ be the initial state. The state (m_0, q_1) of the product automaton has the semantics that the computation is finished, but the parity is incorrect. We call the state (m_0, q_1) *bad*. We want to check that every reachable state $\sigma \in \Sigma^*$ of the family of parity trees satisfies the condition that if the computation is finished in that state, then the *root* process has the correct parity, that is, $\delta(s_0, \sigma) \neq bad$.

Each automaton with the alphabet Σ introduces an abstraction on the set of states Σ^* of the family of parity trees. We will first describe the abstraction function h on the state set Σ of the basic processes root, leaf, and inter. Consider a state $a \in \Sigma$. The abstraction $h(a)$ of a is the function that a induces on the state set Q of the product automaton. Thus, $h(a) : Q \to Q$, where $h(a)(q) = \delta(q, a)$ and δ is the transition function of the automaton.

Now consider an arbitrary state $\sigma = (a_0, a_1, \ldots, a_k) \in \Sigma^k$. The abstraction of σ, $h(\sigma) : Q \to Q$ is given by the following equation:

$$h(\sigma) = h(a_0) \circ h(a_1) \circ \ldots \circ h(a_k),$$

where symbol $\circ$ denotes the function composition.

We will say that σ_1 is equivalent to σ_2 if and only if their abstractions are equal (as functions), that is, if $h(\sigma_1) = h(\sigma_2)$. Note that the number of different functions that can be induced by some state $\sigma \in \Sigma^*$ is bounded by $|Q|^{|Q|}$. Thus, we mapped the infinite state space Σ^* to a finite abstract domain. In practice, the number of different abstract values to which reachable states are mapped will be much smaller.

Example 18.3   *Consider a state $a_0 \in \Sigma$ in which p is true and readyup is true. Then $h(a_0)$ is the following function:*

$$h(a_0)(q_0,m_0) = (q_1,m_0)$$
$$h(a_0)(q_0,m_1) = (q_1,m_1)$$
$$h(a_0)(q_1,m_0) = (q_0,m_0)$$
$$h(a_0)(q_1,m_1) = (q_0,m_1)$$

To see why this is true, consider, for example, $h(a_0)(q_0,m_0)$. In the automaton given in figure 18.11, there is a transition on a_0 from the state q_0 to q_1. Likewise, in the second automaton there is a transition from the state m_0 to m_0 on a_0. Therefore, $h(a_0)(q_0,m_0)$ is (q_1,m_0).

*Consider another state $a_1 \in \Sigma$ in which **not**(p) is true and readyup is true. The abstraction $h(a_1)$ is the following function:*

$$h(a_1)(q_0,m_0) = (q_0,m_0)$$
$$h(a_1)(q_0,m_1) = (q_0,m_1)$$
$$h(a_1)(q_1,m_0) = (q_1,m_0)$$
$$h(a_1)(q_1,m_1) = (q_1,m_1)$$

The abstraction of the state (a_0,a_1) is $h(a_0) \circ h(a_1)$.

The abstract process corresponding to P is denoted by $h(P)$. There is a transition from the abstract state h_1 to the abstract state h_2 in $h(P)$ if and only if there exists two states s_1 and s_2 in P such that $h(s_1) = h_1$, $h(s_2) = h_2$, and there exists a transition from s_1 to s_2 in P. Given two process P_1 and P_2, we say that $P_1 \preceq P_2$ if and only if there exists a relation $\mathcal{E}$ between the states of P_1 and P_2 such that the following conditions hold for all $(s,s') \in \mathcal{E}$:

- $h(s) = h(s')$.
- Given a state s_1 in P_1 and a transition $s \xrightarrow{a} s_1$ in P_1, there exists a transition $s' \xrightarrow{a} s'_1$ in P_2 such that $(s_1,s'_1) \in \mathcal{E}$.

This definition differs from the one given in chapter 11 in two respects:

- Related states have to agree on their abstraction rather than atomic propositions.
- The transitions are labeled by action symbols, and the corresponding transitions have to agree on their labeling.

Given a process P and the corresponding abstract process $h(P)$, define a relation $\mathcal{E}_h$ between the state sets of P and $h(P)$ in the following manner:

$$(s,h_1) \in \mathcal{E}_h \Leftrightarrow h(s) = h_1$$

Using the relation $\mathcal{E}_h$, one can prove that $h(P) \succeq P$. The abstract composition of two processes P_1 and P_2 is defined as follows:

$$P_1 \|_h P_2 = h(P_1 \| P_2)$$

Let h be the abstraction function induced by the product automaton. Let $\|_h$ be the abstract composition operator, and let $\preceq$ be the *simulates* relation. Let I_1, I_2 be abstract processes defined as follows:

$$I_1 = h(inter) \|_h h(leaf) \|_h h(leaf)$$
$$I_2 = h(inter) \|_h I_1 \|_h I_1$$

The following equations can be checked automatically:

$$h(inter) \|_h I_1 \|_h I_1 \npreceq I_1$$
$$I_1 \preceq I_2$$
$$h(inter) \|_h I_2 \|_h I_2 \preceq I_2$$

From the first equation given above, it is clear the I_1 cannot be used as an invariant for the non-terminal SUB. If we select $inv(\text{SUB}) = I_1$, the induction step corresponding to the second rule of the grammar does not hold:

$$\text{SUB} \rightarrow \text{inter} \| \text{SUB} \| \text{SUB}$$

Notice that I_2 was derived from the second rule of the grammar by substituting I_1 for SUB in the right-hand side of the rule. Suppose we use $inv(\text{SUB}) = I_2$ and $inv(\mathcal{S}) = h(\text{root}) \|_h I_2 \|_h I_2$ as the invariants for the nonterminals. From the equations given above, the following inequalities can be derived:

$$inv(\text{SUB}) \succeq h(inter) \|_h inv(\text{SUB}) \|_h inv(\text{SUB})$$
$$inv(\text{SUB}) \succeq h(inter) \|_h h(leaf) \|_h h(leaf)$$

After checking the monotonicity conditions, we can conclude that $H = h(root) \|_h I_2 \|_h I_2$ simulates all the networks generated by the context-free grammar G. After we have constructed H, we can check that all reachable states in H have the desired property. By theorem 11.9 given in chapter 11, we have the result that every network derived using G has the desired property; that is, when the computation is finished the root process has the correct parity. We also checked that from each state we must always reach a state where the computation is finished and is correct, that is, $\mathbf{AF}\mathcal{P}$.

18.5   Undecidability Result for a Family of Token Rings

In this section we prove the undecidability of the verification problem for infinite families of finite-state systems mentioned at the beginning of the chapter. The reader can safely skip this section when reading the chapter for the first time.

Following Suzuki [455], we show how to simulate a Turing machine T by a family of bidirectional rings. A ring of size n simulates n steps of the Turing machine on an empty tape. If the Turing machine halts within n steps, then some process in the ring will enter a special *halt* state and remain there forever. If the Turing machine does not halt within n steps, then no process will ever enter the *halt* state. Thus, the Turing machine does not halt on the empty tape if and only if every ring in the family satisfies the formula $\mathbf{AG} \bigwedge_i \neg halt_i$, where $halt_i$ is true if process i is in the *halt* state.

The Turing machine T is a 5-tuple $T = (Q, \Sigma, \delta, q_0, halt)$, where Q is the set of states, Σ is the tape alphabet, $\delta : Q \times \Sigma \longrightarrow Q \times \Sigma \times \{left, right\}$ is the transition function, q_0 is the initial state, and *halt* is the final state. A ring that simulates n steps of T consists of n processes $P_0, \ldots, P_{n-1}$, each of which represents one cell of the Turing machine tape. We assume that the Turing machine T has a one-way infinite tape extending to the right. Hence, within n steps, it can scan at most n cells of its tape.

Assume that T scans symbol a in cell i when it is in state q. Then process P_i will be in a particular state that represents the combination of symbol a and state q. Process P_i will simulate one move of T and will send the new state q' to the appropriate neighbor according to the move of T. A diagram for process P_i is shown in figure 18.13. Process P_i is connected to process P_{i-1} on its left and to process P_{i+1} on its right, where $i+1$ and $i-1$ are computed modulo n. Input $inright_i$ is connected to $outleft_{i+1}$. Outputs $outright_i$ and $outcolor_i$ are connected to $inleft_{i+1}$ and $incolor_{i+1}$, respectively.

We assume a synchronous model of computation in which every process makes a step at each time and in which the values of the outputs at a certain step are the values of the corresponding inputs in the next step. The current state of P_i is determined by the value of its variables *cell*, *st*, and *color*, which range over Σ, Q, and $\{white, black\}$, respectively. Initially, all variables *cell* are blank; $st_0 = q_0$ and for all $i \geq 1$, $st_i = null$; and $color_0 = black$ and for all $i \geq 1$, $color_i = white$. Also, $outcolor_0 = white$, while all other outputs (and the corresponding inputs) are initially *null*.

The computation on the ring consists of two phases that run in lockstep. One phase (shown in figure 18.14) simulates steps of the Turing machine T on the empty tape while the other phase (shown in figures 18.15 and 18.16) counts until n and then stops the simulation.

The counting phase transfers a colored token around the ring. In each of the n rounds of this phase, the token is propagated from P_0 back to P_0. Initially, all processes are *white*, except P_0, which is *black*. In addition, all processes have $outcolor = null$ except P_0, which has $outcolor = white$. When a process gets a *null* token, it passes the token unchanged to its right neighbor. Similarly, if it gets a token that has the same color as it does, it sends

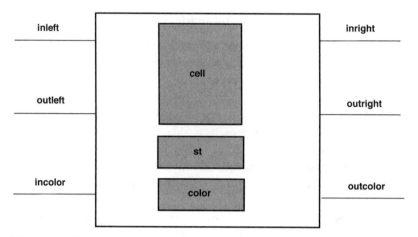

Figure 18.13
Process P_i.

```
while true do
      if incolor ≠ null and st = halt then
            while true do outright := outleft := null;
      end if
      if incolor ≠ null and st ≠ null and δ(st, cell) = (q', a', d) then
            cell := a';
            outright := if d = right then q' else null;
            outleft := if d = left then q' else null;
      else
            outright := outleft := null;
      end if
      st := if inright ≠ null then inright else inleft;
end while
```

Figure 18.14
Simulation program for process P_i for $i \geq 1$.

the token unchanged to the right. If a process gets a *black* token when its color is *white*, it changes its own color to *black* and sends a *white* token to the right.

Process P_0 behaves somewhat differently. Its color is always *black*. In the first round it sends *white* to its right neighbor. If it receives a *null* token, then it sends a *null* token to the right. When it receives a *white* token, it sends a *black* token to the right. Finally, when it receives a *black* token, it changes to an idle phase in which it sends *null* forever.

```
while incolor ≠ black do
    if incolor = null then
        outcolor := null;
    if incolor = white then
        outcolor := black;
end while
while true do outcolor := null;
```

Figure 18.15
Counting program for process P_0.


```
while true do
    if incolor ≠ null then
        outcolor := color;
    else
        outcolor := null;
    end if
    if incolor = black and color = white then
        color := black;
end while
```

Figure 18.16
Counting program for process P_i for $i \geq 1$.

Thus, in any round one more process turns *black* by getting a *black* message from its *black* neighbor on the left. When P_0 gets a *black* message from P_{n-1}, exactly n steps of T have been simulated and the ring moves to an idle phase.

The simulation phase makes sure that exactly one step is performed in each round of the counting phase by activating the appropriate process only when it gets a token (either *black* or *white*). When the head of the Turing machine scans cell i in control state q, process P_i has $st = q$ while all other processes have $st = null$. When P_i gets the token, it simulates $\delta(st, cell) = (q', a', d)$ by setting $cell := a'$, $st := null$ and by sending q' to either its left neighbor or its right neighbor, according to the direction d. The first step of T, $\delta(q_0, blank) = (q', a', right)$, is simulated by P_0 regardless of the value of $incolor_0$.

A subtle case occurs when some P_i has $st \neq null$ and $incolor \neq null$ and the Turing machine moves to the right. Process P_i then simulates one step of the Turing machine by setting $outright = q'$ in order to propagate the new state to P_{i+1}. It also propagates the token to P_{i+1} by setting the value of *outcolor* appropriately. The program ensures that P_{i+1} will not simulate another step of the Turing machine until the next round by having P_{i+1} first check the value of *incolor* together with the *old* value of its variable *st*. Later, P_{i+1} updates the value of *st* according to $inleft_{i+1}$ (which is identical to $outright_i$).

Next, we will describe invariants to establish the correctness of our simulation. There are n rounds in the computation. We number rounds from 0 to $n-1$. Each round has n steps, and we number the steps from 0 to $n-1$ as well. Round i simulates the i-th move of the Turing machine. The following properties can be proved about the computation:

- After step $i-1$ of round i, process P_i changes color from white to black.
- At the end of round i, state of process P_j is equal to $q \neq null$ if and only if after i moves the Turing machine is in state q and is scanning the j-th cell.
- Assume that the process P_j is in state q after round i. All other processes are in state *null*. At step $j-1$ of round $i+1$ the process P_j receives a non-null color from its neighbor. P_j sends the appropriate state to its left or right neighbor (depending on whether the Turing machine moves left or right) and then sets its state to *null*. Notice that P_j can simulate a move only if it receives a non-null color.

Although the problem is undecidable in general, for *specific* families it may be solvable.

Bibliographic Notes

The research on parameterized verification has evolved significantly since this chapter was written. Excellent surveys of recent work on the subject can be found in [215], [6] and in [65]. Another useful source is the chapter on parameterized verification in [136].

Here we briefly describe some of the main trends, followed over the years. Verification problems that often involve an arbitrary number of components include mutual exclusion protocols [415, 143, 3], deadlock freedom [63, 61], distributed algorithms for different network topologies [207, 209], cache coherence protocols [237, 216, 372, 174, 61], multi-threaded programs [38, 296, 297], protocols communicating through a shared register [218] and population protocols [217]. Works that deal with broadcast protocols include [209, 216] and more recently [177, 175, 176].

A large amount of work has been done based on the theory of well-structured transition systems (WSTS) [5, 222, 62, 104, 432, 2], applied to a broad variety of models of parameterized systems [10, 216, 341, 424, 70, 50, 221].

Abstraction is often used to represent the state space of the infinite family in a manageable way. The *cutoff* approach, for instance, reduces parameterized verification to finite-state model checking by identifying a finite set of instances of the family that can represent all of its members. The instances can then be model-checked to verify the entire family [209, 25]. Dynamic cutoff has been introduced in [185]. In [202], decision results for parameterized model checking are obtained using cutoff. Other types of abstractions used in this context include counter abstraction [237], monotonic abstraction [7, 4, 8], view abstraction [9], disjunctive and conjunctive guards [203], and more.

The interesting question of why parametrization can make verification easier is discussed in [294]. An early practical case study is presented in [210]. Tools for designing and verifying parameterized systems are presented in [366] (Neo) and [152] (Cubicle). Parameterized systems can also be modeled as Petri nets, where the number of tokens per node is not bounded. Many interesting safety properties of parameterized systems can then be checked by means of a reduction to the coverability problem in Petri nets. Tools for this purpose include CSC [234], BFC [295], MIST [231], and Petrucchio [379].

19 Discrete Real-Time and Quantitative Temporal Analysis

Computers are frequently used in critical applications where predictable response times are essential for correctness. Such systems are called *real-time systems*. Examples of such applications include controllers for aircraft, industrial machinery, and robots. Because of the nature of such applications, errors in real-time systems can be extremely dangerous, even fatal. Guaranteeing the correctness of a complex real-time system is an important and non-trivial task. Because of this, only conservative and usually ad hoc approaches to design and implementation are routinely used.

Other factors make the validation of real-time systems particularly difficult. The architecture of computer applications is becoming extremely complicated. As a system increases in complexity, so does the probability of introducing an error. Moreover, performance is becoming an important factor in the success of new applications. Due to competition, new products have to fully utilize the available resources. A slow component can affect the performance of the whole system. Consequently, the task of verifying that new applications satisfy their timing specifications is more critical than ever before.

19.1   Real-Time Systems and Rate-Monotonic Scheduling

Because real-time systems are used in critical applications, conservative approaches have been traditionally used in their design. This has frequently led to simple but inefficient implementations. An example of such a technique is *static time slicing*, which divides time equally among all tasks. Each task executes until its time slot has been used and then releases the processor. The resulting program is easy to analyze, but rather inefficient, since all tasks are given equal resources, regardless of their importance or resource utilization. Recently, more powerful techniques to analyze the behavior of a real-time system have been developed. *Rate-monotonic scheduling* (RMS) theory [345, 351, 437] is an example. The RMS theory is applicable to systems described by a set of periodic tasks. Each task corresponds to a concurrent process of the system and is characterized by its periodicity (how often it executes) and its execution time at each instantiation. RMS consists of two components. The first is an algorithm for assigning higher priorities to processes with shorter periods. Optimal response time with respect to static priority algorithms is guaranteed by the RMS theory if priorities are assigned according to this rule [351]. The second component of the RMS theory is a schedulability test based on total CPU utilization; a set of processes (which have priorities assigned according to RMS) is schedulable if the total utilization is below a computed threshold. If the utilization is above this threshold, schedulability is not guaranteed.

RMS is a powerful tool for analyzing real-time systems. It is simple to use, yet it provides very important information for designers. However, this analysis imposes a series of restrictions on the system being verified. Only certain types of processes are considered, with limitations, for example, on periodicity and synchronization. This theory has been extended to more general classes of processes, but limitations still exist [256]. RMS can handle only systems that can be described within the theory. Moreover, the kinds of properties that can be verified are also restricted to properties that can be modeled as task execution times. Verifying distributed systems or systems that do not have a regular communication pattern is not a trivial task in general. In addition, checking for properties that cannot be easily expressed as task execution times such as the number of occurrences of arbitrary events in the system can also be complex.

19.2   Model-Checking Real-Time Systems

It is possible to use symbolic model checking to verify discrete real-time systems. However, the model-checking tools described previously in this book are not suitable to perform this type of verification. It is difficult, for example, to express complex timing properties. It is possible to express the property that "event p will happen in the future," but it is not simple to express the property that "event p will happen within at most n time units" without using the next time operator in convoluted ways. Moreover, quantitative information such as response time or the number of occurrences of events cannot be directly obtained using these techniques. Temporal logic model checking cannot be used in a natural and efficient way to verify many types of real-time systems that occur frequently in practice.

In this chapter we describe a method for specifying and verifying *discrete* real-time systems, which is compatible with symbolic model-checking techniques and can handle large systems [98]. Furthermore, algorithms derived from symbolic model checking are used to compute quantitative information about the model. An important benefit of this approach is that the information produced allows the user to check whether the model satisfies various real-time constraints: schedulability of the tasks of the system can be determined by computing their response time; reaction times to events and several other parameters of the system can also be analyzed by this method. This information provides insight into the behavior of the system and in many cases it can help to identify inefficiencies and suggest optimizations to the design. The same algorithms can then be used to analyze the performance of the modified design. The evaluation of how the optimizations affect the design can be done before the actual implementation. This can significantly reduce development costs.

An important characteristic of this method is that it counts the number of computation steps between events or the number of occurrences of events in an interval. Because of this, it finds application in synchronous systems such as computer circuits and protocols. Real-time systems usually do not execute in lock step and might not seem to be appropriate for our method. However, they are frequently subject to tight timing constraints, which are difficult to satisfy using asynchronous design techniques. Furthermore, programmers often try to reduce asynchronous behavior in their designs in order to ensure predictability. As a result, real-time systems can often be analyzed using techniques based on discrete time. Some systems, however, are inherently asynchronous in nature. For these systems more complex verification techniques based on continuous time are necessary. We discuss methods for verifying continuous real-time systems in chapter 20.

19.3 RTCTL Model Checking

A simple and effective way to allow the verification of time bounded properties is to introduce bounds in the CTL temporal operators. The extended logic is called RTCTL [206]. The expressive power of RTCTL is the same as CTL, since the bounded operators can be translated into nested applications of the **EX** (or **AX**) operators. However, this translation is often impractical, and RTCTL provides a much more compact and convenient way of expressing such properties.

The basic RTCTL temporal operator is the *bounded until* operator, which has the form $\mathbf{U}_{[a,b]}$, where $[a,b]$ defines the time interval in which the property must be true. We say that $f\,\mathbf{U}_{[a,b]}\,g$ is true of some path $\pi = s_0, s_1, \ldots$ if g holds in some future state s on the path, f is true in all states between s_0 and s, and the distance from s_0 to s is within the interval $[a,b]$. The bounded **EG** operator can be defined similarly. Other temporal operators are defined in terms of these two operators. More formally, we extend CTL to include bounded versions of the operators **EU** and **EG** by adding the following clauses to the formal semantics of CTL:

1. $s \models \mathbf{E}[f\,\mathbf{U}_{[a,b]}\,g]$ if and only if there exists a path $\pi = s_0 s_1 s_2 \ldots$ starting at $s = s_0$ and some i such that $a \le i \le b$ and $s_i \models g$ and for all $j < i, s_j \models f$.

2. $s \models \mathbf{EG}_{[a,b]}\,f$ if and only if there exists a path $\pi = s_0 s_1 s_2 \ldots$ starting at $s = s_0$ and for all i such that $a \le i \le b, s_i \models f$.

As an example of the use of the bounded until, consider the property "it is always true that p may be followed by q within 3 time units." This property can be expressed in RTCTL as $\mathbf{AG}(p \rightarrow \mathbf{EF}_{[0,3]}\,q)$, where the bounded **EF** operator is derived from the bounded until just as in the unbounded case. That is, $\mathbf{EF}_{[a,b]}\,f \equiv [true\,\mathbf{U}_{[a,b]}\,f]$.

In order to verify properties written with this operator, we use a modification of the fixpoint computation that is used in CTL model checkers. It is easy to see that the formula $\mathbf{E}[f\,\mathbf{U}_{[a,b]}\,g]$ can be computed in the following manner:

$$\text{if } a > 0 \text{ and } b > 0: \; \mathbf{E}[f\,\mathbf{U}_{[a,b]}\,g] = f \wedge \mathbf{EX}\,\mathbf{E}[f\,\mathbf{U}_{[a-1,b-1]}\,g]$$
$$\text{else, if } b > 0: \quad\quad \mathbf{E}[f\,\mathbf{U}_{[0,b]}\,g] = g \vee (f \wedge \mathbf{EX}\,\mathbf{E}[f\,\mathbf{U}_{[0,b-1]}\,g])$$
$$\text{else:} \quad\quad\quad\quad\quad\quad \mathbf{E}[f\,\mathbf{U}_{[0,0]}\,g] = g$$

Other operators are computed similarly.

19.4   Quantitative Temporal Analysis: Minimum/Maximum Delay

Traditional formal verification algorithms assume that timing constraints are given explicitly in some notation like temporal logic. Typically, the designer provides a constraint on response time for some operation, and the verifier automatically determines if it is satisfied or not. These techniques do not provide any information about how much a system deviates from its expected performance. However, such information can be extremely useful in fine-tuning the behavior of the system. In this section we describe algorithms to compute quantitative timing information, such as exact minimum and maximum delays (in terms of the number of transitions) between a request and the corresponding response. The algorithms are designed to work well with symbolic techniques based on the use of binary decision diagrams and are very efficient in practice.

19.4.1   Minimum Delay Algorithm

The algorithm takes as input a Kripke structure $M = (S,R,L)$ and two sets of states *start* and *final* (figure). It returns the length of (that is, the number of edges in) a shortest path from a state in *start* to a state in *final*. If no such path exists, the algorithm returns infinity. In the algorithm, the function $T(S)$ gives the set of states that are successors of some state in S. In other words, $T(S) = \{s' \mid R(s,s') \text{ holds for some } s \in S\}$. In addition, the variables Z and Z' represent sets of states in the algorithm.

The first algorithm is relatively straightforward. Intuitively, the loop in the algorithm computes the set of states that are reachable from *start*. If at any point we encounter a state satisfying *final*, we return the number of steps taken to reach the state.

19.4.2   Maximum Delay Algorithm

This algorithm also takes *start* and *final* as input (figure 19.2). It returns the length of a longest path from a state in *start* to a state in *final*. If there exists an infinite path beginning in a state in *start* that never reaches a state in *final*, the algorithm returns infinity. The function $T^{-1}(S')$ gives the set of states that are predecessors of some state in S' (that is, $T^{-1}(S') = \{s \mid R(s,s') \text{ holds for some } s' \in S'\}$). Z and Z' will once more be sets of states. Finally, we denote by *not_final* the set of all states that are not in *final*.

procedure *min*(*start*,*final*)
    $i := 0$;
    $Z := start$;
    $Z' := T(Z) \cup Z$;
    while $(Z' \neq Z) \wedge (Z \cap final) = \emptyset$ **do**
        $i := i + 1$;
        $Z := Z'$;
        $Z' := T(Z') \cup Z'$;
    end while
    if $Z \cap final \neq \emptyset$ **then**
        return i;
    else
        return ∞;
    end if
end procedure

Figure 19.1
Minimum delay algorithm.

procedure *max*(*start*,*final*)
    $i := 0$;
    $Z := true$;
    $Z' := not\_final$;
    while $(Z' \neq Z) \wedge (Z' \cap start \neq \emptyset)$ **do**
        $i := i + 1$;
        $Z := Z'$;
        $Z' := T^{-1}(Z') \cap not\_final$;
    end while
    if $Z = Z'$ **then**
        return ∞;
    else
        return i;
    end if
end procedure

Figure 19.2
Maximum delay algorithm.

The upper bound algorithm is more subtle than the previous algorithm. In particular, it must return infinity if there exists a path beginning in *start* that remains within *not_final*. A backward search from the states in *not_final* is more convenient for this purpose than a forward search. At the *i*-th iteration the current *frontier* is the set of states that are the beginning of paths with *i* states completely in *not_final*. Initially, *i* is 0, and the frontier is *not_final*. We then compute the set of predecessors (in *not_final*) of the current frontier. Those states are the beginning of paths with $i+1$ states completely in *not_final*.

The algorithm stops in one of two cases. Either Z' does not contain states from *start* at stage *i*. Since it contained states from *start* at state $i-1$, the size of the longest interval in *not_final* from a state in *start* is $i-1$. Since the transition relation is total, this interval has a continuation to a state outside *not_final*, that is, to a state in *final*. Thus, there is a path of length *i* from *start* to *final* and the algorithm returns *i*. Or, in the other case, a fixpoint is reached and Z still contains some state in *start*. Since the set Z is finite and each state in it has an outgoing edge to a state in Z, each state is the start of an infinite path within Z that is included in *not_final*. Thus, there is an infinite path in *not_final* from a state in *start*. In this case, the algorithm returns infinity.

Next, we argue that the algorithm terminates. Suppose that the condition $Z' \cap start \neq \emptyset$ is never violated. We show that $Z' = Z$ eventually holds. It can be easily seen that if a state is in the *i*-th frontier, it is also in the $i-1$-th frontier, since states that are the beginning of intervals with *i* states completely in *not_final* are also the beginning of intervals of $i-1$ states within *not_final*. Consequently, the frontier at each iteration is contained in the previous one. Since the initial frontier must be finite, there are only a finite number of proper inclusions between the state sets that characterize the frontiers. Therefore, there must be a k such that the frontier at the k-th iteration is the same as the frontier at the $k+1$-th iteration, and the loop cannot execute more than k times without $(Z = Z')$ becoming true.

In many situations we are interested not only in the length of a path leading from a set of starting states to a set of final states but also in the number of states on the path that satisfy a given condition. Thus, we may wish to determine the minimum or maximum number of times a condition *cond* holds on any path from *start* to *final*. These algorithms are called *condition counting algorithms*. We give two examples of how they can be used to analyze the performance of systems. The first example is evaluating the performance of a bus in a complex hardware system. Consider the interval of time between asserting a bus request and the corresponding bus grant. It is important to be able to compute the number of times other transactions are issued in this interval, since this is a measure of the traffic on the bus. The second example is determining the amount of *priority inversion* in a real-time system. Priority inversion occurs when a higher-priority process is blocked by the execution of a lower-priority process [421]. In this case, *start* corresponds to the states where the higher priority process requests execution, *final* corresponds to the states where this process is granted execution, and *cond* characterizes the states where a lower priority process is executed, blocking the process with higher priority. Efficient implementations for these algorithms and additional examples are described in [98, 101].

19.5   Example: An Aircraft Controller

One of the most critical applications of real-time systems is in aircraft control. It is extremely important that time bounds are not violated in such systems. This section briefly describes an aircraft control system used in military airplanes. The example illustrates how timing constraints can be checked using the quantitative algorithms described in section 19.4.

19.5.1   System Description

The control system for an airplane can be characterized by a set of sensors and actuators connected to a central processor. This processor executes the software to analyze sensor data and control the actuators. Our model describes this control program and defines its requirements to ensure that the airplane operating constraints are met. The requirements used are similar to those of existing military aircraft and are derived from those described in [352].

The aircraft controller is divided into systems and subsystems. Each system performs a specific task in controlling a component of the airplane. The most important systems are modeled, including the following:

- Navigation: computes aircraft position; takes into account data such as speed, altitude, and positioning data received from satellites or ground stations.
- Radar Control: receives and processes data from radars; also identifies targets and target position.
- Radar Warning Receiver: identifies possible threats to the aircraft.
- Weapon Control: aims and activates aircraft weapons.
- Display: updates information on the pilot's screen.
- Tracking: updates target position; data from this system are used to aim the weapons.
- Data Bus: provides communication between processor and external devices.

Each system is composed of one or more subsystems. Timing constraints for each subsystem are derived from factors such as required accuracy, human response characteristics, and hardware requirements. For example, the screen must be updated frequently enough so that motion appears continuous. To accomplish this, the update must occur at least once every 50 ms. The table in figure 19.3 gives the subsystems being modeled, as well as their major timing requirements. The priority assignment is explained subsequently.

Concurrent processes are used to implement each subsystem. Communication among the various processes is done indirectly. No data are shared directly by multiple subsystems. Processes communicate only through data servers called *monitor tasks*. Each system maintains a server process that accepts requests for data and returns the desired information.

System	Subsystem	Period	Exec.	% CPU	Priority
Display	status update	200	3	1.50	12
	keyset	200	1	0.50	16
	hook update	80	2	2.50	36
	graphic display	80	9	11.25	40
	store update	200	1	0.50	20
RWR	contact mgmt.	25	5	20.00	72
Radar	target update	50	5	10.00	60
	tracking filter	25	2	8.00	84
NAV	nav update	50	8	16.00	56
	steering cmds.	200	3	1.50	24
Tracking	target update	100	5	5.00	32
Weapon	weapon protocol	200 *	1	0.50	28
	weapon aim	50	3	6.00	64
	weapon release	200 **	3	1.50	98
Data Bus	poll bus devices	40	1	2.50	68

* Weapon protocol is an aperiodic process with a deadline of 200 ms.

** Weapon release has a period of 200 ms, but its deadline is 5 ms.

Figure 19.3
Timing requirements for the aircraft controller.

The various subsystems in each system update the data in the servers. Monitor tasks only accept requests, respond to them, and then enter a waiting state. They are assigned low priority, and priority inheritance is used to maintain predictability [99, 421].

With the exception of the weapon system, all other systems contain only periodic processes, which are scheduled to execute at the beginning of their period. When a process is granted the CPU, it acquires the data it needs through the monitor tasks, executes, updates information on its own data server, and then blocks, waiting for its next execution period.

The weapon system contains a mixture of *periodic* and *aperiodic* processes. It is activated when the display keyset subsystem identifies that the pilot has pressed the firing button. This event causes the weapon protocol subsystem to be activated. It then signals the weapon aim subsystem that had been blocked. Weapon aim is then scheduled to be executed every 50 ms. It aims the aircraft weapons based on the current position of the target. It also decides when to fire and then starts the weapon release subsystem. The firing sequence can be aborted until weapon release is scheduled, but not after this point. Weapon release then executes periodically and fires the weapons five times, once per second.

In order to enforce the different timing constraints of the processes, priority scheduling is used. Predictability is guaranteed by scheduling the processes using RMS [344, 351].

19.5.2 Model of the Aircraft Control System

The aircraft control system has been modeled using the tool VERUS [100]. Model checking has been used to verify its functional correctness, while its timing correctness has been checked using the quantitative algorithms described previously. Most of the characteristics described above have been implemented, although some abstractions have been performed for simplicity. A more detailed description of the implementation follows.

The time for an atomic transition in the model is assumed to be 1 ms. A global timer controls the scheduling of periodic processes. Whenever awakened, a process requests execution and waits until it has been granted the CPU. For each process, an internal counter stores the elapsed execution time. After finishing execution, a process releases the CPU and blocks, waiting for the next period. The time to request data from a monitor task and wait for the response is assumed to be small compared to the total execution time. This is reasonable if we assume an efficient implementation. Sending request and response messages takes only a small amount of time. Processing in the monitor tasks is also fast, considering the limited range of functions performed. The assumption can be violated only if multiple processes access the monitor simultaneously. The access pattern to the monitor tasks, however, minimizes this possibility. They simply receive requests, retrieve data from memory, and return it. There are no nested critical sections. Moreover, priority inheritance protocols [99, 421] have been used to maintain predictability and eliminate the possibility of unbounded blocking due to synchronization.

We consider two scheduling policies, preemptive scheduling and non preemptive scheduling. A preemptive scheduler accepts requests for execution and chooses the highest-priority process requesting the CPU. If a request arrives from a higher-priority process after execution has started, the scheduler preempts the executing process and starts the higher-priority one. When a process finishes executing, it resets its request, and the scheduler chooses another process. However, preemptability is a feature that may not always be available. With a non-preemptive scheduler, once a process starts executing, it continues executing until it voluntarily releases the CPU. If a higher-priority process requests execution, it has to wait until the running process finishes. Non-preemptive schedulers usually cause response time for higher-priority processes to be higher. They are, however, simpler to implement and allow for simpler programs. Modeling both types of schedulers allows us to compare the behavior of the system under different conditions. The results obtained can be used to assist in deciding whether preemption is necessary for system correctness in this case.

Subsystem	Deadline	Execution Times			
		Preemptive		Nonpreemptive	
		Min	Max	Min	Max
Weapon release	5	3	3	3	9
Radar tracking filter	25	2	5	2	10
RWR contact mgmt.	25	7	10	7	15
Data bus poll	40	1	11	1	14
Weapon aim	50	10	14	2	18
Radar target update	50	12	19	12	19
NAV update	50	20	34	20	27
Display graphic	80	10	44	10	43
Display hook update	80	14	46	14	47
Tracking target update	100	26	51	26	51
Weapon protocol	200	1	21	3	46
NAV steering cmds.	200	35	85	36	74
Display store update	200	36	95	37	97
Display keyset	200	37	96	38	98
Display status update	200	40	99	41	101

Figure 19.4
Aircraft controller schedulability results.

19.5.3   Verification Results

Schedulability is one of the most important properties of a real-time system. It states that no process will miss its deadline. In this example the deadlines are the same as the periods (except for the weapon release subsystem). The table in figure 19.4 summarizes the execution times computed by the quantitative analysis performed. Processes are shown in decreasing order of priority. Deadlines are also shown so that schedulability can be easily checked. Minimum and maximum execution times are given for both preemptive and nonpreemptive schedulers.

   We can see from the table in figure 19.4 that the process set is schedulable using preemptive scheduling. From our results we can also identify many important parameters of the system. For example, the response time is usually very low for best-case computations, but it is also good for the worst case. Most processes take less than half of their permitted time to execute. This indicates that the system is still not close to saturation, although the total CPU utilization is high.

Notice also that preemption does not have a big impact on response times. Except for the most critical process, all others maintain their schedulability if a nonpreemptive scheduler is used. Although nonpreemptive scheduling causes weapon release to miss its deadline, the extra delay is small. If preemptive scheduling were expensive, reducing the CPU utilization slightly might make the complete system schedulable without changing the scheduler. By having such information, the designer can easily assess the impact on various alternatives to improve the performance.

To see how the designer can use these results, we can analyze the response time for the display graphic subsystem. The period of this subsystem is 80 ms, and a shorter period might be desired to make motion look continuous. However, the response time of this process can be as high as 44 ms. Changing the period to 40 ms would make it miss its deadline. The designer may choose to decrease the period to 50 ms, for example. To test the effect of this change, the model can be analyzed again in order to check schedulability.

This kind of analysis can also be used to determine execution times for more complex sequences of events. For example, when a pilot presses the firing button, many subsystems are involved in identifying and responding to this event. Analysis of the system using the algorithms in section 19.4 shows that the minimum time between detecting that the fire button has been depressed and the end of execution of weapon release is 120 ms while the maximum time is 167 ms. By examining these times, the designer is able to determine if the weapon system responds quickly enough to satisfy the aircraft requirements.

In this section we have shown how a system with complex timing constraints can be analyzed with a tool like VERUS. We have been able to determine the schedulability of the system and understand its behavior in detail. We have also been able to determine information about its behavior, such as the response time of the weapons subsystem that might be difficult to obtain using other methods.

Bibliographic Notes

Other approaches to schedulability analysis include algorithms for computing the set of reachable states of a finite-state system [118, 226, 236]. A model for the real-time system is constructed with the added constraint that whenever an exception occurs (for example, a deadline is missed) the system transitions to a special exception state. Verification consists of computing the set of reachable states and checking whether the exception state is in this set. Unlike RMS, no restrictions are imposed on the model in this approach, but the algorithm checks only if exceptions can occur or not. Other types of properties cannot be verified, unless encoded in the model as exceptions. Even though most properties can be encoded as exceptions, this can sometimes be difficult and error-prone. Symbolic model-checking techniques have also been extended to handle real-time systems [148, 149, 489]. However, these methods as well as the others mentioned determine only if the system satisfies a given property and do not provide detailed information on its behavior. Restricted quantitative analysis on discrete-time models can be performed [150], but only to the extent of computing minimum/maximum delays.

20 Continuous Real Time

In chapter 19, we assumed that time is *discrete*. When time is modeled in this manner, possible clock values are non-negative integers, and events can occur only at integer time values. This type of model is appropriate for *synchronous systems*, where all of the components are synchronized by a single global clock. The duration between successive clock ticks is chosen as the basic unit for measuring time. This model has been successfully used for reasoning about the correctness of synchronous hardware designs for many years.

Continuous time, on the other hand, is the natural model for *asynchronous systems*, since the separation of events can be arbitrarily small. This ability is desirable for representing causally independent events in an asynchronous system. Moreover, no assumptions need to be made about the speed of the environment when this model of time is assumed [20].

In order to model asynchronous systems using discrete time, it is necessary to discretize time by choosing some fixed time quantum so that the delay between any two events will be a multiple of this time quantum. This is difficult to do a priori and may limit the accuracy with which systems can be modeled. Brzozowski and Seger [89] have shown, for example, that theoretically the reachability problem for asynchronous circuits with bounded delays cannot be solved correctly when time is assumed to be discrete. Also, the choice of a sufficiently small time quantum to model an asynchronous system accurately may blow up the state space so that verification is no longer feasible (this may be more of a problem for explicit state model checkers than for symbolic model checkers, however).

In this chapter we introduce the *timed automata model* of Alur, Courcoubetis, and Dill [19, 181], which is the standard for modeling asynchronous timed systems. We discuss the properties of timed automata and explain the major techniques that have been developed for verifying them. Because so much research has been done in this area, we restrict this brief survey to the *reachability* problem for such automata. Algorithms for a broader range of properties are briefly discussed in the bibliographic notes for this chapter.

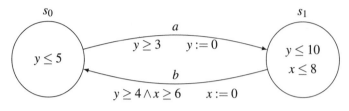

Figure 20.1
A simple timed automaton.

20.1   Timed Automata

A *timed automaton* [19, 181] is a finite automaton augmented with a finite set of real-valued *clocks*. We assume that transitions are instantaneous. However, time can elapse when the automaton is in a state or *location*. When a transition occurs, some of the clocks may be reset to zero. At any instant, the reading of a clock is equal to the time that has elapsed since the last time the clock was reset. We assume that time passes at the same rate for all clocks. In order to prevent pathological behaviors, we consider only automata that are *non-Zeno*, that is, in which only a finite number of transitions can happen within a finite amount of time.

A clock constraint, called a *guard*, is associated with each transition. The transition can be taken only if the current values of the clocks satisfy the clock constraint. A clock constraint is also associated with each location of the automaton. This constraint is called the *invariant* of the location. Time can elapse in the location only as long as the invariant of the location is true. An example of a timed automaton is given in figure 20.1.

The automaton consists of two locations s_0 and s_1, two clocks x and y, an "*a*" transition from s_0 to s_1, and a "*b*" transition from s_1 to s_0. The automaton starts in location s_0. It can remain in that location as long as the clock y is less than or equal to 5. As soon as the value of y is greater than or equal to 3, the automaton can make an "*a*" transition to location s_1 and reset the clock y to 0. The automaton can remain in location s_1 as long as y is less than or equal to 10 and x is less than or equal to 8. When y is at least 4 and x is at least 6, it can make a "*b*" transition back to location s_0 and reset x.

The remainder of this section contains a formal semantics for timed automata in terms of infinite state transition graphs [20, 19]. We begin with a precise definition of clock constraints. Let X be a set of *clock variables*, ranging over the nonnegative real numbers $\mathbb{R}^+$. Define the set of *clock constraints* $C(X)$ as follows:

- All inequalities of the form $x \prec c$ or $c \prec x$ are in $C(X)$, where $\prec$ is either $<$ or $\leq$ and c is a nonnegative rational number.
- If φ_1 and φ_2 are in $C(X)$, then $\varphi_1 \wedge \varphi_2$ is in $C(X)$.

Note that if X contains k clocks, then each clock constraints is a *convex* subset of k-dimensional Euclidean space. Thus, if two points satisfy a clock constraint, then all of the points on the line segment connecting these points satisfy the clock constraint.

A *timed automaton* is a 6-tuple $A = (\Sigma, S, S_0, X, I, T)$ such that

- Σ is a finite *alphabet*;
- S is a finite set of *locations*;
- $S_0 \subseteq S$ is a set of *starting locations*;
- X is a set of clocks;
- $I : S \to \mathcal{C}(X)$ is a mapping from locations to clock constraints, called the *location invariant*; and
- $T \subseteq S \times \Sigma \times \mathcal{C}(X) \times 2^X \times S$ is a set of transitions.

The 5-tuple $(s, a, \varphi, \lambda, s')$ corresponds to a transition from location s to location s' labeled with a, a constraint φ that specifies when the transition is enabled, and a set of clocks $\lambda \subseteq X$ that are reset when the transition is executed.

We will require that time be allowed to progress to infinity; that is, at each location the upper bound imposed on the clocks be either infinity, or smaller than the maximum bound imposed the invariant and by the transitions outgoing from the location. In other words, either it is possible to stay at a location forever, or the invariant will force the automaton to leave the location, and at that point at least one transition will be enabled. For timed automata, these constraints can be imposed syntactically.

A model for a timed automaton A is an infinite state transition graph $\mathcal{T}(A) = (\Sigma, Q, Q_0, R)$. Each state in Q is a pair (s, v) where $s \in S$ is a location and $v : X \to \mathbb{R}^+$ is a *clock assignment*, mapping each clock to a nonnegative real value. The set of *initial states* Q_0 is given by $\{(s, v) | s \in S_0 \wedge \forall x \in X[v(x) = 0]\}$.

In order to define the state transition relation for $\mathcal{T}(A)$, we must first introduce some notation. For $\lambda \subseteq X$, define $v[\lambda := 0]$ to be the clock assignment that is the same as v for clocks in $X - \lambda$ and maps the clocks in λ to 0. For $d \in \mathbb{R}$, define $v + d$ as the clock assignment that maps each clock $x \in X$ to $v(x) + d$. The clock assignment $v - d$ is defined in the same manner.

From the brief discussion in the introduction, we know that a timed automaton has two basic types of transitions:

- *Delay transitions* correspond to the elapsing of time while staying at some location. We write $(s, v) \xrightarrow{d} (s, v + d)$, where $d \in \mathbb{R}^+$, provided that for every $0 \le e \le d$, the invariant $I(s)$ holds for $v + e$.
- *Action transitions* correspond to the execution of a transition from T. We write $(s, v) \xrightarrow{a} (s', v')$, where $a \in \Sigma$, provided that there is a transition $\langle s, a, \varphi, \lambda, s' \rangle$ such that v satisfies φ and $v' = v[\lambda := 0]$.

The transition relation R of $\mathcal{T}(A)$ is obtained by combining the delay and action transitions. We write $(s, v)\, R\, (s', v')$ or $(s, v) \stackrel{a}{\Longrightarrow} (s', v')$ if there exists s'' and v'' such that $(s, v) \stackrel{d}{\longrightarrow} (s'', v'') \stackrel{a}{\longrightarrow} (s', v')$ for some $d \in \mathbb{R}$.

In this chapter we describe an algorithm for solving the *reachability problem* for $\mathcal{T}(A)$: Given a set of initial states Q_0, we show how to compute the set of all states $q \in Q$ that are reachable from Q_0 by transitions in R. This problem is nontrivial because $\mathcal{T}(A)$ has an infinite number of states. In order to accomplish this goal, it is necessary to use a finite representation for the infinite state space of $\mathcal{T}(A)$. Developing such representations is the main topic of the following sections.

20.2   Parallel Composition

Before we consider the reachability problem, we show how real-time systems can be modeled as parallel compositions of timed automata [20, 21]. We assume an interleaving or asynchronous semantics for this operation. Let $A_1 = (\Sigma_1, S_1, S_0^1, X_1, I_1, T_1)$ and $A_2 = (\Sigma_2, S_2, S_0^2, X_2, I_2, T_2)$ be two timed automata. Assume that the two automata have disjoint sets of clocks; that is, $X_1 \cap X_2 = \emptyset$. Then, the *parallel composition* of A_1 and A_2 is the timed automaton

$$A_1 \parallel A_2 = \langle \Sigma_1 \cup \Sigma_2, S_1 \times S_2, S_0^1 \times S_0^2, X_1 \cup X_2, I, T \rangle,$$

where $I(s_1, s_2) = I_1(s_1) \wedge I_2(s_2)$ and the edge relation T is given by the following rules:

1. For $a \in \Sigma_1 \cap \Sigma_2$, if $\langle s_1, a, \varphi_1, \lambda_1, s_1' \rangle \in T_1$ and $\langle s_2, a, \varphi_2, \lambda_2, s_2' \rangle \in T_2$, then T will contain the transition $\langle (s_1, s_2), a, \varphi_1 \wedge \varphi_2, \lambda_1 \cup \lambda_2, (s_1', s_2') \rangle$.

2. For $a \in \Sigma_1 - \Sigma_2$, if $\langle s, a, \varphi, \lambda, s' \rangle \in T_1$ and $t \in S_2$, then T will contain the transition $\langle (s, t), a, \varphi, \lambda, (s', t) \rangle$.

3. For $a \in \Sigma_2 - \Sigma_1$, if $\langle s, a, \varphi, \lambda, s' \rangle \in T_2$ and $t \in S_1$, then T will contain the transition $\langle (t, s), a, \varphi, \lambda, (t, s') \rangle$.

Thus, the locations of the parallel composition are pairs of locations from the component automata, and the invariant of such a location is the conjunction of the invariants of the component locations. There will be a transition in the parallel composition for each pair of transitions from the individual timed automata with the same action. The source location of the transition will be the composite location obtained from the source locations of the individual transitions. The target location will be the composite location obtained from the target locations of the individual transitions. The guard will be the conjunction of the guards for the individual transitions, and the set of clocks that are reset will be the union of the sets that are reset by the individual transitions. If the action of a transition is an action of only one of the two processes, then there will be a transition in the parallel composition for each location of the other timed automaton. The source and target locations of these transitions will be obtained from the source and target locations of the original transition

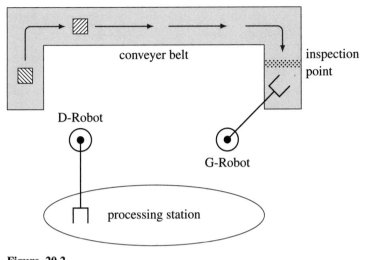

Figure 20.2
A manufacturing example.

and the location from the other automaton. All of the other components of the transition will remain the same.

20.3 Modeling with Timed Automata

To illustrate how timed automata can be used to model real-time systems, we consider a simple manufacturing plant taken from Daws and Yovine [169]. The plant consists of a conveyer belt that moves from left to right, a processing station, and two robots that move boxes between the station and the belt, as shown in figure 20.2. The first robot (called the "D-Robot") takes a box from the station and *deposits* it on the left end of the belt. The second robot (called the "G-Robot") *gets* a box from the right end of the belt and transfers it to the station where boxes are processed. Below, we describe each of these components in more detail.

The timed automaton for the D-Robot is shown in figure 20.3. The robot waits by the station (in location D-Wait) until a box is ready (indicated by the action s-ready). Next, it picks the box up (D-Pick), turns right (D-Turn-R), and puts the box on the moving belt (D-Put). It then turns left (D-Turn-L) and returns to its initial position. Picking up the box or putting it down requires between 1 and 2 seconds. Turning left or right takes between 5 and 6 seconds.

The timed automaton for the G-Robot is given in figure 20.4. This robot waits (in location G-Inspect) at an inspection point near the right end of the belt until a box passes this point. The robot must pick up the box (G-Pick) before it falls off the end of the belt. Next, it turns right (G-Turn-R), waits for the station to finish processing the previous box (G-Wait),

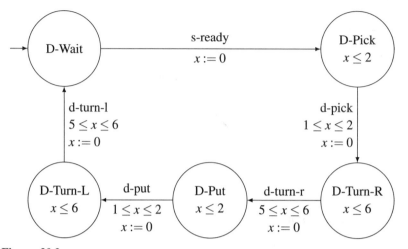

Figure 20.3
Timed automaton for D-Robot.

and then places the box at the station (G-Put). Finally, it turns left (G-Turn-L) back to the inspection point. It takes the robot between 3 and 8 seconds to pick up the box and between 6 and 10 seconds to turn right. It requires between 1 and 2 seconds to place the box at the station and between 8 and 10 seconds to return to the inspection point.

The timed automaton for the processing station is shown in figure 20.5. The station is initially empty (S-Empty). Once a box arrives at the station, it requires between 8 and 10 seconds to be processed. The box is then ready for the D-Robot to pick it up.

The timed automaton for the box is described in figure 20.6. Initially the box is moving (B-Mov) from the left end of the belt to the inspection point. Once it passes the inspection point (B-Inspect), the box will fall off the belt (B-Fall) unless it is picked up by the G-Robot (B-on-G). In the latter case, the box is then placed at the station (B-on-S), picked up by the D-Robot (B-on-D) and put back on the left end of the belt. It takes between 133 and 134 seconds for the box to reach the inspection point from the left end of the belt. The box will fall off the belt if it is not picked up between 20 and 21 seconds after passing the inspection point.

The timed automaton for the system is the parallel composition of the four individual timed automata described above.

20.4   Clock Regions

In the definition of timed automata, we allowed the clock constraints that serve as the invariants of locations and the guards of transitions to contain arbitrary rational constants. We can multiply the constants in each clock constraint by the least common multiple m of the denominators of all the constants that appear in all of the constraints [20]. This converts

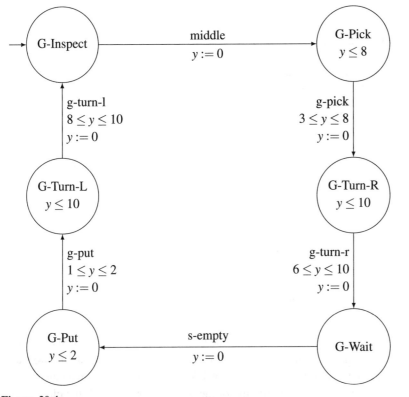

Figure 20.4
Timed automaton for G-Robot.

all of the constants to integers. The value of a clock can still be an arbitrary nonnegative real number. Note that applying this transformation can change the clock assignments in the set of reachable states of $\mathcal{T}(A)$. Fortunately, this does not cause a major problem. The reachable states of the original automaton can be obtained from the locations of the transformed automaton by applying the inverse transformation, that is, dividing each clock value by m.

The largest constant in the transformed automaton is the product of m and the largest constant in the original automaton. Thus, the transformation at worst results in a quadratic blowup in the length of the encodings of the clock constraints [20]. This increase in complexity is acceptable, since the transformation simplifies certain operations on clock constraints that will be needed later in the chapter. We will apply this transformation uniformly to all of the clock constraints that appear in the timed automata that we study. Consequently, in the future we can assume without loss of generality that all constants in clock constraints that we encounter are integers.

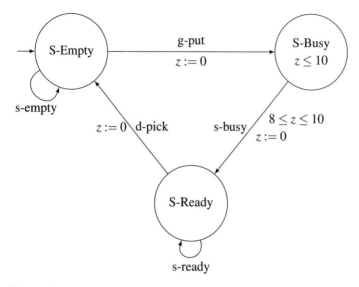

Figure 20.5
Timed automaton for processing station.

In order to obtain a finite representation for the infinite state space of a timed automaton, we define *clock regions* [17, 19], which represent sets of clock assignments. If two states, which correspond to the same location of the timed automaton A, agree on the integral parts of all clock values and also on the ordering of the fractional parts of all the clocks, then the states will behave in a similar manner. The integral parts of the clock values determine whether a clock constraint in the invariant of a location or in the guard of a transition is satisfied or not. The ordering of the fractional parts of the clock values determines which clock will change its integral part first. This is because clock constraints can only involve integers, and all clocks increase at the same rate.

For example, let A be a timed automaton with two clocks x_1 and x_2. Let s be a location in A with an outgoing transition e to some other location. Consider two states (s, v) and (s, v') in $\mathcal{T}(A)$ that correspond to location s. Suppose that $v(x_1) = 5.3$, $v(x_2) = 7.5$, $v'(x_1) = 5.5$, and $v'(x_2) = 7.9$. Assume that the guard φ associated with e is $x_1 \geq 8 \land x_2 \geq 10$. It is easy to see that if (s, v) eventually satisfies the guard, then so will (s, v').

The value of a clock can get arbitrarily large; however, if the clock is never compared to a constant greater than c, then the value of the clock will have no effect on the computation of A once it exceeds c. Suppose, for instance, that the clock x is never compared to a constant greater than 100 in the invariant associated with a location or in the guard of a transition. Then, based on the behavior of A, it is impossible to distinguish between x having the value 101 and x having the value 1001.

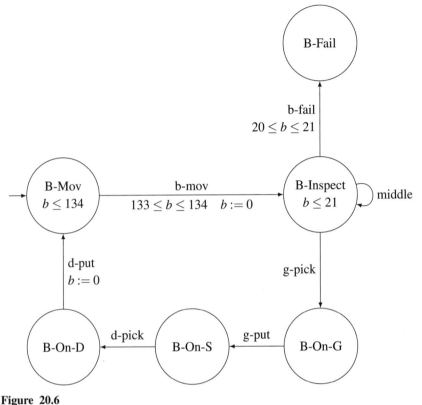

Figure 20.6
Timed automaton for box.

Alur, Courcoubetis, and Dill [17, 19] show how to formalize this reasoning. For each clock $x \in X$, let c_x be the largest constant that x is compared with in the invariant of any location or in the guard of any transition. For $t \in \mathbb{R}^+$, let $fr(t)$ be the fractional part of t, and let $\lfloor t \rfloor$ be the integral part of t. Thus, $t = \lfloor t \rfloor + fr(t)$. We define an equivalence relation $\cong$ on the set of possible clock assignments as follows: Let v and v' be two clock assignments. Then, $v \cong v'$ if and only if three conditions are satisfied:

1. For all $x \in X$, either $v(x) \geq c_x$ and $v'(x) \geq c_x$ or $\lfloor v(x) \rfloor = \lfloor v'(x) \rfloor$.
2. For all $x, y \in X$ such that $v(x) \leq c_x$ and $v(y) \leq c_y$,

$$fr(v(x)) \leq fr(v(y)) \quad \text{if and only if} \quad fr(v'(x)) \leq fr(v'(y)).$$

3. For all $x \in X$ such that $v(x) \leq c_x$,

$$fr(v(x)) = 0 \quad \text{if and only if} \quad fr(v'(x)) = 0.$$

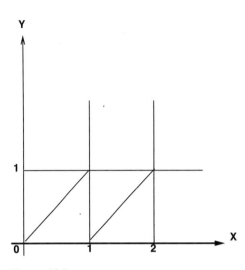

Figure 20.7
Clock region example.

It is easy to see that $\cong$ does indeed define an equivalence relation. The equivalence classes of $\cong$ are called *regions* [17, 19]. We write $[v]$ to denote the region that contains the clock assignment v. Each region can be represented by specifying

1. for every clock $x \in X$, one clock constraint from the set

$$\{x = c \mid c = 0, \ldots, c_x\} \cup \{c - 1 < x < c \mid c = 1, \ldots, c_x\} \cup \{x > c_x\};$$

2. for every pair of clocks $x, y \in X$ such that $c - 1 < x < c$ and $d - 1 < y < d$ are clock constraints in the first condition, whether $fr(x)$ is less than, equal to, or greater than $fr(y)$.

Figure 20.7, which is taken from [19], shows the clock regions for a timed automaton with two clocks x and y where $c_x = 2$ and $c_y = 1$. In this example, there are a total of 28 regions: 6 corner points (for example, $[(1,0)]$), 14 open line segments (for example, $[1 < x < 2 \wedge y = x - 1]$), and 8 open regions (for example, $[1 < x < 2 \wedge 0 < y < x - 1]$).

We will use this observation to show that $\cong$ has finite index and, consequently, that the number of regions is finite. Our proof of this fact is based on the proof given in [19].

Lemma 20.1 *The number of equivalence classes (that is, clock regions) that $\cong$ induces on $\mathcal{C}(X)$ is bounded by*

$$|X|! \cdot 2^{|X|} \cdot \prod_{x \in X} (2c_x + 2).$$

Proof   An equivalence class $[v]$ of $\cong$ can be described by a triple of arrays $\langle \alpha, \beta, \gamma \rangle$ in the following manner: For each clock $x \in X$, the array α tells which of the intervals

$$\{[0,0], (0,1), [1,1], \dots, (c_x - 1, c_x), [c_x, c_x], (c_x, \infty)\}$$

contains the value $v(x)$. Thus, the array α represents the clock assignment v if and only if for each clock $x \in X$, $v(x) \in \alpha(x)$. The number of ways to choose α is $\prod_{x \in X}(2c_x + 2)$.

Let X_α be the set of clocks x such that $\alpha(x)$ has the form $(i, i+1)$ for some $i \leq c_x$. Thus, X_α is the set of clocks with nonzero fractional part. The array $\beta : X_\alpha \to \{1, \dots, |X_\alpha|\}$ is a permutation of X_α, which gives the ordering of the fractional parts of the clocks in X_α with respect to $\leq$. Thus, the array β represents a clock assignment v if and only if, for each pair $x, y \in X_\alpha$, if $\beta(x) < \beta(y)$ then $fr(v(x)) \leq fr(v(y))$. For a given α, the number of ways to choose β is bounded by $|X_\alpha|!$, which is bounded by $|X|!$.

The third component γ is a Boolean array indexed by X_α that is used to specify which clocks in X_α have the same fractional part. For each clock x, $\gamma(x)$ tells whether or not the fractional part of $v(x)$ equals the fractional part of its predecessor in the array β. Thus, the array γ represents a clock assignment v if and only if, for each $x \in X_\alpha$, $\gamma(x)$ equals 0 exactly when there is a clock $y \in X_\alpha$ such that $\beta(y) = \beta(x) + 1$ and $fr(v(x)) = fr(v(y))$. The number of ways of choosing γ is bounded by the number of Boolean arrays over X_α, which is bounded by $2^{|X|}$.

Hence, α encodes the integral parts of the clock assignments, and β together with γ encodes the ordering of their fractional parts. It is easy to see that the sets represented by triples are equivalence classes of $\cong$ and that every equivalence class is represented by some triple. The bound given in the statement of the lemma is the product of the bounds associated with α, β, and γ. $\quad\square$

The following properties of the equivalence relation $\cong$ are used later in this chapter.

Lemma 20.2   *Let v_1 and v_2 be two clock assignments, let φ be a clock constraint, and let $\lambda \subseteq X$ be a set of clocks.*

1. *If $v_1 \cong v_2$ and t is a non-negative integer, then $v_1 + t \cong v_2 + t$.*
2. *If $v_1 \cong v_2$, then $\forall t_1 \in \mathbb{R} \, \exists t_2 \in \mathbb{R} \, [v_1 + t_1 \cong v_2 + t_2]$.*
3. *If $v_1 \cong v_2$, then v_1 satisfies φ if and only if v_2 satisfies φ.*
4. *If $v_1 \cong v_2$, then $v_1[\lambda := 0] \cong v_2[\lambda := 0]$.*

Note that the first property may not hold if t is not an integer. For example, $(.2, .8) \cong (.1, .2)$, but $(.2, .8) + .3$ is not equivalent to $(.1, .2) + .3$. All of the properties except the second are straightforward to prove and are left to the reader. A proof of the second property is sketched below. The proof is not difficult, but it is somewhat tedious. It can be safely skipped when this chapter is read for the first time.

Proof Assume that $v_1 \cong v_2$. We can assume that $t_1 > 0$, since otherwise we can simply choose $t_2 = 0$. Let $X = \{x_1, x_2, \ldots, x_n\}$. We can treat v_1 as a vector $v_1 = \langle a_1, \ldots, a_n \rangle$, where a_i is the value of clock x_i in v_1. Similarly, we let $v_2 = \langle b_1, \ldots, b_n \rangle$. Since corresponding clocks have the same integer part, we can assume without loss of generality that $0 \le a_i < 1$ and $0 \le b_i < 1$. Also, assume that the clock values are sorted into increasing order so that $a_1 \le a_2 \le \ldots \le a_n$ and $b_1 \le b_2 \le \ldots \le b_n$.

Case 1: Assume that the largest element in $v_1 + t_1$ is less than or equal to 1. This case is trivial. We can easily choose t_2 so that $v_1 + t_1 \cong v_2 + t_2$.

Case 2: Assume that $0 \le t_1 < 1$. Let the first element of $v_1 + t_1$ that is greater than or equal to 1 be $a_k + t_1$. Choose ε so that $\varepsilon = 0$ if $a_k + t_1 = 1$ and so that $0 < \varepsilon < b_k - b_{k-1}$ if $a_k + t_1 > 1$. Note that $b_{k-1} < b_k$. If $b_k = b_{k-1}$, then $a_k = a_{k-1}$ and $a_k + t_1$ is not the first element of $v_1 + t_1$ that is greater than or equal to 1. We show that $v_1 + t_1 \cong v_2 + (1 + \varepsilon - b_k)$. In order to show this, we split the vectors into two parts. Let

$$L_1 = \langle a_1 + t_1, \ldots, a_{k-1} + t_1 \rangle, \text{ and}$$
$$L_2 = \langle b_1 + (1 + \varepsilon - b_k), \ldots, b_{k-1} + (1 + \varepsilon - b_k) \rangle.$$

In each case it is straightforward to show that

1. all of the elements are positive,
2. the elements are sorted in increasing order, and
3. all of the elements are less than 1.

Because of these conditions, it is easy to see that $L_1 \cong L_2$. Similarly, let

$$R_1 = \langle a_k + t_1, \ldots, a_n + t_1 \rangle, \text{ and}$$
$$R_2 = \langle b_k + (1 + \varepsilon - b_k), \ldots, b_n + (1 + \varepsilon - b_k) \rangle.$$

All of the elements in R_1 and R_2 are greater than or equal to 1. The fractional parts are given by $R_1 - 1$ and $R_2 - 1$, respectively. For these vectors it is straightforward to show that

1. all of the elements are nonnegative,
2. the elements are sorted in increasing order, and
3. all of the elements are less than 1.

Moreover, an element in one vector is 0 if and only if the corresponding element in the other vector is 0. Thus, $R_1 - 1 \cong R_2 - 1$. It follows immediately that $R_1 \cong R_2$.

It is not difficult to see that the fractional parts of R_2 precede the fractional parts of L_2. Let $i \ge k$, and let $j < k$. Then

$$b_i + (1 + \varepsilon - b_k) - 1 \le b_j + (1 + \varepsilon - b_k).$$

is equivalent to $b_i - b_j \leq 1$, which is obviously true. The same relationship holds for the fractional parts of R_1 and L_1; that is,

$$a_i + t_1 - 1 \leq a_j + t_1.$$

Hence, we obtain $R_1 \cdot L_1 \cong R_2 \cdot L_2$, where "·" is concatenation of vectors. This shows that for all t_1 with $0 \leq t_1 < 1$, there exists a t_2 such that $v_1 + t_1 \cong v_2 + t_2$ and completes the proof of case 2.

Case 3: Suppose that $t_1 \geq 1$. Let $t_1' = t_1 - \lfloor t_1 \rfloor$, so that $0 \leq t_1' < 1$. Find t_2' such that $v_1 + t_1' \cong v_2 + t_2'$. Then

$$v_1 + t_1' + \lfloor t_1 \rfloor \cong v_2 + t_2' + \lfloor t_1 \rfloor.$$

If we choose $t_2 = t_2' + \lfloor t_1 \rfloor$, then we have $v_1 + t_1 \cong v_2 + t_2$ as required. This completes the proof of the second property. □

The equivalence relation $\cong$ over clock assignments can be extended to an equivalence relation over the state space of $\mathcal{T}(A)$ by requiring that equivalent states have identical locations and equivalent clock assignments: $(s, v) \cong (s', v')$ if and only if $s = s'$ and $v \cong v'$. The key property of the equivalence relation $\cong$ is given by the following lemma [21].

Lemma 20.3 *If $v_1 \cong v_2$ and $(s, v_1) \overset{a}{\Longrightarrow} (s', v_1')$, then there exists a clock assignment v_2' such that $v_1' \cong v_2'$ and $(s, v_2) \overset{a}{\Longrightarrow} (s', v_2')$.*

Proof Assume that $v_1 \cong v_2$ and $(s, v_1) \overset{a}{\Longrightarrow} (s', v_1')$. The transition $\langle s, a, \varphi, \lambda, s' \rangle$ that takes state (s, v_1) to state (s', v_1') corresponds to two transitions of the timed automaton:

- a delay transition $(s, v_1) \overset{d_1}{\longrightarrow} (s, v_1 + d_1)$, for some $d_1 \geq 0$; and
- an action transition $(s, v_1 + d_1) \overset{a}{\longrightarrow} (s', v_1')$ such that $v_1 + d_1$ satisfies φ and $v_1' = (v_1 + d_1)[\lambda := 0]$.

Since $v_1 \cong v_2$ and v_1 satisfies $I(s)$, v_2 also satisfies $I(s)$. Furthermore, there exists $d_2 \geq 0$ such that $v_1 + d_1 \cong v_2 + d_2$. Since $v_1 + d_1$ satisfies $I(s)$, $v_2 + d_2$ also satisfies $I(s)$. Because the clock constraint $I(s)$ is convex and is satisfied by both v_2 and $v_2 + d_2$, $I(s)$ must be satisfied by $v_2 + e$ for all e such that $0 \leq e \leq d_2$. Consequently, the delay transition $(s, v_2) \overset{d_2}{\longrightarrow} (s, v_2 + d_2)$ is legal.

Since $v_1 + d_1 \cong v_2 + d_2$, both $v_1 + d_1$ and $v_2 + d_2$ must satisfy the clock constraint for the guard φ. Thus, the transition $\langle s, a, \varphi, \lambda, s' \rangle$ must also be enabled in the state $(s, v_2 + d_2)$. Let $v_2' = (v_2 + d_2)[\lambda := 0]$. Then v_2' is equivalent to v_1'. Hence, there is an action transition $(s, v_2 + d_2) \overset{a}{\longrightarrow} (s', v_2')$. Combining the delay transition with the action transition, we get $(s, v_2) \overset{a}{\Longrightarrow} (s', v_2')$ as required. □

As a result of the lemma, we can construct a finite state transition graph that is bisimulation equivalent to the infinite state transition graph $\mathcal{T}(A)$. The finite state transition graph is called the *region graph* of A [17, 19] and is denoted by $\mathcal{R}(A)$. A *region* is a pair $(s, [v])$. Since $\cong$ has finite index, there are only a finite number of regions. The states of the region graph are the regions of A. The construction of $\mathcal{R}(A)$ will have the property that whenever (s, v) is a state of $\mathcal{T}(A)$, the region $(s, [v])$ will be a state of $\mathcal{R}(A)$. The initial states of the region graph have the form $(s_0, [v_0])$ where s_0 is an initial state of A and v_0 is a clock assignment that assigns 0 to every clock. The transition relation of $\mathcal{R}(A)$ is defined so that bisimulation equivalence is guaranteed. There will be a transition labeled with a from the region $(s, [v])$ to the region $(s', [v'])$ if and only if there are assignments $\omega \in [v]$ and $\omega' \in [v']$ such that (s, ω) can make a transition to (s', ω').

We summarize the construction of the region graph $\mathcal{R}(A)$ below. Let $A = (\Sigma, S, S_0, X, I, T)$ be a timed automaton. Then we have the following:

- The states of $\mathcal{R}(A)$ have the form $(s, [v])$, where $s \in S$ and $[v]$ is a clock region.
- The initial states have the form $(s_0, [v])$, where $s_0 \in S_0$ and $v(x) = 0$ for all $x \in X$.
- $\mathcal{R}(A)$ has a transition $((s, [v]), a, (s', [v']))$ if and only if $(s, \omega) \overset{a}{\Longrightarrow} (s', \omega')$ for some $\omega \in [v]$ and some $\omega' \in [v']$.

We can use lemma 20.3 to prove bisimulation equivalence.

Theorem 20.4 *The state transition graph $\mathcal{T}(A)$ and the region graph $\mathcal{R}(A)$ are bisimilar as transition systems.*

Proof We show that $\mathcal{T}(A)$ and $\mathcal{R}(A)$ are bisimilar. Define the bisimulation relation B by $(s, v)B(s, [v])$. It is easy to see that the initial state (s_0, v_0) corresponds to the state $(s_0, [v_0])$. Next, we show that for each transition of $\mathcal{T}(A)$, there is a corresponding transition of $\mathcal{R}(\mathcal{A})$, and vice versa. Suppose first that $(s, v)B(s, [v])$ and that $(s, v) \overset{a}{\Longrightarrow} (s', v')$. It follows immediately that $(s, [v]) \overset{a}{\Longrightarrow} (s', [v'])$ and that $(s', v')B(s', [v'])$. Suppose, on the other hand, that $(s, v)B(s, [v])$ and that $(s, [v]) \overset{a}{\Longrightarrow} (s', [v'])$. Then, there exists $\omega \cong v$ and $\omega' \cong v'$ such that $(s, \omega) \overset{a}{\Longrightarrow} (s', \omega')$. Since $(s, \omega) \cong (s, v)$, by lemma 20.3 there exists (s', v'') such that $(s', \omega') \cong (s', v'')$ and $(s, v) \overset{a}{\Longrightarrow} (s', v'')$. Hence, $v'' \cong \omega' \cong v'$, so $[v''] = [v']$. By the definition of B, $(s', v'')B(s', [v''])$, it follows that $(s', v'')B(s', [v'])$. $\square$

20.5   Clock Zones

An alternative way to obtain a finite representation for the infinite state space $\mathcal{T}(A)$ is to define *clock zones* [20], which also represent sets of clock assignments. A clock zone is a conjunction of inequalities that compare either a clock value or the difference between two clock values to an integer. We allow inequalities of the following types:

$$x \prec c, c \prec x, x - y \prec c,$$

where $\prec$ is $<$ or $\leq$.

By introducing a special clock x_0 that is always 0, it is possible to obtain a more uniform notation for clock zones. Since the value of a clock is always non-negative, we will assume that constraints involving only one clock have the form

$$-c_{0,i} \prec x_i \prec c_{i,0},$$

where $-c_{0,i}$ and $c_{i,0}$ are both non-negative. Using the special clock x_0, we will replace this constraint by the conjunction of two inequalities

$$x_0 - x_i \prec c_{0,i} \wedge x_i - x_0 \prec c_{i,0}.$$

Thus, the general form of a clock zone is

$$x_0 = 0 \wedge \bigwedge_{0 \le i \ne j \le n} x_i - x_j \prec c_{i,j}.$$

The following operations will be used to construct more complicated clock zones from simpler ones [20]. Let φ be a clock zone. If $\lambda \subseteq X$ is a set of clocks, then define $\varphi[\lambda := 0]$ to be the set of all clock assignments $v[\lambda := 0]$, where $v \in \varphi$. If $d \in \mathbb{R}^+$, then we define $\varphi + d$ to be the set of all clock assignments $v + d$ where $v \in \varphi$. The set $\varphi - d$ is defined similarly.

Let φ be a clock zone expressed in terms of the clocks in X. The conjunction φ will represent a set of assignments to the clocks in X. If X contains k elements, then φ will be a convex subset of k-dimensional Euclidean space. The following lemma shows that the projection of a clock zone onto a lower dimensional subspace is also a clock zone.

Lemma 20.5 *If φ is a clock zone with free clock variable x, then $\exists x[\varphi]$ is also a clock zone.*

This lemma turns out to be quite valuable in working with clock zones and is proved at the end of this section.

Note that the assignment of values to the clocks in an initial state of timed automaton A is easily expressed as a clock zone since $v(x) = 0$ for every clock $x \in X$. Moreover, every clock constraint used in the invariant of an automaton location or in the guard of a transition is a clock zone. Because of this observation, clock zones can be used as the basis for various state reachability analysis algorithms for timed automata. These algorithms are usually expressed in terms of three operations on clock zones [20].

Intersection   If φ and ψ are two clock zones, then the intersection $\varphi \wedge \psi$ is a clock zone. This is easy to see. Since φ and ψ are clock zones, they can be expressed as conjunctions of clock constraints. Hence, $\varphi \wedge \psi$ is also a conjunction of clock constraints and, therefore, a clock zone.

Clock reset   If φ is a clock zone and λ is a set of clocks, then $\varphi[\lambda := 0]$ is a clock zone. We show that this is true when λ contains a single clock x. In this case, $\varphi[x := 0]$ is equivalent to $\exists x[\varphi \wedge x = 0]$, and the result follows immediately by lemma 20.5. The result can easily be extended by induction to sets with more than one clock.

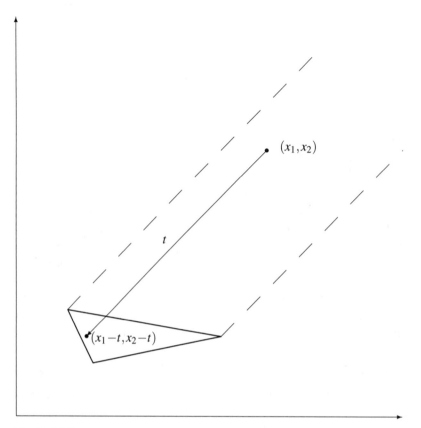

Figure 20.8
The clock zones φ and $\varphi^{\Uparrow}$.

Elapsing of time   We illustrate this operation first with a geometric example (see figure 20.8). The triangular-shaped area represents a simple clock zone φ. The area above the triangle φ is unbounded, and its sides (the dashed lines) make $45°$ angles with the horizontal axis. The triangle and the area above it represent the clock assignments that can be reached by time elapsing from an assignment in φ. This region is denoted by $\varphi^{\Uparrow}$.

Formally, if φ is a clock zone, then a clock assignment v will be an element of $\varphi^{\Uparrow}$, if v satisfies the formula $\exists t \geq 0[(v - t) \in \varphi]$ or, equivalently, $\exists t \geq 0[v \in (\varphi + t)]$. This region is a clock zone. In order to demonstrate this, we assume that t is a new clock and show that $\varphi + t$ is a clock zone that depends on the clocks in X and on t. We consider three types of inequalities:

1. $-c_{0,i} \prec x_i$: This inequality will become $-c_{0,i} \prec x_i - t$, which can be rewritten as $t - x_i \prec c_{0,i}$.

2. $x_i \prec c_{i,0}$: This inequality will become $x_i - t \prec c_{i,0}$, which is already in the appropriate form.

3. $x_i - x_j \prec c_{i,j}$: This inequality will become $(x_i - t) - (x_j - t) \prec c_{i,j}$. Since the two occurrences of the variable t cancel each other out, this inequality also has the appropriate form.

Since $\varphi + t$ is a clock zone, we can use lemma 20.5 to show that $\varphi^{\Uparrow} = \exists t \geq 0 [\varphi + t]$ is a clock zone that depends on X.

In principle, the three operations on clock zones described above can be used to construct a finite representation of the transition graph $\mathcal{T}(A)$ corresponding to a timed automaton. In the next section we describe how this algorithm can be implemented efficiently by using *difference-bound matrices* [20, 181]. In this section states are represented by *zones* [20]. A zone is a pair (s, φ) where s is a location of the timed automaton and φ is a clock zone. Consider a timed automaton A with transition $e = (s, a, \psi, \lambda, s')$. Assume that the current zone is (s, φ). Thus, s is a location of A, and φ is a clock zone. The clock zone $succ(\varphi, e)$ will denote the set of clock assignments v' such that for some $v \in \varphi$, the state (s', v') can be reached from the state (s, v) by letting time elapse and then executing the transition e. The pair $(s', succ(\varphi, e))$ will represent the set of successors of (s, φ) under the transition e. The clock zone $succ(\varphi, e)$ is obtained by the following steps [20]:

1. Intersect φ with the invariant of location s to find the set of possible clock assignments for the current state.
2. Let time elapse in location s using the operator $\Uparrow$ described above.
3. Take the intersection with the invariant of location s again to find the set of clock assignments that still satisfy the invariant.
4. Take the intersection with the guard ψ of the transition e to find the clock assignments that are permitted by the transition.
5. Set all of the clocks in λ that are reset by the transition to 0.

Combining all of the above steps into one formula, we obtain

$$succ(\varphi, e) = ((\varphi \wedge I(s))^{\Uparrow} \wedge I(s) \wedge \psi)[\lambda := 0]).$$

Since clock zones are closed under the operations of intersection, elapsing of time, and resetting of clocks, the set $succ(\varphi, e)$ is also a clock zone.

Finally, we describe how to construct a transition system for a timed automaton A. The transition system is called the *zone graph* and is denoted by $Z(A)$. The states of $Z(A)$ are the zones of A. If s is an initial location of A, then $(s, [X := 0])$ will be an initial state of $Z(A)$. There will be a transition from the zone (s, φ) in $Z(A)$ to the zone $(s', succ(\varphi, e))$ in $Z(A)$ labeled with the action a for each transition of the form $e = (s, a, \psi, \lambda, s')$ of the timed automaton A. Since each step in the construction of the zone graph is effective, this gives an algorithm for determining state reachability in the state transition graph $\mathcal{T}(A)$. In the next section we show how to make this construction more efficient.

Before concluding this section, we will prove lemma 20.5, which was stated without proof earlier in this section. The proof is not difficult but can be safely skipped when reading the section for the first time.

Proof Assume that the clock zone φ is given by

$$x_0 = 0 \wedge \bigwedge_{0 \le i \ne j \le n} x_i - x_j \prec c_{i,j},$$

where each instance of $\prec$ represents either $<$ or $\le$. Without loss of generality, we prove that $\exists x_n[\varphi]$ is a clock zone when $n > 0$. In particular, we will show that $\exists x_n[\varphi]$ is given by

$$x_0 = 0 \wedge \bigwedge_{0 \le i \ne j < n} x_i - x_j \prec c_{i,j} \wedge \bigwedge_{0 \le i \ne j < n} x_i - x_j \prec c_{i,n} + c_{n,j}.$$

In describing the proof we will normally omit writing the constraint $x_0 = 0$ since this equality is part of every formula and quantification over x_0 is not allowed. We first prove that if an assignment to the variables $x_0, \ldots, x_{n-1}$ satisfies

$$\exists x_n \left[\bigwedge_{0 \le i \ne j \le n} x_i - x_j \prec c_{i,j} \right],$$

then it also satisfies

$$\bigwedge_{0 \le i \ne j < n} x_i - x_j \prec c_{i,j} \wedge \bigwedge_{0 \le i \ne j < n} x_i - x_j \prec c_{i,n} + c_{n,j}.$$

In order to see why this is true, we rewrite

$$\bigwedge_{0 \le i \ne j \le n} x_i - x_j \prec c_{i,j}$$

as

$$\bigwedge_{0 \le i \ne j < n} x_i - x_j \prec c_{i,j} \wedge \bigwedge_{0 \le i < n} x_i - x_n \prec c_{i,n} \wedge \bigwedge_{0 \le j < n} x_n - x_j \prec c_{n,j}$$

and consider the following chain of implications:

$$\bigwedge_{0 \le i < n} x_i - x_n \prec c_{i,n} \wedge \bigwedge_{0 \le j < n} x_n - x_j \prec c_{n,j}$$

$$\Rightarrow \bigwedge_{0 \le i \ne j < n} x_i - x_n \prec c_{i,n} \wedge x_n - x_j \prec c_{n,j}$$

$$\Rightarrow \bigwedge_{0 \le i \ne j < n} (x_i - x_n) + (x_n - x_j) \prec c_{i,n} + c_{n,j}$$

$$\Rightarrow \bigwedge_{0 \le i \ne j < n} x_i - x_j \prec c_{i,n} + c_{n,j}$$

Since the last formula does not contain x_n, we see that

$$\exists x_n \left[\bigwedge_{0 \le i \ne j \le n} x_i - x_j \prec c_{i,j} \right]$$

implies

$$\bigwedge_{0 \le i \ne j < n} x_i - x_j \prec c_{i,j} \wedge \bigwedge_{0 \le i \ne j < n} x_i - x_j \prec c_{i,n} + c_{n,j}.$$

Next, we must show the reverse implication. We show that any assignment to $x_0, \ldots, x_{n-1}$ that makes

$$\bigwedge_{0 \le i \ne j < n} x_i - x_j \prec c_{i,j} \wedge \bigwedge_{0 \le i \ne j < n} x_i - x_j \prec c_{i,n} + c_{n,j}$$

true will also make

$$\exists x_n \left[\bigwedge_{0 \le i \ne j \le n} x_i - x_j \prec c_{i,j} \right]$$

true. In other words, we must find a nonnegative value for the variable x_n so that

$$\bigwedge_{0 \le i \ne j \le n} x_i - x_j \prec c_{i,j}$$

is true. If

$$\bigwedge_{0 \le i \ne j < n} x_i - x_j \prec c_{i,j} \wedge \bigwedge_{0 \le i \ne j < n} x_i - x_j \prec c_{i,n} + c_{n,j}$$

is true, then

$$\bigwedge_{0 \le i \ne j < n} x_i - x_j \prec c_{i,n} + c_{n,j}$$

will also be true. This formula can be rewritten as

$$\bigwedge_{0 \le i \ne j < n} x_i - c_{i,n} \prec x_j + c_{n,j}.$$

It follows that

$$\max_{0 \le i < n} (x_i - c_{i,n}) \prec \min_{0 \le j < n} (x_j + c_{n,j}).$$

We will choose the value for x_n so that

$$\max_{0 \le i < n} (x_i - c_{i,n}) \prec x_n \prec \min_{0 \le j < n} (x_j + c_{n,j}).$$

In particular, we will have $0 - c_{0,n} \prec x_n \prec 0 + c_{n,0}$. Since $-c_{0,n}$ and $c_{n,0}$ are both nonnegative, the value of x_n will also be non-negative as required. It follows that

$$\bigwedge_{0 \le i \ne j < n} x_i - c_{i,n} \prec x_n \prec x_j + c_{n,j}$$

is also true. We can rewrite this formula as

$$\bigwedge_{0 \le i < n} x_i - c_{i,n} \prec x_n \wedge \bigwedge_{0 \le j < n} x_n \prec x_j + c_{n,j}.$$

Rearranging terms, we get

$$\bigwedge_{0 \le i < n} x_i - x_n \prec c_{i,n} \wedge \bigwedge_{0 \le j < n} x_n - x_j \prec c_{n,j}.$$

Consequently, if

$$\bigwedge_{0 \le i \ne j < n} x_i - x_j \prec c_{i,j} \wedge \bigwedge_{0 \le i \ne j < n} x_i - x_j \prec c_{i,n} + c_{n,j}.$$

is true, then

$$\bigwedge_{0 \le i \ne j < n} x_i - x_j \prec c_{i,j} \wedge \bigwedge_{0 \le i < n} x_i - x_n \prec c_{i,n} \wedge \bigwedge_{0 \le j < n} x_n - x_j \prec c_{n,j}$$

will also be true. The last formula reduces to

$$\bigwedge_{0 \le i \ne j \le n} x_i - x_j \prec c_{i,j}.$$

This shows that

$$\exists x_n \left[\bigwedge_{0 \le i \ne j \le n} x_i - x_j \prec c_{i,j} \right]$$

is also true and completes the proof of the second half of the lemma.   □

20.6   Difference-Bound Matrices

A clock zone can be represented by a *difference-bound matrix* as described by Dill [181]
This matrix is indexed by the clocks in X together with a special clock x_0 whose value is
always 0. This clock plays exactly the same role as the clock x_0 in the previous section.
Each entry $\mathcal{D}_{i,j}$ in the matrix $\mathcal{D}$ has the form $(d_{i,j}, \prec_{i,j})$ and represents the inequality
$x_i - x_j \prec_{i,j} d_{i,j}$, where $\prec_{i,j}$ is either $<$ or $\le$, or $(\infty, <)$, if no such bound is known. Since the
variable x_0 is always 0, it can be used for expressing constraints that only involve a single
variable. Thus, $\mathcal{D}_{j,0} = (d_{j,0}, \prec)$, means that we have the constraint $x_j \prec d_{j,0}$. Likewise,
$\mathcal{D}_{0,j} = (d_{0,j}, \prec)$, means that we have the constraint $0 - x_j \prec d_{0,j}$ or $-d_{0,j} \prec x_j$.

   To illustrate the use of difference-bound matrices, consider the clock zone given by the
formula

$$x_1 - x_2 < 2 \wedge 0 < x_2 \le 2 \wedge 1 \le x_1.$$

In this case we obtain the follow matrix D:

	0	1	2
0	$(0,\leq)$	$(-1,\leq)$	$(0,<)$
1	$(\infty,<)$	$(0,\leq)$	$(2,<)$
2	$(2,\leq)$	$(\infty,<)$	$(0,\leq)$

The representation of a clock zone by a difference-bound matrix is not unique. In the above example, there are some implied constraints that are not reflected in the matrix D. For example, since $x_1 - x_2 < 2$ and $x_2 - x_0 \leq 2$, it must be the case $x_1 - x_0 < 4$. Since $x_0 = 0$, we see that $x_1 < 4$. Thus, we can change $\mathcal{D}_{1,0}$ to $(4,<)$ and obtain an alternative difference-bound matrix for the same clock zone:

	0	1	2
0	$(0,\leq)$	$(-1,\leq)$	$(0,<)$
1	$(4,<)$	$(0,\leq)$	$(2,<)$
2	$(2,\leq)$	$(\infty,<)$	$(0,\leq)$

Clearly, the new matrix represents the same set of clock interpretations as the original matrix D.

In general, the sum of the upper bounds on the clock differences $x_i - x_j$ and $x_j - x_k$ is an upper bound on the clock difference $x_i - x_k$. This observation can be used to progressively tighten the difference-bound matrix. If $x_i - x_j \prec_{i,j} d_{i,j}$ and $x_j - x_k \prec_{j,k} d_{j,k}$, then it is possible to conclude that $x_i - x_k \prec'_{i,k} d'_{i,k}$, where

$$d'_{i,k} = d_{i,j} + d_{j,k}$$

and

$$\prec'_{i,k} = \begin{cases} \leq & \text{if } \prec_{i,j} = \leq \text{ and } \prec_{j,k} = \leq, \\ < & \text{otherwise.} \end{cases}$$

Thus, if $(d'_{i,k}, \prec'_{i,k})$ is a tighter bound than $(d_{i,k}, \prec_{i,k})$, we should replace the latter by the former so that $\mathcal{D}_{i,k} = (d'_{i,k}, \prec'_{i,k})$. This operation is called *tightening* the difference-bound matrix. We can repeatedly apply tightening to a difference bound matrix until further application of this operation does not change the matrix. The resulting matrix is a *canonical* representation for the clock zone under consideration. By following this procedure for the clock zone in the above example, we obtain the canonical difference-bound matrix:

	0	1	2
0	$(0,\leq)$	$(-1,\leq)$	$(0,<)$
1	$(4,<)$	$(0,\leq)$	$(2,<)$
2	$(2,\leq)$	$(1,\leq)$	$(0,\leq)$

Note that a canonical difference-bound matrix will satisfy the inequality $d_{i,k} \prec_{i,k} d_{i,j} + d_{j,k}$ for all possible values of the indices i, j, and k.

Finding the canonical form of a difference-bound matrix can be automated by using the Floyd–Warshall algorithm [155], which has cubic complexity. The algorithm guarantees that all the possible combinations of indices are systematically checked to determine if further tightening is possible. We determine if a tighter bound can be obtained for $\mathcal{D}_{i,k}$ by checking if the inequality $d_{i,k} \prec_{i,k} d_{i,j} + d_{j,k}$ holds for all possible values of j. If the inequality does not hold for some value of j, then we replace $\mathcal{D}_{i,k}$ by $(d'_{i,k}, \prec'_{i,k})$ as described in the preceding paragraph.

After the difference-bound matrix has been converted to canonical form, we can determine if the corresponding clock zone is nonempty by examining the entries on the main diagonal of the matrix. If the clock zone described by the matrix is nonempty, all of the entries along the main diagonal will have the form $(0, \leq)$. If the clock zone is empty or unsatisfiable, there will be at least one negative entry on the main diagonal.

We describe now three operations on difference-bound matrices [20, 181]. These operations correspond to the three operations defined on clock zones in the previous section.

- **Intersection**. We define $\mathcal{D} = \mathcal{D}^1 \wedge \mathcal{D}^2$. Let $\mathcal{D}^1_{i,j} = (c_1, \prec_1)$, and let $\mathcal{D}^2_{i,j} = (c_2, \prec_2)$. Then $\mathcal{D} = (\min(c_1, c_2), \prec)$, where $\prec$ is defined as follows:

  - If $c_1 < c_2$, then $\prec = \prec_1$.
  - If $c_2 < c_1$, then $\prec = \prec_2$.
  - If $c_1 = c_2$ and $\prec_1 = \prec_2$, then $\prec = \prec_1$.
  - If $c_1 = c_2$ and $\prec_1 \neq \prec_2$, then $\prec = <$.

- **Clock reset**. Define $\mathcal{D}' = \mathcal{D}[\lambda := 0]$, where $\lambda \subseteq X$ as follows:

  - If $x_i, x_j \in \lambda$, then $\mathcal{D}'_{i,j} = (0, \leq)$.
  - If $x_i \in \lambda, x_j \notin \lambda$, then $\mathcal{D}'_{i,j} = \mathcal{D}_{0,j}$.
  - If $x_j \in \lambda, x_i \notin \lambda$, then $\mathcal{D}'_{i,j} = \mathcal{D}_{i,0}$.
  - If $x_i, x_j \notin \lambda$, then $\mathcal{D}'_{i,j} = \mathcal{D}_{i,j}$.

- **Elapsing of time**. Define $\mathcal{D}' = \mathcal{D}^{\Uparrow}$ as follows:

  - $\mathcal{D}'_{i,0} = (\infty, <)$ for any $i \neq 0$.
  - $\mathcal{D}'_{i,j} = \mathcal{D}_{i,j}$ if $i = 0$ or $j \neq 0$.

In each case the resulting matrix may fail to be in canonical form. Thus, as a final step we must reduce the matrix to canonical form. All three of the operations can be implemented efficiently. Moreover, the implementation of these operations is relatively straightforward to program.

We now see how the construction of the zone graph described in the previous section can be made more efficient. Clock zones are represented by difference-bound matrices, and the set $succ(\varphi, e)$ is computed by the three operations on difference-bound matrices described above rather than by operations directly on clock zones. We will illustrate this procedure with the timed automaton in figure 20.1. The initial state is given by (s_0, Z_0), where Z_0 is the clock zone $x = 0 \wedge y = 0$, which corresponds to the following difference-bound matrix:

	x_0	x	y
x_0	$(0, \leq)$	$(0, \leq)$	$(0, \leq)$
x	$(0, \leq)$	$(0, \leq)$	$(0, \leq)$
y	$(0, \leq)$	$(0, \leq)$	$(0, \leq)$

We follow the sequence of five steps given in section 20.5. Only the normalized difference-bound matrix obtained in each step is shown.

1. The invariant $I(s_0)$ is $0 \leq x \wedge 0 \leq y \leq 5$, which is given by the following matrix:

	x_0	x	y
x_0	$(0, \leq)$	$(0, \leq)$	$(0, \leq)$
x	$(\infty, <)$	$(0, \leq)$	$(\infty, <)$
y	$(5, \leq)$	$(5, \leq)$	$(0, \leq)$

   We intersect D_0 with $I(s_0)$ to obtain the zero matrix again.

2. Next, we let time elapse in the location s_0 using the operator $\Uparrow$. The matrix for $(D_0 \wedge I(s_0))^{\Uparrow}$ is

	x_0	x	y
x_0	$(0, \leq)$	$(0, \leq)$	$(0, \leq)$
x	$(\infty, <)$	$(0, \leq)$	$(0, \leq)$
y	$(\infty, <)$	$(0, \leq)$	$(0, \leq)$

3. We intersect with $I(s)$ again to find the set of clock assignments that still satisfy the invariant. The matrix for $(D_0 \wedge I(s_0))^{\Uparrow} \wedge I(s_0)$ is

	x_0	x	y
x_0	$(0, \leq)$	$(0, \leq)$	$(0, \leq)$
x	$(5, \leq)$	$(0, \leq)$	$(0, \leq)$
y	$(5, \leq)$	$(0, \leq)$	$(0, \leq)$

4. The guard g_a for the a transition from location s_0 to location s_1 is

	x_0	x	y
x_0	$(0, \leq)$	$(0, \leq)$	$(-3, \leq)$
x	$(\infty, <)$	$(0, \leq)$	$(\infty, <)$
y	$(\infty, <)$	$(\infty, \leq)$	$(0, \leq)$

   We intersect the current set of states with the guard g_a to obtain $((D_0 \wedge I(s_0))^{\Uparrow} \wedge I(s_0)) \wedge g_a$:

	x_0	x	y
x_0	$(0,\leq)$	$(-3,\leq)$	$(-3,\leq)$
x	$(5,\leq)$	$(0,\leq)$	$(0,<)$
y	$(5,\leq)$	$(0,\leq)$	$(0,\leq)$

5. Finally, we reset the clock y to get the matrix D_1:

	x_0	x	y
x_0	$(0,\leq)$	$(-3,\leq)$	$(0,\leq)$
x	$(5,\leq)$	$(0,\leq)$	$(5,<)$
y	$(0,\leq)$	$(-3,\leq)$	$(0,\leq)$

Note that the last difference-bound matrix corresponds to the clock zone

$$Z_1 \equiv 3 \leq x \leq 5 \wedge 3 \leq x - y \leq 5 \wedge y = 0.$$

Consequently, the successor state in the zone automaton is (s_1, Z_1). Repeating the same sequence of steps, we obtain the remaining states of the zone automaton:

1. $(s_0,\ 4 \leq y \leq 5 \wedge 4 \leq y - x \leq 5 \wedge x = 0)$
2. $(s_1,\ 0 \leq x \leq 1 \wedge 0 \leq x - y \leq 1 \wedge y = 0)$
3. $(s_0,\ 5 \leq y \leq 8 \wedge 5 \leq y - x \leq 8 \wedge x = 0)$
4. $(s_1,\ x = 0 \wedge y = 0)$

The reachability computation terminates at this point since the state

$$(s_1,\ x = 0 \wedge y = 0)$$

is contained in

$$(s_1,\ 0 \leq x \leq 1 \wedge 0 \leq x - y \leq 1 \wedge y = 0).$$

Thus, no new states of $\mathcal{T}(A)$ will be obtained by computing successor states in the zone automaton.

20.7   Complexity Considerations

Because of lemma 20.1 the complexity of checking reachability using the region graph construction is exponential in the number of clocks and also in the magnitude of the clocks. Similar complexity results can be obtained for temporal logic model checking. In practice, the region graph construction can be combined with symbolic model checking techniques based on BDDs. In this case the number of state variables can be quite large. However, the number of clocks will usually be small (probably less than 20).

Difference bound matrices are normally implemented using an explicit state representation. Consequently, the number of states that can be handled is much smaller in this approach. The number of clocks typically reflects the number of components operating concurrently and will also be small. The advantage of this approach is that constraints are represented in terms of linear inequalities and therefore can be easily manipulated.

Bibliographic Notes

Although a number of different models of continuous time have been proposed [19, 181, 266, 338, 423, 448, 490, 491], the timed automata model of Alur, Courcoubetis, and Dill [19, 181] has become the standard, and most of the research on continuous time model checking is based on this model. The key approach to the analysis of timed automata are clock zones [20], as explained in section 20.5. The best known implementation is UPPAAL [339]. Algorithms for CTL model checking [19], LTL model checking [17], and testing inclusion between timed ω-automata [20, 21] have been proposed. Tools based on these algorithms have been developed and tested on realistic examples [23, 168]. The interested reader should consult the papers referenced above to learn more about these techniques.

Various techniques discussed elsewhere in this book can be used to avoid the state explosion problem for continuous real-time systems. In particular, there is research on combining partial order reduction with these algorithms [423, 490, 491]. In addition, approximation techniques that can be used in conjunction with these algorithms have also been investigated [254]. Additional reading can be found in Baier and Katoen [35].

Bibliography

[1] F. Aarts, B. Jonsson, and J. Uijen. Generating models of infinite-state communication protocols using regular inference with abstraction. In *Testing Software and Systems – 22nd IFIP WG 6.1 International Conference, ICTSS*, volume 6435 of *Lecture Notes in Computer Science*, pages 188–204. Springer, 2010.

[2] P. A. Abdulla. Well (and better) quasi-ordered transition systems. *Bull. Symbolic Logic*, 16(4):457–515, 2010.

[3] P. A. Abdulla, M. F. Atig, Y.-F. Chen, C. Leonardsson, and A. Rezine. Counter-example guided fence insertion under TSO. In *Tools and Algorithms for the Construction and Analysis of Systems, TACAS*, volume 7214 of *Lecture Notes in Computer Science*, pages 204–219. Springer, 2012.

[4] P. A. Abdulla, J. Cederberg, and T. Vojnar. Monotonic abstraction for programs with multiply-linked structures. *Int. J. Found. Comput. Sci.*, 24(2):187–210, 2013.

[5] P. A. Abdulla, K. Cerans, B. Jonsson, and Y. Tsay. General decidability theorems for infinite-state systems. In *Logic in Computer Science, LICS*, pages 313–321. IEEE Computer Society, 1996.

[6] P. A. Abdulla and G. Delzanno. Parameterized verification. *STTT*, 18(5):469–473, 2016.

[7] P. A. Abdulla, G. Delzanno, and A. Rezine. Monotonic abstraction in action. In *International Colloquium on Theoretical Aspects of Computing*, volume 5160 of *Lecture Notes in Computer Science*, pages 50–65. Springer, 2008.

[8] P. A. Abdulla, G. Delzanno, O. Rezine, A. Sangnier, and R. Traverso. Parameterized verification of time-sensitive models of ad hoc network protocols. *Theor. Comput. Sci.*, 612:1–22, 2016.

[9] P. A. Abdulla, F. Haziza, and L. Holík. All for the price of few. In *Verification, Model Checking, and Abstract Interpretation, VMCAI*, volume 7737 of *Lecture Notes in Computer Science*, pages 476–495. Springer, 2013.

[10] P. A. Abdulla and B. Jonsson. Verifying networks of timed processes (extended abstract). In *Tools and Algorithms for Construction and Analysis of Systems, TACAS*, volume 1384 of *Lecture Notes in Computer Science*, pages 298–312. Springer, 1998.

[11] S. Aggarwal, R. P. Kurshan, and K. Sabnani. A calculus for protocol specification and validation. In H. Rudin and C. H. West, editors, *Protocol Specification, Testing and Verification*, pages 19–34. North Holland, 1983.

[12] A. V. Aho, J. E. Hopcroft, and J. D. Ullman. *The Design and Analysis of Computer Algorithms.* Addison-Wesley, 1974.

[13] S. B. Akers. Binary decision diagrams. *IEEE Trans. Computers*, C-27(6):509–516, 1978.

[14] F. A. Aloul, I. L. Markov, and K. A. Sakallah. FORCE: a fast and easy-to-implement variable-ordering heuristic. In *Great Lakes Symposium on VLSI*, pages 116–119, 2003.

[15] F. A. Aloul, A. Ramani, K. A. Sakallah, and I. L. Markov. Solution and optimization of systems of pseudo-Boolean constraints. *IEEE Trans. Computers*, 56(10):1415–1424, 2007.

[16] B. Alpern and F. Schneider. Defining liveness. *Inform. Proc. Lett.*, 21:181–185, 1985.

[17] R. Alur. *Techniques for Automatic Verification of Real-Time Systems.* PhD thesis, Stanford University, 1991.

[18] R. Alur, R. K. Brayton, T. A. Henzinger, S. Qudeer, and S. Rajamani. Partial–order reduction in symbolic state space explosion. In O. Grumberg, editor, *Computer Aided Verification, CAV*, volume 1254 of *Lecture Notes in Computer Science*, pages 340–351. Springer, 1997.

[19] R. Alur, C. Courcoubetis, and D. Dill. Model-checking for real-time systems. In *Logic in Computer Science, LICS*, pages 414–425. IEEE Computer Society Press, 1990.

[20] R. Alur and D. L. Dill. A theory of timed automata. *Theor. Comput. Sci.*, 126(2):183–235, 1994.

[21] R. Alur and D. L. Dill. Automata-theoretic verification of real-time systems. In C. Heitmeyer and D. Mandrioli, editors, *Formal Methods for Real-Time Computing*, pages 55–80. Wiley, 1996.

[22] R. Alur and T. A. Henzinger. Reactive modules. *Formal Methods Syst. Design*, 15(1):7–48, 1999.

[23] R. Alur and R. P. Kurshan. Timing analysis in COSPAN. In *Hybrid Systems III. Verification and Control*, volume 1066 of *Lecture Notes in Computer Science*, pages 220–231. Springer, 1995.

[24] R. Alur, P. Madhusudan, and W. Nam. Symbolic compositional verification by learning assumptions. In *Computer Aided Verification, CAV*, volume 3576 of *Lecture Notes in Computer Science*, pages 548–562. Springer, 2005.

[25] B. Aminof, T. Kotek, S. Rubin, F. Spegni, and H. Veith. Parameterized model checking of rendezvous systems. In *Concurrency Theory, CONCUR*, volume 8704 of *Lecture Notes in Computer Science*, pages 109–124. Springer, 2014.

[26] H. R. Andersen. Model checking and Boolean graphs. In B. Krieg-Bruckner, editor, *European Symposium on Programming, ESOP*, volume 582 of *Lecture Notes in Computer Science*, pages 1–19. Springer, 1992.

[27] D. Angluin. Learning regular sets from queries and counterexamples. *Inf. Comput.*, 75(2):87–106, 1987.

[28] K. Apt and D. Kozen. Limits for automatic verification of finite-state systems. *IPL*, 15:307–309, 1986.

[29] A. Armando, C. Castellini, and E. Giunchiglia. SAT-based procedures for temporal reasoning. In S. Biundo and M. Fox, editors, *Recent Advances in AI Planning, 5th European Conference on*

Planning, ECP, volume 1809 of *Lecture Notes in Computer Science*, pages 97–108. Springer, 2000.

[30] R. Armoni, L. Fix, A. Flaisher, R. Gerth, B. Ginsburg, T. Kanza, A. Landver, S. Mador-Haim, E. Singerman, A. Tiemeyer, M. Vardi, and Y. Zbar. The ForSpec temporal logic: A new temporal property-specification logic. In *Tools and Algorithms for the Construction and Analysis of Systems, TACAS*, volume 2280 of *Lecture Notes in Computer Science*, pages 196–211. Springer, 2002.

[31] R. Armoni, L. Fix, R. Fraer, S. Huddleston, N. Piterman, and M. Y. Vardi. SAT-based induction for temporal safety properties. *Electr. Notes Theor. Comput. Sci.*, 119(2):3–16, 2005.

[32] G. Audemard and L. Simon. Predicting learnt clauses quality in modern SAT solvers. In C. Boutilier, editor, *International Joint Conference on Artificial Intelligence, IJCAI*, pages 399–404, 2009.

[33] A. Aziz, V. Singhal, F. Balarin, R. K. Brayton, and A. L. Sangiovanni-Vincentelli. Equivalences for fair Kripke structures. In S. Abiteboul and E. Shamir, editors, *International Colloquium on Automata, Languages and Programming, ICALP*, volume 820 of *Lecture Notes in Computer Science*, pages 364–375. Springer, 1994.

[34] F. Bacchus and J. Winter. Effective preprocessing with hyper-resolution and equality reduction. In E. Giunchiglia and A. Tacchella, editors, *Theory and Applications of Satisfiability Testing, SAT*, volume 2919 of *Lecture Notes in Computer Science*, pages 341–355. Springer, 2004.

[35] C. Baier and J. Katoen. *Principles of Model Checking*. MIT Press, 2008.

[36] F. Balarin and A. Sangiovanni-Vincentelli. On the automatic computation of network invariants. In D. L. Dill, editor, *Computer Aided Verification, CAV*, volume 818 of *Lecture Notes in Computer Science*, pages 235–246. Springer, 1994.

[37] T. Ball, E. Bounimova, B. Cook, V. Levin, J. Lichtenberg, C. McGarvey, B. Ondrusek, S. K. Rajamani, and A. Ustuner. Thorough static analysis of device drivers. In *Proceedings of the 2006 EuroSys Conference*, pages 73–85. ACM, 2006.

[38] T. Ball, S. Chaki, and S. K. Rajamani. Parameterized verification of multithreaded software libraries. In *Tools and Algorithms for the Construction and Analysis of Systems, TACAS*, volume 2031 of *Lecture Notes in Computer Science*, pages 158–173. Springer, 2001.

[39] T. Ball, A. Podelski, and S. K. Rajamani. Boolean and Cartesian abstraction for model checking C programs. In T. Margaria and W. Yi, editors, *Tools and Algorithms for the Construction and Analysis of Systems, TACAS*, volume 2031 of *Lecture Notes in Computer Science*, pages 268–283. Springer, 2001.

[40] T. Ball and S. Rajamani. Boolean programs: A model and process for software analysis. Technical Report 2000-14, Microsoft Research, 2000.

[41] T. Ball and S. K. Rajamani. The SLAM toolkit. In *Computer Aided Verification, CAV*, volume 2102 of *Lecture Notes in Computer Science*, pages 260–264. Springer, 2001.

[42] S. Barner, D. Geist, and A. Gringauze. Symbolic localization reduction with reconstruction layering and backtracking. In *Computer Aided Verification, CAV*, volume 2404 of *Lecture Notes in Computer Science*, pages 65–77. Springer, 2002.

[43] D. L. Beatty, R. E. Bryant, and C.-J. Seger. Formal hardware verification by symbolic ternary trajectory evaluation. In *Design Automation Conference, DAC*, pages 397–402. IEEE Computer Society Press, 1991.

[44] I. Beer, S. Ben-David, C. Eisner, D. Geist, L. Gluhovsky, T. Heyman, A. Landver, P. Paanah, Y. Rodeh, G. Ronin, and Y. Wolfsthal. RuleBase: Model checking at IBM. In *Computer Aided Verification, CAV*, volume 1254 of *Lecture Notes in Computer Science*, pages 480–483. Springer, 1997.

[45] M. Ben-Ari, Z. Manna, and A. Pnueli. The temporal logic of branching time. In *Principles of Programming Languages, POPL*, pages 164–176. ACM, 1981.

[46] M. Ben-Ari, Z. Manna, and A. Pnueli. The temporal logic of branching time. *Acta Inf.*, 20:207–226, 1983.

[47] S. Bensalem, A. Bouajjani, C. Loiseaux, and J. Sifakis. Property preserving simulations. In G. V. Bochmann and D. K. Probst, editors, *Computer Aided Verification, CAV*, volume 663 of *Lecture Notes in Computer Science*, pages 260–273. Springer, 1992.

[48] J. Bergstra, A. Ponse, and S. Smolka, editors. *Handbook of Process Algebra*. Elsevier, 2001.

[49] O. Bernholtz, M. Y. Vardi, and P. Wolper. An automata theoretic approach to branching time model checking. In D. L. Dill, editor, *Computer Aided Verification, CAV*, volume 818 of *Lecture Notes in Computer Science*, pages 142–155. Springer, 1994.

[50] N. Bertrand, G. Delzanno, B. König, A. Sangnier, and J. Stückrath. On the decidability status of reachability and coverability in graph transformation systems. In *Rewriting Techniques and Applications, RTA*, volume 15 of *Leibniz International Proceedings in Informatics*, pages 101–116. Schloss Dagstuhl–Leibniz Center for Informatics, 2012.

[51] D. Beyer, A. Chlipala, T. A. Henzinger, R. Jhala, and R. Majumdar. The BLAST query language for software verification. In R. Giacobazzi, editor, *SAS*, volume 3148 of *Lecture Notes in Computer Science*, pages 2–18. Springer, 2004.

[52] D. Beyer, T. A. Henzinger, and G. Théoduloz. Configurable software verification: Concretizing the convergence of model checking and program analysis. In W. Damm and H. Hermanns, editors, *Computer Aided Verification, CAV*, volume 4590 of *Lecture Notes in Computer Science*, pages 504–518. Springer, 2007.

[53] G. Bhat, R. Cleaveland, and O. Grumberg. Efficient on-the-fly model checking for CTL*. In *Logic in Computer Science, LICS*, pages 388–397. IEEE Computer Society, 1995.

[54] A. Biere. μcke—efficient μ-calculus model checking. In *Computer Aided Verification, CAV*, volume 1254 of *Lecture Notes in Computer Science*, pages 468–471. Springer, 1997.

[55] A. Biere. Adaptive restart strategies for conflict driven SAT solvers. In H. K. Büning and X. Zhao, editors, *Theory and Applications of Satisfiability Testing, SAT*, volume 4996 of *Lecture Notes in Computer Science*, pages 28–33. Springer, 2008.

[56] A. Biere, C. Artho, and V. Schuppan. Liveness checking as safety checking. *Electr. Notes Theor. Comput. Sci.*, 66(2):160–177, 2002.

[57] A. Biere, A. Cimatti, E. M. Clarke, M. Fujita, and Y. Zhu. Symbolic model checking using SAT procedures instead of BDDs. In *Design Automation Conference, DAC*, pages 317–320. IEEE Computer Society, 1999.

[58] A. Biere, A. Cimatti, E. M. Clarke, and Y. Zhu. Symbolic model checking without BDDs. In R. Cleaveland, editor, *Tools and Algorithms for Construction and Analysis of Systems, TACAS*, volume 1579 of *Lecture Notes in Computer Science*, pages 193–207. Springer, 1999.

[59] A. Biere and A. Fröhlich. Evaluating CDCL variable scoring schemes. In *Theory and Applications of Satisfiability Testing, SAT*, volume 9340 of *Lecture Notes in Computer Science*, pages 405–422. Springer, 2015.

[60] A. Biere, M. Heule, H. van Maaren, and T. Walsh, editors. *Handbook of Satisfiability*, volume 185 of *Frontiers in Artificial Intelligence and Applications*. IOS Press, 2009.

[61] B. D. Bingham, M. R. Greenstreet, and J. D. Bingham. Parameterized verification of deadlock freedom in symmetric cache coherence protocols. In *Formal Methods in Computer-Aided Design, FMCAD*, pages 186–195, 2011.

[62] J. D. Bingham. A new approach to upward-closed set backward reachability analysis. *Electr. Notes Theor. Comput. Sci.*, 138(3):37–48, 2005.

[63] J. D. Bingham. Automatic non-interference lemmas for parameterized model checking. In *Formal Methods in Computer-Aided Design, FMCAD*, pages 1–8. IEEE, 2008.

[64] P. Bjesse and K. Claessen. SAT-based verification without state space traversal. In W. A. J. Hunt and S. D. Johnson, editors, *Formal Methods in Computer-Aided Design, FMCAD*, volume 1954 of *Lecture Notes in Computer Science*, pages 372–389. Springer, 2000.

[65] R. Bloem, S. Jacobs, A. Khalimov, I. Konnov, S. Rubin, H. Veith, and J. Widder. Decidability in parameterized verification. *SIGACT News*, 47(2):53–64, 2016.

[66] M. G. Bobaru, C. S. Pasareanu, and D. Giannakopoulou. Automated assume-guarantee reasoning by abstraction refinement. In *Computer Aided Verification, CAV*, volume 5123 of *Lecture Notes in Computer Science*, pages 135–148. Springer, 2008.

[67] G. V. Bochmann. Hardware specification with temporal logic: An example. *IEEE Trans. Computers*, 31(3):223–231, 1982.

[68] M. Bojańczyk. The common fragment of ACTL and LTL. In *Foundations of Software Science and Computational Structures, FOSSACS*, volume 4962 of *Lecture Notes in Computer Science*, pages 172–185. Springer, 2008.

[69] P. Bokor, M. Serafini, N. Suri, and H. Veith. Brief announcement: Efficient model checking of fault-tolerant distributed protocols using symmetry reduction. In *Distributed Computing, DISC*, volume 5805 of *Lecture Notes in Computer Science*, pages 289–290. Springer, 2009.

[70] R. Bonnet. The reachability problem for vector addition system with one zero-test. In *Mathematical Foundations of Computer Science, MFCS*, volume 6907 of *Lecture Notes in Computer Science*, pages 145–157. Springer, 2011.

[71] S. Bose and A. L. Fisher. Automatic verification of synchronous circuits using symbolic logic simulation and temporal logic. In L. Claesen, editor, *Proceedings of the IMEC-IFIP International Workshop on Applied Formal Methods for Correct VLSI Design*. Organizing Committe of the IMEC-IFIP, 1989.

[72] D. Bosnacki, E. Elkind, B. Genest, and D. A. Peled. On commutativity based edge lean search. *Ann. Math. Artif. Intell.*, 56(2):187–210, 2009.

[73] A. Bouajjani, J. Fernandez, and N. Halbwachs. Minimal model generation. In E. M. Clarke and R. P. Kurshan, editors, *Computer Aided Verification, CAV*, volume 531 of *Lecture Notes in Computer Science*, pages 197–203. Springer, 1990.

[74] A. Bouali and R. de Simone. Symbolic bisimulation minimisation. In G. von Bochmann and D. K. Probst, editors, *Computer Aided Verification, CAV*, volume 663 of *Lecture Notes in Computer Science*, pages 96–108. Springer, 1993.

[75] K. S. Brace, R. L. Rudell, and R. E. Bryant. Efficient implementation of a BDD package. In *Design Automation Conference, DAC*, pages 40–45. IEEE Computer Society Press, 1990.

[76] A. R. Bradley. SAT-based model checking without unrolling. In R. Jhala and D. A. Schmidt, editors, *Verification, Model Checking, and Abstract Interpretation, VMCAI*, volume 6538 of *Lecture Notes in Computer Science*, pages 70–87. Springer, 2011.

[77] A. R. Bradley. Understanding IC3. In A. Cimatti and R. Sebastiani, editors, *Theory and Applications of Satisfiability Testing, SAT*, volume 7317 of *Lecture Notes in Computer Science*, pages 1–14. Springer, 2012.

[78] A. R. Bradley and Z. Manna. Checking safety by inductive generalization of counterexamples to induction. In *Formal Methods in Computer-Aided Design, FMCAD*, pages 173–180. IEEE Computer Society, 2007.

[79] M. C. Browne and E. M. Clarke. SML: A high level language for the design and verification of finite state machines. In *IFIP WG 10.2 Working Conference from HDL Descriptions to Guaranteed Correct Circuit Designs*, pages 269–292. International Federation for Information Processing, 1987.

[80] M. C. Browne, E. M. Clarke, and D. Dill. Checking the correctness of sequential circuits. In *International Conference on Computer Design*, pages 545–548. IEEE, 1985.

[81] M. C. Browne, E. M. Clarke, and D. L. Dill. Automatic circuit verification using temporal logic: Two new examples. In *Formal Aspects of VLSI Design*. Elsevier, 1986.

[82] M. C. Browne, E. M. Clarke, D. L. Dill, and B. Mishra. Automatic verification of sequential circuits using temporal logic. *IEEE Trans. Comput.*, C-35(12):1035–1044, 1986.

[83] M. C. Browne, E. M. Clarke, and O. Grumberg. Characterizing finite Kripke structures in propositional temporal logic. *Theor. Comput. Sci.*, 59(1–2):115–131, 1988.

[84] M. C. Browne, E. M. Clarke, and O. Grumberg. Reasoning about networks with many identical finite state processes. *Inf. Comput.*, 81(1):13–31, 1989.

[85] R. E. Bryant. Graph-based algorithms for Boolean function manipulation. *IEEE Trans. Comput.*, 35(8):677–691, 1986.

[86] R. E. Bryant. On the complexity of VLSI implementations and graph representations of Boolean functions with application to integer multiplication. *IEEE Trans. Comput.*, 40(2):205–213, 1991.

[87] R. E. Bryant. Symbolic Boolean manipulation with ordered binary-decision diagrams. *ACM Comput. Surv.*, 24(3):293–318, 1992.

[88] R. E. Bryant and C.-J. Seger. Formal verification of digital circuits using symbolic ternary system models. In R. P. Kurshan and E. M. Clarke, editors, *Computer Aided Verification, CAV*, volume 531, pages 33–43. Springer, 1990.

[89] J. A. Brzozowski and C. J. H. Seger. Advances in asynchronous circuit theory. Part II: Bounded inertial delay models, MOS circuits, design techniques. *Bull. Eur. Assoc. Theor. Comput. Sci.*, 43(3):199–263, 1991.

[90] J. R. Büchi. On a decision method in restricted second order arithmetic. In *International Congress on Logic, Methodology and Philosophy of Science*, pages 1–12. Stanford University Press, 1962.

[91] J. R. Burch, E. M. Clarke, and D. E. Long. Representing circuits more efficiently in symbolic model checking. In *Design Automation Conference, DAC*, pages 403–407. ACM, 1991.

[92] J. R. Burch, E. M. Clarke, and D. E. Long. Symbolic model checking with partitioned transition relations. In A. Halaas and P. B. Denyer, editors, *Very Large Scale Integration, VLSI*, volume A-1 of *IFIP Transactions*, pages 49–58. North-Holland, 1991.

[93] J. R. Burch, E. M. Clarke, D. E. Long, K. L. McMillan, and D. L. Dill. Symbolic model checking for sequential circuit verification. *IEEE Trans. CAD Integr. Circuits Syst.*, 13(4):401–424, 1994.

[94] J. R. Burch, E. M. Clarke, K. L. McMillan, D. L. Dill, and L. J. Hwang. Symbolic model checking: 10^{20} states and beyond. *Inform. and Comput.*, 98(2):142–170, 1992. Originally presented at the 1990 Symposium on Logic in Computer Science (LICS).

[95] R. M. Burstall. Program proving as hand simulation with a little induction. In *IFIP Congress 74*, pages 308–312. North Holland, 1974.

[96] D. Bustan and O. Grumberg. Simulation-based minimization. *ACM Trans. Comput. Logic*, 4(2):181–206, 2003.

[97] C. Cadar, D. Dunbar, and D. R. Engler. KLEE: Unassisted and automatic generation of high-coverage tests for complex systems programs. In R. Draves and R. van Renesse, editors, *Operating Systems Design and Implementation, OSDI*, pages 209–224. USENIX Association, 2008.

[98] S. V. Campos. *A Quantitative Approach to the Formal Verification of Real-Time System*. PhD thesis, School of Computer Science, Carnegie Mellon University, 1996.

[99] S. V. Campos and E. M. Clarke. Real-time symbolic model checking for discrete time models. In T. Rus and C. Rattray, editors, *Theories and Experiences for Real-time System Development*, pages 129–145. World Scientific, 1994.

[100] S. V. Campos, E. M. Clarke, W. Marrero, and M. Minea. Verus: A tool for quantitative analysis of finite-state real-time systems. In *Languages, Compilers and Tools for Real-Time Systems*, pages 70–78. ACM, 1995.

[101] S. V. Campos, E. M. Clarke, W. Marrero, M. Minea, and H. Hiraishi. Computing quantitative characteristics of finite-state real-time systems. In *Real-Time Systems Symposium, RTSS*, pages 266–270. IEEE Computer Society, 1994.

[102] S. Chaki, E. M. Clarke, A. Groce, S. Jha, and H. Veith. Modular verification of software components in C. In L. A. Clarke, L. Dillon, and W. F. Tichy, editors, *International Conference on Software Engineering, ICSE*, pages 385–395. IEEE Computer Society, 2003.

[103] S. Chaki, E. M. Clarke, N. Sinha, and P. Thati. Automated assume-guarantee reasoning for simulation conformance. In *Computer Aided Verification, CAV*, volume 3576 of *Lecture Notes in Computer Science*, pages 534–547. Springer, 2005.

[104] P. Chambart and P. Schnoebelen. Mixing lossy and perfect Fifo channels. In *Concurrency Theory, CONCUR*, volume 5201 of *Lecture Notes in Computer Science*, pages 340–355. Springer, 2008.

[105] P. Chauhan, E. Clarke, J. Kukula, S. Sapra, H. Veith, and D.Wang. Automated abstraction refinement for model checking large state spaces using SAT based conflict analysis. In *Formal*

Methods in Computer Aided Design, FMCAD, volume 2517 of *Lecture Notes in Computer Science*, pages 33–51. Springer, 2002.

[106]   H. Chen, C. David, D. Kroening, P. Schrammel, and B. Wachter. Synthesising interprocedural bit-precise termination proofs. In M. B. Cohen, L. Grunske, and M. Whalen, editors, *Automated Software Engineering, ASE*, pages 53–64. IEEE, 2015.

[107]   Y.-F. Chen, E. M. Clarke, A. Farzan, M.-H. Tsai, Y.-K. Tsay, and B.-Y. Wang. Automated assume-guarantee reasoning through implicit learning. In *Computer Aided Verification, CAV*, volume 6174 of *Lecture Notes in Computer Science*, pages 511–526. Springer, 2010.

[108]   Y.-F. Chen, A. Farzan, E. M. Clarke, Y.-K. Tsay, and B.-Y. Wang. Learning minimal separating DFA's for compositional verification. In *Tools and Algorithms for the Construction and Analysis of Systems, TACAS*, volume 5505 of *Lecture Notes in Computer Science*, pages 31–45. Springer, 2009.

[109]   W. Choi, G. C. Necula, and K. Sen. Guided GUI testing of Android apps with minimal restart and approximate learning. In *Object Oriented Programming Systems Languages & Applications, OOPSLA*, pages 623–640. ACM, 2013.

[110]   C.-T. Chou and D. Peled. Verifying a model-checking algorithm. In *Tools and Algorithms for the Construction and Analysis of Systems, TACAS*, volume 1055 of *Lecture Notes in Computer Science*, pages 241–257. Springer, 1996.

[111]   Y. Choueka. Theories of automata on ω-tapes: A simplified approach. *J. Comput. Syst. Sci.*, 8:117–141, 1974.

[112]   T. S. Chow. Testing software design modeled by finite-state machines. *IEEE Trans. Software Eng.*, 4(3):178–187, 1978.

[113]   A. Cimatti, E. M. Clarke, E. Giunchiglia, F. Giunchiglia, M. Pistore, M. Roveri, R. Sebastiani, and A. Tacchella. NuSMV 2: An opensource tool for symbolic model checking. In *Computer Aided Verification, CAV*, volume 2404 of *Lecture Notes in Computer Science*, pages 359–364. Springer, 2002.

[114]   A. Cimatti, E. M. Clarke, F. Giunchiglia, and M. Roveri. NuSMV: A new symbolic model checker. *STTT*, 2(4):410–425, 2000.

[115]   A. Cimatti and A. Griggio. Software model checking via IC3. In *Computer Aided Verification, CAV*, volume 7358 of *Lecture Notes in Computer Science*, pages 277–293. Springer, 2012.

[116]   A. Cimatti, A. Griggio, A. Micheli, I. Narasamdya, and M. Roveri. Kratos—a software model checker for SystemC. In G. Gopalakrishnan and S. Qadeer, editors, *CAV*, volume 6806 of *Lecture Notes in Computer Science*, pages 310–316. Springer, 2011.

[117]   A. Cimatti, I. Narasamdya, and M. Roveri. Software model checking SystemC. *IEEE Trans. CAD Integr. Circuits Syst.*, 32(5):774–787, 2013.

[118]   D. Clarke, H. Ben-Abdallah, I. Lee, H. Xie, and O. Sokolsky. XVERSA: An integrated graphical and textual toolset for the specification and analysis of resource-bound real-time systems. In *Computer Aided Verification, CAV*, volume 1102 of *Lecture Notes in Computer Science*, pages 402–405. Springer, 1996.

[119]   E. M. Clarke and I. A. Draghicescu. Expressibility results for linear time and branching time logics. In *Linear Time, Branching Time, and Partial Order in Logics and Models for*

Concurrency, volume 354 of *Lecture Notes in Computer Science*, pages 428–437. Springer, 1988.

[120] E. M. Clarke, I. A. Draghicescu, and R. P. Kurshan. A unified approach for showing language containment and equivalence between various types of ω-automata. In A. Arnold, editor, *Colloquium on Trees in Algebra and Programming, CAAP*, volume 431 of *Lecture Notes in Computer Science*, pages 103–116. Springer, 1990.

[121] E. M. Clarke and E. A. Emerson. Design and synthesis of synchronization skeletons using branching time temporal logic. In D. Kozen, editor, *Logic of Programs: Workshop*, volume 131 of *Lecture Notes in Computer Science*, pages 52–71. Springer, 1981.

[122] E. M. Clarke, E. A. Emerson, and A. P. Sistla. Automatic verification of finite-state concurrent systems using temporal logic specifications. In *Principles of Programming Languages, POPL*, pages 117–126. ACM, 1983.

[123] E. M. Clarke, E. A. Emerson, and A. P. Sistla. Automatic verification of finite-state concurrent systems using temporal logic specifications. *ACM Trans. Program. Lang. Syst.*, 8(2):244–263, 1986.

[124] E. M. Clarke, R. Enders, T. Filkorn, and S. Jha. Exploiting symmetry in temporal logic model checking. *Formal Methods Syst. Design*, 9:77–104, 1996.

[125] E. M. Clarke, T. Filkorn, and S. Jha. Exploiting symmetry in temporal logic model checking. In *Computer Aided Verification, CAV*, volume 697 of *Lecture Notes in Computer Science*, pages 450–462. Springer, 1993.

[126] E. M. Clarke, O. Grumberg, and H. Hamaguchi. Another look at LTL model checking. *Formal Methods Syst. Design*, 10(1):47–71, 1997.

[127] E. M. Clarke, O. Grumberg, H. Hiraishi, S. Jha, D. E. Long, K. L. McMillan, and L. A. Ness. Verification of the Futurebus+ cache coherence protocol. In L. Claesen, editor, *International Symposium on Computer Hardware Description Languages and Their Applications*, pages 15–30. North-Holland, 1993.

[128] E. M. Clarke, O. Grumberg, and S. Jha. Veryfying parameterized networks using abstraction and regular languages. In S. Smolka and I. Lee, editors, *Concurrency Theory, CONCUR*, volume 962 of *Lecture Notes in Computer Science*, pages 395–407. Springer, 1995.

[129] E. M. Clarke, O. Grumberg, and S. Jha. Verifying parametrized networks. *ACM Trans. Progr. Lang. Syst.*, 19(5):726–750, 1997.

[130] E. M. Clarke, O. Grumberg, S. Jha, Y. Lu, and H. Veith. Counterexample-guided abstraction refinement for symbolic model checking. *J. ACM*, 50(5):752–794, 2003.

[131] E. M. Clarke, O. Grumberg, and R. P. Kurshan. A synthesis of two approaches for verifying finite state concurrent systems. In *Logic at Botik '89, Symposium on Logical Foundations of Computer Science*, volume 363 of *Lecture Notes in Computer Science*, pages 81–90. Springer, 1989.

[132] E. M. Clarke, O. Grumberg, and D. E. Long. Model checking and abstraction. In *Principles of Programming Languages, POPL*, pages 342–354. ACM, 1992.

[133] E. M. Clarke, O. Grumberg, and D. E. Long. Model checking and abstraction. *ACM Trans. Progr. Lang. Syst.*, 16(5):1512–1542, 1994.

[134] E. M. Clarke, O. Grumberg, and D. A. Peled. *Model Checking*. MIT Press, 1999.

[135] E. M. Clarke, A. Gupta, J. Kukula, and O. Strichman. SAT based abstraction-refinement using ILP and machine learning techniques. In *Computer-Aided Verification, CAV*, volume 2404 of *Lecture Notes in Computer Science*, pages 265–279. Springer, 2002.

[136] E. M. Clarke, T. A. Henzinger, H. Veith, and R. Bloem. *Handbook of Model Checking*. Springer, 2018.

[137] E. M. Clarke, S. Jha, Y. Lu, and H. Veith. Tree-like counterexamples in model checking. In *Logic in Computer Science, LICS*, pages 19–29. IEEE Computer Society, 2002.

[138] E. M. Clarke, D. Kroening, and F. Lerda. A tool for checking ANSI-C programs. In K. Jensen and A. Podelski, editors, *Tools and Algorithms for the Construction and Analysis of Systems, TACAS*, volume 2988 of *Lecture Notes in Computer Science*, pages 168–176. Springer, 2004.

[139] E. M. Clarke, D. Kroening, N. Sharygina, and K. Yorav. Predicate abstraction of ANSI-C programs using SAT. *Formal Methods Syst. Design*, 25(2-3):105–127, 2004.

[140] E. M. Clarke, D. Kroening, N. Sharygina, and K. Yorav. SATABS: SAT-based predicate abstraction for ANSI-C. In N. Halbwachs and L. D. Zuck, editors, *Tools and Algorithms for the Construction and Analysis of Systems, TACAS*, volume 3440 of *Lecture Notes in Computer Science*, pages 570–574. Springer, 2005.

[141] E. M. Clarke, D. E. Long, and K. L. McMillan. A language for compositional specification and verification of finite state hardware controllers. In J. A. Darringer and F. J. Rammig, editors, *Computer Hardware Description Languages and Their Applications*, pages 281–295. North-Holland, 1989.

[142] E. M. Clarke and B. H. Schlingloff. Model checking. In J. Robinson and A. Voronkov, editors, *Handbook of Automated Reasoning*, pages 1635–1790. Elsevier and MIT Press, 2001.

[143] E. M. Clarke, M. Talupur, and H. Veith. Environment abstraction for parameterized verification. In *Verification, Model Checking, and Abstract Interpretation, VMCAI*, volume 3855 of *Lecture Notes in Computer Science*, pages 126–141. Springer, 2006.

[144] R. Cleaveland. Tableau-based model checking in the propositional mu-calculus. *Acta Inf.*, 27(8):725–747, 1990.

[145] R. Cleaveland, M. Klein, and B. Steffen. Faster model checking for the modal mu-calculus. In G. V. Bochmann and D. K. Probst, editors, *Computer Aided Verification, CAV*, volume 663 of *Lecture Notes in Computer Science*, pages 410–422. Springer, 1992.

[146] R. Cleaveland, J. Parrow, and B. Steffen. The concurrency workbench. In J. Sifakis, editor, *Automatic Verification Methods for Finite State Systems*, volume 407 of *Lecture Notes in Computer Science*, pages 24–37. Springer, 1989.

[147] R. Cleaveland and B. Steffen. A linear-time model-checking algorithm for the alternation-free modal mu-calculus. *Formal Methods Syst. Design*, 2(2):121–147, 1993.

[148] R. W. Cleaveland, P. Lewis, S. Smolka, and O. Sokolsky. The concurrency factory: A development environment for concurrent systems. In R. Alur and T. A. Henzinger, editors, *Computer Aided Verification, CAV*, volume 1102 of *Lecture Notes in Computer Science*, pages 398–401. Springer, 1996.

[149] R. W. Cleaveland and S. Sims. The NCSU concurrency workbench. In R. Alur and T. A. Henzinger, editors, *Computer Aided Verification, CAV*, volume 1102 of *Lecture Notes in Computer Science*, pages 394–397. Springer, 1996.

[150] P. Clements, C. Heitmeyer, G. Labaw, and A. Rose. MT: A toolset for specifying and analyzing real-time systems. In *Real-Time Systems Symposium, RTSS*, pages 12–22. IEEE Computer Society, 1993.

[151] J. M. Cobleigh, D. Giannakopoulou, and C. S. Pasareanu. Learning assumptions for compositional verification. In *Tools and Algorithms for the Construction and Analysis of Systems, TACAS*, volume 2619 of *Lecture Notes in Computer Science*, pages 331–346. Springer, 2003.

[152] S. Conchon, A. Goel, S. Krstic, A. Mebsout, and F. Zaïdi. Cubicle: A parallel SMT-based model checker for parameterized systems. In *Computer Aided Verification, CAV*, volume 7358 of *Lecture Notes in Computer Science*, pages 718–724. Springer, 2012.

[153] B. Cook, D. Kroening, P. Rümmer, and C. M. Wintersteiger. Ranking function synthesis for bit-vector relations. *Formal Methods Syst. Design*, 43(1):93–120, 2013.

[154] B. Cook, A. Podelski, and A. Rybalchenko. Termination proofs for systems code. In M. I. Schwartzbach and T. Ball, editors, *Programming Language Design and Implementation, PLDI*, pages 415–426. ACM, 2006.

[155] T. H. Corman, C. E. Leiserson, and R. L. Rivest. *Introduction to Algorithms*. McGraw Hill, 1989.

[156] O. Coudert, C. Berthet, and J. C. Madre. Verification of synchronous sequential machines based on symbolic execution. In J. Sifakis, editor, *Automatic Verification Methods for Finite State Systems*, volume 407 of *Lecture Notes in Computer Science*, pages 365–373. Springer, 1989.

[157] O. Coudert, J. C. Madre, and C. Berthet. Verifying temporal properties of sequential machines without building their state diagrams. In R. P. Kurshan and E. M. Clarke, editors, *Computer Aided Verification, CAV*, volume 531, pages 23–32. Springer, 1990.

[158] C. Courcoubetis, M. Y. Vardi, P. Wolper, and M. Yannakakis. Memory efficient algorithms for the verification of temporal properties. *Formal Methods Syst. Design*, 1:275–288, 1992.

[159] P. Cousot. Abstract interpretation. *ACM Comput. Surv.*, 28:324–328, 1996.

[160] P. Cousot and R. Cousot. Abstract interpretation: A unified lattice model for static analysis of programs by construction or approximation of fixpoints. In *Principles of Programming Languages, POPL*, pages 238–252. ACM, 1977.

[161] W. Craig. Linear reasoning: A new form of the Herbrand-Gentzen theorem. *J. Symbolic Logic*, 22(3):250–268, 1957.

[162] D. W. Currie, A. J. Hu, and S. P. Rajan. Automatic formal verification of DSP software. In *Design Automation Conference, DAC*, pages 130–135. ACM, 2000.

[163] D. Dams, R. Gerth, and O. Grumberg. Generation of reduced models for checking fragments of CTL. In *Computer Aided Verification, CAV*, volume 697 of *Lecture Notes in Computer Science*, pages 479–490. Springer, 1993.

[164] D. Dams, R. Gerth, and O. Grumberg. Abstract interpretation of reactive systems. *ACM Trans. Progr. Lang. Syst.*, 19(2):253–291, 1997.

[165] C. David, D. Kroening, and M. Lewis. Unrestricted termination and non-termination arguments for bit-vector programs. In J. Vitek, editor, *Programming Languages and Systems, 24th European Symposium on Programming, ESOP*, volume 9032 of *Lecture Notes in Computer Science*, pages 183–204. Springer, 2015.

[166] M. Davis, G. Logemann, and D. W. Loveland. A machine program for theorem-proving. *Commun. ACM*, 5(7):394–397, 1962.

[167] M. Davis and H. Putnam. A computing procedure for quantification theory. *J. ACM*, 7(3):201–215, 1960.

[168] C. Daws, A. Olivero, S. Tripakis, and S. Yovine. The tool KRONOS. In *Hybrid Systems III: Verification and Control*, volume 1066 of *Lecture Notes in Computer Science*, pages 208–219. Springer, 1996.

[169] C. Daws and S. Yovine. Two examples of verification of multirate timed automata with KRONOS. In *Real-Time Systems Symposium, RTSS*, pages 66–75. IEEE Computer Society Press, 1995.

[170] L. M. de Moura and N. Bjørner. Z3: An efficient SMT solver. In C. R. Ramakrishnan and J. Rehof, editors, *Tools and Algorithms for the Construction and Analysis of Systems, TACAS*, volume 4963 of *Lecture Notes in Computer Science*, pages 337–340. Springer, 2008.

[171] R. De Nicola. Extensional equivalences for transition systems. *Acta Inf.*, 24(2):211–237, 1987.

[172] R. De Nicola and F. W. Vaandrager. Three logics for branching bisimulation. *J. ACM*, 42(2):458–487, 1995.

[173] P. Della Vigna and C. Ghezzi. Context-free graph grammars. *Inf. Control*, 37:207–233, 1978.

[174] G. Delzanno. Constraint-based verification of parameterized cache coherence protocols. *Formal Methods Syst. Design*, 23(3):257–301, 2003.

[175] G. Delzanno, A. Sangnier, and R. Traverso. Parameterized verification of broadcast networks of register automata. In *Reachability Problems, RP*, volume 8169 of *Lecture Notes in Computer Science*, pages 109–121. Springer, 2013.

[176] G. Delzanno, A. Sangnier, and R. Traverso. Adding data registers to parameterized networks with broadcast. *Fundam. Inf.*, 143(3-4):287–316, 2016.

[177] G. Delzanno, A. Sangnier, R. Traverso, and G. Zavattaro. On the complexity of parameterized reachability in reconfigurable broadcast networks. In *Foundations of Software Technology and Theoretical Computer Science, FSTTCS*, volume 18 of *Leibniz International Proceedings in Informatics*, pages 289–300. Schloss Dagstuhl – Leibniz-Zentrum fuer Informatik, 2012.

[178] S. Demri and P. Gastin. Specification and verification using temporal logics. In *Modern Applications of Automata Theory*, volume 2 of *IISc Research Monographs*, pages 457–494. World Scientific, 2012.

[179] S. Demri, V. Goranko, and M. Lange. *Temporal Logics in Computer Science: Finite-State Systems*. Cambridge University Press, 2016.

[180] E. W. Dijkstra. Guarded commands, nondeterminacy and formal derivation of programs. *Commun. ACM*, 18(8):453–457, 1975.

[181] D. L. Dill. Timing assumptions and verification of finite-state concurrent systems. In J. Sifakis, editor, *Automatic Verification Methods for Finite State Systems*, volume 407 of *Lecture Notes in Computer Science*, pages 197–212. Springer, 1989.

[182] D. L. Dill and E. M. Clarke. Automatic verification of asynchronous circuits using temporal logic. *IEE Proceedings E*, 133(5):276–282, 1986.

[183] D. Dolev, M. Klawe, and M. Rodeh. An $O(n \log n)$ unidirectional distributed algorithm for extrema finding in a circle. *J. Algorithms*, 3:245–260, 1982.

[184] A. F. Donaldson, L. Haller, D. Kroening, and P. Rümmer. Software verification using k-induction. In E. Yahav, editor, *Static Analysis, SAS*, volume 6887 of *Lecture Notes in Computer Science*, pages 351–368. Springer, 2011.

[185] A. F. Donaldson, A. Kaiser, D. Kroening, and T. Wahl. Symmetry-aware predicate abstraction for shared-variable concurrent programs. In *Computer Aided Verification, CAV*, volume 6806 of *Lecture Notes in Computer Science*, pages 356–371. Springer, 2011.

[186] A. F. Donaldson, D. Kroening, and P. Rümmer. Automatic analysis of scratch-pad memory code for heterogeneous multicore processors. In J. Esparza and R. Majumdar, editors, *Tools and Algorithms for the Construction and Analysis of Systems, TACAS*, volume 6015 of *Lecture Notes in Computer Science*, pages 280–295. Springer, 2010.

[187] V. D'Silva, D. Kroening, M. Purandare, and G. Weissenbacher. Interpolant strength. In G. Barthe and M. V. Hermenegildo, editors, *Verification, Model Checking, and Abstract Interpretation, VMCAI*, volume 5944 of *Lecture Notes in Computer Science*, pages 129–145. Springer, 2010.

[188] N. Eén and A. Biere. Effective preprocessing in SAT through variable and clause elimination. In F. Bacchus and T. Walsh, editors, *Theory and Applications of Satisfiability Testing, SAT*, volume 3569 of *Lecture Notes in Computer Science*, pages 61–75. Springer, 2005.

[189] N. Eén, A. Mishchenko, and N. Amla. A single-instance incremental SAT formulation of proof- and counterexample-based abstraction. In R. Bloem and N. Sharygina, editors, *Proceedings of 10th International Conference on Formal Methods in Computer-Aided Design, FMCAD*, pages 181–188. IEEE, 2010.

[190] N. Eén and N. Sörensson. Temporal induction by incremental SAT solving. *Electr. Notes Theor. Comput. Sci.*, 89(4):543–560, 2003.

[191] N. Eén and N. Sörensson. An extensible SAT-solver. In E. Giunchiglia and A. Tacchella, editors, *Theory and Applications of Satisfiability Testing, SAT*, volume 2919 of *Lecture Notes in Computer Science*, pages 502–518. Springer, 2004.

[192] C. Eisner and D. Fisman. *A Practical Introduction to PSL*. Springer, 2006.

[193] K. A. Elkader, O. Grumberg, C. S. Pasareanu, and S. Shoham. Automated circular assume-guarantee reasoning. In *Formal Methods, FM*, volume 9109 of *Lecture Notes in Computer Science*, pages 23–39. Springer, 2015.

[194] K. A. Elkader, O. Grumberg, C. S. Pasareanu, and S. Shoham. Automated circular assume-guarantee reasoning with N-way decomposition and alphabet refinement. In *Computer Aided Verification, CAV*, volume 9779 of *Lecture Notes in Computer Science*, pages 329–351. Springer, 2016.

[195] E. Elkind, B. Genest, D. A. Peled, and H. Qu. Grey-box checking. In *Formal Techniques for Networked and Distributed Systems, FORTE*, volume 4229 of *Lecture Notes in Computer Science*, pages 420–435. Springer, 2006.

[196] E. A. Emerson. *Branching Time Temporal Logic and the Design of Correct Concurrent Programs*. PhD thesis, Harvard University, 1981.

[197] E. A. Emerson. Temporal and modal logic. In J. V. Leeuwen, editor, *Handbook of Theoretical Computer Science*, volume B, pages 997–1072. Elsevier and MIT Press, 1990.

[198] E. A. Emerson and E. M. Clarke. Characterizing correctness properties of parallel programs using fixpoints. In *Automata, Languages and Programming, 7th Colloquium*, volume 85 of *Lecture Notes in Computer Science*, pages 169–181. Springer, 1980.

[199] E. A. Emerson and J. Y. Halpern. "Sometimes" and "Not Never" revisited: On branching time versus linear time. *J. ACM*, 33(1):151–178, 1986.

[200] E. A. Emerson, S. Jha, and D. A. Peled. Combining partial order and symmetry reductions. In *Tools and Algorithms for Construction and Analysis of Systems, TACAS*, volume 1217 of *Lecture Notes in Computer Science*, pages 19–34. Springer, 1997.

[201] E. A. Emerson, C. S. Jutla, and A. P. Sistla. On model-checking for fragments of μ-calculus. In C. Courcoubetis, editor, *Computer Aided Verification, CAV*, volume 697 of *Lecture Notes in Computer Science*, pages 385–396. Springer, 1993.

[202] E. A. Emerson and V. Kahlon. Reducing model checking of the many to the few. In *Conference on Automated Deduction, CADE*, volume 1831 of *Lecture Notes in Computer Science*, pages 236–254. Springer, 2000.

[203] E. A. Emerson and V. Kahlon. Parameterized model checking of ring-based message passing systems. In *Computer Science Logic, CSL*, volume 3210 of *Lecture Notes in Computer Science*, pages 325–339. Springer, 2004.

[204] E. A. Emerson and C.-L. Lei. Modalities for model checking: Branching time strikes back. In M. S. V. Deusen, Z. Galil, and B. K. Reid, editors, *Twelfth Symposium on Principles of Programming Languages*, pages 84–96. ACM Press, 1985.

[205] E. A. Emerson and C.-L. Lei. Efficient model checking in fragments of the propositional mu-calculus. In *Logic in Computer Science, LICS*, pages 267–278. IEEE Computer Society, 1986.

[206] E. A. Emerson, A. K. Mok, A. P. Sistla, and J. Srinivasen. Quantitative temporal reasoning. In R. P. Kurshan and E. M. Clarke, editors, *Computer Aided Verification, CAV*, volume 531, pages 136–145. Springer, 1990.

[207] E. A. Emerson and K. S. Namjoshi. Reasoning about rings. In *Principles of Programming Languages, POPL*, pages 85–94. ACM, 1995.

[208] E. A. Emerson and K. S. Namjoshi. Automatic verification of parameterized synchronous systems. In R. Alur and T. A. Henzinger, editors, *Computer Aided Verification, CAV*, volume 1102 of *Lecture Notes in Computer Science*, pages 87–98. Springer, 1996.

[209] E. A. Emerson and K. S. Namjoshi. On model checking for non-deterministic infinite-state systems. In *Logic in Computer Science, LICS*, pages 70–80. IEEE Computer Society, 1998.

[210] E. A. Emerson and K. S. Namjoshi. Verification of parameterized bus arbitration protocol. In *Computer Aided Verification, CAV*, volume 1427 of *Lecture Notes in Computer Science*, pages 452–463. Springer, 1998.

[211] E. A. Emerson and A. P. Sistla. Symmetry and model checking. In C. Courcoubetis, editor, *Computer Aided Verification, CAV*, volume 697 of *Lecture Notes in Computer Science*, pages 463–478. Springer, 1993.

[212] E. A. Emerson and A. P. Sistla. Utilizing symmetry when model checking under fairness assumptions: An automata-theoretic approach. In *Computer Aided Verification, CAV*, volume 939 of *Lecture Notes in Computer Science*, pages 309–324. Springer, 1995.

[213] E. A. Emerson and R. J. Trefler. Model checking real-time properties of symmetric systems. In L. Brim, J. Gruska, and J. Zlatuska, editors, *Mathematical Foundations of Computer Science, MFCS*, volume 1450 of *Lecture Notes in Computer Science*, pages 427–436. Springer, 1998.

[214] E. A. Emerson and R. J. Trefler. From asymmetry to full symmetry: New techniques for symmetry reduction in model checking. In *Correct Hardware Design and Verification Methods, CHARME*, volume 1703 of *Lecture Notes in Computer Science*, pages 142–156. Springer, 1999.

[215] J. Esparza. Keeping a crowd safe: On the complexity of parameterized verification (invited talk). In E. W. Mayr and N. Portier, editors, *Symposium on Theoretical Aspects of Computer Science, STACS*, volume 25 of *LIPIcs*, pages 1–10. Schloss Dagstuhl – Leibniz-Zentrum fuer Informatik, 2014.

[216] J. Esparza, A. Finkel, and R. Mayr. On the verification of broadcast protocols. In *Logic in Computer Science, LICS*, pages 352–359. IEEE Computer Society, 1999.

[217] J. Esparza, P. Ganty, J. Leroux, and R. Majumdar. Verification of population protocols. *Acta Inf.*, 54(2):191–215, 2017.

[218] J. Esparza, P. Ganty, and R. Majumdar. Parameterized verification of asynchronous shared-memory systems. *J. ACM*, 63(1):10:1–10:48, 2016.

[219] J. Esparza and K. Heljanko. *Unfoldings—A Partial-Order Approach to Model Checking*. Springer, 2008.

[220] J. C. Fernandez, C. Jard, T. Jeron, and G. Viho. Using on-the-fly verification techniques for the generation of test suites. In R. Alur and T. A. Henzinger, editors, *Computer Aided Verification, CAV*, volume 1102 of *Lecture Notes in Computer Science*, pages 348–359. Springer, 1996.

[221] A. Finkel and J. Leroux. Recent and simple algorithms for Petri nets. *Softw. Syst. Model.*, 14(2):719–725, 2015.

[222] A. Finkel and P. Schnoebelen. Well-structured transition systems everywhere! *Theor. Comput. Sci.*, 256(1-2):63–92, 2001.

[223] C. Flanagan and P. Godefroid. Dynamic partial-order reduction for model checking software. In *Principles of Programming Languages, POPL*, pages 110–121. ACM, 2005.

[224] S. Fogarty, O. Kupferman, M. Vardi, and T. Wilke. Unifying Büchi complementation constructions. In *Annual Conference of the European Association for Computer Science Logic*, volume 12 of *Leibniz International Proceedings in Informatics*, pages 248–263. Schloss Dagstuhl – Leibniz-Zentrum fuer Informatik, 2011.

[225] N. Francez. *The Analysis of Cyclic Programs*. PhD thesis, Weizmann Institute of Science, 1976.

[226] A. N. Fredette and R. W. Cleaveland. RTSL: A language for real-time schedulability analysis. In *Real-Time Systems Symposium, RTSS*, pages 274–283. IEEE Computer Society, 1993.

[227] M. Fujita, H. Fujisawa, and N. Kawato. Evaluation and improvements of Boolean comparison method based on binary decision diagrams. In *International Conference on Computer-Aided Design, ICCAD*, pages 2–5. IEEE Computer Society Press, 1988.

[228] M. Fujita, H. Tanaka, and T. Moto-oka. Logic design assistance with temporal logic. In *Conference on Hardware Description Languages and Their Applications, CHDL*, pages 129–137, 1985.

[229] D. Gabbay, A. Pnueli, S. Shelah, and J. Stavi. On the temporal analysis of fairness. In *Principles of Programming Languages, POPL*, pages 163–173. ACM, 1980.

[230] M. K. Ganai, P. Ashar, A. Gupta, L. Zhang, and S. Malik. Combining strengths of circuit-based and CNF-based algorithms for a high-performance SAT solver. In *Design Automation Conference, DAC*, pages 747–750. ACM, 2002.

[231] P. Ganty, J. Raskin, and L. V. Begin. From many places to few: Automatic abstraction refinement for Petri nets. *Fundam. Inf.*, 88(3):275–305, 2008.

[232] M. R. Garey and D. S. Johnson. *Computers and Intractability: A Guide to the Theory of NP-Completeness*. Freeman, 1979.

[233] P. Gastin and D. Oddoux. Fast LTL to Büchi automata translation. In *Computer Aided Verification, CAV*, volume 2102 of *Lecture Notes in Computer Science*, pages 53–65. Springer, 2001.

[234] G. Geeraerts, J. Raskin, and L. V. Begin. On the efficient computation of the minimal coverability set for Petri nets. In K. S. Namjoshi, T. Yoneda, T. Higashino, and Y. Okamura, editors, *Automated Technology for Verification and Analysis*, volume 4762 of *Lecture Notes in Computer Science*, pages 98–113. Springer, 2007.

[235] D. Geist and I. Beer. Efficient model checking by automated ordering of transition relation partitions. In *Computer Aided Verification, CAV*, volume 818 of *Lecture Notes in Computer Science*, pages 299–310. Springer, 1994.

[236] R. Gerber and I. Lee. CCSR: A calculus for communicating shared resources. In *Theories of Concurrency: Unification and Extension, CONCUR*, volume 458 of *Lecture Notes in Computer Science*, pages 263–277. Springer, 1990.

[237] S. M. German and A. P. Sistla. Reasoning about systems with many processes. *J. ACM*, 39(3):675–735, 1992.

[238] R. Gerth, R. Kuiper, D. Peled, and W. Penczek. A partial order approach to branching time logic model checking. In *Israel Symposium on the Theory of Computing and Systems, ISTCS*, pages 130–140. IEEE Computer Society Press, 1995.

[239] R. Gerth, D. Peled, M. Y. Vardi, and P. Wolper. Simple on-the-fly automatic verification of linear temporal logic. In *Protocol Specification Testing and Verification*, pages 3–18. Chapman and Hall, 1995.

[240] D. Giannakopoulou, C. S. Pasareanu, and H. Barringer. Assumption generation for software component verification. In *Automated Software Engineering, ASE*, pages 3–12. IEEE Computer Society, 2002.

[241] P. Godefroid. Using partial orders to improve automatic verification methods. In *Computer Aided Verification, CAV*, volume 531 of *Lecture Notes in Computer Science*, pages 176–185. Springer, 1990.

[242] P. Godefroid, J. de Halleux, A. V. Nori, S. K. Rajamani, W. Schulte, N. Tillmann, and M. Y. Levin. Automating software testing using program analysis. *IEEE Softw.*, 25(5):30–37, 2008.

[243] P. Godefroid, N. Klarlund, and K. Sen. DART: Directed automated random testing. In V. Sarkar and M. W. Hall, editors, *Programming Language Design and Implementation, PLDI*, pages 213–223. ACM, 2005.

[244] P. Godefroid and D. Pirottin. Refining dependencies improves partial-order verification methods. In *Computer Aided Verification, CAV*, volume 697 of *Lecture Notes in Computer Science*, pages 438–449. Springer, 1993.

[245] E. Goldberg and Y. Novikov. BerkMin: A fast and robust Sat-solver. In *Design, Automation and Test in Europe Conference and Exposition, DATE*, pages 142–149. IEEE Computer Society, 2002.

[246] S. Graf and H. Saïdi. Construction of abstract state graphs with PVS. In O. Grumberg, editor, *Computer Aided Verification, CAV*, volume 1254 of *Lecture Notes in Computer Science*, pages 72–83. Springer, 1997.

[247] S. Graf and B. Steffen. Compositional minimization of finite state processes. In R. P. Kurshan and E. M. Clarke, editors, *Computer Aided Verification, CAV*, volume 531, pages 186–196. Springer, 1990.

[248] A. Groce, D. A. Peled, and M. Yannakakis. Adaptive model checking. In *Tools and Algorithms for the Construction and Analysis of Systems, TACAS*, volume 2280 of *Lecture Notes in Computer Science*, pages 357–370. Springer, 2002.

[249] O. Grumberg and D. E. Long. Model checking and modular verification. *ACM Trans. Progr. Lang. Syst.*, 16:843–872, 1994.

[250] E. L. Gunter and D. A. Peled. Path exploration tool. In *Tools and Algorithms for Construction and Analysis of Systems, TACAS*, volume 1579 of *Lecture Notes in Computer Science*, pages 405–419. Springer, 1999.

[251] E. L. Gunter and D. A. Peled. Model checking, testing and verification working together. *Formal Asp. Comput.*, 17(2):201–221, 2005.

[252] A. Gupta, K. L. McMillan, and Z. Fu. Automated assumption generation for compositional verification. *Formal Methods Syst. Design*, 32(3):285–301, 2008.

[253] T. Hafer and W. Thomas. Computation tree logic CTL* and path quantifiers in the monadic theory of the binary tree. In *International Colloquium on Automata, Languages, and Programming, ICALP*, volume 267 of *Lecture Notes in Computer Science*, pages 269–279. Springer, 1987.

[254] N. Halbwachs, Y. E. Proy, and P. Roumanoff. Verification of real-time systems using linear relation analysis. *Formal Methods Syst. Design*, 11(2):157–185, 1997.

[255] J. Y. Halpern. *Reasoning about Uncertainty*. MIT Press, 2005.

[256] M. G. Harbour, M. H. Klein, and J. P. Lehoczky. Timing analysis for fixed-priority scheduling of hard real-time systems. *IEEE Trans. Software Engineering*, 20(1):13–28, 1994.

[257] R. Hardin, Z. Har'El, and R. P. Kurshan. COSPAN. In R. Alur and T. A. Henzinger, editors, *Computer Aided Verification, CAV*, volume 1102 of *Lecture Notes in Computer Science*, pages 423–427. Springer, 1996.

[258] D. Harel. *First-Order Dynamic Logic*, volume 68 of *Lecture Notes in Computer Science*. Springer, 1979.

[259] Z. Har'El and R. P. Kurshan. Software for analytical development of communications protocols. *AT&T Tech. J.*, 69(1):45–59, 1990.

[260] Z. Hassan, A. R. Bradley, and F. Somenzi. Incremental, inductive CTL model checking. In P. Madhusudan and S. A. Seshia, editors, *Computer Aided Verification, CAV*, volume 7358 of *Lecture Notes in Computer Science*, pages 532–547. Springer, 2012.

[261] Z. Hassan, A. R. Bradley, and F. Somenzi. Better generalization in IC3. In *Formal Methods in Computer-Aided Design, FMCAD*, pages 157–164. IEEE, 2013.

[262] M. Hennessy and R. Milner. Algebraic laws for nondeterminism and concurrency. *J. ACM*, 32(1):137–161, 1985.

[263] M. Henzinger, T. A. Henzinger, and P. Kopke. Computing simulations on finite and infinite graphs. In *Foundations of Computer Science, FOCS*, pages 453–462. IEEE Computer Society Press, 1995.

[264] T. A. Henzinger, R. Jhala, R. Majumdar, and K. L. McMillan. Abstractions from proofs. In N. D. Jones and X. Leroy, editors, *Principles of Programming Languages, POPL*, pages 232–244. ACM, 2004.

[265] T. A. Henzinger, R. Jhala, R. Majumdar, and G. Sutre. Lazy abstraction. In *Principles of Programming Languages, POPL*, pages 58–70. ACM Press, 2002.

[266] T. A. Henzinger, X. Nicollin, J. Sifakis, and S. Yovine. Symbolic model checking for real-time systems. *Inf. Comput.*, 111(2):193–244, 1994.

[267] M. Heule and H. van Maaren. Look-ahead based SAT solvers. In *Handbook of Satisfiability*, volume 185 of *Frontiers in Artificial Intelligence and Applications*, pages 155–184. IOS Press, 2009.

[268] C. A. R. Hoare. *Communicating Sequential Processes*. Prentice-Hall, 1985.

[269] G. Holzmann. The model checker SPIN. *IEEE Trans. Software Engineering*, 23(5):279–295, 1997.

[270] G. J. Holzmann. *Design and Validation of Computer Protocols*. Prentice-Hall, 1991.

[271] G. J. Holzmann, P. Godefroid, and D. Pirottin. Coverage preserving reduction strategies for reachability analysis. In *Protocol Specification, Testing and Verification*, pages 349–363. North-Holland, 1992.

[272] G. J. Holzmann and D. Peled. An improvement in formal verification. In *Formal Description Techniques*, pages 197–211. Chapman and Hall, 1994.

[273] G. J. Holzmann and D. Peled. The state of SPIN. In *Computer Aided Verification, CAV*, volume 1102 of *Lecture Notes in Computer Science*, pages 385–389. Springer, 1996.

[274] G. J. Holzmann, D. Peled, and M. Yannakakis. On nested depth first search. In *Second SPIN Workshop*, pages 23–32. AMS, 1996.

[275] J. N. Hooker. Solving the incremental satisfiability problem. *J. Logic Progr.*, 15(1–2):177–186, 1993.

[276] J. E. Hopcroft and J. D. Ullman. *Introduction to Automata Theory, Languages, and Computation*. Addison-Wesley, 1979.

[277] F. Howar and B. Steffen. Learning models for verification and testing. In *Leveraging Applications of Formal Methods, Verification and Validation, ISoLA*, volume 8802 of *Lecture Notes in Computer Science*, pages 199–201. Springer, 2014.

[278] G. Huang. Constructing Craig interpolation formulas. In *Computing and Combinatorics, COCOON*, volume 959 of *Lecture Notes in Computer Science*, pages 181–190. Springer, 1995.

[279] P. Huber, A. M. Jensen, L. O. Jepsen, and K. Jensen. Towards reachability trees for high-level Petri nets. In *Advances in Petri Nets 1984, European Workshop on Applications and Theory in Petri Nets*, volume 188 of *Lecture Notes in Computer Science*, pages 215–233. Springer, 1984.

[280] G. Hughes and M. Cresswell. *A New Introduction to Modal Logic*. Routledge, 1996.

[281] G. E. Hughes and M. J. Creswell. *Introduction to Modal Logic*. Methuen, 1977.

[282] IEEE Computer Society. *IEEE Standard for Futurebus+—Logical Protocol Specification*, 1992. IEEE Standard 896.1–1991.

[283] C. W. Ip and D. L. Dill. Better verification through symmetry. In L. Claesen, editor, *Computer Hardware Description Languages and Their Applications, CHDL*, pages 97–111. North-Holland, 1993.

[284] M. Isberner, F. Howar, and B. Steffen. The TTT algorithm: A redundancy-free approach to active automata learning. In *Runtime Verification, RV*, volume 8734 of *Lecture Notes in Computer Science*, pages 307–322. Springer, 2014.

[285] H. Jain, C. Bartzis, and E. M. Clarke. Satisfiability checking of non-clausal formulas using general matings. In A. Biere and C. P. Gomes, editors, *Theory and Applications of Satisfiability Testing, SAT*, volume 4121 of *Lecture Notes in Computer Science*, pages 75–89. Springer, 2006.

[286] H. Jain, F. Ivancic, A. Gupta, I. Shlyakhter, and C. Wang. Using statically computed invariants inside the predicate abstraction and refinement loop. In T. Ball and R. B. Jones, editors, *Computer Aided Verification, CAV*, volume 4144 of *Lecture Notes in Computer Science*, pages 137–151. Springer, 2006.

[287] H. Jain, D. Kroening, N. Sharygina, and E. M. Clarke. Word-level predicate-abstraction and refinement techniques for verifying RTL Verilog. *IEEE Trans. CAD Integr. Circuits Syst.*, 27(2):366–379, 2008.

[288] R. Jhala and K. L. McMillan. Array abstractions from proofs. In *Computer Aided Verification, CAV*, volume 4590 of *Lecture Notes in Computer Science*, pages 193–206. Springer, 2007.

[289] C. B. Jones. Specification and design of (parallel) programs. In *Proceedings of IFIP'83*, pages 321–332. North-Holland, 1983.

[290] B. Josko. Verifying the correctness of AADL-modules using model checking. In J. W. de Bakker, W.-P. de Roever, and G. Rozenberg, editors, *Proceedings of the REX Workshop on Stepwise Refinement of Distributed Systems, Models, Formalisms, Correctness*, volume 430 of *Lecture Notes in Computer Science*, pages 386–400. Springer, 1989.

[291] D. Jovanovic and B. Dutertre. Property-directed k-induction. In *Formal Methods in Computer-Aided Design, FMCAD*, pages 85–92. IEEE, 2016.

[292] J. J. Joyce and C. H. Seger. The HOL-Voss system: Model-checking inside a general-purpose theorem-prover. In *Higher Order Logic Theorem Proving and its Applications, HUG*, volume 780 of *Lecture Notes in Computer Science*, pages 185–198. Springer, 1994.

[293] M. Jurdzinski, M. Paterson, and U. Zwick. A deterministic subexponential algorithm for solving parity games. *SIAM J. Comput.*, 38(4):1519–1532, 2008.

[294] V. Kahlon. Parameterization as abstraction: A tractable approach to the dataflow analysis of concurrent programs. In *Logic in Computer Science, LICS*, pages 181–192. IEEE Computer Society, 2008.

[295] A. Kaiser, D. Kroening, and T. Wahl. Efficient coverability analysis by proof minimization. In M. Koutny and I. Ulidowski, editors, *Concurrency Theory, CONCUR*, volume 7454 of *Lecture Notes in Computer Science*, pages 500–515. Springer, 2012.

[296] A. Kaiser, D. Kroening, and T. Wahl. A widening approach to multithreaded program verification. *ACM Trans. Progr. Lang. Syst.*, 36(4):14:1–14:29, 2014.

[297] A. Kaiser, D. Kroening, and T. Wahl. Lost in abstraction: Monotonicity in multi-threaded programs. *Inf. Comput.*, 252:30–47, 2017.

[298] M. Kaminski. A branching time logic with past operators. *J. Comput. Syst. Sci.*, 49(2):223–246, 1994.

[299] S. Katz. Techniques for increasing coverage of formal verification. Master's thesis, Department of Computer Science, Technion – Israel Institute of Technology, 2001.

[300] S. Katz and D. A. Peled. An efficient verification method for parallel and distributed programs. In *Workshop on Linear Time, Branching Time and Partial Order in Logics and Models for Concurrency*, volume 354 of *Lecture Notes in Computer Science*, pages 489–507. Springer, 1988.

[301] S. Katz and D. A. Peled. Defining conditional independence using collapses. *Theor. Comput. Sci.*, 101(2):337–359, 1992.

[302] B. W. Kernighan and D. M. Ritchie. *The C Programming Language*. Prentice-Hall, 1978.

[303] Y. Kesten, O. Maler, M. Marcus, A. Pnueli, and E. Shahar. Symbolic model checking with rich assertional laguages. In O. Grumberg, editor, *Computer Aided Verification, CAV*, volume 1254 of *Lecture Notes in Computer Science*, pages 424–435. Springer, 1997.

[304] S. Khurshid, C. S. Pasareanu, and W. Visser. Generalized symbolic execution for model checking and testing. In *Tools and Algorithms for the Construction and Analysis of Systems, TACAS*, volume 2619 of *Lecture Notes in Computer Science*, pages 553–568. Springer, 2003.

[305] J. C. King. A new approach to program testing. In C. Hackl, editor, *Programming Methodology*, volume 23 of *Lecture Notes in Computer Science*, pages 278–290. Springer, 1975.

[306] N. Klarlund. Progress measures for complementation of ω-automata with applications to temporal logic. In *Foundations of Computer Science, FOCS*, pages 358–367. IEEE, 1991.

[307] D. E. Knuth. *The Art of Computer Programming: Fascicle 6 Volume 4B: Satisfiability*. Addison Wesley, 2015.

[308] D. Kozen. Lower bounds for natural proof systems. In *Foundations of Computer Science, FOCS*, pages 254–266. IEEE, 1977.

[309] D. Kozen. Results on the propositional μ-calculus. *Theor. Comput. Sci.*, 27:333–354, 1983.

[310] J. Krajíček. Interpolation theorems, lower bounds for proof systems, and independence results for bounded arithmetic. *J. Symbolic Logic*, 62(2):457–486, 1997.

[311] D. Kroening, J. Ouaknine, O. Strichman, T. Wahl, and J. Worrell. Linear completeness thresholds for bounded model checking. In G. Gopalakrishnan and S. Qadeer, editors, *Computer*

Aided Verification, CAV, volume 6806 of *Lecture Notes in Computer Science*, pages 557–572. Springer, 2011.

[312] D. Kroening and O. Strichman. Efficient computation of recurrence diameters. In L. D. Zuck, P. C. Attie, A. Cortesi, and S. Mukhopadhyay, editors, *Verification, Model Checking, and Abstract Interpretation, VMCAI*, volume 2575 of *Lecture Notes in Computer Science*, pages 298–309. Springer, 2003.

[313] D. Kroening and G. Weissenbacher. Interpolation-based software verification with Wolverine. In G. Gopalakrishnan and S. Qadeer, editors, *Computer-Aided Verification, CAV*, volume 6806 of *Lecture Notes in Computer Science*, pages 573–578. Springer, 2011.

[314] F. Kröger. LAR: A logic of algorithmic reasoning. *Acta Inf.*, 8(3):243–266, 1977.

[315] O. Kullmann. Fundaments of branching heuristics. In *Handbook of Satisfiability*, volume 185 of *Frontiers in Artificial Intelligence and Applications*, pages 205–244. IOS Press, 2009.

[316] O. Kupferman and O. Grumberg. Branching-time temporal logic and tree automata. *Inf. Comput.*, 125(1):62–69, 1996.

[317] O. Kupferman and A. Pnueli. Once and for all. In *Logic in Computer Science, LICS*, pages 25–35. IEEE, 1995.

[318] O. Kupferman and M. Vardi. Weak alternating automata are not that weak. *ACM Trans. Computational Logic*, 2(2):408–429, 2001.

[319] O. Kupferman and M. Y. Vardi. Verification of fair transition systems. In R. Alur and T. A. Henzinger, editors, *Computer Aided Verification, CAV*, volume 1102 of *Lecture Notes in Computer Science*, pages 372–382. Springer, 1996.

[320] O. Kupferman and M. Y. Vardi. Model checking of safety properties. *Formal Methods Syst. Design*, 19(3):291–314, 2001.

[321] O. Kupferman, M. Y. Vardi, and P. Wolper. An automata-theoretic approach to branching-time model checking. *J. ACM*, 47(2):312–360, 2000.

[322] R. Kurshan. Complementing deterministic Büchi automata in polynomial time. *Journal of Computer and Systems Science*, 35:59–71, 1987.

[323] R. P. Kurshan. Analysis of discrete event coordination. In J. W. de Bakker, W.-P. de Roever, and G. Rozenberg, editors, *Proceedings of the REX Workshop on Stepwise Refinement of Distributed Systems, Models, Formalisms, Correctness*, volume 430 of *Lecture Notes in Computer Science*, pages 414–453. Springer, 1989.

[324] R. P. Kurshan. *Computer-Aided Verification of Coordinating Processes: The Automata-Theoretic Approach*. Princeton University Press, 1994.

[325] R. P. Kurshan. Formal verification in a commercial setting. In *Design Automation Conference, DAC*, pages 258–262. ACM, 1997.

[326] R. P. Kurshan, V. Levin, M. Minea, D. A. Peled, and H. Yenigün. Static partial order reduction. In *Tools and Algorithms for the Construction and Analysis of Systems, TACAS*, volume 1384 of *Lecture Notes in Computer Science*, pages 345–357. Springer, 1998.

[327] R. P. Kurshan and K. L. McMillan. A structural induction theorem for processes. In *Principles of Distributed Computing*, pages 239–247. ACM, 1989.

[328] M. Z. Kwiatkowska, G. Norman, and D. Parker. Symmetry reduction for probabilistic model checking. In *Computer Aided Verification, CAV*, volume 4144 of *Lecture Notes in Computer Science*, pages 234–248. Springer, 2006.

[329] M. Z. Kwiatkowska, G. Norman, and D. Parker. PRISM 4.0: Verification of probabilistic real-time systems. In *Computer Aided Verification, CAV*, volume 6806 of *Lecture Notes in Computer Science*, pages 585–591. Springer, 2011.

[330] S. K. Lahiri, T. Ball, and B. Cook. Predicate abstraction via symbolic decision procedures. *Logical Methods Comput. Sci.*, 3(2), 2007.

[331] A. Lal and S. Qadeer. Powering the Static Driver Verifier using Corral. In S. Cheung, A. Orso, and M. D. Storey, editors, *Foundations of Software Engineering, FSE*, pages 202–212. ACM, 2014.

[332] A. Lal, S. Qadeer, and S. K. Lahiri. A solver for reachability modulo theories. In P. Madhusudan and S. A. Seshia, editors, *Computer Aided Verification, CAV*, volume 7358 of *Lecture Notes in Computer Science*, pages 427–443. Springer, 2012.

[333] L. Lamport. "Sometimes" is sometimes "Not Never". In *Principles of Programming Languages, POPL*, pages 174–185. ACM Press, 1980.

[334] L. Lamport. What good is temporal logic? In *IFIP Congress*, pages 657–668. Elsevier, 1983.

[335] F. Laroussinie and P. Schnoebelen. Specification in CTL+past for verification in CTL. *Inf. Comput.*, 156(1-2):236–263, 2000.

[336] K. G. Larsen. Modal specifications. In J. Sifakis, editor, *Automatic Verification Methods for Finite State Systems*, volume 407 of *Lecture Notes in Computer Science*, pages 232–246. Springer, 1989.

[337] K. G. Larsen. Efficient local correctness checking. In G. V. Bochmann and D. K. Probst, editors, *Computer Aided Verification, CAV*, volume 663 of *Lecture Notes in Computer Science*, pages 30–43. Springer, 1992.

[338] K. G. Larsen, P. Pettersson, and W. Yi. Compositional and symbolic model-checking of real-time systems. In *Real-Time Systems Symposium, RTSS*, pages 76–87. IEEE, 1995.

[339] K. G. Larsen, P. Pettersson, and W. Yi. UPPAAL: Status & developments. In *Computer Aided Verification, CAV*, volume 1254 of *Lecture Notes in Computer Science*, pages 456–459. Springer, 1997.

[340] T. Latvala, A. Biere, K. Heljanko, and T. A. Junttila. Simple bounded LTL model checking. In A. J. Hu and A. K. Martin, editors, *Formal Methods in Computer-Aided Design, FMCAD*, volume 3312 of *Lecture Notes in Computer Science*, pages 186–200. Springer, 2004.

[341] R. Lazić, T. Newcomb, J. Ouaknine, A. W. Roscoe, and J. Worrell. Nets with tokens which carry data. *Fundam. Inf.*, 88(3):251–274, 2008.

[342] C. Y. Lee. Representation of switching circuits by binary-decision programs. *Bell System Tech. J.*, 38:985–999, 1959.

[343] D. Lee and M. Yannakakis. Online minimization of transition systems (extended abstract). In S. R. Kosaraju, M. Fellows, A. Wigderson, and J. A. Ellis, editors, *Annual ACM Symposium on Theory of Computing*, pages 264–274. ACM, 1992.

[344] J. P. Lehoczky. Fixed priority scheduling of periodic task sets with arbitrary deadlines. In *Real-Time Systems Symposium, RTSS*, pages 201–209. IEEE Computer Society, 1990.

[345] J. P. Lehoczky, L. Sha, J. K. Strosnider, and H. Tokuda. Fixed priority scheduling theory for hard real-time systems. In *Foundations of Real-Time Computing—Scheduling and Resource Management*, pages 1–30. Kluwer, 1991.

[346] B. Li, C. Wang, and F. Somenzi. Abstraction refinement in symbolic model checking using satisfiability as the only decision procedure. *STTT*, 7(2):143–155, 2005.

[347] O. Lichtenstein and A. Pnueli. Checking that finite state concurrent programs satisfy their linear specification. In *Principles of Programming Languages, POPL*, pages 97–107. ACM, 1985.

[348] O. Lichtenstein, A. Pnueli, and L. Zuck. The glory of the past. In *Logics of Programs*, volume 193 of *Lecture Notes in Computer Science*, pages 196–218. Springer, 1985.

[349] C. J. Lillieroth and S. Singh. Formal verification of FPGA cores. *Nord. J. Comput.*, 6(3):299–319, 1999.

[350] B. Lin and A. R. Newton. Efficient symbolic manipulation of equvialence relations and classes. In *International Workshop on Formal Methods in VLSI Design*, pages 46–61. ACM, 1991.

[351] C. L. Liu and J. W. Layland. Scheduling algorithms for multiprogramming in a hard real-time environment. *J. ACM*, 20(1):46–61, 1973.

[352] C. D. Locke, D. R. Vogel, and T. J. Mesler. Building a predictable avionics platform in Ada: A case study. In *Real-Time Systems Symposium, RTSS*, pages 181–189. IEEE, 1991.

[353] C. Loiseaux, S. Graf, J. Sifakis, A. Bouajjani, and S. Bensalem. Property preserving abstractions for the verification of concurrent systems. *Formal Methods Syst. Design*, 6:11–45, 1995.

[354] D. E. Long. *Model Checking, Abstraction, and Compositional Reasoning*. PhD thesis, Carnegie Mellon University, 1993.

[355] D. E. Long, A. Browne, E. M. Clarke, S. Jha, and W. R. Marrero. An improved algorithm for the evaluation of fixpoint expressions. In D. L. Dill, editor, *Computer Aided Verification, CAV*, volume 818 of *Lecture Notes in Computer Science*, pages 338–350. Springer, 1994.

[356] S. MacLane and G. Birkhoff. *Algebra*. MacMillan, 1968.

[357] A. Mader. Tableau recycling. In G. V. Bochmann and D. K. Probst, editors, *Computer Aided Verification, CAV*, volume 663 of *Lecture Notes in Computer Science*, pages 330–342. Springer, 1992.

[358] P. Maier. Compositional circular assume-guarantee rules cannot be sound and complete. In *Foundations of Software Science and Computational Structures, FOSSACS*, volume 2620 of *Lecture Notes in Computer Science*, pages 343–357. Springer, 2003.

[359] Y. Malachi and S. S. Owicki. Temporal specifications of self-timed systems. In H. T. Kung, B. Sproull, and G. Steele, editors, *VLSI Systems and Computations*, pages 203–212. Springer, 1981.

[360] S. Malik, A. Wang, R. Brayton, and A. Sangiovanni-Vincenteli. Logic verification using binary decision diagrams in a logic synthesis environment. In *International Conference on Computer-Aided Design*, pages 6–9. IEEE, 1988.

[361] M. Mandrykin, V. Mutilin, E. Novikov, A. V. Khoroshilov, and P. Shved. Using Linux device drivers for static verification tools benchmarking. *Prog. Comput. Softw.*, 38(5):245–256, 2012.

[362] Z. Manna and A. Pnueli. *The Temporal Logic of Reactive and Concurrent Systems: Specification*. Springer, 1992.

[363] Z. Manna and A. Pnueli. *Temporal Verifications of Reactive Systems: Safety*. Springer, 1995.

[364] R. Marelly and O. Grumberg. GORMEL—Grammar ORiented ModEL checker. Technical Report 697, Technion, 1991.

[365] J. P. Marques Silva and K. A. Sakallah. GRASP—a new search algorithm for satisfiability. In *International Conference on Computer-Aided Design, ICCAD*, pages 220–227. IEEE Computer Society, 1996.

[366] O. Matthews, J. D. Bingham, and D. J. Sorin. Verifiable hierarchical protocols with network invariants on parametric systems. In *Formal Methods in Computer-Aided Design, FMCAD*, pages 101–108. IEEE, 2016.

[367] A. W. Mazurkiewicz. Basic notions of trace theory. In *Linear Time, Branching Time and Partial Order in Logics and Models for Concurrency*, volume 354 of *Lecture Notes in Computer Science*, pages 285–363. Springer, 1988.

[368] K. McMillan. Using unfolding to avoid the state explosion problem in the verification of asynchronous circuits. In *Computer Aided Verification, CAV*, volume 663 of *Lecture Notes in Computer Science*, pages 164–174. Springer, 1992.

[369] K. L. McMillan. *Symbolic Model Checking: An Approach to the State Explosion Problem*. Kluwer, 1993.

[370] K. L. McMillan. Circular compositional reasoning about liveness. In *Correct Hardware Design and Verification Methods, CHARME*, volume 1703 of *Lecture Notes in Computer Science*, pages 342–345. Springer, 1999.

[371] K. L. McMillan. Verification of infinite state systems by compositional model checking. In *Correct Hardware Design and Verification Methods, CHARME*, volume 1703 of *Lecture Notes in Computer Science*, pages 219–234. Springer, 1999.

[372] K. L. McMillan. Parameterized verification of the FLASH cache coherence protocol by compositional model checking. In *Correct Hardware Design and Verification Methods*, volume 2144 of *Lecture Notes in Computer Science*, pages 179–195. Springer, 2001.

[373] K. L. McMillan. Applying SAT methods in unbounded symbolic model checking. In E. Brinksma and K. G. Larsen, editors, *Computer Aided Verification, CAV*, volume 2404 of *Lecture Notes in Computer Science*, pages 250–264. Springer, 2002.

[374] K. L. McMillan. Interpolation and SAT-based model checking. In W. A. J. Hunt and F. Somenzi, editors, *Computer Aided Verification, CAV*, volume 2725 of *Lecture Notes in Computer Science*, pages 1–13. Springer, 2003.

[375] K. L. McMillan. An interpolating theorem prover. *Theor. Comput. Sci.*, 345(1):101–121, 2005.

[376] K. L. McMillan. Lazy abstraction with interpolants. In T. Ball and R. B. Jones, editors, *CAV*, volume 4144 of *Lecture Notes in Computer Science*, pages 123–136. Springer, 2006.

[377] K. L. McMillan and N. Amla. Automatic abstraction without counterexamples. In H. Garavel and J. Hatcliff, editors, *Tools and Algorithms for the Construction and Analysis of Systems, TACAS*, volume 2619 of *Lecture Notes in Computer Science*, pages 2–17. Springer, 2003.

[378] T. F. Melham. Abstraction mechanisms for hardware verification. In G. Birtwistle and P. A. Subrahmanyam, editors, *VLSI Specification, Verification and Synthesis*, volume SECS35, pages 267–291. Kluwer, 1988.

[379] R. Meyer and T. Strazny. Petruchio: From dynamic networks to nets. In T. Touili, B. Cook, and P. B. Jackson, editors, *Computer Aided Verification, CAV*, volume 6174 of *Lecture Notes in Computer Science*, pages 175–179. Springer, 2010.

[380] R. Milner. An algebraic definition of simulation between programs. In D. C. Cooper, editor, *International Joint Conference on Artificial Intelligence, IJCAI*, pages 481–489. Kaufmann, 1971.

[381] R. Milner. *A Calculus of Communicating Systems*, volume 92 of *Lecture Notes in Computer Science*. Springer, 1980.

[382] S. Minato. Techniques of BDD/ZDD: brief history and recent activity. *IEICE Transactions*, 96-D(7):1419–1429, 2013.

[383] A. Miné. A few graph-based relational numerical abstract domains. In M. V. Hermenegildo and G. Puebla, editors, *Static Analysis, SAS*, volume 2477 of *Lecture Notes in Computer Science*, pages 117–132. Springer, 2002.

[384] A. Miné. The octagon abstract domain. *Higher-Order Symbolic Comput.*, 19(1):31–100, 2006.

[385] B. Mishra and E. Clarke. Hierarchical verification of asynchronous circuits using temporal logic. *Theor. Comput. Sci.*, 38:269–291, 1985.

[386] J. Misra and K. M. Chandy. Proofs of networks of processes. *IEEE Trans. Software Engineering*, 7(4):417–426, 1981.

[387] M. W. Moskewicz, C. F. Madigan, Y. Zhao, L. Zhang, and S. Malik. Chaff: Engineering an efficient SAT solver. In *Design Automation Conference, DAC*, pages 530–535. ACM, 2001.

[388] R. Mukherjee, D. Kroening, and T. Melham. Hardware verification using software analyzers. In *2015 IEEE Computer Society Annual Symposium on VLSI, ISVLSI*, pages 7–12. IEEE Computer Society, 2015.

[389] G. J. Myers. *The Art of Software Testing*. Wiley, 2nd edition, 2004.

[390] A. Nadel, V. Ryvchin, and O. Strichman. Efficient MUS extraction with resolution. In *Formal Methods in Computer-Aided Design, FMCAD*, pages 197–200. IEEE, 2013.

[391] K. S. Namjoshi and R. J. Trefler. On the competeness of compositional reasoning. In *Computer Aided Verification, CAV*, volume 1855 of *Lecture Notes in Computer Science*, pages 139–153. Springer, 2000.

[392] W. T. Overman. *Verification of Concurrent Systems: Function and Timing*. PhD thesis, University of California at Los Angeles, 1981.

[393] R. Paige and R. E. Tarjan. Three efficient algorithms based on partition refinement. *SIAM J. Comput.*, 16(6):973–989, 1987.

[394] D. Park. Concurrency and automata on infinite sequences. In *5th GI-Conference on Theoretical Computer Science*, volume 104 of *Lecture Notes in Computer Science*, pages 167–183. Springer, 1981.

[395] C. S. Pasareanu, D. Giannakopoulou, M. G. Bobaru, J. M. Cobleigh, and H. Barringer. Learning to divide and conquer: Applying the L* algorithm to automate assume-guarantee reasoning. *Formal Methods Syst. Design*, 32(3):175–205, 2008.

[396] J.-P. Pécuchet. On the complementation of Büchi automata. *Theor. Comput. Sci.*, 47(1):95–98, 1986.

[397] D. Peled. All from one, one for all: on model checking using representatives. In C. Courcoubetis, editor, *Computer Aided Verification, CAV*, volume 697 of *Lecture Notes in Computer Science*, pages 409–423. Springer, 1993.

[398] D. Peled. Combining partial order reductions with on-the-fly model-checking. In D. L. Dill, editor, *Computer Aided Verification, CAV*, volume 818 of *Lecture Notes in Computer Science*, pages 377–390. Springer, 1994.

[399] D. Peled. Verification for robust specification. In E. Gunter, editor, *Conference on Theorem Proving in Higher Order Logic*, volume 1275 of *Lecture Notes in Computer Science*, pages 231–241. Springer, 1997.

[400] D. Peled and T. Wilke. Stutter-invariant temporal properties are expressible without the nexttime operator. *Inform. Proc. Lett.*, 63(5):243–246, 1997.

[401] D. Peled, T. Wilke, and P. Wolper. An algorithmic approach for checking closure properties of ω-regular languages. In *Concurrency Theory, CONCUR*, volume 1119 of *Lecture Notes in Computer Science*, pages 596–610. Springer, 1996.

[402] D. A. Peled and A. Pnueli. Proving partial order liveness properties. In *International Colloquium on Automata, Languages and Programming, ICALP*, volume 443 of *Lecture Notes in Computer Science*, pages 553–571. Springer, 1990.

[403] D. A. Peled, A. Valmari, and I. Kokkarinen. Relaxed visibility enhances partial order reduction. *Formal Methods Syst. Design*, 19(3):275–289, 2001.

[404] D. A. Peled, M. Y. Vardi, and M. Yannakakis. Black box checking. In *Formal Methods for Protocol Engineering and Distributed Systems, FORTE*, volume 156 of *IFIP Conference Proceedings*, pages 225–240. Kluwer, 1999.

[405] W. Penczek, B. Wozna, and A. Zbrzezny. Bounded model checking for the universal fragment of CTL. *Fundam. Inf.*, 51(1-2):135–156, 2002.

[406] N. Piterman. From nondeterministic Büchi and Streett automata to deterministic parity automata. *Logical Methods Comput. Sci.*, 3(3):5, 2007.

[407] C. Pixley. Introduction to a computational theory and implementation of sequential hardware equivalence. In R. P. Kurshan and E. M. Clarke, editors, *Computer Aided Verification, CAV*, volume 531, pages 54–64. Springer, 1990.

[408] C. Pixley, G. Beihl, and E. Pacas-Skewes. Automatic derivation of FSM specification to implementation encoding. In *International Conference on Computer Design, ICCD*, pages 245–249. IEEE Computer Society, 1991.

[409] C. Pixley, S.-W. Jeong, and G. D. Hachtel. Exact calculation of synchronization sequences based on binary decision diagrams. In *Design Automation Conference, DAC*, pages 620–623. IEEE Computer Society Press, 1992.

[410] A. Pnueli. The temporal logic of programs. In *Foundations of Computer Science, FOCS*, pages 46–57. IEEE Computer Society, 1977.

[411] A. Pnueli. The temporal semantics of concurrent programs. In *Semantics of Concurrent Computation*, volume 70 of *Lecture Notes in Computer Science*, pages 1–20. Springer, 1979.

[412] A. Pnueli. A temporal logic of concurrent programs. *Theor. Comput. Sci.*, 13:45–60, 1981.

[413] A. Pnueli. In transition for global to modular temporal reasoning about programs. In K. R. Apt, editor, *Logics and Models of Concurrent Systems*, volume 13 of *NATO ASI. Series F, Computer and System Sciences*. Springer, 1984.

[414] A. Pnueli, Y. Rodeh, O. Strichman, and M. Siegel. Deciding equality formulas by small domains instantiations. In N. Halbwachs and D. A. Peled, editors, *Computer Aided Verification, CAV*, volume 1633 of *Lecture Notes in Computer Science*, pages 455–469. Springer, 1999.

[415] A. Pnueli, J. Xu, and L. D. Zuck. Liveness with $(0, 1, \infty)$-counter abstraction. In *Computer Aided Verification, CAV*, Lecture Notes in Computer Science, pages 107–122. Springer, 2002.

[416] V. R. Pratt. A practical decision method for propositional dynamic logic: Preliminary report. In *Symposium on Theory of Computing, STOC*, pages 326–337. ACM, 1978.

[417] P. Pudlák. Lower bounds for resolution and cutting plane proofs and monotone computations. *J. Symbolic Logic*, 62(3):981–998, 1997.

[418] J. P. Quielle and J. Sifakis. Specification and verification of concurrent systems in CESAR. In M. Dezani-Ciancaglini and U. Montanari, editors, *International Symposium on Programming*, volume 137 of *Lecture Notes in Computer Science*, pages 337–350, 1982.

[419] M. O. Rabin and D. Scott. Finite automata and their decision problems. *IBM Journal of Research and Development*, 3(2):114–125, 1959.

[420] S. Rajan, N. Shankar, and M. K. Srivas. An integration of model checking with automated proof checking. In P. Wolper, editor, *Computer Aided Verification, CAV*, volume 939 of *Lecture Notes in Computer Science*, pages 84–97. Springer, 1995.

[421] R. Rajkumar. *Task Synchronization in Real-Time Systems*. PhD thesis, ECE, Carnegie Mellon University, 1989.

[422] A. Rauzy. Toupie = μ-calculus + constraints. In P. Wolper, editor, *Computer Aided Verification, CAV*, volume 939 of *Lecture Notes in Computer Science*, pages 114–126. Springer, 1995.

[423] T. G. Rokicki and C. J. Myers. Automatic verification of timed circuits. In D. L. Dill, editor, *Computer Aided Verification, CAV*, volume 818 of *Lecture Notes in Computer Science*, pages 468–480. Springer, 1994.

[424] F. Rosa-Velardo and D. Frutos-Escrig. Decidability results for restricted models of Petri nets with name creation and replication. In *International Conference on Applications and Theory of Petri Nets*, volume 5606 of *Lecture Notes in Computer Science*, pages 63–82. Springer, 2009.

[425] A. W. Roscoe. Model-checking CSP. In A. W. Roscoe, editor, *A Classical Mind: Essays in Honour of C. A. R. Hoare*, pages 353–378. Prentice-Hall, 1994.

[426] V. Roy and R. de Simone. Auto/Autograph. In R. P. Kurshan and E. M. Clarke, editors, *Computer Aided Verification, CAV*, volume 531, pages 235–250. Springer, 1990.

[427] R. Rudell. Dynamic variable ordering for ordered binary decision diagrams. In *International Conference on Computer Aided Design, ICCAD*, pages 42–47. IEEE Computer Society / ACM, 1993.

[428] S. Safra. On the complexity of ω-automata. In *Foundations of Computer Science, FOCS*, pages 319–327. IEEE Computer Society, 1988.

[429] H. Saïdi. Model checking guided abstraction and analysis. In *Static Analysis, SAS*, volume 1824 of *Lecture Notes in Computer Science*, pages 377–396. Springer, 2000.

[430] H. Saïdi and N. Shankar. Abstract and model check while you prove. In *Computer Aided Verification, CAV*, volume 1633 of *Lecture Notes in Computer Science*, pages 443–454. Springer, 1999.

[431] S. Schewe. Tighter bounds for the determinisation of Büchi automata. In *Foundations of Software Science and Computation Structures, FOSSACS*, volume 5504 of *Lecture Notes in Computer Science*, pages 167–181. Springer, 2009.

[432] P. Schnoebelen. Revisiting Ackermann-hardness for lossy counter machines and reset Petri nets. In *Mathematical Foundations of Computer Science*, volume 6281 of *Lecture Notes in Computer Science*, pages 616–628. Springer, 2010.

[433] V. Schuppan and A. Biere. Shortest counterexamples for symbolic model checking of LTL with past. In *Tools and Algorithms for the Construction and Analysis of Systems, TACAS*, volume 3440 of *Lecture Notes in Computer Science*, pages 493–509. Springer, 2005.

[434] V. Schuppan and A. Biere. Liveness checking as safety checking for infinite state spaces. *Electr. Notes Theor. Comput. Sci.*, 149(1):79–96, 2006.

[435] C. H. Seger, R. B. Jones, J. W. O'Leary, T. F. Melham, M. Aagaard, C. Barrett, and D. Syme. An industrially effective environment for formal hardware verification. *IEEE Trans. CAD Integr. Circuits Syst.*, 24(9):1381–1405, 2005.

[436] K. Sen and G. Agha. CUTE and jCUTE: Concolic unit testing and explicit path model-checking tools. In T. Ball and R. B. Jones, editors, *CAV*, volume 4144 of *Lecture Notes in Computer Science*, pages 419–423. Springer, 2006.

[437] L. Sha, M. H. Klein, and J. B. Goodenough. Rate monotonic analysis for real-time systems. In *Foundations of Real-Time Computing — Scheduling and Resource Management*, pages 129–155. Kluwer, 1991.

[438] M. Sheeran, S. Singh, and G. Stålmarck. Checking safety properties using induction and a SAT-solver. In W. A. J. Hunt and S. D. Johnson, editors, *Formal Methods in Computer Aided Design, FMCAD*, volume 1954 of *Lecture Notes in Computer Science*, pages 108–125. Springer, 2000.

[439] M. Sheeran and G. Stålmarck. A tutorial on Stålmarck's proof procedure for propositional logic. *Formal Methods Syst. Design*, 16(1):23–58, 2000.

[440] S. Shoham and O. Grumberg. A game-based framework for CTL counterexamples and 3-valued abstraction-refinement. *ACM Trans. Computer Logic (TOCL)*, 9(1), 2007.

[441] Z. Shtadler and O. Grumberg. Network grammars, communication behaviors and automatic verification. In *Automatic Verification Methods for Finite State Systems, International Workshop*, volume 407 of *Lecture Notes in Computer Science*, pages 151–165. Springer, 1990.

[442] G. Shu and D. Lee. Testing security properties of protocol implementations—a machine learning based approach. In *International Conference on Distributed Computing Systems, ICDCS*. IEEE Computer Society, 2007.

[443] G. Shurek and O. Grumberg. The modular framework of computer-aided verification: Motivation, solutions and evaluation criteria. In R. P. Kurshan and E. M. Clarke, editors, *Computer Aided Verification, CAV*, volume 531, pages 214–223. Springer, 1990.

[444] D. Sieling. The nonapproximability of OBDD minimization. *Inf. Comput.*, 172(2):103–138, 2002.

[445] A. P. Sistla. *Theoretical Issues in the Design and Verification of Distributed Systems*. PhD thesis, Harvard University, 1983.

[446] A. P. Sistla and E. M. Clarke. The complexity of propositional linear temporal logics. *J. ACM*, 32(3):733–749, 1985.

[447] A. P. Sistla, M. Y. Vardi, and P. Wolper. The complementation problem for Büchi automata with applications to temporal logic. *Theor. Comput. Sci.*, 49:217–237, 1987.

[448] R. H. Sloan and U. Buy. Stubborn sets for real-time Petri nets. *Formal Methods Syst. Design*, 11(1):23–40, 1997-07.

[449] A. Slobodová, J. Davis, S. Swords, and W. A. J. Hunt. A flexible formal verification framework for industrial scale validation. In S. Singh, B. Jobstmann, M. Kishinevsky, and J. Brandt, editors, *Formal Methods and Models for Codesign, MEMOCODE*, pages 89–97. IEEE, 2011.

[450] F. Somenzi. CUDD: Colorado University decision diagram package. Technical report, Colorado University, 1996.

[451] C. Stirling. Bisimulation, modal logic and model checking games. *Logic J. IGPL*, 7(1):103–124, 1999.

[452] C. Stirling. *Modal and Temporal Properties of Processes*. Springer, 2001.

[453] C. Stirling and D. Walker. CCS, liveness, and local model checking in the linear time mu-calculus. In J. Sifakis, editor, *Automatic Verification Methods for Finite State Systems*, volume 407 of *Lecture Notes in Computer Science*, pages 166–178. Springer, 1989.

[454] C. Stirling and D. Walker. Local model checking in the modal mu-calculus. *Theor. Comput. Sci.*, 89(1):161–177, 1991.

[455] I. Suzuki. Proving properties of a ring of finite-state machines. *IPL*, 28:213–214, 1988.

[456] N. Suzuki, editor. *Symbolic Computation Algorithms on Shared Memory Multiprocessors*. MIT Press, 1992.

[457] Z.-H. Tao, C.-H. Zhou, Z. Chen, and L.-F. Wang. Bounded model checking of CTL*. *J. Comput. Sci. Technol.*, 22(1):39–43, 2007.

[458] R. E. Tarjan. Depth first search and linear graph algorithms. *SIAM J. Comput.*, 1:146–160, 1972.

[459] A. Tarski. A lattice-theoretical fixpoint theorem and its applications. *Pacific J. Math*, 5:285–309, 1955.

[460] W. Thomas. Automata on infinite objects. In *Handbook of Theoretical Computer Science, Volume B: Formal Models and Sematics (B)*, pages 133–192. Elsevier and MIT Press, 1990.

[461] W. Thomas. Complementation of Büchi automata revisited. In J. Karhumäki, H. Maurer, G. Paun, and G. Rozenberg, editors, *Jewels are Forever, Contributions on Theoretical Computer Science in Honor of Arto Salomaa*, pages 109–122. Springer, 1999.

[462] G. S. Tseitin. On the complexity of derivation in propositional calculus. In *Studies in Constructive Mathematics and Mathematical Logic, Part II*, volume 8 of *Seminars in Mathematics*, pages 234–259. V.A. Steklov Mathematical Institute, 1968. English Translation: Consultants Bureau, New York, 1970, pages 115–125.

[463] J. D. Ullman. *Computational Aspects of VLSI*. Computer Science Press, 1984.

[464] A. Valmari. Stubborn sets for reduced state space generation. In *Applications and Theory of Petri Nets*, volume 483 of *Lecture Notes in Computer Science*, pages 491–515. Springer, 1989.

[465] A. Valmari. A stubborn attack on state explosion. In *Computer Aided Verification, CAV*, volume 531 of *Lecture Notes in Computer Science*, pages 156–165. Springer, 1990.

[466] A. Valmari. Stubborn set methods for process algebras. In *Partial Order Methods in Verification*, volume 29 of *DIMACS Series in Discrete Mathematics and Theoretical Computer Science*, pages 213–232. DIMACS/AMS, 1996.

[467] A. Valmari and H. Hansen. Can stubborn sets be optimal? *Fundam. Inform.*, 113(3–4):377–397, 2011.

[468] T. van Dijk. *Sylvan: multi-core decision diagrams*. PhD thesis, University of Twente, Enschede, Netherlands, 2016.

[469] T. van Dijk, A. Laarman, and J. van de Pol. Multi-core BDD operations for symbolic reachability. *Electr. Notes Theor. Comput. Sci.*, 296:127–143, 2013.

[470] T. van Dijk and J. van de Pol. Sylvan: multi-core framework for decision diagrams. *STTT*, 19(6):675–696, 2017.

[471] M. Y. Vardi and P. Wolper. An automata-theoretic approach to automatic program verification. In *Logic in Computer Science, LICS*, pages 332–344. IEEE Computer Society, 1986.

[472] M. P. Vasilevskii. Failure diagnosis of automata. *Cybernetics*, 9:653–665, 1973.

[473] V. C. Vimjam and M. S. Hsiao. Explicit safety property strengthening in SAT-based induction. In *International Conference on VLSI Design, VLSI*, pages 63–68. IEEE Computer Society, 2007.

[474] Y. Vizel and O. Grumberg. Interpolation-sequence based model checking. In *Formal Methods in Computer-Aided Design, FMCAD*, pages 1–8. IEEE, 2009.

[475] Y. Vizel, O. Grumberg, and S. Shoham. Lazy abstraction and SAT-based reachability in hardware model checking. In *Formal Methods in Computer-Aided Design, FMCAD*, pages 173–181. IEEE, 2012.

[476] Y. Vizel and A. Gurfinkel. Interpolating property directed reachability. In *Computer Aided Verification, CAV*, volume 8559 of *Lecture Notes in Computer Science*, pages 260–276. Springer, 2014.

[477] B. Wachter, D. Kroening, and J. Ouaknine. Verifying multi-threaded software with Impact. In *Formal Methods in Computer-Aided Design, FMCAD*, pages 210–217. IEEE, 2013.

[478] M. Wehrle and M. Helmert. About partial order reduction in planning and computer aided verification. In *International Conference on Automated Planning and Scheduling, ICAPS*. AAAI, 2012.

[479] J. Whittemore, J. Kim, and K. A. Sakallah. SATIRE: A new incremental satisfiability engine. In *Design Automation Conference, DAC*, pages 542–545. ACM, 2001.

[480] B. Willems and P. Wolper. Partial-order methods for model checking: From linear time to branching time. In *Logic in Computer Science, LICS*, pages 294–303. IEEE Computer Society, 1996.

[481] G. Winskel. Event structures. In *Petri Nets: Central Models and Their Properties, Advances in Petri Nets 1986, Part II, Proceedings of an Advanced Course*, volume 255 of *Lecture Notes in Computer Science*, pages 325–392. Springer, 1986.

[482] G. Winskel. A note on model checking in the modal ν-calculus. In *International Colloquium on Automata, Languages and Programming, ICALP*, volume 372 of *Lecture Notes in Computer Science*, pages 761–772. Springer, 1989.

[483] T. Witkowski, N. Blanc, D. Kroening, and G. Weissenbacher. Model checking concurrent Linux device drivers. In R. E. K. Stirewalt, A. Egyed, and B. Fischer, editors, *Automated Software Engineering, ASE*, pages 501–504. ACM, 2007.

[484] P. Wolper. Temporal logic can be more expressive. In *Foundations of Computer Science, FOCS*, pages 340–348. IEEE Computer Society, 1981.

[485] P. Wolper. Specification and synthesis of communicating processes using an extended temporal logic. In *Principles of Programming Languages, POPL*, pages 20–33. ACM, 1982.

[486] P. Wolper. Expressing interesting properties of programs in propositional temporal logic. In *Principles of Programming Languages, POPL*, pages 184–193. ACM, 1986.

[487] P. Wolper and P. Godefroid. Partial-order methods for temporal verification. In *Concurrency Theory, CONCUR*, volume 715 of *Lecture Notes in Computer Science*, pages 233–246. Springer, 1993.

[488] P. Wolper and V. Lovinfosse. Verifying properties of large sets of processes with network invariants. In J. Sifakis, editor, *Automatic Verification Methods for Finite State Systems*, volume 407 of *Lecture Notes in Computer Science*, pages 68–80. Springer, 1989.

[489] J. Yang, A. Mok, and F. Wang. Symbolic model checking for event-driven real-time systems. In *Real-Time Systems Symposium, RTSS*, pages 23–32. IEEE Computer Society, 1993.

[490] T. Yoneda and B.-H. Schlingloff. Efficient verification of parallel real-time systems. *Formal Methods Syst. Design*, 11(2):197–215, 1997.

[491] T. Yoneda, A. Shibayama, B.-H. Schlingloff, and E. M. Clarke. Efficient verification of parallel real-time systems. In C. Courcoubetis, editor, *Computer Aided Verification, CAV*, volume 697 of *Lecture Notes in Computer Science*, pages 321–332. Springer, 1993.

[492] L. Zhang, C. F. Madigan, M. W. Moskewicz, and S. Malik. Efficient conflict driven learning in Boolean satisfiability solver. In R. Ernst, editor, *International Conference on Computer-Aided Design, ICCAD*, pages 279–285. IEEE Computer Society, 2001.

[493] L. Zhang and S. Malik. Conflict driven learning in a quantified Boolean satisfiability solver. In L. T. Pileggi and A. Kuehlmann, editors, *International Conference on Computer-Aided Design, ICCAD*, pages 442–449. ACM / IEEE Computer Society, 2002.

Index

abstract interpretation, 239
abstraction, 12, 182
  appropriateness, 220
  conservative, 219
  data, 219, 224
  existential, 219
  function, 220
  predicate, 219
  relational, 225
action transition, 343
alphabet, 85
alternation depth, 280
always operator, 38
ample set, 214
appropriateness, 220
assertion, 241
assume-guarantee paradigm, 261
assume-guarantee reasoning, 257
asynchronous system, 341
atomic proposition, 17
automaton
  Büchi, 87
  black box, 271
  deterministic, 86
  input, 86
  regular, 85
  run, 86
  timed, 341
automorphism, 292

Büchi automaton, 87
  emptiness checking, 91
  generalized, 95

BCP, *see* Boolean constraint propagation
BDD, *see* binary decision diagram
binary decision diagram, 113
  Apply, 118
  dynamic reordering, 117
bisimulation, 353
  equivalent, 177
  fair, 182
  relation, 177
bisimulation equivalence, 177
black box, 270
BMC, *see* bounded model checking
Boolean constraint propagation, 144
bounded model checking, 153
bounded until, 331
branching heuristic, *see* decision heuristic

cache coherence protocol, 303
canonical representation, 115, 361
CBMC, 256
CDCL, *see* conflict-driven clause learning
CEGAR, *see* counterexample-guided abstraction
    refinement
CFG, *see* control-flow graph
Chaff, 149
characteristic function, 19, 119
circuit, 23
clock, 342
  assignment, 343
  constraint, 342
  region, 348
  variable, 342
  zone, 354

clock zone
  intersection, 355
closure, 98
CNF, *see* conjunctive normal form
complete assignment, 138
completeness threshold, 159, 175
compositional verification, 257, 260
Computation Tree Logic, 43
  fair semantics, 53, 59
  indexed, 307
condition counting, 334
cone of influence, 223
conflict clause, 147
conflict node, 146
conflict-driven clause learning, 146
conjunctive normal form, 137
control-flow graph, 241
counterexample, 6, 125
  spurious, 220, 232
counterexample-guided abstraction refinement,
  220
Craig interpolant, 165
Craig interpolation, 153
CTL, *see* Computation Tree Logic
CTL*, 37

Davis–Putnam–Logemann–Loveland algorithm,
  137
decision heuristic, 140, 148
delay transition, 343
diameter, 160, 170
difference-bound matrix, 357, 360
  tightening, 361
double DFS, 92
DPLL, *see* Davis–Putnam–Logemann–Loveland

EBMC, 136, 175
environment, 18, 278
equivalence query, 257
eventually operator, 38
execution
  interleaved, 28
  synchronous, 28

fair bisimulation, 182
fairness, 7, 34, 47

false negative, 6
formal model, 15
frontier set, 334

globally operator, 6, 38
graph isomorphism problem, 299
GRASP, 149
guard, 342
guarded command, 212

Horn satisfiability, 152

image, 63
implication, 144
implication graph, 146
induction, 12
initial state
  spurious, 237
interleaving semantics, 29
invariance group, 294
invariant, 342
invariant rule, 309

k-induction, 153
Kripke structure, 16, 17
  fair, 34
  logically equivalent, 177

L^* algorithm, 257
labeled transition system, 262
language
  of an automaton, 86
  regular, 86
lasso, 49
leader election algorithm, 212
least fixpoint, 63
left total, 16
linear temporal logic, 46
literal, 137
localization reduction, 219, 223
location invariant, 343
LTL, *see* linear temporal logic

membership query, 257
MiniSat, 150

model, 17
  concrete, 219
model checking
  complexity, 60, 80, 82
  CTL, 53
  local, 110
  on-the-fly, 109, 110
  problem, 41
  symbolic, 155
modeling, 6, 15
μ-calculus, 277
  complexity, 288

negation normal form, 42, 101
nested DFS, *see* double DFS
network grammar, 314
never claim, 213
next time operator, 10, 38
NNF, *see* negation normal form
nondeterminism, 18
NuSMV, 109, 136

ω-automaton
  timed, 365
ω-regular language, 87
orbit, 294
  problem, 299
  relation, 297
overapproximation, 219

parallel composition, 263
partial order reduction, 10, 189
partitioning criterion, 237
path, 16, 17
  fair, 34
  length, 190
path formula, 39
path quantifier, 37
PDR, *see* property-directed reachability
permutation, 291
persistent set, 214
pivot, 147
post image, 63, 164
predicate transformer, 60
PreImage, 237
priority inversion, 334

PRISM, 136
process, 28
program
  concurrent, 28
  sequential, 26
program counter, 26, 203
program location, 26, 241
Promela, 211
property-directed reachability, 153
propositional SAT, 137
  assumptions, 150
  incremental, 150

QBF, *see* quantified Boolean formula
quantified Boolean formula, 122
quantitative analysis, 340
quotient structure, 294

rate-monotonic scheduling, 329
reachability analysis, 62, 164
reactive system, 15
real-time
  continuous, 341
  discrete, 330
real-time system, 344
region graph, 354
regular automaton, 85
regular language
  learning, 257
relational product, 122, 128, 183
release operator, 38
representation
  explicit, 53
requirements engineering, 15
resolution proof, 148
resolution rule, 146, 166
resolvent, 147
restriction, 296
run
  accepting, 86
  ultimately periodic, 91

SAT, *see* satisfiability
satisfiability, 137
satisfiability modulo theories, 150
SCC, *see* strongly connected component

scheduler, 33
sequential composition, 27
Shannon expansion, 118
simulation equivalence, 239
simulation relation, 182, 183
sleep set, 214
SMT, *see* satisfiability modulo theories
SMV, 135, 310
specification, 6
SPIN, 110, 207, 211
splitting refinement, 237
state, 16
  of an automaton, 85
  bad, 232
  dead-end, 232
  failure, 235
  irrelevant, 232
  successor, 101
state formula, 39
state label, 17
strongest postcondition, 243
strongly connected component, 54, 91, 125, 214
structural equivalence, 177
stubborn set, 214
subset construction, 86
Sylvan, 136
symbolic representation, 246
symmetry, 12

table
  closed, 258
  consistent, 258
tableau, 72
  application to BMC, 158
temporal logic, 37
temporal operator, 37
timed automaton, 341, 343
  non-Zeno, 342
  parallel composition, 344
  reachability problem, 344
trace, 246
transition, 16
  atomic, 32
  deterministic, 190
  enabled, 190
  spurious, 237

transition relation, 16
  of an automaton, 85
  conjunctive partitioning, 131
  disjunctive partitioning, 130
  partitioned, 129
transition system, 16
  path, 190
transposition, 292
truth assignment, 138
Tseitin's method, 139

unit clause, 144
unit rule, 144
unsatisfiable core, 150
until operator, 38

variable
  invisible, 223
  shared, 28, 30
  visible, 223
verification, 6
Verilog, 16, 35, 136, 175
  blocking assignment, 35
  non-blocking assignment, 35
VHDL, 16

weak until, 52
well-structured transition system, 326
witness, 125
WSTS, *see* well-structured transition system

Z3, 150
zone graph, 357